Die Grundlehren der mathematischen Wissenschaften

in Einzeldarstellungen
mit besonderer Berücksichtigung
der Anwendungsgebiete

Band 145

Herausgegeben von

J. L. Doob · E. Heinz · F. Hirzebruch · E. Hopf · H. Hopf
W. Maak · S. Mac Lane · W. Magnus · D. Mumford
M. M. Postnikov · F. K. Schmidt · D. S. Scott · K. Stein

Geschäftsführende Herausgeber

B. Eckmann und B. L. van der Waerden

Paul L. Butzer · Hubert Berens

Semi-Groups of Operators and Approximation

Springer-Verlag Berlin Heidelberg New York 1967

Professor Dr. Paul L. Butzer
Rheinisch-Westfälische Technische Hochschule
Aachen

Dr. rer. nat. Hubert Berens
Rheinisch-Westfälische Technische Hochschule
Aachen

Geschäftsführende Herausgeber:

Professor Dr. B. Eckmann
Eidgenössische Technische Hochschule Zürich

Professor Dr. B. L. van der Waerden
Mathematisches Institut der Universität Zürich

Library of Congress Catalog Card Number 68–11980
Printed in Germany
Title No. 5128

Preface

In recent years important progress has been made in the study of semi-groups of operators from the viewpoint of approximation theory. These advances have primarily been achieved by introducing the theory of intermediate spaces. The applications of the theory not only permit integration of a series of diverse questions from many domains of mathematical analysis but also lead to significant new results on classical approximation theory, on the initial and boundary behavior of solutions of partial differential equations, and on the theory of singular integrals.

The aim of this book is to present a systematic treatment of semi-groups of bounded linear operators on Banach spaces and their connections with approximation theoretical questions in a more classical setting as well as within the setting of the theory of intermediate spaces. However, no attempt is made to present an exhaustive account of the theory of semi-groups of operators per se, which is the central theme of the monumental treatise by HILLE and PHILLIPS (1957). Neither has it been attempted to give an account of the theory of approximation as such. A number of excellent books on various aspects of the latter theory has appeared in recent years, so for example CHENEY (1966), DAVIS (1963), LORENTZ (1966), MEINARDUS (1964), RICE (1964), SARD (1963). By contrast, the present book is primarily concerned with those aspects of semi-group theory that are connected in some way or other with approximation. Special emphasis is placed upon the significance of the relationships between the abstract theory and its various applications. This is, in fact, the original aim of the Springer Grundlehren as suggested by the subtitle of the series.

The present book is written for the graduate student as well as for the research mathematician. It can be read by one who is familiar with real variable theory and the elements of functional analysis. To make the exposition self-contained these foundations are collected in the Appendix. The results given are not always presented in their most general form, so that the reader is not distracted by many of the possible, but often irrelevant, complications. Furthermore, an attempt has been made to make the presentation and proofs of the theorems as clear and detailed as practicable so that the book will, in fact, be accessible to the student reader. About two-thirds of the material is treated here for the first time outside of technical papers, and about a half is based upon recent research. Each chapter concludes with a detailed section entitled "Notes and Remarks", containing references and appropriate historical remarks to the principal results treated, as well as information on important topics related to, but not included among those given in the body of the text. In this way the book may furnish additional information for the research mathematician. Any inaccuracy or omission in assigning priorities for important discoveries is unintentional and the writers will appreciate any corrections suggested by colleagues in the field.

Chapter I gives the standard theory of semi-groups of operators on Banach spaces, the presentation being straight-forward, systematic and without unnecessary details, yet sufficiently complete to include the major results. It aims to serve as an introduction to the theory.

Chapter II presents the basic approximation theorems for semi-group operators. Both direct and converse, optimal and non-optimal approximation theorems for such operators are studied in Banach spaces. Special emphasis is placed on the various concepts of generalized derivatives as well as on the applications of the theory to the initial and boundary behavior of solutions of partial differential equations, in particular to the study of Dirichlet's problem for the unit disk and Fourier's problem of the ring. The material of this chapter is largely based upon the research efforts of the writers, initiated by the senior author in 1956—1957, and continued jointly and individually since 1962.

Chapter III is devoted to the incorporation and grouping of the powerful approximation theorems for semi-group operators, as discussed in Chapter II, into the theory of intermediate spaces between the initial Banach space and the domain of definition of powers of the infinitesimal generator of the semi-group, and to deep generalizations of the corresponding theorems in the new setting. These goals are primarily achieved by the development of an interpolation method between Banach spaces, in particular by the K- and J-methods of JAAK PEETRE. There also are applications to Lorentz spaces and interpolation theorems. Although the emphasis here is mainly on the role of intermediate spaces in the study of semi-groups of operators, the theory of intermediate spaces per se is developed to a limited extent. Consequently, Chapter III may provide an introduction to interpolation space theory, especially since this theory, founded in 1959—1963, has not been treated in book-form previously.

Chapter IV outlines and discusses some of the many applications of the general theory presented in Chapter III, emphasizing the semi-group of left translations as well as the singular integrals of Abel-Poisson for periodic functions and of Cauchy-Poisson for functions defined on the real line. Finally, the singular integral of Gauss-Weierstrass on Euclidean n-space is treated in connection with Sobolev and

Besov spaces. This chapter stresses the interplay between functional analysis and "hard" classical analysis such as the theory of Fourier series and that of Fourier and Hilbert transforms.

The references cited are listed in the bibliography and a conventional terminology is used so that it will not be necessary to continually refer to a collection of symbols.

About ten years ago the late JEAN FAVARD suggested to the senior author to attempt a book on approximation, based on the semi-group approach. We are particularly grateful that he was able to participate in the Conference on Approximation Theory conducted by one of us at the Mathematical Research Institute, Oberwolfach, in August of 1963, before his untimely death in January, 1965. His sincere and abiding interest and encouragement over the years are deeply acknowledged. The senior author also wishes to express his gratitude to Professor EINAR HILLE for the opportunity to participate in a highly profitable seminar on semi-groups of operators conducted by Hille at the University of Mainz in 1956/57. Professor JAAK PEETRE kindly sent us his many papers on intermediate spaces even in their preprint form.

We are grateful to Miss URSULA WESTPHAL and Mr. KARL SCHERER for their critical reading of the manuscript, assistance in reading the proofs, and preparation of the index. We also wish to express our appreciation to Mrs. DORIS EWERS for her patient and careful typing of the manuscript. Last but not least, our warm thanks go to Professor BÉLA SZ.-NAGY for his invitation to write this book for the Springer Series as well as to the Springer-Verlag for producing it in accord with their usual high standards of publication.

Aachen, June 1967

P. L. BUTZER · H. BERENS

Contents

Chapter One

Fundamentals of Semi-Group Theory

Chapter Two

Approximation Theorems for Semi-Groups of Operators

Chapter Three

Intermediate Spaces and Semi-Groups

Chapter Four

Applications to Singular Integrals

Chapter One

Fundamentals of Semi-Group Theory

1.0 Introduction

As a motivation for the study of semi-groups of operators, we shall consider the *equation of heat-conduction* for an infinite rod

$$\frac{\partial w}{\partial t} = \frac{\partial^2 w}{\partial x^2} \qquad (-\infty < x < \infty;\ t > 0) \tag{1.0.1}$$

with the given initial temperature distribution

$$w(x, 0) = f(x). \tag{1.0.2}$$

Here we restrict our discussion to the case where $f(x)$ belongs to the space of all bounded, uniformly continuous real-valued functions defined on the real axis, in notation: $f \in \mathsf{UCB}(\mathrm{E}_1)$.

Denoting a "solution" $w(x, t)$ of (1.0.1) associated with the given initial value $f(x)$ by $w(x, t; f)$, it is essential for our study that there exists a unique solution in the sense that $w(x, t; f)$ and its required partial derivatives belong to $\mathsf{UCB}(\mathrm{E}_1)$ for each $t > 0$ and that

$$\lim_{t \to 0+} w(x, t; f) = f(x) \tag{1.0.3}$$

uniformly with respect to x.

The above problem is referred to as *Cauchy's problem* for the particular instance of the heat-conduction equation. In [2] J. HADAMARD pointed out that the classical problem of Cauchy for a linear partial differential equation, if it possesses a unique solution (or as he said, if it is *correctly set*), leads to group theoretical considerations. This he could conclude from an analysis of the implications of the *major premise of Huygens' principle,* which in the case of Cauchy's problem for the equation of heat-conduction takes on the form: *If the temperature distribution $w(x, t)$ of the rod at the time $t > 0$ is uniquely determined by the initial distribution $f(x)$, then $w(x, t)$ can also be obtained by first computing the temperature distribution $w(x, t_0)$ at the intermediate time t_0. The major premise then asserts that these two computations should lead to the same result:*

$$w(x, t; f) = w\big(x, t - t_0; w(\cdot, t_0; f)\big). \tag{1.0.4}$$

For each fixed $t > 0$, $w(x, t; f)$ may be considered as a transformation on f:

(1.0.5) $$w(x, t; f) = [W(t) f](x) \qquad (t > 0),$$

which is *linear* because of the linearity of the problem. In these terms, property (1.0.4) can be restated in the form

(1.0.6) $$W(t_1 + t_2) f = W(t_1)[W(t_2) f] \qquad (0 < t_1, t_2 < \infty),$$

the so-called *semi-group property* of the solution. Also, the initial condition (1.0.3) can be reformulated as

(1.0.7) $$\lim_{t \to 0+} \| W(t) f - f \|_C = 0.$$

(We introduce in $UCB(E_1)$ the norm: $\|f\|_C = \sup_{x \in E_1} |f(x)|$; convergence in norm signifies uniform convergence with respect to x.)

The solution of the heat-conduction equation under consideration is explicitly given by

(1.0.8) $$w(x, t; f) = \frac{1}{\sqrt{4\pi t}} \int_{E_1} \exp\left[-\frac{(x-u)^2}{4t}\right] f(u)\, du,$$

called the *singular integral of Gauss-Weierstrass*, and solves the problem for all functions f in $UCB(E_1)$. Here, $w(x, t; f) = [W(t) f](x)$ is a bounded linear transformation on $UCB(E_1)$ to itself and the semi-group property (1.0.4) is a consequence of the formula concerning the Gaussian distribution:

(1.0.9) $$\frac{1}{\sqrt{4\pi(t_1 + t_2)}} \exp\left(\frac{-x^2}{4t}\right)$$
$$= \frac{1}{4\pi\sqrt{t_1 t_2}} \int_{E_1} \exp\left[\frac{-(x-u)^2}{4t_1}\right] \exp\left[\frac{-u^2}{4t_2}\right] du \qquad (0 < t_1, t_2 < \infty).$$

We now consider the connection between our semi-group of operators $\{W(t); 0 < t < \infty\}$ and the differential equation (1.0.1). We have for $\tau > 0$

(1.0.10) $$\frac{w(\cdot, t+\tau; f) - w(\cdot, t; f)}{\tau} = W(t) \left\{\frac{W(\tau) - I}{\tau}\right\} f$$
$$= \left\{\frac{W(\tau) - I}{\tau}\right\} W(t) f = \left\{\frac{W(\tau) - I}{\tau}\right\} w(\cdot, t; f),$$

where I denotes the identity operator. Hence we may define an operator U, called the *infinitesimal generator* of $\{W(t); 0 < t < \infty\}$, by

(1.0.11) $$U f = \lim_{\tau \to 0+} \frac{W(\tau) - I}{\tau} f$$

for those $f \in UCB(E_1)$ for which this limit exists in the UCB-norm. Now, if we take the limit for $\tau \to 0+$ in (1.0.10), we have that $w(x, t)$

as a function of t is differentiable uniformly with respect to x, $w(x,t)$ belongs to the domain of U for each fixed $t > 0$, and

$$\frac{\partial}{\partial t} w(x,t) = U\, w(x,t). \tag{1.0.12}$$

Comparing this with the differential equation (1.0.1), we see that the operator U is equal to d^2/dx^2. The differential equation (1.0.1) is thus to be understood in the sense of (1.0.12).

The problem considered above is a special case of a quite more general situation. Thus, instead of the special space $\mathsf{UCB}(\mathrm{E}_1)$, let X be any real or complex Banach space with norm $\|\cdot\|$, its elements being denoted by $f, g, \ldots$ Furthermore, let $\{T(t);\, 0 \leqq t < \infty\}$ be a family of bounded linear operators on X to itself with $T(0) = I$ having the semi-group property (1.0.6) as well as property (1.0.7) for all $f \in \mathsf{X}$, the latter being referred to as the $(\mathscr{C}_0)$-property. We then speak of $\{T(t);\, 0 \leqq t < \infty\}$ as a *semi-group of operators of class* $(\mathscr{C}_0)$ on X. Under these assumptions the map $t \to T(t)f$ from $[0,\infty)$ to X is continuous in the norm for all $f \in \mathsf{X}$. The infinitesimal generator A defined by (1.0.11) is a linear operator and it will be shown that although A is in general unbounded, it is a closed operator with domain $\mathsf{D}(A)$ dense in X.

Such a semi-group of operators on a Banach space is closely connected with an *abstract Cauchy problem*, which we may formulate with E. Hille [7; 8; 9] as follows:

Given a Banach space X *and a linear operator* U *whose domain* $\mathsf{D}(U)$ *and range* $\mathsf{R}(U)$ *belong to* X *and given an element* $f_0 \in \mathsf{X}$, *to find a function* $w(t) \equiv w(t; f_0)$ *on* $[0,\infty)$ *to* X *such that*

(1.0.13)
- (i) $w(t)$ *is continuously differentiable on* $[0,\infty)$ *in the norm;*
- (ii) $w(t) \in \mathsf{D}(U)$ *and* $w'(t) = U\,w(t)$ *for each* $t > 0$;
- (iii) $\lim_{t \to 0+} \|w(t) - f_0\| = 0$.

Now, if U is the infinitesimal generator of a semi-group of operators $\{W(t);\, 0 \leqq t < \infty\}$ of class $(\mathscr{C}_0)$ in X (thus U being closed with dense domain), and if $f \in \mathsf{D}(U)$, then we obtain by (1.0.10) that the function $w(t) = W(t)f$ satisfies (i) and (ii) with

$$\frac{d}{dt} w(t) = W(t)\,U f = U\,w(t) \qquad (t \geqq 0),$$

whereas (iii) follows by the $(\mathscr{C}_0)$-property of the semi-group. Thus $w(t) = W(t)f$ solves the Cauchy problem for all $f \in \mathsf{D}(U)$. It can be shown that the solution is unique.

We have studied Cauchy's problem for the heat-conduction equation in $\mathsf{UCB}(\mathrm{E}_1)$ as an instance of this general situation. Here the operator U is defined by

$$(1.0.14)\quad \begin{cases} [U f](x) = f''(x), \\ \mathsf{D}(U) = \{f \in \mathsf{UCB}(E_1);\ f, f' \text{ continuously differentiable}, \\ \qquad\qquad f'' \in \mathsf{UCB}(E_1)\}, \end{cases}$$

and the solution was given by the singular integral (1.0.8) of Gauss-Weierstrass. In this particular case we have seen that the problem has a unique solution for all $f \in \mathsf{UCB}(E_1)$, if condition (i) holds on the open interval $(0, \infty)$.

Of particular interest in Chapter I is the question under what conditions a closed linear operator U generates a semi-group solution of the abstract Cauchy problem. The first result in this direction, and for many purposes the most useful, was obtained independently by E. HILLE and K. YOSIDA in 1948. They studied the spectral properties of the operator U, i.e. the equation

$$\lambda f - U f = g \qquad (\lambda \text{ a complex number})$$

for all $f \in \mathsf{D}(U)$. In this respect one needs to know the *resolvent set* $\varrho(U)$ of U, namely, the set of values of λ for which $\lambda I - U$ has a bounded inverse with domain dense in X. For these values of λ the inverse $(\lambda I - U)^{-1}$ is called the *resolvent* of U and is denoted by $R(\lambda; U)$. In this terminology the *theorem of Hille-Yosida* asserts: *If U is a closed linear operator in X to itself with dense domain and if $R(\lambda; U)$ exists for all real $\lambda > 0$ with $\|R(\lambda; U)\| \leqq 1/\lambda$, then U is the infinitesimal generator of a semi-group of operators $\{T(t); 0 \leqq t < \infty\}$ of class $(\mathscr{C}_0)$ on X such that $\|T(t)\| \leqq 1$ for all $t \geqq 0$. Moreover, U is the infinitesimal generator of exactly one semi-group.* More generally, W. FELLER, I. MIYADERA and R. S. PHILLIPS in 1953 gave necessary and sufficient conditions that a linear operator U be the infinitesimal generator of a semi-group of operators of class $(\mathscr{C}_0)$ on X.

E. HILLE has also given a number of representation formulas of $T(t)$ by the resolvent $R(\lambda; U)$; in particular

$$(1.0.15)\quad T(t) f = \lim_{\lambda \to \infty} e^{-\lambda t} \sum_{k=0}^{\infty} \frac{(\lambda t)^k}{k!} [\lambda R(\lambda; A)]^k f \qquad (f \in \mathsf{X};\ t > 0),$$

giving $T(t)$ if the resolvent is known.

We have seen that if U is the infinitesimal generator of a semi-group of class $(\mathscr{C}_0)$, then the abstract Cauchy problem has a unique solution for all $f \in \mathsf{D}(U)$. Conversely, in 1954 R. S. PHILLIPS was able to show: *If U is a closed linear operator with dense domain $\mathsf{D}(U)$ and non-empty resolvent set $\varrho(U)$ and if for each $f \in \mathsf{D}(U)$ the abstract Cauchy problem has a unique solution, then U is the infinitesimal generator of a semi-group of operators of class $(\mathscr{C}_0)$ on X.*

In order to see how the Hille-Yosida theorem may actually be used to establish the existence of the semi-group solution to our problem (1.0.1)—(1.0.2) (the hypotheses to be understood in the precise form given by (1.0.13) with U defined by (1.0.14)), we may proceed as follows. Clearly, $\mathsf{D}(U)$ is dense in $\mathsf{UCB}(\mathrm{E}_1)$ while $R(\lambda; U)\, g$ is obtained as the solution to $(\lambda I - U)\, f = \lambda f - f'' = g$ with $f \in \mathsf{D}(U)$ so that

$$(1.0.16)\quad [R(\lambda; U)\, g]\,(x) = \frac{1}{2\sqrt{\lambda}} \int_{\mathrm{E}_1} \exp[-\sqrt{\lambda}|x-u|]\, g(u)\, du \quad (\lambda > 0).$$

One readily obtains that

$$\|R(\lambda; U)\, g\|_{\mathsf{C}} \leqq \sup_{x \in \mathrm{E}_1} \frac{\|g\|_{\mathsf{C}}}{2\sqrt{\lambda}} \int_{\mathrm{E}_1} \exp[-\sqrt{\lambda}\,|x-u|]\, du = \lambda^{-1}\, \|g\|_{\mathsf{C}}.$$

The conditions of the Hille-Yosida theorem are therefore satisfied and thus U generates a semi-group solution of class $(\mathscr{C}_0)$.

Finally, making use of the formula (1.0.15), a rather involved calculation (by Fourier transforms) gives the explicit representation of the solution in its classical form (1.0.8).

Thus we have seen in a particular example as well as for an abstract Cauchy problem that the theory of semi-groups of operators on Banach spaces plays an important role in the theory of linear partial differential equations.

We may also introduce semi-groups of operators from a different point of view. It is well-known that the exponential function $e(t) = e^{t\alpha}$, α a real or complex number, is the most general continuous function of $t \geqq 0$ satisfying $e(t_1 + t_2) = e(t_1)\, e(t_2)$ and $e(0) = 1$. By analogy, one would expect the most general continuous operator function $T(t)$ defined for $t \geqq 0$ and satisfying $T(t_1 + t_2) = T(t_1)\, T(t_2)$, $T(0) = I$ $(t_1, t_2 \geqq 0)$ to be, in an appropriate sense, given by

$$(1.0.17)\qquad T(t) = e^{tA},$$

with A the infinitesimal generator.

Since the classical exponential function has the property $e'(t) = \alpha\, e(t)$, we have formally

$$\frac{d}{dt}\, T(t) = A\, T(t) \qquad (t \geqq 0),$$

again showing the connection with Cauchy's problem.

Having given a motivation for the study of semi-groups of operators on Banach spaces, we now indicate the scope of Chapter I which is devoted to an exposition of the basic ideas and fundamental results on semi-group theory.

In Section 1.1 we present the definition and main properties of a one-parameter semi-group of operators $\{T(t); 0 \leqq t < \infty\}$ of class $(\mathscr{C}_0)$

on a Banach space X (for each $t \geqq 0$, $T(t)$ is a bounded linear transformation from X to itself), of the infinitesimal generator A, and its powers A^r (r integral) (Prop. 1.1.2, 1.1.4 and 1.1.6). We then discuss briefly n-parameter semi-groups of operators in $\mathscr{E}(X)$ (Prop. 1.1.8 and 1.1.9) and proceed with a more detailed study of holomorphic semi-groups — Prop. 1.1.11 giving necessary and sufficient conditions such that $\{T(t); 0 \leqq t < \infty\}$ has a holomorphic extension $T(\zeta)$ in a sector of the complex plane.

In Sec. 1.2 the emphasis is upon representation theorems for semi-groups of operators. As we have noted, the first major problem in semi-group theory is to give an appropriate interpretation of (1.0.17). In this respect Theorem 1.2.2 gives "Hille's first exponential formula". The second part is concerned with a general convergence theorem of Bohman-Korovkin type for families of bounded linear operators $\{T(t); 0 \leqq t \leqq 1\}$ not necessarily having the semi-group property (Theorem 1.2.6). A corollary of the latter result applied to the semi-group of left translations in $UCB(\mathrm{E}_1)$ defined by $[T(t)f](x) = f(x+t)$, $0 \leqq t < \infty$, $f \in UCB(\mathrm{E}_1)$, leads to a proof of the Weierstrass approximation theorem using Bernstein polynomials (Theorem 1.2.11). A "generalization" of the Bernstein polynomials to the compactified infinite interval $[0, \infty]$ is given via the transform of (1.2.23), due to J. Favard.

Section 1.3 is devoted to a study of the infinitesimal generator and upon conditions an operator U should possess that it be the generator of a semi-group of class $(\mathscr{C}_0)$. We begin with a classification of the spectral properties of a linear operator U having both domain and range in X. In Theorem 1.3.5 we show that if A is the generator of a semi-group $\{T(t); 0 \leqq t < \infty\}$ of class $(\mathscr{C}_0)$ on X, then the set of complex numbers $\{\lambda; \operatorname{Re}\lambda > \omega_0 \equiv \lim_{t\to 0+} (t^{-1} \log \| T(t) \|) < \infty\}$ belongs to the resolvent set $\varrho(A)$ and its resolvent $R(\lambda; A)$ is the Laplace transform of $T(t)$. Conversely, if $R(\lambda; A)$ is known, we can obtain $T(t)$ by various inversion formulas. One such formula is given by Proposition 1.3.11. Its proof will be seen to follow from Theorem 1.3.6, due to W. Feller, I. Miyadera and R. S. Phillips, which is the principal generation theorem in semi-group theory. The Hille-Yosida theorem follows as Corollary 1.3.7, and likewise another result of E. Hille (Prop. 1.3.10). The fact that a semi-group of operators is uniquely determined by its generator is shown in Prop. 1.3.9. The last part of this section deals with a detailed analysis of the semi-group of left translations on the function spaces $UCB(\mathrm{E}_1)$ and $L^p(\mathrm{E}_1)$, $1 \leqq p < \infty$. The section concludes with a brief discussion on groups of operators $\{T(t); -\infty < t < \infty\}$ on X (Theorem 1.3.15).

Section 1.4 deals with dual semi-groups. Beginning with the definition and the basic properties of the dual operator U^* on the dual space X^* of a linear transformation U with dense domain in X to X, we investigate in detail the dual $\{T^*(t); 0 \leqq t < \infty\}$ of a semi-group of operators of class $(\mathscr{C}_0)$ in $\mathscr{E}(X)$. Propositions 1.4.3 and 1.4.4 show that $\{T^*(t); 0 \leqq t < \infty\}$ is a weakly* continuous semi-group of operators on X^* with the weakly* infinitesimal generator being equal to the dual A^*. In Proposition 1.4.6 we then prove that there is an invariant strongly closed linear subspace X_0^* in X^* (X_0^* being weakly* dense in X^*) upon which the restriction of $\{T^*(t); 0 \leqq t < \infty\}$ is strongly continuous. Denoting this restriction by $\{T_0^*(t); 0 \leqq t < \infty\}$ and its infinitesimal generator by A_0^*, the connections between $\{T_0^*(t); 0 \leqq t < \infty\}$ with A_0^* on X_0^* and $\{T^*(t); 0 \leqq t < \infty\}$ with A^* on X^* are discussed in Prop. 1.4.7. In the second part we continue our investigations of Sec. 1.3.3 concerning the semi-group of left translations on the spaces $UCB(\mathrm{E}_1)$ and $L^p(\mathrm{E}_1)$, $1 \leqq p < \infty$. As a particular result we obtain a theorem of A. Plessner on absolutely continuous functions.

The first part of Section 1.5 is concerned with a summary without proofs of classical theorems in the theory of Fourier series needed in the text. The second part is devoted to a detailed study of Fourier's problem of the ring, the periodic version of the partial differential equation considered at the beginning of the introduction. Using the Hille-Yosida theorem it is shown that this problem has a unique semi-group solution in the function spaces $C_{2\pi}$ or $L_{2\pi}^p$, $1 \leqq p < \infty$, known as the periodic singular integral of Weierstrass (Theorem 1.5.3). In part three we consider strongly continuous semi-groups of operators of factor sequence type on the spaces $C_{2\pi}$, $L_{2\pi}^p$, $1 \leqq p < \infty$, as well as their dual semi-groups on the corresponding dual spaces. The main results here are given in Theorems 1.5.4 and 1.5.7. The final part deals with Dirichlet's problem of the Laplace equation for the unit disk, finite Fourier transform methods being used in the treatment.

Section 1.6 is devoted to "Notes and Remarks".

1.1 Elements of Semi-Group Theory

1.1.1 Basic Properties

Let X be a real or complex Banach space with elements $f, g, \ldots$ having norm $\|f\|, \|g\|, \ldots$ and let $\mathscr{E}(X)$ be the Banach algebra of endomorphisms of X. If $T \in \mathscr{E}(X)$, $\|T\|$ denotes the norm of T.

Definition 1.1.1. *If $T(t)$ is an operator function on the non-negative real axis $0 \leqq t < \infty$ to the Banach algebra $\mathscr{E}(X)$ satisfying the following* *conditions:*

$$(1.1.1) \begin{cases} \text{(i)}\ T(t_1+t_2) = T(t_1)\,T(t_2) & (t_1, t_2 \geqq 0), \\ \text{(ii)}\ T(0) = I & (I = \textit{identity operator}), \end{cases}$$

then $\{T(t);\ 0 \leqq t < \infty\}$ *is called a **one-parameter semi-group of operators** in* $\mathscr{E}(\mathsf{X})$. *The semi-group* $\{T(t);\ 0 \leqq t < \infty\}$ *is said to be **of class** $(\mathscr{C}_0)$ if it satisfies the further property*

$$(1.1.1) \quad \text{(iii)}\ \operatorname*{s-lim}_{t\to 0+} T(t)\,f = f \qquad (f \in \mathsf{X}),$$

*referred to as the **strong continuity** of* $T(t)$ *at the origin.*

In the text we shall generally assume, unless otherwise stated, that the family of bounded linear operators $\{T(t);\ 0 \leqq t < \infty\}$ mapping X to itself is a semi-group of class $(\mathscr{C}_0)$, thus that all three conditions of the above definition are satisfied.

Proposition 1.1.2. (a) $\|T(t)\|$ *is bounded on every finite subinterval of* $[0, \infty)$.

(b) *For each* $f \in \mathsf{X}$, *the vector-valued function* $T(t)\,f$ *on* $[0, \infty)$ *is strongly continuous.*

(c) *One has*

$$(1.1.2) \qquad \omega_0 \equiv \inf_{t>0} \frac{1}{t} \log \|T(t)\| = \lim_{t\to\infty} \frac{1}{t} \log \|T(t)\| < \infty.$$

(d) *For each* $\omega > \omega_0$, *there exists a constant* M_ω *such that for all* $t \geqq 0$

$$(1.1.3) \qquad \|T(t)\| \leqq M_\omega e^{\omega t}.$$

Proof. Regarding (a), we first show that $\|T(t)\|$ is bounded in some neighborhood of the origin, i.e. there are constants $\delta > 0$ and $M = M(\delta) \geqq 1$ such that $\|T(t)\| \leqq M$ for $0 \leqq t \leqq \delta$. Clearly, if this does not hold, then there exists a sequence $\{t_n\}_{n=1}^{\infty}$, $t_n \to 0+$, such that $\|T(t_n)\| \geqq n$. Since $\{\|T(t_n)\|\}$ is unbounded, by the uniform boundedness theorem (App. 1) $\{\|T(t_n)\,f\|\}$ is unbounded for at least one $f \in \mathsf{X}$. But this is a contradiction to (1.1.1) (iii). Now, given any $t > 0$, we have $t = m\,\delta + \tau$ with $0 \leqq \tau < \delta$ (m integral). Hence

$$\|T(t)\| \leqq \|T(\delta)\|^m\, \|T(\tau)\| \leqq M^{1+m} \leqq M\, M^{t/\delta} = M e^{\omega t},$$

where $\omega = \delta^{-1} \log M \geqq 0$.

To prove (b), we have by hypothesis for a fixed $t > 0$ and $s > 0$

$$\|T(t+s)\,f - T(t)\,f\| \leqq \|T(t)\|\, \|T(s)\,f - f\|,$$

and thus $\operatorname*{s-lim}_{s\to 0+} T(t+s)\,f = T(t)\,f$ for each $f \in \mathsf{X}$. On the other hand, for $0 < s < t$ by part (a)

$$\|T(t-s)\,f - T(t)\,f\| \leqq \|T(t-s)\|\, \|T(s)\,f - f\| \leqq M\, e^{\omega t}\, \|T(s)\,f - f\|,$$

which proves (b).

To establish (c), we set $p(t) = \log \| T(t) \|$. Obviously, $-\infty < p(t) < \infty$ and thus we have for $\omega_0 = \inf_{t>0} t^{-1} p(t)$ that $-\infty \leqq \omega_0 < \infty$. First assume ω_0 to be finite. Then, given any $\varepsilon > 0$, there exists a t_0 such that $p(t_0) \leqq (\omega_0 + \varepsilon) t_0$. In view of the semi-group property (1.1.1) (i), it follows that $p(t_1 + t_2) \leqq p(t_1) + p(t_2)$, and thus for any $t = m t_0 + \tau$ $(0 \leqq \tau < t_0;\ m$ integral) we have

$$\omega_0 \leqq \frac{p(t)}{t} \leqq \frac{p(m t_0)}{t} + \frac{p(\tau)}{t} \leqq \frac{m t_0}{t} \frac{p(t_0)}{t_0} + \frac{p(\tau)}{t}$$

$$\leqq \frac{m t_0}{t} (\omega_0 + \varepsilon) + \frac{\omega t_0 + \log M}{t}$$

by making use of part (a). Hence $\limsup_{t \to \infty} t^{-1} p(t) \leqq \omega_0 + \varepsilon$ for each $\varepsilon > 0$. This proves (1.1.2) for finite ω_0. The case $\omega_0 = -\infty$ may be treated similarly.

Regarding (d), if $\omega > \omega_0$, by (c) there exists a t_0 such that $t^{-1} p(t) \leqq \omega$ for $t \geqq t_0$, i.e. $\| T(t) \| \leqq e^{\omega t}$ for $t \geqq t_0$. By part (a) $\| T(t) \| \leqq M_0$ for $0 \leqq t \leqq t_0$. Thus we have (1.1.3) if we set $M_\omega = M_0$ $(\omega \geqq 0)$, $= e^{-\omega t_0} M_0$ $(\omega < 0)$.

In part (b) of the proposition we have seen that the operator function $T(t)$ is continuous on $[0, \infty)$ in the strong operator topology (App. 2). Thus the family $\{T(t); 0 \leqq t < \infty\}$ is often called a *strongly continuous semi-group* in $\mathscr{E}(\mathsf{X})$. If, in addition, the map $t \to T(t)$ is continuous on $[0, \infty)$ in the uniform operator topology (App. 2), then $\{T(t); 0 \leqq t < \infty\}$ is said to be a *uniformly continuous semi-group* in $\mathscr{E}(\mathsf{X})$. In case the norms of the semi-group operators are bounded uniformly with respect to t, i.e. $\| T(t) \| \leqq M$ (M a constant larger than or equal to one) for all $t \geqq 0$, then $\{T(t); 0 \leqq t < \infty\}$ is called an *equi-bounded semi-group of class* $(\mathscr{C}_0)$ in $\mathscr{E}(\mathsf{X})$, and if the constant M is equal to one a *contraction semi-group of class* $(\mathscr{C}_0)$ in $\mathscr{E}(\mathsf{X})$.

Definition 1.1.3. *The infinitesimal generator A of the semi-group $\{T(t); 0 \leqq t < \infty\}$ is defined by*

$$(1.1.4) \qquad A f \equiv \operatorname*{s-lim}_{\tau \to 0+} A_\tau f, \quad A_\tau = \frac{1}{\tau} [T(\tau) - I]$$

whenever the limit exists; the domain of A, in symbols $\mathsf{D}(A)$, being the set of elements f for which this limit exists.

Proposition 1.1.4. (a) *$\mathsf{D}(A)$ is a linear manifold in X and A is a linear operator.*

(b) *If $f \in \mathsf{D}(A)$, then $T(t) f \in \mathsf{D}(A)$ for each $t \geqq 0$ and*

$$(1.1.5) \qquad \frac{d}{dt} T(t) f = A\, T(t) f = T(t) A f \qquad (t \geqq 0);$$

furthermore,

$$T(t)\, f - f = \int_0^t T(u)\, A\, f\, du \qquad (t > 0). \tag{1.1.6}$$

(c) $D(A)$ *is dense in* X, *i.e.* $\overline{D(A)} = X$, *and* A *is a closed operator.*

Proof. Part (a) follows immediately by definition. To prove (b) let $\tau > 0$. For a fixed $t \geqq 0$ we have

$$\frac{T(t+\tau) - T(t)}{\tau}\, f = T(t)\, A_\tau f = A_\tau T(t)\, f.$$

If $f \in D(A)$, then for the middle part of the equation the limit in norm exists as $\tau \to 0+$ and thus the other limits too. In particular $T(t)\, f \in D(A)$, and the strong right derivative of $T(t)\, f$ is equal to $T(t)\, A\, f = A\, T(t)\, f$. On the other hand, for $t > 0$ and τ sufficiently small

$$\frac{T(t-\tau) - T(t)}{-\tau}\, f = T(t-\tau)\, A_\tau f.$$

Applying Proposition 1.1.2 (b), we have $\operatorname{s-lim}_{\tau \to 0+} T(t-\tau)\, A\, f = T(t)\, A\, f$ and thus

$$\operatorname{s-lim}_{\tau \to 0+} \frac{T(t-\tau) - T(t)}{-\tau}\, f = T(t)\, A\, f.$$

Hence, the strong left derivative of $T(t)\, f$ exists for each $f \in D(A)$ and is equal to the strong right derivative. Now, applying linear functionals $f^* \in X^*$ (X^* being the dual space of X) to both sides of (1.1.5) and integrating, we obtain

$$\langle f^*, T(t)\, f - f\rangle = \int_0^t \frac{d}{du} \langle f^*, T(u)\, f\rangle\, du = \int_0^t \langle f^*, \frac{d}{du} T(u)\, f\rangle\, du$$

$$= \int_0^t \langle f^*, T(u)\, A\, f\rangle\, du = \langle f^*, \int_0^t T(u)\, A\, f\, du\rangle.$$

By a corollary of the theorem of Hahn-Banach (App. 1) this proves relation (1.1.6). The integral in (1.1.6) is to be understood as a vector-valued Riemann integral (App. 2).

A proof of part (c) may be given as follows. For any $f \in X$ and $t, \tau > 0$,

$$A_\tau \int_0^t T(u)\, f\, du = \frac{1}{\tau} \int_0^t [T(\tau) - I]\, T(u)\, f\, du \tag{1.1.7}$$

$$= \frac{1}{\tau} \int_\tau^{t+\tau} T(u)\, f\, du - \frac{1}{\tau} \int_0^t T(u)\, f\, du$$

$$= \frac{1}{\tau} \int_0^\tau T(u)\, [T(t) - I]\, f\, du.$$

When $\tau \to 0+$, the right-hand side of the equation tends to $[T(t) - I]f$ in norm, since $T(u)f$ is strongly continuous in $u \geqq 0$ for each $f \in \mathsf{X}$. Thus $\int_0^t T(u) f\, du \in \mathsf{D}(A)$, and using again the fact that $\operatorname{s-lim}_{t\to 0+} \frac{1}{t}\int_0^t T(u) f\, du = f$, this shows that $\mathsf{D}(A)$ is dense in X. To prove that A is closed, let $\{f_n\}_{n=1}^{\infty}$ be a sequence of elements in $\mathsf{D}(A)$ converging to f_0 with $A f_n$ converging to g_0. Then by Proposition 1.1.2 (a)

$$\| T(u)\, A f_n - T(u)\, g_0 \| \leqq M\, e^{\omega t}\, \| A f_n - g_0 \|,$$

which tends to zero uniformly with respect to u in $[0, t]$. Replacing f by f_n in (1.1.6) and passing to the limit in norm as $n \to \infty$, we thus obtain

$$T(t)\, f_0 - f_0 = \int_0^t T(u)\, g_0\, du.$$

Hence, $A_t f_0 = \frac{1}{t}\int_0^t T(u)\, g_0\, du \to g_0$ in norm as $t \to 0+$, giving $f_0 \in \mathsf{D}(A)$ and $A f_0 = g_0$. This proves that A is closed.

A simple consequence of the fact that the infinitesimal generator is closed is that its domain $\mathsf{D}(A)$ is a Banach space under the norm

(1.1.8) $$\| f \|_{\mathsf{D}(A)} = \| f \| + \| A f \|.$$

Clearly, the graph of A, by definition the set of elements

$$\{(f, A f);\ f \in \mathsf{D}(A)\}$$

in the product space $\mathsf{X} \times \mathsf{X}$, is a closed linear manifold in $\mathsf{X} \times \mathsf{X}$ and thus a Banach space itself under the norm of $\mathsf{X} \times \mathsf{X}$, i.e. under the norm given by (1.1.8).

Definition 1.1.5. *For* $r = 0, 1, 2, \ldots$ *the operator* A^r *is defined inductively by the relations* $A^0 = I$, $A^1 = A$, *and*

$$\mathsf{D}(A^r) = \{f;\ f \in \mathsf{D}(A^{r-1}) \text{ and } A^{r-1} f \in \mathsf{D}(A)\}$$
$$A^r f = A(A^{r-1} f) = \operatorname{s-lim}_{\tau\to 0+} A_\tau (A^{r-1} f) \qquad (f \in \mathsf{D}(A^r)).$$

For the operator A^r and its domain $\mathsf{D}(A^r)$ we have the following

Proposition 1.1.6. (a) $\mathsf{D}(A^r)$ *is a linear subspace in* X *and* A^r *is a linear operator.*

(b) *If* $f \in \mathsf{D}(A^r)$, *so does* $T(t) f$ *for each* $t \geqq 0$ *and*

(1.1.9) $$\frac{d^r}{dt^r} T(t)\, f = A^r\, T(t)\, f = T(t)\, A^r f.$$

Moreover

(1.1.10) $$T(t)\, f - \sum_{k=0}^{r-1} \frac{t^k}{k!} A^k f = \frac{1}{(r-1)!} \int_0^t (t-u)^{r-1}\, T(u)\, A^r f\, du$$

and

(1.1.11)

$$[T(t) - I]^r f = \int_0^t \int_0^t \cdots \int_0^t T(u_1 + u_2 + \cdots + u_r)\, A^r f\, du_1\, du_2 \ldots du_r.$$

(c) $\mathsf{D}(A^r)$ *is dense in* X *for each* $r = 1, 2, \ldots$; *furthermore,* $\bigcap_{r=1}^{\infty} \mathsf{D}(A^r)$ *is dense in* X. A^r *is a closed operator.*

Proof. Part (a) is evident. Relation (1.1.9) of part (b) is a generalization of (1.1.5) and follows by induction. Moreover, repeated integration of the formula

$$T(t)\, A^{r-1} f - A^{r-1} f = \int_0^t T(u)\, A^r f\, du$$

leads to *Taylor's formula* (1.1.10), while the equation (1.1.11) is a direct generalization of (1.1.6).

It remains to prove part (c). Let $\mathsf{C}_{00}^{\infty}(\mathrm{E}_1^+)$ be the class of all numerically-valued functions defined on the positive real axis $\mathrm{E}_1^+ = \{t; 0 < t < \infty\}$ having continuous derivatives of all orders and compact support. If $\varphi \in \mathsf{C}_{00}^{\infty}(\mathrm{E}_1^+)$, so is $\varphi^{(r)} \in \mathsf{C}_{00}^{\infty}(\mathrm{E}_1^+)$ for all $r = 1, 2, \ldots$, and the map $u \to \varphi(u)\, T(u)\, f$ defines a strongly continuous vector-valued function on E_1^+ to X for each $f \in \mathsf{X}$. Let X_{00} be the set of all elements of the form

(1.1.12)
$$g = \int_0^{\infty} \varphi(u)\, T(u)\, f\, du \qquad (\varphi \in \mathsf{C}_{00}^{\infty}(\mathrm{E}_1^+),\ f \in \mathsf{X}).$$

(The integral is well defined.) X_{00} is a linear manifold in X. We shall show that $\mathsf{X}_{00} \subset \mathsf{D}(A^r)$ for each $r = 1, 2, \ldots$ and that X_{00} is dense in X.

Now, for τ sufficiently small

$$A_\tau g = \frac{1}{\tau} \int_0^{\infty} \varphi(u)\, \{T(u + \tau)\, f - T(u)\, f\}\, du$$

$$= \frac{1}{\tau} \int_0^{\infty} \{\varphi(u - \tau) - \varphi(u)\}\, T(u)\, f\, du.$$

By assumption, $\tau^{-1}\{\varphi(u - \tau) - \varphi(u)\} \to -\varphi'(u)$ as $\tau \to 0+$ uniformly with respect to u in the support of φ. Thus

$$A\, g = \operatorname*{s-lim}_{\tau \to 0+} A_\tau\, g = -\int_0^{\infty} \varphi'(u)\, T(u)\, f\, du.$$

Repeating the argument we have $g \in \mathsf{D}(A^r)$ for each integer $r > 0$ and

$$A^r g = (-1)^r \int_0^\infty \varphi^{(r)}(u)\, T(u)\, f\, du,$$

which shows that $\mathsf{X}_{00} \subset \bigcap_{r=1}^{\infty} \mathsf{D}(A^r)$.

Let us suppose that X_{00} is not dense in X. Then there exists an element $f_0 \in \mathsf{X}$ having positive distance from X_{00}, and by a corollary of the theorem of Hahn-Banach (App. 1) a bounded linear functional f_0^* on X such that $\langle f_0^*, g\rangle = 0$ for all $g \in \mathsf{X}_{00}$ and $\langle f_0^*, f_0\rangle = 1$. This implies that

$$\langle f_0^*, \int_0^\infty \varphi(u)\, T(u)\, f\, du\rangle = \int_0^\infty \varphi(u)\, \langle f_0^*, T(u)\, f\rangle\, du = 0$$

for each $\varphi \in \mathsf{C}_{00}^\infty(\mathrm{E}_1^+)$ and each $f \in \mathsf{X}$. But $\langle f_0^*, T(u)\, f_0\rangle$ is a continuous function in $u \geqq 0$ with $\langle f_0^*, f_0\rangle = 1$, and it is easy to see that there is a $\varphi \in \mathsf{C}_{00}^\infty(\mathrm{E}_1^+)$ such that $\int_0^\infty \varphi(u)\, \langle f_0^*, T(u)\, f_0\rangle\, du \neq 0$. This is a contradiction to the latter equation. Therefore X_{00} and also $\bigcap_{r=1}^{\infty} \mathsf{D}(A^r)$ are dense in X.

It is readily verified that A^r is a closed operator and that its domain $\mathsf{D}(A^r)$ is a Banach space under the norm

$$\|f\|_{\mathsf{D}(A^r)} = \|f\| + \|A f\| + \cdots + \|A^r f\|. \tag{1.1.13}$$

Indeed, by definition, A^2 is a linear transformation with domain $\mathsf{D}(A^2)$ in $\mathsf{D}(A)$ to X. Thus A^2 is closed if its graph is closed in the product space $\mathsf{D}(A) \times \mathsf{X}$ with norm $\|f\|_{\mathsf{D}(A)} + \|f\|_{\mathsf{X}}$.

Remark. If B is any operator in $\mathscr{E}(\mathsf{X})$, then the operator function

$$T(t) = \exp(t B) \equiv I + \sum_{k=1}^{\infty} \frac{(t B)^k}{k!} \qquad (0 \leqq t < \infty) \tag{1.1.14}$$

defines a semi-group in $\mathscr{E}(\mathsf{X})$. Indeed, by the definition and the properties of the ordinary exponential function one obtains that $\|T(t)\| \leqq \exp(t\, \|B\|)$ for all $t \geqq 0$ and that $\{T(t);\, 0 \leqq t < \infty\}$ satisfies the semi-group properties (1.1.1) (i) and (ii). Moreover, it is not difficult to prove that $T(t)$ is continuous, even continuously differentiable in $0 \leqq t < \infty$ in the uniform operator topology. Thus $\{T(t);\, 0 \leqq t < \infty\}$ forms a uniformly continuous semi-group in $\mathscr{E}(\mathsf{X})$, its infinitesimal generator is given by B and

$$\frac{d}{dt} \exp(t B) = B \exp(t B) = \exp(t B)\, B \qquad (0 \leqq t < \infty).$$

On the other hand, it may be shown that every uniformly continuous semi-group in $\mathscr{E}(\mathsf{X})$ is of the form (1.1.14).

We now consider briefly *n-parameter semi-groups of operators*. Let E_n be the n-dimensional Euclidean space supplied with the usual definitions of arithmetical operations and metric. We write $t = (t_1, t_2, \ldots, t_n)$ and denote the unit vectors by $e_1, \ldots, e_n$, where $e_k = (0, \ldots, 0, 1, 0, \ldots, 0)$ with 1 in the k-th place and zero elsewhere. Furthermore, let $\overline{E_n^+} = \{t \in E_n; t_k \geqq 0, k = 1, 2, \ldots, n\}$, the first closed 2^n-ant in E_n.

Definition 1.1.7. *A familiy of bounded linear operators* $\{T(t); t \in \overline{E_n^+}\}$ *on* X *is called an n-parameter semi-group of class* $(\mathscr{C}_0)$ *in* $\mathscr{E}(X)$ *when the following three conditions are satisfied:*

(i) $$T(t+s) = T(t)\,T(s) \qquad (t, s \in \overline{E_n^+});$$

(ii) $$T(0) = I;$$

(iii) $$\operatorname*{s-lim}_{\substack{t \in \overline{E_n^+} \\ t \to 0}} T(t)\,f = f \qquad (f \in X).$$

Proposition 1.1.8. *If* $\{T(t); t \in \overline{E_n^+}\}$ *is an n-parameter semi-group of operators of class* $(\mathscr{C}_0)$ *in* $\mathscr{E}(X)$, *then* $\{T(t); t \in \overline{E_n^+}\}$ *is the direct product of n one-parameter semi-groups* $\{T_k(t_k); 0 \leqq t_k < \infty\}$ *of class* $(\mathscr{C}_0)$ *in* $\mathscr{E}(X)$ *such that*

$$T(t) = \prod_{k=1}^{n} T_k(t_k), \tag{1.1.15}$$

where $T_k(t_k) = T(t_k e_k)$. *The operators* $T_k(t_k)$, $0 \leqq t_k < \infty$ $(k = 1, 2, \ldots, n)$, *commute with each other.*

The proof follows very easily by a reduction to the one-parameter case.

Using the decomposition (1.1.15) of the n-parameter semi-group $\{T(t); t \in \overline{E_n^+}\}$, one can prove several assertions for this semi-group by applying the preceding propositions on one-parameter semi-groups of operators. For this purpose, let A_k be the infinitesimal generator of $\{T_k(t_k); 0 \leqq t_k < \infty\}$ with domain $D(A_k)$, $k = 1, 2, \ldots, n$.

Proposition 1.1.9. (a) $\|T(t)\|$ *is bounded on every finite subinterval in* $\overline{E_n^+}$, *and* $T(t)$ *is continuous in the strong operator topology on* $\overline{E_n^+}$.

(b) *If* f *belongs to* $D(A_k)$, *so does* $T(t)\,f$ *for each* $t \in \overline{E_n^+}$ *and*

$$A_k\,T(t)\,f = T(t)\,A_k\,f \qquad (k = 1, 2, \ldots, n).$$

(c) $\bigcap_{k=1}^{n} D(A_k)$ *is a dense subspace in* X *and moreover a Banach space with norm*

$$\|f\|_{\bigcap_{k=1}^{n} D(A_k)} = \|f\| + \sum_{k=1}^{n} \|A_k\,f\|.$$

(d) *If* f *belongs to* $\mathsf{D}(A_j)$ *and* $\mathsf{D}(A_j A_k)$, *then* f *is also in* $\mathsf{D}(A_k A_j)$ *and* $A_k A_j f = A_j A_k f (j, k = 1, 2, \ldots, n; j \neq k)$.

We shall not prove this proposition explicitly. Let us only mention that part (d) is related to the well-known theorem of H. A. Schwarz concerning partial derivatives of functions of several variables.

1.1.2 Holomorphic Semi-Groups

In this subsection we shall discuss in greater detail a particular class of semi-groups of operators $\{T(t); 0 \leqq t < \infty\}$ of class $(\mathscr{C}_0)$ in $\mathscr{E}(\mathsf{X})$, namely those for which the range of $T(t)$ in X, denoted by $T(t)[\mathsf{X}]$, belongs to $\mathsf{D}(A)$ for each $t > 0$. Here we assume X to be a complex Banach space.

Proposition 1.1.10. *Let* $\{T(t); 0 \leqq t < \infty\}$ *be of class* $(\mathscr{C}_0)$ *in* $\mathscr{E}(\mathsf{X})$. *If* $T(t)[\mathsf{X}] \subset \mathsf{D}(A)$ *for each* $t > 0$, *then* $T^{(1)}(t) = A\,T(t)$ *exists as a bounded linear operator for all* $t > 0$ *and* $T(t)$ *is continuous in the uniform operator topology in* $0 < t < \infty$. *Moreover,* $T(t)$ *is* r *times continuously differentiable in the uniform operator topology for* $0 < t < \infty$ *and all integers* $r > 0$, *and* $T^{(r)}(t) = A^r T(t)$.

Proof. By assumption $T(t)$ maps X into $\mathsf{D}(A)$ for each $t > 0$. Thus for a $t > 0$, $A\,T(t) f = \underset{\tau \to 0+}{\text{s-lim}}\, A_\tau T(t) f$ exists for all $f \in \mathsf{X}$. Applying the uniform boundedness theorem, $A\,T(t)$ is a bounded linear operator. Furthermore, for any fixed $\delta > 0$

$$T(t+\tau) f - T(t) f = \int_t^{t+\tau} A\,T(u) f\,du \qquad (t, t+\tau > \delta;\ f \in \mathsf{X}),$$

and since $\|A\,T(u)\| \leqq \|T(u-\delta)\|\ \|A\,T(\delta)\|$, $u \geqq \delta$, we have $\|T(t+\tau) - T(t)\| = O(|\tau|)$ as $|\tau| \to 0$. Thus $T(t)$ is continuous in the uniform operator topology for each $t > 0$.

To prove the latter part of the theorem we have for any $t > 0$ and all $f \in \mathsf{X}$ that $T^{(1)}(t) f = T(t/2)\,[A\,T(t/2) f]$ belongs to $\mathsf{D}(A)$ and

$$T^{(2)}(t) f = \underset{\tau \to 0+}{\text{s-lim}}\, A_\tau T(t/2)\,[A\,T(t/2) f] = [A\,T(t/2)]^2 f = A^2 T(t) f.$$

By induction,

$$T^{(r)}(t) f = [A\,T(t/r)]^r f = A^r T(t) f \qquad (t > 0;\ f \in \mathsf{X}).$$

This equation shows that $T^{(r)}(t)$ is a bounded linear operator for each $t > 0$. Furthermore, since $T(t)$ is continuous in the uniform operator topology for $t > 0$, by the equation $T^{(r)}(t) = T(t-\delta)\,A^r T(\delta)$ for $t \geqq \delta$, $\delta > 0$ being arbitrary, the same is true for $T^{(r)}(t)$. Hence

$$T^{(r-1)}(t+\tau) - T^{(r-1)}(t) = \int_t^{t+\tau} T^{(r)}(u)\,du \qquad (t, t+\tau > 0),$$

or $T^{(r-1)}(t)$ is differentiable in the uniform operator topology for all $t > 0$, which proves the theorem.

Under the assumptions of the above proposition the semi-group $\{T(t); 0 \leqq t < \infty\}$ considered as an operator function on $[0, \infty)$ into $\mathscr{E}(\mathsf{X})$ is r times continuously differentiable on $(0, \infty)$ in the uniform operator topology for all $r = 1, 2, \ldots$ From this fact, however, it does not necessarily follow that $T(t)$ is analytic. But the next proposition shows that if in addition $\|A\,T(t)\| = O(t^{-1})$ $(t \to 0+)$, then $T(t)$ admits a holomorphic extension $T(\zeta)$ in a sector of the half-plane $\operatorname{Re}\zeta > 0$. (For the definition and basic properties of a holomorphic operator function see App. 2.) We have:

Proposition 1.1.11. *If $\{T(t); 0 \leqq t < \infty\}$ is of class $(\mathscr{C}_0)$ in $\mathscr{E}(\mathsf{X})$ such that for each $t > 0$ $T(t)[\mathsf{X}] \subset \mathsf{D}(A)$ and if there is a constant $N > 0$ with $t\,\|A\,T(t)\| \leqq N$ $(0 < t \leqq 1)$, then this semi-group has a holomorphic extension $\{T(\zeta); \zeta \in \Delta\}$, where $\Delta = \{\zeta;\ \operatorname{Re}\zeta > 0, |\arg\zeta| < 1/(eN)\}$, thus:*

(i) *$T(\zeta)$ is a holomorphic operator function in Δ with values in $\mathscr{E}(\mathsf{X})$;*

(ii) *$T(\zeta_1)\,T(\zeta_2) = T(\zeta_1 + \zeta_2)$ whenever $\zeta_1, \zeta_2 \in \Delta$;*

(iii) *$\operatorname*{s-lim}_{\zeta \to 0} T(\zeta) f = f$ for all $f \in \mathsf{X}$, where $|\arg\zeta| \leqq \varepsilon/(e\,N)$ $(0 < \varepsilon < 1)$;*

and conversely.

Proof. (i) Let $t_0 > 0$. By Taylor's formula we obtain

$$T(t) = \sum_{k=0}^{r-1} \frac{(t-t_0)^k}{k!} A^k\,T(t_0) + \frac{1}{(r-1)!} \int_{t_0}^{t} (t-u)^{r-1} A^r\,T(u)\,du \qquad (r = 1, 2, \ldots).$$

Since $\|A^r\,T(u)\| \leqq \|A\,T(u/r)\|^r \leqq N^r (r/u)^r$ for $0 < u/r \leqq 1$, the remainder term of Taylor's formula is majorized in the norm by

$$\frac{r^r}{r!} N^r \frac{(t-t_0)^r}{t_0^r} < \left(e\,N\,\frac{t-t_0}{t_0}\right)^r$$

for $t \geqq t_0 > 0$ and r sufficiently large. Therefore, if $t - t_0 < t_0/(e\,N)$, the Taylor expansion converges for these values of t and represents $T(t)$. On the other hand, the Taylor series

$$\sum_{k=0}^{\infty} \frac{(\zeta-t_0)^k}{k!} A^k\,T(t_0) \tag{1.1.16}$$

converges for $|\zeta - t_0| < t_0/(e\,N)$ and defines a holomorphic operator function $T(\zeta)$ in this circle. Since $t_0 > 0$ was arbitrary, this implies that the semi-group operators can be extended to a holomorphic function in Δ.

(ii) We remark that

$$\frac{d}{d\zeta} T(\zeta) = A\,T(\zeta) = \sum_{k=0}^{\infty} \frac{(\zeta - t_0)^k}{k!} A^{k+1} T(t_0) \qquad (\zeta \in \Delta).$$

Now, for a fixed $t > 0$ we have

$$T(t)\,T(\zeta) = \sum_{k=0}^{\infty} \frac{(\zeta - t_0)^k}{k!} A^k T(t_0 + t)$$

$$= \sum_{k=0}^{\infty} \frac{[(\zeta + t) - (t_0 + t)]^k}{k!} A^k T(t_0 + t) = T(\zeta + t).$$

Using this particular result, one obtains by the same argument the semi-group property of the extension $T(\zeta)$ in Δ.

(iii) We first show that $\|T(\zeta)\|$ is bounded uniformly with respect to ζ in any region $\Delta_{\varepsilon, b} = \{\zeta; 0 < \operatorname{Re}\zeta \leqq b, |\arg\zeta| \leqq \varepsilon/(e N)\ (0 < \varepsilon < 1)\}$. Indeed, let ζ belong to this region. Then for $t = \operatorname{Re}\zeta > 0$, $|\zeta - t|/t \leqq \leqq \varepsilon/(e N)$, and consequently by (1.1.16)

$$\|T(\zeta)\| \leqq \|T(t)\| + \sum_{k=1}^{\infty} \frac{|\zeta - t|^k}{k!} \|A^k T(t)\|$$

$$\leqq \|T(t)\| + \sum_{k=1}^{\infty} \varepsilon^k \leqq M_b + \frac{\varepsilon}{1 - \varepsilon} = M_{\varepsilon, b}.$$

The last estimate follows by the fact that $\{T(t); 0 \leqq t < \infty\}$ is of class $(\mathscr{C}_0)$, implying that $\|T(t)\|$ is bounded on every finite subinterval $[0, b]$.

Again by the $(\mathscr{C}_0)$-property of the semi-group one obtains that the union $\mathsf{X}_0 \equiv \bigcup_{0<t<\infty} T(t)[\mathsf{X}]$ is dense in X. Furthermore, $T(\zeta)\,T(t)\,f = T(\zeta + t)\,f \to T(t)\,f$ in norm as $\zeta \to 0$ for all $f \in \mathsf{X}$ and each $t > 0$. Hence, $\|T(\zeta)\|$ being bounded on $\Delta_{\varepsilon, b}$, the assertion follows from the Banach-Steinhaus theorem (App. 1). This proves the proposition in one direction.

Conversely, let $T(\zeta)$ be an operator function in $\Delta = \{\zeta; \operatorname{Re}\zeta > 0, |\arg\zeta| < \alpha_0 \leqq \pi/2\}$ satisfying the conditions (i), (ii) and (iii). Clearly, under the convention $T(0) = I$, we see that for t real $\{T(t); 0 \leqq t < \infty\}$ defines a semi-group of class $(\mathscr{C}_0)$ and $T(t)[\mathsf{X}]$ belongs to $\mathsf{D}(A)$ whenever $t > 0$. Furthermore, by the same reasoning as applied in the proof of Proposition 1.1.2 (a), we can deduce from (iii) that $\|T(\zeta)\| \leqq M_{\alpha, 2}$ in the region $\Delta_{\alpha, 2} = \{0 \leqq \operatorname{Re}\zeta \leqq 2, |\arg\zeta| \leqq \alpha < \alpha_0\}$. Let $0 < t \leqq 1$. By Cauchy's integral formula (App. 2)

$$A\,T(t) = T^{(1)}(t) = \frac{1}{2\pi i} \int_{|\zeta - t| = (\sin\alpha)t} \frac{T(\zeta)}{(\zeta - t)^2}\, d\zeta,$$

and consequently

$$\| A\,T(t) \| \leqq \frac{M_{\alpha,2}}{\sin\alpha}\,\frac{1}{t} = N\,t^{-1}$$

uniformly with respect to t in $(0, 1]$. Thus the proof is complete.

In the following we shall call a semi-group of the class discussed in Proposition 1.1.11 *a holomorphic semi-group of class* $(\mathscr{C}_0)$.

Corollary 1.1.12. *If* $\{T(t); 0 \leqq t < \infty\}$ *is a holomorphic semi-group of class* $(\mathscr{C}_0)$ *with unbounded infinitesimal generator* A, *then*

$$\limsup_{t \to 0+} (t\,\| A\,T(t) \|) \geqq e^{-1}. \tag{1.1.17}$$

Proof. Suppose that $\limsup_{t \to 0+} (e\,t\,\| A\,T(t) \|) < 1$. Then there are constants ϱ, $0 < \varrho < 1$, and $\delta > 0$ such that $t\,\| A\,T(t) \| \leqq \varrho\,e^{-1}$ for $0 < t \leqq \delta$. Consequently, the series (1.1.16) converges for $|\zeta - t_0| < t_0/\varrho$. Since this circle contains the origin, it follows in particular that $T(t)$ is continuous on $[0, \infty)$ in the uniform operator topology, and thus $T(t)$ is given by (1.1.14) with bounded infinitesimal operator.

We shall see later on (e.g. Sec. 1.5.4) that the inequality (1.1.17) is sharp.

1.2 Representation Theorems for Semi-Groups of Operators

1.2.1 First Exponential Formula

In this section we wish to represent the semi-group $\{T(t); 0 \leqq t < \infty\}$ by its infinitesimal generator A. We have seen in the first section that a uniformly continuous semi-group in $\mathscr{E}(\mathsf{X})$ can be expressed by

$$T(t) = \exp(t\,A) \qquad (0 \leqq t < \infty).$$

But as the generator A of a strongly continuous semi-group is in general not defined over the whole space, we show that in this case it is possible to represent $T(t)\,f$ as the strong limit for $\tau \to 0+$ of the exponential formula

$$\exp(t\,A_\tau)\,f \equiv \left\{\sum_{k=0}^{\infty} \frac{t^k}{k!}\,A_\tau^k\right\} f \qquad (f \in \mathsf{X}). \tag{1.2.1}$$

This result is often referred to as *Hille's first exponential formula* and it is the first fundamental theorem in the theory of semi-groups of operators. For the proof of this theorem which follows below and for later applications we need

Lemma 1.2.1. (a) *For* $N > 0$ *and* $u \geqq 0$ *we have*

$$e^{-u} \sum_{|k-u| > N} \frac{u^k}{k!} \leqq \frac{u}{N^2}. \tag{1.2.2}$$

(b) *For* $u \geqq 0$

$$\sum_{k=0}^{\infty} |k-u| \frac{u^k}{k!} \leqq \sqrt{u}\, e^u. \tag{1.2.3}$$

Proof. It follows readily that

$$\sum_{k=0}^{\infty} (k-u)^2 \frac{u^k}{k!} = u\, e^u,$$

giving

$$N^2 \sum_{|k-u|>N} \frac{u^k}{k!} < \sum_{k=0}^{\infty} (k-u)^2 \frac{u^k}{k!} = u\, e^u,$$

which proves (1.2.2). To prove (1.2.3), according to Schwarz's inequality we have

$$\sum_{k=0}^{\infty} |k-u| \frac{u^k}{k!} \leqq \left\{\sum_{k=0}^{\infty} (k-u)^2 \frac{u^k}{k!}\right\}^{1/2} \left\{\sum_{k=0}^{\infty} \frac{u^k}{k!}\right\}^{1/2} = \sqrt{u}\, e^u.$$

Let $\omega(\delta; T(\cdot) f)$ be the *rectified modulus of continuity* of $T(t) f$ in $[0, b]$, i.e.

$$\omega(\delta; T(\cdot) f) = \sup\{\|T(t) f - T(s) f\|;\ 0 \leqq t, s \leqq b, |t-s| \leqq \delta\}.$$

Theorem 1.2.2. *Suppose* $\{T(t); 0 \leqq t < \infty\}$ *is a semi-group of class* $(\mathscr{C}_0)$ *in* $\mathscr{E}(\mathsf{X})$. *Then for each* $f \in \mathsf{X}$ *and each* $t \geqq 0$

$$T(t) f = \operatorname*{s-lim}_{\tau \to 0+} \exp(t A_\tau) f, \tag{1.2.4}$$

the limit existing uniformly with respect to t in any finite interval $[0, b]$. *More specifically, if* $\omega(\delta; T(\cdot) f)$ *is the rectified modulus of continuity of* $T(t) f$ *in* $[0, b+1]$ *and* $\|T(t)\| \leqq M$ *for* $0 \leqq t \leqq 1$ $(M > 1)$, *then for small* $\tau > 0$ *and* $0 \leqq t \leqq b$

$$\|\exp(t A_\tau) f - T(t) f\| \leqq \omega(\tau^{1/3}; T(\cdot) f) + K \tau^{1/3} \|f\|, \tag{1.2.5}$$

where $K = K(b, M)$ *is a positive constant independent of* τ.

Proof. Since A_τ is bounded for each fixed $\tau > 0$, the operator $\exp(t A_\tau)$ defined by (1.2.1) is a bounded linear operator in $\mathscr{E}(\mathsf{X})$. Furthermore, according to the assumption that $\|T(t)\| \leqq M$ for $0 \leqq t \leqq 1$, we have by Proposition 1.1.2 (a) that $\|T(t)\| \leqq M^{1+t}$ for all $t \geqq 0$. Thus

$$\exp(t A_\tau) = e^{-t/\tau} \sum_{k=0}^{\infty} \left(\frac{t}{\tau}\right)^k \frac{[T(\tau)]^k}{k!}$$

and

$$\|\exp(t A_\tau)\| \leqq e^{-t/\tau} M \sum_{k=0}^{\infty} \left(\frac{t}{\tau}\right)^k \frac{(M^\tau)^k}{k!} = M \exp\left\{t \frac{M^\tau - 1}{\tau}\right\}.$$

Consequently, by the inequality

$$\frac{t}{\tau} \leqq \frac{t}{\tau} M^\tau \leqq \frac{t}{\tau} + t(M-1) \qquad (M > 1,\ 0 < \tau \leqq 1) \tag{1.2.6}$$

the norm of $\exp(t A_\tau)$ is uniformly bounded by $M\, e^{b(M-1)}$ for $0 \leqq t \leqq b$ and $0 < \tau \leqq 1$.

We have for each $f \in X$

$$\exp(t A_\tau) f - T(t) f = e^{-t/\tau} \sum_{k=0}^{\infty} \left(\frac{t}{\tau}\right)^k \frac{1}{k!} [T(k\tau) - T(t)] f$$

and thus

$$\|\exp(t A_\tau) f - T(t) f\| \leqq e^{-t/\tau} \sum_{k=0}^{\infty} \left(\frac{t}{\tau}\right)^k \frac{1}{k!} \|T(k\tau) f - T(t) f\|.$$

Let us split the summation on the right-hand side as a sum of two parts: $\sum'$ and $\sum''$, the summations $\sum'$ and $\sum''$ being extended over all $k = 0, 1, 2, \ldots$, subject respectively to the conditions

$$\textstyle\sum'\colon\ |k - t/\tau| \leqq \tau^{-2/3}; \qquad \sum''\colon\ |k - t/\tau| > \tau^{-2/3}.$$

For the sum $\sum'$ we have immediately

$$e^{-t/\tau} \textstyle\sum' \leqq e^{-t/\tau}\, \omega(\tau^{1/3}; T(\cdot) f) \displaystyle\sum_{k=0}^{\infty} \left(\frac{t}{\tau}\right)^k \frac{1}{k!} = \omega(\tau^{1/3}; T(\cdot) f).$$

Regarding $\sum''$,

$$\textstyle\sum'' \leqq \sum'' \displaystyle\left(\frac{t}{\tau}\right)^k \frac{1}{k!} \|T(k\tau)\| \, \|f\| + \textstyle\sum'' \displaystyle\left(\frac{t}{\tau}\right)^k \frac{1}{k!} \|T(t)\| \, \|f\| = \textstyle\sum_1'' + \sum_2'',$$

and in view of the inequality (1.2.6) we have, if τ is small enough $\left(2b(M-1) \leqq \tau^{-2/3}\right)$,

$$\begin{aligned} e^{-t/\tau} \textstyle\sum_1'' &\leqq M\, e^{-t/\tau} \displaystyle\sum_{|k - t/\tau| > \tau^{-2/3}} \left(\frac{t}{\tau}\right)^k \frac{(M^\tau)^k}{k!} \|f\| \\ &\leqq M\, e^{-t/\tau} \sum_{|k - (t/\tau) M^\tau| > \frac{\tau^{-2/3}}{2}} \left(\frac{t\, M^\tau}{\tau}\right)^k \frac{1}{k!} \|f\|. \end{aligned}$$

By the estimate (1.2.2) of Lemma 1.2.1 it follows that

$$e^{-t/\tau} \textstyle\sum_1'' \leqq 4M^2\, b\, e^{b(M-1)}\, \tau^{1/3} \|f\|.$$

Also,

$$e^{-t/\tau} \textstyle\sum_2'' \leqq M^{b+1}\, b\, \tau^{1/3} \|f\|.$$

This proves relation (1.2.5) of the theorem with the constant $K = M\, b(M^b + 4M\, e^{b(M-1)})$ and thus the theorem itself.

The question as to whether the estimate on the right-hand side of (1.2.5) can be improved to the form $\omega(\tau^\gamma; T(\cdot) f) + K \tau^\gamma \|f\|$ with $\gamma > 1/3$ remains undecided.

If, however, an element $f \in X$ is such that $T(t) f$ satisfies the *Lipschitz type condition*

$$\|T(t) f - T(s) f\| \leqq L(f) \frac{|t - s|^\gamma}{|t + s|^{\gamma/2}} \qquad (0 < t, s < \infty), \tag{1.2.7}$$

where $L(f)$ is a constant dependent on f only, with the exponent γ, $0 < \gamma \leqq 1$, and $\{T(t); 0 < t < \infty\}$ a semi-group of operators in $\mathscr{E}(X)$ (thus (1.1.1) (i) holding with zero excluded), then we can prove a more precise estimate of the approximation of $T(t)f$ by $\exp(tA_\tau)f$ than given in (1.2.5) not only for each finite interval within $(0, \infty)$ but even for the whole infinite interval. This is given by the proposition below.

Obviously, the exponent γ of (1.2.7) is bounded by one. For if $\gamma > 1$, then $T(t)f$ is strongly differentiable in $(0, \infty)$ and its (strong) derivative equals θ everywhere in $(0, \infty)$. Thus $T(t)f$ is a constant. In case $\{T(t); 0 \leqq t < \infty\}$ is even of class $(\mathscr{C}_0)$ in $\mathscr{E}(\mathsf{X})$, we have $T(t)f = f$ for all $t \geqq 0$.

Proposition 1.2.3. *Let* $\{T(t); 0 < t < \infty\}$ *be a semi-group of operators in* $\mathscr{E}(\mathsf{X})$. *If* $f \in \mathsf{X}$ *is such that* $T(t)f$ *satisfies the Lipschitz type condition* (1.2.7), *then*

$$\|\exp(tA_\tau)f - T(t)f\| \leqq L(f)\,\tau^{\gamma/2}$$

for all $0 < t < \infty$.

Proof. By assumption we have for each fixed $t > 0$

$$\begin{aligned}\|\exp(tA_\tau)f - T(t)f\| &\leqq L(f)\, e^{-t/\tau} \sum_{k=0}^{\infty} \frac{1}{k!}\left(\frac{t}{\tau}\right)^k \frac{|k\tau - t|^\gamma}{(k\tau + t)^{\gamma/2}} \\ &\leqq L(f)\, e^{-t/\tau} \frac{\tau^\gamma}{t^{\gamma/2}} \sum_{k=0}^{\infty} \frac{1}{k!}\left(\frac{t}{\tau}\right)^k \left|k - \frac{t}{\tau}\right|^\gamma.\end{aligned}$$

For $\gamma = 1$ the inequality (1.2.3) of Lemma 1.2.1 yields

$$\sum_{k=0}^{\infty} \frac{1}{k!}\left(\frac{t}{\tau}\right)^k \left|k - \frac{t}{\tau}\right| \leqq \left(\frac{t}{\tau}\right)^{1/2} e^{t/\tau},$$

which proves the theorem in this case. For $0 < \gamma < 1$, by Hölder's inequality,

$$\begin{aligned}\sum_{k=0}^{\infty} \frac{1}{k!}\left(\frac{t}{\tau}\right)^k \left|k - \frac{t}{\tau}\right|^\gamma &\leqq \left\{\sum_{k=0}^{\infty} \frac{1}{k!}\left(\frac{t}{\tau}\right)^k \left|k - \frac{t}{\tau}\right|\right\}^\gamma \left\{\sum_{k=0}^{\infty} \frac{1}{k!}\left(\frac{t}{\tau}\right)^k\right\}^{1-\gamma} \\ &\leqq e^{(1-\gamma)t/\tau}\left(\frac{t}{\tau}\right)^{\gamma/2} e^{\gamma t/\tau} = \left(\frac{t}{\tau}\right)^{\gamma/2} e^{t/\tau}.\end{aligned}$$

This completes the proof.

Theorem 1.2.2 has an interesting application. Using the usual notation of the calculus of finite differences we denote by

$$\text{(1.2.8)} \qquad \Delta_\tau^r T(t) = \sum_{k=0}^{r} (-1)^{r-k} \binom{r}{k} T(t + k\tau)$$

the r-th right difference of $T(t)$. By the semi-group property this may be rewritten as

$$\frac{\Delta_\tau^r T(t)}{\tau^r} = \left[\frac{T(\tau) - I}{\tau}\right]^r T(t) = [A_\tau]^r\, T(t).$$

We have the following

Corollary 1.2.4. *If* $\{T(t); 0 \leqq t < \infty\}$ *is a semi-group of class* $(\mathscr{C}_0)$ *in* $\mathscr{E}(X)$, *then for each* $f \in X$

$$T(t) f = \operatorname*{s-lim}_{\tau \to 0+} \sum_{k=0}^{\infty} \frac{t^k}{k!} \frac{\Delta_\tau^k T(0) f}{\tau^k} \tag{1.2.9}$$

uniformly with respect to t *in any finite interval* $[0, b]$.

This is a generalized form of Taylor's series expansion.

In the following example we apply Hille's first exponential formula to the semi-group of left translations in the spaces $UCB(E_1)$ and $L^p(E_1)$, $1 \leqq p < \infty$, which is perhaps the simplest example of a semi-group of class $(\mathscr{C}_0)$.

By $UCB(E_1)$ we denote the set of all bounded uniformly continuous real or complex-valued functions $f(x)$ defined on the real axis. Obviously, $UCB(E_1)$ becomes a Banach space under the norm

$$\|f\|_C = \sup_x |f(x)|.$$

The notion of strong convergence in this space coincides with the classical notion of uniform convergence with respect to x in E_1. The Lebesgue space $L^p(E_1)$, where p is fixed, $1 \leqq p < \infty$, is the Banach space of all Lebesgue measurable real or complex-valued functions f on the real axis E_1 for which $\int_{-\infty}^{\infty} |f(x)|^p \, dx$ exists. The norm is defined by

$$\|f\|_p = \left\{ \int_{-\infty}^{\infty} |f(x)|^p \, dx \right\}^{1/p}.$$

(To be more correct we should say the elements of $L^p(E_1)$ are not functions but rather equivalence classes of functions which are equal almost everywhere.)

Example 1.2.5. Let X be one of the spaces $UCB(E_1)$, $L^p(E_1)$, $1 \leqq p < \infty$. The *semi-group of left translations* $\{T(t); 0 \leqq t < \infty\}$ in $\mathscr{E}(X)$ is defined by

$$[T(t) f](x) = f(x + t) \qquad (0 \leqq t < \infty;\ f \in X). \tag{1.2.10}$$

The conditions (1.1.1) (i) and (ii) are trivially satisfied.

In the case $X = UCB(E_1)$, the uniform continuity of f on E_1 implies the $(\mathscr{C}_0)$-property (1.1.1) (iii). Moreover, $\|T(t) f\|_C = \|f\|_C$ for each $t \geqq 0$ and all $f \in UCB(E_1)$, giving $\|T(t)\| = 1$, so that $\{T(t); 0 \leqq t < \infty\}$ forms a contraction semi-group of class $(\mathscr{C}_0)$.

Here $[A_\tau f](x) = (1/\tau)\{f(x+\tau) - f(x)\}$ $(\tau > 0)$, and if $f \in \mathsf{D}(A)$, then there exists a function g in $\mathsf{UCB}(\mathrm{E}_1)$ such that

$$\frac{f(x+\tau)-f(x)}{\tau} \to g(x) \qquad (\tau \to 0+)$$

uniformly with respect to x on E_1. Thus $f(x)$ has a continuous right derivative $d^+f(x)/dx$, and by a well-known lemma f is differentiable and the derivative $f'(x)$ is equal to $g(x)$. On the other hand, if f has a continuous derivative in $\mathsf{UCB}(\mathrm{E}_1)$, then on account of the relation

$$\frac{f(x+\tau)-f(x)}{\tau} - f'(x) = \frac{1}{\tau}\int_0^\tau \{f'(x+u) - f'(x)\}\, du,$$

it is easy to see that f belongs to the domain of A. Thus

$$\mathsf{D}(A) = \{f \in \mathsf{UCB}(\mathrm{E}_1);\ f' \text{ exists and belongs to } \mathsf{UCB}(\mathrm{E}_1)\}$$

and $[A f](x) = f'(x)$. (For a further discussion see Sec. 1.3.3.) Furthermore, for an $f \in \mathsf{UCB}(\mathrm{E}_1)$

$$\frac{[\Delta_\tau^r T(0) f](x)}{\tau^r} = \frac{1}{\tau^r} \sum_{k=0}^{r} (-1)^{r-k} \binom{r}{k} f(x + k\tau).$$

Formula (1.2.9) then asserts that

$$f(x+t) = \lim_{\tau \to 0+} \sum_{k=0}^{\infty} \frac{t^k}{k!} \frac{[\Delta_\tau^k f](x)}{\tau^k}, \tag{1.2.11}$$

where the limit exists uniformly with respect to x in E_1 and uniformly with respect to t in every finite interval $[0, b]$.

Let us compare formula (1.2.11) with Taylor's series expansion of $f(x)$ in a neighborhood of $x = x_0$

$$f(x_0 + t) = \sum_{k=0}^{\infty} \frac{t^k}{k!} f^{(k)}(x_0), \tag{1.2.12}$$

which is valid provided f satisfies suitable sufficient conditions. Simple conditions for this purpose are that $f^{(k)}(x)$ exists with $|f^{(k)}(x)| \leqq M$ for all x in a neighborhood of x_0 and all $k \geqq 1$. (More sophisticated conditions are due to S. Bernstein.) Now, if f has derivatives of all orders at $x = x_0$, then $\lim_{\tau \to 0+} (1/\tau^k)[\Delta_\tau^k f](x_0) = f^{(k)}(x_0)$ $(k = 1, 2, \ldots)$. Thus formula (1.2.11) may be regarded as a deep generalization of Taylor's representation (1.2.12) in view of the fact that the limit in (1.2.11) exists for all x, even uniformly with respect to x and without any differentiability assumptions whatsoever. This is an important result in numerical analysis.

The result treated above may easily be carried over to the space $\mathsf{L}^p(\mathrm{E}_1)$, $1 \leqq p < \infty$, the convergence now being understood in the mean of order p.

1.2.2 General Convergence Theorems

We shall now prove a general convergence theorem.

Let $\{T(t); 0 \leqq t \leqq 1\}$ denote a family of bounded linear transformations which map the Banach space X to itself and such that $T(t)f$ is strongly continuous on $0 \leqq t \leqq 1$ for each $f \in \mathsf{X}$.

Let n be an arbitrary natural number. Divide the interval $[0, 1]$ into n equal parts and to each node k/n, $k = 0, 1, \ldots, n$, let there correspond a bounded real-valued function $\varphi_{k,n}(t) \geqq 0$ defined on $0 \leqq t \leqq 1$. Introducing the sum

$$\Phi_n(t) f = \left\{\sum_{k=0}^{n} \varphi_{k,n}(t)\, T\left(\frac{k}{n}\right)\right\} f \qquad (f \in \mathsf{X}), \tag{1.2.13}$$

the problem is to find necessary and sufficient conditions upon the system $\{\varphi_{k,n}\}$ such that for each $f \in \mathsf{X}$

$$\operatorname*{s-lim}_{n\to\infty} \Phi_n(t) f = T(t) f, \tag{1.2.14}$$

the convergence being uniform with respect to t in $[0, 1]$.

Theorem 1.2.6. *Let $\{T(t); 0 \leqq t \leqq 1\}$ be a family of operators in $\mathscr{E}(\mathsf{X})$ continuous in the strong operator topology on $[0, 1]$. A necessary and sufficient condition upon the system $\{\varphi_{k,n}\}$ such that the limit-relation (1.2.14) holds uniformly with respect to t in $[0, 1]$ for each fixed $f \in \mathsf{X}$ is that*

$$\begin{cases} \lim_{n\to\infty} \sum_{|k/n-t|<\delta} \varphi_{k,n}(t) = 1, \\ \lim_{n\to\infty} \sum_{|k/n-t|\geqq\delta} \varphi_{k,n}(t) = 0 \end{cases} \tag{1.2.15}$$

for each $\delta > 0$ and uniformly with respect to t in $[0, 1]$. Equivalent to this condition is the following:

$$\begin{cases} \lim_{n\to\infty} \sum_{k=0}^{n} \varphi_{k,n}(t) = 1, \\ \lim_{n\to\infty} \sum_{k=0}^{n} \frac{k}{n}\, \varphi_{k,n}(t) = t, \\ \lim_{n\to\infty} \sum_{k=0}^{n} \left(\frac{k}{n}\right)^2 \varphi_{k,n}(t) = t^2 \end{cases} \tag{1.2.16}$$

uniformly with respect to t in $[0, 1]$.

Proof. We suppose that (1.2.15) is satisfied. Since for each $f \in \mathsf{X}$ the vector-valued function $T(t)f$ is strongly continuous on $[0, 1]$, it is bounded there, i.e. there exists a constant $M_f > 0$ such that $\|T(t)f\| \leqq M_f$ on $[0, 1]$. (Actually, by the uniform boundedness principle the norms $\|T(t)\|$ are uniformly bounded on the interval, thus there is a constant $M > 0$ such that $\| T(t) f \| \leqq M \| f \|$ for all $f \in \mathsf{X}$.) Furthermore, since the strong continuity of $T(t) f$ is uniform with respect to t in $[0, 1]$, given any $\varepsilon > 0$ there is a $\delta = \delta(\varepsilon)$ such that $\| T(t_1) f - T(t_2) f \| < \varepsilon$ for $|t_1 - t_2| < \delta$, $0 \leqq t_1, t_2 \leqq 1$. For $0 \leqq t \leqq 1$ and any fixed $f \in \mathsf{X}$ we then have

$$\left\| \left\{ \sum_{k=0}^{n} \varphi_{k,n}(t)\, T\left(\frac{k}{n}\right) \right\} f - T(t) f \right\| \leqq \sum_{|k/n-t| < \delta} \varphi_{k,n}(t) \left\| T\left(\frac{k}{n}\right) f - T(t) f \right\| +$$

$$+ \sum_{|k/n-t| \geqq \delta} \varphi_{k,n}(t) \left\| T\left(\frac{k}{n}\right) f \right\| + \left\| T(t) f - \sum_{|k/n-t| < \delta} \varphi_{k,n}(t)\, T(t) f \right\|$$

$$\leqq \varepsilon \sum_{|k/n-t| < \delta} \varphi_{k,n}(t) + M_f \sum_{|k/n-t| \geqq \delta} \varphi_{k,n}(t) + M_f \left| 1 - \sum_{|k/n-t| < \delta} \varphi_{k,n}(t) \right|.$$

Hence applying the assumption (1.2.15)

$$\limsup_{n \to \infty} \| \Phi_n(t) f - T(t) f \| \leqq \varepsilon$$

for each fixed $f \in \mathsf{X}$ and any $\varepsilon > 0$, uniformly with respect to t, which proves (1.2.14).

Now, if condition (1.2.14) is satisfied for any operator function $T(t)$, $0 \leqq t \leqq 1$, in $\mathscr{E}(\mathsf{X})$, continuous in the strong operator topology, it is satisfied by the particular operators: $T_1(t) = I$, $0 \leqq t \leqq 1$, $T_2(t) = t \cdot I$, $0 \leqq t \leqq 1$, and $T_3(t) = t^2 \cdot I$, $0 \leqq t \leqq 1$, which implies (1.2.16). Finally, suppose that (1.2.16) is satisfied. Then for $n \to \infty$

$$t^2 \sum_{k=0}^{n} \varphi_{k,n}(t) - 2t \sum_{k=0}^{n} \left(\frac{k}{n}\right) \varphi_{k,n}(t) + \sum_{k=0}^{n} \left(\frac{k}{n}\right)^2 \varphi_{k,n}(t)$$

converges to $t^2 - 2t^2 + t^2 = 0$, uniformly with respect to t in $[0, 1]$. On the other hand, this expression equals

$$\sum_{k=0}^{n} \left(t - \frac{k}{n}\right)^2 \varphi_{k,n}(t) \geqq \delta^2 \sum_{|k/n-t| \geqq \delta} \varphi_{k,n}(t) \qquad (\delta > 0),$$

which gives

$$\lim_{n \to \infty} \sum_{|k/n-t| \geqq \delta} \varphi_{k,n}(t) = 0$$

for each $\delta > 0$ uniformly on $[0, 1]$. This and the fact that

$$\sum_{|k/n-t| < \delta} \varphi_{k,n}(t) + \sum_{|k/n-t| \geqq \delta} \varphi_{k,n}(t) = \sum_{k=0}^{n} \varphi_{k,n}(t)$$

converges uniformly to one as $n \to \infty$, implies

$$\lim_{n \to \infty} \sum_{|k/n-t| < \delta} \varphi_{k,n}(t) = 1$$

uniformly on $[0, 1]$ for each $\delta > 0$. Thus the theorem is established by a cyclic argument.

This theorem is interesting, and the surprising fact is that the condition (1.2.16) implies (1.2.14). The method of proof, however, shows clearly that this depends essentially on the fact that the functions $\varphi_{k,n}(t)$ are all non-negative on $[0, 1]$.

We shall study the theorem for a special system of functions $\{\varphi_{k,n}\}$.

Lemma 1.2.7. *The binomial distribution*

(1.2.17)
$$q_{k,n}(t) = \binom{n}{k} t^k (1-t)^{n-k} \quad (0 \leqq t \leqq 1; k = 0, 1, \ldots, n, n = 0, 1, \ldots),$$

satisfies the conditions (1.2.15) *or* (1.2.16) *of Theorem* 1.2.6.

Proof. Obviously, the functions $q_{k,n}$ are non-negative and bounded in $[0, 1]$. For $n = 1, 2, \ldots$ the following identities hold:

(1.2.18)
$$\text{(i)} \quad \sum_{k=0}^{n} q_{k,n}(t) = 1, \qquad \text{(ii)} \quad \sum_{k=0}^{n} \left(\frac{k}{n}\right) q_{k,n}(t) = t,$$
$$\text{(iii)} \quad \sum_{k=0}^{n} \left(\frac{k}{n}\right)^2 q_{k,n}(t) = t^2 + \frac{t(1-t)}{n}.$$

Indeed, (i) follows upon setting $u = t$ and $v = 1 - t$ in

$$\sum_{k=0}^{n} \binom{n}{k} u^k v^{n-k} = (u+v)^n.$$

Differentiating the latter formula with respect to u the same substitution gives (ii). A further differentiation gives (iii). Since $t(1-t) \leqq 1/4$ on $[0, 1]$, it follows immediately from (1.2.18) (i)—(iii) that the system $\{q_{k,n}\}$ satisfies the condition (1.2.16). Furthermore, the above set of identities gives

(1.2.19)
$$\sum_{k=0}^{n} \left(\frac{k}{n} - t\right)^2 q_{k,n}(t) = \frac{t(1-t)}{n},$$

from which the inequality

$$\sum_{\left|\frac{k}{n} - t\right| \geqq \delta} q_{k,n}(t) \leqq \frac{1}{\delta^2} \sum_{k=0}^{n} \left(\frac{k}{n} - t\right)^2 q_{k,n}(t) \leqq \frac{1}{4n\delta^2} \qquad (\delta > 0),$$

follows. Hence

$$\lim_{n \to \infty} \sum_{\left|\frac{k}{n} - t\right| \geqq \delta} q_{k,n}(t) = 0$$

uniformly on $[0, 1]$ for each $\delta > 0$, which together with $\sum q_{k,n}(t) = 1$ proves that the equivalent condition (1.2.15) is also satisfied by the system $\{q_{k,n}\}$.

Using this lemma we immediately obtain by Theorem 1.2.6

Corollary 1.2.8. *Let* $\{T(t); 0 \leqq t \leqq 1\}$ *be a family of operators in* $\mathscr{E}(\mathsf{X})$ *continuous in the strong operator topology. Then for each* $f \in \mathsf{X}$

$$\text{s-}\lim_{n\to\infty}\left\{\sum_{k=0}^{n}\binom{n}{k}t^k(1-t)^{n-k}\,T\left(\frac{k}{n}\right)\right\}f = T(t)\,f, \tag{1.2.20}$$

the convergence being uniform on $[0, 1]$.

If $\{T(t); 0 \leqq t < \infty\}$ *is a semi-group of class* $(\mathscr{C}_0)$ *in* $\mathscr{E}(\mathsf{X})$, *we have*

$$T(t)\,f = \text{s-}\lim_{n\to\infty}\left[(1-t)\,I - t\,T\left(\frac{1}{n}\right)\right]^n f \tag{1.2.21}$$

whenever $0 \leqq t \leqq 1$, *the convergence being uniform in this interval.*

Proof. It only remains to verify relation (1.2.21). But this follows directly from the identity

$$\left[(1-t)\,I - t\,T\left(\frac{1}{n}\right)\right]^n = \sum_{k=0}^{n} T\left(\frac{k}{n}\right)\binom{n}{k}t^k(1-t)^{n-k} \qquad (0 \leqq t \leqq 1).$$

We establish two further propositions.

Proposition 1.2.9. *Let* $T(t)$, $0 \leqq t \leqq 1$, *be an operator function continuous in the strong operator topology. Denoting by* $\omega(\delta; T(\cdot)\,f)$ *the rectified modulus of continuity of* $T(t)\,f$ *in the interval* $[0, 1]$, *then for each* $f \in \mathsf{X}$

$$\left\|\left\{\sum_{k=0}^{n}\binom{n}{k}t^k(1-t)^{n-k}\,T\left(\frac{k}{n}\right)\right\}f - T(t)\,f\right\| \leqq \frac{3}{2}\,\omega\left(\frac{1}{\sqrt{n}}; T(\cdot)f\right).$$

Proof. For each $\lambda > 0$ it follows readily that

$$\omega(\lambda\,\delta; T(\cdot)\,f) \leqq (\lambda+1)\,\omega(\delta; T(\cdot)\,f).$$

This gives

$$\begin{aligned}\left\|\left\{\sum_{k=0}^{n} q_{k,n}(t)\,T\left(\frac{k}{n}\right)\right\}f - T(t)\,f\right\| &\leqq \sum_{k=0}^{n} q_{k,n}(t)\left\|T\left(\frac{k}{n}\right)f - T(t)\,f\right\|\\ &\leqq \sum_{k=0}^{n} q_{k,n}(t)\,\omega\left(\left|\frac{k}{n}-t\right|; T(\cdot)\,f\right)\\ &\leqq \left\{\sqrt{n}\sum_{k=0}^{n}\left|\frac{k}{n}-t\right| q_{k,n}(t) + 1\right\}\omega\left(\frac{1}{\sqrt{n}}; T(\cdot)\,f\right).\end{aligned}$$

By (1.2.19) and the Cauchy-Schwarz inequality we have

$$\left\{\sum_{k=0}^{n}\left|\frac{k}{n}-t\right| q_{k,n}(t)\right\}^2 \leqq \sum_{k=0}^{n}\left(\frac{k}{n}-t\right)^2 q_{k,n}(t)\sum_{k=0}^{n} q_{k,n}(t) \leqq \frac{1}{4n}.$$

This proves the desired estimate.

Proposition 1.2.10. *Under the same hypothesis as Proposition* 1.2.9 *we have*

$$\left\|\int_0^1\left\{\sum_{k=0}^{n}\binom{n}{k}t^k(1-t)^{n-k}\,T\left(\frac{k}{n}\right)\right\}f\,dt - \int_0^1 T(t)\,f\,dt\right\| \leqq \omega\left(\frac{1}{n+1}; T(\cdot)\,f\right).$$

Proof. We have for each $k = 0, 1, 2, \ldots, n$, $\| T(t) f - T\left(\frac{k}{n}\right) f \| \leqq \leqq \omega(1/(n+1); T(\cdot) f)$ in $k/(n+1) \leqq t \leqq (k+1)/(n+1)$. Using the identity $\int_0^1 q_{k,n}(t)\, dt = (n+1)^{-1}$ $(k = 0, 1, 2, \ldots, n)$

$$\left\| \int_0^1 T(t) f\, dt - \int_0^1 \left\{ \sum_{k=0}^{n} q_{k,n}(t)\, T\left(\frac{k}{n}\right) \right\} f\, dt \right\|$$

$$\leqq \sum_{k=0}^{n} \left\| \int_{k/(n+1)}^{(k+1)/(n+1)} \left[T(t) f - T\left(\frac{k}{n}\right) f \right] dt \right\|$$

$$\leqq \sum_{k=0}^{n} \int_{k/(n+1)}^{(k+1)/(n+1)} \omega\left(\frac{1}{n+1}; T(\cdot) f\right) dt = \omega\left(\frac{1}{n+1}; T(\cdot) f\right).$$

1.2.3 Weierstrass Approximation Theorem

Now let g be any real-valued continuous function defined on $[0, 1]$. We set $g_0(x) = g(0)$ in $(-\infty, 0)$, $= g(x)$ in $[0, 1]$, and $= g(1)$ in $(1, \infty)$. Clearly, the function g_0 belongs to $UCB(E_1)$, and if we apply Corollary 1.2.8 to the semi-group of left translations on $UCB(E_1)$, then we obtain

Theorem 1.2.11. *If g is continuous on $[0, 1]$, then the sum*

$$[B_n g](t) = \sum_{k=0}^{n} \binom{n}{k} t^k (1-t)^{n-k} g\left(\frac{k}{n}\right) \tag{1.2.22}$$

converges to $g(t)$ whenever $0 \leqq t \leqq 1$, the convergence being uniform in this interval.

This result gives a proof of the fundamental theorem of Weierstrass which states that any continuous function g defined on a finite closed interval can be uniformly approximated on that interval by algebraic polynomials with any preassigned degree of accuracy. Indeed, the sum in (1.2.22) is a polynomial in t of degree n at most, called the *Bernstein polynomial* corresponding to the function g defined on $[0, 1]$. Thus a sequence of well-defined polynomials (which depend upon the values of the given function g at the rational points k/n, $k = 0, 1, \ldots, n$) has actually been *constructed* as to give uniform approximation to the function g. The original Weierstrass theorem only states that there *exist* polynomials having the desired property.

Remark. There exists a generalized analogue of the theorem of Weierstrass to the infinite interval $[0, \infty]$ giving uniform approximation to g on $[0, \infty]$ by

$$[F_\nu g](t) = e^{-\nu t} \sum_{k=0}^{\infty} g\left(\frac{k}{\nu}\right) \frac{(\nu t)^k}{k!}$$

for $\nu \to \infty$. Indeed, let g be a function continuous at each $t > 0$ for which the one-sided limits $\lim_{t\to 0+} g(t)$ and $\lim_{t\to\infty} g(t)$ exist. Then it may be shown that

$$\lim_{\nu\to\infty} [F_\nu g](t) = g(t) \tag{1.2.23}$$

uniformly on $[0, \infty]$. Although it is not possible to approximate a function g of the above type on $[0, \infty]$ by algebraic polynomials, that is by linear combinations of the powers t^k $(k = 0, 1, 2, \ldots)$, such functions may nevertheless be approximated by linear combinations of the functions e^{-kt} $(k = 0, 1, 2, \ldots)$.

If g satisfies the Lipschitz type condition

$$|g(t) - g(s)| < L \frac{|t-s|^\gamma}{(t+s)^{\gamma/2}} \qquad (0 < t, s < \infty), \tag{1.2.24}$$

where L, γ are constants, $0 < \gamma \leqq 1$, then the method of proof of Proposition 1.2.3 may be used to show that

$$|[F_\nu g](t) - g(t)| \leqq L\, t^{-\gamma/2} \qquad (\nu \to \infty) \tag{1.2.25}$$

uniformly for $0 < t < \infty$.

There exist functions g satisfying the Lipschitz type condition (1.2.24). Indeed, for $\gamma = 1$ the function g defined by $g(t) = c - t$ for $0 < t \leqq c$, c a positive constant, $g(t) = 0$ for $t \geqq c$, satisfies (1.2.24). This at the same time shows that the condition (1.2.7) is meaningful.

Finally, let us restate the formulae (1.2.4) and (1.2.20) of Theorem 1.2.2 and Corollary 1.2.8, respectively, in two ways. In the terminology of summability theory the formula (1.2.4), namely

$$T(t) f = \operatorname*{s-lim}_{\tau\to 0+} e^{-t/\tau} \sum_{k=0}^{\infty} \frac{1}{k!} \left(\frac{t}{\tau}\right)^k T(\tau k) f, \tag{1.2.26}$$

of Theorem 1.2.2 shows that this result is connected with Borel's summability method, while the formula (1.2.20) of Corollary 1.2.8 gives the connection with generalized Euler summability.

On the other hand, in the terminology of probability distribution, the formula (1.2.26) corresponds to the Poisson distribution. Indeed, the distribution function is

$$P_\tau(u, t) = \begin{cases} e^{-t/\tau} \sum\limits_{k \leqq u/\tau} \dfrac{(t/\tau)^k}{k!} & (0 < u < \infty) \\ 0 & (u = 0), \end{cases}$$

and (1.2.26) can be written as

$$T(t) f = \operatorname*{s-lim}_{\tau\to 0+} \int_0^\infty T(u) f \, d_u P_\tau(u, t).$$

With the distribution function

$$B_n(u,t) = \begin{cases} \sum_{k \leqq nu} \binom{n}{k} t^k (1-t)^{n-k} & (0 < u \leqq 1) \\ 0 & (u = 0), \end{cases}$$

which is constant except for jumps of $q_{k,n}(t)$ at the points $t = k/n$, $k = 0, 1, 2, \ldots, n$, (1.2.20) may be written in the form

$$T(t)\, f = \operatorname*{s-lim}_{n\to\infty} \int_0^1 T(u)\, f\, d_u B_n(u,t),$$

showing its relation to the binomial distribution.

1.3 Resolvent and Characterization of the Generator

1.3.1 Resolvent and Spectrum

Let X be a complex Banach space and U a linear (not necessarily bounded) transformation with both domain $\mathsf{D}(U)$ and range $\mathsf{R}(U)$ in X. We begin with a classification of the spectral properties of the operator U. The operator $U_\lambda \equiv \lambda I - U$, where λ is an arbitrary complex number, is also defined on $\mathsf{D}(U)$. Its range will be denoted by $\mathsf{R}(U_\lambda)$. Regarding the distribution of values of λ for which U_λ has an inverse, there are the following possibilities.

(i) The inverse of U_λ does not exist, i.e. there exists an element $f \neq \theta$ such that $U f = \lambda f$. We then call λ an *eigenvalue* of U and f an eigenvector belonging to the eigenvalue λ. The values of λ for which no inverse exists are said to form the *point spectrum* $\mathrm{P}_\sigma(U)$ of U.

(ii) U_λ^{-1} exists with domain $\mathsf{D}(U_\lambda^{-1})$ not dense in X. The corresponding values of λ are said to form the *residual spectrum* $\mathrm{R}_\sigma(U)$ of U.

(iii) U_λ^{-1} exists with $\mathsf{D}(U_\lambda^{-1})$ dense in X but U_λ^{-1} is not bounded. The corresponding values of λ are said to form the *continuous spectrum* $\mathrm{C}_\sigma(U)$ of U.

The *spectrum* $\sigma(U)$ of U is defined by the union of $\mathrm{P}_\sigma(U)$, $\mathrm{R}_\sigma(U)$ and $\mathrm{C}_\sigma(U)$.

(iv) U_λ^{-1} exists with $\mathsf{D}(U_\lambda^{-1})$ dense in X and U_λ^{-1} is bounded. In this case the values of λ are said to form the *resolvent set* $\varrho(U)$ of U; the inverse U_λ^{-1} will then be denoted by $R(\lambda; U)$ and is called the *resolvent* of U.

By definition, the sets $\sigma(U)$ and $\varrho(U)$ are mutually exclusive and their union is the complex plane.

From now on we assume that in addition U is closed. In this case, if $\lambda \in \varrho(U)$, $R(\lambda; U)$ is closed and bounded with domain dense in X. This implies $\mathsf{R}(U_\lambda) = \mathsf{X}$ and thus $R(\lambda; U)$ transforms X one-to-one onto $\mathsf{D}(U)$, i.e.

$$(1.3.1) \qquad \begin{cases} \text{(i)} \ (\lambda I - U)\, R(\lambda; U)\, f = f & (f \in \mathsf{X}), \\ \text{(ii)} \ R(\lambda; U)\, (\lambda I - U)\, f = f & (f \in \mathsf{D}(U)). \end{cases}$$

We next establish the so-called *first resolvent equation*.

Proposition 1.3.1. *If* $\lambda_1, \lambda_2 \in \varrho(U)$, *then*

$$(1.3.2) \qquad R(\lambda_1; U) - R(\lambda_2; U) = (\lambda_2 - \lambda_1)\, R(\lambda_1; U)\, R(\lambda_2; U).$$

Proof. For all $f \in \mathsf{X}$ we have

$$\begin{aligned} R(\lambda_1; U)\, f &= R(\lambda_1; U)\, (\lambda_2 I - U)\, R(\lambda_2; U)\, f \\ &= R(\lambda_1; U)\, [(\lambda_2 - \lambda_1)\, I + (\lambda_1 I - U)]\, R(\lambda_2; U)\, f \\ &= (\lambda_2 - \lambda_1)\, R(\lambda_1; U)\, R(\lambda_2; U)\, f + R(\lambda_2; U)\, f. \end{aligned}$$

It follows immediately from (1.3.2) that $R(\lambda_1; U)$ and $R(\lambda_2; U)$ commute.

Proposition 1.3.2. *If* $\lambda_0 \in \varrho(U)$, *then all values of* λ *satisfying* $|\lambda - \lambda_0|\, \|R(\lambda_0; U)\| < 1$ *belong to* $\varrho(U)$ *and*

$$R(\lambda; U) = \sum_{n=0}^{\infty} (-1)^n\, (\lambda - \lambda_0)^n\, [R(\lambda_0; U)]^{n+1},$$

the series converging in the norm of $\mathscr{E}(\mathsf{X})$. *Furthermore,*

$$\|R(\lambda; U)\| \leqq \frac{\|R(\lambda_0; U)\|}{1 - |\lambda - \lambda_0|\, \|R(\lambda_0; U)\|}.$$

The proof of this proposition will be omitted.

Corollary 1.3.3. *The resolvent set* $\varrho(U)$ *is open and the operator function* $R(\lambda; U)$ *is holomorphic in* $\varrho(U)$ *with*

$$(1.3.3) \qquad \frac{d^n}{d\lambda^n} R(\lambda; U) = (-1)^n\, n!\, [R(\lambda; U)]^{n+1} \qquad (n = 1, 2, \ldots).$$

A lemma concerning Laplace transforms will be needed.

Lemma 1.3.4. *Suppose* F *is a real or complex-valued function defined on* $(0, \infty)$ *and such that* $F \in \mathsf{L}^1(0, R)$ *for every finite* $R > 0$. *If the Laplace transform of* F, *defined by*

$$f(\lambda) = \mathfrak{L}[F]\, (\lambda) \equiv \int_0^\infty e^{-\lambda t}\, F(t)\, dt,$$

converges for $\mathrm{Re}\,\lambda > \omega$ $(\omega < \infty)$, *then* $f(\lambda)$ *is holomorphic in the half-plane* $\mathrm{Re}\,\lambda > \omega$, *and*

$$f^{(r)}(\lambda) = \int_0^\infty (-t)^r e^{-\lambda t} F(t)\, dt \qquad (r = 0, 1, 2, \ldots).$$

Furthermore, $F(t)$ *is uniquely determined by its Laplace transform* $f(\lambda)$ *up to a set of measure zero.*

Now, let $\{T(t); 0 \leqq t < \infty\}$ be a semi-group of class $(\mathscr{C}_0)$ in $\mathscr{E}(\mathsf{X})$. We wish to obtain an expression for the resolvent $R(\lambda; A)$ of the infinitesimal generator A in terms of the semi-group. If the semi-group is continuous in the uniform operator topology on $[0, \infty)$, thus if $T(t) = \exp(tA)$ $(0 \leqq t < \infty)$ with bounded generator A, then it is easy to see that for $\mathrm{Re}\,\lambda$ sufficiently large $(\mathrm{Re}\,\lambda > \|A\|)$

$$R(\lambda; A) = \mathfrak{L}[\exp(tA)](\lambda) = \int_0^\infty e^{-\lambda t} e^{tA}\, dt = (\lambda I - A)^{-1}.$$

Thus the resolvent of A is the Laplace transform of the operator function $T(t)$.

In case $\{T(t); 0 \leqq t < \infty\}$ is a strongly continuous semi-group, we prove the following analogue:

Theorem 1.3.5. *Let* $\{T(t); 0 \leqq t < \infty\}$ *be a semi-group of class* $(\mathscr{C}_0)$ *in* $\mathscr{E}(\mathsf{X})$ *with infinitesimal generator* A. *If* $\omega_0 = \lim_{t\to\infty} t^{-1} \log \|T(t)\|$ *and* $\mathrm{Re}\,\lambda > \omega_0$, *then* λ *belongs to* $\varrho(A)$ *and*

$$(1.3.4) \qquad R(\lambda; A) f = \int_0^\infty e^{-\lambda t} T(t) f\, dt \qquad (f \in \mathsf{X}).$$

Furthermore, for each $f \in \mathsf{X}$

$$(1.3.5) \qquad \operatorname*{s-lim}_{|\lambda|\to\infty} \lambda R(\lambda; A) f = f \qquad (|\arg \lambda| \leqq \alpha_0 < \pi/2).$$

Proof. We introduce the operator

$$R_\lambda f = \int_0^\infty e^{-\lambda t} T(t) f\, dt \qquad (f \in \mathsf{X}; \mathrm{Re}\,\lambda > \omega_0).$$

To show the existence of the integral, we suppose that $\mathrm{Re}\,\lambda \geqq \omega > \omega_0$. By Proposition 1.1.2 (d) there is a constant M_ω such that $\|T(t)\| \leqq M_\omega e^{\omega t}$, $t \geqq 0$. This gives $\|e^{-\lambda t} T(t) f\| \leqq M_\omega e^{-(\sigma-\omega)t} \|f\|$, where $\sigma = \mathrm{Re}\,\lambda$. As the integrand is strongly continuous for $t \geqq 0$, it follows that the integral exists in the sense of Bochner (App. 2). Thus R_λ defines a bounded linear operator on X into itself with norm $\|R_\lambda\| \leqq$ $\leqq M_\omega \int_0^\infty e^{-(\sigma-\omega)t}\, dt = M_\omega/(\sigma - \omega)$. We now show that $\mathsf{R}(R_\lambda) \subset \mathsf{D}(A)$

and that

(1.3.6) $$(\lambda I - A) R_\lambda f = f \qquad (f \in \mathsf{X}).$$

Indeed,

$$A_\tau R_\lambda f = \frac{1}{\tau} \int_0^\infty e^{-\lambda t} [T(t+\tau) f - T(t) f]\, dt$$

$$= \frac{e^{\lambda\tau} - 1}{\tau} \int_\tau^\infty e^{-\lambda t} T(t) f\, dt - \frac{1}{\tau} \int_0^\tau e^{-\lambda t} T(t) f\, dt.$$

Thus

$$A R_\lambda f = \underset{\tau \to 0+}{\text{s-lim}}\, A_\tau R_\lambda f = \lambda R_\lambda f - f$$

for each $f \in \mathsf{X}$, proving at the same time relation (i) of (1.3.1) with $U = A$. Next we show

(1.3.7) $$R_\lambda (\lambda I - A) f = f \qquad (f \in \mathsf{D}(A))$$

(relation (ii) of (1.3.1)), which together with (1.3.6) proves that $R_\lambda = R(\lambda; A)$. Since A is a closed operator, we have (App. 2) for each $f \in \mathsf{D}(A)$

$$R_\lambda A f = \int_0^\infty e^{-\lambda t} T(t) A f\, dt = A \int_0^\infty e^{-\lambda t} T(t) f\, dt = A R_\lambda f.$$

Combining this with the previous relation for $A R_\lambda f$ we have (1.3.7).

To establish (1.3.5), we have to show that the integral

$$\lambda R(\lambda; A) f - f = \lambda \int_0^\infty e^{-\lambda t} [T(t) f - f]\, dt \qquad (\operatorname{Re}\lambda > \max(0, \omega_0))$$

approaches θ in norm as $\lambda \to \infty$, uniformly in λ in any fixed sector $|\arg\lambda| \leqq \alpha_0 < \pi/2$. We split the integral into two parts, corresponding to those values of t for which $0 \leqq t \leqq \delta$ and those for $\delta \leqq t < \infty$, where δ is chosen as follows: given $\varepsilon > 0$, by the strong continuity of $T(t) f$ there is a $\delta = \delta(\varepsilon, f) > 0$ such that $\|T(t) f - f\| < \varepsilon$ for $0 \leqq t \leqq \delta$. Thus

$$|\lambda| \int_0^\delta e^{-\sigma t} \|T(t) f - f\|\, dt < \frac{|\lambda|}{\sigma} \varepsilon \leqq \sqrt{1 + (\tan\alpha_0)^2}\, \varepsilon \qquad (\operatorname{Re}\lambda = \sigma),$$

and for $\operatorname{Re}\lambda = \sigma > \omega > \max(0, \omega_0)$

$$|\lambda| \int_\delta^\infty e^{-\sigma t} \|T(t) f - f\|\, dt \leqq |\lambda| \int_\delta^\infty e^{-\sigma t} [M_\omega e^{\omega t} + 1]\, \|f\|\, dt$$

$$\leqq \sigma \left[\frac{M_\omega}{\sigma - \omega} e^{\omega\delta} + \frac{1}{\sigma}\right] \sqrt{1 + (\tan\alpha_0)^2}\, e^{-\sigma\delta}\, \|f\|,$$

which becomes sufficiently small for σ large enough.

1.3.2 Hille-Yosida Theorem

Our next problem is to find conditions upon a closed linear operator U that it be the infinitesimal generator of a semi-group of class $(\mathscr{C}_0)$ (see the remarks concerning the abstract Cauchy problem in Sec. 1.0). This problem will be solved in general by the following

Theorem 1.3.6. *A necessary and sufficient condition for a closed linear operator U with dense domain $\mathsf{D}(U)$ and range in X to generate a semi-group $\{T(t); 0 \leqq t < \infty\}$ of class $(\mathscr{C}_0)$ is that there exist real numbers M and ω such that for every real $\lambda > \omega$, λ belongs to $\varrho(U)$ and*

$$\|[R(\lambda; U)]^r\| \leqq M(\lambda - \omega)^{-r} \qquad (r = 1, 2, \ldots). \tag{1.3.8}$$

In this case $\|T(t)\| \leqq M\, e^{\omega t}$ for all $t \geqq 0$.

Proof. We first prove the necessity. Suppose that $\{T(t); 0 \leqq t < \infty\}$ is of class $(\mathscr{C}_0)$ in $\mathscr{E}(\mathsf{X})$ with infinitesimal generator A. Then there are constants M and ω such that $\|T(t)\| \leqq M\, e^{\omega t}$ for all $t \geqq 0$. By Theorem 1.3.5 every λ with $\mathrm{Re}\,\lambda > \omega$ belongs to the resolvent set $\varrho(A)$ of the infinitesimal generator A and

$$R(\lambda; A) f = \int_0^\infty e^{-\lambda t}\, T(t) f\, dt \qquad (f \in \mathsf{X};\ \mathrm{Re}\,\lambda > \omega).$$

From this it follows readily by Lemma 1.3.4 that

$$\frac{d^{r-1}}{d\lambda^{r-1}} R(\lambda; A) f \equiv R^{(r-1)}(\lambda; A) f = \int_0^\infty (-t)^{r-1} e^{-\lambda t}\, T(t) f\, dt \qquad (r = 1, 2, \ldots),$$

and thus

$$\|R^{(r-1)}(\lambda; A)\| \leqq M \int_0^\infty t^{r-1} e^{-(\sigma-\omega)t}\, dt = M(r-1)!\,(\sigma-\omega)^{-r} \quad (\mathrm{Re}\,\lambda = \sigma),$$

which together with (1.3.3) proves the relation (1.3.8) for every real $\lambda > \omega$ and $r = 1, 2, \ldots$

To establish the sufficiency, we set $B_\lambda = \lambda^2 R(\lambda; U) - \lambda I$, $\lambda > \omega$, and we shall construct a semi-group $\{T(t); 0 \leqq t < \infty\}$ of class $(\mathscr{C}_0)$ as the strong limit as $\lambda \to \infty$ of the semi-group

$$S_\lambda(t) \equiv \exp(t B_\lambda) = e^{-\lambda t} \sum_{k=0}^\infty \frac{(\lambda^2 t)^k}{k!} [R(\lambda; U)]^k.$$

At first, we show that

$$\underset{\lambda\to\infty}{\text{s-lim}}\, B_\lambda f = U f \qquad (f \in \mathsf{D}(U)). \tag{1.3.9}$$

If $f \in \mathsf{D}(U)$, then

$$(\|\lambda R(\lambda; U) f - f\| = \|R(\lambda; U)\, U f\| \leqq M\, \|U f\| (\lambda - \omega)^{-1},$$

which tends to zero as $\lambda \to \infty$. Since $\| \lambda R(\lambda; U) \| \leqq M \lambda (\lambda - \omega)^{-1} < 2M$ for large λ, the Banach-Steinhaus theorem implies that $\underset{\lambda\to\infty}{\text{s-lim}}\, \lambda R(\lambda; U) f = f$ for all $f \in \mathsf{X}$. Hence $B_\lambda f = \lambda R(\lambda; U) U f$ converges to $U f$ for each $f \in \mathsf{D}(U)$.

We next give an estimate for the norm of the operator $S_\lambda(t)$. We have

$$\| S_\lambda(t) \| \leqq e^{-\lambda t} \sum_{k=0}^{\infty} \frac{(\lambda^2 t)^k}{k!} \frac{M}{(\lambda - \omega)^k} = M \exp[t \lambda \omega (\lambda - \omega)^{-1}].$$

Given $\gamma > 1$, then $\lambda(\lambda - \omega)^{-1} < \gamma$ for $\lambda > \gamma \omega (\gamma - 1)^{-1} = \lambda(\gamma)$ and thus

$$\| S_\lambda(t) \| \leqq M e^{\gamma \omega t} \qquad (\lambda > \lambda(\gamma)). \tag{1.3.10}$$

Thirdly, we show that the limit

$$\underset{\lambda\to\infty}{\text{s-lim}}\, S_\lambda(t) f = T(t) f \tag{1.3.11}$$

exists for each $f \in \mathsf{D}(U)$ and then for each $f \in \mathsf{X}$ uniformly with respect to t in any finite interval $0 \leqq t \leqq b$. Now, since $R(\lambda; U)$ commutes with $R(\nu; U)$ for any λ and ν, we have $B_\lambda B_\nu = B_\nu B_\lambda$. The formula $S_\lambda(t) = \sum_{k=0}^{\infty} (t^k/k!) B_\lambda^k$ then shows that $B_\nu S_\lambda(t) = S_\lambda(t) B_\nu$. Hence, if $f \in \mathsf{D}(U)$ (indeed for $f \in \mathsf{X}$) we have

$$S_\lambda(t) f - S_\nu(t) f = \int_0^t \frac{d}{du} [S_\nu(t - u) S_\lambda(u) f] \, du$$

$$= \int_0^t S_\nu(t - u) [B_\lambda - B_\nu] S_\lambda(u) f \, du = \int_0^t S_\nu(t - u) S_\lambda(u) [B_\lambda - B_\nu] f \, du.$$

Applying (1.3.10), we obtain

$$\| S_\lambda(t) f - S_\nu(t) f \| \leqq M^2 e^{\gamma \omega t} t \| B_\lambda f - B_\nu f \|$$

for $\lambda, \nu > \lambda(\gamma)$. On account of (1.3.9) we have $\lim_{\lambda,\nu\to\infty} \| B_\lambda f - B_\nu f \| = 0$ for each $f \in \mathsf{D}(U)$. Thus $S_\lambda(t) f$ converges strongly to a limit which we denote by $T(t) f$, the convergence being uniform in t in any finite interval $0 \leqq t \leqq b$. Since $\mathsf{D}(U)$ is dense in X and (1.3.10) holds, the theorem of Banach-Steinhaus gives that $\underset{\lambda\to\infty}{\text{s-lim}}\, S_\lambda(t) f = T(t) f$ for each $f \in \mathsf{X}$, uniformly with respect to t in $[0, b]$, proving (1.3.11).

It remains to show that $\{T(t); 0 \leqq t < \infty\}$ defines a semi-group of class $(\mathscr{C}_0)$ in $\mathscr{E}(\mathsf{X})$ with infinitesimal generator U. Since $\{S_\lambda(t); 0 \leqq t < \infty\}$ is a semi-group of class $(\mathscr{C}_0)$ for each $\lambda > \omega$, it follows that

$$T(t_1 + t_2) f = \underset{\lambda\to\infty}{\text{s-lim}}\, S_\lambda(t_1 + t_2) f = \underset{\lambda\to\infty}{\text{s-lim}}\, S_\lambda(t_1) S_\lambda(t_2) f = T(t_1) T(t_2) f$$

for $f \in \mathsf{X}$ and $t_1, t_2 \in [0, \infty)$. Clearly, $T(0) = I$ and the strong continuity of $T(t)f$ in t follows from the uniformity of the convergence of $S_\lambda(t)f$ to $T(t)f$ in any finite interval $[0, b]$. Finally, $\|T(t)\| \leqq M e^{\gamma\omega t}$, $t \geqq 0$, for all $\gamma > 1$ and thus $\|T(t)\| \leqq M e^{\omega t}$. Now, if $f \in \mathsf{D}(U)$, then by (1.3.9) $\underset{\lambda\to\infty}{\text{s-lim}}\, B_\lambda f = Uf$ and on account of the inequality

$$\|S_\lambda(t)\, B_\lambda f - T(t)\, Uf\| \leqq \|S_\lambda(t)\|\, \|B_\lambda f - Uf\| + \|[S_\lambda(t) - T(t)]Uf\|$$

we see that $S_\lambda(t)\, B_\lambda f$ converges strongly to $T(t)\, Uf$ as $\lambda \to \infty$, uniformly with respect to t in $[0, b]$. Thus we may take the limit as $\lambda \to \infty$ on both sides of the equality

$$S_\lambda(t)\, f - f = \int_0^t S_\lambda(u)\, B_\lambda f\, du$$

to deduce

$$T(t)\, f - f = \int_0^t T(u)\, Uf\, du .$$

Hence, by definition of the infinitesimal generator A

$$A f \equiv \underset{\tau\to 0+}{\text{s-lim}}\, A_\tau f = \underset{\tau\to 0+}{\text{s-lim}}\, \frac{1}{\tau} \int_0^\tau T(u)\, Uf\, du = Uf$$

for each $f \in \mathsf{D}(U)$, i.e. $\mathsf{D}(U) \subset \mathsf{D}(A)$ and A is an extension of U. By assumption, λ belongs to $\varrho(U)$ for every $\lambda > \omega$. Using the estimate of the norm of $T(t)$, Theorem 1.3.5 also gives that $\lambda \in \varrho(A)$. Thus for these values of λ we have by the equations $(\lambda I - U)\, [\mathsf{D}(U)] = \mathsf{X}$, $A\, [\mathsf{D}(U)] = U[\mathsf{D}(U)]$ and $(\lambda I - A)\, [\mathsf{D}(A)] = \mathsf{X}$ that $\mathsf{D}(U) = \mathsf{D}(A)$, and consequently $U = A$, which proves the theorem.

The Hille-Yosida theorem is an immediate corollary. This gives sufficient conditions on U that it generates a semi-group of class $(\mathscr{C}_0)$.

Corollary 1.3.7. *If U is a closed linear operator with domain $\mathsf{D}(U)$ dense in X and if $R(\lambda; U)$ exists for all λ larger than some real number ω and satisfies the inequality*

$$\|R(\lambda; U)\| \leqq (\lambda - \omega)^{-1} \qquad (\lambda > \omega), \tag{1.3.12}$$

then U is the infinitesimal generator of a semi-group $\{T(t); 0 \leqq t < \infty\}$ of class $(\mathscr{C}_0)$ such that $\|T(t)\| \leqq e^{\omega t}$ for all $t \geqq 0$.

Proof. Since

$$\|[R(\lambda; U)]^r\| \leqq \|R(\lambda; U)\|^r \leqq (\lambda - \omega)^r \quad (r = 1, 2, \ldots; \lambda > \omega),$$

the sufficiency hypothesis of Theorem 1.3.6 is satisfied and the result follows.

There is an advantage in using criterion (1.3.12) rather than (1.3.8) since the former requires a bound only for the first power of the resolvent operator whereas the latter requires a bound for all of the positive integral powers of the resolvent.

Corollary 1.3.8. *A necessary and sufficient condition for a closed linear operator A in a Banach space X to itself with dense domain to generate a contraction semi-group of class $(\mathscr{C}_0)$ in $\mathscr{E}(\mathsf{X})$ is that $\{\lambda;\ \lambda > 0\}$ belongs to $\varrho(A)$ and $\lambda R(\lambda; A)$ is a contraction operator for each $\lambda > 0$.*

We next establish the uniqueness of the generation problem.

Proposition 1.3.9. *A closed linear operator U with domain $\mathsf{D}(U)$ dense in X is the infinitesimal generator of at most one semi-group of class $(\mathscr{C}_0)$.*

Proof. Suppose U is the infinitesimal generator of two semi-groups $\{T_1(t); 0 \leqq t < \infty\}$ and $\{T_2(t); 0 \leqq t < \infty\}$, each of class $(\mathscr{C}_0)$. If $f \in \mathsf{D}(U)$, then $V(s) f = T_1(t-s)\, T_2(s) f$ is strongly differentiable with respect to s in $0 < s < t$ for each fixed $t > 0$ and

$$\frac{d}{ds} V(s) f = T_1(t-s)\, U\, T_2(s) f - T_1(t-s)\, U\, T_2(s) f = \theta.$$

Thus, $V(s) f = V(t) f = V(0) f$, which shows that $T_1(t) f = T_2(t) f$ for all $t \geqq 0$ and each $f \in \mathsf{D}(U)$. Since $\mathsf{D}(U)$ is dense in X, this statement holds for all $f \in \mathsf{X}$ and thus the two semi-groups coincide.

In Theorem 1.3.5 we have seen that the resolvent $R(\lambda; A)$ of the infinitesimal generator A of a strongly continuous semi-group $\{T(t); 0 \leqq t < \infty\}$ is the Laplace transform of $T(t)$, whenever $\operatorname{Re}\lambda > \omega_0$ $(= \lim_{t\to\infty} (t^{-1} \log \|T(t)\|) < \infty)$. By Theorem 1.3.6 we can prove the following converse.

Proposition 1.3.10. *A necessary and sufficient condition for a closed linear operator U with dense domain and range in X to be the infinitesimal generator of a semi-group of class $(\mathscr{C}_0)$ is that there exists a family of bounded linear operators $\{S(t); 0 \leqq t < \infty\}$ continuous in the strong operator topology for $t \geqq 0$ satisfying $\|S(t)\| \leqq M e^{\omega t}$ for real numbers M and ω, and such that*

$$R(\lambda; U) f = \int_0^\infty e^{-\lambda t} S(t) f\, dt \qquad (f \in \mathsf{X};\ \lambda > \omega). \tag{1.3.13}$$

In this case $\{S(t); 0 \leqq t < \infty\}$ is the semi-group with infinitesimal generator U.

Proof. The necessity follows readily from Theorem 1.3.5. Conversely, if (1.3.13) is satisfied, then as in the necessity argument of Theorem 1.3.6

we have for each $f \in X$

$$[R(\lambda; U)]^r f = \frac{(-1)^{r-1}}{(r-1)!} R^{(r-1)}(\lambda; U) f = \frac{(-1)^{r-1}}{(r-1)!} \int_0^\infty (-t)^{r-1} e^{-\lambda t} S(t) f \, dt \qquad (r = 1, 2, \ldots).$$

This gives

$$\| [R(\lambda; U)]^r \| \leqq \frac{M}{(r-1)!} \int_0^\infty t^{r-1} e^{-\lambda t} e^{\omega t} \, dt = M(\lambda - \omega)^{-r}$$

for all $\lambda > \omega$ and $r = 1, 2, \ldots$ Thus, by the sufficiency hypothesis of Theorem 1.3.6, there exists a semi-group $\{T(t); 0 \leqq t < \infty\}$ of class $(\mathscr{C}_0)$ with $\|T(t)\| \leqq M e^{\omega t}$ having U as its infinitesimal generator. Moreover,

$$R(\lambda; U) f = \int_0^\infty e^{-\lambda t} T(t) f \, dt \qquad (f \in X;\ \lambda > \omega).$$

Thus for $f^* \in X^*$ we have

$$\int_0^\infty e^{-\lambda t} \langle f^*, T(t) f - S(t) f \rangle \, dt = 0 \qquad (\lambda > \omega).$$

The last assertion of Lemma 1.3.4 together with the strong continuity of the functions $T(t) f$ and $S(t) f$ implies that $\langle f^*, T(t) f \rangle = \langle f^*, S(t) f \rangle$ for each $t \geqq 0$ and all $f^* \in X^*$ and $f \in X$. Hence $T(t) \equiv S(t)$, $t \geqq 0$.

As a final consequence of Theorem 1.3.6 we obtain

Proposition 1.3.11. *If $\{T(t); 0 \leqq t < \infty\}$ is a semi-group of class $(\mathscr{C}_0)$ in $\mathscr{E}(X)$, then for each $f \in X$ and $t \geqq 0$,*

$$T(t) f = \underset{\lambda \to \infty}{\text{s-lim}}\, e^{-\lambda t} \sum_{k=0}^{\infty} \frac{(\lambda t)^k}{k!} [\lambda R(\lambda; A)]^k f, \tag{1.3.14}$$

the limit existing uniformly with respect to t in any finite interval $[0, b]$.

The proof follows readily from the proof of Theorem 1.3.6, in particular from relation (1.3.11), noting that

$$e^{-\lambda t} \sum_{k=0}^{\infty} \frac{(\lambda t)^k}{k!} [\lambda R(\lambda; A)]^k = \exp\{t[\lambda^2 R(\lambda; A) - \lambda I]\}.$$

1.3.3 Translations; Groups of Operators

In this subsection we shall go into a detailed discussion of the semi-group of left translations on the function spaces $UCB(\mathrm{E}_1)$ and $L^p(\mathrm{E}_1)$, $1 \leqq p < \infty$, defined in Example 1.2.5.

We start with the following definition:

Let $AC_{\mathrm{loc}}(\mathrm{E}_1)$ denote the space of all locally absolutely continuous real or complex-valued functions f on E_1, i.e. the space of those functions on E_1 which are absolutely continuous on each bounded closed subinterval of E_1.

Proposition 1.3.12. *Let* X *be one of the spaces* $\mathsf{UCB}(E_1)$, $\mathsf{L}^p(E_1)$, $1 \leq p < \infty$, *and let*

$$\mathsf{D}(A) = \{f \in \mathsf{X};\, f \in \mathsf{AC}_{\mathrm{loc}}(E_1) \text{ and } f' \in \mathsf{X}\} \tag{1.3.15}$$

be the domain of the operator of differentiation $A f = f'$.

(a) *A is a closed linear operator and* $\mathsf{D}(A)$ *is dense in* X.

(b) *The spectrum of A is given by*

$$\sigma(A) = \{\lambda;\, \mathrm{Re}\,\lambda = 0\} = \begin{cases} \mathrm{P}_\sigma(A) & (\mathsf{X} = \mathsf{UCB}(E_1)), \\ \mathrm{R}_\sigma(A) & (\mathsf{X} = \mathsf{L}^1(E_1)), \\ \mathrm{C}_\sigma(A) & (\mathsf{X} = \mathsf{L}^p(E_1),\ 1 < p < \infty). \end{cases} \tag{1.3.16}$$

The resolvent set $\varrho(A)$ *is equal to* $\{\lambda;\, \mathrm{Re}\,\lambda \neq 0\}$ *and* $R(\lambda; A)$ *has the representation*

$$\begin{cases} [R(\lambda; A) f](x) = \int_0^\infty e^{-\lambda t} f(x+t)\, dt & (\mathrm{Re}\,\lambda > 0), \\ [R(\lambda; A) f](x) = \int_{-\infty}^0 e^{-\lambda t} f(x+t)\, dt & (\mathrm{Re}\,\lambda < 0). \end{cases} \tag{1.3.17}$$

Finally, $\|R(\lambda; A)\| \leq 1/|\sigma|$ $(\lambda = \sigma + i\tau,\ \sigma \neq 0)$, *equality holding if λ is real.*

Proof. Regarding the proof of (a), A is obviously a linear operator. To prove that A is closed, assume there is a sequence of elements $\{f_n\}_{n=1}^\infty$ in $\mathsf{D}(A)$ with $f_n \to f$ and $f_n' \to g$ in norm as $n \to \infty$. Now

$$f_n(y) - f_n(x) = \int_x^y f_n'(u)\, du$$

for every x and y in E_1, and using classical arguments of the theory of Lebesgue integration, there exists a subsequence f_{n_k} converging to $f(y) - f(x)$ almost everywhere as $n_k \to \infty$. On the other hand, the right-hand side of the above equation tends to $\int_x^y g(u)\, du$ as $n \to \infty$. This gives $\int_x^y g(u)\, du = f(y) - f(x)$ for almost all x and y, proving that $f \in \mathsf{AC}_{\mathrm{loc}}(E_1)$ and $f'(x) = g(x)$ a.e. Consequently A is closed.

The function space $\mathsf{C}_{00}^\infty(E_1)$, the space of all real or complex-valued continuous functions φ on E_1 with compact support which have continuous derivatives of all orders, is a dense subset in $\mathsf{L}^p(E_1)$, $1 \leq p < \infty$. Moreover, since $\mathsf{C}_{00}^\infty(E_1) \subset \mathsf{D}(A) \subset \mathsf{L}^p(E_1)$, it follows that $\mathsf{D}(A)$ is dense in $\mathsf{L}^p(E_1)$, $1 \leq p < \infty$.

Regarding the case $X = UCB(\mathrm{E}_1)$, $C_{00}^{\infty}(\mathrm{E}_1)$ is a subspace of $UCB(\mathrm{E}_1)$, but its closure in $UCB(\mathrm{E}_1)$ is equal to the proper subspace

$$C_0(\mathrm{E}_1) = \{f \in UCB(\mathrm{E}_1);\ \{x \in \mathrm{E}_1;\ |f(x)| \geqq \varepsilon\} \text{ is compact, every } \varepsilon > 0\}.$$

However, the set of functions in $UCB(\mathrm{E}_1)$ defined by

$$g(x) = \int_{-\infty}^{\infty} \varphi(u)\, f(x+u)\, du \qquad (\varphi \in C_{00}^{\infty}(\mathrm{E}_1),\, f \in UCB(\mathrm{E}_1)),$$

belongs to $D(A)$ and is dense in $UCB(\mathrm{E}_1)$ (see the proof of Proposition 1.1.6 (c)).

To prove part (b), we first restrict the discussion to the function space $UCB(\mathrm{E}_1)$.

For λ to belong to the point spectrum of A, the homogeneous differential equation

$$(1.3.18) \qquad \lambda f(x) - f'(x) = 0$$

should have a non-trivial solution in $UCB(\mathrm{E}_1)$. Its solution is given by $c\, e^{\lambda x}$ which belongs to $UCB(\mathrm{E}_1)$ if $\mathrm{Re}\,\lambda = 0$ and only for these values of λ. Thus $\mathrm{P}_\sigma(A) = \{\lambda;\ \mathrm{Re}\,\lambda = 0\}$ and $f_\tau(x) = e^{i\tau x}$ $(\lambda = i\tau,\ -\infty < \tau < \infty)$ is an eigenfunction corresponding to the eigenvalue $i\tau$.

It follows that for all $\mathrm{Re}\,\lambda \neq 0$ the inhomogeneous differential equation

$$(1.3.19) \qquad \lambda f(x) - f'(x) = g(x)$$

has a unique solution for some $g \in UCB(\mathrm{E}_1)$, precisely for all $g \in R(\lambda I - A)$. Suppose $\mathrm{Re}\,\lambda > 0$. One verifies without difficulty that the solution of (1.3.19) is given by

$$f(x) = [R_\lambda g](x) = \int_x^{\infty} e^{\lambda(x-u)}\, g(u)\, du = \int_0^{\infty} e^{-\lambda u}\, g(x+u)\, du,$$

the integral existing as a Lebesgue integral. Thus

$$f = R_\lambda g = R_\lambda[\lambda I - A] f \qquad (f \in D(A)),$$

proving the second equation of (1.3.1).

Furthermore, R_λ defines a bounded linear transformation on $UCB(\mathrm{E}_1)$ into itself with $\|R_\lambda\| \leqq 1/\sigma$ $(\lambda = \sigma + i\tau,\, \sigma > 0)$, $R_\lambda[UCB(\mathrm{E}_1)] \subset D(A)$ and

$$[\lambda I - A]\, R_\lambda g = g \qquad (g \in UCB(\mathrm{E}_1)).$$

Indeed, for an arbitrary $g \in UCB(\mathrm{E}_1)$ the integral

$$[R_\lambda g](x) = \int_0^{\infty} e^{-\lambda u}\, g(x+u)\, du$$

exists for each real x and

$$|[R_\lambda g](x)| \leqq \frac{1}{\sigma}\, \|g\|_C \qquad (\mathrm{Re}\,\lambda = \sigma),$$

proving that the function $[R_\lambda g](x)$ is bounded. The estimate

$$|[R_\lambda g](y) - [R_\lambda g](x)| \leqq \frac{1}{\sigma} \|g(y+\cdot) - g(x+\cdot)\|_C$$

further shows that it is uniformly continuous on E_1 since g is uniformly continuous. Thus $R_\lambda \in \mathscr{E}(\mathsf{UCB}(E_1))$ and, as already has been proven, the norm $\|R_\lambda\| \leqq 1/\sigma$ $(\lambda = \sigma + i\tau, \sigma > 0)$, equality holding for real λ. By the representation of R_λ one easily verifies that its range belongs to $\mathsf{D}(A)$ and that

$$[R_\lambda g]'(x) = \lambda [R_\lambda g](x) - g(x) \qquad (g \in \mathsf{UCB}(E_1)),$$

establishing the first equation of (1.3.1). As a consequence, the set $\{\lambda; \operatorname{Re}\lambda > 0\} \subset \varrho(A)$ and the resolvent $R(\lambda; A)$ is equal to the operator R_λ.

By the same method one shows that $\{\lambda; \operatorname{Re}\lambda < 0\} \subset \varrho(A)$ too, and that the given representation in (1.3.17) is valid for the resolvent $R(\lambda; A)$. This proves part (b) for the space $\mathsf{UCB}(E_1)$.

To continue the proof for the Lebesgue spaces $\mathsf{L}^p(E_1)$, $1 \leqq p < \infty$, we need some further properties for these spaces.

The space of all essentially bounded complex-valued Lebesgue measurable functions $F(x)$ on E_1 will be denoted by $\mathsf{L}^\infty(E_1)$. It becomes a Banach space under the norm

$$\|F\|_\infty = \operatorname*{ess\,sup}_x |F(x)| = \inf\{M; \operatorname{meas}\{x \in E_1; |F(x)| > M\} = 0\}.$$

Clearly, $\mathsf{UCB}(E_1)$ is a closed subspace of $\mathsf{L}^\infty(E_1)$. Furthermore, the dual space of $\mathsf{L}^p(E_1)$, $1 \leqq p < \infty$, the Banach space of all bounded linear functionals on $\mathsf{L}^p(E_1)$, is by the Riesz representation theorem isometrically isomorphic to the space $\mathsf{L}^{p'}(E_1)$, $p^{-1} + p'^{-1} = 1$, and the natural pairing between the elements of $\mathsf{L}^p(E_1)$ and its dual $\mathsf{L}^{p'}(E_1)$ is given by

$$\langle F, f\rangle = \int_{-\infty}^{\infty} \bar{F}(x) f(x)\, dx \qquad (f \in \mathsf{L}^p(E_1), F \in \mathsf{L}^{p'}(E_1)),$$

where $\bar{F}$ denotes the complex conjugate of F. (By Hölder's inequality the product $\bar{F} f \in \mathsf{L}^1(E_1)$ and $|\langle F, f\rangle| \leqq \|F\|_{p'} \|f\|_p$.) $\mathsf{L}^p(E_1)$ is reflexive for $1 < p < \infty$, while $\mathsf{L}^1(E_1)$ and $\mathsf{L}^\infty(E_1)$ are not.

If $k \in \mathsf{L}^1(E_1)$, then for every $f \in \mathsf{L}^p(E_1)$, $1 \leqq p \leqq \infty$, the convolution integral

$$[K f](x) = \int_{-\infty}^{\infty} k(u) f(x+u)\, du$$

exists for almost all x, belongs to $\mathsf{L}^p(E_1)$ and $\|K f\|_p \leqq \|k\|_1 \|f\|_p$. If, in addition, $k \in \mathsf{L}^{p'}(E_1)$ for all $1 \leqq p' \leqq \infty$, then $[K f](x)$ exists for all x, moreover, it defines a function in $\mathsf{UCB}(E_1)$.

Returning to the proof of part (b) of the proposition, we remark that the homogeneous differential equation (1.3.18) only has the trivial solution in $L^p(E_1)$, $1 \leqq p < \infty$, proving that $P_\sigma(A) = \emptyset$ (the empty set). Moreover, using the properties of the convolution integral defined above, one verifies easily by the same method as in the proof for the space $UCB(E_1)$ that the set $\{\lambda; \operatorname{Re}\lambda \neq 0\} \subset \varrho(A)$ and that the representations (1.3.17) hold for the resolvent $R(\lambda; A)$. Thus it only remains to investigate the set $\{\lambda; \operatorname{Re}\lambda = 0\}$.

At first we turn to the space $L^1(E_1)$. Since the point spectrum is empty, the operator $i\tau I - A$ $(\lambda = i\tau; -\infty < \tau < \infty)$ has an inverse, but $D([i\tau I - A]^{-1})$, or equivalently, $R(i\tau I - A)$ is not dense in $L^1(E_1)$. Indeed, the bounded linear functional

$$\langle F_\tau, f\rangle = \int_{-\infty}^{\infty} e^{-i\tau x} f(x)\, dx \qquad (f \in L^1(E_1))$$

does not vanish identically on $L^1(E_1)$. However, $\langle F_\tau, i\tau f - f'\rangle = 0$ for all $f \in D(A)$. This proves that the set $\{\lambda; \operatorname{Re}\lambda = 0\}$ belongs to the residual spectrum $R_\sigma(A)$ of A.

The proposition will be proved if we show that for the space $L^p(E_1)$, $1 < p < \infty$, the set $\{\lambda; \operatorname{Re}\lambda = 0\}$ belongs to the continuous spectrum $C_\sigma(A)$ of A. We know already that $P_\sigma(A) = \emptyset$. Thus the operator $i\tau I - A$ $(-\infty < \tau < \infty)$ has an inverse. If $i\tau \in C_\sigma(A)$, then the domain of $[i\tau I - A]^{-1}$ is dense in $L^p(E_1)$ and the norm $\|[i\tau I - A]^{-1}\|$ is unbounded. The first of these assertions will follow if we can show that any bounded linear functional F_τ vanishing on $D([i\tau I - A]^{-1})$ vanishes identically. Let $F_\tau \in L^{p'}(E_1)$, $p^{-1} + p'^{-1} = 1$, be such that $\langle F_\tau, i\tau f - f'\rangle = 0$ for all $f \in D(A)$. Using Fubini's theorem, we then obtain

$$\begin{aligned}\int_{-\infty}^{\infty}\left((i\tau)\int_0^t \bar F_\tau(x+u)\,du\right) f(x)\,dx &= \int_0^t du\,(i\tau)\int_{-\infty}^{\infty} \bar F_\tau(x) f(x-u)\,dx\\ &= \int_0^t du \int_{-\infty}^{\infty} \bar F_\tau(x) f'(x-u)\,dx = \int_{-\infty}^{\infty} \bar F_\tau(x)\left(\int_0^t f'(x-u)\,du\right)dx\\ &= \int_{-\infty}^{\infty} \bar F_\tau(x)\,(f(x) - f(x-t))\,dx = \int_{-\infty}^{\infty}(\bar F_\tau(x) - \bar F_\tau(x+t))\,f(x)\,dx\end{aligned}$$

for each fixed $t \neq 0$ and all $f \in D(A)$. Since $D(A)$ is dense in $L^p(E_1)$, the equation

$$\int_{-\infty}^{\infty}(\bar F_\tau(x+t) - \bar F_\tau(x))\,f(x)\,dx = \int_{-\infty}^{\infty}\left((-i\tau)\int_0^t \bar F_\tau(x+u)\,du\right) f(x)\,dx$$

holds for all $f \in L^p(\mathrm{E}_1)$ and thus

$$F_\tau(x+t) - F_\tau(x) = i\tau \int_0^t F_\tau(x+u)\,du,$$

proving that $F_\tau \in AC_{\mathrm{loc}}(\mathrm{E}_1)$ and that $(i\tau)\,F'_\tau - F_\tau = \theta$. But the homogeneous differential equation (1.3.18) has only the trivial solution in $L^{p'}(\mathrm{E}_1)$, $1 < p' < \infty$; this means $F_\tau = \theta$, and as a consequence the range of $i\tau I - A$ is dense in $L^p(\mathrm{E}_1)$.

Finally, the functions

$$f_n(x) = \left(\frac{1}{2n}\right)^{1/p} \begin{cases} e^{(i\tau - 1/np)x} & (x > 0) \\ 1 & (x = 0) \\ e^{(i\tau + 1/np)x} & (x < 0) \end{cases}$$

belong to $D(A)$ for all $n = 1, 2, \ldots$, and their norms $\|f_n\|_p = 1$. Since the norms of

$$i\tau f_n(x) - f'_n(x) = i\tau f_n(x) - \left(i\tau - \frac{\operatorname{sgn} x}{np}\right) f_n(x) = \left(\frac{\operatorname{sgn} x}{np}\right) f_n(x)$$

tend to zero as $n \to \infty$, the operator $[i\tau I - A]^{-1}$ is necessarily unbounded. This completes the proof of the proposition.

Using this proposition we are able to prove the following theorem for the semi-group of left translations on $UCB(\mathrm{E}_1)$, $L^p(\mathrm{E}_1)$, $1 \leqq p < \infty$.

Theorem 1.3.13. *Let X be one of the spaces $UCB(\mathrm{E}_1)$, $L^p(\mathrm{E}_1)$, $1 \leqq p < \infty$. The family of left translations $\{T(t); 0 \leqq t < \infty\}$ in $\mathscr{E}(X)$ defined by*

$$[T(t)\,f](x) = f(x+t) \qquad (f \in X)$$

forms a contraction semi-group of class $(\mathscr{C}_0)$ with

$$D(A) = \{f \in X;\, f \in AC_{\mathrm{loc}}(\mathrm{E}_1) \text{ and } f' \in X\}$$

and $A f = f'$.

Furthermore, for each integer $r > 0$

$$D(A^r) = \{f \in X;\, f, f', \ldots, f^{(r-1)} \in AC_{\mathrm{loc}}(\mathrm{E}_1) \cap X \text{ and } f^{(r)} \in X\}$$

and $A^r f = f^{(r)}$.

Proof. By Proposition 1.3.12 we obtain that the operator A satisfies the assumptions of the Hille-Yosida theorem (Corollary 1.3.7) and thus generates a contraction semi-group of class $(\mathscr{C}_0)$. By the representation (1.3.17) of the resolvent $R(\lambda; A)$ $(\mathrm{Re}\,\lambda > 0)$ and Proposition 1.3.10 we obtain that the generated semi-group is equal to the semi-group of left translations.

Thus we have a detailed proof of the statements given in Example 1.2.5.

At this stage it is necessary to say something about *groups of operators* in $\mathscr{E}(X)$.

Definition 1.3.14. *If the map $t \to T(t)$ from the real axis into the Banach algebra $\mathscr{E}(\mathsf{X})$ satisfies the conditions*

$$(1.3.20) \quad \begin{cases} \text{(i)} & T(t_1 + t_2) = T(t_1)\,T(t_2) \qquad (-\infty < t_1, t_2 < \infty), \\ \text{(ii)} & T(0) = I, \end{cases}$$

then the family $\{T(t); -\infty < t < \infty\}$ is called a one-parameter group of operators in $\mathscr{E}(\mathsf{X})$. The group is said to be of class $(\mathscr{C}_0)$ if it is continuous at the origin in the strong operator topology, i.e. if

$$(1.3.20) \qquad \text{(iii)} \quad \operatorname*{s-lim}_{t\to 0} T(t)\,f = f \qquad (f \in \mathsf{X}).$$

As we have seen in Sec. 1.1.1, a uniformly continuous semi-group $\{T(t); 0 \leqq t < \infty\}$ in $\mathscr{E}(\mathsf{X})$ can always be extended to a uniformly continuous group on $-\infty < t < \infty$, moreover to a holomorphic group on the complex ζ-plane. Indeed $T(\zeta) = \exp(\zeta A)$, where A is the bounded infinitesimal generator.

By definition, $\{T^+(t) = T(t);\ 0 \leqq t < \infty\}$ and $\{T^-(t) = T(-t);\ 0 \leqq t < \infty\}$ are both semi-groups of class $(\mathscr{C}_0)$ in $\mathscr{E}(\mathsf{X})$. Consequently, if we define

$$\omega_+ \equiv \lim_{t\to\infty} t^{-1} \log \| T^+(t) \|, \qquad \omega_- \equiv \lim_{t\to\infty} t^{-1} \log \| T^-(t) \|,$$

then by Proposition 1.1.2 for each $\omega > \max(\omega_+, \omega_-)$ there exists a constant M_ω such that

$$\| T(t) \| \leqq M_\omega\, e^{\omega |t|} \qquad (-\infty < t < \infty).$$

The infinitesimal generator A of the group $\{T(t); -\infty < t < \infty\}$ is defined by the limit in norm as $\tau \to 0$ of

$$A_\tau f \equiv \frac{T(\tau) - I}{\tau}\, f \qquad (\tau \neq 0),$$

whenever it exists. A is a closed linear operator with domain $\mathsf{D}(A)$ dense in X.

The question as to whether a closed linear operator U with dense domain generates a group of operators of class $(\mathscr{C}_0)$ in $\mathscr{E}(\mathsf{X})$ will be answered in the following theorem.

Theorem 1.3.15. *A necessary and sufficient condition that a closed linear operator U with domain $\mathsf{D}(U)$ dense in X generates a group of operators $\{T(t); -\infty < t < \infty\}$ in $\mathscr{E}(\mathsf{X})$ of class $(\mathscr{C}_0)$ is that there exist real numbers M and $\omega \geqq 0$ such that for every real λ, $|\lambda| > \omega$,*

$$(1.3.21) \qquad \| [R(\lambda; U)]^r \| \leqq M (|\lambda| - \omega)^{-r} \qquad (r = 1, 2, \ldots).$$

Furthermore, $\| T(t) \| \leqq M\, e^{\omega |t|}$ for all t.

We shall not prove this theorem, since the proof easily follows from Theorem 1.3.6.

By means of this theorem and Proposition 1.3.12 it is obvious that the operator of differentiation $A = (d/dx)$ defined in (1.3.15) for the function spaces $UCB(E_1)$ and $L^p(E_1)$, $1 \leqq p < \infty$, not only generates the semi-group of left translations, as was stated in Theorem 1.3.13, but even the group of translations

$$[T(t) f](x) = f(x+t) \qquad (-\infty < t < \infty;\ f \in X),$$

which is a contraction group of class $(\mathscr{C}_0)$ in $\mathscr{E}(X)$.

We shall conclude with a discussion of the semi-group of left translations on the function spaces $UCB(E_1^+)$ and $L^p(E_1^+)$, $1 \leqq p < \infty$, E_1^+ being the positive real number system.

Theorem 1.3.16. *Let X be one of the spaces $UCB(E_1^+)$, $L^p(E_1^+)$, $1 \leqq p < \infty$. The semi-group of left translations*

$$[T(t) f](x) = f(x+t) \qquad (f \in X;\ 0 \leqq t < \infty)$$

is generated by the operator of differentiation $Af = f'$ with domain

$$D(A) = \{f \in X; f \in AC_{\text{loc}}(E_1^+) \text{ and } f' \in X\}.$$

$\{T(t); 0 \leqq t < \infty\}$ is a contraction semi-group of class $(\mathscr{C}_0)$ in $\mathscr{E}(X)$. Furthermore, the spectrum of A is given by

$$\sigma(A) = \{\lambda;\ \mathrm{Re}\,\lambda \leqq 0\}.$$

In particular, for the space $UCB(E_1^+)$ the spectrum $\sigma(A) = P_\sigma(A)$, and for $L^p(E_1^+)$, $1 \leqq p < \infty$, $\sigma(A)$ is the union of $P_\sigma(A) = \{\lambda; \mathrm{Re}\,\lambda < 0\}$ and $C_\sigma(A) = \{\lambda;\ \mathrm{Re}\,\lambda = 0\}$. Also, $\varrho(A) = \{\lambda;\ \mathrm{Re}\,\lambda > 0\}$ and the resolvent is given by

$$[R(\lambda; A) f](x) = \int_0^\infty e^{-\lambda t} f(x+t)\, dt.$$

For the norm of the resolvent we have the estimate $\| R(\lambda;\ A) \| \leqq 1/\sigma$ $(\mathrm{Re}\,\lambda = \sigma > 0)$.

We will not prove this theorem explicitly.

1.4 Dual Semi-Groups

1.4.1 Theory

As in the foregoing sections, X will be a real or complex Banach space and $\{T(t); 0 \leqq t < \infty\}$ a semi-group of class $(\mathscr{C}_0)$ in $\mathscr{E}(X)$. Let X^* be the dual (or adjoint) space of all bounded linear functionals f^* on X. X^* is again a Banach space under the norm

$$\| f^* \| = \sup_{\|f\| \leqq 1,\ f \in X} |\langle f^*, f \rangle|.$$

Definition 1.4.1. *Let U be a linear operator with domain $\mathsf{D}(U)$ dense in X to X. The* d u a l *(or adjoint) operator U^* of U is a transformation whose domain $\mathsf{D}(U^*)$ consists of the set of all $f^* \in \mathsf{X}^*$ for which there exists a $g^* \in \mathsf{X}^*$ such that*

$$\langle g^*, f\rangle = \langle f^*, U f\rangle \tag{1.4.1}$$

for all $f \in \mathsf{D}(U)$; in this case we set $U^* f^* = g^*$.

Proposition 1.4.2. *Let U be a linear operator with domain $\mathsf{D}(U)$ dense in X to X.*

(a) *The dual U^* is a weakly* closed linear operator. If in addition U is bounded, then $U^* \in \mathscr{E}(\mathsf{X}^*)$ and $\|U^*\| = \|U\|$.*

(b) *If U is closed, then $\mathsf{D}(U^*)$ is weakly* dense in X^* and, if X is reflexive, $\mathsf{D}(U^*)$ is strongly dense in X^*.*

Proof. (a) Since $\mathsf{D}(U)$ is a dense subset in X, the functional $\langle f^*, U f\rangle$ has a unique bounded extension on X whenever it is bounded on $\mathsf{D}(U)$ (App. 1), and so g^* is uniquely determined. Thus the dual operator U^* is well-defined; obviously, it is a linear operator. To prove that U^* is weakly* closed, we remark that the graph of U^* in $\mathsf{X}^* \times \mathsf{X}^* = (\mathsf{X} \times \mathsf{X})^*$:

$$\operatorname{graph} U^* = \{(U^* f^*, f^*) \in \mathsf{X}^* \times \mathsf{X}^*;\, f^* \in \mathsf{D}(U^*)\},$$

by Definition 1.4.1 is equal to the annihilator of the graph of U in $(\mathsf{X} \times \mathsf{X})^*$, i.e.

$$\operatorname{graph} U^* = (\operatorname{graph} U)^0 = \{(g^*, f^*) \in \mathsf{X}^* \times \mathsf{X}^*;\, \langle g^*, f\rangle - \langle f^*, U f\rangle = 0 \text{ for all } (f, U f) \in \operatorname{graph} U \text{ in } \mathsf{X} \times \mathsf{X}\},$$

where the natural pairing between $\mathsf{X} \times \mathsf{X}$ and its dual $\mathsf{X}^* \times \mathsf{X}^*$ is defined by $\langle f^*, f\rangle - \langle h^*, h\rangle$ for all $(f, h) \in \mathsf{X} \times \mathsf{X}$ and $(f^*, h^*) \in \mathsf{X}^* \times \mathsf{X}^*$. Then, by a corollary concerning annihilators the graph of U^* is a saturated subspace of $\mathsf{X}^* \times \mathsf{X}^*$ and thus weakly* closed (App. 1).

If U is bounded, then for an arbitrary $f^* \in \mathsf{X}^*$ the mapping $f \to \langle f^*, U f\rangle$ defines a bounded linear functional on $\mathsf{D}(U)$. Thus $\mathsf{D}(U^*) = \mathsf{X}^*$. Moreover, U^* is bounded and

$$\begin{aligned} \|U^*\| &= \sup_{\|f^*\| \leq 1} \|U^* f^*\| = \sup_{\|f^*\| \leq 1} \sup_{\|f\| \leq 1} |\langle U^* f^*, f\rangle| \\ &= \sup_{\|f\| \leq 1} \sup_{\|f^*\| \leq 1} |\langle f^*, U f\rangle| = \sup_{\|f\| \leq 1} \|U f\| = \|U\| \\ &\qquad (f \in \mathsf{D}(U),\ f^* \in \mathsf{X}^*). \end{aligned}$$

(b) If $\mathsf{D}(U^*)$ were not weakly* dense in X^*, then there would exist an element $f_0 \in \mathsf{X}$, $f_0 \neq \theta$ such that $\langle f^*, f_0\rangle = 0$ for all $f^* \in \mathsf{D}(U^*)$. Now, since U is a closed operator, graph U is a closed linear manifold in $\mathsf{X} \times \mathsf{X}$ and (θ, f_0) does not belong to it. By a corollary of the theorem of Hahn-Banach there then exists an element $(g_0^*, f_0^*) \in \mathsf{X}^* \times \mathsf{X}^*$ such that $\langle g_0^*, f\rangle - \langle f_0^*, U f\rangle = 0$ for all $f \in \mathsf{D}(U)$ and $\langle g_0^*, \theta\rangle - \langle f_0^*, f_0\rangle \neq 0$. Hence we obtain from the first of these assertions that $f_0^* \in \mathsf{D}(U^*)$ and from the second one that $\langle f_0^*, f_0\rangle \neq 0$, which is impossible by the way in which f_0 was chosen.

If X is reflexive, then the weak and weak* topologies of X^* coincide, and thus the strong and weak closures of $\mathsf{D}(U^*)$ are equal (App. 1).

It is the purpose of this subsection to investigate the dual semi-group operators $T^*(t), t \geqq 0$, as well as the dual infinitesimal generator A^* on X^* and to establish their fundamental properties.

Proposition 1.4.3. *Let $\{T(t); 0 \leqq t < \infty\}$ be a semi-group of operators of class $(\mathscr{C}_0)$ in $\mathscr{E}(\mathsf{X})$. Then $T^*(t)$ is an operator function on the interval $0 \leqq t < \infty$ into the Banach algebra $\mathscr{E}(\mathsf{X}^*)$ with $\| T^*(t) \| = \| T(t) \|$ for each $t \geqq 0$. Moreover,*

$$(1.4.2)\quad \begin{cases} \text{(i)*} & T^*(t_1)\, T^*(t_2) = T^*(t_1 + t_2) \qquad (t_1, t_2 \geqq 0); \\ \text{(ii)*} & T^*(0) = I^* \ \textit{(identity operator on } \mathsf{X}^*\textit{)}; \\ \text{(iii)*} & \text{w*-}\lim_{t\to 0+} T^*(t) f^* = f^* \ \textit{for all } f^* \in \mathsf{X}^* \ \textit{(weak* continuity} \\ & \textit{of } T^*(t) \textit{ at the origin)}. \end{cases}$$

Proof. For each fixed $t \geqq 0$ the dual $T^*(t)$ defines (by Proposition 1.4.2 (a)) a bounded linear transformation from X^* to itself with $\| T^*(t) \| = \| T(t) \|$, proving the first part of this proposition. The relations (i)* and (ii)* of (1.4.2) are immediate consequences of the definition of a dual operator, whereas the third property in (1.4.2) follows from the fact that $\{T(t); 0 \leqq t < \infty\}$ is a strongly continuous semi-group. Indeed,

$$\langle T^*(t) f^* - f^*, f\rangle = \langle f^*, T(t) f - f\rangle,$$

which tends to zero as $t \to 0+$ for each $f^* \in \mathsf{X}^*$ and all $f \in \mathsf{X}$.

By the properties (i)* and (ii)* of (1.4.2) we see that $\{T^*(t); 0 \leqq t < \infty\}$ defines a semi-group of operators in $\mathscr{E}(\mathsf{X}^*)$ which, however, does not necessarily belong to the class $(\mathscr{C}_0)$ in general. Nevertheless, the map $t \to T^*(t)$ on $[0, \infty)$ into $\mathscr{E}(\mathsf{X}^*)$ is continuous in the weak* operator topology (App. 2). This follows readily from property (iii)* of (1.4.2). Thus we call $\{T^*(t); 0 \leqq t < \infty\}$ a weakly* continuous semi-group or a *semi-group of operators of class $(\mathscr{C}_0)^*$ in $\mathscr{E}(\mathsf{X}^*)$*.

As a first result concerning dual semi-groups we obtain

Proposition 1.4.4. *Under the hypothesis of the foregoing proposition we have*

(a) *The dual A^* of the infinitesimal generator A of the given semi-group $\{T(t); 0 \leqq t < \infty\}$ is a weakly* closed linear operator and its domain $\mathsf{D}(A^*)$ is weakly* dense in X^*.*

(b) *If f^* belongs to $\mathsf{D}(A^*)$, so does $T^*(t) f^*$ for each $t \geqq 0$ and $A^* T^*(t) f^* = T^*(t) A^* f^*$. Furthermore,*

$$(1.4.3) \qquad \langle T^*(t) f^* - f^*, f\rangle = \int_0^t \langle T^*(u) A^* f^*, f\rangle \, du \qquad (f \in \mathsf{X};\ t > 0).$$

(c) *An element $f^* \in \mathsf{X}^*$ belongs to the domain of A^* if and only if*

$$(1.4.4.) \qquad A_\tau^* f^* \equiv \frac{T^*(\tau) - I^*}{\tau} f^* \qquad (f^* \in \mathsf{X}^*;\ \tau > 0)$$

converges in the weak topology of X^* as $\tau \to 0+$, and the weak* limit is equal to $A^* f^*$.*

Proof. (a) Under the given hypothesis upon the semi-group $\{T(t); 0 \leqq t < \infty\}$ its infinitesimal generator A is a closed linear operator with domain $\mathsf{D}(A)$ dense in X. Thus A has a dual A^* which by Proposition 1.4.2 satisfies the properties given in part (a).

(b) If $f^* \in \mathsf{D}(A^*)$, then we have for each fixed $t \geqq 0$ and all $f \in \mathsf{D}(A)$ by the definition of the dual A^* and by Proposition 1.1.4 (b) that

$$\langle T^*(t) A^* f^*, f\rangle = \langle A^* f^*, T(t) f\rangle = \langle f^*, A T(t) f\rangle$$
$$= \langle f^*, T(t) A f\rangle = \langle T^*(t) f^*, A f\rangle,$$

proving that $T^*(t) f^* \in \mathsf{D}(A^*)$ and $A^* T^*(t) f^* = T^*(t) A^* f^*$. Moreover, for any fixed $f^* \in \mathsf{D}(A^*)$, the numerically-valued function $\langle T^*(u) A^* f^*, f\rangle = \langle A^* f^*, T(u) f\rangle$ on $[0, \infty)$ is continuous for each $f \in \mathsf{X}$. Hence, for an arbitrary $t > 0$

$$\int_0^t \langle T^*(u) A^* f^*, f\rangle \, du = \int_0^t \langle A^* f^*, T(u) f\rangle \, du = \langle A^* f^*, \int_0^t T(u) f \, du\rangle$$
$$= \langle f^*, A\left(\int_0^t T(u) f \, du\right)\rangle = \langle f^*, T(t) f - f\rangle = \langle T^*(t) f^* - f^*, f\rangle,$$

using the fact that the vector-valued function $T(u) f$ on $[0, \infty)$ is strongly continuous and that the integral $\int_0^t T(u) f \, du \in \mathsf{D}(A)$ with $A\left(\int_0^t T(u) f \, du\right) = T(t) f - f$. This shows relation (1.4.3).

(c) Assume $f^* \in \mathsf{X}^*$ is such that $A_\tau^* f^*$ converges to an element g^* in the weak* topology of X^* as $\tau \to 0+$. Then for all $f \in \mathsf{D}(A)$

$$\langle g^*, f\rangle = \lim_{\tau \to 0+} \langle A_\tau^* f^*, f\rangle = \lim_{\tau \to 0+} \langle f^*, A_\tau f\rangle = \langle f^*, A f\rangle,$$

proving that $f^* \in \mathsf{D}(A^*)$ and $A^* f^* = g^*$. Conversely, for any fixed $f^* \in \mathsf{D}(A^*)$ one obtains by relation (1.4.3)

$$\langle A^*_\tau f^*, f\rangle = \frac{1}{\tau}\langle T^*(\tau) f^* - f^*, f\rangle = \frac{1}{\tau}\int_0^\tau \langle T^*(u)\, A^* f^*, f\rangle\, du$$

$$= \frac{1}{\tau}\int_0^\tau \langle A^* f^*, T(u)\, f\rangle\, du = \langle A^* f^*, \frac{1}{\tau}\int_0^\tau T(u)\, f\, du\rangle$$

for all $f \in \mathsf{X}$. Since $(1/\tau)\int_0^\tau T(u)\, f\, du \to f$ in the strong topology of X as $\tau \to 0+$, we have that the limit of $\langle A^*_\tau f^*, f\rangle$ exists as $\tau \to 0+$ and is equal to $\langle A^* f^*, f\rangle$ for all $f \in \mathsf{X}$, which concludes the proof of this proposition.

Corollary 1.4.5. *The dual operator A^* is equal to the weak* infinitesimal generator of the dual semi-group.*

Remark. In Theorem 1.3.5 we have seen that all complex numbers λ with $\operatorname{Re}\lambda > \omega_0$ $(= \lim_{t\to 0+} t^{-1} \log \| T(t)\| < \infty)$ belong to the resolvent set $\varrho(A)$ and that $R(\lambda; A)\, f = \int_0^\infty e^{-\lambda t}\, T(t)\, f\, dt$ $(f \in \mathsf{X})$. Regarding the dual operator A^*, we have that $\{\lambda; \operatorname{Re}\lambda > \omega_0\}$ also belongs to $\varrho(A^*)$ and that the resolvent $R(\lambda; A^*)$ is equal to $R(\lambda; A)^*$. Indeed, $(\lambda I - A)^* = \lambda I^* - A^*$ and, using the resolvent relations(1.3.6) and (1.3.7),

$$\begin{aligned}
\langle f^*, f\rangle &= \langle f^*, (\lambda I - A)\, R(\lambda; A)\, f\rangle = \langle(\lambda I^* - A^*)\, f^*, R(\lambda; A)\, f\rangle\\
&= \langle R(\lambda; A)^* (\lambda I^* - A^*)\, f^*, f\rangle \qquad (f \in \mathsf{X},\ f^* \in \mathsf{D}(A^*)),\\
\langle f^*, f\rangle &= \langle f^*, R(\lambda; A)\, (\lambda I - A)\, f\rangle\\
&= \langle R(\lambda; A)^* f^*, (\lambda I - A)\, f\rangle \qquad (f \in \mathsf{D}(A),\ f^* \in \mathsf{X}^*),
\end{aligned}$$

which proves the assertion.

Furthermore, if in addition to the hypothesis of Proposition 1.4.3 $\{T(t); 0 \leqq t < \infty\}$ is holomorphic, then the dual semi-group has a *holomorphic extension* $T^*(\zeta)$ in a sector $\Delta = \{\zeta; \operatorname{Re}\zeta > 0, |\arg\zeta| < \alpha_0 \leqq \pi/2\}$ of the complex plane, thus:

(i)* $T^*(\zeta)$ is a holomorphic operator function in Δ with values in $\mathscr{E}(\mathsf{X}^*)$;

(ii)* $T^*(\zeta_1)\, T^*(\zeta_2) = T^*(\zeta_1 + \zeta_2)$ whenever $\zeta_1, \zeta_2 \in \Delta$;

(iii)* $\text{w*-}\lim_{\zeta\to 0} T^*(\zeta)\, f^* = f^*$ for all $f^* \in \mathsf{X}^*$, where $|\arg\zeta| \leqq \alpha < \alpha_0$.

This is readily shown by Proposition 1.1.11.

We denote by X_0^* the set of all elements $f^* \in \mathsf{X}^*$, for which the map $t \to T^*(t) f^*$ from $[0, \infty)$ to X^* is strongly continuous at the origin, i.e.

$$\mathsf{X}_0^* = \{f^* \in \mathsf{X}^*; \lim_{t \to 0+} \| T^*(t) f^* - f^* \| = 0\}. \tag{1.4.5}$$

Obviously, X_0^* is non-empty; it contains at least the zero-element θ^*. Actually, X_0^* is larger. We can prove

Proposition 1.4.6. (a) *X_0^* is a strongly closed invariant linear manifold in X^*.*

(b) $\mathsf{D}(A^*) \subset \mathsf{X}_0^*$. *Moreover,*

$$\| T^*(t)f^* - f^* \| \leqq \sup_{0 \leqq u \leqq t} \{\| T(u) \|\} \cdot \| A^* f^* \| \, t \qquad (f^* \in \mathsf{D}(A^*)). \tag{1.4.6}$$

Proof. (a) That X_0^* is a linear subspace in X^* is obvious. To prove that it is strongly closed, suppose that $\{f_n^*\}_{n=1}^{\infty}$ is a sequence of elements in X_0^* converging in norm to an $f_0^* \in \mathsf{X}^*$ as $n \to \infty$, i.e. for each $\varepsilon > 0$ there is an $n = n(\varepsilon)$ such that $\| f_n^* - f_0^* \| < \varepsilon/2(M + 1)$, where the constant M is given by $\| T^*(t) \| = \| T(t) \| \leqq M$ on $[0, 1]$. Then

$$\begin{aligned} \| T^*(t) f_0^* - f_0^* \| &\leqq \| T^*(t) f_0^* - T^*(t) f_n^* \| + \| T^*(t) f_n^* - f_n^* \| + \| f_n^* - f_0^* \| \\ &\leqq (M + 1) \| f_n^* - f_0^* \| + \| T^*(t) f_n^* - f_n^* \|. \end{aligned}$$

By assumption there is a $\delta = \delta(\varepsilon, n) > 0$ $(0 < \delta \leqq 1)$ such that $\| T^*(t) f_n^* - f_n^* \| < \varepsilon/2$ for all $0 \leqq t < \delta$, and consequently $\| T^*(t) f_0^* - f_0^* \| < \varepsilon$ for $0 \leqq t < \delta$, which proves that X_0^* is a closed subspace in X^*.

From the semi-group property of $\{T^*(t); 0 \leqq t < \infty\}$ it follows readily that $f^* \in \mathsf{X}_0^*$ if and only if the function $T^*(t) f^*$ is strongly continuous on $[0, \infty)$; this implies at the same time that X_0^* is an invariant linear manifold under the dual semi-group, i.e. $T^*(t) [\mathsf{X}_0^*] \subset \mathsf{X}^*$ for all $t \geqq 0$.

(b) If $f^* \in \mathsf{D}(A^*)$, then relation (1.4.3) gives

$$\begin{aligned} |\langle T^*(t) f^* - f^*, f \rangle| &\leqq \int_0^t |\langle T^*(u) A^* f^*, f \rangle| \, du \\ &\leqq \sup_{0 \leqq u \leqq t} \{\| T(u) \|\} \cdot \| A^* f^* \| \, \| f \| \, t, \end{aligned}$$

proving relation (1.4.6).

As a consequence of this proposition we obtain that X_0^* itself becomes a Banach space under the norm of X^* and that the restriction $\{T_0^*(t); 0 \leqq t < \infty\}$ of the dual semi-group $\{T^*(t); 0 \leqq t < \infty\}$ on X_0^* defines a semi-group of class $(\mathscr{C}_0)$ in $\mathscr{E}(\mathsf{X}_0^*)$. We denote the infinitesimal generator of $\{T_0^*(t); 0 \leqq t < \infty\}$ by A_0^* and its domain by $\mathsf{D}(A_0^*)$. Clearly, the semi-group $\{T_0^*(t); 0 \leqq t < \infty\}$ and its infinitesimal generator A_0^* have all the properties stated in the foregoing sections.

In the following proposition we study the connections between the dual semi-group $\{T^*(t); 0 \leqq t < \infty\}$ on X^* and its restriction $\{T_0^*(t); 0 \leqq t < \infty\}$ on X_0^*.

Proposition 1.4.7. (a) $\mathsf{D}(A_0^*) \subset \mathsf{D}(A^*) \subset \mathsf{X}_0^*$. *$\mathsf{X}_0^*$ is equal to the strong closure of $\mathsf{D}(A^*)$ in X^*, while $\mathsf{D}(A_0^*)$ is weakly* dense in X^*.*

(b) *A_0^* is equal to the largest restriction of A^* with both domain and range in X_0^*. On the other hand, A^* is equal to the weak* closure of A_0^*, i.e. the graph of A^* is equal to the weak* closure of the graph of A_0^* in $\mathsf{X}^* \times \mathsf{X}^*$.*

Proof. (a) If $f^* \in \mathsf{D}(A_0^*)$ then, by definition, $A_\tau^* f^* \to A_0^* f^*$ in the strong sense as $\tau \to 0+$. But strong convergence implies weak and weak* convergence, and thus by Proposition 1.4.4 (c) f^* belongs to $\mathsf{D}(A^*)$. The inclusion $\mathsf{D}(A^*) \subset \mathsf{X}_0^*$ has already been shown. Furthermore, since $\mathsf{D}(A_0^*)$ is strongly dense in X_0^*, so is the larger subspace $\mathsf{D}(A^*)$ of X_0^*. At the same time this proves together with Proposition 1.4.4 (a) that $\mathsf{D}(A_0^*)$ is weakly* dense in X^*.

(b) The first part will be proved if one can show that an element $f^* \in \mathsf{D}(A^*)$ belongs to $\mathsf{D}(A_0^*)$ if $A^* f^* \in \mathsf{X}_0^*$. Now, if $A^* f^* \in \mathsf{X}_0^*$, then the map $u \to T_0^*(u) A^* f^*$ is strongly continuous on $[0, \infty)$ into X_0^* and by (1.4.3)

$$\langle T_0^*(t) f^* - f^*, f\rangle = \int_0^t \langle T_0^*(u) A^* f^*, f\rangle\, du = \langle \int_0^t T_0^*(u) A^* f^*\, du, f\rangle$$

for all $f \in \mathsf{X}$ and any fixed $t > 0$. Applying a corollary of the theorem of Hahn-Banach we obtain

$$T_0^*(t) f^* - f^* = \int_0^t T_0^*(u) A^* f^*\, du,$$

proving that $f^* \in \mathsf{D}(A_0^*)$ and $A_0^* f^* = A^* f^*$.

Since A^* is a weakly* closed operator, it suffices to show that the graph of A_0^*: $\operatorname{graph} A_0^* = \{(A_0^* f^*, f^*) \in \mathsf{X}^* \times \mathsf{X}^*; f^* \in \mathsf{D}(A_0^*)\}$, is weakly* dense in the graph of A^*. Thus we need only prove that any weakly* continuous linear functional on $\mathsf{X}^* \times \mathsf{X}^*$ that vanishes on the graph of A_0^* also vanishes on the graph of A^*. Now, since the space of all weakly* continuous linear functionals on $\mathsf{X}^* \times \mathsf{X}^*$ is given by $\mathsf{X} \times \mathsf{X}$, let (f, g) be an ordered pair in $\mathsf{X} \times \mathsf{X}$ such that

$$\langle A_0^* f^*, f\rangle - \langle f^*, g\rangle = 0 \tag{1.4.7}$$

for all $f^* \in \mathsf{D}(A_0^*)$. Using the relation $T_0^*(t) f^* - f^* = \int_0^t T_0^*(u) A_0^* f^*\, du$

for all $f^* \in \mathsf{D}(A_0^*)$ and any fixed $t > 0$ as well as relation (1.4.7), we then obtain

$$\langle f^*, T(t)\, f - f\rangle = \langle T_0^*(t)\, f^* - f^*, f\rangle = \langle \int_0^t T_0^*(u)\, A_0^*\, f^*\, du, f\rangle$$

$$= \int_0^t \langle A_0^*\, T_0^*(u)\, f^*, f\rangle\, du = \int_0^t \langle T_0^*(u)\, f^*, g\rangle\, du$$

$$= \int_0^t \langle f^*, T(u)\, g\rangle\, du = \langle f^*, \int_0^t T(u)\, g\, du\rangle.$$

Since $\mathsf{D}(A_0^*)$ is weakly* dense in X^* the equation

$$\langle f^*, T(t)\, f - f\rangle = \langle f^*, \int_0^t T(u)\, g\, du\rangle$$

holds for all $f^* \in \mathsf{X}^*$ and any fixed $t > 0$, and as a consequence $T(t)\, f - f = \int_0^t T(u)\, g\, du$. But then $f \in \mathsf{D}(A)$ and $A\, f = g$, proving that the linear functional on $\mathsf{X}^* \times \mathsf{X}^*$ defined in (1.4.7) vanishes for all $f^* \in \mathsf{D}(A^*)$. This completes the proof of part (b).

Corollary 1.4.8. *If X is reflexive, then $\mathsf{X}_0^* = \mathsf{X}^*$. The two operators A_0^* and A^* are equal.*

Proof. If X is reflexive, then by Proposition 1.4.2(b) $\mathsf{D}(A^*)$ is strongly dense in X^*, which together with Proposition 1.4.7 proves this corollary.

1.4.2 Applications

Here we shall continue our investigations of Sec. 1.3.3 concerning translations in the function spaces $\mathsf{UCB}(\mathrm{E}_1)$ and $\mathsf{L}^p(\mathrm{E}_1)$, $1 \leqq p < \infty$.

Thus let X be one of the spaces $\mathsf{C}_0(\mathrm{E}_1)$ or $\mathsf{L}^p(\mathrm{E}_1)$, $1 \leqq p < \infty$, and let $\{T(t);\, 0 \leqq t < \infty\}$ be the semi-group of right translations on X:

$$[T(t)\, f](x) = f(x - t) \qquad (f \in \mathsf{X};\ t \geqq 0). \tag{1.4.8}$$

By methods used in Sec. 1.3.3 one verifies easily that $\{T(t);\, 0 \leqq t < \infty\}$ forms a contraction semi-group of class $(\mathscr{C}_0)$ in $\mathscr{E}(\mathsf{X})$ and that its infinitesimal generator A is defined by $[A\, f](x) = -f'(x)$ with domain

$$\mathsf{D}(A) = \{f \in \mathsf{X};\ f \in \mathsf{AC}_{\mathrm{loc}}(\mathrm{E}_1) \text{ and } f' \in \mathsf{X}\}.$$

We now wish to study the dual of the semi-group of right translations on X^*. But before going into details, we need some further results on these function spaces.

The dual space of $C_0(E_1)$ is isometrically isomorphic to the space $NBV(E_1)$, the space of all normalized real or complex-valued functions μ of bounded variation on the real axis. By saying that μ is normalized we mean that $\mu(x) = \{\mu(x+) + \mu(x-)\}/2$ for each real x, $\mu(-\infty) = \lim_{x\to-\infty} \mu(x) = 0$ and $\mu(\infty) = \lim_{x\to\infty} \mu(x)$. $NBV(E_1)$ is a Banach space under the norm defined by its total variation on E_1:

$$\|\mu\|_V \equiv [\mathrm{Var}\,\mu]\,(E_1) = \int_{-\infty}^{\infty} |d\mu(x)|.$$

The natural representation of the bounded linear functionals on $C_0(E_1)$ is given by

$$\langle \mu, f\rangle = \int_{-\infty}^{\infty} f(x)\, d\bar{\mu}(x) \qquad (f \in C_0(E_1),\ \mu \in NBV(E_1)),$$

where $\bar{\mu}$ denotes the complex conjugate of μ.

The space of all absolutely continuous functions μ on E_1, the space $AC(E_1)$, is a closed linear subspace of $NBV(E_1)$, and there is an isometric isomorphism between $AC(E_1)$ and $L^1(E_1)$ given by the correspondence $\mu' \leftrightarrow f$ with $\|\mu\|_V = \|f\|_1$.

In Sec. 1.3.3 we have already noted that the dual of $L^p(E_1)$, $1 \leqq p < \infty$, is equal to $L^{p'}(E_1)$, $p^{-1} + p'^{-1} = 1$, and

$$\langle F, f\rangle = \int_{-\infty}^{\infty} f(x)\, \bar{F}(x)\, dx \qquad (f \in L^p(E_1),\ F \in L^{p'}(E_1)).$$

Furthermore, $L^p(E_1)$ is reflexive for $1 < p < \infty$.

Theorem 1.4.9. *The dual of the semi-group of right translations $\{T(t);\ 0 \leqq t < \infty\}$ on $[C_0(E_1)]^*$, i.e. on $NBV(E_1)$, is given by the semi-group of left translations*

$$(1.4.9) \qquad [T^*(t)\,\mu]\,(x) = \mu(x+t) \quad (\mu \in NBV(E_1);\ 0 \leqq t < \infty).$$

The dual generator A^* has domain

$$(1.4.10) \qquad D(A^*) = \{\mu \in NBV(E_1);\ \mu \in AC(E_1) \text{ and } \mu' \in NBV(E_1)\}$$

and $[A^*\mu]\,(x) = \mu'(x)$. $\{T^*(t);\ 0 \leqq t < \infty\}$ is of class $(\mathscr{C}_0)^*$ in $\mathscr{E}(NBV(E_1))$. Furthermore, the subspace $[C_0(E_1)]_0^*$, the space of all elements in $[C_0(E_1)]^*$ which are continuous under left translations in NBV-norm, is isometrically isomorphic to $AC(E_1)$.

By the correspondence between $AC(E_1)$ and $L^1(E_1)$, the restriction $\{T_0^*(t);\ 0 \leqq t < \infty\}$ of the dual semi-group is equal to the strongly continuous semi-group of left translations on $L^1(E_1)$ as defined in Theorem 1.3.13.

Proof. By the definition of the dual semi-group we have for each operator $T^*(t)$, $0 \leqq t < \infty$,

$$\langle \mu, T(t) f \rangle = \int_{-\infty}^{\infty} f(x - t)\, d\bar{\mu}(x) = \int_{-\infty}^{\infty} f(x)\, d_x \bar{\mu}(x + t) = \langle T^*(t)\, \mu, f \rangle$$

for all $f \in C_0(E_1)$ and all $\mu \in NBV(E_1)$, proving relation (1.4.9). Now, if $\mu \in D(A^*)$, then there exists an element $\nu \in NBV(E_1)$ such that

$$\langle \mu, A f \rangle = -\int_{-\infty}^{\infty} f'(x)\, d\bar{\mu}(x) = \int_{-\infty}^{\infty} f(x)\, d\bar{\nu}(x) = \langle \nu, f \rangle$$

for all $f \in D(A)$. Since $C_{00}^{\infty}(E_1) \subset D(A)$, we have for each real $\tau \neq 0$

$$\int_{\infty}^{\infty} \varphi(x)\, d_x\{\bar{\mu}(x+\tau) - \bar{\mu}(x)\} = \int_0^{\tau} du \int_{-\infty}^{\infty} (-\varphi'(x - u))\, d\bar{\mu}(x)$$

$$= \int_0^{\tau} du \int_{-\infty}^{\infty} \varphi(x - u)\, d\bar{\nu}(x) = \int_{-\infty}^{\infty} \varphi(x)\, \{\bar{\nu}(x+\tau) - \bar{\nu}(x)\}\, dx.$$

By assumption the above functional is bounded on $C_{00}^{\infty}(E_1)$, and since this subspace is dense in $C_0(E_1)$ we obtain for arbitrary but fixed x and y

$$\int_x^y d_u\{\mu(u+\tau) - \mu(u)\} = \int_x^y \{\nu(u+\tau) - \nu(u)\}\, du.$$

The limit as $\tau \to -\infty$ then gives

$$\mu(y) - \mu(x) = \int_x^y \nu(u)\, du,$$

which proves that $\mu \in AC(E_1)$ and $\mu'(x) = \nu(x)$ a.e.

The characterization of $D(A^*)$ given in (1.4.10) shows that its strong closure is equal to $AC(E_1)$. This proves together with Proposition 1.4.7 the rest of the theorem.

We note that the space $C_{00}^{\infty}(E_1)$, considered as a subspace of $NBV(E_1)$ by the correspondence $\phi' \leftrightarrow \varphi$ (all $\varphi \in C_{00}^{\infty}(E_1)$), is weakly* dense in $NBV(E_1)$.

Remark 1.4.10. Theorem 1.4.9 contains a famous theorem of A. Plessner: A function $\mu(x)$ of bounded variation on the finite interval $a \leqq x \leqq b$ is absolutely continuous if and only if μ is continuous under translations in norm, i.e. if and only if

$$\lim_{\tau \to 0} \int_a^b |d_x\{\mu(x+\tau) - \mu(x)\}| = 0, \tag{1.4.11}$$

where $\mu(x) = \mu(a)$ for $x < a$ and $\mu(x) = \mu(b)$ for $x > b$. Indeed, by Theorem 1.4.9 the normalized function μ_0 of the extended μ belongs to $AC(E_1)$ if and only if $\| \mu_0(\cdot + \tau) - \mu_0(\cdot) \|_V$ tends to zero as $\tau \to 0$. This means that relation (1.4.11) is valid.

For the dual of $\{T(t); 0 \leqq t < \infty\}$ on $[\mathsf{L}^1(\mathrm{E}_1)]^*$ we have

Theorem 1.4.11. *The semi-group of left translations on* $\mathsf{L}^\infty(\mathrm{E}_1)$*:*

$$[T^*(t)\, F]\,(x) = F(x+t) \qquad (F \in \mathsf{L}^\infty(\mathrm{E}_1);\ 0 \leqq t < \infty),$$

forms a contraction semi-group of class $(\mathscr{C}_0)^*$ *in* $\mathscr{E}(\mathsf{L}^\infty(\mathrm{E}_1))$ *with*

$$\mathsf{D}(A^*) = \{F \in \mathsf{L}^\infty(\mathrm{E}_1);\ F \in \mathsf{AC}_{\mathrm{loc}}(\mathrm{E}_1) \text{ and } F' \in \mathsf{L}^\infty(\mathrm{E}_1)\}$$

and $[A^*\, F]\,(x) = F'(x)$ *a.e.*

Moreover, the space $[\mathsf{L}^1(\mathrm{E}_1)]_0^*$ *is isometrically isomorphic to* $\mathsf{UCB}(\mathrm{E}_1)$.

The reader will have little difficulty to transfer the method of proof of Theorem 1.4.9 to this theorem.

It remains to discuss the case of the reflexive function spaces $\mathsf{L}^p(\mathrm{E}_1)$, $1 < p < \infty$. Because of the reflexivity we have by Corollary 1.4.8 that the dual of $\{T(t); 0 \leqq t < \infty\}$ on $[\mathsf{L}^p(\mathrm{E}_1)]^*$ is given by the semi-group of left translations on $\mathsf{L}^{p'}(\mathrm{E}_1)$, $p^{-1} + p'^{-1} = 1$: $[T^*(t)\, F]\,(x) = F(x+t)$ $(F \in \mathsf{L}^{p'}(\mathrm{E}_1); 0 \leqq t < \infty)$. $\{T^*(t); 0 \leqq t < \infty\}$ is a contraction semi-group of class $(\mathscr{C}_0)$ in $\mathscr{E}(\mathsf{L}^{p'}(\mathrm{E}_1))$ and its infinitesimal generator is equal to the dual of A, where $\mathsf{D}(A^*) = \{F \in \mathsf{L}^{p'}(\mathrm{E}_1);$ $F \in \mathsf{AC}_{\mathrm{loc}}(\mathrm{E}_1)$ and $F' \in \mathsf{L}^{p'}(\mathrm{E}_1)\}$ and $[A^*\, F]\,(x) = F'(x)$ a.e. (see Sec. 1.3.3, Theorem 1.3.13).

1.5 Trigonometric Semi-Groups

In this section we are concerned exclusively with the function spaces $\mathsf{C}_{2\pi}$ and $\mathsf{L}^p_{2\pi}$, $1 \leqq p < \infty$, and with their dual spaces $\mathsf{NBV}_{2\pi}$ and $\mathsf{L}^{p'}_{2\pi}$, $p^{-1} + p'^{-1} = 1$, respectively.

The spaces $\mathsf{C}_{2\pi}$, $\mathsf{L}^p_{2\pi}$ $(1 \leqq p \leqq \infty)$ and $\mathsf{NBV}_{2\pi}$ are the periodic analogues of the spaces $\mathsf{UCB}(\mathrm{E}_1)$, $\mathsf{L}^p(\mathrm{E}_1)$ $(1 \leqq p \leqq \infty)$ and $\mathsf{NBV}(\mathrm{E}_1)$ defined previously. Their norms are defined by

$$\|f\|_{\mathsf{C}} = \max_x |f(x)|,$$

$$\|f\|_p = \begin{cases} \left\{ \dfrac{1}{2\pi} \displaystyle\int_0^{2\pi} |f(x)|^p\, dx \right\}^{1/p} & (1 \leqq p < \infty) \\ \operatorname*{ess\,sup}_x |f(x)| & (p = \infty), \end{cases}$$

and

$$\|\mu\|_{\mathsf{V}} = (1/2\pi)\, [\mathrm{Var}\, \mu]_0^{2\pi},$$

respectively. The natural representation of the bounded linear functionals on $\mathsf{C}_{2\pi}$ by elements of $\mathsf{NBV}_{2\pi}$ is given by

$$\langle \mu, f \rangle = \frac{1}{2\pi} \int_0^{2\pi} f(x)\, d\bar{\mu}(x) \qquad (f \in \mathsf{C}_{2\pi},\ \mu \in \mathsf{NBV}_{2\pi}),$$

and on $L^p_{2\pi}$, $1 \leq p < \infty$, by elements of $L^{p'}_{2\pi}$, $p^{-1} + p'^{-1} = 1$, by

$$\langle F, f\rangle = \frac{1}{2\pi}\int_0^{2\pi} f(x)\,\bar{F}(x)\,dx \qquad (f \in L^p_{2\pi},\ F \in L^{p'}_{2\pi}).$$

Concerning the space $NBV_{2\pi}$ we remark that the elements μ are normalized by $\mu(0) = 0$, $\mu(x) = \{\mu(x+) + \mu(x-)\}/2$ and that $\mu(x+2\pi) - \mu(x) = \mu(2\pi)$ for all x. By $AC_{2\pi}$ we mean the closed subspace of functions $\mu \in NBV_{2\pi}$ which are absolutely continuous. The correspondence $\mu' \leftrightarrow f$ with $\|\mu\|_V = \|f\|_1$ defines an isometric isomorphism between $AC_{2\pi}$ and $L^1_{2\pi}$. Finally, we denote by $P_{2\pi}$ the set of all trigonometric polynomials $p(x) = \sum_{k=-n}^{n} p_k e^{ikx}$, $n = 0, 1, 2, \ldots$ $P_{2\pi}$ forms a dense subset in $C_{2\pi}$ and $L^p_{2\pi}$, $1 \leq p < \infty$. The latter spaces are known to be separable while $L^\infty_{2\pi}$ and $NBV_{2\pi}$ are non-separable. The spaces $L^p_{2\pi}$, $1 < p < \infty$, are reflexive.

1.5.1 Classical Results on Fourier Series

The trigonometric system of functions $\{e_k(x) = e^{ikx};\ k = 0, \pm 1, \pm 2, \ldots\}$ forms an *orthonormal system* on the interval $[0, 2\pi]$ with respect to the measure $dx/2\pi$, i.e.

$$\langle e_k, e_j\rangle = \frac{1}{2\pi}\int_0^{2\pi} e^{ijx}\,e^{-ikx}\,dx = \delta_{jk} = \begin{cases} 1, & j = k,\\ 0, & j \neq k.\end{cases}$$

This system is complete in the function spaces $C_{2\pi}$, $L^p_{2\pi}$, $1 \leq p \leq \infty$, and $NBV_{2\pi}$. If X represents anyone of these spaces, this means that the system $\{e_k; k = 0, \pm 1, \pm 2, \ldots\} \subset X \cap X^*$ and $\langle e_k, f\rangle = 0$ for all $k = 0, \pm 1, \pm 2, \ldots$ implies that $f = \theta$. Thus each $f \in X$ has a unique representation as a formal series

$$f \sim \sum_{k=-\infty}^{\infty} \langle e_k, f\rangle\, e_k.$$

For the spaces $C_{2\pi}$ and $L^p_{2\pi}$, $1 \leq p \leq \infty$, we denote by

$$f(x) \sim \sum_{k=-\infty}^{\infty} f^\wedge(k)\, e^{ikx}, \qquad f^\wedge(k) = \frac{1}{2\pi}\int_0^{2\pi} e^{-ikx} f(x)\,dx$$

the *Fourier series* of f with the *Fourier coefficients* $f^\wedge(k)$, $k = 0, \pm 1, \pm 2, \ldots$ If we set the n-th partial sum of the Fourier series of f by

$$s_n(f)(x) = \sum_{k=-n}^{n} f^\wedge(k)\, e^{ikx} \qquad (n = 0, 1, 2, \ldots),$$

then we have for the first arithmetic means of $s_n(f)$, or more familiarly for the n-th *Fejér mean* of f,

$$\sigma_n(f)(x) = \frac{1}{n+1}\sum_{k=0}^{n} s_k(f)(x) = \sum_{k=-n}^{n}\left(1 - \frac{|k|}{n+1}\right) f^\wedge(k)\, e^{ikx}$$

$$= \frac{1}{2\pi}\int_0^{2\pi} f(u)\,\frac{1}{n+1}\,\frac{\sin^2\{(n+1)(x-u)/2\}}{\sin^2(x-u)/2}\,du$$

that $\sigma_n(f)(x)$ converges to $f(x)$ as $n \to \infty$ at every point of continuity of f, to $\{f(x+) + f(x-)\}/2$ whenever this expression has a meaning, and to $f(x)$ at every Lebesgue point of f, in particular almost everywhere. Furthermore, $\sigma_n(f)$ converges to f as $n \to \infty$ in the norm of the spaces $C_{2\pi}$ and $L^p_{2\pi}$, $1 \leqq p < \infty$, whereas for $L^\infty_{2\pi}$ the convergence of $\sigma_n(f)$ to f as $n \to \infty$ is in the weak* topology.

For the space $NBV_{2\pi}$ we denote by

$$d\mu(x) \sim \sum_{k=-\infty}^{\infty} \mu^\vee(k)\, e^{ikx}, \qquad \mu^\vee(k) = \frac{1}{2\pi}\int_0^{2\pi} e^{-ikx}\, d\mu(x)$$

the *Fourier-Stieltjes series* of μ with the *Fourier-Stieltjes coefficients* $\mu^\vee(k)$. Here we have that $\sigma_n(d\mu)(x)$ converges to $\mu'(x)$ as $n \to \infty$ for almost every x, and $\sigma_n(d\mu) \to d\mu$ as $n \to \infty$ in the weak* topology.

Remark. The properties mentioned above for the Fejér means of f are in general not valid for the partial sums $s_n(f)$. However, for an f in the space $L^2_{2\pi}$ one has that

$$\lim_{n\to\infty} \| s_n(f) - f \|_2 = 0.$$

Moreover, the famous *Parseval's formula* holds:

$$\|f\|_2^2 = \frac{1}{2\pi}\int_0^{2\pi} |f(x)|^2\, dx = \sum_{k=-\infty}^{\infty} |f^\wedge(k)|^2.$$

If f and g are two functions in $L^1_{2\pi}$, we call the integral

$$[f * g](x) = \frac{1}{2\pi}\int_0^{2\pi} f(x-u)\, g(u)\, du$$

the *convolution* of f and g. One has that $f * g = g * f$ exists almost everywhere, belongs to $L^1_{2\pi}$ and $\|f * g\|_1 \leqq \|f\|_1 \|g\|_1$. Moreover, for the Fourier coefficients of the convolution integral:

$$[f * g]^\wedge(k) = f^\wedge(k)\, g^\wedge(k) \quad (k = 0, \pm 1, \pm 2, \ldots).$$

If in particular $f \in L^p_{2\pi}$ and $g \in L^{p'}_{2\pi}$, $1 \leqq p < \infty$, $p^{-1} + p'^{-1} = 1$, then the convolution $f * g$ defines a continuous function. In case $1 < p < \infty$

one further obtains that

$$[f * g](x) = \lim_{n\to\infty} \sum_{k=-n}^{n} f^\wedge(k)\, g^\wedge(k)\, e^{ikx}$$

for all x. This limit relation remains true even in case $p = 1$ if in addition g is of bounded variation. Analogously, for an $f \in C_{2\pi}$ and $\mu \in NBV_{2\pi}$ the *Stieltjes convolution*

$$[f * d\mu](x) = \frac{1}{2\pi} \int_0^{2\pi} f(x-u)\, d\mu(u)$$

represents a continuous function in $C_{2\pi}$.

Now, let f be an element in $L^1_{2\pi}$. We denote by

$$\sum_{k=-\infty}^{\infty} (-i \operatorname{sgn} k)\, f^\wedge(k)\, e^{ikx}$$

the *conjugate Fourier series* of f, where $\operatorname{sgn} k = k/|k|$ for all integers $k \neq 0$, and $\operatorname{sgn} 0 = 0$. This series need not necessarily be a Fourier series at all. However, if $\sigma_n^\sim(f)$ denotes the n-th Fejér mean of the conjugate Fourier series of f, then for almost every x

$$\lim_{n\to\infty} \left\{ \sigma_n^\sim(f)(x) - \left(-\frac{1}{\pi} \int_{1/n}^{\pi} [f(x+u) - f(x-u)] \frac{1}{2} \cot \frac{u}{2}\, du \right) \right\} = 0.$$

For $f \in L^1_{2\pi}$, we define the *conjugate function* $f^\sim$ by

$$f^\sim(x) = \lim_{\varepsilon\to 0+} -\frac{1}{\pi} \int_{\varepsilon}^{\pi} [f(x+u) - f(x-u)] \frac{1}{2} \cot \frac{u}{2}\, du.$$

The limit exists almost everywhere, but in general $f^\sim$ does not belong to $L^1_{2\pi}$. If, however, $f^\sim$ is a function in $L^1_{2\pi}$, then the conjugate Fourier series of f is equal to the Fourier series of the conjugate function $f^\sim$. Furthermore, by the famous theorem of M. Riesz (see Ch. IV, Theorem 4.2.5 for functions in $L^p(E_1)$, $1 < p < \infty$) we have that for all $f \in L^p_{2\pi}$, $1 < p < \infty$, also $f^\sim \in L^p_{2\pi}$, while for $f \in C_{2\pi}$ the conjugate function in general is not necessarily continuous.

For a $\mu \in NBV_{2\pi}$ we denote by

$$\sum_{k=-\infty}^{\infty} (-i \operatorname{sgn} k)\, \mu^\vee(k)\, e^{ikx}$$

the *conjugate Fourier-Stieltjes series* of μ. One has

$$\sigma_n^\sim(d\mu)(x) - \left(-\frac{1}{\pi} \int_{1/n}^{\pi} \frac{\mu(x+u) - 2\mu(x) + \mu(x-u)}{4 \sin^2 u/2}\, du \right) \to 0$$

for almost every x.

We conclude this subsection with some remarks on *factor sequences*. Let X and Y be anyone of the spaces $C_{2\pi}$, $L^p_{2\pi}$, $1 \leqq p \leqq \infty$, or $NBV_{2\pi}$. A sequence of complex numbers $\{\chi_k; k = 0, \pm 1, \pm 2, \ldots\}$ is said to be a factor sequence of type (X, Y) if for each $f \in X$ the formal series

$$\sum_{k=-\infty}^{\infty} \chi_k f^\wedge(k)\, e^{ikx}$$

is the Fourier series of some function in Y. Each factor sequence of type (X, Y) defines a bounded linear transformation T from X to Y.

If for a sequence $\{\chi_k; k = 0, \pm 1, \pm 2, \ldots\}$ the series $\sum_{k=-\infty}^{\infty} \chi_k e^{ikx}$ is the Fourier-Stieltjes series of a function $\chi \in NBV_{2\pi}$, then one can readily see that the sequence forms a factor sequence of type $(C_{2\pi}, C_{2\pi})$ or $(L^p_{2\pi}, L^p_{2\pi})$, $1 \leqq p < \infty$, and the transformation T is given by

$$[T f](x) = \frac{1}{2\pi} \int_0^{2\pi} f(x-u)\, d\chi(u) \sim \sum_{k=-\infty}^{\infty} \chi_k f^\wedge(k)\, e^{ikx},$$

where the integral exists in the Lebesgue-Stieltjes sense for almost all x and $\|T\| \leqq (1/2\pi)\, [\mathrm{Var}\,\chi]_0^{2\pi}$.

For the spaces $C_{2\pi}$ and $L^1_{2\pi}$ the above condition is not only sufficient but also necessary and the norm of T is equal to $(1/2\pi)\, [\mathrm{Var}\,\chi]_0^{2\pi}$. Furthermore, the complex conjugate sequence $\{\bar{\chi}_k; k = 0, \pm 1, \pm 2, \ldots\}$ represents the dual operator T^* and thus this sequence is of type $(NBV_{2\pi}, NBV_{2\pi})$ or $(L^{p'}_{2\pi}, L^{p'}_{2\pi})$, $p^{-1} + p'^{-1} = 1$.

In particular, a sequence $\{\chi_k; k = 0, \pm 1, \pm 2, \ldots\}$ is of type $(L^2_{2\pi}, L^2_{2\pi})$ if and only if the sequence is bounded. In this case $\|T\| = \sup_k |\chi_k|$.

1.5.2 Fourier's Problem of the Ring

Given a homogeneous isotropic ring of unit radius whose diameter is small in comparison to its length. Let $f(x)$, $0 \leqq x < 2\pi$, be a given initial temperature distribution at the time $t = 0$. The problem is to determine the temperature at any point x of the ring at time $t > 0$ under the hypothesis that there is no radiation at the surface. This temperature function $w(x, t)$ satisfies the normalized differential equation of heat-conduction

$$\frac{\partial w}{\partial t} = \frac{\partial^2 w}{\partial x^2} \qquad (0 < x < 2\pi;\ t > 0)$$

with the boundary conditions

$$w(0, t) = w(2\pi, t), \qquad \frac{\partial w}{\partial x}(0, t) = \frac{\partial w}{\partial x}(2\pi, t)$$

and the initial condition

$$\lim_{t\to 0+} w(x, t) = f(x).$$

This is the so-called *Fourier problem of the ring* (see also Sec. 1.0).

More specifically, we are interested in a solution of the following *Cauchy problem:*

Let X *be one of the spaces* $C_{2\pi}$, $L^p_{2\pi}$, $1 \leqq p < \infty$, *and let*

$$D(U) = \{f \in X; f, f' \in AC_{2\pi} \text{ and } f'' \in X\} \tag{1.5.1}$$

be the domain of the operator U *defined by* $Uf = f''$.

Given an element $f_0 \in X$, *find a function* $w(t) = w(t; f_0)$ *on* $[0, \infty)$ *to* X *such that*

(i) $w(t)$ *is strongly continuously differentiable in* $(0, \infty)$;

(ii) *for each* $t > 0$, $w(t) \in D(U)$ *and* $w'(t) = U w(t)$;

(iii) $\operatorname{s-lim}_{t\to 0+} w(t; f_0) = f_0$.

If the initial value f_0 is equal to the zero element θ we call a solution $w(t, \theta) \neq \theta$ of this Cauchy problem a (proper) null solution. Clearly, the non-existence of a null solution is necessary and sufficient for the uniqueness of the problem.

We shall show that this problem has exactly one solution which is given by

$$w(t; f_0) = W(t) f_0, \tag{1.5.2}$$

where $\{W(t); 0 \leqq t < \infty\}$ is a semi-group of operators of class $(\mathscr{C}_0)$ in $\mathscr{E}(X)$. The existence will be established by two different methods. The first method will mainly consist of semi-group theoretical arguments. It will be shown that the operator U satisfies the hypotheses of the Hille-Yosida theorem (Corollary 1.3.8) and thus generates a semi-group of operators of class $(\mathscr{C}_0)$. By the second method we shall prove by *finite Fourier transform* arguments that a solution will be given by (1.5.2), where $\{W(t); 0 \leqq t < \infty\}$ is a family of factor sequence operators in $\mathscr{E}(X)$.

Proposition 1.5.1. (a) *U is a closed linear operator with domain $D(U)$ dense in X.*

(b) *An equivalent characterization of the domain of U is given by*

$$\{f \in X; \sim \sum_{k=-\infty}^{\infty} k^2 f^\wedge(k)\, e^{ikx} \in X\}^{1} \tag{1.5.3}$$

and

$$[Uf]^\wedge(k) = -k^2 f^\wedge(k) \quad (k = 0, \pm 1, \pm 2, \ldots).$$

---

[1] The notation $\sim \sum_{k=-\infty}^{\infty} g_k e^{ikx} \in X$ means that the series represents an element g belonging to X.

Proof. (a) Obviously, U is a linear operator. To prove that U is closed, we have to show that whenever $\{f_n\}_{n=1}^{\infty}$ is a sequence of elements in $\mathsf{D}(U)$ such that $f_n \to f_0$ and $U f_n = f_n'' \to g_0$ in norm as $n \to \infty$, then $f_0 \in \mathsf{D}(U)$ and $U f_0 = f_0'' = g_0$. From the equation

$$f_n(x+t) - f_n(x) - t f_n'(x) = \int_0^t (t-u) f_n''(x+u)\, du$$

holding for all x, all $n = 1, 2, \ldots$, and any real t, we have that f_n' is also strongly convergent as $n \to \infty$, say to the element h_0. But then f_0 and h_0 belong to $\mathsf{AC}_{2\pi}$, $f_0' = h_0$ and $h_0' = g_0$, proving that U is closed. Finally, since $\mathsf{P}_{2\pi} \subset \mathsf{D}(U)$ and since $\mathsf{P}_{2\pi}$ is dense in X, we have immediately that $\mathsf{D}(U)$ is a dense subset of X.

(b) If $f \in \mathsf{D}(U)$, then we obtain by integration by parts

$$[U f]^{\wedge}(k) = \frac{1}{2\pi} \int_0^{2\pi} e^{-ikx} f''(x)\, dx = \frac{(ik)^2}{2\pi} \int_0^{2\pi} e^{-ikx} f(x)\, dx = -k^2 f^{\wedge}(k)$$

for all $k = 0, \pm 1, \pm 2, \ldots$, proving that $\mathsf{D}(U)$ belongs to the set of elements defined in (1.5.3). Conversely, if f is a function in the set of (1.5.3), then one has for the Fejér-means of the Fourier series

$$f(x) \sim \sum_{k=-\infty}^{\infty} f^{\wedge}(k)\, e^{ikx}, \qquad g(x) \sim \sum_{k=-\infty}^{\infty} (-k^2) f^{\wedge}(k)\, e^{ikx}$$

that

$$U \sigma_n(f) = [\sigma_n(f)]'' = \sigma_n(g).$$

Since U is closed and since $\sigma_n(f) \to f$ and $U \sigma_n(f) = \sigma_n(g) \to g$ in norm as $n \to \infty$, it follows that $f \in \mathsf{D}(U)$ and $U f = g$.

Proposition 1.5.2. *The spectrum of U is given by the point spectrum*

$$\mathrm{P}_\sigma(U) = \{\lambda;\, \lambda = -k^2,\, k = 0, \pm 1, \pm 2, \ldots\}.$$

Also, the resolvent set

$$\varrho(U) = \{\lambda;\, \lambda \neq -k^2,\, k = 0, \pm 1, \pm 2, \ldots\}$$

and the resolvent

$$[R(\lambda; U) f](x) \sim \sum_{k=-\infty}^{\infty} \frac{f^{\wedge}(k)}{\lambda + k^2} e^{ikx} \qquad (f \in \mathsf{X}). \tag{1.5.4}$$

Moreover for positive λ, $R(\lambda; U)$ has the representation

$$[R(\lambda; U) f](x) = \frac{1}{2\pi} \int_0^{2\pi} f(u)\, r(\lambda; x-u)\, du \tag{1.5.5}$$

with kernel

$$r(\lambda; u) = \frac{\pi}{\sqrt{\lambda}} \frac{\cosh \sqrt{\lambda}\,(u-\pi)}{\sinh \sqrt{\lambda}\,\pi} \qquad (0 \leq u < 2\pi) \tag{1.5.6}$$

and

$$\|R(\lambda; U)\| = 1/\lambda.$$

Proof. By part (b) of the foregoing proposition the homogeneous equation $\lambda f - U f = \theta$ is equivalent to

$$\lambda f^\wedge(k) + k^2 f^\wedge(k) = 0 \qquad (k = 0, \pm 1, \pm 2, \ldots).$$

Thus λ belongs to the point spectrum $P_\sigma(U)$ if and only if $\lambda = -k^2$ and the eigenvectors corresponding to the eigenvalue $-k^2$ are given by e^{ikx} and e^{-ikx}. Consequently, for all $\lambda \neq -k^2$, k integral, the operator $\lambda I - U$ has a unique inverse.

Therefore, we obtain for an $f \in \mathsf{D}(U)$ by $\lambda f - U f = g$, or equivalently by

$$\lambda f^\wedge(k) + k^2 f^\wedge(k) = g^\wedge(k) \quad (k = 0, \pm 1, \pm 2, \ldots),$$

that

$$f(x) = [(\lambda I - U)^{-1} g](x) \sim \sum_{k=-\infty}^{\infty} \frac{g^\wedge(k)}{\lambda + k^2} e^{ikx}.$$

Since the range $\mathsf{R}(\lambda I - U)$ contains the trigonometric polynomials, it is a dense subset of X, and the representation of $(\lambda I - U)^{-1}$ given in the latter equation shows that its norm is bounded. Thus, according to the definition of the resolvent, λ belongs to $\varrho(U)$ and the resolvent $R(\lambda; U)$ is given by (1.5.4).

It remains to prove the special representation of $R(\lambda; U)$ for positive λ. Since the trigonometric series

$$\sum_{k=-\infty}^{\infty} \frac{1}{\lambda + k^2} e^{ikx}$$

is uniformly convergent for a fixed λ, it is the Fourier series of a function in $\mathsf{C}_{2\pi}$. It is easily verified that this function is given by $r(\lambda; x)$ defined in (1.5.6), its Fourier coefficients $r^\wedge(\lambda; k)$ being $1/(\lambda + k^2)$, $k = 0, \pm 1, \pm 2, \ldots$ Thus

$$\frac{1}{2\pi} \int_0^{2\pi} f(u)\, r(\lambda; x - u)\, du = \sum_{k=-\infty}^{\infty} \frac{1}{\lambda + k^2} f^\wedge(k)\, e^{ikx},$$

which proves (1.5.5). Since the kernel $k(\lambda; \cdot)$ of the convolution integral is non-negative, we have

$$\| R(\lambda; U) f \| \leqq r^\wedge(\lambda; 0) \| f \| = (1/\lambda) \| f \|.$$

The norm is in fact equal to $1/\lambda$ as the particular function $f(x) = 1$, all x, shows.

Theorem 1.5.3. *The given Cauchy problem has a unique solution*

$$w(t; f) = W(t) f \qquad (f \in \mathsf{X}; t \geqq 0),$$

where $\{W(t); 0 \leqq t < \infty\}$ *is the contraction semi-group of operators of class* $(\mathscr{C}_0)$ *in* $\mathscr{E}(\mathsf{X})$ *generated by* U, U *being its infinitesimal generator.*

The solution is the well-known ***periodic singular integral of Weierstrass***

$$(1.5.7)\qquad [W(t)\,f]\,(x) = \sum_{k=-\infty}^{\infty} e^{-k^2 t}\, f^\wedge(k)\, e^{ikx}$$

$$= \frac{1}{2\pi}\int_0^{2\pi} f(u)\,\vartheta_3(x-u;t)\,du \qquad (t>0),$$

the kernel $\vartheta_3(\cdot\,;t)$ *being the so-called Jacobi theta function*

$$(1.5.8)\qquad \sum_{k=-\infty}^{\infty} e^{-k^2 t}\, e^{ikx} = \sqrt{\frac{\pi}{t}}\sum_{k=-\infty}^{\infty}\exp\left\{-\frac{(2\pi k - x)^2}{4t}\right\} \qquad (t>0).$$

Finally, $\{W(t);\, 0 \leqq t < \infty\}$ *forms a holomorphic semi-group.*

Proof. In the foregoing propositions we have shown that the operator U satisfies the hypotheses of Corollary 1.3.8 and thus generates a strongly continuous contraction semi-group of operators $\{W(t);\, 0 \leqq t < \infty\}$ in $\mathscr{E}(\mathsf{X})$. By semi-group theory it then follows that the function $w(t;f) = W(t)\,f$ on $[0,\infty)$ to X solves the Cauchy problem for all $f \in \mathsf{D}(U)$.

Having established the existence of a semi-group solution to our problem for all $f \in \mathsf{D}(U)$ we shall now determine its explicit representation. Applying the representation formula (1.3.14) of Proposition 1.3.11 we then obtain for the k-th Fourier coefficient of $W(t)\,f$

$$[W(t)\,f]^\wedge(k) = \lim_{\lambda\to\infty} e^{-\lambda t}\sum_{j=0}^{\infty}\frac{(\lambda^2 t)^j}{j!}\,[\{R(\lambda;U)\}^j f]^\wedge(k)$$

$$= \lim_{\lambda\to\infty} e^{-\lambda t}\sum_{j=0}^{\infty}\frac{(\lambda^2 t)^j}{j!}\,\frac{f^\wedge(k)}{(\lambda+k^2)^j}$$

$$= \lim_{\lambda\to\infty}\exp\left\{-\lambda t + \frac{\lambda^2 t}{\lambda+k^2}\right\} f^\wedge(k) = e^{-k^2 t} f^\wedge(k)$$

$$(t>0;\ k=0,\pm1,\pm2,\ldots).$$

Now, $\sum_{k=-\infty}^{\infty} e^{-k^2 t}\, e^{ikx}$ $(t>0)$ is the Fourier series of Jacobi's theta function $\vartheta_3(x,t)$ defined in (1.5.8), which proves the desired representation of $W(t)\,f$ in (1.5.7). Furthermore, we obtain by the representation (1.5.7) that $W(t)\,[\mathsf{X}] \subset \mathsf{D}(U)$ for all $t>0$ and that

$$[U\,W(t)\,f]\,(x) = \sum_{k=-\infty}^{\infty}(-k^2)\, e^{-k^2 t}\, f^\wedge(k)\, e^{ikx}$$

$$= \frac{1}{2\pi}\int_0^{2\pi} f(u)\,\vartheta_3''(x-u;t)\,du \qquad (f\in\mathsf{X};\ t>0),$$

giving

$$\| U\, W(t) \| \leqq \frac{1}{2\pi} \int_0^{2\pi} |\vartheta_3''(u; t)|\, du \leqq t^{-1}.$$

Thus, the semi-group is holomorphic, and consequently the function $w(t) = W(t) f$ solves the problem for all $f \in \mathsf{X}$.

It remains to prove the uniqueness. Suppose there exists a proper null solution $w_0(t) = w(t; \theta)$. Since $w_0(s) \in \mathsf{D}(U)$ is strongly differentiable in $(0, \infty)$, the same is true for the function $W(t-s)\, w_0(s)$ in $(0, t)$ for any fixed $t > 0$ and

$$\frac{d}{ds} \{W(t-s)\, w_0(s)\} = W(t-s)\, \{w_0'(s) - U\, w_0(s)\} = \theta.$$

Thus $w_0(t) = W(0)\, w_0(t) - W(t)\, w_0(0) = \theta$ for each $t > 0$. Consequently, the periodic singular integral of Weierstrass is the unique solution of the Cauchy problem as asserted.

We shall conclude with a sketch of the finite Fourier transform method in solving Fourier's problem of the ring. If there exists a solution $w(t) = w(t; f)$, then by the required properties (i), (ii) and (iii) the Fourier coefficients of $w(t)$ have to fulfil

$$\frac{d}{dt} w^\wedge(t; k) = [U\, w(t)]^\wedge(k) = -k^2\, w^\wedge(t; k) \qquad (0 < t < \infty)$$

and

$$\lim_{t \to 0+} w^\wedge(t; k) = f^\wedge(k)$$

for all integers k. This gives $w^\wedge(t; k) = e^{-k^2 t} f^\wedge(k)$ $(0 \leqq t < \infty;\ k$ integral) and thus

$$[w(t)](x) \sim \sum_{k=-\infty}^{\infty} e^{-k^2 t} f^\wedge(k)\, e^{ikx}.$$

From this it follows immediately that Fourier's ring problem has only the trivial null solution, which proves the uniqueness too.

1.5.3 Semi-Groups of Factor Sequence Type

In solving Fourier's problem of the ring for the space $\mathsf{C}_{2\pi}$ and $\mathsf{L}^p_{2\pi}$, $1 \leqq p < \infty$, respectively, we have seen that the solution $w(t; f_0)$ is given by a semi-group of operators $\{W(t);\, 0 \leqq t < \infty\}$ acting on the initial value f_0. In terms of the finite Fourier transform the semi-group operators themselves are characterized by the sequences of real numbers

$$\left\{w_k(t) = e^{-|k|^2 t},\ k = 0, \pm 1, \pm 2, \ldots;\ 0 \leqq t < \infty\right\},$$

satisfying

(i) $w_k(t_1 + t_2) = w_k(t_1)\, w_k(t_2)$ $\quad (k = 0, \pm 1, \pm 2, \ldots;\, 0 \leqq t_1, t_2 < \infty)$

(ii) $w_k(0) = 1$ $\quad (k = 0, \pm 1, \pm 2, \ldots)$.

Thus $\{W(t); 0 \leqq t < \infty\}$ is represented by a semi group of factor sequences of type $(C_{2\pi}, C_{2\pi})$ and $(L^p_{2\pi}, L^p_{2\pi})$, $1 \leqq p < \infty$, respectively.

The object of this subsection is a general study of *semi-groups of factor sequence type*.

Let X be one of the spaces $C_{2\pi}$, $L^p_{2\pi}$, $1 \leqq p < \infty$, and let $\{T(t); 0 \leqq t < \infty\}$ be a family of factor sequence operators of type (X, X) of the special form

$$[T(t)\, f]\,(x) \sim \sum_{k=-\infty}^{\infty} e^{\lambda_k t} f^{\wedge}(k)\, e^{ikx}, \tag{1.5.9}$$

where λ_k, $k = 0, \pm 1, \pm 2, \ldots$, are complex numbers.

Theorem 1.5.4. *A necessary and sufficient condition such that the family of operators* (1.5.9) *forms a semi-group of class* $(\mathscr{C}_0)$ *in* $\mathscr{E}(X)$ *is that there exists a constant* $M \geqq 1$ *such that* $\|T(t)\| \leqq M$ *for* $0 \leqq t \leqq 1$. *Furthermore, the infinitesimal generator* A *is defined by*

$$[A\, f]^{\wedge}(k) = \lambda_k f^{\wedge}(k) \quad (k = 0, \pm 1, \pm 2, \ldots; f \in D(A)) \tag{1.5.10}$$

and

$$D(A) = \left\{ f \in X;\ \sim \sum_{k=-\infty}^{\infty} \lambda_k f^{\wedge}(k)\, e^{ikx} \in X \right\}. \tag{1.5.11}$$

Proof. Obviously, the family of operators $\{T(t); 0 \leqq t < \infty\}$ forms a semi-group in $\mathscr{E}(X)$. If $\{T(t); 0 \leqq t < \infty\}$ is of class $(\mathscr{C}_0)$ in $\mathscr{E}(X)$, then by Proposition 1.1.2 there exists a constant $M \geqq 1$ such that $\|T(t)\| \leqq M$ for $0 \leqq t \leqq 1$. Conversely, setting $e_k(x) = e^{ikx}$ we have that $\underset{t \to 0+}{\text{s-lim}}\, T(t)\, e_k = \underset{t \to 0+}{\text{s-lim}}\, e^{\lambda_k t} e_k = e_k$ for all integers k. Thus the semi-group satisfies the $(\mathscr{C}_0)$-property for every trigonometric polynomial in $P_{2\pi}$. Since $P_{2\pi}$ is dense in X and the norms $\|T(t)\|$ are uniformly bounded by M in $0 \leqq t \leqq 1$, we obtain by the Banach-Steinhaus theorem that $\underset{t \to 0+}{\text{s-lim}}\, T(t)\, f = f$ for all $f \in X$, proving the first part of the theorem.

Now suppose $f \in D(A)$. Then by definition

$$[A\, f]^{\wedge}(k) = \lim_{\tau \to 0+} \frac{1}{2\pi} \int_0^{2\pi} \tau^{-1} \{[T(\tau)\, f]\,(x) - f(x)\}\, e^{-ikx}\, dx$$

$$= \lim_{\tau \to 0+} \tau^{-1} \{e^{\lambda_k \tau} - 1\}\, f^{\wedge}(k) = \lambda_k f^{\wedge}(k) \qquad (k = 0, \pm 1, \pm 2, \ldots),$$

proving relation (1.5.10) and

$$D(A) \subset \left\{ f \in X;\ \sim \sum_{k=-\infty}^{\infty} \lambda_k f^{\wedge}(k)\, e^{ikx} \in X \right\}.$$

On the other hand, if f belongs to the set on the right-hand side of the latter relation, we obtain for the n-th Fejér sum of the element

$g(x) \sim \sum_{k=-\infty}^{\infty} \lambda_k f^\wedge(k)\, e^{ikx}$ that $A\,\sigma_n(f) = \sigma_n(g)$ $(n = 1, 2, \ldots)$. Since A is a closed operator and since $\sigma_n(f)$ and $A\,\sigma_n(f)$ converge in norm to f and g, respectively, as $n \to \infty$, this proves that $f \in \mathsf{D}(A)$ and $A\,f = g$, which completes the proof.

Remark. The operators defined by (1.5.9) commute with the group of translations. This follows directly by definition.

Example 1.5.5. For the spaces X equal to $C_{2\pi}$ or $L^p_{2\pi}$, $1 \leqq p < \infty$, the sequence of constants $\{\lambda_k = i\,k;\, k = 0, \pm 1, \pm 2, \ldots\}$ generates the semi-group of left translations

$$[T(t)\,f]\,(x) = f(x+t) \sim \sum_{k=-\infty}^{\infty} f^\wedge(k)\, e^{ik(x+t)}$$

and

$$\mathsf{D}(A) = \{f \in \mathsf{X};\ f \in AC_{2\pi} \text{ and } f' \in \mathsf{X}\}$$
$$= \left\{f \in \mathsf{X};\ \sim \sum_{k=-\infty}^{\infty} (i\,k)\, f^\wedge(k)\, e^{ikx} \in \mathsf{X}\right\},$$

where

$$[A\,f]^\wedge(k) = (i\,k)\, f^\wedge(k) \qquad (k = 0, \pm 1, \pm 2, \ldots).$$

Let $\{T(t);\, 0 \leqq t < \infty\}$ be a strongly continuous semi-group of factor sequence operators of type (1.5.9) on the spaces $C_{2\pi}$ and $L^p_{2\pi}$, $1 \leqq p < \infty$. In Theorem 1.5.4 we proved that the domain of A is characterized by (1.5.11) and $[A\,f]^\wedge(k) = \lambda_k f^\wedge(k)$ (all integers k). Now, for a particular choice of $\{\lambda_k\}$ the problem is to find a direct characterization of the domain $\mathsf{D}(A)$ in terms of f which does not involve Fourier coefficients. In this respect the following lemma is very useful for further applications.

Lemma 1.5.6. *Let X be one of the spaces $C_{2\pi}$, $L^p_{2\pi}$, $1 \leqq p < \infty$, and r be any fixed integer >0. The following properties are equivalent for an element $f \in \mathsf{X}$:*

(i) $\sim \sum_{k=-\infty}^{\infty} |k|^r f^\wedge(k)\, e^{ikx} \in \mathsf{X}$;

(ii) $\begin{cases} f, f', \ldots, f^{(r-1)} \in AC_{2\pi} \text{ and } f^{(r)} \in \mathsf{X}, \text{ if } r \text{ is even,} \\ f^\sim, (f^\sim)', \ldots, (f^\sim)^{(r-1)} \in AC_{2\pi} \text{ and } (f^\sim)^{(r)} \in \mathsf{X}, \text{ if } r \text{ is odd.} \end{cases}$

($f^\sim$ denotes the conjugate function of f.)

Proof. We shall sketch the proof only for the case $r = 1$.

If f is such that (i) holds, then we have for the n-th Fejér mean of $g(x) \sim \sum_{k=-\infty}^{\infty} |k|\, f^\wedge(k)\, e^{ikx}$

$$\sigma_n^\sim(f)\,(x) - \sigma_n^\sim(f)\,(y) = \int_y^x \sigma_n(g)\,(u)\, du.$$

Since $\sigma_n(g) \to g$ in norm as $n \to \infty$, the right-hand side of the latter equation converges to $\int_x^y g(u)\,du$ as $n \to \infty$ for all x and y. As $\sigma_n^\sim(f)(x)$ tends to $f^\sim(x)$ for almost all x, this gives

$$f^\sim(x) - f^\sim(y) = \int_y^x g(u)\,du$$

a. e., i.e. $f^\sim \in \mathsf{AC}_{2\pi}$ and $(f^\sim)' \in \mathsf{X}$. Conversely, if (ii) is valid, then it is easy to see by the properties of the finite Fourier transform that $[(f^\sim)']^\wedge(k) = (i\,k)\,[f^\sim]^\wedge(k) = (i\,k)\,(-i\,\mathrm{sgn}\,k)\,f^\wedge(k) = |k|\,f^\wedge(k)$ for all $k = 0, \pm 1, \pm 2, \ldots$, proving (i).

In the following theorem we discuss the dual of a semi-group of factor sequence operators of type (1.5.9).

Theorem 1.5.7. *The dual semi-group* $\{T^*(t); 0 \leqq t < \infty\}$ *on* X^* *(i.e. on the spaces* $\mathsf{NBV}_{2\pi}$, $\mathsf{L}_{2\pi}^{p'}$, $1 < p' \leqq \infty$*) is again a family of factor sequence operators of type* $(\mathsf{X}^*, \mathsf{X}^*)$, *and*

$$[T^*(t)\,f^*](x) \sim \sum_{k=-\infty}^{\infty} e^{\bar{\lambda}_k t}\,[f^*]^\wedge(k)\,e^{ikx} \qquad (t > 0).^1 \tag{1.5.12}$$

If $\{T(t); 0 \leqq t < \infty\}$ *is of class* $(\mathscr{C}_0)$ *in* $\mathscr{E}(\mathsf{X})$, *then* $\{T^*(t); 0 \leqq t < \infty\}$ *is of class* $(\mathscr{C}_0)^*$ *in* $\mathscr{E}(\mathsf{X}^*)$,

$$\mathsf{D}(A^*) = \left\{f^* \in \mathsf{X}^*; \sim \sum_{k=-\infty}^{\infty} \bar{\lambda}_k\,[f^*]^\wedge(k)\,e^{ikx} \in \mathsf{X}^*\right\} \tag{1.5.13}$$

and

$$[A^*\,f^*]^\wedge(k) = \bar{\lambda}_k\,[f^*]^\wedge(k) \quad (k = 0, \pm 1, \pm 2, \ldots). \tag{1.5.14}$$

Proof. By definition, $\langle T^*(t)\,f^*, f\rangle = \langle f^*, T(t)\,f\rangle$ for all $f \in \mathsf{X}$ and all $f^* \in \mathsf{X}^*$. Thus for $f = e_k$ $(e_k(x) = e^{ikx})$ we have

$$\overline{[T^*(t)\,f^*]^\wedge(k)} = \langle T^*(t)\,f^*, e_k\rangle = \langle f^*, T(t)\,e_k\rangle$$
$$= \langle f^*, e^{\lambda_k t}\,e_k\rangle = e^{\lambda_k t}\,\langle f^*, e_k\rangle = e^{\lambda_k t}\,\overline{[f^*]^\wedge(k)},$$

i.e. for all integers k

$$[T^*(t)\,f^*]^\wedge(k) = e^{\bar{\lambda}_k t}\,[f^*]^\wedge(k),$$

proving (1.5.12).

By the same method one obtains for each $f^* \in \mathsf{D}(A^*)$ that the relation (1.5.14) is valid for the Fourier coefficients of $A^*\,f^*$. Thus $\mathsf{D}(A^*)$ belongs to the set of elements

$$\left\{f^* \in \mathsf{X}^*; \sim \sum_{k=-\infty}^{\infty} \bar{\lambda}_k\,[f^*]^\wedge(k)\,e^{ikx} \in \mathsf{X}^*\right\}.$$

---

[1] In case $\mathsf{X} = \mathsf{C}_{2\pi}$ and thus $\mathsf{X}^* = \mathsf{NBV}_{2\pi}$, $[f^*]^\wedge(k)$ stands for $\mu^\vee(k)$ in view of the correspondence $f^* \leftrightarrow \mu$. Analogously for $\mathsf{X} = \mathsf{L}_{2\pi}^p$, $1 \leqq p < \infty$.

On the other hand, if f^* belongs to the latter subset then we have for the n-th Fejér mean of $g^*(x) \sim \sum_{k=-\infty}^{\infty} \bar{\lambda}_k [f^*]^\wedge(k)\, e^{ikx}$ that $A^* \sigma_n(f^*) = \sigma_n(g^*)$, and since $\sigma_n(f^*) \to f^*$ and $A^* \sigma_n(f^*) \to g^*$ in the weak* topology as $n \to \infty$ and since A^* is weakly* closed, we have that $f^* \in \mathsf{D}(A^*)$ with $A^* f^* = g^*$.

There is a further lemma of interest.

Lemma 1.5.8. *Under the hypotheses of Lemma 1.5.6 we have the following equivalent characterizations for an element $f^* \in \mathsf{X}^*$:*

(i) $\sim \sum_{k=-\infty}^{\infty} |k|^r [f^*]^\wedge(k)\, e^{ikx} \in \mathsf{X}^*$,

(ii) $\begin{cases} f^*, (f^*)', \ldots, (f^*)^{(r-1)} \in \mathsf{AC}_{2\pi} \text{ and } (f^*)^{(r)} \in \mathsf{X}^*, \text{ if } r \text{ is even,} \\ (f^*)^\sim, [(f^*)^\sim]', \ldots, [(f^*)^\sim]^{(r-1)} \in \mathsf{AC}_{2\pi} \text{ and } [(f^*)^\sim]^{(r)} \in \mathsf{X}^*, \text{ if } r \text{ is odd.} \end{cases}$

Proof. As in Lemma 1.5.6 we shall prove this lemma only for $r = 1$ and only for the space $[\mathsf{C}_{2\pi}]^* = \mathsf{NBV}_{2\pi}$. Let $\mu \in \mathsf{NBV}_{2\pi}$ be such that $d\nu(x) \sim \sum_{k=-\infty}^{\infty} |k|\, \mu^\vee(k)\, e^{ikx} \in \mathsf{NBV}_{2\pi}$. Then we have for the Fejér means of the functions $\mu_0(x) = \mu(x) - \mu^\vee(0) \cdot x$ and $\nu(x)$ (which belong to $\mathsf{L}^1_{2\pi}$)

$$[\sigma_n^\sim(\mu_0)]'(x) - [\sigma_n^\sim(\mu_0)]'(y) = \sigma_n^\sim(d\mu)(x) - \sigma_n^\sim(d\mu)(y)$$

$$= \int_y^x \sigma_n(d\nu)(u)\, du = \int_y^x [\sigma_n(\nu)]'(u)\, du = \sigma_n(\nu)(x) - \sigma_n(\nu)(y)$$

for all x, y on the real axis and each $n = 1, 2, \ldots$ Thus

$$\sigma_n^\sim(\mu_0)(x) - \sigma_n^\sim(\mu_0)(y) = \int_y^x \{\sigma_n(\nu)(u) - \nu^\wedge(0)\}\, du,$$

and as $n \to \infty$

$$\mu_0^\sim(x) - \mu_0^\sim(y) = \int_y^x \{\nu(u) - \nu^\wedge(0)\}\, du,$$

proving that $\mu_0^\sim = \mu^\sim$ (by definition) belongs to $\mathsf{AC}_{2\pi}$ and $(\mu^\sim)'(x) = \nu(x) - \nu^\wedge(0)$ a.e. Finally, since $(\mu^\sim)'$ and ν are normalized, $\nu^\wedge(0)$ is equal to zero, which proves the fact that (i) implies (ii). The proof of the converse will be omitted.

Example 1.5.9. In Example 1.5.5 we studied the semi-group of left-translations on the space $\mathsf{C}_{2\pi}$. By Theorem 1.5.7 the dual semi-group $\{T^*(t); 0 \leq t < \infty\}$ on $\mathsf{NBV}_{2\pi}$ will be the semi-group of right translations, i.e.

$$d[T^*(t)\,\mu](x) = d_x\mu(x-t) \sim \sum_{k=-\infty}^{\infty} \mu^\vee(k)\, e^{ik(x-t)} \qquad (t > 0).$$

Furthermore,

$$D(A^*) = \left\{\mu \in NBV_{2\pi};\ \sim \sum_{k=-\infty}^{\infty} (-ik)\, \mu^\vee(k)\, e^{ikx} \in NBV_{2\pi}\right\}$$

$$= \{\mu \in NBV_{2\pi};\ \mu \in AC_{2\pi} \text{ and } \mu' \in NBV_{2\pi}\}$$

and $[A^* \mu]^\vee (k) = (-ik)\, \mu^\vee(k)$ for all $k = 0, \pm 1, \pm 2, \ldots$

By Proposition 1.4.3 the semi-group $\{T^*(t);\, 0 \leqq t < \infty\}$ is continuous in the weak* operator topology on $NBV_{2\pi}$. It is strongly continuous on the closed subspace $[C_{2\pi}]_0^*$, equal to the strong closure of $D(A^*)$. This subspace $[C_{2\pi}]_0^*$ is isometrically isomorphic to $AC_{2\pi}$, or equivalently, to $L^1_{2\pi}$. We have thus shown that the set of all functions in $NBV_{2\pi}$ with continuous right translations is precisely the set of all absolutely continuous functions, i.e. the subset $AC_{2\pi}$. This is the periodic version of Plessner's theorem given in Remark 1.4.10.

Plessner's original proof, which is quite different to that given above, is also of interest. Indeed, suppose $\mu \in NBV_{2\pi}$ is strongly continuous under translation. Then we have for the Fejér means of $\mu_0(x) = \mu(x) - \mu^\vee(0)\, x$

$$\sigma_n(\mu_0)(x) - \mu_0(x) = \frac{1}{2\pi} \int_0^{2\pi} \{\mu_0(x+u) - \mu_0(x)\} \frac{1}{n+1} \frac{\sin^2 (n+1) u/2}{\sin^2 u/2}\, du \qquad (n = 1, 2, \ldots)$$

and setting $\omega(u) = \|\mu_0(\cdot + u) - \mu_0(\cdot)\|_V$,

$$\|\sigma_n(\mu_0) - \mu_0\|_V \leqq \frac{1}{2\pi} \int_0^{2\pi} \omega(u) \frac{1}{n+1} \frac{\sin^2 (n+1) u/2}{\sin^2 u/2}\, du.$$

By assumption $\omega(u)$ is a continuous 2π-periodic function with $\omega(0) = 0$. Thus

$$\lim_{n \to \infty} \|\sigma_n(\mu_0) - \mu_0\|_V = 0.$$

Since the Fejér means $\sigma_n(\mu_0)$ belong to $AC_{2\pi}$ and since $AC_{2\pi}$ is a strongly closed subspace in $NBV_{2\pi}$, the latter limit relation proves that μ_0, and consequently μ are absolutely continuous. The converse of this statement is obvious.

1.5.4 Dirichlet's Problem for the Unit Disk

There is a further famous application of semi-groups of factor sequence operators, known as *Abel's method of summation.*

Let X be one of the spaces $C_{2\pi}$, $L^p_{2\pi}$, $1 \leqq p < \infty$. For an element $f \in X$ we denote by

$$[V(\varrho) f](x) = \sum_{k=-\infty}^{\infty} \varrho^{|k|} f^\wedge(k)\, e^{ikx} \qquad (0 \leqq \varrho < 1) \tag{1.5.15}$$

Abel's sum of the Fourier series of f. Clearly, since $|f^\wedge(k)| \leqq \|f\|$ for all integers k, the sum is absolutely and uniformly convergent for each fixed $0 \leqq \varrho < 1$. If we set $V(1) = I$ and replace the parameter ϱ by e^{-t} $(0 \leqq t \leqq \infty)$ in (1.5.15), then we see that Abel's summation process forms a semi-group of factor sequence operators of type (1.5.9) with $\{\lambda_k = -|k|;\, k = 0, \pm 1, \pm 2, \ldots\}$.

On the other hand, $v(\varrho; f) = V(\varrho) f$ $(0 \leqq \varrho \leqq 1)$ is known as the solution of *Dirichlet's problem for the unit disk*:

Let X be one of the spaces $\mathsf{C}_{2\pi}$, $\mathsf{L}^p_{2\pi}$ $(1 \leqq p < \infty)$ and let

$$\mathsf{D}(U) = \{f \in \mathsf{X};\ f, f' \in \mathsf{AC}_{2\pi} \text{ and } f'' \in \mathsf{X}\}$$

be the domain of the operator U defined by $U f = f''$.

Given any element $f_0 \in \mathsf{X}$, find a function $v(\varrho) = v(\varrho; f_0)$ on $0 \leqq \varrho \leqq 1$ to X such that

(i) *$v(\varrho)$ is twice strongly continuously differentiable in $[0, 1)$;*

(ii) *for each $\varrho \in [0, 1)$, $v(\varrho) \in \mathsf{D}(U)$ and*

$$\varrho^2 v''(\varrho) + \varrho v'(\varrho) + U v(\varrho) = 0 \qquad (0 \leqq \varrho < 1);$$

(iii) $\operatorname*{s-lim}_{\varrho \to 1-} v(\varrho; f_0) = f_0$.

That the unique solution of this classical boundary value problem will be given by $v(\varrho; f_0) = V(\varrho) f_0$ (any $f_0 \in \mathsf{X}; 0 \leqq \varrho \leqq 1$) may be proved by semi-group theoretical methods as pointed out in the second part of this section concerning the solution of Fourier's ring problem for the unit circle. But it will be more convenient to use the finite Fourier transform method. An explicit proof will be omitted.

Considered as the solution of Dirichlet's problem the vector-valued function $V(\varrho) f$ is often known as the *singular integral of Abel-Poisson*, because of its integral representation

$$[V(\varrho) f](x) = \frac{1}{2\pi} \int_0^{2\pi} f(u)\, p(\varrho; x - u)\, du \tag{1.5.16}$$

with the *Abel-Poisson kernel*

$$p(\varrho; u) = \frac{1 - \varrho^2}{1 - 2\varrho \cos u + \varrho^2} \qquad (0 \leqq \varrho < 1). \tag{1.5.17}$$

Theorem 1.5.10. *If X is one of the spaces $\mathsf{C}_{2\pi}$ or $\mathsf{L}^p_{2\pi}$, $1 \leqq p < \infty$, the singular integral of Abel-Poisson $\{V(e^{-t}); 0 \leqq t < \infty\}$ defines a contraction semi-group of class $(\mathscr{C}_0)$ in $\mathscr{E}(\mathsf{X})$, the domain of the infinitesimal generator A being given by*

$$\mathsf{D}(A) = \left\{f \in \mathsf{X};\ \sim \sum_{k=-\infty}^{\infty} |k|\, f^\wedge(k)\, e^{ikx} \in \mathsf{X}\right\} = \{f \in \mathsf{X}; f^\sim \in \mathsf{AC}_{2\pi} \text{ and } (f^\sim)' \in \mathsf{X}\}$$

and $A f = -(f^\sim)'$. *In general, for* $r = 1, 2, \ldots$

$$(1.5.18)\quad \mathsf{D}(A^r) = \left\{f \in \mathsf{X};\ \sim \sum_{k=-\infty}^{\infty} |k|^r f^\wedge(k)\, e^{ikx} \in \mathsf{X}\right\}$$

$$= \left\{f \in \mathsf{X};\ \begin{matrix} f, f', \ldots, f^{(r-1)} \in \mathsf{AC}_{2\pi} \text{ and } f^{(r)} \in \mathsf{X} \ (r \text{ even}) \\ f^\sim, (f^\sim)', \ldots, (f^\sim)^{(r-1)} \in \mathsf{AC}_{2\pi} \text{ and } (f^\sim)^{(r)} \in \mathsf{X} \ (r \text{ odd}) \end{matrix}\right\}$$

and

$$(1.5.19)\qquad A^r f = (-1)^{[(r+1)/2]} \begin{cases} f^{(r)} & (r \text{ even}) \\ (f^\sim)^{(r)} & (r \text{ odd}). \end{cases}$$

Furthermore, $\{V(e^{-t}); 0 \leqq t < \infty\}$ *forms a holomorphic semi-group.*

Proof. Since the Poisson kernel $p(\varrho; \cdot)$ is non-negative for each fixed $0 \leqq \varrho < 1$, we have that $\|p(\varrho; \cdot)\|_1 = p^\wedge(\varrho; 0) = 1$ and thus

$$\|V(\varrho) f\| \leqq \|f\| \qquad (f \in \mathsf{X})$$

In particular, for the function $f_0(x) \equiv 1$ one obtains $V(\varrho) f_0 = f_0$ for all $0 \leqq \varrho < 1$ and thus $\|V(\varrho)\| \equiv 1$.

By Theorem 1.5.4 it follows that $\{V(e^{-t}); 0 \leqq t < \infty\}$ forms a contraction semi-group of class $(\mathscr{C}_0)$ in $\mathscr{E}(\mathsf{X})$ and an element $f \in \mathsf{X}$ belongs to $\mathsf{D}(A)$ if and only if $\sim \sum_{k=-\infty}^{\infty} (-|k|)\, f^\wedge(k)\, e^{ikx} \in \mathsf{X}$, but this implies by Lemma 1.5.6 that $f^\sim \in \mathsf{AC}_{2\pi}$ and $(f^\sim)' \in \mathsf{X}$. The generalizations (1.5.18) and (1.5.19) are also consequences of Lemma 1.5.6.

Thus it remains to prove that $\{V(e^{-t}); 0 \leqq t < \infty\}$ is holomorphic. From the representation (1.5.15) it follows immediately that $V(e^{-t})[\mathsf{X}] \subset \mathsf{D}(A)$ for all $t > 0$ and

$$[A\, V(e^{-t}) f](x) = \sum_{k=-\infty}^{\infty} (-|k|)\, e^{-|k|t} f^\wedge(k)\, e^{ikx}$$

$$= -\frac{1}{2\pi} \int_0^{2\pi} f(u)\, q'(e^{-t}; x - u)\, du,$$

where $q'(\varrho; u)$ is the derivative with respect to u of the conjugate Poisson kernel

$$(1.5.20)\qquad q(\varrho; u) = \frac{2\varrho \sin u}{1 - 2\varrho \cos u + \varrho^2} \qquad (0 \leqq \varrho < 1).$$

One verifies without difficulty that the $\mathsf{L}^1_{2\pi}$-norm of $q'(\varrho; \cdot)$ can be estimated by $\|q'(\varrho; \cdot)\|_1 \leqq 2\varrho/(1-\varrho)$, and on account of the fact that $1 - \varrho \leqq \log\frac{1}{\varrho} \leqq (1-\varrho)/\varrho$ $(0 < \varrho < 1)$ we obtain that

$$(1.5.21)\qquad \|A\, V(e^{-t})\| \leqq \|q'(e^{-t}; \cdot)\|_1 \leqq 2t^{-1} \qquad (0 < t < \infty).$$

In case $X = L^2_{2\pi}$ we have a sharper estimate given by

$$\|A\, V(e^{-t})\| = \sup_k\{|k|\, e^{-|k|t}\} \leqq (e\,t)^{-1} \qquad (0 < t < \infty),$$

equality holding for all $t = 1/|k|$ $(k = \pm 1, \pm 2, \ldots)$.

Theorem 1.5.11. *The singular integral of Abel-Poisson* $\{V^*(\varrho);\ 0 \leqq \varrho \leqq 1\}$ *on* $NBV_{2\pi}$ *defined by*

$$(1.5.22)\quad d[V^*(\varrho)\,\mu](x) \sim \sum_{k=-\infty}^{\infty} \varrho^{|k|}\mu^{\vee}(k)\, e^{ikx} = \frac{1}{2\pi}\int_0^{2\pi} p(\varrho; x-u)\, d\mu(u)$$

forms a contraction semi-group of class $(\mathscr{C}_0)^*$ *in* $\mathscr{E}(NBV_{2\pi})$ *(if we replace* ϱ *by* e^{-t}*) with*

$$(1.5.23)\quad D(A^*) = \left\{\mu \in NBV_{2\pi};\ \sim \sum_{k=-\infty}^{\infty} (-|k|)\, \mu^{\vee}(k)\, e^{ikx} \in NBV_{2\pi}\right\}$$
$$= \{\mu \in NBV_{2\pi};\ \mu^{\sim} \in AC_{2\pi} \text{ and } (\mu^{\sim})' \in NBV_{2\pi}\}$$

and $A^*\mu = -(\mu^{\sim})' = -(\mu')^{\sim}$.

Furthermore, the closed subspace of $NBV_{2\pi}$ *upon which the restriction* $\{V^*_0(\varrho);\ 0 \leqq \varrho \leqq 1\}$ *defines a semi-group of class* $(\mathscr{C}_0)$, *is given by* $AC_{2\pi}$ *(= isometrically isomorphic to* $L^1_{2\pi}$*) and*

$$(1.5.24)\qquad D(A^*_0) = \{\mu \in AC_{2\pi};\ (\mu^{\sim})' \in AC_{2\pi}\}.$$

Proof. Since $NBV_{2\pi}$ is isometrically isomorphic to $[C_{2\pi}]^*$, the first part of this theorem follows by Theorem 1.5.7 and Lemma 1.5.8. By Proposition 1.4.7 the subspace $[C_{2\pi}]^*_0$ is given by the strong closure of $D(A^*)$ in $[C_{2\pi}]^*$, proving together with the representation (1.5.23) of $D(A^*)$ that $[C_{2\pi}]^*_0$ is equal to $AC_{2\pi}$. Moreover, we know by Proposition 1.4.7 that $D(A^*_0)$ is given by those elements μ of $D(A^*)$ for which $A^*\mu \in [C_{2\pi}]^*_0$, which proves (1.5.24).

An equivalent result is valid for the $L^\infty_{2\pi}$-space too. In this case we have

Theorem 1.5.12. *The singular integral of Abel-Poisson* $\{V^*(\varrho);\ 0 \leqq \varrho \leqq 1\}$ *on* $L^\infty_{2\pi}$ *defined by*

$$(1.5.25)\qquad [V^*(\varrho)\,F](x) = \sum_{k=-\infty}^{\infty} \varrho^{|k|} F^{\wedge}(k)\, e^{ikx}$$
$$= \frac{1}{2\pi}\int_0^{2\pi} F(u)\, p(\varrho; x-u)\, du \qquad (0 \leqq \varrho < 1)$$

forms a contraction semi-group of class $(\mathscr{C}_0)^*$ *in* $\mathscr{E}(L^\infty_{2\pi})$ *with*

$$(1.5.26)\qquad D(A^*) = \{F \in L^\infty_{2\pi};\ F^{\sim} \in AC_{2\pi} \text{ and } (F^{\sim})' \in L^\infty_{2\pi}\}$$

and $A^*F = -(F^{\sim})'$.

Furthermore, $\{V_0^*(\varrho); 0 \leqq \varrho \leqq 1\}$ *is defined on* $[\mathsf{L}^1_{2\pi}]_0^* = \mathsf{C}_{2\pi}$ *and*

$$D(A_0^*) = \{F \in \mathsf{C}_{2\pi};\ F^{\sim} \in \mathsf{AC}_{2\pi} \text{ and } (F^{\sim})' \in \mathsf{C}_{2\pi}\}. \tag{1.5.27}$$

The proof of this theorem is exactly the same as that given for Theorem 1.5.11 and is therefore omitted.

1.6 Notes and Remarks

1.6.1 There are a number of expositions on semi-group theory which treat the major portion covered by Chapter I of this book. The standard book on the subject is the monumental treatise of E. HILLE [4] published in 1948 and its revised edition written together with R. S. PHILLIPS [1] of 1957. The following books contain at least one chapter on semi-group theory: F. RIESZ-B. SZ.-NAGY [1], N. DUNFORD-J. SCHWARTZ [1], E. B. DYNKIN [2], K. YOSIDA [10]. One may also consult lecture notes on the subject by R. S. PHILLIPS [7], K. YOSIDA [7] and L.SCHWARTZ [2].

E. HILLE begins his treatment from an algebraic point of view, by defining an *abstract semi-group* $\mathscr{S}$ (an associative groupoid under a binary operation $\circ$). In analysis $\mathscr{S}$ is always a *topological semi-group*: $\mathscr{S}$ is a Hausdorff space and the binary operation $\circ$ is separately continuous. He then introduces a family of transformations $\mathscr{T}$ defined on an *abstract space* $\mathfrak{X}$ to itself considered as a *realization* of the abstract semi-group $\mathscr{S}$, i.e. to every element $a \in \mathscr{S}$ there corresponds an element $T(a) \in \mathscr{T}$ such that $T(a \circ b) = T(a)\,T(b)$. The realization is said to be faithful if $a \neq b$ implies $T(a) \neq T(b)$. This family $\mathscr{T} = \{T(a); a \in \mathscr{S}\}$ is then called a *transformation semi-group* on $\mathfrak{X}$.

The positive real axis $\mathrm{E}_1^+ = \{t; 0 < t < \infty\}$ endowed with the arithmetical operation $+$ of addition is e.g. one of the simplest examples of a semi-group. If X is a Banach space, $\mathscr{E}(\mathsf{X})$ the corresponding Banach algebra of endomorphisms of X, then the family of operators $\{T(t); 0 < t < \infty\}$ in $\mathscr{E}(\mathsf{X})$, considered as a realization of E_1^+, defines a transformation semi-group on X.

It is the theory of this simple instance, more or less, which one understands under *semi-group theory*, or more precisely, under the theory of one-parameter semi-groups of operators on Banach spaces. This instance has many important applications.

The definition of a semi-group of operators in $\mathscr{E}(\mathsf{X})$ given in Definition 1.1.1 is sometimes replaced by a different and weaker one in the various expositions on the subject. Thus, HILLE-PHILLIPS [1, Ch. X] assume to begin with that $\{T(t); 0 < t < \infty\}$ is a one-parameter semi-group of operators in $\mathscr{E}(\mathsf{X})$ (i.e. fulfils (1.1.1) (i) with $t=0$ excluded) such that (a) $T(t)$ is strongly measurable (from which may be shown that $T(t)$ is strongly continuous) on E_1^+ and (b) $\mathsf{X}_0 \equiv \bigcup_{0<t<\infty} T(t)[\mathsf{X}]$ is dense in X. It can be shown that a semi-group in the above sense of H.-Ph. is of class $(\mathscr{C}_0)$ (i.e. fulfils (1.1.1) (ii) and (iii)) if and only if (c) there is a constant $M>0$ such that $\|T(t)\| \leqq M$ for $0<t\leqq 1$ (cf. H.-Ph. [1, p. 319]). In the hypotheses of many of their theorems, however, apart from the conditions (a) and (b), H.-Ph. assume an additional condition concerning the convergence of $T(t)$ in some sense to the identity I as $t \to 0+$. Indeed, instead of the $(\mathscr{C}_0)$-property they often take $T(t)f$ to be either strongly $(\mathscr{C}_1)$ or Abel-summable to f as $t \to 0+$ for all $f \in \mathsf{X}$, thus

$$(\mathscr{C}_1):\quad \underset{t\to 0+}{\text{s-lim}}\, \frac{1}{t}\int_0^t T(u)\, f\, du = f;$$

$$(\mathscr{A}):\quad \underset{\lambda\to\infty}{\text{s-lim}}\, \lambda \int_0^\infty e^{-\lambda u}\, T(u)\, f\, du = f.$$

Obviously, if $\{T(t);\, 0\leqq t<\infty\}$ is of class $(\mathscr{C}_0)$, then $T(t)f$ is $(\mathscr{C}_1)$-summable to f as $t\to 0+$ which, in turn, implies that $T(t)f$ is $(\mathscr{A})$-summable to f as $\lambda\to\infty$. However, most of the important examples of semi-group operators are of class $(\mathscr{C}_0)$. For a freak counterexample, see e.g. H.-Ph. [1, p. 552].

Concerning Definition 1.1.1 we further remark that the strong $(\mathscr{C}_0)$-property is equivalent to the weak $(\mathscr{C}_0)$-property

$$\text{(1.1.1)} \qquad \text{(iii)}' \quad \underset{t\to 0+}{\text{w-lim}}\, T(t)f = f \qquad (f\in \mathsf{X}).$$

See H.-Ph. [1, p. 324] or K. Yosida [10, p. 233]. Furthermore, K. Yosida [7, p. 58] noted that the infinitesimal generator A (Definition 1.1.3) may also be defined by the weak limit of $A_\tau f$ as $\tau\to 0+$, and one obtains the same operator.

Regarding the proofs of the Propositions 1.1.2, 1.1.4 and 1.1.6 we just remark that they may be found in any of the expositions cited above. Concerning Proposition 1.1.2 (a), the three conditions of Definition 1.1.1 imply that $\|T(t)\|$ is measurable and bounded on every finite subinterval of $[0,\infty)$ (cf. Dunford-Schwartz [1, p. 616]). The proof of Proposition 1.1.6 (c) is based upon a construction due to I. Gelfand in the case of one-parameter groups (cf. H.-Ph. [1, p. 308]). For uniformly continuous semi-groups in $\mathscr{E}(\mathsf{X})$ see H.-Ph. [1, pp. 338–342] or Dunford-Schwartz [1, p. 621].

The discussion on n-parameter semi-groups $\{T(t);\, t\in \overline{\mathrm{E}_n^+}\}$ of class $(\mathscr{C}_0)$ in $\mathscr{E}(\mathsf{X})$ can be considered from a more general point of view. To each vector $t \in \overline{E_n^+}$, $t \neq 0$ (zero vector) there is associated an infinitesimal generator $A(t)$ defined by

$$A(t)\, f = \operatorname*{s-lim}_{\tau \to 0+} \frac{T(\tau t) - I}{\tau} f$$

whenever it exists. Clearly, $A_k = A(e_k)$, $k = 1, 2, \ldots, n$. $A(t)$ is an additive, positive-homogeneous function of t. More precisely, all generators are of the form

$$A(t) = \sum_{k=1}^{n} t_k A_k \qquad (t = (t_1, t_2, \ldots, t_n)).$$

Thus the set of generators $\{A(t); t \in \overline{E_n^+}, t \neq 0\}$ itself is an additive abelian semi-group of closed operators. For a detailed study of the theory of n-parameter semi-groups of operators, developed by E. Hille in 1944, we refer to H.-Ph. [1, pp. 327—336], in particular to Chapter XXV on Lie Semi-Groups, ibidem. For recent results see also R. P. Langlands [1], O. A. Ivanova [1].

Concerning holomorphic semi-groups of operators in a sector $\Delta = \{\zeta; \operatorname{Re}\zeta > 0, |\arg \zeta| < \alpha_0 \leqq \pi/2\}$ we refer to E. Hille [5], H.-Ph. [1, p. 325 and Ch. XVII], as well as to K. Yosida [10, pp. 254—259].

A few words on the history of the subject. The algebraic theory of semi-groups seems to go back to a treatise of J. A. de Séguier [1] on abstract groups (which are of older origin), but the main progress took place in the early thirties (cf. H.-Ph. [1, p. 261]). See e. g. the treatises by A. H. Clifford–G. B. Preston [1], E. S. Ljapin [1] and K. H. Hofmann–P. S. Mostert [1]. One-parameter transformation groups were first considered by M. H. Stone [1; 2] and J. von Neumann [1] in 1929—1932 for the case of unitary groups in Hilbert space. General groups in a Banach space were treated by I. Gelfand [1] and M. Fukamiya [1] in 1939—1940. The earliest investigations on one-parameter transformation semi-groups date back to papers by E. Hille [1] and B. Sz.-Nagy [1] of 1936, the former discussing some interesting special semi-groups. The representation theorem (cf. Sec. 1.2) for semi-groups of bounded linear self-adjoint operators on a Hilbert space was discovered independently by B. Sz.-Nagy [2] and E. Hille [2] in 1938 (cf. also K. Yosida [1]). On the other hand, it should be noted that the semi-group property of the solution (1.0.8) of the heat-conduction equation appears to have been noticed first by P. Appell [1] in 1892. J. Hadamard [1; 3] in his analysis of *Huygens' principle* observed as early as 1903 that Cauchy's problem for the wave equation leads to certain transformation groups and that the group properties imply and are implied by certain *transcendental addition theorems* satisfied by the elementary solutions used in constructing the solution. The investigations by F. Bernstein [1] and G. Doetsch [1; 2] in 1920—1923 on the heat equation must be mentioned. See also G. Doetsch [3; 5].

In the period 1938—1948 the theory of semi-groups and its applications made vigorous progress and were built up as a new mathematical discipline especially in the hands of E. Hille. Here we must also mention the contributions of N. Dunford [1] (cf. also E. Hille [4, p. 182]). There is, moreover, a paper by N. P. Romanov [1] of 1947 giving another approach to the subject.

It was in 1948 that the first of K. Yosida's contributions [2; 3; 4; 5] to the theory appeared. Indeed, K. Yosida found the basic generation theorem for semi-groups (Corollary 1.3.7) independently of E. Hille in 1948. Soon thereafter, W. Feller [1; 2; 3; 4] and R. S. Phillips [1; 2; 3; 4; 5; 6; 8; 9] became interested in the field and began with their penetrating investigations.

There are several important fields of research on semi-groups that will not be considered in this book. These are semi-groups on Hilbert spaces, on locally convex spaces, and distribution semi-groups. But a few words on each topic.

For a study of groups and semi-groups of transformations on *Hilbert spaces* we refer to the famous book of F. Riesz-B. Sz.-Nagy [1, Ch. X] or to H.-Ph. [1, Ch. XXII]. For such semi-groups of contractions an operator B called the *cogenerator* of $T(t)$, defined by $B = (A + I) \times \times (A - I)^{-1}$ and introduced by B. Sz.-Nagy-C. Foiaş and studied by them in a series of papers [1; 2], plays an essential role (cf. also W. Mlak [1, pp. 71—78]).

The extension of semi-group theory to the case that $\mathscr{X}$ is a *locally convex linear Hausdorff space* which, in addition, is sequentially complete has been considered by L. Schwartz [2], H. G. Tillmann [1], H. Komatsu [1], K. Yosida [10, Ch. IX] and K. Singbal-Vedak [1]. In particular, K. Yosida in his book studies *equi-continuous* semi-groups of class $(\mathscr{C}_0)$ on such spaces. If $\mathscr{X}$ is a Banach space this concept agrees with what we have called an *equi-bounded* semi-group of class $(\mathscr{C}_0)$. Recent research on the theory of partial differential equations (cf. the survey-article by L. Gårding [1] as well as the book of R. E. Edwards [1]) shows that there is a considerable loss of subtility if one forces the theory into the bodice of Banach space theory. This is one reason why it is of interest to presuppose that $\mathscr{X}$ is locally convex but not normable.

The theory of one-parameter semi-groups of operators may also be generalized through the introduction of *distribution semi-groups of operators* on a Banach space X. We give a brief outline. Let $\mathfrak{D}_+$ be the convolution algebra of all functions φ in $\mathsf{C}_{00}^{\infty}(\mathrm{E}_1^+)$ provided with the topology of L. Schwartz [1].

Definition. *A distribution semi-group in $\mathscr{E}(\mathsf{X})$ is a linear mapping G from $\mathfrak{D}_+$ to $\mathscr{E}(\mathsf{X})$ such that*

(i) $G(\varphi * \psi) = G(\varphi)\, G(\psi)$ $\quad(\varphi, \psi \in \mathfrak{D}_+;\ *$ *means convolution);*

(ii) $G(\varphi) \to G(\varphi_0)$ *uniformly as* $\varphi \to \varphi_0$ *in* $\mathfrak{D}_+$*;*

(iii) $\mathsf{X}_{00} = \{g \in \mathsf{X};\ g = G(\varphi)\, f,$ *all* $f \in \mathsf{X}$ *and* $\varphi \in \mathfrak{D}_+\}$ *is dense in* X*;*

(iv) *if* $f \in \mathsf{X}$ *and* $G(\varphi)\, f = 0$ *for all* $\varphi \in \mathfrak{D}_+$, *then* $f = \theta$.

If $\{T(t);\ 0 < t < \infty\}$ is a strongly continuous semi-group in $\mathscr{E}(\mathsf{X})$ in the sense of H.-Ph. with the additional condition that if for an $f \in \mathsf{X}$ $T(t)\, f = \theta$ for all $t > 0$ implies $f = \theta$, then by the relation

$$G(\varphi)\, f = \int_0^\infty \varphi(t)\, T(t)\, f\, dt \qquad (f \in \mathsf{X},\ \varphi \in \mathfrak{D}_+) \tag{1.6.1}$$

the mapping G from $\mathfrak{D}_+$ to $\mathscr{E}(\mathsf{X})$ is a distribution semi-group.

Now, let $\overline{\mathfrak{E}'_+}$ be the convolution algebra of distributions on E_1 with compact support contained in $\overline{\mathrm{E}_1^+}$ (in the sense of L. Schwartz). As is well known, $\mathfrak{D}_+$ is an ideal in $\overline{\mathfrak{E}'_+}$. If $S \in \overline{\mathfrak{E}'_+}$, the operator $G(S)$ with domain X_{00} is defined by

$$G(S)\, g = G(S * \varphi)\, f \qquad (g \in \mathsf{X}_{00}),$$

where $g = G(\varphi)\, f$ for some $f \in \mathsf{X}$ and $\varphi \in \mathfrak{D}_+$. It can be shown that $G(S)$ is a uniquely defined linear operator (in general unbounded) on X_{00} to itself; moreover, $G(S)$ has a smallest closed linear extension $\overline{G(S)}$ in X with dense domain. If, in particular, S is the *Dirac distribution* δ_0 at the point $t = 0$, then $\overline{G(\delta_0)} = I$. The operator $\overline{G(-\delta_0')}$ is defined to be the *infinitesimal generator* of the distribution semi-group G.

A distribution semi-group G in $\mathscr{E}(\mathsf{X})$ is said to be *regular* if and only if $G(\phi)$ is bounded for every $\phi \in \overline{\mathfrak{D}_+}$; $\overline{\mathfrak{D}_+}$ denotes the space of all infinitely often differentiable functions ϕ on $\overline{\mathrm{E}_1^+}$ with compact support.

More specifically, a distribution semi-group G in $\mathscr{E}(\mathsf{X})$ is said to be of *class* $(\mathscr{C}_0)$ if and only if for every $\varphi \in \mathfrak{D}_+$ with $\int_0^\infty \varphi(t)\, dt = 1$,

$$\operatorname*{s-lim}_{s \to 0+} G(\varphi_s)\, f = f, \qquad \varphi_s(t) = (1/s)\, \varphi(t/s) \qquad (s > 0)$$

for all $f \in \mathsf{X}$.

A distribution semi-group of class $(\mathscr{C}_0)$ automatically satisfies the conditions (iii) and (iv) of the above definition. Furthermore, any semi-group $\{T(t);\ 0 \leqq t < \infty\}$ of class $(\mathscr{C}_0)$ in $\mathscr{E}(\mathsf{X})$ also forms a distribution semi-group G of class $(\mathscr{C}_0)$ by (1.6.1) and its infinitesimal generator A is equal to $\overline{G(-\delta_0')}$.

In 1960 J. L. Lions [4] introduced the concept of a regular distribution semi-group. However, we have mainly followed the presentation given by J. PEETRE [5]. For further generalizations as well as for applications we refer to the cited papers, also to C. FOIAȘ [1], K. YOSHINAGA [1; 2].

1.6.2 Theorem 1.2.2 is due to E. HILLE [3]. Several proofs have been given, for the earliest, see E. HILLE [3]. The present proof, giving a slightly stronger form through the inequality (1.2.5), is adapted from L. C. HSU [1] and is modelled upon arguments typical for the special case of the semi-group of left translations in $UCB(E_1^+)$ (defined in Example 1.2.5). For the particular case that $\{T(t); 0 \leqq t < \infty\}$ is a semi-group of contraction operators, a very simple proof has been given by N. DUNFORD-I. E. SEGAL [1]. Moreover, Theorem 1.2.2 possesses a basic generalization, due to B. Sz.-Nagy (see F. RIESZ–B. SZ.-NAGY [1, p. 400]): *Let $\{T(t); 0 \leqq t < \infty\}$ be a semi-group of operators of class $(\mathscr{C}_0)$ in $\mathscr{E}(X)$ with generator A, and let $\{B_\tau; 0 < \tau \leqq \tau_0\}$ be a family of operators in $\mathscr{E}(X)$ satisfying*

(i) *B_τ commutes with $T(t)$;*

(ii) $\sup_{0 \leqq t \leqq b} \|\exp(t B_\tau)\| \leqq N_b$ *(a constant independent of τ);*

(iii) $\text{s-lim}_{\tau \to 0+} B_\tau f = A f$ *for each $f \in D(A)$.*

Then for each $f \in X$ and each $t \geqq 0$

$$T(t) f = \text{s-lim}_{\tau \to 0+} \exp(t B_\tau) f,$$

the convergence being uniform in t, $0 \leqq t \leqq b < \infty$. For $B_\tau = A_\tau = \tau^{-1}[T(\tau) - I]$ this result reduces to Hille's first exponential formula. For a further generalization see C. FOIAȘ–G. GUSSI–V. POENARU [1].

Proposition 1.2.3 for the special case of the semi-group of left translations in $UCB(E_1^+)$ is due to O. SZÁSZ [1]. Theorem 1.2.6 appears for the first time in book-form, the particular case of the semi-group of left translations being due to H. BOHMAN [1]. Corollary 1.2.8, in particular formula (1.2.21), is due to D. G. KENDALL [1]. K. L. CHUNG [1] has given a simple unified approach in the language of probability theory to the formulae (1.2.4) of E. HILLE and (1.2.21) of D. G. KENDALL, both of which give representations for semi-groups (see also formula (1.3.14)). The classical theorem on the approximation of continuous functions by polynomials was given by K. WEIERSTRASS [1] in 1885. Very many proofs of this theorem and many generalizations thereof have been given; see e.g. the literature cited by E. W. CHENEY [1, p. 226] and DUNFORD-SCHWARTZ [1, pp. 383–385]. The polynomials defined by (1.2.22) were introduced by S. BERNSTEIN [1] in 1912 and give perhaps the simplest constructive proof of the Weierstrass theorem. These polynomials have applications to the theory of divergent series, moment problems and probability theory. See the monograph by

G. G. LORENTZ [3] on the subject. The transform appearing in (1.2.23) is due to J. FAVARD [1]. For results on pointwise convergence for this transform see O. SZÁSZ [1] and P. L. BUTZER [1], also M. GOLOMB [1, p. 237]. For generalizations see E. W. CHENEY–A. SHARMA [1], A. LUPAŞ–M. MÜLLER [1]. If a function $g(x)$ is continuous on $[0, \infty)$ with $\lim_{x\to\infty} g(x) = 0$, then M. H. STONE [3] has shown that $g(x)$ can be uniformly approximated by functions of the form $e^{-\alpha x} p(x)$, α being a fixed positive number and $p(x)$ an algebraic polynomial. For summability theory we refer to the monograph by K. ZELLER [1].

1.6.3 The material of Sec. 1.3 is standard in the theory of semi-group operators and is to be found in any of the revelant texts, e.g. H.-PH. [1, pp. 337—377], DUNFORD—SCHWARTZ [1, pp. 622—630] and K. YOSIDA [10, pp. 240—250]. Regarding a proof of Proposition 1.3.2 and Lemma 1.3.4 see e.g. A. E. TAYLOR [1, p. 256] and D. V. WIDDER [1, Ch. II], respectively. The first sufficient conditions that a closed linear operator generates a semi-group of class $(\mathscr{C}_0)$ were obtained independently by E. HILLE [4] and K. YOSIDA [2] in 1948. This is the so-called Hille-Yosida theorem (Corollary 1.3.7). The complete characterization of the infinitesimal generator given in Theorem 1.3.6 was published almost simultaneously by W. FELLER [4], I. MIYADERA [1], and R. S. PHILLIPS [4] in 1952—1953. It is one of the cornerstones of semi-group theory. The resolvent of the generator being available, Proposition 1.3.11 gives a third representation formula for $T(t)$ (the others being formulae (1.2.4) and (1.2.21)). Formula (1.3.14), due to R. S. PHILLIPS [5], goes back to K. YOSIDA [2] and is related to still earlier work of W. B. CATON–E. HILLE [1]. For another proof of Proposition 1.3.11 in terms of the unified approach of probability theory, see the cited paper by K. L. CHUNG [1]. For further representation formulae see the list given by H.-PH. [1, p. 354]. We state two more explicitly. If $\{T(t); 0 \leqq t < \infty\}$ is a semi-group of class $(\mathscr{C}_0)$, then for each $f \in \mathsf{X}$ and $t > 0$ it can be shown that

$$T(t) f = \underset{n\to\infty}{\text{s-lim}} \left[\frac{n}{t} R\left(\frac{n}{t}; A\right)\right]^n f.$$

In view of the fact that

$$\frac{(-1)^n}{n!} \left(\frac{n}{t}\right)^{n+1} R^{(n)}\left(\frac{n}{t}; A\right) = \left[\frac{n}{t} R\left(\frac{n}{t}; A\right)\right]^{n+1},$$

we see the connection with the Post-Widder real inversion formula for the Laplace transform. The other inversion formula is given by

$$T(t) f = \underset{\gamma\to\infty}{\text{s-lim}} \frac{1}{2\pi i} \int_{\omega - i\gamma}^{\omega + i\gamma} e^{\lambda t} R(\lambda; A) f \, d\lambda$$

holding for each $f \in \mathsf{D}(A)$ and $t > 0$ with $\omega > \max(0, \omega_0)$.

For the proof of Theorem 1.3.15 see H.-PH. [1, p. 364]. For further material on groups of operators we refer to the latter book as well as to RIESZ-NAGY [1]. For a proof of Theorem 1.3.16 we may mention K. YOSIDA [10, p. 235, p. 242] and H.-PH. [1, Ch. XIX].

The extension of Theorem 1.3.6 to the case that X is a locally convex, sequentially complete, linear Hausdorff space is due to L. SCHWARTZ [2], see K. YOSIDA [10, p. 246] or H. KOMATSU [1]. For a version of Corollary 1.3.8 for regular distribution semi-groups in $\mathscr{E}(\mathsf{X})$, see J. L. LIONS [4], also J. PEETRE [5], G. DA PRATO–U. MOSCO [1; 2], and K. YOSHINAGA [1; 2].

1.6.4 The definition of the dual semi-group given in Sec. 1.4 is not equivalent with what R. S. PHILLIPS calls the "adjoint semi-group", see H.-PH. [1, Ch. XIV]. R. S. PHILLIPS [9] begins his treatment with the dual A^* of the infinitesimal generator A of a semi-group $\{T(t); 0 \leqq t < \infty\}$ of class $(\mathscr{C}_0)$ in $\mathscr{E}(\mathsf{X})$. Denoting the strong closure of $\mathsf{D}(A^*)$ in X^* by X^+, he shows that the restrictions $T^+(t)$ of the dual semi-group operators $T^*(t)$ on X^* form a strongly continuous semi-group of operators on X^+ with infinitesimal generator A^+ being equal to the largest restriction of A^* with domain and range in X^+. He then calls X^+ the "adjoint space" of X with respect to the semi-group $\{T(t); 0 \leqq t < \infty\}$ and $\{T^+(t); 0 \leqq t < \infty\}$ the "adjoint semi-group". By Proposition 1.4.7 (a) the space X^+ is identically equal to the space X_0^* defined in (1.4.5), and thus the restriction $\{T_0^*(t); 0 \leqq t < \infty\}$ of the dual semi-group on X_0^* with generator A_0^*, of our approach, coincides with $\{T^+(t); 0 \leqq t < \infty\}$ and A^+. Thus the two different ways of constructing these strongly continuous semi-groups lead to the same result. For further information on "adjoint theory" we again refer to H.-PH. [1, Ch. XIV].

W. FELLER [3] treats semi-groups of operators on Banach spaces in general weak topologies from a very general point of view. Although W. FELLER does not employ a precise notion of the dual of an unbounded operator the results of Proposition 1.4.3 and 1.4.4 can be reduced from those of W. FELLER. In an earlier paper [1] on parabolic differential equations W. FELLER had already demonstrated the usefulness of dual semi-groups.

Our approach to dual theory has its roots in papers [1; 2] by K. DE LEEUW and the methods of the proofs of the propositions presented are based upon these papers. See also E. B. DYNKIN [1; 2, Ch. I]. Corollary 1.4.8 was proved by R. S. PHILLIPS [9].

In [2] K. DE LEEUW introduced the useful notion of a *smooth subspace* with respect to a semi-group $\{T(t); 0 \leqq t < \infty\}$: A linear subspace Y of X will be called *smooth* if it is dense in X, contained in $\mathsf{D}(A)$ and $T(t)[\mathsf{Y}] \subset \mathsf{Y}$ for all $t \geqq 0$. He then proves: *If B is the restric-*

tion of A on a smooth subspace Y of X, then the dual of B is equal to A^*. Furthermore, A is the closure of B. Equivalently, a linear subspace Y^* of X^* is said to be *weakly* smooth* if it is weakly* dense in X^*, contained in $\mathsf{D}(A^*)$ and $T^*(t)\,[\mathsf{Y}^*] \subset \mathsf{Y}^*$ for all $t \geqq 0$. *If B^* is the restriction of A^* on Y^*, then A^* is the weakly* closure of B^*.* These two assertions are easily verified by the methods of proof given in Sec. 1.4. We only mention that $\mathsf{D}(A_0^*)$ is a weakly* smooth subspace of X^*.

The dual theory for semi-groups on locally convex linear Hausdorff spaces was given by H. KOMATSU [1], see K. YOSIDA [10, pp. 272–274]. For the original proof of Plessner's theorem see A. PLESSNER [1], also we refer to H.-PH. [1, p. 534].

1.6.5 Concerning Sec. 1.5.1, the most convenient reference to the classical results on Fourier series is A. ZYGMUND's two-volume *Trigonometrical Series* [5], which contains essentially the important work on the subject. A short and elegant treatment of Fourier series is given by G. H. HARDY–W. W. ROGOSINSKI [1].

For a study of Fourier's problem of the ring from the classical point of view of the theory of partial differential equations see e.g. H. S. CARSLAW [1, pp. 211–217]. One may also consult S. BOCHNER [3], E. HILLE [4, p. 402], and S. MINAKSHISUNDARAM [1]. The detailed treatment of Fourier's problem via the Hille-Yosida theorem given in Sec. 1.5.2 seems to be new in book-form. For the representation of the kernel $r(\lambda;\cdot)$ of the resolvent (1.5.5), which is actually the Laplace transform of Jacobi's theta function $\vartheta_3(\cdot;t)$, see also G. DOETSCH [6, Bd. I, p. 281]. It was also G. DOETSCH [4] who in 1935 first considered the application of finite Fourier transforms, thus Fourier coefficients, in solving partial differential equations in which one or more of the independent variables range over a finite interval. These methods have been extended by I. N. SNEDDON [1].

For the material on semi-groups of factor sequence type on the spaces $C_{2\pi}$ and $L_{2\pi}^p$, $1 \leqq p < \infty$, of Sec. 1.5.3 see H.-PH [1, Ch. XX]. Theorem 1.5.7 on the corresponding dual semi-groups is new. For complete proofs of Lemmata 1.5.6 and 1.5.8 see E. GÖRLICH [1]. Dirichlet's problem for the Laplace equation in the unit disk considered in Sec. 1.5.4 is actually a specific instance of a general abstract Cauchy problem of higher order. For a treatment of this problem which is a natural generalization of the abstract Cauchy problem discussed in Sec. 1.0, we refer to H.-PH [1, pp. 623–633]. For the determination of the infinitesimal generator of the singular integral of Abel-Poisson on the spaces $C_{2\pi}$ and $L_{2\pi}^p$, $1 \leqq p < \infty$, given in Theorem 1.5.10 see H.-PH. [1, p. 556], also for the corresponding results for the spaces $NBV_{2\pi}$ and $L_{2\pi}^\infty$ (Theorems 1.5.11 and 1.5.12) see K. DE LEEUW [2].

Let us recall the abstract Cauchy problem of E. HILLE defined and considered in Sec. 1.0. We studied the equation of heat-conduction for an infinite rod in Sec. 1.0 and the corresponding Cauchy problem for a circular wire in great detail in Sec. 1.5.2 so as to reveal the importance of the Hille-Yosida theorem and thus of semi-group methods in the theory of linear partial differential equations. For a general treatment of partial differential equations of the heat equation type in the spaces $L^1(\mathrm{E}_n)$ and $UCB(\mathrm{E}_n)$, which is connected with the names of W. FELLER, E. HILLE and K. YOSIDA, as well as for equations of the wave equation type in $L^2(\mathrm{E}_n)$ studied by K. YOSIDA, J. L. LIONS and R. S. PHILLIPS, we refer to H.-PH. [1, Ch. XXIII] and K. YOSIDA [10, Ch. XIII to XIV]. The exact references may be found in the bibliography of these books. For the development in the Soviet Union we refer to YU. I. LJUBICH [1] and the literature cited there.

However, in the case of the wave equation in $L^p(\mathrm{E}_n)$ $(p \neq 2; n \geqq 2)$ the Hille-Yosida theorem fails completely. Indeed, from recent work of W. LITTMAN [1] it follows that there are data in $L^p(\mathrm{E}_n)$ at the time $t = 0$ such that for the solution the data, for any time $t > 0$, are not in $L^p(\mathrm{E}_n)$, but only distributions. The result of W. LITTMAN indicates from the point of view of Cauchy's problem that the concept of strongly continuous semi-groups is somewhat narrow, and one is thus led to generalize it. This is one reason for the introduction of distribution semi-groups of operators. For further details see J. PEETRE [5].

There are many other fields where one encounters one-parameter transformation semi-groups. We just mention three very important instances: *Ergodic theory*, the *theory of stochastic processes* and *perturbation theory*. For ergodic theory we refer to the accounts in H.-PH. [1, Ch. XVIII], DUNFORD–SCHWARTZ [1, pp. 657—730], RIESZ-NAGY [1, Ch. X], K. YOSIDA [10, Ch. XIII]. For semi-group theory and stochastic processes we refer to the basic paper by W. FELLER [1] and to the treatments in H.-PH. [1, pp. 633—663], E. B. DYNKIN [2], J. NEVEU [1], K. ITÔ–H. MCKEAN [1] and W. FELLER [5]. For perturbation theory, see H.-PH. [1, Ch. XIII] and T. KATO [3]; for scattering theory, see P. D. LAX–R. S. PHILLIPS [1].

Chapter Two

Approximation Theorems for Semi-Groups of Operators

2.0 Introduction

In the applications to the previous chapter, in particular in Sec. 1.5, we discussed the existence, uniqueness and explicit representation of the semi-group solution of the diffusion as well as Laplace equation for the circle. The main concern of the applications to the general theory to be studied in the present chapter is the behavior of the solutions in question in their dependence upon the given initial or boundary conditions.

For reasons of precision and as a motivation let us return to the example of the heat-conduction equation for an infinite rod considered in Sec. 1.0. We have seen that the solution $w(x, t; f)$ for an initial value function $f(x)$ belonging to $UCB(E_1)$ is given by a contraction semi-group of operators $\{W(t); 0 \leqq t < \infty\}$ of class $(\mathscr{C}_0)$ on $UCB(E_1)$ acting on f: $w(x, t; f) = [W(t) f](x)$, whereby its infinitesimal generator is $[U f](x) = f''(x)$ with domain $D(U) = \{f \in UCB(E_1); f, f'$ continuously differentiable with $f'' \in UCB(E_1)\}$. By the $(\mathscr{C}_0)$-property it follows that

$$\lim_{t \to 0+} \| W(t) f - f \|_C = 0 \qquad (f \in UCB(E_1)).$$

Let us now consider approximation theoretical questions for the semi-group solution $W(t) f$. In 1936 E. Hille [1] showed that if an initial value function f in $UCB(E_1)$ is such that

$$\| W(t) f - f \|_C = o(t) \qquad (t \to 0+), \tag{2.0.1}$$

then $f(x)$ is equal to a constant. Indeed, if the assertion (2.0.1) holds for an $f \in UCB(E_1)$, then $f \in D(U)$ and $[U f](x) = f''(x) = 0$, which implies that $f(x)$ is constant or $W(t) f = f$ for all $t \geqq 0$. Thus for all non-constant functions f in $UCB(E_1)$ the solution $W(t) f$ approximates its initial value f in the UCB-norm with an order of at most $O(t)$ $(t \to 0+)$. Furthermore, E. Hille [4, p. 323] has shown that this order of approximation is reached for all functions in $D(U)$:

$$\| W(t) f - f \|_C = O(t) \qquad (t \to 0+; f \in D(U)). \tag{2.0.2}$$

Moreover, the behavior of $\| W(t) f - f \|_C$ for small values of t is closely connected with that of $\| \lambda R(\lambda; U) f - f \|_C$ for large values of λ, where $R(\lambda; U)$, $\lambda > 0$, is the resolvent of U given by (1.0.16). In particular, if for an $f \in \mathsf{UCB}(\mathrm{E}_1)$

$$\| \lambda R(\lambda; U) f - f \|_C = o(\lambda^{-1}) \qquad (\lambda \to \infty),$$

then $f \in \mathsf{D}(U)$ and $U f = \theta$, or $\lambda R(\lambda; U) f = f$ for all $\lambda > 0$. Thus if $f(x) \neq$ const. in $\mathsf{UCB}(\mathrm{E}_1)$, then the approximation of f by $\lambda R(\lambda; U) f$ in the norm as $\lambda \to \infty$ is at most of order $O(\lambda^{-1})$. One easily sees that this order is attained when $f \in \mathsf{D}(U)$:

$$\| \lambda R(\lambda; U) f - f \|_C = \| R(\lambda; U) U f \|_C = O(\lambda^{-1}) \qquad (\lambda \to \infty; f \in \mathsf{D}(U)).$$

In this respect we remark that the operation $\lambda R(\lambda; U) f$, $f \in \mathsf{UCB}(\mathrm{E}_1)$, as defined through (1.0.16), is referred to as the singular integral of Picard.

It is not difficult to see that this special instance has an analogue, when $\mathsf{UCB}(\mathrm{E}_1)$ is replaced by an arbitrary Banach space X and $\{W(t); 0 \leq t < \infty\}$ by any strongly continuous semi-group $\{T(t); 0 \leq t < \infty\}$ in $\mathscr{E}(\mathsf{X})$ with generator A.

Now the first problem in this respect is to give a complete characterization of the class of elements $f \in \mathsf{X}$ for which the "optimal" order of approximation of f by $T(t) f$, namely $O(t)$ $(t \to 0+)$, is precisely attained. This is the so-called *saturation problem* in semi-group theory and the associated class of elements is said to be the *Favard class* with respect to the semi-group. Correspondingly, the saturation problem may also be stated for the approximation process $\lambda R(\lambda; A)$ for $\lambda \to \infty$, where $R(\lambda; A)$ is now the resolvent of the infinitesimal generator A of the semi-group.

The second problem is concerned with the question of "non-optimal" approximation, in particular finding necessary and sufficient conditions upon an element $f \in \mathsf{X}$ such that

$$\text{(2.0.3)} \qquad \| T(t) f - f \| = O(t^{\alpha}) \qquad (0 < \alpha < 1;\ t \to 0+).$$

One of the major aims of this chapter is to study these two general and significant problems.

For the example of the singular integral of Gauss-Weierstrass $W(t) f$ on $\mathsf{UCB}(\mathrm{E}_1)$ in case of saturation the general theorems obtained will give:

$$\| W(t) f - f \|_C = O(t)\ (t \to 0+) \iff \| \lambda R(\lambda; U) f - f \|_C = O(\lambda^{-1})\ (\lambda \to \infty)$$
$$\iff f'' \in \mathsf{L}^{\infty}(\mathrm{E}_1) \iff f \in \mathrm{Lip}^* 2,$$

where $\mathrm{Lip}^* \beta = \{f \in \mathsf{UCB}(\mathrm{E}_1); \| f(\cdot + u) - 2 f(\cdot) + f(\cdot - u) \|_C = O(|u|^{\beta}), u \to 0\}$, $0 < \beta \leq 2$, and in case of "non-optimal" approximation for $0 < \alpha < 1$:

$$\| W(t) f - f \|_C = O(t^{\alpha}) \quad (t \to 0+) \iff f \in \mathrm{Lip}^* 2\alpha.$$

Furthermore, the operational calculus suggests writing the solution $W(t)f$ in the symbolic form

$$[W(t)f](x) = [\exp\{t(d/dx)^2\}f](x) = \sum_{k=0}^{\infty} \frac{t^k}{k!} f^{(2k)}(x).$$

For this purpose it is of interest to determine the class of functions $f \in \mathsf{UCB}(\mathrm{E}_1)$ which is equivalent to

$$\left\| W(t)f - \sum_{k=0}^{r-1} \frac{t^k}{k!} f^{(2k)} \right\|_{\mathsf{C}} = o\left(\frac{t^k}{r!}\right) \qquad (t \to 0+;\ r = 1, 2, \ldots).$$

This class may be represented in the form: $f, f', \ldots, f^{(2r-1)}$ are locally absolutely continuous and $f^{(2r)} \in \mathsf{L}^\infty(\mathrm{E}_1)$. Problems of this type and generalizations thereof are also considered in a general setting.

As already noted, the principal aim of this chapter is the study of approximation theorems for semi-groups of operators on Banach spaces. Sec. 2.1 is concerned with the saturation problem and thus with the determination of the Favard class. This problem is solved for general strongly continuous semi-groups of operators on reflexive spaces (Theorem 2.1.2) as well as for the dual semi-groups (Theorem 2.1.4). There are applications to classical theorems of Titchmarsh and Hardy-Littlewood on the identification of Lipschitz classes of functions. The results here are formulated and established for the spaces $\mathsf{UCB}(\mathrm{E}_1^+)$ and $\mathsf{L}^p(\mathrm{E}_1^+)$, $1 \leqq p < \infty$.

Sec. 2.2 is devoted to a detailed study of higher powers of the infinitesimal generator, and of generalizations and equivalent representations for them. Taylor, Peano and Riemann operators are treated. Theorems 2.2.13, 2.2.14 and 2.2.18 are the important and useful theorems from which spring many of the applications. This section concludes with a discussion of generalized derivatives of scalar-valued functions, connected with the names of Riemann, Peano and Taylor. We mention here especially Theorems 2.2.25 and 2.2.26.

Sec. 2.3 is concerned with direct, converse and associated equivalence theorems on non-optimal approximation by holomorphic semi-groups of operators (Theorem 2.3.5 and Corollary 2.3.6).

Sec. 2.4 is devoted to applications, in particular to Dirichlet's problem for the Laplace equation on the unit disk and to Fourier's problem. In the first two subsections the singular integral of Abel-Poisson is treated from the point of view of saturation (Theorems 2.4.1, 2.4.3 and 2.4.5) — Neumann's problem also being discussed at this point — as well as non-optimal approximation. Of particular interest is Theorem 2.4.13. Sec. 2.4 is also concerned with the approximation by Weierstrass' singular integral.

In Sec. 2.5 the emphasis is on the study of approximation theorems for the family of resolvent operators $\{\lambda R(\lambda; A); \lambda > \omega_0\}$ of a semi-group $\{T(t); 0 \leqq t < \infty\}$ of class $(\mathscr{C}_0)$ in $\mathscr{E}(X)$ with generator A. Prop. 2.5.2 and 2.5.3 deal with convergence, while Theorems 2.5.4 and 2.5.7 treat saturation problems. The results obtained are then applied to the semi-group of left translations on the function spaces $UCB(E_1^+)$ and $L^p(E_1^+)$, $1 \leqq p < \infty$, as well as to the periodic singular integral of Weierstrass for functions in $C_{2\pi}$, $L^p_{2\pi}$ $(1 \leqq p < \infty)$. Of particular interest is Theorem 2.5.13 giving necessary and sufficient conditions upon a family of operators $\{S(\lambda); \lambda > \omega\}$ in $\mathscr{E}(X)$ such that for each $\lambda > \omega$, $S(\lambda)$ is the resolvent of an operator A which generates a semi-group of class $(\mathscr{C}_0)$ in $\mathscr{E}(X)$.

Sec. 2.6 is devoted to a boundary-value problem of the heat-conduction equation for a semi-infinite rod. This problem, however, will be treated in a more general setting by solving the Cauchy problem for the differential equation of fractional order $(\partial/\partial x)\, w(x, t) = -(\partial/\partial t)^\gamma\, w(x, t)$ $(0 < \gamma < 1; x, t > 0)$ with $w(0, t) = f(t)$ for functions $f \in L^p(E_1^+)$, $1 \leqq p < \infty$. The case $\gamma = 1/2$ leads to the heat equation. The solution of the Cauchy problem is given in Theorem 2.6.6, Laplace transform methods being used. In Theorem 2.6.7 the saturation problem for the solution is formulated.

Chapter II concludes with Sec. 2.7 on "Notes and Remarks".

2.1 Favard Classes and the Fundamental Approximation Theorems

2.1.1 Theory

Let X be a Banach space, and let $\{T(t); 0 < t < \infty\}$ be a family of operators in $\mathscr{E}(X)$ converging to the identity operator I in the strong operator topology as $t \to 0+$. It is the aim of this section to discuss the degree of approximation of a given element f in X by $T(t)f$ in the X-norm for small values of the parameter t, that is, the order of magnitude of

$$D_t(f; T(\cdot)) \equiv \|T(t)f - f\|$$

as a function of t for $t \to 0+$.

In this respect there are three questions to be considered:

(i) *Given a non-trivial class of elements $\mathscr{K} \subset X$, to find an estimate of $D_t(f; T(\cdot))$ if $f \in \mathscr{K}$. Results of this type are called* d i r e c t *theorems.*

(ii) *Given a positive non-increasing function ϕ on $(0, \infty)$ such that $\phi(s) \to 0$ as $s \to \infty$, to determine a class $\mathscr{K} \subset X$ such that $D_t(f; T(\cdot)) = O[\phi(1/t)]$ $(t \to 0+)$ implies $f \in \mathscr{K}$. Results of this type are called* c o n v e r s e *theorems.*

(iii) *To fix a non-trivial class* $\mathscr{K} \subset \mathsf{X}$ *and a function* ϕ *on* $(0, \infty)$ *such that for the pair* $(\mathscr{K}, \phi)$ *both a direct and converse theorem hold simultaneously for* $\{T(t); 0 < t < \infty\}$. *Results of this type are called* *equivalence theorems.*

There are the following two possibilities for question (iii): The order of approximation $O[\phi(1/t)]$ $(t \to 0+)$ in a given equivalence theorem may be "optimal" for some specific class $\mathscr{F}$ of the possible classes $\mathscr{K} \subset \mathsf{X}$. This means that for the pair $(\mathscr{F}, \phi)$ corresponding to the approximation process $\{T(t); 0 < t < \infty\}$ there holds an equivalence theorem

$$D_t(f; T(\cdot)) = O[\phi(1/t)] \ (t \to 0+) \iff f \in \mathscr{F},$$

and, moreover,

$$D_t(f; T(\cdot)) = o[\phi(1/t)] \ (t \to 0+) \implies f \text{ is } \textit{invariant} \text{ under } \{T(t); 0 < t < \infty\} \text{ for small values of } t.$$

Here $T(t) f$ furnishes an approximation of f of order $O[\phi(1/t)]$ and no higher order of approximation can occur except for the invariant elements, i.e. for which $D_t(f; T(\cdot)) = 0$ for t small enough. This order is reached for all elements of $\mathscr{F}$, which is called its *saturation* or *Favard class.* We then speak of the equivalence theorem as the *saturation theorem.* The other alternative is that the order of approximation $O[\phi(1/t)]$ $(t \to 0+)$ in an equivalence theorem is "non-optimal".

After these preliminaries, let us give a formal definition of the notion of saturation associated with an approximation process $\{T(t); 0 < t < \infty\}$.

Definition 2.1.1. *Let* X *be a Banach space and* $\{T(t); 0 < t < \infty\}$ *a family of operators in* $\mathscr{E}(\mathsf{X})$ *converging to the identity* I *in the strong operator topology as* $t \to 0+$. *Suppose there exists a positive non-increasing function* ϕ on $(0, \infty)$ *such that* $\phi(s) \to 0$ *as* $s \to \infty$ *and a class of functions* $\mathscr{F} \subset \mathsf{X}$ *such that for* $f \in \mathsf{X}$ *as* $t \to 0+$

(i) $D_t(f; T(\cdot)) = o[\phi(1/t)]$ *implies* $T(t) f = f$ *for small* t,

(ii) $D_t(f; T(\cdot)) = O[\phi(1/t)]$ *implies* $f \in \mathscr{F}$,

and conversely

(iii) $f \in \mathscr{F}$ *implies* $D_t(f; T(\cdot)) = O[\phi(1/t)]$,

where $\mathscr{F}$ *contains at least one element which is not invariant. Then the approximation process* $\{T(t); 0 < t < \infty\}$ *is said to have optimal approximation order* $O[\phi(1/t)]$ $(t \to 0+)$ *or to be saturated in* X *with order* $O[\phi(1/t)]$ *and* $\mathscr{F}$ *is called its saturation or Favard class.*

This concept was introduced into classical approximation theory by J. Favard. It is sometimes convenient to have another definition of saturation. Indeed, Definition 2.1.1 may easily be shown to be equivalent to the following: The approximation process $\{T(t); 0<t<\infty\}$ is said to be saturated in X if there exists a positive non-increasing function ϕ on $(0, \infty)$ with $\phi(s) \to 0$ as $s \to \infty$ such that for each $f \in X$ which is not invariant under the given process

$$D_t(f; T(\cdot)) > C_1\, \phi(1/t),$$

where $C_1 > 0$ depends only upon f, and if there exists at least one non-invariant element $f_0 \in X$ such that

$$D_t(f_0; T(\cdot)) < C_2\, \phi(1/t),$$

where C_2 is another constant depending only upon f_0. The class of non-invariant elements $f \in X$ with

$$D_t(f; T(\cdot)) = O[\phi(1/t)] \qquad (t \to 0+),$$

is called the saturation class of the given approximation process in X.

Our fundamental approximation theorem in this section will be the following saturation theorem for semi-groups of operators of class $(\mathscr{C}_0)$ in $\mathscr{E}(X)$. The result is of importance in the theory of approximation, in particular, in the study of singular integrals and the initial and boundary behavior of solutions of partial differential equations.

Theorem 2.1.2. *Suppose $\{T(t); 0 \leqq t < \infty\}$ is a semi-group of class $(\mathscr{C}_0)$ in $\mathscr{E}(X)$.*

(a) *Let f and g be fixed elements in X such that*

$$\liminf_{\tau \to 0+} \left\| \frac{T(\tau) f - f}{\tau} - g \right\| = 0. \tag{2.1.1}$$

Then $f \in D(A)$ and $A f = g$. In case $g = \theta$ we have $T(t) f = f$ for all $t \geqq 0$, i.e. f is an invariant element of the semi-group.

(b) *For all $f \in D(A)$ we have*

$$\|T(t) f - f\| \leqq \sup_{0 \leqq u \leqq t} \{\|T(u)\|\}\, \|A f\|\, t. \tag{2.1.2}$$

(c) *If X is reflexive and $f \in X$ such that*

$$\liminf_{\tau \to 0+} \left\| \frac{T(\tau) f - f}{\tau} \right\| < \infty, \tag{2.1.3}$$

then $f \in D(A)$, i.e. there is a $g \in X$ such that

$$\operatorname*{s-lim}_{\tau \to 0+} \frac{T(\tau) f - f}{\tau} = g.$$

Proof. (a) Let $\tau > 0$. For a fixed $t > 0$ we have by formula (1.1.7)

$$\int_0^t T(u)\, A_\tau f\, du = \frac{1}{\tau} \int_0^\tau T(u)\, \{T(t) f - f\}\, du, \tag{2.1.4}$$

and by the strong continuity of the semi-group it follows that

$$\operatorname*{s-lim}_{\tau\to 0+} \int_0^t T(u)\, A_\tau f\, du = T(t)\, f - f \qquad (t > 0).$$

Furthermore,

$$\left\| \int_0^t T(u)\, \{A_\tau f - g\}\, du \right\| \leqq \sup_{0 \leqq u \leqq t} \{\| T(u) \|\}\, \| A_\tau f - g \|\, t.$$

By assumption, the limit inferior of the right-hand side of the latter inequality tends to zero as $\tau \to 0+$, giving

$$(2.1.5) \qquad T(t)\, f - f = \int_0^t T(u)\, g\, du$$

for all $t \geqq 0$. Therefore, $f \in \mathsf{D}(A)$ and $A f = g$. Moreover, equation (2.1.5) shows that in case $g = \theta$, f is an invariant element of the semi-group.

(b) The relation (2.1.2) is an immediate consequence of relation (1.1.6) which is valid for all $f \in \mathsf{D}(A)$ and $t > 0$.

(c) If relation (2.1.3) holds, then there exists a sequence $\{\tau_n\}_{n=1}^{\infty}$, $\tau_n \to 0+$, such that $A_{\tau_n} f$ is bounded. In a reflexive Banach space bounded subsets are conditionally sequentially weakly compact (App. 1), i.e. there exists a subsequence $\{\tau_n'\}$ such that the sequence $\{A_{\tau_n'} f\}$ converges weakly to a limit $g \in \mathsf{X}$. Thus

$$\lim_{n\to\infty} \langle f^*, A_{\tau_n'} f\rangle = \langle f^*, g\rangle$$

for all $f^* \in \mathsf{X}^*$.

Furthermore, by definition of dual operators it follows that

$$\lim_{n\to\infty} \langle f^*, T(u)\, A_{\tau_n'} f\rangle = \langle f^*, T(u)\, g\rangle$$

for each $u \geqq 0$ and all $f^* \in \mathsf{X}^*$. Since $|\langle f^*, T(u)\, A_{\tau_n'} f\rangle| \leqq \| f^* \| \times \times \| T(u) \|\, \| A_{\tau_n'} f \| \leqq \| f^* \| \sup_{0 \leqq u \leqq t} \{\| T(u) \|\}\, \| A_{\tau_n'} f \|$ is bounded in each finite interval $0 \leqq u \leqq t$ uniformly with respect to n ($t > 0$ being arbitrary, but fixed), it follows that $\langle f^*, T(u)\, A_{\tau_n'} f\rangle$ converges dominatedly to $\langle f^*, T(u)\, g\rangle$ in $[0, t]$ and by Lebesgue's dominated convergence theorem we have for each $f^* \in \mathsf{X}^*$

$$(2.1.6) \qquad \lim_{n\to\infty} \langle f^*, \int_0^t T(u)\, A_{\tau_n'} f\, du\rangle = \lim_{n\to\infty} \int_0^t \langle f^*, T(u)\, A_{\tau_n'} f\rangle\, du$$

$$= \int_0^t \langle f^*, T(u)\, g\rangle\, du = \langle f^*, \int_0^t T(u)\, g\, du\rangle.$$

On the other hand, as strong convergence implies weak convergence, we have by (2.1.4)

$$\lim_{n\to\infty} \langle f^*, \int_0^t T(u)\, A_{\tau_n'} f\, du\rangle = \langle f^*, T(t) f - f\rangle \tag{2.1.7}$$

for each $f^* \in X^*$. Comparing the relations (2.1.6) and (2.1.7), this gives for each $t > 0$ and all $f^* \in X^*$

$$\langle f^*, T(t) f - f\rangle = \langle f^*, \int_0^t T(u)\, g\, du\rangle .$$

Upon applying a corollary of the theorem of Hahn-Banach we obtain (2.1.5). Thus $f \in D(A)$ and $A f = g$, which completes the proof of the theorem.

In the terminology of saturation theory we have the following

Corollary 2.1.3. *Let X be a reflexive Banach space and $\{T(t); 0 \leqq t < \infty\}$ a semi-group of class $(\mathscr{C}_0)$ in $\mathscr{E}(X)$. Then the semi-group $\{T(t); 0 \leqq t < \infty\}$ is saturated with order $O(t)$ $(t \to 0+)$ and the Favard class $\mathscr{F} = \mathscr{F}\{T(t) - I; X\}$ is equal to the domain of the infinitesimal generator A.*

The proof of this corollary is an immediate consequence of theorem 2.1.2. Indeed, in case $g = \theta$, part (a) states in particular that if $\|T(t) f - f\| = o(t)$ $(t \to 0+)$, then $T(t) f = f$ for all $t \geqq 0$. So if f is not an invariant element under the semi-group, the order of approximation of f by $T(t) f$ cannot exceed $O(t)$ $(t \to 0+)$ and this order is reached for all elements of $D(A)$, which, as we recall, is dense in X. This follows by part (b). Conversely, part (c) gives that if the Banach space X is in addition reflexive and if the order of approximation of f by $T(t) f$ is $O(t)$ $(t \to 0+)$, then necessarily $f \in D(A)$.

Thus we have solved the saturation problem for strongly continuous semi-groups of operators on reflexive spaces. But there are important examples of non-reflexive Banach spaces. It is even then possible to treat the saturation problem. For this purpose let us consider the counterpart of Theorem 2.1.2 for dual semi-groups.

Theorem 2.1.4. *Suppose X_0^* is the maximal closed linear subspace of X^* upon which the restriction of the dual semi-group $\{T^*(t); 0 \leqq t < \infty\}$ is of class $(\mathscr{C}_0)$ in $\mathscr{E}(X_0^*)$.*

(a) *Let f^* and g^* be elements in X_0^* such that*

$$\liminf_{\tau\to 0+} \left\| \frac{T^*(\tau) f^* - f^*}{\tau} - g^* \right\| = 0 . \tag{2.1.8}$$

Then $f \in D(A_0^*)$ and $A_0^* f = g^*$. In case $g^* = \theta^*$, we have $T^*(t) f^* = f^*$ for all $t \geqq 0$.

(b) *For all* $f^* \in \mathsf{D}(A^*)$

$$\|T^*(t)f^* - f^*\| \leqq \sup_{0 \leqq u \leqq t} \{\|T(u)\|\} \|A^* f^*\| t. \tag{2.1.9}$$

(c) *If* $f^* \in \mathsf{X}_0^*$ *and*

$$\liminf_{\tau \to 0+} \left\| \frac{T^*(\tau) f^* - f^*}{\tau} \right\| < +\infty, \tag{2.1.10}$$

then $f^* \in \mathsf{D}(A^*)$.

Proof. Part (a) is nothing but a special case of Theorem 2.1.2 (a), whereas part (b) has already been shown in Proposition 1.4.6 (b). Thus it only remains to prove part (c). By assumption (2.1.10), there is a constant $C > 0$ and a sequence $\{\tau_j\}_{j=1}^{\infty}$, $\tau_j \to 0+$ as $j \to \infty$, such that

$$\left\| \frac{T^*(\tau_j) f^* - f^*}{\tau_j} \right\| \leqq C$$

for all $j = 1, 2, \ldots$ Now, for each integer $n > 0$ let S_n be the weak* closure of the set

$$\left\{ \frac{T^*(\tau_j) f^* - f^*}{\tau_j}; \quad j \geqq n \right\}$$

in X^*. By a corollary of the theorem of Alaoglu bounded weakly* closed sets in X^* are compact in the weak* topology (App. 1), and since the sequence

$$S_1 \supset S_2 \supset S_3 \supset \cdots$$

has the finite intersection property (App. 1), there must be an element $g^* \in \mathsf{X}^*$ such that

$$g^* \in \bigcap_{n=1}^{\infty} S_n.$$

If f is an arbitrary, but fixed element in $\mathsf{D}(A)$, then because of the choice of g^* there exists a subsequence $\{\tau_j'\}_{j=1}^{\infty}$ depending upon the given element $f \in \mathsf{D}(A)$ with $\tau_j' \to 0+$ as $j \to \infty$ such that

$$\begin{aligned} \langle f^*, Af \rangle &= \lim_{j \to \infty} \langle f^*, \frac{T(\tau_j') f - f}{\tau_j'} \rangle \\ &= \lim_{j \to \infty} \langle \frac{T^*(\tau_j') f^* - f^*}{\tau_j'}, f \rangle = \langle g^*, f \rangle. \end{aligned} \tag{2.1.11}$$

But this holds for each $f \in \mathsf{D}(A)$, which shows that f^* belongs to $\mathsf{D}(A^*)$ and $A^* f^* = g^*$. This completes the proof of the theorem.

Remark. If X is separable, the above proof is considerably simpler. Indeed, in this case there exists a countably dense subset $\{f_n\}_{n=1}^{\infty}$ of elements in X which generates the weak* topology on X^* (App. 1). Consequently, by a diagonal process there is a subsequence $\tau_j' \to 0+$ as $j \to \infty$ such that $(1/\tau_j') \{T(\tau_j') f - f\}$ converges weakly* to an element g^* in S_1. Thus relation (2.1.11) holds for this subsequence $\{\tau_j'\}$ and for all $f \in \mathsf{D}(A)$, which proves part (c) of the theorem for separable Banach spaces X.

Corollary 2.1.5. *Under the hypotheses of Theorem* 2.1.4 *we have*

(a) *If an element* $f^* \in X_0^*$ *satisfies*

$$\| T^*(t) f^* - f^* \| = o(t) \qquad (t \to 0+),$$

then f^* *is invariant under the dual semi-group.*

(b) *For an element* $f^* \in X_0^*$ *the following assertions are equivalent:*

(i) $f^* \in D(A^*)$;

(ii) $\text{w*-}\lim_{t\to 0+} \frac{T^*(t) f^* - f^*}{t} = g^*$, *where* $g^* \in X^*$;

(iii) $\| T^*(t) f^* - f^* \| = O(t) \qquad (t \to 0+)$.

The equivalence of (i) and (ii) follows by Corollary 1.4.5, that of (i) and (iii) by the latter theorem.

Corollary 2.1.5 solves the saturation problem for the restriction of the dual semi-group $\{T^*(t); 0 \leqq t < \infty\}$ on the subspace X_0^* of X^*. Furthermore, this corollary contains Corollary 2.1.3. Indeed, if X is reflexive, then by Corollary 1.4.8 X_0^* is equal to X^*, and consequently the two operators A_0^* and A^* are equal too.

2.1.2 Applications to Theorems of Titchmarsh and Hardy-Littlewood

In this subsection we apply Theorems 2.1.2 and 2.1.4 to the semi-group of left translations on the Banach spaces $UCB(\mathrm{E}_1^+)$ and $L^p(\mathrm{E}_1^+)$, $1 \leqq p < \infty$. For the definition and basic properties of these operators see Theorem 1.3.16 at the end of Sec. 1.3.3. This will give a unified approach to some classical theorems of Titchmarsh and Hardy-Littlewood. In view of the definition of saturation it will be seen that the theorem of Titchmarsh gives the order of saturation, while the theorem of Hardy-Littlewood determines the Favard class for the left translations on these function spaces. These results may easily be carried over to the group of translations defined on the various function spaces on E_1 (see Sec. 1.3.3, 1.4.2 and 1.5.3).

Theorem 2.1.6. *Let* X *be one of the spaces* $UCB(\mathrm{E}_1^+)$, $L^p(\mathrm{E}_1^+)$, $1 \leqq p < \infty$, *and* $f \in X$. *If there is a* $g \in X$ *such that*

$$\liminf_{t\to 0+} \left\| \frac{f(\cdot + t) - f(\cdot)}{t} - g(\cdot) \right\| = 0, \tag{2.1.12}$$

then $f \in AC_{\mathrm{loc}}(\mathrm{E}_1^+)$, $f' \in X$ *and* $f' = g$. *In particular, if*

$$\| f(\cdot + t) - f(\cdot) \| = o(t) \qquad (t \to 0+), \tag{2.1.13}$$

then $f(x) = \text{const.}$ *in case* $X = UCB(\mathrm{E}_1^+)$ *and* $f(x) = 0$ *a.e. in case* $X = L^p(\mathrm{E}_1^+)$.

Proof. The result follows immediately by applying Theorems 1.3.16 and 2.1.2 (a).

Note that the original theorem of Titchmarsh states that if $\int_a^b |f(x+t) - f(x)|\, dx = o(t)\ (t \to 0)$, the interval (a, b) being finite, then $f(x) = \text{const. a.e.}$

Now the question arises what can be said about the functions f if „small" $o(t)$ is replaced by „large" $O(t)$ in (2.1.13). In this direction we have the following theorem.

Theorem 2.1.7. (a) *The following assertions are equivalent for an element* $f \in \mathsf{UCB}(\mathrm{E}_1^+)$*:*

(i) $$\|f(\cdot + t) - f(\cdot)\|_{\mathsf{C}} = O(t) \qquad (t \to 0+);$$

(ii) *there is a* $g \in \mathsf{L}^\infty(\mathrm{E}_1^+)$ *such that for all* $\psi \in \mathsf{C}_{00}^\infty(\mathrm{E}_1^+)$

$$\lim_{t\to 0+} \int_0^\infty \frac{f(x+t) - f(x)}{t}\, \psi(x)\, dx = \int_0^\infty g(x)\, \psi(x)\, dx;$$

(iii) $f \in \mathsf{AC}_{\mathrm{loc}}(\mathrm{E}_1^+)$ *and* $f' \in \mathsf{L}^\infty(\mathrm{E}_1^+)$.

(b) *The following assertions are equivalent for an element* $f \in \mathsf{L}^1(\mathrm{E}_1^+)$*:*

(i) $$\|f(\cdot + t) - f(\cdot)\|_1 = O(t) \qquad (t \to 0+);$$

(ii) *there is a* $\mu \in \mathsf{NBV}(\mathrm{E}_1^+)$ *such that for all* $\psi \in \mathsf{C}_{00}^\infty(\mathrm{E}_1^+)$

$$\lim_{t\to 0+} \int_0^\infty \frac{f(x+t) - f(x)}{t}\, \psi(x)\, dx = \int_0^\infty \psi(x)\, d\mu(x);$$

(iii) $f \in \mathsf{NBV}(\mathrm{E}_1^+)$.

(c) *Let* f *be in* $\mathsf{L}^p(\mathrm{E}_1^+)$, $1 < p < \infty$. *Then the following assertions are equivalent:*

(i) $$\|f(\cdot + t) - f(\cdot)\|_p = O(t) \qquad (t \to 0+);$$

(ii) *there is a* $g \in \mathsf{L}^p(\mathrm{E}_1^+)$ *such that for all* $\psi \in \mathsf{C}_{00}^\infty(\mathrm{E}_1^+)$

$$\lim_{t\to 0+} \int_0^\infty \frac{f(x+t) - f(x)}{t}\, \psi(x)\, dx = \int_0^\infty g(x)\, \psi(x)\, dx;$$

(iii) $f \in \mathsf{AC}_{\mathrm{loc}}(\mathrm{E}_1^+)$ *and* $f' \in \mathsf{L}^p(\mathrm{E}_1^+)$;

(iv) *there is a* $g \in \mathsf{L}^p(\mathrm{E}_1^+)$ *such that*

$$\lim_{t\to 0+} \left\| \frac{f(\cdot + t) - f(\cdot)}{t} - g(\cdot) \right\|_p = 0.$$

Proof. We only prove part (a). In Theorem 1.4.11 we have shown that $\mathsf{UCB}(\mathrm{E}_1^+)$ is the largest subspace in $\mathsf{L}^\infty(\mathrm{E}_1^+)$ upon which the restriction of the semi-group of left translations is of class $(\mathscr{C}_0)$. The equivalence of (i) and (iii) then follows by Corollary 2.1.5 (b). Furthermore, this corollary gives that (i) or (iii) is equivalent to

(ii)* *there is a* $g \in \mathsf{L}^\infty(\mathrm{E}_1^+)$ *such that for all* $h \in \mathsf{L}^1(\mathrm{E}_1^+)$

$$\lim_{t\to 0+} \int_0^\infty \frac{f(x+t)-f(x)}{t} h(x)\,dx = \int_0^\infty g(x)\,h(x)\,dx.$$

Thus it remains to show the equivalence of (ii) and (ii)*. Evidently, (ii)* implies (ii) as $\mathsf{C}_{00}^\infty(\mathrm{E}_1^+)$ is a subspace of $\mathsf{L}^1(\mathrm{E}_1^+)$. Conversely, if (ii) holds, then for all $\psi \in \mathsf{C}_{00}^\infty(\mathrm{E}_1^+)$

$$\lim_{t\to 0+} \int_0^\infty \frac{f(x+t)-f(x)}{t} \psi(x)\,dx = \lim_{t\to 0+} \int_0^\infty f(x) \frac{\psi(x-t)-\psi(x)}{t}\,dx$$

$$= -\int_0^\infty f(x)\,\psi'(x)\,dx = \int_0^\infty g(x)\,\psi(x)\,dx.$$

From this it follows by methods similar to those given in Sec. 1.4.2, in particular see the proof of Theorem 1.4.9, that

$$f(x+t)-f(x) = \int_0^t g(x+u)\,du.$$

Thus $\|f(\cdot+t)-f(\cdot)\|_{\mathsf{C}} \leqq \|g\|_\infty t$, proving (i), which in turn gives (ii)*. Parts (b) and (c) follow similarly by Corollaries 2.1.5 and 2.1.3, respectively.

Remark. It should be remarked that by the theorem of Banach-Steinhaus the directed set of bounded linear functionals $\{(1/t)\,(f(\cdot+t) - - f(\cdot));\, 0 < t < \infty\}$ on $\mathsf{L}^1(\mathrm{E}_1^+)$ with $f \in \mathsf{UCB}(\mathrm{E}_1^+)$ converges to a bounded linear functional $g \in \mathsf{L}^\infty(\mathrm{E}_1^+)$ as $t \to 0+$, i.e. (ii)* holds, if and only if

(i) $$\left\|\frac{f(\cdot+t)-f(\cdot)}{t}\right\|_{\mathsf{C}} = O(1) \qquad (t\to 0+)$$

and

(ii) for a dense subset in $\mathsf{L}^1(\mathrm{E}_1^+)$ (here the space $\mathsf{C}_{00}^\infty(\mathrm{E}_1^+)$)

$$\lim_{t\to 0+} \int_0^\infty \frac{f(x+t)-f(x)}{t} \psi(x)\,dx = \int_0^\infty g(x)\,\psi(x)\,dx \qquad (\psi \in \mathsf{C}_{00}^\infty(\mathrm{E}_1^+)).$$

Thus by the Banach-Steinhaus theorem one only obtains that assertion (ii)* is equivalent to the assertions (i) and (ii) together, whereas the previous semi-group argument shows, that both (i) and (ii) are independently equivalent to (ii)*.

2.2 Taylor, Peano, and Riemann Operators Generated by Semi-Groups of Operators

The object of the first subsection below is to study generalizations and equivalent representations of the r-th power of the infinitesimal generator A, where r is some fixed positive integer. The second is devoted to saturation theorems, while in Sec. 2.2.3 the results obtained will be applied to the semi-group of left translations for the classical function spaces on E_1^+.

2.2.1 Generalizations of Powers of the Infinitesimal Generator

As previously X will be a real or complex Banach space and $\{T(t);\ 0 \leqq t < \infty\}$ a strongly continuous semi-group in $\mathscr{E}(\mathsf{X})$. Throughout this and the following two subsections we further assume that r is any fixed positive integer.

Definition 2.2.1. *The r-th Taylor operator B^r of the semi-group $\{T(t);\ 0 \leqq t < \infty\}$ having domain $\mathsf{D}(B^r)$ in $\mathsf{D}(A^{r-1})$ and range in X is defined by*

$$\operatorname*{s-lim}_{t\to 0+} B_t^r f = B^r f,$$

whenever this limit exists, where B_t^r is given by

$$B_t^r f \equiv \frac{r!}{t^r}\left[T(t) - \sum_{k=0}^{r-1} \frac{t^k}{k!} A^k\right] f \qquad (t > 0;\ f \in \mathsf{D}(A^{r-1})). \tag{2.2.1}$$

Obviously, B_t^r defines a bounded linear transformation on $\mathsf{D}(A^{r-1})$ into X for each fixed $t > 0$. $\mathsf{D}(B^r)$ is a linear subspace in $\mathsf{D}(A^{r-1})$ and B^r a linear operator. Furthermore, in case $r = 1$ we have $B^1 = A$.

A connection between the operators A^r and B^r is given by

Proposition 2.2.2. *If $f \in \mathsf{D}(A^r)$, then $\operatorname*{s-lim}_{t\to 0+} B_t^r f = A^r f$, or $f \in \mathsf{D}(B^r)$ and $B^r f = A^r f$.*

Proof. For all $f \in \mathsf{D}(A^r)$ we have by relation (1.1.10)

$$B_t^r f = \frac{r}{t^r}\int_0^t (t-u)^{r-1}\, T(u)\, A^r f\, du.$$

Thus

$$\| B_t^r f - A^r f \| \leqq \frac{r}{t^r}\int_0^t (t-u)^{r-1} \| [T(u) - I]\, A^r f \|\, du = o(1) \quad (t \to 0+)$$

giving $\mathsf{D}(A^r) \subset \mathsf{D}(B^r)$ and $B^r f = A^r f$, which establishes the result.

Thus we have seen that B^r is an extension of A^r. Now the question arises whether the extension is proper. The answer is negative. To prove this, we need the following

Lemma 2.2.3. *If $f \in \mathsf{D}(A^{r-1})$, then for an arbitrary fixed $s > 0$ we have*

$$\text{(2.2.2)} \qquad \operatorname*{s-lim}_{t\to 0+} \int_0^s T(u)\, B_t^r f\, du = [T(s) - I]\, A^{r-1} f.$$

Proof. Under the hypothesis that $f \in \mathsf{D}(A^{r-1})$ we first establish the important identity:

$$\text{(2.2.3)} \qquad \int_0^s T(u)\, B_t^r f\, du = \frac{r}{t^r} \int_0^t u^{r-1} B_u^{r-1} [T(s) - I] f\, du$$

$(t, s > 0$ being arbitrary, fixed).

Indeed, the left-hand member of (2.2.3) equals

$$\frac{r!}{t^r}\left\{\int_0^s T(u)\,[T(t) - I]\, f\, du - \sum_{k=1}^{r-1} \frac{t^k}{k!} \int_0^s T(u)\, A^k f\, du\right\}$$

$$= \frac{r!}{t^r}\left\{\int_0^t T(u)\,[T(s) - I]\, f\, du - \sum_{k=1}^{r-1} \frac{t^k}{k!} A^{k-1}\,[T(s) - I]\, f\right\}$$

$$= \frac{r!}{t^r} \int_0^t \left\{T(u) - \sum_{k=0}^{r-2} \frac{u^k}{k!} A^k\right\}[T(s) - I]\, f\, du,$$

which in turn is equal to the right-hand member of the identity (2.2.3). Then, we have

$$\left\| \int_0^s T(u)\, B_t^r f\, du - [T(s) - I]\, A^{r-1} f \right\|$$

$$= \left\| \frac{r}{t^r} \int_0^t u^{r-1} [T(s) - I]\, \{B_u^{r-1} f - A^{r-1} f\}\, du \right\|,$$

which tends to zero as $t \to 0+$ in view of the proof of Proposition 2.2.2. The proof is thus completed.

Proposition 2.2.4. *An element $f \in \mathsf{D}(A^{r-1})$ belongs to $\mathsf{D}(B^r)$ if and only if $f \in \mathsf{D}(A^r)$. Moreover, $B^r f = A^r f$.*

Proof. The "if" part has been shown in Proposition 2.2.2. Hence assume $f \in \mathsf{D}(B^r)$. In view of Lemma 2.2.3 it follows that

$$[T(s) - I]\, A^{r-1} f - \int_0^s T(u)\, B^r f\, du = \operatorname*{s-lim}_{t\to 0+} \int_0^s T(u)\, \{B_t^r f - B^r f\}\, du$$

for any $s > 0$. Since $B_t^r f - B^r f \to \theta$ in norm as $t \to 0+$, the same is true for the right-hand integral of this equation. Thus

$$\frac{T(s) - I}{s} A^{r-1} f = \frac{1}{s} \int_0^s T(u)\, B^r f\, du \qquad (s > 0),$$

which proves that $f \in \mathsf{D}(A^r)$ and $A^r f = B^r f$. This completes the proof.

Next we study the behavior of the r-th *Peano operator* P^r of the semi-group $\{T(t); 0 \leqq t < \infty\}$.

Definition 2.2.5. *Let f be an element of X. If there exist elements $g_{k,r} \in \mathsf{X}$ $(k = 0, 1, 2, \ldots, r-1)$ such that*

$$(2.2.4) \qquad P_t^r f \equiv \frac{r!}{t^r} \left\{ T(t) f - \sum_{k=0}^{r-1} \frac{t^k}{k!} g_{k,r} \right\} \qquad (t > 0;\ f \in \mathsf{X})$$

converges in norm as $t \to 0+$, then we write $f \in \mathsf{D}(P^r)$ and denote the limit by $P^r f$. More precisely, we should denote the limit by $P^r(g_{0,r}, \ldots, g_{r-1,r}) f$, because it may depend on the special choice of the elements $g_{k,r}$.

It follows by definition that $\mathsf{D}(P^r)$ is a linear manifold in X, but the operator P^r may not be uniquely defined on $\mathsf{D}(P^r)$. Furthermore, in case $r = 1$ we have $P^1 = A$, which implies that the element $g_{0,1}$ is always equal to f.

Proposition 2.2.6. *If $f \in \mathsf{X}$ belongs to $\mathsf{D}(P^r)$, then $f \in \mathsf{D}(P^k)$ for each $k = 1, 2, \ldots, r-1$.*

Proof. For $k = r - 1$ we have, putting $g_{j,r-1} = g_{j,r}$ $(j = 0, 1, 2, \ldots, r-2)$,

$$\| P_t^{r-1} f - g_{r-1,r} \| = \left\| \frac{(r-1)!}{t^{r-1}} \left\{ T(t) f - \sum_{j=0}^{r-1} \frac{t^j}{j!} g_{j,r} \right\} \right\| = \frac{t}{r} \| P_t^r f \|.$$

Since $\| P_t^r f \| \to \| P^r f \|$ as $t \to 0+$, the right-hand side of the equation tends to zero as $t \to 0+$ and $P^{r-1}(g_{0,r}, \ldots, g_{r-2,r}) f = g_{r-1,r}$. Applying this argument succesively we have $f \in \mathsf{D}(P^k)$ for all $k = 1, 2, \ldots, r-1$.

It is evident that the r-th Peano operator P^r is by definition more general than the r-th Taylor operator B^r. Indeed, if $f \in \mathsf{D}(B^r)$, then with $g_{k,r} = A^k f$ $(k = 0, 1, 2, \ldots, r-1)$ one obtains $P_t^r f = B_t^r f$ for all $t > 0$ and thus $\operatorname{s-lim}_{t \to 0+} P_t^r f = B^r f$, proving $\mathsf{D}(B^r) \subset \mathsf{D}(P^r)$. The next proposition shows, that the converse is valid too, proving at the same time that the operator P^r is uniquely defined (which justifies the fact that one may actually call P^r an operator) and that P^r and B^r are equal to another.

Proposition 2.2.7. *An element $f \in \mathsf{X}$ belongs to $\mathsf{D}(P^r)$ if and only if $f \in \mathsf{D}(B^r)$ (or if and only if $f \in \mathsf{D}(A^r)$). Moreover, $P^r f = B^r f = A^r f$.*

Proof. It only remains to prove the result in one direction. Assume $f \in \mathsf{D}(P^r)$. Then there exist elements $g_{j,r}$ $(j = 0, 1, 2, \ldots, r-1)$ such that

$$P_t^r f = \frac{r!}{t^r}\left\{T(t) f - \sum_{j=0}^{r-1} \frac{t^j}{j!} g_{j,r}\right\}$$

converges in norm as $t \to 0+$. By Proposition 2.2.6 f belongs to $\mathsf{D}(P^k)$ $(k = 1, 2, \ldots, r-1)$ and $P^k(g_{0,r}, \ldots, g_{k-1,r}) f = g_{k,r}$. Thus we have to prove that $f \in \mathsf{D}(A^{r-1})$ and that $g_{k,r} = A^k f$ for $k = 1, 2, \ldots, r-1$. Since the first Peano operator P^1 is equal to A, the elements $g_{0,r}$ and $g_{1,r}$ are uniquely determined by f and $A f$, respectively. Hence

$$P_t^2 f = 2!\, t^{-2}\{T(t) f - g_{0,r} - t g_{1,r}\} = 2!\, t^{-2}\{T(t) f - f - t A f\} = B_t^2 f$$

converges in norm to $g_{2,r}$ as $t \to 0+$. Applying Proposition 2.2.4, we have $f \in \mathsf{D}(A^2)$ and $A^2 f = g_{2,r}$. Proceeding successively, this completes the proof.

There is another natural generalization of the definition of the r-th power of the infinitesimal generator A.

Definition 2.2.8. *The r-th Riemann operator C^r with domain and range in X is defined by*

$$\operatorname*{s-lim}_{t \to 0+} C_t^r f = C^r f$$

whenever this limit exists, where C_t^r is given by

$$(2.2.5)\quad C_t^r f \equiv [A_t]^r f = \frac{1}{t^r}\left\{\sum_{k=0}^{r} (-1)^{r-k} \binom{r}{k} T(kt) f\right\} \qquad (t > 0;\ f \in \mathsf{X}).$$

The domain of C^r is denoted by $\mathsf{D}(C^r)$.

Again, $\mathsf{D}(C^r)$ is a linear subspace of X and C^r a linear operator, $C^1 = A$.

At first sight the r-th Riemann operator C^r is by definition the most general relative to A^r, to the r-th Taylor and the r-th Peano operator. Indeed,

Proposition 2.2.9. *If $f \in \mathsf{D}(P^r)$, then $f \in \mathsf{D}(C^r)$ and $C^r f = P^r f$.*

Proof. For the proof we need the following identities:

$$(2.2.6)\quad \begin{cases} [T(t) - I]^r = \sum_{j=1}^{r} (-1)^{r-j} \binom{r}{j} [T(jt) - I] & (r = 1, 2, \ldots), \\ \sum_{j=1}^{r} (-1)^{r-j} \binom{r}{j} j^k = \begin{cases} 0, & k = 1, 2, \ldots, r-1 \\ r!, & k = r \end{cases} & (r = 1, 2, \ldots). \end{cases}$$

The first identity is evident. To prove the second one, we remark that

$$(e^t - 1)^r = \sum_{j=0}^{r} (-1)^{r-j} \binom{r}{j} e^{jt}.$$

Differentiating the latter formula with respect to t and setting $t = 0$, we have the second identity.

Now assume $f \in \mathsf{D}(P^r)$. By definition there exist elements $g_{k,r} \in \mathsf{X}$ $(k = 0, 1, \ldots, r-1)$ such that

$$P_t^r f = \frac{r!}{t^r}\left\{T(t) f - \sum_{k=0}^{r-1} \frac{t^k}{k!} g_{k,r}\right\} \qquad (t > 0)$$

converges in norm to $P^r f$ as $t \to 0+$. By the identities (2.2.6) we have

$$C_t^r f - P^r f = \frac{[T(t) - I]^r}{t^r} f - P^r f$$

$$= \frac{1}{r!} \sum_{j=1}^{r} (-1)^{r-j} \binom{r}{j} j^r \left\{\frac{r!}{(j\,t)^r}\left(T(j\,t) f - \sum_{k=0}^{r-1} \frac{(j\,t)^k}{k!} g_{k,r}\right) - P^r f\right\}.$$

Thus, the limit in norm as $t \to 0+$ of $C_t^r f$ exists and is equal to $P^r f$.

The next proposition shows that, even for the Riemann operator, f belongs to $\mathsf{D}(C^r)$ if and only if $f \in \mathsf{D}(A^r)$. To prove this, we need two lemmas.

Lemma 2.2.10. *For each $f \in \mathsf{X}$ we have*

(2.2.7)
$$[T(t_r) - I][T(t_{r-1}) - I] \ldots [T(t_1) - I] f$$
$$= \operatorname*{s-lim}_{t \to 0+} \int_0^{t_r} T(u_r)\, du_r \int_0^{t_{r-1}} T(u_{r-1}) \ldots du_2 \int_0^{t_1} T(u_1)\, C_t^r f\, du_1$$

($t_k \geq 0$ being arbitrary, $k = 1, 2, \ldots, r$).

Proof. By the fact that $C_t^r = [A_t]^r$, $t > 0$, we obtain

$$\int_0^{t_r} T(u_r)\, du_r \int_0^{t_{r-1}} T(u_{r-1}) \ldots du_2 \int_0^{t_1} T(u_1)\, [A_t]^r f\, du_1$$

$$= \frac{1}{t^r} \int_0^{t} T(u_r)\, du_r \int_0^{t} T(u_{r-1}) \ldots du_2 \int_0^{t} T(u_1)\, [T(t_r) - I][T(t_{r-1}) - I] \ldots$$
$$\ldots [T(t_1) - I] f\, du_1$$

$$= \frac{1}{t^r} \int_0^{t}\int_0^{t} \ldots \int_0^{t} T(u_r + u_{r-1} + \cdots + u_1)[T(t_r) - I][T(t_{r-1}) - I] \ldots$$
$$\ldots [T(t_1) - I] f\, du_r\, du_{r-1} \ldots du_1,$$

from which the desired relation (2.2.7) follows immediately.

Lemma 2.2.11. *Let f and g be two elements in X such that*

$$[T(t_r) - I][T(t_{r-1}) - I] \ldots [T(t_1) - I] f$$
$$= \int_0^{t_r} T(u_r)\, du_r \int_0^{t_{r-1}} T(u_{r-1}) \ldots du_2 \int_0^{t_1} T(u_1)\, g\, du_1 \qquad (r = 1, 2, \ldots),$$

$t_k \geqq 0$ $(k = 1, 2, \ldots, r)$ *being arbitrary. Then* $f \in \mathsf{D}(A^r)$ *with* $A^r f = g$, *and consequently*

$$[T(t) - I]\, f = \sum_{k=1}^{r-1} \frac{t^k}{k!} A^k f + \frac{1}{(r-1)!} \int_0^t (t-u)^{r-1}\, T(u)\, g\, du.$$

Proof. We prove this lemma by induction. For $r = 1$ the assertion is already known. Now assume that the assertion is valid for $r - 1$. Then, putting $f_1(t_1) = [T(t_1) - I]\, f$ and $g_1(t_1) = \int_0^{t_1} T(u_1)\, g\, du_1$, we have $f_1(t_1) \in \mathsf{D}(A^{r-1})$ and $A^{r-1} f_1(t_1) = g_1(t_1)$ for each fixed $t_1 \geqq 0$. Furthermore,

(2.2.8)
$$[T(t) - I]\, f_1(t_1) = \sum_{k=1}^{r-2} \frac{t^k}{k!} A^k f_1(t_1) + \frac{1}{(r-2)!} \int_0^t (t-u)^{r-2}\, T(u)\, g_1(t_1)\, du.$$

One sees easily that the vector-valued functions $A^k f_1(t_1)$ $(k = 0, 1, 2, \ldots, r-1)$ are strongly continuous on every finite interval $0 \leqq t_1 \leqq s$. Indeed, $f_1(t_1)$ and $g_1(t_1)$ are strongly continuous on $[0, s]$. By Taylor's formula we have

$$[T(t) - I]\, A^{r-3} f_1(t_1) - t\, A^{r-2} f_1(t_1) = \int_0^t (t-u)\, T(u)\, g_1(t_1)\, du$$

for each $t_1 \in [0, s]$ and all $t > 0$. Thus for $t = 1$

$$A^{r-2} f_1(t_1) = [T(t_1) - I]\, A^{r-3} f_1(1) - \int_0^{t_1} T(u_1)\, du_1 \int_0^1 g_1(u)\, du.$$

But the right-hand side of the equality is strongly continuous on $[0, s]$. Applying this argument successively, the desired result follows for all $A^k f_1(t_1)$ $(k = 0, 1, \ldots, r-1)$.

Now integration of both sides of equality (2.2.8) relative to t_1 over $[0, s]$, followed by division by t, gives

$$\frac{1}{t} \int_0^s [T(t) - I]\, f_1(t_1)\, dt_1 = \frac{1}{t} \int_0^t T(t_1)\, [T(s) - I]\, f\, dt_1 - s\, \frac{T(t) - I}{t} f$$

$$= \int_0^s A\, f_1(t_1)\, dt_1 + \sum_{k=2}^{r-2} \frac{t^{k-1}}{k!} \int_0^s A^k f_1(t_1)\, dt_1 +$$

$$+ \frac{1}{t} \frac{1}{(r-2)!} \int_0^t (t-u)^{r-2}\, T(u)\, du \int_0^s g_1(t_1)\, dt_1.$$

Then taking the limit in norm as $t \to 0+$,

$$[T(s) - I]\, f - s\left(\underset{t\to 0+}{\text{s-lim}} \frac{T(t) - I}{t} f\right) = \int_0^s A\, f_1(t_1)\, dt_1,$$

which proves that $f \in \mathsf{D}(A)$ and thus by induction $f \in \mathsf{D}(A^r)$ and $A^r f = g$. This completes the proof.

Proposition 2.2.12. *An element $f \in \mathsf{X}$ belongs to $\mathsf{D}(C^r)$ if and only if it belongs to $\mathsf{D}(A^r)$.*

Proof. It remains to prove the "only if" part. Supposing $f \in \mathsf{D}(C^r)$, then $C_t^r f \to g$ in norm as $t \to 0+$. Hence, applying Lemma 2.2.10

$$[T(t_r) - I]\,[T(t_{r-1}) - I] \ldots [T(t_1) - I]\, f -$$

$$- \int_0^{t_r} T(u_r)\, du_r \int_0^{t_{r-1}} T(u_{r-1}) \ldots du_2 \int_0^{t_1} T(u_1)\, g\, du_1$$

$$= \underset{t\to 0+}{\text{s-lim}} \int_0^{t_r} T(u_r)\, du_r \int_0^{t_{r-1}} T(u_{r-1}) \ldots du_2 \int_0^{t_1} T(u_1) \{C_t^r f - g\}\, du_1 = \theta$$

for arbitrary, but fixed $t_k \geqq 0$ $(k = 1, 2, \ldots, r)$. Thus by Lemma 2.2.11 $f \in \mathsf{D}(A^r)$ and $A^r f = g$.

Combining the results of the foregoing propositions we have the following theorem, giving that all the operators are equal to another.

Theorem 2.2.13. *For an element $f \in \mathsf{X}$ and any fixed integer $r > 0$ the following statements are equivalent:*

(i) *$f \in \mathsf{D}(A^r)$, i.e. $f \in \mathsf{D}(A^{r-1})$ and $A_t(A^{r-1} f)$ converges in norm as $t \to 0+$;*

(ii) *$f \in \mathsf{D}(B^r)$, i.e. $f \in \mathsf{D}(A^{r-1})$ and*

$$B_t^r f \equiv \frac{t^r}{r!} \left\{T(t)\, f - \sum_{k=0}^{r-1} \frac{t^k}{k!} A^k f\right\}$$

converges in norm as $t \to 0+$;

(iii) *$f \in \mathsf{D}(P^r)$, i.e. there exist elements $g_{k,r} \in \mathsf{X}$ $(k = 0, 1, \ldots, r-1)$ such that*

$$P_t^r f \equiv \frac{t^r}{r!} \left\{T(t)\, f - \sum_{k=0}^{r-1} \frac{t^k}{k!} g_{k,r}\right\}$$

converges in norm as $t \to 0+$;

(iv) *$f \in \mathsf{D}(C^r)$, i.e.*

$$C_t^r f \equiv \frac{1}{t^r} \sum_{k=0}^{r} (-1)^{r-k} \binom{r}{k} T(k t)\, f$$

converges in norm as $t \to 0+$.

Furthermore, if f is an element in anyone of the four domains, then

$$A^r f = B^r f = P^r f = C^r f.$$

Remark. In order to assure that f belongs to $\mathsf{D}(A^r)$ it is sufficient to assume that there exists at least one sequence $\{t_n\}_{n=1}^{\infty}$, $t_n \to 0+$ as $n \to \infty$ such that $B^r_{t_n} f$, $P^r_{t_n} f$ and $C^r_{t_n} f$, respectively, converge in norm as $n \to \infty$.

Remark. The preceding definitions generalizing the higher powers of the infinitesimal generator A are classical in case X is equal to the Banach space $\mathsf{UCB}(\mathrm{E}_1^+)$ and $\{T(t); 0 \leqq t < \infty\}$ to the semi-group of left translations. Indeed, for this special case Definition 2.2.1 is nothing but the definition of the r-th Taylor derivative in norm of a function f in $\mathsf{UCB}(\mathrm{E}_1^+)$, and the Definitions 2.2.5 and 2.2.8 are those of the r-th Peano and the r-th Riemann derivatives in norm, respectively. For a detailed discussion of the semi-group of left translations on the space $\mathsf{UCB}(\mathrm{E}_1^+)$ and $\mathsf{L}^p(\mathrm{E}_1^+)$, $1 \leqq p < \infty$, see Sec. 2.2.3 below.

2.2.2 Saturation Theorems

In this subsection we shall discuss the saturation behavior of the family of operators $\{[T(t) - I]^r\}$ as $t \to 0+$. The basic theorem is the following generalization of Theorem 2.1.2.

Theorem 2.2.14. *Suppose $\{T(t); 0 \leqq t < \infty\}$ is a semi-group of class $(\mathscr{C}_0)$ on X.*

(a) *Let f and g be two elements in X such that*

$$\liminf_{\tau \to 0+} \| C^r_\tau f - g \| = 0. \tag{2.2.9}$$

Then $f \in \mathsf{D}(A^r)$ and $A^r f = g$. In case $g = \theta$, then $A^r f = \theta$, i.e. for all $t \geqq 0$

$$T(t) f = \sum_{k=0}^{r-1} \frac{t^k}{k!} A^k f \quad \text{or equivalently} \quad [T(t) - I]^r f = \theta.$$

(b) *For each $f \in \mathsf{D}(A^r)$ one has*

$$\| C^r_t f \| \leqq \sup_{0 \leqq u \leqq rt} \{\| T(u) \|\} \, \| A^r f \| \qquad (t > 0). \tag{2.2.10}$$

(c) *If X is reflexive and $f \in \mathsf{X}$ such that*

$$\liminf_{\tau \to 0+} \| C^r_\tau f \| < +\infty, \tag{2.2.11}$$

then $f \in \mathsf{D}(A^r)$. In this case, $\operatorname{s-lim}_{\tau \to 0+} C^r_\tau f = A^r f$.

Proof. (a) If the limit inferior in condition (2.2.9) is replaced by the limit, then we have the "only if" part of Proposition 2.2.12. Since the proof is only a slight modification of the one given there it will be omitted. In the special case $g = \theta$ and thus $A^r f = \theta$ the desired representations follow by the relations (1.1.10) and (1.1.11), respectively.

(b) This part is a direct consequence of (1.1.11).

(c) If the condition (2.2.11) is valid for an element f in X, then by the same reasoning as in the proof of Theorem 2.1.2(c) there exist a sequence $\{\tau_k'\}$ and an element $g \in \mathsf{X}$ such that

$$\lim_{k\to\infty} \langle f^*, T(u)\, C^r_{\tau_k'} f\rangle = \langle f^*, T(u)\, g\rangle$$

for all $f^* \in \mathsf{X}^*$ and all $u \geqq 0$.

Applying Lemma 2.2.10 and Lebesgue's dominated convergence theorem we obtain

$$\langle f^*, [T(t_r) - I]\,[T(t_{r-1}) - I] \ldots [T(t_1) - I]\, f\rangle$$

$$= \lim_{k\to\infty} \langle f^*, \int_0^{t_r} T(u_r)\, du_r \int_0^{t_{r-1}} T(u_{r-1}) \ldots du_2 \int_0^{t_1} T(u_1)\, C^r_{\tau_k'} f\, du_1\rangle$$

$$= \lim_{k\to\infty} \int_0^{t_r}\int_0^{t_{r-1}} \ldots \int_0^{t_1} \langle f^*, T(u_r + u_{r-1} + \cdots + u_1)\, C^r_{\tau_k'} f\rangle\, du_r\, du_{r-1} \ldots du_1$$

$$= \int_0^{t_r}\int_0^{t_{r-1}} \ldots \int_0^{t_1} \langle f^*, T(u_r + u_{r-1} + \cdots + u_1)\, g\rangle\, du_r\, du_{r-1} \ldots du_1$$

$$= \langle f^*, \int_0^{t_r} T(u_r)\, du_r \int_0^{t_{r-1}} T(u_{r-1}) \ldots du_2 \int_0^{t_1} T(u_1)\, g\, du_1\rangle$$

for each $f^* \in \mathsf{X}^*$ and arbitrary but fixed $t_k \geqq 0$ $(k = 1, 2, \ldots, r)$. Thus

$$[T(t_r) - I]\,[T(t_{r-1}) - I] \ldots [T(t_1) - I]\, f$$
$$= \int_0^{t_r} T(u_r)\, du_r \int_0^{t_{r-1}} T(u_{r-1}) \ldots du_2 \int_0^{t_1} T(u_1)\, g\, du_1$$

for any $t_k \geqq 0$ $(k = 1, 2, \ldots, r)$. Finally, Lemma 2.2.11 applies and we have $f \in \mathsf{D}(A^r)$ and $A^r f = g$, which completes the proof.

The following saturation theorem is an immediate consequence of the foregoing theorem.

Corollary 2.2.15. *Let X be a reflexive space and $\{T(t); 0 \leqq t < \infty\}$ a semi-group of class $(\mathscr{C}_0)$ in $\mathscr{E}(\mathsf{X})$. The family of operators $\{[T(t) - I]^r\}$ in $\mathscr{E}(\mathsf{X})$ is saturated with order $O(t^r)$ $(t \to 0+)$ and the Favard class $\mathscr{F}\{[T(t) - I]^r; \mathsf{X}\}$ is given by $\mathsf{D}(A^r)$.*

Remark. In the first part of Sec. 2.1.1 we have defined approximation problems for an element f in X by elements $T(t) f$ as $t \to 0+$, where $\{T(t); 0 < t < \infty\}$ is a given approximation process. In particular, we have studied the saturation problem for semi-group operators. To generalize these questions to the r-th Riemann difference $[T(t) - I]^r$ it is more appropriate to ask with what order does $\|[T(t) - I]^r f\|$ converge to zero as $t \to 0+$ for a given element $f \in \mathsf{X}$. This explains what we mean by saying "the family of operators $\{[T(t) - I]^r\}$ in $\mathscr{E}(\mathsf{X})$ is saturated with order $O(t^r)$ $(t \to 0+)$ and the Favard class $\mathscr{F}\{[T(t) - I]^r; \mathsf{X}\}$ is given by $\mathsf{D}(A^r)$" in Corollary 2.2.15.

The following corollary is a definite generalization of Theorem 2.2.13 for reflexive spaces X and gives rather weak conditions such that any element f of X belongs to $\mathsf{D}(A^r)$.

Corollary 2.2.16. *Under the hypotheses of Corollary* 2.2.15 *the following statements are equivalent for an element* $f \in \mathsf{X}$:

(i) $f \in \mathsf{D}(A^r)$;

(ii) $f \in \mathsf{D}(A^{r-1})$ *and*

$$\left\| \left[T(t) - \sum_{j=0}^{k-1} \frac{t^j}{j!} A^j\right] A^{r-k} f \right\| = O\left(\frac{t^k}{k!}\right)$$

(*any fixed* k, $1 \leqq k \leqq r$; $t \to 0+$);

(iii) $f \in \mathsf{D}(A^{r-k})$ *and there exist elements* $g_{j,k} \in \mathsf{X}$, $j = 0, 1, \ldots, k-1$, *such that*

$$\left\| T(t) A^{r-k} f - \sum_{j=0}^{k-1} \frac{t^j}{j!} g_{j,k} \right\| = O\left(\frac{t^k}{k!}\right)$$

(*any fixed* k, $1 \leqq k \leqq r$; $t \to 0+$);

(iv) $f \in \mathsf{D}(A^{r-k})$ *and*

$$\|[T(t) - I]^k A^{r-k} f\| = O(t^k)$$

(*any fixed* k, $1 \leqq k \leqq r$; $t \to 0+$).

Proof. Let k be any fixed integer, $1 \leqq k \leqq n$. If (i) holds, then by (1.1.10)

$$\left[T(t) - \sum_{j=0}^{k-1} \frac{t^j}{j!} A^j\right] A^{r-k} f = \frac{1}{(k-1)!} \int_0^t (t-u)^{k-1} T(u) A^r f \, du$$

for all $t > 0$. Thus

$$\left\| \left[T(t) - \sum_{j=0}^{k-1} \frac{t^j}{j!} A^j\right] A^{r-k} f \right\| \leqq \sup_{0 \leqq u \leqq t} \{\|T(u)\|\} \, \|A^r f\| \frac{t^k}{k!},$$

proving (ii). Putting $g_{j,k} = A^{r-k+j} f$, $j = 0, 1, \ldots, k-1$, then (ii) implies (iii). The fact that (iii) implies (iv) can be obtained by the identities (2.2.6). To conclude the cyclic argument of proof we have to show that (i) follows by (iv), but this is part (c) of Theorem 2.2.14.

Remark. If we replace the "O" conditions in the statements (ii) – (iv) of Corollary 2.2.16 by the "o" ones, then the resulting statements are equivalent to (i) with $A^r f = \theta$. This does not only hold for reflexive spaces, but is true for arbitrary Banach spaces.

With the help of Corollary 2.2.16 and the latter remark one can formulate saturation theorems similar to Corollary 2.2.15 for the r-th Taylor and Peano operator. In particular we have

Corollary 2.2.17. *Let* X *be a reflexive space and* $\{T(t); 0 \leqq t < \infty\}$ *a semi-group of class* $(\mathscr{C}_0)$ *in* $\mathscr{E}(\mathsf{X})$. *The family of operators* $\left\{T(t) - \sum_{k=0}^{r-1} \frac{t^k}{k!} A^k\right\}$ *defined on* $\mathsf{D}(A^{r-1})$ *is saturated with order* $O(t^r/r!)$ $(t \to 0+)$ *and the Favard class* $\mathscr{F}\left\{T(t) - \sum_{k=0}^{r-1} \frac{t^k}{k!} A^k; \mathsf{X}\right\}$ *is given by* $\mathsf{D}(A^r)$.

It is possible to formulate and prove without any difficulties the corresponding saturation theorems for the dual semi-group $\{T^*(t); 0 \leqq t < \infty\}$. We shall formulate only the most general result, namely for the r-th Riemann operator, the proof being left to the reader.

Theorem 2.2.18. *Let* X_0^* *be the maximal closed linear subspace in* X^* *upon which the restriction of* $\{T^*(t); 0 \leqq t < \infty\}$ *is of class* $(\mathscr{C}_0)$.

(a) *If* $f^* \in \mathsf{X}_0^*$ *and if*

$$\|[T^*(t) - I^*]^r f^*\| = o(t^r) \qquad (t \to 0+),$$

then $f^* \in \mathsf{D}((A_0^*)^r)$ *and* $(A_0^*)^r f^* = \theta^*$, *or equivalently* $[T^*(t) - I^*]^r f^* = \theta^*$ *for all* $t \geqq 0$.

(b) *For an element* $f^* \in \mathsf{X}_0^*$ *the following statements are equivalent:*

(i) $f^* \in \mathsf{D}((A_0^*)^{r-1})$ *and* $(A_0^*)^{r-1} f^* \in \mathsf{D}(A^*)$;

(ii) $f^* \in \mathsf{D}((A^r)^*)$;

(iii) $\|[T^*(t) - I^*]^r f^*\| = O(t^r) \qquad (t \to 0+)$.

Finally, we have seen in Sec. 2.1.1 that the approximation of an element f in a Banach space X by $T(t) f$, $\{T(t); 0 \leqq t < \infty\}$ being a strongly continuous semi-group in $\mathscr{E}(\mathsf{X})$, cannot exceed the order $O(t)$ $(t \to 0+)$ unless f is an invariant element under the semi-group. We can, however, improve the approximation if we introduce certain linear combinations of the semi-group operators.

For the family of operators $\{T_r(t); 0 \leqq t < \infty\}$ in $\mathscr{E}(\mathsf{X})$, defined by

$$T_r(t) = \sum_{k=1}^{r} (-1)^{k-1} \binom{r}{k} T(k t), \tag{2.2.12}$$

we have the following approximation theorem.

Theorem 2.2.19. *Under the hypotheses of Theorem* 2.2.14 *we have*

(a) *If* $f \in \mathsf{X}$ *is such that* $\|T_r(t) f - f\| = o(t^r)$ $(t \to 0+)$, *then* $T_r(t) f = f$ *for all* $t \geqq 0$.

(b) *For all* $f \in D(A^r)$ *one has the estimate*

(2.2.13) $$\|T_r(t) f - f\| = O(t^r) \qquad (t \to 0+).$$

(c) *If* X *is reflexive, then* (2.2.13) *for an element* $f \in X$ *implies that* $f \in D(A^r)$.

The proof of this theorem follows immediately by Theorem 2.2.14.

2.2.3 Generalized Derivatives of Scalar-valued Functions

It is the purpose of this subsection to study connections between the classical pointwise derivative $f^{(r)}(x)$ of order r $(r = 1, 2, \ldots)$ of a function $f(x)$, which is defined successively by means of the derivatives of lower orders at the point x, and generalized derivatives of order r such as those of Riemann, Peano and Taylor in the spaces $UCB(\mathrm{E}_1^+)$ and $L^p(\mathrm{E}_1^+)$, $1 \leqq p < \infty$.

Let X be anyone of the spaces $UCB(\mathrm{E}_1^+)$, $L^p(\mathrm{E}_1^+)$, $1 \leqq p < \infty$, and $r = 1, 2, \ldots$

Definition 2.2.20. *If* $f \in X$ *and if there is an element* $f^{[r]}$ *in* X *such that*

(2.2.14) $$\operatorname*{s-lim}_{t\to 0+} \frac{1}{t^r} \Delta_t^r f = f^{[r]},$$

then we speak of $f^{[r]}$ *as the* Riemann derivative *of order* r *of* f *in the* X*-norm, where* $\Delta_t^r f$ *is given through* (1.2.11).

Definition 2.2.21. *If* $f \in X$ *and if there are elements* $g_{k,r} \in X$, $k = 0, 1, \ldots, r$, *such that*

(2.2.15) $$\operatorname*{s-lim}_{t\to 0+} \frac{r!}{t^r} \Diamond_t^r f = g_{r,r},$$

where

$$[\Diamond_t^r f](x) = f(x+t) - \sum_{k=0}^{r-1} \frac{t^k}{k!} g_{k,r}(x) \qquad (t > 0),$$

then $g_{r,r} = f^{\langle r\rangle}$ *is called the* Peano derivative *of order* r *of* f *in the* X*-norm. More exactly,* $f^{\langle r\rangle} = f^{\langle r\rangle}(g_{0,r}, \ldots, g_{r-1,r})$.

Definition 2.2.22. *Let* f *and its first* $(r-2)$ *ordinary derivatives* $f^{(1)}, f^{(2)}, \ldots, f^{(r-2)}$ *belong to* $AC_{\mathrm{loc}}(\mathrm{E}_1^+) \cap X$.[1] *If* $f^{(r-1)} \in X$ *and if there is an* $f^{\textcircled{r}} \in X$ *such that*

$$\operatorname*{s-lim}_{t\to 0+} \frac{r!}{t^r} V_t^r f = f^{\textcircled{r}},$$

where

$$[V_t^r f](x) = f(x+t) - \sum_{k=0}^{r-1} \frac{t^k}{k!} f^{(k)}(x),$$

then we call $f^{\textcircled{r}}$ *the* Taylor derivative *of order* r *of* f *in the* X*-norm.*

[1] In case $X = L^1(\mathrm{E}_1^+)$ here and in the following $AC_{\mathrm{loc}}(\mathrm{E}_1^+) \cap X$ may be replaced by $AC(\mathrm{E}_1^+)$.

For $r = 1$ all three definitions are equal to another. In this case norm-convergence and saturation problems have been investigated in Sec. 2.1.2.

Our first result in this subsection will reveal that the existence of the r-th Riemann derivative of a function f in the X-norm is equivalent to the existence of the r-th ordinary derivative belonging to X.

Theorem 2.2.23. (a) *If the functions f and g defined on E_1^+ belong to X and if*

$$\operatorname*{s-lim}_{t\to 0+} \frac{1}{t^r} \Delta_t^r f = g,$$

then $f, f', \ldots, f^{(r-1)}$ belong to $AC_{loc}(E_1^+) \cap X$, $f^{(r)} \in X$ and $f^{(r)} = g$. In particular, $g = \theta$ implies $f(x) =$ const. in case $X = UCB(E_1^+)$ and $f(x) = 0$ a.e. in case $X = L^p(E_1^+)$, $1 \leqq p < \infty$.

(b) *If $f \in X$, then the r-th Riemann derivative $f^{[r]}$ exists in the X-norm if and only if $f, f', \ldots, f^{(r-1)}$ belong to $AC_{loc}(E_1^+) \cap X$ and $f^{(r)} \in X$. In this case $f^{(r)} = f^{[r]}$.*

The proof is a consequence of Theorem 1.3.16 and Proposition 2.2.12.

In case $X = UCB(E_1^+)$, part (b) of Theorem 2.2.23 is related to a result of A. Marchaud [1] who has shown that if $f \in C[a, b]$ and $\lim_{t\to 0} t^{-r}[\Delta_t^r f](x) = g(x)$ uniformly on the finite interval $[a, b]$, then

$$f(x) = p_{r-1}(x) + \int_a^x dx_1 \int_a^{x_1} \ldots dx_{r-1} \int_a^{x_{r-1}} g(x_r)\, dx_r \tag{2.2.16}$$

for all $x \in [a, b]$, $p_{r-1}(x)$ being a polynomial of degree $\leqq r - 1$. One may replace uniform convergence in the latter result by convergence in $L^1(a, b)$-norm or by weak convergence as was shown by P. L. Butzer-W. Kozakiewicz [1]. The particular case $g(x) = 0$ for the $L^1(a, b)$-norm is due to W. T. Reid [1].

Regarding Theorem 2.2.23 (b), it is important to note that if one replaces norm-convergence by *pointwise* convergence, then the existence of the r-th Riemann derivative $f^{[r]}(x)$ at a point $x = x_0$, i.e. of

$$f^{[r]}(x_0) = \lim_{t\to 0} \frac{1}{t^r} [\Delta_t^r f](x_0),$$

does not necessarily imply the existence of the r-th ordinary derivative $f^{(r)}(x)$ at $x = x_0$. Indeed, for the function $f(x) = x^{r-1}|x|$ defined on the whole real axis, there exist Riemann derivatives of every order except of order r at the origin, but the r-th and every further ordinary derivative do not exist at $x = 0$. Thus the pointwise Riemann derivative is a much more general concept than the pointwise ordinary derivative. Furthermore, there is a fundamental difference between the r-th Riemann derivative whether considered in the UCB-norm or in the L^p-norm, i.e. in the uniform sense or in the norm of order p.

Finally, we remark that if one replaces the r-th "right" difference $\Delta_t^r f$ of a function f with increment t in Definition 2.2.20 by the *central* difference defined by

$$[\bar{\Delta}_t^r f](x) = \sum_{k=0}^{r} (-1)^k \binom{r}{k} f\left[x + t\left(\frac{r}{2} - k\right)\right],$$

then all statements of Theorem 2.2.23 may be carried over to the r-th "central" Riemann derivative. In particular, if $f, g \in UCB(\mathrm{E}_1^+)$ and $\lim_{t\to 0+} (1/t^r)\, \bar{\Delta}_t^r f = g$ in the UCB-norm, then $f^{(r)} = g$ on E_1^+. But if one replaces norm-convergence by pointwise convergence in the latter result, then the situation is very different, especially for $r \geqq 3$. In this respect there is a result stating that if $f(x)$ belongs to $C(a, b)$ and has at every point of the finite interval (a, b) a finite "central" Riemann derivative $g(x)$ of order r which is integrable, then (2.2.16) holds, provided that $f^{(r-2)}(x)$ exists everywhere on (a, b). For $r = 2$ this is a theorem of Ch. de la Vallée Poussin which includes a well-known lemma of H. A. Schwarz for $g(x) = 0$ (cf. E. C. Titchmarsh [2, p. 153; 3, p. 431]). For $r = 3$ and $r = 4$ the result is due to S. Saks [1] and S. Verblunsky [1], respectively. For $r \geqq 5$ the result seems to be unknown (see C. Kassimatis [1]). The fact that one must assume the existence of $f^{(r-2)}(x)$ for $r \geqq 3$ even in case $g(x) = 0$ can be seen from the counterexample $f(x) = x^{r-3}|x|$. In fact, the first $r - 3$ ordinary derivatives of this function exist, but the $(r - 2)$-th ordinary derivative does not exist at $x = 0$, while the "central" Riemann derivative of order r is zero everywhere. But if one replaces pointwise convergence by uniform convergence, then the derivative $f^{(r-2)}$ need not exist for $r \geqq 3$ as follows from the result of A. Marchaud [1] cited above, which may also be stated for the central Riemann derivative.

Concerning the Peano derivatives we have the following results.

Theorem 2.2.24. (a) *If $f \in X$ and if there are elements $g_{k,r} \in X$, $k = 0, 1, \ldots, r$, such that*

$$\text{s-}\lim_{t\to 0+} \frac{r!}{t^r} \Diamond_t^r f = g_{r,r},$$

then $f, f', \ldots, f^{(r-1)}$ belong to $AC_{\text{loc}}(\mathrm{E}_1^+) \cap X$, $f^{(r)} \in X$ and $f^{(r)} = g_{r,r}$. In particular, $g = \theta$ implies $f(x) = \text{const.}$ and $f(x) = 0$ a.e. for $X = UCB(\mathrm{E}_1^+)$ and $X = L^p(\mathrm{E}_1^+)$, $1 \leqq p < \infty$, respectively.

(b) *If $f \in X$, then the r-th Peano derivative $f^{\langle r\rangle}$ exists in the X-norm if and only if $f, f', \ldots, f^{(r-1)}$ belong to $AC_{\text{loc}}(\mathrm{E}_1^+) \cap X$ and $f^{(r)} \in X$. In this case $f^{\langle r\rangle} = f^{(r)}$.*

The proof of this theorem follows immediately from Theorem 1.3.16 and Proposition 2.2.7.

The Peano derivative, considered as a pointwise limit, is also a true generalization of the ordinary derivative. If $f^{(r)}(x)$ exists at a point x_0, so does $f^{\langle r\rangle}(x_0)$ and $f^{\langle r\rangle}(x_0) = f^{(r)}(x_0)$. But the function

$$(2.2.17) \qquad f(x) = \begin{cases} \exp(-x^{-2}) \sin \exp(x^{-2}) & (x \neq 0) \\ 0 & (x = 0) \end{cases}$$

has Peano derivatives of every order at $x = 0$ ($f^{\langle k\rangle}(0) = 0$, $k = 1, 2, \ldots$), though not even the second ordinary derivative exists at $x = 0$.

If we compare the Peano derivative with the Riemann derivative, one may show that the existence of the Peano derivative $f^{\langle r\rangle}(x)$ at a point $x = x_0$ implies that of the Riemann derivative $f^{[r]}(x)$ at x_0 and $f^{[r]}(x_0) = f^{\langle r\rangle}(x_0)$. But the converse is not true in general. For instance, the function $f(x) = x^{r-1}|x|$ possesses only the first $(r-1)$ Peano derivatives $f^{\langle k\rangle}(0)$ $(= 0$, $k = 1, 2, \ldots, r-1)$, but the Riemann derivatives of all orders except of order r exist at $x = 0$ and equal zero.

Turning now to the Taylor derivative we only mention that results analogous to those given in the preceding theorems also hold for this type of a generalized derivative. We further note that the concept of the Taylor derivative at a point is more general than the ordinary but less general than the Peano concept of a derivative. The function defined by (2.2.17) possesses Peano derivatives of every order at $x = 0$ though its Taylor derivative of order 3 already does not exist at the origin. Finally, the function

$$(2.2.18) \qquad f(x) = \begin{cases} x^{3(r-1)} \sin(x^{-2}) & (x \neq 0) \\ 0 & (x = 0) \end{cases} \qquad (r = 2, 3, \ldots)$$

possesses only the first $(r-1)$ ordinary derivatives at $x = 0$ but the r-th Taylor derivative $f^{Ⓡ}(0)$ exists and is equal to zero.

We collect some of the results of this subsection in the following

Theorem 2.2.25. *If f belongs to X, then for each positive integer r the following assertions are equivalent:*

(i) *$f, f', \ldots, f^{(r-1)}$ belong to $\mathsf{AC}_{\text{loc}}(\mathrm{E}_1^+) \cap \mathsf{X}$ and $f^{(r)} \in \mathsf{X}$;*

(ii) *the r-th Riemann derivative $f^{[r]}$ exists in the X-norm;*

(iii) *there are functions $g_{k,r} \in \mathsf{X}$, $k = 0, 1, \ldots, r-1$, such that the r-th Peano derivative $f^{\langle r\rangle}$ exists in the X-norm;*

(iv) *$f, f', \ldots, f^{(r-2)} \in \mathsf{AC}_{\text{loc}}(\mathrm{E}_1^+) \cap \mathsf{X}$, $f^{(r-1)} \in \mathsf{X}$ and the r-th Taylor derivative $f^{Ⓡ}$ exists in the X-norm.*

If anyone of the four derivatives of the same order r exists, so does each of the others and $f^{(r)} = f^{[r]} = f^{\langle r \rangle} = f^{ⓡ}$.

As a final contribution to this subsection we wish to extend the results of Hardy-Littlewood on the first difference $\{f(\cdot + t) - f(\cdot)\}$ of a function f (as given in Theorem 2.1.7) to the Riemann, Peano and Taylor differences of order r defined above.

Theorem 2.2.26. *Let* X *be one of the spaces* $\mathsf{UCB}(\mathrm{E}_1^+)$, $\mathsf{L}^p(\mathrm{E}_1^+)$, $1 \leqq p < \infty$, *and* f *a function in* X. *For* $r = 1, 2, \ldots$ *the assertion* (a) *is equivalent to each of the assertions* (b), (c) *or* (d) *given below:*

(a) *for* $\mathsf{X} = \mathsf{UCB}(\mathrm{E}_1^+)$: $f, f', \ldots, f^{(r-1)} \in \mathsf{AC}_{\mathrm{loc}}(\mathrm{E}_1^+) \cap \mathsf{UCB}(\mathrm{E}_1^+)$ *and* $f^{(r)} \in \mathsf{L}^\infty(\mathrm{E}_1^+)$;

for $\mathsf{X} = \mathsf{L}^1(\mathrm{E}_1^+)$: $f, f', \ldots, f^{(r-2)} \in \mathsf{AC}(\mathrm{E}_1^+)$ *and* $f^{(r-1)} \in \mathsf{NBV}(\mathrm{E}_1^+)$;

for $\mathsf{X} = \mathsf{L}^p(\mathrm{E}_1^+)$, $1 < p < \infty$: $f, f', \ldots, f^{(r-1)} \in \mathsf{AC}_{\mathrm{loc}}(\mathrm{E}_1^+) \cap \mathsf{L}^p(\mathrm{E}_1^+)$ *and* $f^{(r)} \in \mathsf{L}^p(\mathrm{E}_1^+)$;

(b)
$$\|\Delta_t^r f\| = O(t^r) \qquad (t \to 0+);$$

(c) *there are elements* $g_{k,r} \in \mathsf{X}$ *such that*
$$\|\Diamond_t^r f\| = O\left(\frac{t^r}{r!}\right) \qquad (t \to 0+);$$

(d) $f, f', \ldots, f^{(r-2)} \in \mathsf{AC}_{\mathrm{loc}}(\mathrm{E}_1^+) \cap \mathsf{X}$, $f^{(r-1)} \in \mathsf{X}$ *and*
$$\|\nabla_t^r f\| = O\left(\frac{t^r}{r!}\right) \qquad (t \to 0+).$$

Remark. We note that the assertion (b) of Theorem 2.2.26, for instance, may be replaced by the following assertion

(b′) *for* $\mathsf{X} = \mathsf{UCB}(\mathrm{E}_1^+)$: *there is a* $g \in \mathsf{L}^\infty(\mathrm{E}_1^+)$ *such that*
$$\lim_{t \to 0+} \int_0^\infty \frac{1}{t^r} [\Delta_t^r f](x)\, \psi(x)\, dx = \int_0^\infty g(x)\, \psi(x)\, dx \qquad (\psi \in \mathsf{C}_{00}^\infty(\mathrm{E}_1^+));$$

for $\mathsf{X} = \mathsf{L}^1(\mathrm{E}_1^+)$: *there is a* $\mu \in \mathsf{NBV}(\mathrm{E}_1^+)$ *such that*
$$\lim_{t \to 0+} \int_0^\infty \frac{1}{t^r} [\Delta_t^r f](x)\, \psi(x)\, dx = \int_0^\infty \psi(x)\, d\mu(x) \qquad (\psi \in \mathsf{C}_{00}^\infty(\mathrm{E}_1^+));$$

for $\mathsf{X} = \mathsf{L}^p(\mathrm{E}_1^+)$, $1 < p < \infty$: *there is a* $g \in \mathsf{L}^p(\mathrm{E}_1^+)$ *such that*
$$\lim_{t \to 0+} \int_0^\infty \frac{1}{t^r} [\Delta_t^r f](x)\, \psi(x)\, dx = \int_0^\infty g(x)\, \psi(x)\, dx \qquad (\psi \in \mathsf{C}_{00}^\infty(\mathrm{E}_1^+)).$$

Corresponding equivalences are valid for the statements (c) and (d), respectively.

Finally, we mention that the assertion (b) may also be replaced by: $\liminf_{t\to 0+} \| t^{-r} \Delta_t^r f \|$ is finite. A similar remark applies to (c) and (d). Likewise, the limites in (b′) may be replaced by the limites inferiores for $t \to 0+$.

Corollary 2.2.27. *An element* $f \in \mathsf{X}$ *is constant in case* $\mathsf{X} = UCB(\mathrm{E}_1^+)$, *and equal to zero almost everywhere in case* $\mathsf{X} = L^p(\mathrm{E}_1^+)$, $1 \leqq p < \infty$, *if and only if the assertions* (b), (c), *or* (d) *are valid for the large "O", replaced by the small "o".*

Obviously, the results obtained for the semi-group of left-translations on the spaces $UCB(\mathrm{E}_1^+)$ and $L^p(\mathrm{E}_1^+)$, $1 \leqq p < \infty$, have their analogues for the group of translations defined on the function spaces in consideration. The same is true for the periodic spaces.

2.3 Theorems of Non-optimal Approximation

2.3.1 Equivalence Theorems for Holomorphic Semi-Groups

Throughout this subsection $\{T(t); 0 \leqq t < \infty\}$ will be a strongly continuous semi-group in $\mathscr{E}(\mathsf{X})$ satisfying the additional assumption that $T(t)[\mathsf{X}] \subset \mathsf{D}(A)$ for each $t > 0$.

It has been shown in Proposition 1.1.10 that under these hypotheses the operator function $T(t)$ on $[0, \infty)$ is r-times continuously differentiable in the uniform operator topology for all $t > 0$ and all integers $r > 0$. A simple consequence of this fact is that

$$T(t) f - f = \operatorname*{s-lim}_{\varepsilon \to 0+} \int_\varepsilon^t A\, T(u) f \, du \tag{2.3.1}$$

for each $t > 0$ and all $f \in \mathsf{X}$, the integral being understood in the sense of Riemann.

Proposition 2.3.1. *Let* $\{T(t); 0 \leqq t < \infty\}$ *be a strongly continuous semi-group in* $\mathscr{E}(\mathsf{X})$ *with* $T(t)[\mathsf{X}] \subset \mathsf{D}(A)$ *for each* $t > 0$. *The following assertions are equivalent for an element* $f \in \mathsf{X}$:

(i) $\| T(t) f - f \| = O(t) \qquad (t \to 0+)$;

(ii) $\| A\, T(t) f \| = O(1) \qquad (t \to 0+)$.

In case X *is reflexive, these assertions are equivalent to*

(iii) $f \in \mathsf{D}(A)$.

Proof. If condition (i) holds for an element $f \in \mathsf{X}$, then there exists a constant $C_0 > 0$ such that $\| A_\tau f \| \leqq C_0$ for all $0 < \tau \leqq 1$. Thus for an arbitrary, but fixed $0 < t \leqq 1$,

$$\| A\,T(t)\,f \| = \lim_{\tau \to 0+} \| A_\tau\,T(t)\,f \| \leqq \sup_{0 \leqq t \leqq 1} \{\| T(t) \|\}\, C_0\,,$$

proving (ii). On the other hand, condition (ii) means that there is a constant $C_1 > 0$ such that $\| A\,T(u)\,f \| \leqq C_1$ for $0 < u \leqq 1$. Thus by (2.3.1) we obtain

$$\| T(t)\,f - f \| = \lim_{\varepsilon \to 0+} \left\| \int_\varepsilon^t A\,T(u)\,f\,du \right\| \leqq C_1 \cdot t \qquad (0 < t \leqq 1).$$

The equivalence of (iii) and (i) for reflexive spaces has been shown in Theorem 2.1.2.

More generally, we have the following

Theorem 2.3.2. *Under the hypothesis of Proposition 2.3.1 the following two assertions are equivalent for an element $f \in X$ and $r = 1, 2, \ldots$:*

(i) $\| [T(t) - I]^r f \| = O(t^r)$ $\qquad (t \to 0+)$;

(ii) $\| A^r\,T(t)\,f \| = O(1)$ $\qquad (t \to 0+)$.

In case $f \in D(A^{r-1})$, these assertions are equivalent to

(iii) $$\left\| \left[T(t) - \sum_{k=0}^{r-1} \frac{t^k}{k!} A^k \right] f \right\| = O\left(\frac{t^r}{r!}\right) \qquad (t \to 0+).$$

Moreover, if X is reflexive, then (i), (ii) *or* (iii) *are equivalent to*

(iv) $f \in D(A^r)$.

The proof of the equivalence of (i) and (ii) is similar to that given in Proposition 2.3.1 and is omitted. The rest follows by Corollary 2.2.16.

In Sec. 2.1.1 we have seen that unless f is an invariant element of the semi-group, the optimal order of approximation of f by $T(t)\,f$ is at most $O(t)$, and, in case X is reflexive, this order is reached precisely by all elements f in X which belong to $D(A)$. Furthermore, under the hypothesis of Proposition 2.3.1, this set of elements is also uniquely characterized by the condition $\| A\,T(t)\,f \| = O(1)$ $(t \to 0+)$. The aim of this subsection is to study the corresponding equivalence theorems (direct and converse theorems) for non-optimal approximation, i.e. to characterize those elements f in X for which $T(t)\,f$ does not furnish the saturation order $O(t)$ for small values of t. Thus, in view of Proposition 2.3.1, one might expect that for $0 < \alpha < 1$, $f \in X$ we have $\| T(t)\,f - f \| = O(t^\alpha)$ $(t \to 0+)$ if and only if $\| A\,T(t)\,f \| = O(t^{\alpha-1})$ $(t \to 0+)$. The following converse theorem shows under what general assumptions this conjecture is valid.

Proposition 2.3.3. *Let $\{T(t); 0 \leqq t < \infty\}$ be a holomorphic semi-group of class $(\mathscr{C}_0)$ in $\mathscr{E}(\mathsf{X})$. For an element $f \in \mathsf{X}$ the relation*

$$(2.3.2) \qquad \|T(t)f - f\| = O[\phi(1/t)] \qquad (t \to 0+),$$

$\phi(s)$ being a positive, non-increasing function on $(0, \infty)$ with $\lim_{s\to\infty} \phi(s) = 0$, implies

$$(2.3.3) \quad \|A\,T(t)f\| \leqq M_1 + M_2 t^{-1} \phi(1/t) + M_3 \int_1^{t^{-1}} \phi(u)\,du \quad (0 < t \leqq 1),$$

where M_1, M_2 and M_3 are constants.

Proof. By Proposition 1.1.11, $T(t)[\mathsf{X}] \subset \mathsf{D}(A)$ for each $t > 0$ and there is a constant C_1 such that $\|A\,T(t)\| \leqq C_1 t^{-1}$ in $0 < t \leqq 1$. Also the condition (2.3.2) upon f can be rewritten in the form $\|T(t)f - f\| \leqq$ $\leqq C_2 \phi(t^{-1})$, $0 < t \leqq 1$, where C_2 is a second constant.

Setting $t_k = 1/2^k$, $k = 0, 1, 2, \ldots$, we denote by U_k the operator $T(t_k) - T(t_{k-1})$. Then by the semi-group property

$$A\,U_k f = A\,T(t_k)\{f - T(t_{k-1})f\} - A\,T(t_{k-1})\{f - T(t_k)f\}$$

for all $k = 1, 2, \ldots$, and making use of the assumptions one obtains

$$\begin{aligned} \|A\,U_k f\| &\leqq \|A\,T(t_k)\|\,\|f - T(t_{k-1})f\| + \|A\,T(t_{k-1})\|\,\|f - T(t_k)f\| \\ &\leqq C_1 C_2\{t_k^{-1}\phi(t_{k-1}^{-1}) + t_{k-1}^{-1}\phi(t_k^{-1})\} \\ &\leqq 3C_0\, 2^{k-1}\phi(2^{k-1}) \qquad (C_0 = C_1 C_2; \quad k = 1, 2, \ldots). \end{aligned}$$

Now, given any t in $(0, 1)$, we can choose an integer n such that $t_n < t \leqq t_{n-1}$. Then

$$(2.3.4) \quad \begin{aligned} \|A\,T(t_n)f - A\,T(t_{n_0})f\| &\leqq \sum_{k=n_0+1}^{n} \|A\,U_k f\| \leqq 3C_0 \sum_{k=n_0+1}^{n} 2^{k-1}\phi(2^{k-1}) \\ &\leqq 6C_0 \int_{2^{n_0}-1}^{2^n-1} \phi(u)\,du \leqq 6C_0 \int_{2^{n_0}-1}^{t^{-1}} \phi(u)\,du, \end{aligned}$$

where n_0 is some fixed integer > 0. Similarly, we obtain

$$(2.3.5) \quad \begin{aligned} \|A\,T(t)f - A\,T(t_n)f\| &\leqq \|A\,T(t)\|\,\|f - T(t_n)f\| + \|A\,T(t_n)\| \times \\ &\times \|f - T(t)f\| \leqq C_0\{t^{-1}\phi(t_n^{-1}) + t_n^{-1}\phi(t^{-1})\} \leqq 3C_0 t^{-1}\phi(t^{-1}). \end{aligned}$$

On the other hand,

$$\begin{aligned} \|A\,T(t)f\| \leqq \|A\,T(t_{n_0})f\| &+ \|A\,T(t_n)f - A\,T(t_{n_0})f\| + \\ &+ \|A\,T(t)f - A\,T(t_n)f\|, \end{aligned}$$

which gives for $n_0 = 1$ by the inequalities (2.3.4) and (2.3.5) the desired estimate (2.3.3). The constants M_1, M_2 and M_3 are given by $\|A\,T(1/2)f\|$, $3C_0$ and $6C_0$, respectively.

Remark. The preceding proposition is actually valid under the following more general assumptions: $\{T(t); 0 < t < \infty\}$ a family of commutative operators in $\mathscr{E}(\mathsf{X})$ converging to the identity I in the strong operator topology as $t \to 0+$; B a closed linear operator with domain and range in X such that $T(t)[\mathsf{X}] \subset \mathsf{D}(B)$ for each $t > 0$ and $\|B\,T(t)\| = O(t^{-1})$ $(t \to 0+)$.

Corollary 2.3.4. *Under the hypothesis of Proposition* 2.3.3 *we have for an element* $f \in \mathsf{X}$:

(a) $\|T(t)f - f\| = O(t^\alpha)$ $(0 < \alpha < 1;\, t \to 0+)$ *if and only if* $\|A\,T(t)f\| = O(t^{\alpha-1})$ $(t \to 0+)$;

(b) *if* $\|T(t)f - f\| = O(t)$ $(t \to 0+)$, *then* $\|A\,T(t)f\| = O(\log 1/t)$ $(t \to 0+)$.

Proof. To prove part (a), we remark that the "only if" part follows by Proposition 2.3.3 for the particular function $\phi(u) = u^{-\alpha}$. Now suppose the "if" part is valid. Then there exists a constant C such that $\|A\,T(u)f\| \leqq C\,u^{\alpha-1}$ for all $0 < u \leqq 1$. Thus by relation (2.3.1) we obtain

$$\|T(t)f - f\| = \lim_{\varepsilon \to 0+} \left\| \int_\varepsilon^t A\,T(u)f\,du \right\| \leqq \frac{C}{\alpha} t^\alpha \qquad (0 < t \leqq 1).$$

Part (b) follows by Proposition 2.3.3 upon setting $\phi(u) = u^{-1}$.

Proposition 2.3.3 has the following generalization.

Theorem 2.3.5. *Under the assumptions of Proposition* 2.3.3 *we have for an element* $f \in \mathsf{X}$ *satisfying* (2.3.2)

$$\|A^r\,T(t)f\| \leqq M_1 + M_2\,t^{-r}\phi(1/t) + M_3 \int_1^{t^{-1}} u^{r-1}\phi(u)\,du \tag{2.3.6}$$

$$(r = 1, 2, \ldots;\ 0 < t \leqq 1),$$

where M_1, M_2 *and* M_3 *are constants.*

Proof. For $r = 1$ we have exactly Proposition 2.3.3. Now let r be some fixed integer > 1. By hypothesis, there exists a constant $C_1 > 0$ such that $\|A\,T(t)\| \leqq C_1\,t^{-1}$ in $0 < t \leqq 1/r$. Since $A^r\,T(t) = [A\,T(t/r)]^r$, we obtain $\|A^r\,T(t)\| \leqq C_r\,t^{-r}$ in $(0, 1]$, where the constant $C_r = (r\,C_1)^r$. Making use of this estimate for the norms of the operators $A^r\,T(t)$ in $(0, 1]$, by the method of proof given in Proposition 2.3.3 it is not difficult to verify relation (2.3.6). The constants M_1, M_2 and M_3 depend in general upon the given element f and upon the choice of the integer r.

Corollary 2.3.6. *Under the hypothesis of Proposition* 2.3.3 *we have for an element* $f \in \mathsf{X}$:

(a) *For* $0 < \alpha < 1$ *the following assertions are equivalent:*

(i) $\|T(t)f - f\| = O(t^\alpha)$ $(t \to 0+)$;

(ii) $\|A\,T(t)f\| = O(t^{\alpha-1})$ $(t \to 0+)$;

(iii) $\|A^2\,T(t)f\| = O(t^{\alpha-2})$ $(t \to 0+)$.

(b) *If* $\|T(t)f - f\| = O(t)$ $(t \to 0+)$, *then* $\|A^2\,T(t)f\| = O(t^{-1})$ *and further* $\|A\,T(t)f\| = O(\log 1/t)$ $(t \to 0+)$.

Proof. (a) If relation (i) is valid, then (iii) follows by Theorem 2.3.5 for $r = 2$ and $\phi(u) = u^{-\alpha}$. Now suppose relation (iii) holds. Then

$$A\,T(1)f - A\,T(t)f = \int_t^1 A^2\,T(u)f\,du \qquad (0 < t \leqq 1),$$

$$\|A\,T(t)f\| \leqq \|A\,T(1)f\| + \int_t^1 \|A^2\,T(u)f\|\,du = O(t^{\alpha-1}) \qquad (t \to 0+),$$

proving (ii). That (ii) implies (i) has already been shown in part (a) of Corollary 2.3.4.

(b) If $\|T(t)f - f\| = O(t)$ $(t \to 0+)$, then we obtain by Theorem 2.3.5 for $r = 2$ and $\phi(u) = u^{-1}$ that $\|A^2\,T(t)f\| = O(t^{-1})$ $(t \to 0+)$, which in turn implies $\|A\,T(t)f\| = O(\log 1/t)$ $(t \to 0+)$.

In part (a) of Corollary 2.3.4 it has been shown that the assertions (i) and (ii) of Corollary 2.3.6 are equivalent. The further equivalence (iii) can be proved without using Theorem 2.3.5. Indeed, that (iii) implies (ii) has been shown in the above proof. On the other hand, the equation

$$A^2\,T(t)f = A\,T(t/2)\{A\,T(t/2)f\} \qquad (t > 0) \tag{2.3.7}$$

shows that (iii) follows by (ii). Indeed, $\|A^2\,T(t)f\| \leqq \|A\,T(t/2)\| \times \times \|A\,T(t/2)f\| = O(t^{-1} \cdot t^{\alpha-1})$ $(t \to 0+)$.

Part (a) of Corollary 2.3.4 is an equivalence theorem for non-optimal approximation by holomorphic semi-group operators $\{T(t); 0 \leqq t < \infty\}$ with order $O(t^\alpha)$, $0 < \alpha < 1$. Part (b) is a converse theorem in the case of optimal approximation, leading to the estimate (*) $\|A\,T(t)f\| = O(\log 1/t)$ $(t \to 0+)$, which is not best possible according to Proposition 2.3.1. If we apply relation (2.3.7) and the estimate (*), we obtain $\|A^2\,T(t)f\| = O(t^{-1}\log 1/t)$ $(t \to 0+)$, which however is weaker than the estimate given by Corollary 2.3.6. One can also prove part (b) of Corollary 2.3.6 by applying Proposition 2.3.1 and relation (2.3.7).

Finally, it may be noted that the methods of proof of the equivalence theorems for non-optimal approximation of this section and the saturation theorems of Sec. 2.1.1 are entirely different, each, however, giving within its own sphere the best possible results.

2.3.2 Lipschitz Classes

This section is concerned with the definition and a few remarks on Lipschitz classes of functions in $C_{2\pi}$ and $L^p_{2\pi}$, $1 \leqq p < \infty$, respectively. In Example 1.5.5 of Sec. 1.5.3 we have defined the semi-group of left translations on these function spaces: If X is one of the spaces in question and f a function in X, then

$$f(x+t) \sim \sum_{k=-\infty}^{\infty} e^{ikt} f^{\wedge}(k)\, e^{ikx} \qquad (0 \leqq t < \infty),$$

where $f^{\wedge}(k)$, $k = 0, \pm 1, \pm 2, \ldots$, are the Fourier coefficients of f. The infinitesimal generator is equal to d/dx with domain $\{f \in X;\, f \in AC_{2\pi}$ and $f' \in X\}$. On the other hand, we have also seen that d/dx generates the group of translations in $\mathscr{E}(X)$.

Definition 2.3.7. *Let $0 < \alpha \leqq 1$. A function f in X with the property*

$$\|f(\cdot + t) - f(\cdot)\| = O(|t|^{\alpha}) \qquad (t \to 0) \tag{2.3.8}$$

is said to satisfy a Lipschitz condition of order α with respect to the X-norm, or to belong to the class $\mathrm{Lip}(\alpha; X)$. *If the large "O" in* (2.3.8) *is replaced by small "o", then we write* $f \in \mathrm{lip}(\alpha; X)$.

We know from the periodic versions of Theorems 2.1.6 and 2.1.7 that if $f \in \mathrm{lip}(1; X)$ then f is equal to a constant. Thus $\mathrm{lip}(1; X)$ reduces to the trivial class of constant functions. Furthermore, $\mathrm{Lip}(1; C_{2\pi}) = \{f \in C_{2\pi};\, f \in AC_{2\pi}$ and $f' \in L^{\infty}_{2\pi}\}$, $\mathrm{Lip}(1; L^1_{2\pi}) = \{f \in L^1_{2\pi};\, f \in NBV_{2\pi}\}$ and $\mathrm{Lip}(1; L^p_{2\pi}) = \{f \in L^p_{2\pi};\, f \in AC_{2\pi}$ and $f' \in L^p_{2\pi}\}$ when $1 < p < \infty$. These are the classical results of Titchmarsh and Hardy-Littlewood treated in Sec. 2.1.2.

More generally than defined above we have

Definition 2.3.8. *Let $0 < \alpha \leqq 2$. An element $f \in X$ satisfying*

$$\|f(\cdot + t) - 2f(\cdot) + f(\cdot - t)\| = O(|t|^{\alpha}) \qquad (t \to 0)$$

is said to belong to the generalized Lipschitz class of order α in the X-norm, briefly: $f \in \mathrm{Lip}^*(\alpha; X)$. If

$$\|f(\cdot + t) - 2f(\cdot) + f(\cdot - t)\| = o(|t|^{\alpha}) \qquad (t \to 0),$$

then we write $f \in \mathrm{lip}^*(\alpha; X)$. In case $\alpha = 1$, $\mathrm{Lip}^*(1; X)$ is more familiarly known as the Zygmund class of functions.

In Theorem 2.2.26 and Corollary 2.2.27 we have seen that f belongs to $\mathrm{lip}^*(2; X)$ if and only if f is equal to a constant, $\mathrm{Lip}^*(2; C_{2\pi}) = \{f \in C_{2\pi};\, f, f' \in AC_{2\pi}$ and $f'' \in L^{\infty}_{2\pi}\}$, $\mathrm{Lip}^*(2; L^1_{2\pi}) = \{f \in L^1_{2\pi};\, f \in AC_{2\pi}$ and $f' \in NBV_{2\pi}\}$ and $\mathrm{Lip}^*(2, L^p_{2\pi}) = \{f \in L^p_{2\pi};\, f, f' \in AC_{2\pi}$ and $f'' \in L^p_{2\pi}\}$ $(1 < p < \infty)$. Furthermore, for $0 < \alpha < 1$ the classes $\mathrm{Lip}(\alpha; X)$

and Lip* $(\alpha; \mathsf{X})$ are equal and for $1 < \alpha < 2$, Lip* $(\alpha; \mathsf{X}) = \{f \in \mathsf{X}; f \in \mathsf{AC}_{2\pi}$ and $f' \in \mathrm{Lip}(\alpha - 1; \mathsf{X})\}$, while Lip $(1; \mathsf{X})$ is a proper subset of Lip* $(1; \mathsf{X})$. For the proof of the latter assertions see Sec. 4.1.1 below. There we shall give a thorough treatment of Lipschitz classes and generalizations thereof.

2.4 Applications to Periodic Singular Integrals

In this section we return to Fourier's problem of the ring and Dirichlet's problem for the unit disk considered in Sec. 1.5.2 and 1.5.4, respectively. We study the initial and boundary behavior of the solutions in question and examine the rate at which the solutions approximate the initial and boundary conditions for time $t \to 0+$ and radius $\varrho \to 1-$, respectively.

2.4.1 The Boundary Behavior of the Solution of Dirichlet's Problem; Saturation

At first we consider the singular integral of Abel-Poisson on the spaces $\mathsf{C}_{2\pi}$ and $\mathsf{L}^p_{2\pi}$, $1 \leqq p < \infty$. Thus for $0 \leqq \varrho < 1$

$$[V(\varrho) f](x) = \frac{1}{2\pi} \int_0^{2\pi} f(u)\, p(\varrho; x - u)\, du, \qquad p(\varrho; u) = \frac{1 - \varrho^2}{1 - 2\varrho \cos u + \varrho^2},$$

where f is a function in X, X being one of the given spaces. We know from Sec. 1.5.4 that $v(\varrho, x) = [V(\varrho) f](x)$ solves Dirichlet's problem for the unit disk in these function spaces. This means $v(\varrho, x)$ is the solution of the Laplace equation (in polar coordinate form)

$$\frac{\partial^2 v}{\partial \varrho^2} + \frac{1}{\varrho} \frac{\partial v}{\partial \varrho} + \frac{1}{\varrho^2} \frac{\partial^2 v}{\partial x^2} = 0 \qquad (0 < x < 2\pi; \quad 0 \leqq \varrho < 1)$$

in the interior of the unit circle about the origin, taking on the given boundary value $f(x)$ on the circumference:

$$\lim_{\varrho \to 1-} v(\varrho, x) = f(x),$$

the problem being understood in the sense as explained in Sec. 1.5.4.

If we define $V(1) = I$ and replace the parameter ϱ by e^{-t}, $0 \leqq t < \infty$, then by Theorem 1.5.10 $\{V(e^{-t}); 0 \leqq t < \infty\}$ is a semi-group of factor sequence operators of type (X, X) of the form

$$[V(e^{-t}) f](x) \sim \sum_{k=-\infty}^{\infty} e^{-|k|t} f^\wedge(k)\, e^{ikx} \qquad (f \in \mathsf{X}),$$

$f^\wedge(k)$ $(k = 0, \pm 1, \pm 2, \ldots)$ being the Fourier coefficients of f. $\{V(e^{-t});\ 0 \leqq t < \infty\}$ is holomorphic and of class $(\mathscr{C}_0)$ with $\|V(e^{-t})\| \equiv 1$, and its infinitesimal generator A is given by $Af = -(f^\sim)'$ with domain

$$\mathsf{D}(A) = \{f \in \mathsf{X};\ f^\sim \in \mathsf{AC}_{2\pi} \text{ and } (f^\sim)' \in \mathsf{X}\} = \left\{f \in \mathsf{X};\ \sim \sum_{k=-\infty}^{\infty} |k| f^\wedge(k)\, e^{ikx} \in \mathsf{X}\right\},$$

where $f^\sim$ denotes the conjugate function of f.

Theorem 2.4.1. I. *If f and g belong to X with*

$$\lim_{\varrho \to 1-} \left\| \frac{1}{1-\varrho} [V(\varrho) f - f] - g \right\| = 0,$$

then $f^\sim \in \mathsf{AC}_{2\pi}$, $(f^\sim)' \in \mathsf{X}$ and $(f^\sim)' = -g$. In particular, if $\|V(\varrho) f - f\| = o(1-\varrho)$ $(\varrho \to 1-)$, then $f = \text{const}$.

II. *The following assertions are equivalent for a function $f \in \mathsf{X}$:*

(a) $$\|V(\varrho) f - f\| = O(1-\varrho) \qquad (\varrho \to 1-);$$

(b) $$\|[V^\sim(\varrho) f]'\| = O(1) \qquad (\varrho \to 1-);$$

(c) *for $\mathsf{X} = \mathsf{C}_{2\pi}$: there is a $g \in \mathsf{L}^\infty_{2\pi}$ such that*

$$-|k| f^\wedge(k) = g^\wedge(k) \qquad (k = 0, \pm 1, \pm 2, \ldots),$$

for $\mathsf{X} = \mathsf{L}^1_{2\pi}$: there is a $\mu \in \mathsf{NBV}_{2\pi}$ such that

$$-|k| f^\wedge(k) = \mu^\vee(k) \qquad (k = 0, \pm 1, \pm 2, \ldots),$$

for $\mathsf{X} = \mathsf{L}^p_{2\pi}$, $1 < p < \infty$: there is a $g \in \mathsf{L}^p_{2\pi}$ such that

$$-|k| f^\wedge(k) = g^\wedge(k) \qquad (k = 0, \pm 1, \pm 2, \ldots);$$

(d) *$f^\sim$ belongs to X and as a function of X to $\mathrm{Lip}(1; \mathsf{X})$;*

(e) *for $\mathsf{X} = \mathsf{C}_{2\pi}$: $f^\sim \in \mathsf{AC}_{2\pi}$ and $(f^\sim)' \in \mathsf{L}^\infty_{2\pi}$,*
for $\mathsf{X} = \mathsf{L}^1_{2\pi}$: $f^\sim \in \mathsf{NBV}_{2\pi}$,
for $\mathsf{X} = \mathsf{L}^p_{2\pi}$, $1 < p < \infty$: $f^\sim \in \mathsf{AC}_{2\pi}$ and $(f^\sim)' \in \mathsf{L}^p_{2\pi}$.

The proof of this theorem is a consequence of Theorems 1.5.10, 1.5.11, 1.5.12, 2.1.2, 2.1.4, the analogue of Theorem 2.1.7 for the periodic function spaces and the fact that $t = \log(1/\varrho)$ and $1-\varrho$ are asymptotically equal to another as $\varrho \to 1-$.

Theorem 2.4.1 has the following

Corollary 2.4.2. *The singular integral $V(\varrho) f$, $0 \leqq \varrho < 1$, of Abel-Poisson associated with the function $f \in \mathsf{X}$ is saturated with order $O(1-\varrho)$ $(\varrho \to 1-)$, and the Favard class is given by anyone of the characterisations (c)—(e) of Theorem 2.4.1.*

So far we have studied Dirichlet's problem for the Laplace equation on the unit disk. The *second boundary value problem* or *Neumann's problem* is defined as follows:

Given any element $g_0 \in \mathsf{X}$, *to find a function* $v_N(\varrho) = v_N(\varrho; g_0)$[1] *on* $0 \leqq \varrho < 1$ *to* X *such that*

(i) $v_N(\varrho)$ *is twice strongly continuously differentiable in* $[0, 1)$;

(ii) *for each* $\varrho \in [0, 1)$, $v_N(\varrho) \in \mathsf{D}(U)$ *and*

$$\varrho^2 \frac{d^2}{d\varrho^2} v_N(\varrho) + \varrho \frac{d}{d\varrho} v_N(\varrho) + U v_N(\varrho) = \theta \qquad (0 \leqq \varrho < 1),$$

where the operator U *is defined by* $U f = f''$ *and* $\mathsf{D}(U) = \{f \in \mathsf{X}; f, f' \in \mathsf{AC}_{2\pi}$ *and* $f'' \in \mathsf{X}\}$;

(iii) $$\operatorname*{s-lim}_{\varrho \to 1-} \frac{d}{d\varrho} v_N(\varrho; g_0) = g_0.$$

Applying the finite Fourier transform method one may prove without major difficulties that Neumann's problem for the unit disk has a solution if and only if $g_0^\wedge(0) = 0$, the solution then being uniquely determined except for an additive constant c_0, and given by

$$[v_N(\varrho; g_0)](x) = c_0 + \frac{1}{2\pi} \int_0^{2\pi} g_0(u) \log \frac{1}{1 - 2\varrho \cos(x-u) + \varrho^2} du$$

or $$(0 \leqq \varrho < 1)$$

$$[v_N(\varrho; g_0)](x) \sim c_0 + \sum_{k=-\infty}^{\infty}{}' \frac{g_0^\wedge(k)}{|k|} e^{ikx} \varrho^{|k|},$$

the prime indicating summation over all integers k except $k = 0$.

We are now able to give an interpretation of Theorem 2.4.1, part I:

If $v(\varrho)$, $0 \leqq \varrho < 1$, *is the solution of Dirichlet's problem for a given boundary function* $f_0 \in \mathsf{X}$, *i.e.* $v(\varrho) = V(\varrho) f_0$, *then* $v(\varrho)$ *also solves Neumann's problem for a function* $g_0 \in \mathsf{X}$ *if and only if* $\tilde{f_0} \in \mathsf{AC}_{2\pi}$, $(\tilde{f_0})' \in \mathsf{X}$ *and* $(\tilde{f_0})' = g_0$, *i.e.* f_0 *belongs to the domain* $\mathsf{D}(A)$ *of the infinitesimal generator.*

Conversely, if $v_N(\varrho)$, $0 \leqq \varrho < 1$, *is the solution of Neumann's problem for a given element* $g_0 \in \mathsf{X}$, *then* $v_N(\varrho)$ *solves Dirichlet's problem for a function* $f_0 \in \mathsf{X}$, *i.e.* $v_N(\varrho; g_0) = V(\varrho) f_0$, f_0 *being uniquely determined except for an additive constant. Furthermore,* $\tilde{f_0} \in \mathsf{AC}_{2\pi}$ *and* $(\tilde{f_0})' = g_0$.

Both assertions are immediate consequences of part *I* of the theorem. Indeed, by the properties of $\{V(\varrho); 0 \leqq \varrho < 1\}$, the relation

$$\lim_{\varrho \to 1-} \left\| \frac{f_0 - V(\varrho) f_0}{1 - \varrho} - g_0 \right\| = 0$$

[1] The index N in $v_N(\varrho; g_0)$ stands for Neumann to distinguish $v_N(\varrho; g_0)$ from the solution $v(\varrho; f_0)$ of Dirichlet's problem.

is equivalent to

$$\lim_{\varrho \to 1-} \left\| \frac{d}{d\varrho} V(\varrho) f_0 - g_0 \right\| = 0.$$

In case $X = C_{2\pi}$ (and similarly in case $X = L^1_{2\pi}$) we have the following essential generalization of Neumann's problem:

Given an element $g_0 \in L^\infty_{2\pi}$, *to find a function* $v_N(\varrho) = v_N(\varrho; g_0)$ *on* $0 \leqq \varrho < 1$ *to* $C_{2\pi}$ *such that*

(i) $v_N(\varrho)$ *is twice strongly continuously differentiable on* $[0, 1)$ *in* $C_{2\pi}$;

(ii) *for each* $\varrho \in [0, 1)$, $v_N(\varrho) \in D(U)$ *and*

$$\varrho^2 \frac{d^2}{d\varrho^2} v_N(\varrho) + \varrho \frac{d}{d\varrho} v_N(\varrho) + U v_N(\varrho) = \theta \qquad (0 \leqq \varrho < 1),$$

where the operator U *is defined by* $Uf = f''$ *and* $D(U) = \{f \in C_{2\pi}; f, f' \in AC_{2\pi}$ *and* $f'' \in C_{2\pi}\}$;

(iii) $$\text{w*-}\lim_{\varrho \to 1-} \frac{d}{d\varrho} v_N(\varrho; g_0) = g_0 \qquad (\textit{weak* convergence in } L^\infty_{2\pi})$$

$\left(\textit{or } \frac{d}{d\varrho} v_N(\varrho; g_0) \textit{ converges boundedly and almost everywhere as } \varrho \to 1-\right)$.

Regarding the existence and uniqueness of the solution of the *generalized Neumann problem* in $C_{2\pi}$, there hold the same conclusions as for the classical one except for the fact that g_0 now belongs to $L^\infty_{2\pi}$.

As for the interpretation of part II, the saturation case, we have:

If $v(\varrho)$, $0 \leqq \varrho < 1$, *is a solution of Dirichlet's problem for a given boundary function* $f_0 \in C_{2\pi}$, *then* $v(\varrho)$ *also solves the generalized Neumann problem for a function* $g_0 \in L^\infty_{2\pi}$ *if and only if* $f_0^\sim \in AC_{2\pi}$, $(f_0^\sim)' \in L^\infty_{2\pi}$ *and* $(f_0^\sim)' = g_0$, *i.e.* f_0 *belongs to the Favard class* $\mathscr{F}\{V(\varrho) - I; C_{2\pi}\}$.

Conversely, if $v_N(\varrho)$, $0 \leqq \varrho < 1$, *is the solution of the generalized Neumann problem in* $C_{2\pi}$ *for an element* $g_0 \in L^\infty_{2\pi}$, *then* $v_N(\varrho)$ *solves Dirichlet's problem, where the boundary function* $f_0 \in C_{2\pi}$ *is uniquely determined except for an additive constant. Furthermore, the approximation of* f_0 *by* $V(\varrho) f_0$ *is of order* $O(1 - \varrho)$.

An equivalent generalization is valid for $X = L^1_{2\pi}$, whereas for $X = L^p_{2\pi}$, $1 < p < \infty$, the generalized and the classical Neumann problem are identical, since these spaces are reflexive and the strong limit in condition (iii) of Neumann's problem is equal to the weak limit.

Below we set $f^{\{k\}} = f^{(k)}$, if k is even, and $= (f^\sim)^{(k)}$, if k is odd.

Theorem 2.4.3. *Let* $f \in X$ *and* r *be any fixed integer* > 0. *The following assertions are equivalent:*

(a) $f \in \mathsf{D}(A^r)$, *i.e.*

$$\begin{cases} f, f', \ldots, f^{(r-1)} \in \mathsf{AC}_{2\pi} \text{ and } f^{(r)} \in \mathsf{X}, \text{ if } r \text{ is even,} \\ f^{\sim}, (f^{\sim})', \ldots, (f^{\sim})^{(r-1)} \in \mathsf{AC}_{2\pi} \text{ and } (f^{\sim})^{(r)} \in \mathsf{X}, \text{ if } r \text{ is odd;} \end{cases}$$

(b)
$$\frac{1}{(1-\varrho)^r} \sum_{k=0}^{r} (-1)^{r-k} \binom{r}{k} V(\varrho^k) f$$

converges in X*-norm as* $\varrho \to 1-$;

(c) *there are functions* $g_{k,r} \in \mathsf{X}$, $k = 0, 1, \ldots, r-1$, *such that*

$$\frac{r!}{(1-\varrho)^r} \left\{ V(\varrho) f - \sum_{k=0}^{r-1} \frac{(1-\varrho)^k}{k!} g_{k,r} \right\}$$

converges in X*-norm as* $\varrho \to 1-$;

(d) $f \in \mathsf{D}(A^{r-1})$ *and*

$$\frac{r!}{(1-\varrho)^r} \left\{ V(\varrho) f - \sum_{k=0}^{r-1} \frac{(1-\varrho)^k}{k!} (-1)^{[(k+1)/2]} f^{\{k\}} \right\}$$

converges in X*-norm as* $\varrho \to 1-$.

The proof of this theorem follows by Theorems 1.5.10 and 2.2.13. One simple consequence of Theorem 2.4.3 is

Corollary 2.4.4. *A function* f *in* X *is equal to a constant if and only if*

$$\left\| \sum_{k=0}^{r} (-1)^{r-k} \binom{r}{k} V(\varrho^k) f \right\| = o[(1-\varrho)^r] \qquad (r = 1, 2, \ldots; \ \varrho \to 1-).$$

Similar conditions are valid for the Peano and Taylor differences, respectively. Furthermore, as a definite generalization of Theorem 2.4.3 we have

Theorem 2.4.5. *Let* $f \in \mathsf{X}$ *and* r *a fixed integer* ≥ 1. *The following are equivalent:*

(a) $f \in \mathsf{D}(A^{r-1})$ *and* $(f^{\{r-1\}})^{\sim}$ *belongs to* X *and as a function of* X *to* $\mathrm{Lip}(1; \mathsf{X})$;

(b) $$\left\| \sum_{k=0}^{r} (-1)^{r-k} \binom{r}{k} V(\varrho^k) f \right\| = O[(1-\varrho)^r] \qquad (\varrho \to 1-);$$

(c) $\|[V(\varrho) f]^{\{r\}}\| = O(1) \qquad (\varrho \to 1-)$;

(d) *there are functions* $g_{k,r} \in \mathsf{X}$ $(k = 0, 1, \ldots, r-1)$ *such that*

$$\left\| V(\varrho) f - \sum_{k=0}^{r-1} \frac{(1-\varrho)^k}{k!} g_{k,r} \right\| = O\left[\frac{(1-\varrho)^r}{r!}\right] \qquad (\varrho \to 1-);$$

(e) $f \in \mathsf{D}(A^{r-1})$ *and*

$$\left\| V(\varrho) f - \sum_{k=0}^{r-1} \frac{(1-\varrho)^k}{k!} (-1)^{[(k+1)/2]} f^{\{k\}} \right\| = O\left[\frac{(1-\varrho)^r}{r!}\right] \qquad (\varrho \to 1-);$$

(f) *for* $\mathsf{X} = \mathsf{C}_{2\pi}$: *there is a* $g \in \mathsf{L}^\infty_{2\pi}$ *such that*

$$(-|k|)^r f^\wedge(k) = g^\wedge(k) \qquad (k = 0, \pm 1, \pm 2, \ldots),$$

for $\mathsf{X} = \mathsf{L}^1_{2\pi}$: *there is a* $\mu \in \mathsf{NBV}_{2\pi}$ *such that*

$$(-|k|)^r f^\wedge(k) = \mu^\vee(k) \qquad (k = 0, \pm 1, \pm 2, \ldots),$$

for $\mathsf{X} = \mathsf{L}^p_{2\pi}$, $1 < p < \infty$: *there is a* $g \in \mathsf{L}^p_{2\pi}$ *such that*

$$(-|k|)^r f^\wedge(k) = g^\wedge(k) \qquad (k = 0, \pm 1, \pm 2, \ldots).$$

We know that in case $\mathsf{X} = \mathsf{L}^p_{2\pi}$, $1 < p < \infty$, condition (a) of Theorem 2.4.5 states that $f \in \mathsf{D}(A^r)$, which is nothing but condition (a) of Theorem 2.4.3. Thus Theorem 2.4.5 generalizes Theorem 2.4.3 essentially.

2.4.2 The Boundary Behavior for Dirichlet's Problem; Non-optimal Approximation

In this subsection we continue with a detailed investigation of equivalence theorems for non-optimal approximation for the solution of Dirichlet's problem.

To prove the following proposition we need a lemma concerning some properties of the Abel-Poisson kernel.

Lemma 2.4.6. *Let* $p(\varrho; u)$ *be the Abel-Poisson kernel* (1.5.17).

(i) $p(\varrho; u)$ *is even and non-negative for all* u *and* $0 \leqq \varrho < 1$;

(ii) $p(\varrho; u) \leqq \dfrac{2}{1-\varrho}$ *for all* u *and* $0 \leqq \varrho < 1$;

(iii) $p(\varrho; u) \leqq \pi^2 \dfrac{1-\varrho}{u^2}$ *for* $0 \leqq u \leqq \pi$ *and* $\dfrac{1}{2} \leqq \varrho < 1$.

Proof. The proof of this lemma is obvious by the following representation of the kernel

$$p(\varrho; u) = \frac{1-\varrho^2}{2\varrho(1-\cos u) + (1-\varrho)^2},$$

and the fact that $(1 - \cos u) \geqq (2/\pi^2)\, u^2$ for $0 \leqq u \leqq \pi$.

Proposition 2.4.7. *Let* $f \in \mathsf{X}$. *If* $f \in \mathrm{Lip}^*(\alpha; \mathsf{X})$ $0 < \alpha \leqq 1$, *then for the order of approximation of* f *by* $V(\varrho) f$ *as* $\varrho \to 1-$

$$(2.4.1) \qquad \| V(\varrho) f - f \| = \begin{cases} O[(1-\varrho)^\alpha] & (0 < \alpha < 1), \\ O\left[(1-\varrho) \log \dfrac{1}{1-\varrho}\right] & (\alpha = 1). \end{cases}$$

Proof. Since the Poisson kernel is non-negative and even, we obtain, setting $g(x, u) = f(x + u) - 2f(x) + f(x - u)$

$$[V(\varrho) f](x) - f(x) = \frac{1}{2\pi} \int_0^\pi g(x, u)\, p(\varrho; u)\, du,$$

and furthermore

$$\| V(\varrho) f - f \| \leqq \int_0^\pi \| g(\cdot, u) \| \, p(\varrho; u)\, du$$

$$= \frac{1}{2\pi} \left\{ \int_0^{1-\varrho} + \int_{1-\varrho}^{\pi} \right\} \| g(\cdot, u) \| \, p(\varrho; u)\, du = I_1 + I_2 .$$

Using the estimates (ii) and (iii) of Lemma 2.4.6 for the integrals I_1 and I_2, respectively, we have the desired result (2.4.1), where the large "O" depends on the given function f and on α.

Remark. In the next proposition we shall prove that Proposition 2.4.7 has a converse for $0 < \alpha < 1$. Thus the estimate (2.4.1) is best possible for this class. Even for $\alpha = 1$ the order of approximation deduced in (2.4.1) cannot be improved in general. Indeed, if $\mathsf{X} = \mathsf{C}_{2\pi}$, then it is known that the function

$$f_0(x) = \sum_{k=1}^{\infty} \frac{\cos k x}{k^2} \tag{2.4.2}$$

belongs to $\mathrm{Lip}(1; \mathsf{C}_{2\pi})$ and thus to $\mathrm{Lip}^*(1; \mathsf{C}_{2\pi})$ too. But

$$\| V(\varrho) f_0 - f_0 \| \geqq | [V(\varrho) f_0](0) - f_0(0) | = \sum_{k=1}^{\infty} \frac{1 - \varrho^k}{k^2}$$

$$= (1 - \varrho) \sum_{k=1}^{\infty} \frac{1}{k^2} \sum_{j=0}^{k-1} \varrho^j = (1 - \varrho) \sum_{j=0}^{\infty} \varrho^j \sum_{k=j+1}^{\infty} \frac{1}{k^2}$$

$$\geqq (1 - \varrho) \sum_{j=0}^{\infty} \frac{\varrho^j}{j+1} = \frac{1-\varrho}{\varrho} \log \frac{1}{1-\varrho} \qquad (0 \leqq \varrho < 1).$$

We need a further lemma.

Lemma 2.4.8. *If B denotes the operator d/dx with domain $\mathsf{D}(B) = \{f \in \mathsf{X};\ f \in \mathsf{AC}_{2\pi}$ and $f' \in \mathsf{X}\}$, then $V(\varrho) B f = B V(\varrho) f$ for all $f \in \mathsf{D}(B)$, $0 \leqq \varrho < 1$, and $V(\varrho)[\mathsf{X}] \subset \mathsf{D}(B)$ for all $0 \leqq \varrho < 1$. Furthermore,*

$$\| B V(\varrho) \| \leqq \frac{1}{2\pi} \int_0^{2\pi} | p'(\varrho; u) | \, du \leqq \frac{4}{\pi} \frac{1}{1-\varrho} \qquad (0 \leqq \varrho < 1), \tag{2.4.3}$$

and

$$\| B^2 V(\varrho) \| \leqq \frac{1}{2\pi} \int_0^{2\pi} | p''(\varrho; u) | \, du \leqq 4 \frac{1}{(1-\varrho)^2} \qquad (0 \leqq \varrho < 1). \tag{2.4.4}$$

Proof. By the definition of B and the known properties of $\{V(\varrho); 0 \leqq \varrho < 1\}$ it follows immediately that for an f in $\mathsf{D}(B)$ $V(\varrho) B f = B V(\varrho) f$ $(0 \leqq \varrho < 1)$ and that $V(\varrho)[\mathsf{X}] \subset \mathsf{D}(B)$ for all $0 \leqq \varrho < 1$. By the representations

$$[B V(\varrho) f](x) = [V(\varrho) f]'(x) = \frac{1}{2\pi} \int_0^{2\pi} f(u)\, p'(\varrho; x-u)\, du$$

and

$$[B^2 V(\varrho) f](x) = [V(\varrho) f]''(x) = \frac{1}{2\pi} \int_0^{2\pi} f(u)\, p''(\varrho; x-u)\, du$$

valid for all $f \in \mathsf{X}$ and $0 \leqq \varrho < 1$, one easily verifies the inequalities (2.4.3) and (2.4.4).

Proposition 2.4.9. *If f is a function in X such that*

$$(2.4.5) \qquad \| V(\varrho) f - f \| = O[(1-\varrho)^\alpha] \qquad (0 < \alpha \leqq 1;\ \varrho \to 1-),$$

then for $0 < \delta \leqq \pi$

$$(2.4.6) \qquad \omega^*(\delta; f; \mathsf{X}) = \sup_{0<|u|<\delta} \| f(\cdot + u) - 2f(\cdot) + f(\cdot - u) \| = O(\delta^\alpha).$$

Proof. By assumption (2.4.5) and the fact that $\| V(\varrho) f \| \leqq \| f \|$ for all $f \in \mathsf{X}$ and $0 \leqq \varrho < 1$, it follows that there is a constant $C > 0$ such that $\| V(\varrho) f - f \| \leqq C(1-\varrho)^\alpha$, $0 \leqq \varrho < 1$. Now we choose a sequence $\{\varrho_k\}_{k=0}^\infty$ such that $1 - \varrho_k = 1/2^k$ and denote by U_k the operator $V(\varrho_k) - V(\varrho_{k-1})$ for $k = 1, 2, \ldots$ Then

$$\| U_k f \| = \| V(\varrho_k) f - V(\varrho_{k-1}) f \| \leqq \| V(\varrho_k) f - f \| + \| V(\varrho_{k-1}) f - f \|$$
$$\leqq C\{2^{-\alpha k} + 2^{-\alpha(k-1)}\} \leqq 3C\, 2^{-\alpha k}.$$

Therefore,

$$V(\varrho_n) f = V(\varrho_0) f + \sum_{k=1}^n \{V(\varrho_k) f - V(\varrho_{k-1}) f\}$$
$$= f^\wedge(0) + \sum_{k=1}^n U_k f \qquad (V(\varrho_0) f = f^\wedge(0))$$

converges in norm to f as $n \to \infty$, i.e.

$$f = f^\wedge(0) + \sum_{k=1}^\infty U_k f.$$

To prove the proposition we have to estimate the second symmetrical difference of f

$$f(\cdot + u) - 2f(\cdot) + f(\cdot - u) = \sum_{k=1}^\infty \{[U_k f](\cdot + u) - 2[U_k f](\cdot) +$$
$$+ [U_k f](\cdot - u)\} = \sum_{k=1}^m \{\cdots\} + \sum_{k=m+1}^\infty \{\cdots\} = \Sigma_1 + \Sigma_2,$$

where m is some natural number.

First consider $\sum_1$. Applying Lemma 2.4.8, we obtain from

$$U_k f = V(\varrho_k) f - V(\varrho_{k-1}) f = V(\varrho_k)\{f - V(\varrho_{k-1}) f\} - V(\varrho_{k-1})\{f - V(\varrho_k) f\}$$

for $k = 1, 2, \ldots$

$$\begin{aligned}\|[U_k f]''\| &\leqq \|B^2 V(\varrho_k)\| \, \|f - V(\varrho_{k-1}) f\| + \|B^2 V(\varrho_{k-1})\| \, \|f - V(\varrho_k) f\| \\ &\leqq 4C\{2^{2k}\, 2^{-\alpha(k-1)} + 2^{2(k-1)}\, 2^{-\alpha k}\} \leqq 9C\, 2^{(2-\alpha)k}.\end{aligned}$$

Thus we obtain for $\sum_1$ by the mean value theorem and by the latter estimate

$$\begin{aligned}\left\|\sum\nolimits_1\right\| &\leqq u^2 \sum_{k=1}^{m} \|[U_k f]''(\cdot + \vartheta_k u)\| \qquad (-1 < \vartheta_k < 1) \\ &\leqq 9C\, u^2 \sum_{k=1}^{m} 2^{(2-\alpha)k} \leqq 9C\, u^2 \int_2^{2^{m+1}} s^{1-\alpha}\, ds.\end{aligned}$$

For $\sum_2$ we have the estimate

$$\left\|\sum\nolimits_2\right\| \leqq 4 \sum_{k=m+1}^{\infty} \|U_k f\| \leqq 12C \sum_{k=m+1}^{\infty} 2^{-\alpha k} \leqq 24C \int_{2^m}^{\infty} s^{-1-\alpha}\, ds.$$

Now, for a given δ, $0 < \delta \leqq 1$, we choose m such that $2^{m-1} \leqq 1/\delta < 2^m$. Consequently,

$$\omega^*(\delta; f; X) \leqq 9C\, \delta^2 \int_0^{4/\delta} s^{1-\alpha}\, ds + 24C \int_{1/\delta}^{\infty} s^{-1-\alpha}\, ds = O(\delta^\alpha),$$

where the O-constant depends on the given function f and on α. This proves the proposition.

Corollary 2.4.10. (a) *$V(\varrho) f$ approximates an element $f \in X$ with order $O[(1-\varrho)^\alpha]$ $(0 < \alpha < 1;\ \varrho \to 1-)$ if and only if $f \in \mathrm{Lip}(\alpha; X)$.*

(b) *If for an element $f \in X$ we have $\|V(\varrho) f - f\| = O(1-\varrho)$ $(\varrho \to 1-)$, then $f \in \mathrm{Lip}^*(1; X)$.*

Corollary 2.4.10 (a) is an equivalence theorem for non-optimal approximation. On the other hand, the method of proof of Proposition 2.4.9 is not strong enough to solve the saturation problem. Indeed, we know by Corollary 2.4.2 that the Favard class is given by the class of functions f in X for which $f^\sim$ belongs to X as well as to $\mathrm{Lip}(1; X)$. But the Favard class is a proper subspace of $\mathrm{Lip}^*(1; X)$. Indeed, for $X = C_{2\pi}$ this follows by the example given in (2.4.2).

Next we study the behavior of the derivatives of Poisson's integral.

Proposition 2.4.11. *Under the hypothesis of Proposition 2.4.9 we have*

$$(2.4.7)\qquad \|[V(\varrho) f]'\| = \begin{cases} O[(1-\varrho)^{\alpha-1}] & (0 < \alpha < 1;\ \varrho \to 1-) \\ O\left[\log \dfrac{1}{1-\varrho}\right] & (\alpha = 1;\ \varrho \to 1-), \end{cases}$$

and

(2.4.8) $\|[V(\varrho) f]''\| = O[(1-\varrho)^{\alpha-2}] \qquad (0<\alpha\leqq 1;\ \varrho\to 1-)$,

where the large "O"-constants depend on the function f and the index α.

Proof. We only show relation (2.4.7). As in the proof of Proposition 2.4.9 we obtain by (2.4.3) for the family of functions $\{U_k f\}_{k=1}^{\infty}$

$$\|[U_k f]'\| \leqq \|B\,V(\varrho_k)\|\,\|f - V(\varrho_{k-1}) f\| + \|B\,V(\varrho_{k-1})\|\,\|f - V(\varrho_k) f\|$$
$$\leqq \frac{4}{\pi} C\{2^k\, 2^{-\alpha(k-1)} + 2^{k-1}\, 2^{-\alpha k}\} \leqq 4C\, 2^k\, 2^{-\alpha k}.$$

Now, given a ϱ in $0\leqq\varrho<1$, we choose an n such that $2^n \leqq 1/(1-\varrho) < 2^{n+1}$. Then by the latter estimate

$$\|[V(\varrho_n) f]' - [V(\varrho_0) f]'\| = \Big\|\sum_{k=1}^{n} [U_k f]'\Big\| \leqq 4C \sum_{k=1}^{n} 2^k\, 2^{-\alpha k} \leqq 8C \int_1^{1/(1-\varrho)} s^{-\alpha}\, ds.$$

Furthermore,

$$\|[V(\varrho) f]' - [V(\varrho_n) f]'\| \leqq \|B\,V(\varrho)\|\,\|f - V(\varrho_n) f\| + \|B\,V(\varrho_n)\|\,\|f - V(\varrho) f\|$$
$$\leqq \frac{4}{\pi} C\{(1-\varrho)^{-1}\, 2^{-\alpha n} + 2^n (1-\varrho)^{\alpha}\}$$
$$\leqq 4C(1-\varrho)^{\alpha-1}.$$

Thus, because $V(\varrho_0) f = f^{\wedge}(0)$,

$$\|[V(\varrho) f]'\| \leqq \|[V(\varrho_0) f]'\| + \|[V(\varrho_n) f]' - [V(\varrho_0) f]'\| + \|[V(\varrho) f]' - [V(\varrho_n) f]'\| \leqq 4C(1-\varrho)^{\alpha-1} + 8C \int_1^{1/(1-\varrho)} s^{-\alpha}\, ds,$$

which proves the estimate (2.4.7).

Remark. The estimates given in (2.4.7) and (2.4.8) are of best possible order. For $0<\alpha<1$ this follows by Theorem 2.4.13 below. If e.g. $\mathsf{X} = \mathsf{C}_{2\pi}$, then the function

(2.4.9) $$g_0(x) = \sum_{k=1}^{\infty} \frac{\sin k x}{k^2}$$

is an element of the Favard class $\mathscr{F}\{V(\varrho) - I;\ \mathsf{C}_{2\pi}\}$, because its conjugate function belongs to $\mathrm{Lip}(1;\ \mathsf{C}_{2\pi})$ (cf. remark to Proposition 2.4.7). Thus $\|V(\varrho) g_0 - g_0\| = O(1-\varrho)$ $(\varrho\to 1-)$. But the derivative of $[V(\varrho) g_0](x)$ at the origin is equal to

$$[V(\varrho) g_0]'(0) = \sum_{k=1}^{\infty} \frac{\varrho^k}{k} = \log\frac{1}{1-\varrho}.$$

For the second derivative we have

$$[V(\varrho) g_0]''(x) = -\sum_{k=1}^{\infty} (\sin k x)\, \varrho^k = -\frac{\varrho \sin x}{1 - 2\varrho\cos x + \varrho^2}.$$

The extrema are at the points $x_0 = \arccos(2\varrho/(1+\varrho^2))$ and

$$|[V(\varrho)\, g_0]''(x_0)| = \frac{\varrho}{1+\varrho}\,\frac{1}{1-\varrho}.$$

Since the singular integral of Abel-Poisson defines a holomorphic semi-group operator we have upon applying Corollary 2.3.6 the following equivalence theorem for non-optimal approximation.

Proposition 2.4.12. *Let* $0<\alpha<1$. *The following assertions are equivalent for an element* $f \in \mathsf{X}$:

(i) $\|V(\varrho)f - f\| = O[(1-\varrho)^\alpha]$ $(\varrho \to 1-)$;

(ii) $\|[V^\sim(\varrho)f]'\| = O[(1-\varrho)^{\alpha-1}]$ $(\varrho \to 1-)$;

(iii) $\|[V(\varrho)f]''\| = O[(1-\varrho)^{\alpha-2}]$ $(\varrho \to 1-)$.

Indeed, this proposition follows by the fact that $A\,V(\varrho)f = -[V^\sim(\varrho)f]'$ and $A^2\,V(\varrho)f = -[V(\varrho)f]''$ for all $f \in \mathsf{X}$ and $0 \leqq \varrho < 1$.

Finally, combining all of the results for non-optimal approximation of a function $f \in \mathsf{X}$ by the singular integral $V(\varrho)f$, $0 \leqq \varrho < 1$, we have

Theorem 2.4.13. *Let* $0<\alpha<1$. *The following assertions are equivalent for an element* $f \in \mathsf{X}$ *as* $\varrho \to 1-$:

(a) $f \in \mathrm{Lip}(\alpha;\mathsf{X})$; (b) $f^\sim$ *belongs to* X *as well as to* $\mathrm{Lip}(\alpha;\mathsf{X})$;

(c) $\|[V(\varrho)f]'\| = O[(1-\varrho)^{\alpha-1}]$; (d) $\|[V^\sim(\varrho)f]'\| = O[(1-\varrho)^{\alpha-1}]$;

(e) $\|[V(\varrho)f]''\| = O[(1-\varrho)^{\alpha-2}]$; (f) $\|[V^\sim(\varrho)f]''\| = O[(1-\varrho)^{\alpha-2}]$;

(g) $\|V(\varrho)f - f\| = O[(1-\varrho)^\alpha]$; (h) $f^\sim \in \mathsf{X}$ *and* $\|V^\sim(\varrho)f - f^\sim\| = O[(1-\varrho)^\alpha]$.

The equivalence of (a) and (b) is a classical result of I. I. Privalov, the rest following from this assertion and the foregoing propositions.

2.4.3 Initial Behavior of the Solution of Fourier's Ring Problem

As the second example we consider again the solution $w(x,t)$ of the partial differential equation

$$\frac{\partial w}{\partial t} = \frac{\partial^2 w}{\partial x^2} \qquad (0 < x < 2\pi;\ t > 0)$$

with the boundary conditions

$$w(0,t) = w(2\pi,t), \qquad \frac{\partial w}{\partial x}(0,t) = \frac{\partial w}{\partial x}(2\pi,t)$$

and the initial condition

$$\lim_{t\to 0+} w(x,t) = f(x)$$

on the function space X, being equal to $C_{2\pi}$ or $L^p_{2\pi}$, $1 \le p < \infty$. We have seen in Sec. 1.5.2, specifically Theorem 1.5.3, that this problem is uniquely solved by the so-called singular integral of Weierstrass

$$w(x,t) \equiv [W(t)\,f](x) = \frac{1}{2\pi}\int_0^{2\pi} f(u)\,\vartheta_3(x-u;t)\,du \qquad (t>0),$$

where $\vartheta_3(\cdot;t)$ is Jacobi's theta function. Furthermore, the operator function $\{W(t); 0 < t < \infty\}$ defines a holomorphic contraction semi-group of operators of class $(\mathscr{C}_0)$ in $\mathscr{E}(X)$ with infinitesimal generator $[U\,f](x) = f''(x)$ having domain $D(U) = \{f \in X;\ f, f' \in AC_{2\pi}$ and $f'' \in X\} = \left\{f \in X; \sim \sum_{k=-\infty}^{\infty} k^2 f^\wedge(k)\,e^{ikx} \in X\right\}$.

Theorem 2.4.14. I. *If f and g belong to X such that*

$$\lim_{t\to 0+}\left\|\frac{W(t)f - f}{t} - g\right\| = 0,$$

then f and f' belong to $AC_{2\pi}$, $f'' \in X$ and $f'' = g$. In particular, if $\|W(t)\,f - f\| = o(t)$ $(t \to 0+)$, then $f =$ const.

II. *For an element $f \in X$ the following are equivalent:*

(a) $\|W(t)\,f - f\| = O(t) \qquad (t \to 0+)$;

(b) $\|[W(t)\,f]''\| = O(1) \qquad (t \to 0+)$;

(c) *for $X = C_{2\pi}$: there is a $g \in L^\infty_{2\pi}$ such that*

$$-k^2 f^\wedge(k) = g^\wedge(k) \qquad (k = 0, \pm 1, \pm 2, \ldots),$$

for $X = L^1_{2\pi}$: there is a $\mu \in NBV_{2\pi}$ such that

$$-k^2 f^\wedge(k) = \mu^\vee(k) \qquad (k = 0, \pm 1, \pm 2, \ldots),$$

for $X = L^p_{2\pi}$, $1 < p < \infty$: there is a $g \in L^p_{2\pi}$ such that

$$-k^2 f^\wedge(k) = g^\wedge(k) \qquad (k = 0, \pm 1, \pm 2, \ldots);$$

(d) $f \in \mathrm{Lip}^*(2; X)$, *i.e.* $\|f(\cdot + t) - 2f(\cdot) + f(\cdot - t)\| = O(t^2) \qquad (t \to 0+)$;

(e) $f \in AC_{2\pi}$, $f' \in X$ *and* $\|f(\cdot + t) - f(\cdot) - t\,f'(\cdot)\| = O(t^2) \qquad (t \to 0+)$;

(f) $f \in AC_{2\pi}$ *and* $f' \in \mathrm{Lip}(1; X)$;

(g) *for $f \in C_{2\pi}$: $f, f' \in AC_{2\pi}$ and $f'' \in L^\infty_{2\pi}$,*
for $f \in L^1_{2\pi}$: $f \in AC_{2\pi}$ and $f' \in NBV_{2\pi}$,
for $f \in L^p_{2\pi}$, $1 < p < \infty$: $f, f' \in AC_{2\pi}$ and $f'' \in L^p_{2\pi}$.

As a consequence we have

Corollary 2.4.15. *The singular integral of Weierstrass* $\{W(t);\ 0 \leqq t < \infty\}$ *defined on* X *is saturated with order* $O(t)$ $(t \to 0+)$ *and the Favard class* $\mathcal{F}\{W(t) - I;\, X\}$ *is given by anyone of the characterizations* (c)—(g) *of Theorem* 2.4.14.

As a generalization of Theorem 2.4.14 we have

Theorem 2.4.16. *Let* $f \in X$ *and* r *be any fixed integer* $\geqq 1$. *The following are equivalent:*

(a) *for* $X = C_{2\pi}$: $f^{(k)} \in AC_{2\pi}$, $k = 0, 1, \ldots, 2r-1$, *and* $f^{(2r)} \in L^{\infty}_{2\pi}$,
for $X = L^1_{2\pi}$: $f^{(k)} \in AC_{2\pi}$, $k = 0, 1, \ldots, 2r-2$, *and* $f^{(2r-1)} \in NBV_{2\pi}$,
for $X = L^p_{2\pi}$, $1 < p < \infty$: $f^{(k)} \in AC_{2\pi}$, $k = 0, 1, \ldots, 2r-1$, *and* $f^{(2r)} \in L^p_{2\pi}$;

(b) $$\left\| \sum_{k=0}^{r} (-1)^{r-k} \binom{r}{k} W(k\,t)\, f \right\| = O(t^r) \qquad (t \to 0+);$$

(c) $$\| [W(t)\, f]^{(2r)} \| = O(1) \qquad (t \to 0+);$$

(d) *there are functions* $g_{k,r} \in X$ $(k = 0, 1, \ldots, r-1)$ *such that*
$$\left\| W(t)\, f - \sum_{k=0}^{r-1} \frac{t^k}{k!}\, g_{k,r} \right\| = o\left(\frac{t^r}{r!}\right) \qquad (t \to 0+);$$

(e) $f^{(k)} \in AC_{2\pi}$ $(k = 0, 1, \ldots, 2r-3)$, $f^{(2r-2)} \in X$ *and*
$$\left\| W(t)\, f - \sum_{k=0}^{r-1} \frac{t^k}{k!}\, f^{(2k)} \right\| = o\left(\frac{t^r}{r!}\right) \qquad (t \to 0+);$$

(f) *for* $X = C_{2\pi}$: *there is a* $g \in L^{\infty}_{2\pi}$ *such that*
$$(-k^2)^r f^\wedge(k) = g^\wedge(k) \qquad (k = 0, \pm 1, \pm 2, \ldots),$$
for $X = L^1_{2\pi}$: *there is a* $\mu \in NBV_{2\pi}$ *such that*
$$(-k^2)^r f^\wedge(k) = \mu^\vee(k) \qquad (k = 0, \pm 1, \pm 2, \ldots),$$
for $X = L^p_{2\pi}$, $1 < p < \infty$: *there is a* $g \in L^p_{2\pi}$ *such that*
$$(-k^2)^r f^\wedge(k) = g^\wedge(k) \qquad (k = 0, \pm 1, \pm 2, \ldots);$$

(g) $$\|\Delta_t^{2r} f(\cdot)\| = O(t^{2r}) \qquad (t \to 0+);$$

(h) *there are elements* $h_{k,2r} \in X$ $(k = 0, 1, \ldots, 2r-1)$ *such that*
$$\|\Diamond_t^{2r} f(\cdot)\| = o\left(\frac{t^{2r}}{(2r)!}\right) \qquad (t \to 0+);$$

(i) $f^{(k)} \in AC_{2\pi}$, $k = 0, 1, \ldots, 2r-2$, $f^{(2r-1)} \in X$ *and*
$$\|\nabla_t^{2r} f(\cdot)\| = o\left(\frac{t^{2r}}{(2r)!}\right) \qquad (t \to 0+).$$

Theorem 2.4.16 contains the saturation theorems for the r-th Riemann difference of $\{W(t);\, 0 \leqq t < \infty\}$ as well as for the r-th Peano and Taylor differences, respectively.

Turning now to non-optimal approximation we have the following

Theorem 2.4.17. *Let* $0 < \alpha < 1$. *The following assertions are equivalent for an element* $f \in X$:

(a) $\| W(t) f - f \| = O(t^{\alpha})$ $(t \to 0+)$;

(b) $\| [W(t) f]'' \| = O(t^{\alpha - 1})$ $(t \to 0+)$;

(c) $f \in \mathrm{Lip}^*(2\alpha; X)$;

(d) *for* $0 < \alpha < 1/2$: $f \in \mathrm{Lip}(2\alpha; X)$,
for $1/2 < \alpha < 1$: $f \in AC_{2\pi}$ *and* $f' \in \mathrm{Lip}(2\alpha - 1; X)$.

The proofs of Theorems 2.4.14 and 2.4.16 are immediate consequences of the properties of the Weierstrass singular integral as given in Sec. 1.5.2 as well as of the results established in the previous sections of this chapter. The proof of Theorem 2.4.17 is similar to that of Theorem 2.4.13 for the integral of Abel-Poisson and shall be omitted (see also Corollary 4.1.16 of Sec. 4.1.3).

2.5 Approximation Theorems for Resolvent Operators

2.5.1 The Basic Theorems

It is the purpose of this section to study a number of connections existing between the semi-group of operators $\{T(t); 0 \leq t < \infty\}$ of class $(\mathscr{C}_0)$ in $\mathscr{E}(X)$ and the family of resolvent operators $\{\lambda R(\lambda; A); \lambda > \omega_0\}$ of the infinitesimal generator A, where $\omega_0 = \lim_{t \to \infty} t^{-1} \log \| T(t) \| < \infty$. Immediate connections follow by the inverse relations

$$\lambda R(\lambda; A) f = \lambda \int_0^\infty e^{-\lambda t} T(t) f \, dt \qquad (\lambda > \omega_0;\ f \in X)$$

and

$$T(t) f = \operatorname*{s\text{-}lim}_{\lambda \to \infty} e^{-\lambda t} \sum_{k=0}^{\infty} \frac{(\lambda t)^k}{k!} [\lambda R(\lambda; A)]^k f \qquad (t > 0;\ f \in X),$$

which result from Theorems 1.3.5 and 1.3.6, respectively. They are formulated in the following

Proposition 2.5.1. *Let* $\{T(t); 0 \leq t < \infty\}$ *be a semi-group of class* $(\mathscr{C}_0)$ *in* $\mathscr{E}(X)$. *A necessary and sufficient condition that* $T(t)$ *for all* $t > 0$

(i) *leave an element* $f \in X$ *invariant,*

(ii) *be a contraction operator,*

(iii) *be a positive operator,*

is that $\lambda R(\lambda; A)$ *have the corresponding property for all* $\lambda > \omega_0$.

Concerning condition (iii) of this proposition, we have to note that a subspace X_+ of X is called a *positive cone* if it is subject to the following conditions: (i) $f_1, f_2 \in X_+$ implies $f_1 + f_2 \in X_+$, (ii) $f \in X_+$, $\alpha \geqq 0$ implies $\alpha f \in X_+$, (iii) $\{f_n\}_{n=1}^{\infty} \in X_+$, $\text{s-lim}_{n\to\infty} f_n = f_0$ implies $f_0 \in X_+$. An operator $T \in \mathscr{E}(X)$ is then said to be *positive* if it maps X_+ into itself.

The main object here is to consider connections between semi-group operators and resolvent operators from the viewpoint of approximation. Thus we shall for example discuss the order of magnitude of $\|\lambda R(\lambda; A) f - f\|$, or more generally of $\|\lambda R(\lambda; A) f - \sum_{k=0}^{r-1} (A/\lambda)^k f\|$, as a function of λ for large values of λ, where f is some fixed element of X, or $D(A^{r-1})$, $r = 1, 2, \ldots$ More specifically, we shall compare the order of magnitude of the latter two quantities for large values of λ with those of $\|T(t) f - f\|$ and $\left\|T(t) f - \sum_{k=1}^{r-1} (tA)^k f/k!\right\|$, respectively, as a function of t for small values of t. In this respect we have as a first result

Proposition 2.5.2. *Let $\{T(t); 0 \leqq t < \infty\}$ be of class $(\mathscr{C}_0)$ in $\mathscr{E}(X)$, and let n be an arbitrary, but fixed positive integer.*

(a) *For all $f \in X$*

$$\lim_{\lambda\to\infty} \|\lambda R(\lambda; A) f - f\| = 0 \tag{2.5.1}$$

and, more generally,

$$\lim_{\lambda\to\infty} \|[\lambda R(\lambda; A)]^n f - f\| = 0. \tag{2.5.2}$$

(b) *If $f \in D(A)$, then*

$$\lim_{\lambda\to\infty} \left\|\frac{\lambda}{n}\{[\lambda R(\lambda; A)]^n f - f\} - A f\right\| = 0. \tag{2.5.3}$$

(c) *If $f \in D(A^r)$, r integral $\geqq 1$, then*

$$\lim_{\lambda\to\infty} \left\|\lambda^r \left\{\lambda R(\lambda; A) f - \sum_{k=0}^{r-1} \frac{A^k}{\lambda^k} f\right\} - A^r f\right\| = 0. \tag{2.5.4}$$

Proof. The limit-relation (2.5.2) follows by (2.5.1) (cf. (1.3.5) of Theorem 1.3.5) and by the identity

$$[\lambda R(\lambda; A)]^n f - f = \sum_{k=0}^{n-1} [\lambda R(\lambda; A)]^k \{\lambda R(\lambda; A) f - f\} \quad (f \in X), \tag{2.5.5}$$

since $\|[\lambda R(\lambda; A)]^k\|$ is uniformly bounded (cf. (1.3.8)). The proof of (2.5.3) in case $n = 1$ follows in view of the fact that $\|\lambda\{\lambda R(\lambda; A) f - f\} - A f\| = \|\lambda R(\lambda; A) A f - A f\|$, which tends to zero by (2.5.1) as $\lambda \to \infty$, and for general $n \geqq 1$ by the identity

$$[\lambda R(\lambda; A)]^n f - f - \frac{n}{\lambda} A f = \frac{1}{\lambda} \sum_{k=1}^{n} \{[\lambda R(\lambda; A)]^k A f - A f\} \quad (f \in D(A)), \tag{2.5.6}$$

making use of (2.5.2). Finally, relation (2.5.4) proceeds by the identity

$$\lambda R(\lambda; A) f - \sum_{k=0}^{r-1} \frac{A^k}{\lambda^k} f = \lambda^{-r+1} R(\lambda; A) A^r f \tag{2.5.7}$$

$$(\lambda > \max(0, \omega_0);\ f \in \mathsf{D}(A^r))$$

and (2.5.1) applied to $A^r f$ instead of f.

At this point we recall that the resolvent $R(\lambda; A)$ defines a holomorphic operator function in $\operatorname{Re}\lambda > \omega_0$, and thus in the foregoing proposition as well as in the following results the limit $\lambda \to \infty$, λ real, may be generalized to $|\lambda| \to \infty$ in any sector $|\arg \lambda| \leq \alpha_0 < \pi/2$. Yet there is no great loss in generality if we restrict the discussion to real λ.

Proposition 2.5.3. *Under the hypotheses of the foregoing proposition we have:*

(a) *If f belongs to X and if there is a $g \in \mathsf{X}$ such that*

$$\liminf_{\lambda\to\infty} \| \lambda\{\lambda R(\lambda; A) f - f\} - g \| = 0, \tag{2.5.8}$$

then $f \in \mathsf{D}(A)$ and $A f = g$. In case $g = \theta$, then $A f = \theta$ and $\lambda R(\lambda; A) f = f$ for all $\lambda > \omega_0$. The same conclusion holds if (2.5.8) *is replaced by the more general limit-condition*

$$\liminf_{\lambda\to\infty} \left\| \frac{\lambda}{n} \{[\lambda R(\lambda; A)]^n f - f\} - g \right\| = 0. \tag{2.5.9}$$

(b) *If f and g belong to X with $f \in \mathsf{D}(A^{r-1})$ such that*

$$\liminf_{\lambda\to\infty} \left\| \lambda^r \left\{\lambda R(\lambda; A) f - \sum_{k=0}^{r-1} \frac{A^k}{\lambda^k} f\right\} - g \right\| = 0, \tag{2.5.10}$$

then $f \in \mathsf{D}(A^r)$ and $A^r f = g$. If $g = \theta$, then $A^r f = \theta$ and $\lambda R(\lambda; A) f = \sum_{k=0}^{r-1} (A/\lambda)^k f$ for all $\lambda > \max(0, \omega_0)$.

Proof. (a) We prove at once the general case. To this end we investigate the expression

$$I(f; g) \equiv \frac{\lambda}{n} \{[\lambda R(\lambda; A)]^n - I\} \int_0^t T(u) f\, du - \int_0^t T(u) g\, du \qquad (t > 0).$$

Since

$$\|I(f; g)\| = \left\| \int_0^t T(u) \left[\frac{\lambda}{n} \{[\lambda R(\lambda; A)]^n f - f\} - g\right] du \right\|$$

$$\leq t \sup_{0\leq u\leq t} \|T(u)\| \left\| \frac{\lambda}{n} \{[\lambda R(\lambda; A)]^n f - f\} - g \right\|,$$

and since the last term tends to zero for at least one sequence $\{\lambda_k\}_{k=1}^{\infty}$, $\lambda_k \to \infty$, this yields

$$\underset{\lambda_k\to\infty}{\text{s-lim}} \frac{\lambda_k}{n} \{[\lambda_k R(\lambda_k; A)]^n - I\} \int_0^t T(u) f\, du = \int_0^t T(u)\, g\, du,$$

for each fixed $t > 0$. On the other hand, by Proposition 2.5.2 (b) the limit on the left-hand side equals $A \int_0^t T(u) f\, du = T(t) f - f$ since $\int_0^t T(u) f\, du \in D(A)$. Thus for each $t > 0$ $T(t) f - f = \int_0^t T(u)\, g\, du$ or $A f = g$ with $f \in D(A)$.

Regarding part (b), in view of the identity (2.5.7), the hypothesis (2.5.10) may be rewritten in the form

$$\liminf_{\lambda\to\infty} \| \lambda \{\lambda R(\lambda; A) A^{r-1} f - A^{r-1} f\} - g \| = 0.$$

Hence, the element $A^{r-1} f \in X$ satisfies the case $n = 1$ of relation (2.5.9), giving $A^{r-1} f \in D(A)$ and $A^r f = g$. If $g = \theta$ or $A^r f = \theta$, then on account of the identity (2.5.7) it follows that $\lambda R(\lambda; A) f = \sum_{k=0}^{r-1} (A/\lambda)^k f$ for all $\lambda > \max(0, \omega_0)$, and the proof of part (b) is complete.

A first significant result is the following

Theorem 2.5.4. *Let $\{T(t); 0 \leqq t < \infty\}$ be of class $(\mathscr{C}_0)$ in $\mathscr{E}(X)$. The following three assertions are equivalent for an element $f \in X$:*

(i) $\| T(t) f - f \| = O(t)$ $\quad (t \to 0+)$;

(ii) $\| \lambda R(\lambda; A) f - f \| = O(\lambda^{-1})$ $\quad (\lambda \to \infty)$;

(iii) $\| [\lambda R(\lambda; A)]^n f - f \| = O(\lambda^{-1})$ $\quad (\lambda \to \infty;$ *any fixed* $n \geqq 1)$.

If X is reflexive, then any of the latter three assertions is equivalent to

(iv) $f \in D(A)$.

In the course of the proof we need

Lemma 2.5.5. *Let $H(t)$ be a vector-valued function on $[0, \infty)$ to X, integrable in the sense of Bochner on every finite interval $[0, b]$, $b > 0$. If furthermore $\| H(t) \| \leqq C e^{\omega t}$ for any fixed $\omega \geqq 0$ and all $t \geqq 0$, C being a positive constant, then the condition*

(2.5.11) $$H(t) = O(t^{\gamma}) \quad (t \to 0+;\ \gamma > 0 \text{ fixed})$$

implies

(2.5.12) $$\left\| \lambda^n \frac{d^{n-1}}{d\lambda^{n-1}} h(\lambda) \right\| = O(\lambda^{-\gamma}) \quad (\lambda \to \infty;\ n \text{ any fixed integer} \geqq 1),$$

where $h(\lambda) = \int_0^{\infty} e^{-\lambda t} H(t)\, dt$ is the Laplace transform of $H(t)$.

Proof of the lemma. Under the given assumptions $h(\lambda)$ exists for $\lambda > \omega$ (moreover, $h(\lambda)$ defines a holomorphic vector function in the half-plane $\mathrm{Re}\,\lambda > \omega$, cf. Lemma 1.3.4 as well as App. 2). Now, in view of (2.5.11), there exist a $\delta > 0$ and a constant $M_1 = M_1(\delta) > 0$ such that $\|H(t)\| \leqq M_1 t^\gamma$ for all $0 < t \leqq \delta$. Hence

$$\left\| \lambda^n \frac{d^{n-1}}{d\lambda^{n-1}} h(\lambda) \right\| \leqq \lambda^n \left(\int_0^\delta + \int_\delta^\infty \right) t^{n-1} e^{-\lambda t} \|H(t)\| \, dt = I_1 + I_2 .$$

Applying the estimate available we have for $\lambda \to \infty$

$$I_1 \leqq M_1 \lambda^n \int_0^\delta t^{n-1} e^{-\lambda t} t^\gamma \, dt \leqq M_1 \lambda^n \int_0^\infty t^{\gamma+n-1} e^{-\lambda t} \, dt = O(\lambda^{-\gamma}) .$$

Regarding I_2, there is a constant $M_2 = M_2(\gamma, \delta) > 0$ with $C \leqq M_2 t^\gamma$ for $t \geqq \delta$. Therefore for $\lambda \to \infty$

$$I_2 \leqq C \lambda^n \int_\delta^\infty t^{n-1} e^{-\lambda t} e^{\omega t} \, dt \leqq M_2 \lambda^n \int_0^\infty t^{\gamma+n-1} e^{-(\lambda-\omega)t} \, dt = O(\lambda^{-\gamma}),$$

which proves the lemma.

Proof of Theorem 2.5.4. We first show that (i) implies (iii). From Corollary 1.3.3 and formula (1.3.4) of Theorem 1.3.5 we obtain immediately

$$[\lambda R(\lambda; A)]^n f - f = \frac{\lambda^n}{(n-1)!} \int_0^\infty e^{-\lambda t} t^{n-1} \{T(t) f - f\} \, dt .$$

We then apply Lemma 2.5.5 with $H(t) = T(t) f - f$ and $\lambda^n (d^{n-1}/d\lambda^{n-1}) h(\lambda) = (-1)^{n-1} \cdot (n-1)! \{[\lambda R(\lambda; A)]^n f - f\}$, where $\lambda > \max(0, \omega_0)$, $C = 2M_\omega \|f\|$ (cf. Proposition 1.1.2 (d)) and $\gamma = 1$. The result now follows.

Next we show that (iii) implies (ii). On account of the fact that the norm of $\mu R(\mu; A)$ is uniformly bounded for $\mu \geqq \omega > \omega_0$ we have

$$\left\| \frac{\lambda}{n} \{[\lambda R(\lambda; A)]^n - I\} \mu R(\mu; A) f \right\|$$
$$\leqq \|\mu R(\mu; A)\| \left\| \frac{\lambda}{n} \{[\lambda R(\lambda; A)]^n f - f\} \right\| = O(1)$$

as $\lambda \to \infty$ uniformly with respect to $\mu \geqq \omega$. Furthermore, since $\mu R(\mu; A) f$ belongs to $\mathsf{D}(A)$, by Proposition 2.5.2 (b)

$$\|\mu A R(\mu; A) f\| = \lim_{\lambda \to \infty} \left\| \frac{\lambda}{n} \{[\lambda R(\lambda; A)]^n - I\} \mu R(\mu; A) f \right\| = O(1)$$

for $\mu \geqq \omega > \omega_0$, or $\|\mu R(\mu; A) f - f\| = O(\mu^{-1})$ $(\mu \to \infty)$ giving (ii)

Finally, if (ii) holds, then equivalently $\| \lambda A R(\lambda; A) f \| = O(1)$ for $\lambda \geqq \omega > \omega_0$. Thus for a fixed $t > 0$

$$\| T(t) f - f \| = \lim_{\lambda\to\infty} \| [T(t) - I] \lambda R(\lambda; A) f \|$$

$$= \lim_{\lambda\to\infty} \left\| \int_0^t \lambda T(u) A R(\lambda; A) f \, du \right\|$$

$$\leqq t \sup_{0 \leqq u \leqq t} \| T(u) \| \sup_{\lambda \geqq \omega} \| \lambda A R(\lambda; A) f \| = O(t) \qquad (t \to 0+).$$

Hence (ii) implies (i). If X is reflexive, the equivalence between (i) and (iv) is given by Theorem 2.1.2, and the proof of the theorem is complete.

Corollary 2.5.6. *The family of resolvent operators* $\{\lambda R(\lambda; A); \lambda > \omega_0\}$ *on* X *is saturated with order* $O(\lambda^{-1})$ $(\lambda \to \infty)$, *the Favard class being equal to* $\mathscr{F}\{T(t) - I; \mathsf{X}\}$. *If* X *is reflexive, then the Favard class is* $\mathsf{D}(A)$.

The next theorem generalizes the results of Theorem 2.5.4 to the r-th Taylor difference.

Theorem 2.5.7. *The following assertions are equivalent for an element* $f \in \mathsf{D}(A^{r-1})$, $r = 1, 2, \ldots$:

(i) $$\left\| T(t) f - \sum_{k=0}^{r-1} \frac{t^k}{k!} A^k f \right\| = O\left(\frac{t^r}{r!}\right) \qquad (t \to 0+);$$

(ii) $$\left\| \lambda R(\lambda; A) f - \sum_{k=0}^{r-1} \frac{A^k}{\lambda^k} f \right\| = O(\lambda^{-r}) \qquad (\lambda \to \infty).$$

If X *is reflexive,* (i) *as well as* (ii) *is equivalent to*

(iii) $f \in \mathsf{D}(A^r)$.

Proof. At first we remark that for $\lambda > \max(0, \omega_0)$ and $f \in \mathsf{D}(A^{r-1})$

$$\lambda R(\lambda; A) f - \sum_{k=0}^{r-1} \frac{A^k}{\lambda^k} f = \lambda \int_0^\infty e^{-\lambda t} \left\{ T(t) f - \sum_{k=0}^{r-1} \frac{t^k}{k!} A^k f \right\} dt. \tag{2.5.13}$$

Now, setting $H(t) = T(t) f - \sum_{k=0}^{r-1} (t A)^k f / k!$, and consequently $\lambda h(\lambda) = \lambda R(\lambda; A) f - \sum_{k=0}^{r-1} (A/\lambda)^k f$, then Lemma 2.5.5 with $\gamma = r$ yields that (i) implies (ii). Conversely, the fact that (ii) implies (i) follows by the identity (2.5.7) and

$$T(t) f - \sum_{k=0}^{r-1} \frac{t^k}{k!} A^k f = \operatorname*{s-lim}_{\lambda\to\infty} \frac{\lambda}{(r-1)!} \int_0^t (t - u)^{r-1} T(u) A^r R(\lambda; A) f \, du.$$

If X is reflexive, the equivalence of (iii) and (i) is shown in Corollary 2.2.16.

2.5.2 Resolvents as Approximation Processes

We first consider the semi-group of left translations on the function spaces $UCB(\mathrm{E}_1^+)$ and $L^p(\mathrm{E}_1^+)$, $1 \leqq p < \infty$. Let X denote one of these spaces. As a companion to Theorems 2.1.6 and 2.2.25 as well as to Theorems 2.1.7 and 2.2.26, we may formulate

Theorem 2.5.8. (a) *If f is a function in X and if there is a $g \in X$ such that*

$$\liminf_{\lambda\to\infty} \left\| \frac{\lambda}{n} \left\{ \frac{\lambda^n}{(n-1)!} \int_0^\infty t^{n-1} e^{-\lambda t} f(\cdot + t)\, dt - f(\cdot) \right\} - g(\cdot) \right\| = 0$$

for any fixed integer $n \geqq 1$, then $f \in AC_{\mathrm{loc}}(\mathrm{E}_1^+)$, $f' \in X$ and $f' = g$. If $g(x) = 0$, then $\lambda \int_0^\infty e^{-\lambda t} f(x+t)\, dt = f(x)$, or $f(x) =$ const. in case $X = UCB(\mathrm{E}_1^+)$ and $f(x) = 0$ a.e. in case $X = L^p(\mathrm{E}_1^+)$.

(b) *If $f, f', \ldots, f^{(r-2)} \in AC_{\mathrm{loc}}(\mathrm{E}_1^+) \cap X$ and $f^{(r-1)} \in X$, $r = 1, 2, \ldots$, and if there is a $g \in X$ with*

$$\liminf_{\lambda\to\infty} \left\| \lambda^r \left\{ \lambda \int_0^\infty e^{-\lambda t} f(\cdot + t)\, dt - \sum_{k=0}^{r-1} \lambda^{-k} f^{(k)}(\cdot) \right\} - g(\cdot) \right\| = 0,$$

then $f^{(r-1)} \in AC_{\mathrm{loc}}(\mathrm{E}_1^+)$ and $f^{(r)} \in X$.

The proof follows by Theorem 1.3.16 and Proposition 2.5.3.

Theorem 2.5.9. (a) *The following assertions are equivalent for an $f \in X$:*

(i) $f \in \mathrm{Lip}(1; X)$, *i.e.* $\|f(\cdot + t) - f(\cdot)\| = O(t) \qquad (t \to 0+)$;

(ii) $$\left\| \frac{\lambda^n}{(n-1)!} \int_0^\infty t^{n-1} e^{-\lambda t} f(\cdot + t)\, dt - f(\cdot) \right\| = O(\lambda^{-1}) \qquad (\lambda \to \infty),$$

n being any fixed integer $\geqq 1$.

(b) *If $f, f', \ldots, f^{(r-2)} \in AC_{\mathrm{loc}}(\mathrm{E}_1^+) \cap X$ and $f^{(r-1)} \in X$, $r = 1, 2, \ldots$, then the following are equivalent:*

(i) $$\left\| f(\cdot + t) - \sum_{k=0}^{r-1} \frac{t^k}{k!} f^{(k)}(\cdot) \right\| = O\left(\frac{t^r}{r!}\right) \qquad (t \to 0+);$$

(ii) $$\left\| \lambda \int_0^\infty e^{-\lambda t} f(\cdot + t)\, dt - \sum_{k=0}^{r-1} \lambda^{-k} f^{(k)}(\cdot) \right\| = O(\lambda^{-r}) \qquad (\lambda \to \infty).$$

The proof is a direct consequence of Theorems 2.5.4 and 2.5.7. The assertions of parts (a) and (b) are moreover equivalent to those of Theorems 2.1.7 and 2.2.26, respectively.

We now return to the periodic singular integral of Weierstrass considered in Sec. 1.5.2 and 2.4.3. Under the notations and conventions of these sections, according to Proposition 1.5.2 the corresponding resolvent operator is given by

$$[R(\lambda; U) f](x) = \sum_{k=-\infty}^{\infty} \frac{1}{\lambda + k^2} f^\wedge(k)\, e^{ikx} \qquad (\lambda > 0;\ f \in \mathsf{X}), \tag{2.5.14}$$

which may be rewritten as the convolution integral

$$[R(\lambda; U) f](x) = \frac{1}{2\pi} \int_0^{2\pi} f(u)\, r(\lambda; x - u)\, du,$$

$$r(\lambda; u) = \frac{\pi}{\sqrt{\lambda}} \frac{\cosh \sqrt{\lambda}\,(u - \pi)}{\sinh \sqrt{\lambda}\,\pi}.$$

This leads us to a consideration of the singular integral $w^\dagger(\lambda, \cdot; f) = W^\dagger(\lambda) f = \lambda R(\lambda; U) f$, thus

$$w^\dagger(\lambda, x; f) = \frac{1}{2\pi} \int_0^{2\pi} f(u)\, r^\dagger(\lambda; x - u)\, du \qquad (\lambda > 0;\ f \in \mathsf{X}) \tag{2.5.15}$$

with parameter $\lambda \to \infty$ and kernel $r^\dagger(\lambda; u) = \lambda\, r(\lambda; u)$, $0 \leqq u \leqq 2\pi$, which is positive and satisfies $\int_0^{2\pi} r^\dagger(\lambda; u)\, du = 2\pi$. In view of (2.5.14) and the fact that

$$\lim_{\lambda \to \infty} \| w^\dagger(\lambda; f) - f \| = 0 \qquad (f \in \mathsf{X}),$$

which follows by Proposition 2.5.2 (a), $w^\dagger(\lambda, \cdot; f)$ may be regarded as a method of summation of the Fourier series of the function $f \in \mathsf{X}$ with convergence factor $\{\lambda/(\lambda + k^2);\ k = 0, \pm 1, \pm 2, \ldots\}$ for $\lambda \to \infty$. Furthermore, $w^\dagger(\lambda, x; f)$ satisfies the differential equation

$$\frac{\partial^2}{\partial x^2} w^\dagger = \lambda\, w^\dagger - \lambda f \qquad (0 < x < 2\pi;\ \lambda > 0)$$

with $\lim_{\lambda \to \infty} w^\dagger(\lambda, x) = f(x)$. Also, $w^\dagger(\lambda; f) = W^\dagger(\lambda) f$ fulfils the functional equation

$$\lambda_1 W^\dagger(\lambda_2) - \lambda_2 W^\dagger(\lambda_1) = (\lambda_1 - \lambda_2)\, W^\dagger(\lambda_1)\, W^\dagger(\lambda_2) \qquad (\lambda_1, \lambda_2 > 0).$$

More generally, we introduce for $f \in \mathsf{X}$, $n = 1, 2, \ldots$

$$w_n^\dagger(\lambda, x; f) = \frac{1}{2\pi} \int_0^{2\pi} f(u)\, r_n^\dagger(\lambda; x - u)\, du, \tag{2.5.16}$$

$$r_n^\dagger(\lambda; u) = \frac{(-1)^{n-1}}{(n-1)!} \lambda^n \frac{\partial^{n-1}}{\partial \lambda^{n-1}} \{\lambda^{-1} r^\dagger(\lambda; u)\}.$$

Obviously, $w_n^\dagger(\lambda; f) = [W^\dagger(\lambda)]^n f$ and $w_1^\dagger(\lambda; f)$ equals $w^\dagger(\lambda; f)$. For these singular integrals the fundamental approximation theorems read as follows, their proofs being obvious by Proposition 2.5.3 and Theorem 2.5.7.

Theorem 2.5.10. (a) *Let* $f \in X$. *If there is a* $g \in X$ *with*

$$\liminf_{\lambda\to\infty} \left\| \frac{\lambda}{n} \{w_n^\dagger(\lambda; f) - f\} - g \right\| = 0$$

for any fixed integer $n \geqq 1$, *then* $f, f' \in AC_{2\pi}$, $f'' \in X$, *and* $f'' = g$. *In particular if* $g(x) = 0$, *then* $f(x) = \text{const.}$

(b) *If* $f^{(k)} \in AC_{2\pi}$, $k = 0, 1, \ldots, 2r-3$, $f^{(2r-2)} \in X$, *and if for a* $g \in X$

$$\liminf_{\lambda\to\infty} \left\| \lambda^r \left\{ w^\dagger(\lambda; f) - \sum_{k=0}^{r-1} \frac{f^{(2k)}}{\lambda^k} \right\} - g \right\| = 0,$$

then $f^{(2r-2)}, f^{(2r-1)} \in AC_{2\pi}$, $f^{(2r)} \in X$ *and* $f^{(2r)} = g$.

Theorem 2.5.11. *Let* $f^{(k)} \in AC_{2\pi}$, $k = 0, 1, \ldots, 2r-3$, *and* $f^{(2r-2)} \in X$, $r = 1, 2, \ldots$ *The following assertions are equivalent:*

(i) $$\left\| w(t; f) - \sum_{k=0}^{r-1} \frac{t^k}{k!} f^{(2k)} \right\| = O\left(\frac{t^r}{r!}\right) \qquad (t \to 0+);$$

(ii) $$\left\| w^\dagger(\lambda; f) - \sum_{k=0}^{r-1} \frac{f^{(2k)}}{\lambda^k} \right\| = O(\lambda^{-r}) \qquad (\lambda \to \infty).$$

Combining this result with Theorem 2.4.16 we see immediately that the assertion (ii) is equivalent to any of the assertions (a)—(i) of the cited theorem. Finally, in the terminology of saturation theory the case $r = 1$ of Theorem 2.5.11 takes on the form

Corollary 2.5.12. *The singular integral* $w^\dagger(\lambda; f)$ *defined by* (2.5.15) *and associated with the function* $f \in X$ *is saturated with order* $O(\lambda^{-1})$ $(\lambda \to \infty)$. *The Favard class is characterized by the statements* (c)—(g) *of Theorem* 2.4.14 II.

In the foregoing considerations we compared the behavior of a semi-group of operators $\{T(t); 0 \leqq t < \infty\}$ of class $(\mathscr{C}_0)$ in $\mathscr{E}(X)$ with that of the family of resolvent operators $\{\lambda R(\lambda; A); \lambda > \omega_0\}$ of the infinitesimal generator A. In particular, if the saturation class of a specific semi-group is known, so is the saturation class of the corresponding family of resolvent operators and both classes are identical (Corollary 2.5.6).

Let us now begin with an operator function $\lambda \to S(\lambda)$ defined on the interval (ω, ∞) to $\mathscr{E}(X)$, ω being an arbitrary but fixed real number, i.e. let us consider a one-parameter family $\{S(\lambda); \lambda > \omega\}$ of bounded linear operators on X to itself. The question is to find conditions upon $S(\lambda)$ such that $\lambda S(\lambda)$, considered as an approximation process for $\lambda \to \infty$, may be connected with a suitable operator $T(t)$, $t \geqq 0$, satisfying the semi-group property with respect to t. More precisely, we wish to determine necessary and sufficient conditions upon the family

$\{S(\lambda); \lambda > \omega\}$ such that for each $\lambda > \omega$ $S(\lambda)$ is the resolvent of a closed linear operator A with domain $\mathsf{D}(A)$ dense in X, which generates a semi-group $\{T(t); 0 \leqq t < \infty\}$ of class $(\mathscr{C}_0)$ in $\mathscr{E}(\mathsf{X})$. In this respect we have

Theorem 2.5.13. *Necessary and sufficient conditions for a given family $\{S(\lambda); \lambda > \omega\}$ of operators in $\mathscr{E}(\mathsf{X})$ to be a family of resolvents of a closed linear operator A with dense domain in X to itself such that A generates a semi-group $\{T(t); 0 \leqq t < \infty\}$ of class $(\mathscr{C}_0)$ in $\mathscr{E}(\mathsf{X})$ are:*

(i) $S(\lambda_1) - S(\lambda_2) = (\lambda_2 - \lambda_1)\, S(\lambda_1)\, S(\lambda_2) \qquad (\lambda_1, \lambda_2 > \omega)$;

(ii) $\lim_{\lambda \to \infty} \| \lambda S(\lambda) f - f \| = 0 \qquad (f \in \mathsf{X})$;

(iii) *there is a constant $M > 0$ such that*

$$\| [S(\lambda)]^n \| \leqq M (\lambda - \omega)^{-n} \qquad (\lambda > \omega;\ n = 1, 2, \ldots).$$

In this case $\| T(t) \| \leqq M e^{\omega t}$ and

$$S(\lambda) f = \int_0^\infty e^{-\lambda t}\, T(t)\, f\, dt \qquad (\lambda > \omega;\ f \in \mathsf{X}).$$

Remark. If condition (iii) in the foregoing theorem is replaced by

(iii)′ $\lambda \| S(\lambda) \| \leqq 1 \qquad (\lambda > 0)$,

then the operator A generates a contraction semi-group.

For a proof we refer to the literature cited in Sec. 2.7.5. Note that condition (i) of the theorem is the resolvent equation for $\{S(\lambda); \lambda > \omega\}$, the essential condition (ii) assures the existence of an operator A such that $\{\lambda; \lambda > \omega\} \subset \varrho(A)$ with $R(\lambda; A) = S(\lambda)$, while condition (iii) finally gives that A generates the semi-group $\{T(t); 0 \leqq t < \infty\}$ (via Theorem 1.3.6). We observe that $T(t)$ may be obtained by anyone of the known inversion formulas.

As an example let us briefly discuss the singular integral

$$\text{(2.5.16)} \qquad v^\dagger(\lambda, x; f) = \frac{1}{2\pi} \int_0^{2\pi} f(u)\, p^\dagger(\lambda; x - u)\, du$$

$$\sim \sum_{k=-\infty}^{\infty} \frac{1}{\lambda + |k|} f^\wedge(k)\, e^{ikx} \qquad (\lambda > 0)$$

with kernel

$$\text{(2.5.17)} \qquad p^\dagger(\lambda; u) = \int_0^1 \frac{\varrho^{\lambda - 1}(1 - \varrho^2)}{1 - 2\varrho \cos u + \varrho^2}\, d\varrho$$

and associated with the function $f \in \mathsf{X}$, X being one of the spaces $\mathsf{C}_{2\pi}$

or $L^p_{2\pi}$, $1 \leqq p < \infty$. It may be shown that the integral $v^\dagger(\lambda; f)$ defines an operator $V^\dagger(\lambda)$ on X to itself: $v^\dagger(\lambda; f) = V^\dagger(\lambda) f$, which satisfies the relations (i), (ii) and (iii)′ of the aforesaid theorem. Thus there is a closed linear operator A with domain dense in X satisfying $\{\lambda; \lambda > 0\} \subset \varrho(A)$ and $R(\lambda; A) = V^\dagger(\lambda)$. This operator may easily be determined by $[A f]^\wedge(k) = -|k| f^\wedge(k)$, $k = 0, \pm 1, \pm 2, \ldots$, with $D(A) = \left\{f \in X; \sim \sum_{k=-\infty}^{\infty} |k| f^\wedge(k) e^{ikx} \in X\right\}$, or by Lemma 1.5.6: $A f = -(f^\sim)'$ with $D(A) = \{f \in X; f^\sim \in AC_{2\pi}$ and $(f^\sim)' \in X\}$, $f^\sim$ denoting the conjugate function of f. The corresponding semi-group operator may then be evaluated by an inversion formula and is given by $V(\varrho) f$, $0 \leqq \varrho < 1$, the singular integral of Abel-Poisson considered in Sec. 1.5.4, 2.4.1, and 2.4.2.

It follows that the theory of Sec. 2.5.1 may be applied to the singular integral $\lambda v^\dagger(\lambda; f)$. As a counterpart to the results of Sec. 2.4.1 we have

Theorem 2.5.14. (a) *If f and g belong to X with*

$$\liminf_{\lambda \to \infty} \| \lambda\{\lambda v^\dagger(\lambda; f) - f\} - g \| = 0,$$

then $f^\sim \in AC_{2\pi}$, $(f^\sim)' \in X$ and $(f^\sim)' = -g$; $g = \theta$ implies $f =$ const.

(b) *The following are equivalent for an $f \in X$:*

(i) $\| \lambda v^\dagger(\lambda; f) - f \| = O(\lambda^{-1}) \qquad (\lambda \to \infty)$;

(ii) *$f^\sim$ belongs to X and as a function of X to* $\mathrm{Lip}(1; X)$.

These considerations may also be applied to the singular integral

$$\lambda^n v_n^\dagger(\lambda; x; f) = \frac{(-1)^{n-1} \lambda^n}{2\pi(n-1)!} \int_0^{2\pi} f(u) \left\{ \int_0^1 \frac{(1-\varrho^2)\, \varrho^{\lambda-1} (\log \varrho)^{n-1}}{1 - 2\varrho \cos(x-u) + \varrho^2}\, d\varrho \right\} du,$$

n being any fixed positive integer.

2.6 Laplace Transforms in Connection with a Generalized Heat Equation

In this section we shall briefly discuss Cauchy's problem for a linear partial differential equation containing a derivative of fractional order, which includes as a particular case a boundary-value problem of the heat-conduction equation for a semi-infinite rod. This problem will be solved via the Hille-Yosida theorem (Corollary 1.3.8), this time using the Laplace transform as an important auxiliary means. Although the treatment of this broad field is rather fragmentary, the reader will obtain some ideas on the theory of fractional integration and differentiation in connection with semi-group theory.

In contrast to our notation introduced in Lemma 1.3.4, we denote the Laplace transform of a function $f \in L^1(0, b)$, each $b > 0$, by

$$f^\wedge(\lambda) = \mathfrak{L}[f](\lambda) \equiv \int_0^\infty e^{-\lambda t} f(t)\, dt \qquad (\lambda \textit{ complex}).$$

Also we must introduce the *Laplace convolution:* If f and g are two functions in $L^1(0, b)$, each $b > 0$, the integral

$$[f * g](t) = \int_0^t f(t-u)\, g(u)\, du = \int_0^t g(t-u)\, f(u)\, du$$

is called the (Laplace) convolution of f and g. $[f * g](t)$ exists for almost all $t > 0$ and
$$[f * g]^\wedge(\lambda) = f^\wedge(\lambda)\, g^\wedge(\lambda)$$
whenever each side is meaningful.

Furthermore, we need the concepts of fractional integration and differentiation.

Definition 2.6.1. *Let f be a real or complex-valued function defined on the positive real axis, and let $\gamma > 0$. The integral of order γ of f is defined by the convolution integral*

$$[J^\gamma f](t) = \frac{1}{\Gamma(\gamma)} \int_0^t (t-u)^{\gamma-1} f(u)\, du \qquad (t > 0). \tag{2.6.1}$$

Obviously, if f belongs to $L^1(0, b)$, each $b > 0$, then $J^\gamma f$ exists almost everywhere and belongs to the same space. The derivative of order $\gamma > 0$ of a function f is now defined indirectly through fractional integration.

Definition 2.6.2. *The derivative $J^{-\gamma} f$ of a function f of order γ, $n \leqq \gamma < n+1$ $(n = 0, 1, 2, \ldots)$, is defined by*

$$[J^{-\gamma} f](t) = \frac{d^{n+1}}{dt^{n+1}} [J^{n-\gamma+1} f](t), \tag{2.6.2}$$

whenever it exists.

In the following we shall restrict the discussion to functions f belonging to $L^p(E_1^+)$, $1 \leqq p < \infty$; moreover, we restrict the parameter γ to $0 < \gamma < 1$. The lemma below determines the connection of the fractional integral or derivative of a function with its Laplace transform.

Lemma 2.6.3. *Let $f, g \in L^p(E_1^+)$, $1 \leqq p < \infty$ and $0 < \gamma < 1$.*

(a) *The Laplace transform of the fractional integral $J^\gamma f$ is absolutely convergent for each λ,* $\mathrm{Re}\,\lambda > 0$, *and satisfies*

$$[J^\gamma f]^\wedge(\lambda) = \lambda^{-\gamma} f^\wedge(\lambda) \qquad (\mathrm{Re}\,\lambda > 0), \tag{2.6.3}$$

where the branch of λ^γ is taken such that $\mathrm{Re}\,\lambda^\gamma > 0$ *when* $\mathrm{Re}\,\lambda > 0$.

(b) *The representation*

$$\lambda^\gamma f^\wedge(\lambda) = g^\wedge(\lambda) \qquad (\mathrm{Re}\,\lambda > 0) \tag{2.6.4}$$

holds if and only if $J^{1-\gamma} f \in \mathsf{AC}_{\mathrm{loc}}(\overline{\mathrm{E}_1^+})$ *with* $[J^{1-\gamma} f](0) = 0$, $J^{-\gamma} f \in \mathsf{L}^p(\mathrm{E}_1^+)$ *and* $J^{-\gamma} f = g$.

We may now formulate and solve the Cauchy problem under discussion:

Let the operator B_γ, $0 < \gamma < 1$, with domain

$$\mathsf{D}(B_\gamma) = \{f \in \mathsf{L}^p(\mathrm{E}_1^+);\ J^{1-\gamma} f \in \mathsf{AC}_{\mathrm{loc}}(\overline{\mathrm{E}_1^+}),\ [J^{1-\gamma} f](0) = 0 \ \text{and}\ J^{-\gamma} f \in \mathsf{L}^p(\mathrm{E}_1^+)\} \tag{2.6.5}$$

and range in $\mathsf{L}^p(\mathrm{E}_1^+)$, $1 \leqq p < \infty$, be defined by

$$B_\gamma f = -J^{-\gamma} f. \tag{2.6.6}$$

Given an element $f_0 \in \mathsf{L}^p(\mathrm{E}_1^+)$, *to find a function* $w_\gamma(x) = w_\gamma(x; f_0)$ *on* $[0, \infty)$ *to* $\mathsf{L}^p(\mathrm{E}_1^+)$ *such that:*

(i) $w_\gamma(x)$ *is strongly continuously differentiable on* $(0, \infty)$;

(ii) *for each* $x > 0$, $w_\gamma(x) \in \mathsf{D}(B_\gamma)$ *and* $w'_\gamma(x) = B_\gamma w_\gamma(x)$;

(iii) $\lim_{x \to 0+} \| w_\gamma(x) - f_0 \|_p = 0$.

The method of solution of this problem is pointed out by the Hille-Yosida theorem. But first of all an intermediate result.

Proposition 2.6.4. *An equivalent characterization of the operator* B_γ *and its domain is given by*

$$[B_\gamma f]^\wedge(\lambda) = -\lambda^\gamma f^\wedge(\lambda) \qquad (\mathrm{Re}\,\lambda > 0) \tag{2.6.7}$$

with

$$\mathsf{D}(B_\gamma) = \{f \in \mathsf{L}^p(\mathrm{E}_1^+);\ \lambda^\gamma f^\wedge(\lambda) = g^\wedge(\lambda) \ \textit{where}\ g \in \mathsf{L}^p(\mathrm{E}_1^+)\}. \tag{2.6.8}$$

The proof is obvious by Lemma 2.6.3.

Proposition 2.6.5. (a) B_γ *is a closed linear operator with domain dense in* $\mathsf{L}^p(\mathrm{E}_1^+)$ *to* $\mathsf{L}^p(\mathrm{E}_1^+)$.

(b) *The set* $\{\sigma; \sigma$ *real* $> 0\}$ *belongs to the resolvent set* $\varrho(B_\gamma)$ *of* B_γ, *and the resolvent* $R(\sigma; B_\gamma)$ *is given by*

$$[R(\sigma; B_\gamma) f](t) = \int_0^t f(t-u)\, q_\gamma(u; \sigma)\, du \qquad (\sigma > 0;\ f \in \mathsf{L}^p(\mathrm{E}_1^+)) \tag{2.6.9}$$

where

$$q_\gamma(t; \sigma) = \frac{\sin \gamma\pi}{\pi} \int_0^\infty e^{-tu} \frac{u^\gamma}{\sigma^2 - 2u^\gamma \sigma \cos \gamma\pi + u^{2\gamma}}\, du. \tag{2.6.10}$$

Moreover,

$$\| R(\sigma; B_\gamma) f \| \leqq \frac{1}{\sigma} \| f \| \qquad (\sigma > 0;\ f \in \mathsf{L}^p(\mathrm{E}_1^+)). \tag{2.6.11}$$

Proof. (a) The linearity of B_γ is obvious by definition. To prove that B_γ is closed, suppose there is a sequence $\{f_n\}_{n=1}^\infty$ in $\mathsf{D}(B_\gamma)$ such that f_n and $B_\gamma f_n$ converge in L^p-norm to an f_0 and g_0 in $\mathsf{L}^p(\mathrm{E}_1^+)$, respectively. Then for each fixed λ, $\mathrm{Re}\,\lambda > 0$,

$$\lim_{n\to\infty} f_n^\wedge(\lambda) = f_0^\wedge(\lambda) \quad \text{and} \quad \lim_{n\to\infty} -\lambda^\gamma f_n^\wedge(\lambda) = g_0^\wedge(\lambda),$$

i.e. $-\lambda^\gamma f_0^\wedge(\lambda) = g_0^\wedge(\lambda)$, $\mathrm{Re}\,\lambda > 0$, or by Proposition 2.6.4, $f_0 \in \mathsf{D}(B_\gamma)$ and $B_\gamma f_0 = g_0$. Finally, it is easy to see that $\mathsf{C}_{00}^\infty(\mathrm{E}_1^+)$ is contained in $\mathsf{D}(B_\gamma)$. Thus, $\mathsf{D}(B_\gamma)$ is dense in $\mathsf{L}^p(\mathrm{E}_1^+)$.

(b) At first we shall prove that $\{\sigma; \sigma > 0\} \subset \varrho(B_\gamma)$, i.e. we have to show that for each $\sigma > 0$ the operator $\sigma I - B_\gamma$ on $\mathsf{D}(B_\gamma)$ to $\mathsf{L}^p(\mathrm{E}_1^+)$ has an inverse $[\sigma I - B_\gamma]^{-1}$ such that its domain $\mathsf{D}([\sigma I - B_\gamma]^{-1})$ is equal to $\mathsf{L}^p(\mathrm{E}_1^+)$ (since B_γ is closed). Obviously, $[\sigma I - B_\gamma]^{-1}$ exists for $\sigma > 0$, since the equation

$$\sigma f - B_\gamma f = \theta, \quad \text{or} \quad \sigma f^\wedge(\lambda) + \lambda^\gamma f^\wedge(\lambda) = 0 \qquad (\mathrm{Re}\,\lambda > 0),$$

implies $f(t)$ is equal to zero almost everywhere. Thus it remains to prove that for a given $g \in \mathsf{L}^p(\mathrm{E}_1^+)$ there is an $f \in \mathsf{D}(B_\gamma)$ such that

$$\text{(2.6.12)} \qquad \sigma f - B_\gamma f = g, \quad \text{or} \quad (\sigma + \lambda^\gamma) f^\wedge(\lambda) = g^\wedge(\lambda) \qquad (\mathrm{Re}\,\lambda > 0).$$

But the function $1/(\sigma + \lambda^\gamma)$ $(\mathrm{Re}\,\lambda > 0)$ is the Laplace transform of the function $q_\gamma(\cdot;\sigma)$ defined by (2.6.10):

$$\text{(2.6.13)} \qquad \mathfrak{L}[q_\gamma(\cdot;\sigma)](\lambda) = (\sigma + \lambda^\gamma)^{-1} \qquad (\mathrm{Re}\,\lambda > 0),$$

where $q_\gamma(u;\sigma)$ is non-negative, belongs to $\mathsf{L}^1(\mathrm{E}_1^+)$ and $\|q_\gamma(\cdot;\sigma)\|_1 = \sigma^{-1}$. Thus,

$$\text{(2.6.14)} \qquad f(t) = [R_\sigma g](t) = \int_0^t g(t-u)\, q_\gamma(u;\sigma)\, du$$

is the solution of the differential equation (2.6.12), i.e.

$$[\sigma I - B_\gamma] R_\sigma g = g \qquad (g \in \mathsf{L}^p(\mathrm{E}_1^+)).$$

Obviously,

$$R_\sigma [\sigma I - B_\gamma] f = f \qquad (f \in \mathsf{D}(B_\gamma)),$$

which proves that $\{\sigma; \sigma > 0\} \subset \varrho(B_\gamma)$ and $R(\sigma; B_\gamma) = R_\sigma$. Finally

$$\|R_\sigma g\|_p \leqq \|q_\gamma(\cdot;\sigma)\|_1 \|g\|_p = \sigma^{-1} \|g\|_p \qquad (g \in \mathsf{L}^p(\mathrm{E}_1^+)),$$

proving the estimate (2.6.11).

Theorem 2.6.6. *The given Cauchy problem has a unique solution* $w_\gamma(x;f) = W_\gamma(x) f$, $x \geqq 0$, *for each* $f \in \mathsf{L}^p(\mathrm{E}_1^+)$, *where* $\{W_\gamma(x); 0 \leqq x < \infty\}$ *is a contraction semi-group of class* $(\mathscr{C}_0)$ *in* $\mathscr{E}(\mathsf{L}^p(\mathrm{E}_1^+))$ *generated by* B_γ. *The solution is given by the singular convolution integral*

$$\text{(2.6.15)} \qquad [W_\gamma(x) f](t) = \int_0^t f(t-u)\, p_\gamma(u;x)\, du \qquad (f \in \mathsf{L}^p(\mathrm{E}_1^+))$$

with kernel

(2.6.16) $$p_\gamma(t;x)=\frac{1}{\pi}\int\limits_0^\infty \exp(t\,u\cos\theta - x\,u^\gamma\cos\gamma\,\theta)\times$$
$$\times\sin(t\,u\sin\theta - x\,u^\gamma\sin\gamma\,\theta+\theta)\,du \quad (x>0,\ t\geqq 0;\ \pi/2\leqq\theta\leqq\pi)$$

$0<\gamma<1$, *known as the Lévy stable density function on* E_1^+. *Furthermore,* $\{W_\gamma(x);\, 0\leqq x<\infty\}$ *is holomorphic.*

Proof. Since by Proposition 2.6.5 the operator B_γ on $\mathsf{D}(B_\gamma)$ to $\mathsf{L}^p(\mathrm{E}_1^+)$ satisfies the assumptions of the Hille-Yosida theorem, there exists by Corollary 1.3.8 a unique contraction semi-group $\{W_\gamma(x);\, 0\leqq x<\infty\}$ of class $(\mathscr{C}_0)$ in $\mathscr{E}(\mathsf{L}^p(\mathrm{E}_1^+))$ with infinitesimal generator B_γ. Via the inversion formula (1.3.14) we have for the operator $W_\gamma(x)$, $x\geqq 0$:

$$[W_\gamma(x)\,f]^\wedge(\lambda)=\lim_{\sigma\to\infty} e^{-\sigma x}\sum_{k=0}^\infty \frac{(\sigma^2 x)^k}{k!}\,[\{R(\sigma;B_\gamma)\}^k f]^\wedge(\lambda)$$
$$=\lim_{\sigma\to\infty} e^{-\sigma x}\sum_{k=0}^\infty \frac{(\sigma^2 x)^k}{k!}\,\frac{f^\wedge(\lambda)}{(\sigma+\lambda^\gamma)^k}$$
$$=\lim_{\sigma\to\infty}\exp\left\{-\sigma x+\frac{\sigma^2 x}{\sigma+\lambda^\gamma}\right\} f^\wedge(\lambda)=e^{-x\lambda^\gamma} f^\wedge(\lambda)$$

for each fixed λ, $\mathrm{Re}\,\lambda>0$, and all $f\in\mathsf{L}^p(\mathrm{E}_1^+)$.

Since

(2.6.17) $$\mathfrak{L}[p_\gamma(\cdot;x)](\lambda)=\exp(-x\,\lambda^\gamma)\qquad(x>0;\ \mathrm{Re}\,\lambda>0),$$

the representation (2.6.15) of the solution $W_\gamma(x)\,f$ follows. We remark that the density function $p_\gamma(t;x)$ is non-negative and arbitrarily often continuously differentiable on E_1^+ for each $x>0$, moreover, $p_\gamma(\cdot;x)\in\mathsf{L}^1(\mathrm{E}_1^+)$ and $\int_0^\infty p_\gamma(t;x)\,dt=1$ for each $x>0$. It remains to prove that $\{W_\gamma(x);\,0\leqq x<\infty\}$ is holomorphic, but this is omitted.

Finally, let us verify the uniqueness of the solution $w_\gamma(x;f)$ of the Cauchy problem by Laplace transform methods. Suppose there exists a non-trivial null-solution $w_{\gamma,0}(x)=w_\gamma(x;\theta)$. Hence for each fixed λ, $\mathrm{Re}\,\lambda>0$,

$$(d/dx)\,[w_{\gamma,0}(x)]^\wedge(\lambda)=[B_\gamma\,w_{\gamma,0}(x)]^\wedge(\lambda)=-\lambda^\gamma\,[w_{\gamma,0}(x)]^\wedge(\lambda)\quad(0<x<\infty)$$

and

$$\lim_{x\to 0+}[w_{\gamma,0}(x)]^\wedge(\lambda)=0.$$

The solution of the latter differential equation is given by $c(\lambda)\exp(-x\,\lambda^\gamma)$, where $c(\lambda)$ is determined by the foregoing limit-condition. This implies that $c(\lambda)=0$ for each λ, $\mathrm{Re}\,\lambda>0$, and consequently, $[w_{\gamma,0}(x)]^\wedge(\lambda)=0$ or $w_{\gamma,0}(x)=\theta$ for all $x\geqq 0$, which is a contradiction, proving the theorem.

For the particular case $\gamma = 1/2$ the Lévy stable density function is explicitly known:

$$p_{1/2}(x; t) = \frac{x}{\sqrt{4\pi}} \frac{\exp(-x^2/4t)}{t^{3/2}} \qquad (x > 0;\ t \in E_1^+), \tag{2.6.18}$$

and so the solution $w_{1/2}(x, t; f) = [W_{1/2}(x) f](t)$ of the Cauchy problem takes on the form

$$w_{1/2}(x, t; f) = \frac{x}{\sqrt{4\pi}} \int_0^t f(t-u) \frac{\exp(-x^2/4u)}{u^{3/2}}\, du \qquad (f \in L^p(E_1^+)). \tag{2.6.19}$$

The semi-group property of $w_{1/2}(x, \cdot; f)$ with respect to x is reflected in the functional equation satisfied by the kernel:

$$\frac{x_1 + x_2}{\sqrt{4\pi}} \frac{\exp[-(x_1+x_2)^2/4t]}{t^{3/2}} \tag{2.6.20}$$

$$= \frac{x_1 x_2}{4\pi} \int_0^t \frac{\exp[-x_1^2/4(t-u)]}{(t-u)^{3/2}} \frac{\exp[x_2^2/4u]}{u^{3/2}}\, du \qquad (x_1, x_2 > 0,\ t \in E_1^+).$$

Moreover, the corresponding resolvent operator is given by

$$[R(\sigma; B_{1/2}) f](t) = \int_0^t f(t-u) \left\{\frac{1}{\sqrt{\pi u}} - \sigma e^{\sigma^2 u} \operatorname{Erfc}(\sigma \sqrt{u})\right\} du \tag{2.6.21}$$

$$(\sigma > 0;\ f \in L^p(E_1^+)),$$

where $\operatorname{Erfc} u = (2/\sqrt{\pi}) \int_u^\infty e^{-v^2}\, dv$ is the complementary error function. The singular integral (2.6.19) is known to be the solution of the classical heat-conduction equation for a semi-infinite rod:

$$\frac{\partial w}{\partial t} = \frac{\partial^2 w}{\partial x^2} \qquad (x, t > 0)$$

with the initial condition

$$w(x, 0) = 0,$$

and the boundary conditions

$$w(0, t) = f(t) \quad \text{and} \quad \lim_{x \to \infty} w(x, t) = 0.$$

This is a proper boundary value problem. To be correct, the singular integral $w(x, t; f)$ is the unique solution of this problem in the following precise form:

Let the operator B with domain

$$D(B) = \{f \in L^p(E_1^+);\ f \in AC_{\text{loc}}(\overline{E_1^+}),\ f(0) = 0 \text{ and } f' \in L^p(E_1^+)\}$$

in $\mathsf{L}^p(\mathrm{E}_1^+)$ *to* $\mathsf{L}^p(\mathrm{E}_1^+)$ *be defined by* $B f = f'$. *Given any function* $f \in \mathsf{L}^p(\mathrm{E}_1^+)$, *find a function* $w(x) = w(x, \cdot; f)$ *on* $[0, \infty)$ *to* $\mathsf{L}^p(\mathrm{E}_1^+)$ *such that*

(i) $w(x)$ *is twice continuously differentiable in the norm on* $(0, \infty)$;

(ii) *for each* $x > 0$, $w(x) \in \mathsf{D}(B)$ *and* $w''(x) = B\, w(x)$;

(iii) *there is a constant* $M = M_f > 0$ *such that* $\| w(x) \|_p \leqq M$ *uniformly with respect to* x;

(iv) $\lim_{x \to 0+} \| w(x) - f \|_p = 0$.

Indeed, it is easy to see that $B = [B_{1/2}]^2$ with $\mathsf{D}(B) = \mathsf{D}([B_{1/2}]^2)$. Now, since $\{W_{1/2}(x); 0 \leqq x < \infty\}$ is a holomorphic contraction semi-group of class $(\mathscr{C}_0)$ in $\mathscr{E}(\mathsf{L}^p(\mathrm{E}_1^+))$ (Theorem 2.6.6), $w(x, \cdot; f) = W_{1/2}(x) f$ satisfies the conditions (i)—(iv) with $M_f = \| f \|$. Finally, condition (iii) guarantees the uniqueness of the solution.

We shall conclude with a brief consideration of the saturation problem for the semi-group $\{W_\gamma(x); 0 \leqq x < \infty\}$ in $\mathsf{L}^p(\mathrm{E}_1^+)$ as well as for the corresponding family $\{\sigma R(\sigma; B_\gamma); \sigma > 0\}$ of resolvent operators multiplied by the factor σ.

Theorem 2.6.7. I. *For an element* $f \in \mathsf{L}^p(\mathrm{E}_1^+)$, *the following assertions are equivalent:*

(i) $f \in \mathsf{D}(B_\gamma)$, *i.e. there exists a* $g \in \mathsf{L}^p(\mathrm{E}_1^+)$ *such that*

$$\lim_{x \to 0+} \left\| \frac{W_\gamma(x) f - f}{x} - g \right\|_p = 0;$$

(ii) *there is a* $g \in \mathsf{L}^p(\mathrm{E}_1^+)$ *with*

$$\lim_{\sigma \to \infty} \| \sigma \{\sigma R(\sigma; B_\gamma) f - f\} - g \|_p = 0;$$

(iii)
$$-\lambda^\gamma f^\wedge(\lambda) = g^\wedge(\lambda) \qquad (\mathrm{Re}\,\lambda > 0)$$

for some function $g \in \mathsf{L}^p(\mathrm{E}_1^+)$;

(iv) *there is a* $g \in \mathsf{L}^p(\mathrm{E}_1^+)$ *such that*

$$\lim_{\varepsilon \to 0+} \left\| \frac{1}{-\Gamma(-\gamma)} \int_\varepsilon^\infty \frac{f(\cdot - u) - f(\cdot)}{u^{1+\gamma}}\, du - g(\cdot) \right\|_p = 0;$$

(v) $J^{1-\gamma} f \in \mathsf{AC}_{\mathrm{loc}}(\overline{\mathrm{E}_1^+})$, $[J^{1-\gamma} f](0) = 0$ *and* $J^{-\gamma} f \in \mathsf{L}^p(\mathrm{E}_1^+)$.

Moreover, the function g *occurring in the assertions* (i)—(iv) *is equal to* $-J^{-\gamma} f$. *If, in particular,* $g(t) = 0$ *a.e., then* $f(t)$ *is also equal to zero almost everywhere.*

II. *A function* $f \in \mathsf{L}^p(\mathrm{E}_1^+)$ *belongs to the Favard class* $\mathscr{F}\{W_\gamma(x) - I; \mathsf{L}^p(\mathrm{E}_1^+)\}$ *if and only if anyone of the following conditions is satisfied:*

(i) $\|W_\gamma(x) f - f\|_p = O(x) \qquad (x \to 0+)$;

(ii) $\|\sigma R(\sigma; B_\gamma) f - f\|_p = O(\sigma^{-1}) \qquad (\sigma \to \infty)$;

(iii) $$\left\| \frac{1}{-\Gamma(-\gamma)} \int\limits_\varepsilon^\infty \frac{f(\cdot - u) - f(\cdot)}{u^{1+\gamma}}\, du \right\|_p = O(1) \qquad (\varepsilon \to 0+);$$

moreover, for $p = 1$:

(iv) *there is a* $\mu \in \mathsf{BV}(\overline{\mathrm{E}_1^+})$ *such that*

$$-\lambda^\gamma f^\wedge(\lambda) = \mu^\vee(\lambda) \equiv \int\limits_0^\infty e^{-\lambda t}\, d\mu(t) \qquad (\mathrm{Re}\,\lambda > 0);$$

(v) $J^{1-\gamma} f \in \mathsf{BV}(\overline{\mathrm{E}_1^+})$ *with* $[J^{1-\gamma} f](0) = 0$,

while for $1 < p < \infty$: *anyone of the conditions* (i)—(v) *of part I of the theorem.*

The theorem is partially proven by the results obtained in this section as well as by the general saturation theorems of this chapter. For the remaining parts we refer to the literature given in Sec. 2.7.6 on "Notes and Remarks".

2.7 Notes and Remarks

2.7.1 The material of this chapter, treating approximation theoretical questions for semi-groups of operators on Banach spaces has, apart from Theorem 2.1.2, not appeared in book-form before.

The concept of saturation was first introduced by the late French mathematician J. FAVARD [2; 3] in 1947 for summation methods of Fourier series. It was formulated for semi-group operators on Banach spaces by P. L. BUTZER [3; 4] in 1956. Theorem 2.1.2 as a whole was first given by P. L. BUTZER [4], while parts (a) (in case $g = \theta$) and (b) go back to E. HILLE [4, pp. 323—324]. As a matter of fact, part (a) was already established by E. HILLE [1] in 1936 for some special semi-groups and actually led Hille to his first investigations of the theory. Theorem 2.1.2, which plays a central role in the chapter, has also been incorporated into the revised edition of Hille's book, see H.-PH. [1, p. 326]. The hypothesis of reflexivity of the space X in Corollary 2.1.3, which solves the saturation problem for strongly continuous semi-groups of operators on such spaces, is indispensable. The counterpart of Theorem 2.1.2 for dual semi-groups, namely Theorem 2.1.4, is due to K. DE LEEUW [2]. In particular, this theorem solves the saturation problem for certain non-reflexive Banach spaces, namely those which are isometrically isomorphic to the restriction X_0^* of X^* with respect to the semi-group. But all the examples considered in our monograph have this property.

The original theorem of Titchmarsh cited in Sec. 2.1.2 may be found in E. C. TITCHMARSH [1], with a shorter proof in E. C. TITCHMARSH [3, p. 371]. For the periodic version see A. ZYGMUND [5, Vol. I p. 45]. The equivalence of the assertions (i) and (iii) of parts (b) and (c) of Theorem 2.1.7 for periodic functions was shown by G. H. HARDY-J. E. LITTLEWOOD [1, I. p. 599; 2, p. 619]. See also E. C. TITCHMARSH [3, p. 372] in the case of functions defined on a finite interval. For a different proof in the periodic case see also A. ZYGMUND [5, Vol. I p. 180]. For further classical proofs of such results we refer to V. P. IL'IN [1] and L. CUPELLO [1]. The semi-group approach to Theorems 2.1.6 and 2.1.7(c) is brought up in P. L. BUTZER [8] and gives a general and unified presentation of the results as well as of the proofs.

There is another method in proving Theorems 2.1.6 and 2.1.7 for functions belonging either to $L^p(E_1)$, $1 \leqq p \leqq 2$, or to $C_{2\pi}$ and $L^p_{2\pi}$, $1 \leqq p < \infty$, respectively. In the former case it is the Fourier transform method, introduced into approximation theory by P. L. BUTZER [5; 6; 7; 11; 12], and in the latter case it is the dual finite Fourier transform (or Fourier coefficient) method of G. SUNOUCHI-C. WATARI [1] (see also G. SUNOUCHI [2]). For Fourier transform methods in solving problems of approximation we refer the reader to the monograph by P. L. BUTZER–R. J. NESSEL [3].

2.7.2 The material of Sec. 2.2.1 and 2.2.2 is largely taken from P. L. BUTZER-H. G. TILLMANN [1; 2] and H. BERENS [2]. The definition of the r-th Taylor operator B^r ($r = 1, 2, \ldots$) through (2.2.1) was suggested by some work of TH. CHAUNDY [1, p. 117] on "umbral" derivatives. It should be compared with Definition 2.2.22 of the r-th Taylor derivative of a scalar-valued function. The r-th Peano operator P^r, given by H. BERENS [2], naturally has its roots in the concept of the Peano derivative of order r (Definition 2.2.21), due to G. PEANO [1, pp. 204—209]. The notion of the classical Riemann derivative of order r (cf. (2.2.14)), which plays an important role in the uniqueness theory of trigonometric series (see e.g. A. ZYGMUND [5, Vol. I Ch. IX]), suggested the introduction of the r-th Riemann operator C^r of Definition 2.2.8.

The fundamental saturation theorem for the family of operators $\{[T(t) - I]^r\}$ connected with C^r (Corollary 2.2.15) is due to H. BERENS [2], while Corollary 2.2.17, the counterpart for the family $\{T(t) - \sum_{k=0}^{r-1} (t^k/k!)\, A^k\}$, goes back to an earlier paper by P. L. BUTZER-H. G.

TILLMANN [2]. For generalizations of Corollary 2.2.17 to semi-groups on locally convex spaces as well as to distribution semi-groups on Banach spaces see H. G. TILLMANN [1] and J. LÖFSTRÖM [1], respectively. Concerning Theorem 2.2.19 we remark that the idea of using linear combinations of approximation processes is not novel. A famous example is the summation method of Ch. de La Vallée-Poussin of a Fourier series (cf. A. ZYGMUND [5, Vol. I p. 115]). Linear combinations of singular convolution integrals have been studied by I. P. NATANSON [2] as well as by P. L. BUTZER [6], so as to give a proof of D. Jackson's "direct theorem" in the theory of best trigonometric approximation (see the remarks in Sec. 2.7.3).

The material of Sec. 2.2.3 has its origin in a paper by P. L. BUTZER [10]. For the proofs of the theorems of this section using the semi-group approach, see H. BERENS [2]. Theorem 2.2.23 was proven for the spaces $L^p(E_1)$, $1 \leq p \leq 2$, and $C_{2\pi}$, $L^p_{2\pi}$ $(1 \leq p < \infty)$ by P. L. BUTZER [10] using Fourier transform and Fourier coefficient methods, respectively. Theorem 2.2.25 for the various function spaces has been shown by E. GÖRLICH-R. J. NESSEL [1] by distribution theoretical methods. The examples (2.2.17) and (2.2.18) are given in TH. CHAUNDY [1, p. 119 and p. 137]. The importance of Theorem 2.2.26 lies not only in the fact that it is a deep generalization of the results of Hardy-Littlewood but also that the same proofs deliver analogous results for the function spaces defined on E_1 as well as for the periodic case. For questions involving the derivative of a function of one variable and its generalizations we also refer to the expository article by A. M. BRUCKNER–J. L. LEONARD [1] which contains a lengthy bibliography.

2.7.3 Direct and converse theorems concerning non-optimal approximation in semi-group theory as well as associated equivalence theorems were first considered in the doctoral dissertation [1] of H. BERENS (see also H. BERENS–P. L. BUTZER [2]). This problem was posed by P. L. BUTZER [4] in 1957, while a simple direct result was already formulated in HILLE [4, p. 324]: *If $\{T(t);\ 0 < t < \infty\}$ is a strongly continuous semi-group on a Banach space X and if $g \in X$ is of the form*

$$g = \int_a^b (b-u)^{\alpha-1}\, T(u)\, f\, du \qquad \text{with } f \in X,$$

where a, b and α are fixed $0 < a < b$, $0 < \alpha < 1$, then $\|T(t)\,g - g\| = O(t^\alpha)$ $(t \to 0+)$. Actually one can prove that $\|T(t)\,g - g\| = o(t^\alpha)$ $(t \to 0+)$. Special results, in particular for the singular integral of Abel-Poisson on the periodic function spaces were already treated in 1928–1932 by G. H. HARDY–J. E. LITTLEWOOD [1] and in 1945–1946 by A. ZYGMUND [3] and R. SALEM–A. ZYGMUND [1]. See Sec. 2.4.2 as well as the remarks in Sec. 2.7.4 below.

The method of proof of the major converse theorem (Theorem 2.3.5) was, in fact, suggested by a result on derivatives of trigonometric polynomials due to M. ZAMANSKY [1].

The Lipschitz classes of periodic functions defined in Sec. 2.3.2 play an important role in the theory of best approximation of functions by trigonometric polynomials. If X is one of the spaces $C_{2\pi}$ or $L^p_{2\pi}$, $1 \leqq p < \infty$, and if $E_n[f; X]$, $n = 0, 1, \ldots$, denotes the best approximation of $f \in X$ by such polynomials of order n in the X-metric:

$$E_n[f; X] = \inf\left\{\|f - p_n\|;\ p_n(x) = \sum_{k=-n}^{n} c_k\, e^{ikx}\right\},$$

then for $0 < \alpha < 1$ the class $\mathrm{Lip}(\alpha; X)$ is identical to the class of functions $f \in X$ with $E_n[f; X] = O(n^{-\alpha})$. More precisely, there are two positive constants C_1 and C_2, such that for all $f \in \mathrm{Lip}(\alpha; X)$

$$C_1 \sup_{n=1,2,\ldots} (n^\alpha E_n[f; X]) \leqq \sup_{0<|t|<\pi} (|t|^{-\alpha} \|f(\cdot + t) - f(\cdot)\|) \leqq C_2 \sup_{n=1,2,\ldots} (n^\alpha E_n[f; X]).$$

The left and right-hand inequalities here are the fundamental direct and converse theorems of classical approximation theory due to D. Jackson and S. Bernstein, respectively, dating back to 1911—1912. (cf. CH. J. DE LA VALLÉE-POUSSIN [1, Ch. III—IV], N. I. ACHIESER [1], I. P. NATANSON [1], A. F. TIMAN [1], E. W. CHENEY [1] and G. G. LORENTZ [5]) (Actually the method of proof of the result of M. Zamansky mentioned above is based upon that of Bernstein's theorem). On the other hand, the class $\mathrm{Lip}^*(1; X)$ appears in a natural way if one attempts to generalize the preceding results to $\alpha = 1$. Indeed, A. ZYGMUND [2] has shown in 1945 that the class $\mathrm{Lip}^*(1; X)$ is identical with the class $\{f \in X;\ E_n[f; X] = O(n^{-1})\}$, or for all $f \in \mathrm{Lip}^*(1; X)$

$$C_3 \sup_{n=1,2,\ldots} (n\, E_n[f; X]) \leqq \sup_{0<|t|<\pi} (|t|^{-1} \|f(\cdot + t) - 2f(\cdot) + f(\cdot - t)\|) \leqq C_4 \sup_{n=1,2,\ldots} (n\, E_n[f; X]) \quad (C_3, C_4 \text{ constants}).$$

Moreover, f is in $\mathrm{lip}(\alpha; X)$, $0 < \alpha < 1$, if and only if $E_n[f; X] = o(n^{-\alpha})$ $(n \to \infty)$, while $f \in \mathrm{lip}^*(1; X)$ precisely when $E_n[f; X] = o(n^{-1})$ $(n \to \infty)$. For further details see the remarks in Sec. 4.4.1.

Finally, let us mention some interesting recent results in connection with Lipschitz classes. It is known that the classes $\mathrm{Lip}(\alpha; X)$, $0 < \alpha \leqq 1$, become Banach spaces under the norm

$$\|f\| + \sup_{0<|t|<\pi} (|t|^{-\alpha} \|f(\cdot + t) - f(\cdot)\|).$$

In [1] H. MIRKIL has in particular shown that a function $f \in \mathrm{Lip}(\alpha; X)$, $0 < \alpha < 1$, belongs to $\mathrm{lip}(\alpha; X)$ if and only if f is continuous under translations in the $\mathrm{Lip}(\alpha; X)$-norm, while a function f is in $AC_{2\pi}$ with $f' \in X$ if and only if $f \in \mathrm{Lip}(1; X)$ and f is continuous under translations in the $\mathrm{Lip}(1; X)$-norm (see also Sec. 4.1.1 for a proof). Furthermore, K. DE LEEUW [3] proved that the second dual of $\mathrm{lip}(\alpha; C_{2\pi})$, $0 < \alpha < 1$, is isometrically isomorphic to $\mathrm{Lip}(\alpha; C_{2\pi})$ (see also Z. CIESIELSKI [1]); he also studied the extreme points of the unit sphere in $(\mathrm{lip}(\alpha; C_{2\pi}))^*$. Let us at last indicate a result of Z. CIESIELSKI [1] stating that a function $f \in C[0, 1]$ belongs to $\mathrm{Lip}(\alpha; C[0, 1])$ for $0 < \alpha < 1$ if and only if its Schauder polygonal expansion is given by

$$f(x) \sim \sum a_n n^{-\alpha+1/2} \varphi_n(x),$$

where $\{a_n\}$ is a bounded sequence. The functions φ_n are integrals of the Haar orthogonal functions. Hence, the map $f \to \{a_n\}$ is an isomorphism from $\mathrm{Lip}(\alpha; C[0, 1])$ onto m, the space of bounded sequences. Ciesielski also proved that $\mathrm{lip}(\alpha; C[0, 1])$, $0 < \alpha < 1$, is isomorphic to c_0, the space of bounded sequences tending to zero. The fact that $\mathrm{Lip}(1; C[0, 1])$, and m are isomorphic is due to A. PEŁCZYŃSKI [1]. In this direction there is an old result of H. LEBESGUE (see e.g. A. ZYGMUND [5, Vol. I p. 46]) stating that if $f \in \mathrm{Lip}(\alpha; X)$, $0 < \alpha \leqq 1$, then the Fourier coefficients satisfy $f^\wedge(k) = O(|k|^{-\alpha})$ $(|k| \to \infty)$. Any converse result is as far as we know still open except for the case $X = L^2_{2\pi}$, where $f \in \mathrm{Lip}(\alpha; L^2_{2\pi})$, $0 < \alpha < 1$, if and only if $\{\sum_{|k| \geqq n+1} |f^\wedge(k)|^2\}^{1/2} = O(n^{-\alpha})$ (cf. N. I. ACHIESER [1, p. 170]). Here $\{\sum_{k \geqq n+1} |f^\wedge(k)|^2\}^{1/2}$ is equal to $E_n[f; L^2_{2\pi}]$. See furthermore R. P. BOAS, JR. [1].

2.7.4 Part I of Theorem 2.4.1 was shown by A. ZYGMUND [3] in 1945 using an elementary Fourier coefficient device (see also E. HILLE [4, p. 352]). Furthermore, the fact that (c) implies (a) (but not the converse) of part II of this theorem is due to E. HILLE [4, p. 352], while the saturation theorem itself, namely the equivalence of the assertions (a), (c) and (e) for the reflexive spaces $L^p_{2\pi}$, $1 < p < \infty$, was first shown by P. L. BUTZER [3; 4] in 1956 as an application of Theorem 2.1.2. The corresponding results for the non-reflexive spaces $C_{2\pi}$ and $L^1_{2\pi}$ were supplied by K. DE LEEUW [2] in 1960 using Theorem 2.1.4. In the meantime the latter results were also obtained by G. SUNOUCHI–C. WATARI [1] by means of the Fourier coefficient method. One may also consult the papers by H. BUCHWALTER [1], R. TABERSKI [1], A. H. TURECKIĬ [1] and furthermore P. L. BUTZER [10; 12], P. L. BUTZER–E. GÖRLICH [1], G. SUNOUCHI [1; 2], etc. The interpretation of Theorem 2.4.1 via the Neumann problem for the Laplace equation in the unit disk seems to be new. For the classical treatment of Neumann's problem as well as for its generalization see e.g. G. C. EVANS [1], W. J. STERNBERG–T. L. SMITH [1], R. COURANT–D. HILBERT [1].

Theorems 2.4.3 and 2.4.5 for $L^p_{2\pi}$, $1 < p < \infty$, are due to P. L. BUTZER–H. G. TILLMANN [2] and H. BERENS [2] using the semi-group approach, and to P. L. BUTZER–G. SUNOUCHI [1] who discussed the behavior of the r-th Taylor operator of the singular integral of Abel-Poisson on $C_{2\pi}$ and $L^p_{2\pi}$, $1 \leqq p < \infty$, by finite Fourier transform methods (see also H. BERENS–E. GÖRLICH [1]). These results concerning the circle have been extended to smooth surfaces in E_3 by R. LEIS [1; 2; 3].

For Proposition 2.4.7 see R. SALEM–A. ZYGMUND [1], while the converse theorem (Proposition 2.4.9) was first proven by N. DU PLESSIS [2], who actually treated the Poisson singular integral on the unit n-sphere for continuous functions. It was rediscovered in the form given by H. BERENS [1]. The method of proof again has its origin in the proof of S. Bernstein's "converse theorem" (see the remarks in Sec. 2.7.3). Proposition 2.4.12, due to H. BERENS [1], is a direct application of semi-group theory, thus of Corollary 2.3.6. Theorem 2.4.13 collecting the results established on non-optimal approximation for the singular integral of Abel-Poisson follows by Propositions 2.4.7, 2.4.9 and 2.4.12 together with a result of I. I. PRIVALOV [1]. The equivalence of the assertions (a)—(f) of this theorem is mainly due to G. H. HARDY–J. E. LITTLEWOOD [1; 3] (see A. ZYGMUND [5, Vol. I Ch. VII]). Their proofs, in contrast to ours, used complex methods and thus cannot be extended to n-dimensional space. For the examples (2.4.2) and (2.4.9) see e.g. I. P. NATANSON [1, p. 92]. For the Theorems 2.4.14 and 2.4.16 concerning the singular integral of Weierstrass, the results of which are partially new, see P. L. BUTZER–G. SUNOUCHI [1], H. BERENS–E. GÖRLICH [1] and S. PAWELKE [1]. For the connections with results due to M. H. TAIBLESON [2, I] see the remarks in Sec. 4.4.

2.7.5 The material of Sec. 2.5 is taken from P. L. BUTZER–S. PAWELKE [1]. This paper also contains a number of other results, partially described below. The close similarity between the properties of $T(t)$, $t \geqq 0$, and those of $\lambda R(\lambda; A)$, $\lambda > \omega_0$, seems to have been first noted by K. YOSIDA [3]. See also E. HILLE [6] and H.–PH. [1, p. 353]. These results are collected in Prop. 2.5.1. Prop. 2.5.2 (c) and 2.5.3 (b) lead to a further equivalent definition (cf. Sec. 2.2.1) of the r-th power of the infinitesimal generator A (r any positive integer) via the strong limit of

$$\lambda^r \left\{\lambda R(\lambda; A) f - \sum_{k=0}^{r-1} \frac{A^k}{\lambda^k} f\right\} \qquad (f \in D(A^{r-1})) \tag{2.7.1}$$

as $\lambda \to \infty$, whenever it exists. The same result may be obtained when the Taylor expansion (2.7.1) is replaced by that of Peano

$$\lambda^r \left\{\lambda R(\lambda;A) f - \sum_{k=0}^{r-1} \lambda^{-k} g_{k,r}\right\} \quad (f, g_{k,r} \in \mathsf{X}; k = 0, 1, \ldots, r-1), \tag{2.7.2}$$

or by

$$\frac{\lambda^r}{r!} \left\{\prod_{k=1}^{r} \left[\frac{\lambda}{k} R\left(\frac{\lambda}{k}; A\right) - I\right]\right\} f = \frac{\lambda^r}{r!} \left\{\lambda \int_0^\infty e^{-\lambda t} [T(t) - I]^r f\, dt\right\} \quad (f \in \mathsf{X}), \tag{2.7.3}$$

or even by

$$\lambda^r [\lambda R(\lambda; A) - I]^r f \qquad (f \in \mathsf{X}). \tag{2.7.4}$$

We have: *If anyone of the limits of* (2.7.1) – (2.7.4) *as* $\lambda \to \infty$ *exists, then all limits exist, are equal and define* $A^r f$.

The definition of A^r via (2.7.2) is due to H. Komatsu [2, p. 289]. In this paper Komatsu also reproved some well-known theorems on approximation by semi-group operators, including Theorem 2.1.2.

There are further results similar to those of Theorem 2.5.7 for the other differences. Let us formulate the following.

If $\{T(t); 0 \leqq t < \infty\}$ *is of class* $(\mathscr{C}_0)$ *in* $\mathscr{E}(\mathsf{X})$, *then the following statements are equivalent for a fixed* $f \in \mathsf{X}$:

(i) $\|[T(t) - I]^r f\| = O(t^r) \qquad (t \to 0+)$;

(ii) *there are elements* $g_{k,r} \in \mathsf{X}$ $(k = 0, 1, \ldots, r-1)$ *such that*

$$\left\| \lambda R(\lambda; A) f - \sum_{k=0}^{r-1} \lambda^{-k} g_{k,r} \right\| = O(\lambda^{-r}) \qquad (\lambda \to \infty);$$

(iii) $\left\| \left\{\prod_{k=1}^{r} \left[\frac{\lambda}{k} R\left(\frac{\lambda}{k}; A\right) - I\right]\right\} f \right\| = O(r!\, \lambda^{-r}) \qquad (\lambda \to \infty)$;

(iv) $\|[\lambda R(\lambda; A) - I]^r f\| = O(\lambda^{-r}) \qquad (\lambda \to \infty)$.

In case $f \in \mathsf{D}(A^{r-1})$, *these statements are equivalent to those of Theorem* 2.5.7.

Lemma 2.5.5 is given in a more general form for real-valued functions by D. V. Widder [1, p. 182].

One essential advantage of the theorems of Sec. 2.5.1 is that they enable one to treat saturation theorems for singular integrals which do not define semi-group operators but which, apart from a factor, are resolvents of the infinitesimal generator of a semi-group. The singular integral $w^\dagger(\lambda; f)$ defined by (2.5.15), or its generalization (2.5.16), does not seem to have been considered from the point of view of approximation previously.

For a proof of Theorem 2.5.13, which is a fundamental result on the representation of a one-parameter family of operators as a family of resolvents of a closed linear operator, we refer to P. L. BUTZER–S. PAWELKE [1]. In this proof, results of H.–PH. [1, p. 183], T. KATO [1], and K. YOSIDA [9] (gathered in K. YOSIDA [10, Ch. VIII § 4]) are used.

2.7.6 The material of Sec. 2.6 is taken from H. BERENS–U. WESTPHAL [2]. The definitions of integration and differentiation of fractional order of scalar-valued functions go back to J. LIOUVILLE, B. RIEMANN, and H. WEYL. In connection with Laplace transform theory these notions are intensively treated in G. DOETSCH [6, Bd. III Kap. 25], see also D. V. WIDDER [1, Ch. II]. For recent literature see the papers cited in H. BERENS–U. WESTPHAL [2] as well as the monograph by P. L. BUTZER–W. TREBELS [1] on the subject. Lemma 2.6.3 is e.g. proved (even in a more general form) in D. V. WIDDER [1, Ch. II § 8].

Let us introduce the semi-group of right translations on $L^p(E_1^+)$, $1 \leqq p < \infty$:

$$[W(x) f](t) = \begin{cases} 0 & 0 < t < x \\ f(t-x) & x < t < \infty, \end{cases} \tag{2.7.5}$$

with infinitesimal generator $-J^{-1} = -(d/dt)$ having domain $D(-J^{-1}) = \{f \in L^p(E_1^+);\, f \in AC_{\text{loc}}(\overline{E_1^+})$ with $f(0) = 0$ and $f' \in L^p(E_1^+)\}$. Trivially, the function $w(x, t; f) = [W(x) f](t)$ is the unique solution of the Cauchy problem

$$\frac{\partial w(x,t)}{\partial x} = -J^{-1} w(x,t), \quad w(0,t) = f(t) \qquad (x, t > 0) \tag{2.7.6}$$

for all $f \in D(-J^{-1})$. The Cauchy problem considered in Sec. 2.6 may then be regarded as a generalization of that of (2.7.6), whereby the differential operator J^{-1} is replaced by $J^{-\gamma}$, $0 < \gamma < 1$. The solution $w_\gamma(x, \cdot; f) = W_\gamma(x) f$ obtained in Theorem 2.6.6 is then connected with that of (2.7.6) by the integral

$$W_\gamma(x) f = \int_0^\infty p_\gamma(u; x)\, W(u) f\, du. \tag{2.7.7}$$

For a verification of the fact that the semi-group $\{W_\gamma(x);\, 0 \leqq x < \infty\}$ in $\mathscr{E}(L^p(E_1^+))$ is holomorphic see e.g. K. YOSIDA [10, Ch. IX § 11].

On the other hand, the Cauchy problem for the differential equation

$$\frac{\partial^2 w(x,t)}{\partial x^2} = B\, w(x,t) \qquad (x, t > 0), \tag{2.7.8}$$

where the operator B is equal to $[-J^{-\gamma}]^2 \equiv J^{-2\gamma}$, $0 < \gamma \leqq 1$, is in the case $\gamma = 1$ a paraphrase of the boundary value problem of the

wave equation
$$\frac{\partial^2 w(x,t)}{\partial x^2} = \frac{\partial^2 w(x,t)}{\partial t^2} \qquad (x, t > 0)$$
with the initial conditions
$$w(x,0) = \left.\frac{\partial w(x,t)}{\partial t}\right|_{t=0} = 0 \qquad (x > 0)$$
and the boundary conditions
$$w(0,t) = f(t), \qquad \lim_{x\to\infty} w(x,t) = 0 \qquad (t > 0).$$
The solution of the latter wave equation is given for all $f \in \mathsf{D}(J^{-2})$ by (2.7.5). (For a general treatment of linear partial differential equations of wave equation type see E. HILLE [7; 4, Sec. 20.3 – 20.6] as well as K. YOSIDA [10, Ch. XIV § 3].) Now for $B = J^{-1}$ (the case $\gamma = 1/2$), the Cauchy problem for (2.7.8) reduces to the boundary value problem of the heat-conduction equation for a semi-infinite rod, as treated in Sec. 2.6. Thus we may also regard its solution (2.6.19) as the solution of the *generalized wave equation* (2.7.8) for $\gamma = 1/2$.

The Cauchy problem for the heat equation as well as its solution (2.6.19) are well-known in the literature. E. CESÀRO [1] already noted in 1902 that the kernel (2.6.18) satisfies the semi-group property (2.6.20) with respect to x, as G. DOETSCH [3; 6 Bd. III pp. 81 and 267] remarks. Furthermore, Theorem 2.6.7 part I gives in case $\gamma = 1/2$ a number of equivalent characterizations of the domain of $-J^{-1/2}$ in $L^p(E_1^+)$, while part II solves the saturation problem. For an explicit proof of Theorem 2.6.7 see H. BERENS–U. WESTPHAL [1]. One of the interesting characterizations of $-J^{-\gamma}f$ is that given by the integral

$$(2.7.9) \qquad \frac{1}{-\Gamma(-\gamma)} \int_{\varepsilon}^{\infty} \frac{f(t-u) - f(t)}{u^{1+\gamma}}\, du \qquad (\varepsilon > 0),$$

which may be interpreted as a fractional differential quotient of f of order γ.

The representation (2.7.7) of the semi-group $\{W_\gamma(x); 0 \leqq x < \infty\}$, $0 < \gamma < 1$, in $\mathscr{E}(L^p(E_1^+))$ with infinitesimal generator $-J^{-\gamma}$ via the semi-group of right translations with generator $-J^{-1}$ and the density function $p_\gamma(\cdot\,; x)$ is a particular instance of a quite more general situation. Indeed, let X be a Banach space and $\{T(t); 0 \leqq t < \infty\}$ an equi-bounded semi-group of class $(\mathscr{C}_0)$ in $\mathscr{E}(\mathsf{X})$ with generator A. Then the family of operators

$$(2.7.10) \qquad S_\gamma(t) f = \begin{cases} \int_0^\infty p_\gamma(u; t)\, T(u) f\, du & (0 < \gamma < 1;\ t > 0) \\ f & (t = 0) \end{cases}$$

in $\mathscr{E}(\mathsf{X})$ again forms an equi-bounded semi-group of class $(\mathscr{C}_0)$, which is in addition holomorphic. The infinitesimal generator A_γ of $\{S_\gamma(t);$

$0 \leqq t < \infty\}$ is connected with the generator A of $\{T(t); 0 \leqq t < \infty\}$ by $A_\gamma = -(-A)^\gamma$, and for all $f \in \mathsf{D}(A)$

$$(2.7.11)\qquad (-A)^\gamma f = \frac{1}{\Gamma(-\gamma)} \int_0^\infty \frac{[T(u) - I] f}{u^{1+\gamma}}\, du$$

or

$$(2.7.12)\qquad (-A)^\gamma f = -\frac{\sin\gamma\pi}{\pi} \int_0^\infty \lambda^{\gamma-1} R(\lambda; A)\, A f\, d\lambda.$$

Moreover, the resolvent of A_γ is given by

$$(2.7.13)\quad R(\lambda; A_\gamma) = \frac{\sin\gamma\pi}{\pi} \int_0^\infty R(\sigma; A) \frac{\sigma^\gamma}{\lambda^2 - 2\lambda\sigma^\gamma\cos\gamma\pi + \sigma^{2\gamma}}\, d\sigma.$$

The semi-group $\{S_\gamma(t); 0 \leqq t < \infty\}$ was defined by R. S. PHILLIPS [3], and these investigations had their origin in papers by S. BOCHNER [2] and W. FELLER [2] on fractional powers of the Laplacian operator. This work was then carried on by A. V. BALAKRISHNAN [1; 2] and also T. KATO [2], K. YOSIDA [8]. The representations (2.7.11) and (2.7.12) are due to Balakrishnan, while (2.7.13) goes back to T. Kato. For a more detailed discussion see K. YOSIDA [10, Ch. IX § 11].

In connection with (2.7.11) the exact domain of definition of $(-A)^\gamma$ for $0 < \gamma < 1$ is characterized by the set of elements $f \in \mathsf{X}$ for which

$$\operatorname*{s-lim}_{\varepsilon \to 0+} \frac{1}{\Gamma(-\gamma)} \int_\varepsilon^\infty \frac{[T(u) - I] f}{u^{1+\gamma}}\, du$$

exists, the strong limit being equal to $(-A)^\gamma f$. More generally, an $f \in \mathsf{X}$ belongs to $\mathsf{D}((-A)^\gamma)$, $0 < \gamma < r$ $(r = 1, 2, \ldots)$, if and only if

$$\operatorname*{s-lim}_{\varepsilon \to 0+} \frac{1}{C_{\gamma,r}} \int_\varepsilon^\infty \frac{[T(u) - I]^r f}{u^{1+\gamma}}\, du$$

exists, the limit being equal to $(-A)^\gamma f$. Here, $C_{\gamma,r} = \int_0^\infty u^{-1-\gamma}(e^{-u} - 1)^r\, du$. In case $\gamma = 1, 2, \ldots, r-1$, this is a result due to J. L. LIONS–J. PEETRE [2] (see also Sec. 3.6.4), while for arbitrary $0 < \gamma < r$, see H. BERENS–P. L. BUTZER–U. WESTPHAL [1].

Finally we remark that A. V. BALAKRISHNAN [2] studied the abstract Cauchy problem

$$\frac{d^2}{dx^2} w(x) \pm A\, w(x) = 0,$$

where the operator A itself need not be an infinitesimal generator. A treatment of problems of this type is one main motivation for the study of fractional powers of operators, as we have seen in Sec. 2.6.

Chapter Three

Intermediate Spaces and Semi-Groups

3.0 Scope of the Chapter

In Chapter II we discussed necessary and sufficient condition supon an element $f \in \mathsf{X}$ such that $\| [T(t) - I]^r f \|$ (r any fixed positive integer) is precisely of optimal order $O(t^r)$ $(t \to 0+)$—the saturation problem (Theorem 2.2.14)—as well as conditions such that $\| [T(t) - I]^r f \|$ is of order $O(t^\alpha)$ $(0 < \alpha < r, t \to 0+)$ in the special case $r = 1$—the problem of non-optimal approximation (Corollary 2.3.6)—where $\{T(t);\ 0 \leqq t < \infty\}$ is a strongly continuous semi-group of operators on the Banach space X.

In this chapter we study these problems and essential generalizations thereof through intermediate space theory. The emphasis is principally upon the presentation of one of the various possible approaches to the theory of intermediate spaces and some of its many applications to mathematical analysis.

Without any essential loss of generality we may assume $\{T(t);\ 0 \leqq t < \infty\}$ to be equi-bounded. Setting

$$\|f\|_{\alpha,r;q} = \begin{cases} \|f\| + \left\{ \displaystyle\int_0^\infty (t^{-\alpha} \| [T(t) - I]^r f \|)^q \frac{dt}{t} \right\}^{1/q} \\ \qquad\qquad\qquad (0 < \alpha < r;\ 1 \leqq q < \infty) \\ \|f\| + \sup\limits_{0<t<\infty} (t^{-\alpha} \| [T(t) - I]^r f \|) \\ \qquad\qquad (0 \leqq \alpha \leqq r;\ q = \infty) \qquad (r = 1, 2, \ldots), \end{cases} \tag{3.0.1}$$

we say an element $f \in \mathsf{X}$ belongs to the space $\mathsf{X}_{\alpha,r;q}$ if the functional $\|f\|_{\alpha,r;q}$ is finite. These spaces, generated by the semi-group $\{T(t);\ 0 \leqq t < \infty\}$, are meaningful for the parameters α, q and r in question; moreover, they become Banach spaces with respect to the norm (3.0.1) and

$$\mathsf{D}(A^r) \subset \mathsf{X}_{\alpha,r;q} \subset \mathsf{X} \tag{3.0.2}$$

with continuous injections. In this sense $\mathsf{X}_{\alpha,r;q}$ is said to form an *intermediate space* between $\mathsf{D}(A^r)$ and X.

In particular, $X_{0,r;\infty} = X$, but in all other cases the inclusions (3.0.2) are in general proper. This will be shown in Sec. 3.1 by elementary methods. Moreover, we prove there that $D(A^r)$ is dense in $X_{\alpha,r;q}$ for $0 < \alpha < r$, $1 \leqq q < \infty$. If X is reflexive, then Corollary 2.2.15—the saturation theorem for the r-th Riemann difference of the semi-group—interpreted from the point of view of intermediate spaces states that $X_{r,r;\infty} = D(A^r)$ with equivalent norms.

Now, let $\{T(t); 0 \leqq t < \infty\}$ be in addition a holomorphic semi-group. Defining

$$(3.0.3)\qquad \|f\|'_{\alpha,r;q} = \begin{cases} \|f\| + \left\{\int\limits_0^\infty (t^{r-\alpha}\|A^r T(t) f\|)^q \frac{dt}{t}\right\}^{1/q} \\ \qquad\qquad (0 < \alpha < r,\ 1 \leqq q < \infty) \\ \|f\| + \sup\limits_{0<t<\infty} (t^{r-\alpha}\|A^r T(t) f\|) \\ \qquad\qquad (0 \leqq \alpha \leqq r,\ q = \infty), \end{cases}$$

then an $f \in X$ belongs to the space $X'_{\alpha,r;q}$ if $\|f\|'_{\alpha,r;q} < \infty$. Again, $X'_{\alpha,r;q}$ is a Banach space under the norm (3.0.3) and intermediate between X and $D(A^r)$, see Sec. 3.5.

In this terminology Theorem 2.3.2 states that the intermediate spaces $X_{r,r;\infty}$ and $X'_{r,r;\infty}$ are equal with equivalent norms (cf. Corollary 3.5.7). But the massive Theorem 3.5.3 shows that in general the spaces $X_{\alpha,r;q}$ and $X'_{\alpha,r;q}$ are equal with equivalent norms. In particular, for non-optimal approximation, namely the case $0 < \alpha < r$, $1 \leqq q \leqq \infty$, this is a fundamental generalization of Corollary 2.3.6 (a), the special instance for $0 < \alpha < 1$, $q = \infty$.

The preceding results which are part of the facts treated in Sec. 3.1, 3.4 and 3.5 are directly attached to the theorems stated at the beginning of this section and illustrate these in their new setting. This gives us an orientation into Chap. III.

The theory of intermediate spaces as developed in this chapter is an indispensable tool for the treatment of the spaces $X_{\alpha,r;q}$, especially in Sec. 3.4 and 3.5. This is one motivation for a particular study of this theory for which we have reserved Sec. 3.2. While in Sec. 3.2.1 the basic definitions are formulated, Sec. 3.2.2 is devoted to the significant K- and J-methods of interpolation of J. Peetre for generating intermediate spaces between Banach spaces. Sec. 3.2.3 is concerned with the equivalence of these two methods—we mention here especially Theorem 3.2.12—and Sec. 3.2.4 with the theorem of reiteration (Theorem 3.2.20). Finally, Sec. 3.2.5 treats an abstract version of the M. Riesz–Thorin as well as Marcinkiewicz interpolation theorems.

Sec. 3.3, which may be postponed until Sec. 4.2 without disrupting the continuity of the presentation, is devoted to an application of the theory of intermediate spaces, namely to the Lorentz spaces and the classical interpolation theorems of M. Riesz–Thorin and Marcinkiewicz.

Sec. 3.4 deals with equivalent characterizations for the spaces $X_{\alpha,r;q}$ by the K- and J-methods of interpolation. The most important results here are the two theorems of reduction for non-optimal as well as optimal approximation (Theorems 3.4.6 and 3.4.10). These theorems in particular state that

$$f \in X_{\alpha,r;q} \iff f \in D(A^k) \ (\alpha = k + \beta;\ k = 0, 1, \ldots, r-1,\ 0 < \alpha < r,\ 1 \leqq q \leqq \infty) \quad 0 < \beta \leqq 1)$$

$$\text{and } A^k f \in \begin{cases} X_{\beta,1;q} & (0 < \beta < 1) \\ X_{1,2;q} & (\beta = 1), \end{cases}$$

and that

$$f \in X_{r,r;\infty} \iff f \in D(A^{r-1}) \text{ and } A^{r-1} f \in X_{1,1;\infty}.$$

The counterparts of these theorems for the Taylor and Peano differences are also presented.

Apart from these results Chap. III is also concerned with problems of Plessner type in intermediate space setting. Defining

$$X^0_{\alpha,r;q} = \{f \in X_{\alpha,r;q};\ \lim_{t\to 0+} \|T(t) f - f\|_{\alpha,r;q} = 0\}, \tag{3.0.4}$$

it is shown in Sec. 3.1 that $X^0_{\alpha,r;q}$ is a closed linear subspace of $X_{\alpha,r;q}$ with $D(A^r)$ as a dense subset (Proposition 3.1.6). As a consequence one obtains that $X^0_{\alpha,r;q} = X_{\alpha,r;q}$ for $0 < \alpha < r$, $1 \leqq q < \infty$ and $X^0_{r,r;\infty} = D(A^r)$, the latter being the Plessner type characterization of $D(A^r)$. For the remaining case $0 < \alpha < r$, $q = \infty$ Theorem 3.4.14 gives that

$$f \in X^0_{\alpha,r;\infty} \iff f \in D(A^k) \qquad (\alpha = k + \beta;\ k = 0, 1, \ldots, r-1, 0 < \beta \leqq 1)$$

$$\text{and } \begin{cases} \|[T(t) - I]\, A^k f\| = o(t^\beta) & (0 < \beta < 1;\ t \to 0+) \\ \|[T(t) - I]^2\, A^k f\| = o(t) & (\beta = 1;\ t \to 0+). \end{cases}$$

Finally, Sec. 3.5 deals with the extensions of these results to holomorphic semi-groups. Ch. III concludes with Sec. 3.6 on "Notes and Remarks".

3.1 Banach Subspaces of *X* Generated by Semi-Groups of Operators

Throughout this chapter X will be a real or complex Banach space and $\{T(t); 0 \leqq t < \infty\}$ an equi-bounded semi-group (with bound M) of class $(\mathscr{C}_0)$ in $\mathscr{E}(X)$; any further specialization will be stated explicitly.

Definition 3.1.1. *Let r be an arbitrary, but fixed integer >0. We denote by $X_{\alpha,r;q}$, $0 < \alpha < r$, $1 \leqq q \leqq \infty$, the set of elements $f \in X$ for* *which the expressions*

$$\int_0^\infty \left(s^{-\alpha} \| [T(s) - I]^r f \|\right)^q \frac{ds}{s} \qquad (1 \leqq q < \infty),$$

$$\sup_{0<s<\infty} \left(s^{-\alpha} \| [T(s) - I]^r f \|\right) \qquad (q = \infty)$$

are finite.

Definition 3.1.2. *The Favard class* $X_{r,r;\infty}$ *of order* r $(r = 1, 2, \ldots)$ *of the semi-group* $\{T(t); 0 \leqq t < \infty\}$ *in* X *is defined as the set of elements* $f \in X$ *for which*

$$\sup_{0<s<\infty} \left(s^{-r} \| [T(s) - I]^r f \|\right) < +\infty.$$

Remark. In Sec. 2.2.2 we have defined and studied the saturation problem for the family of operators $\{[T(t) - I]^r; 0 \leqq t < \infty\}$ on X as $t \to 0+$. Under the above hypothesis upon the semi-group we have by Theorem 2.2.14 (a):

(i) $\| [T(t) - I]^r f \| = o(t^r) \quad (t \to 0+) \qquad \Longrightarrow [T(t) - I]^r f \equiv \theta;$

(ii) $\| [T(t) - I]^r f \| = O(t^r) \quad (t \to 0+) \qquad \Longleftrightarrow f \in X_{r,r;\infty}.$

This justifies the terminology in saying that $X_{r,r;\infty}$ is the Favard class of order r of $\{T(t); 0 \leqq t < \infty\}$ in X.

Proposition 3.1.3. *The sets* $X_{\alpha,r;q}$, $0 < \alpha < r$, $1 \leqq q \leqq \infty$ *and/or* $\alpha = r$, $q = \infty$, *are linear subspaces in* X. *They are Banach spaces under the norms*

$$(3.1.1) \quad \|f\|_{\alpha,r;q} = \begin{cases} \|f\| + \left\{\int_0^\infty \left(s^{-\alpha} \| [T(s) - I]^r f \|\right)^q \frac{ds}{s}\right\}^{1/q} \\ \qquad\qquad (0 < \alpha < r,\ 1 \leqq q < \infty), \\ \|f\| + \sup_{0<s<\infty} \left(s^{-\alpha} \| [T(s) - I]^r f \|\right) \\ \qquad\qquad (0 < \alpha \leqq r,\ q = \infty). \end{cases}$$

Furthermore,

$$(3.1.2) \qquad D(A^r) \subset X_{\alpha,r;q} \subset X.$$

Here and in the following the notation "$\subset$" means "the identity mapping of the subspace into the whole space is a bounded transformation", briefly: "is a continuously embedded subspace of".

Proof. The spaces $X_{\alpha,r;q}$ are obviously normed linear spaces under the norms described. To prove that they are Banach spaces one merely has to verify completeness. We restrict the discussion to the case $1 \leqq q < \infty$. Suppose that $\{f_n\}_{n=1}^\infty$ is a Cauchy sequence in $X_{\alpha,r;q}$. Then by the definition of the norm (3.1.1) $\{f_n\}$ is also a Cauchy sequence in X and therefore converges strongly to a limit f in X. Furthermore, for each fixed $0 < s < \infty$

$$s^{-\alpha}[T(s) - I]^r f = \operatorname{s-lim}_{n\to\infty} s^{-\alpha}[T(s) - I]^r f_n,$$

and by the lemma of Fatou

$$\int_0^\infty (s^{-\alpha} \|[T(s) - I]^r f\|)^q \frac{ds}{s} \leqq \liminf_{n\to\infty} \int_0^\infty (s^{-\alpha} \|[T(s) - I]^r f_n\|)^q \frac{ds}{s} < \infty.$$

Thus f belongs to $\mathsf{X}_{\alpha,r;q}$. It remains to prove that $f_n \to f$ as $n \to \infty$ in $\mathsf{X}_{\alpha,r;q}$-norm. Given $\varepsilon > 0$, by assumption there is an N such that $\|f_n - f_m\|_{\alpha,r;q} < \varepsilon$ for all $n, m \geqq N$. Consequently

$$\int_0^\infty (s^{-\alpha} \|[T(s) - I]^r (f_n - f_m)\|)^q \frac{ds}{s} < \varepsilon^q \quad (n, m \geqq N),$$

and applying Fatou's lemma again with $m \to \infty$

$$\int_0^\infty (s^{-\alpha} \|[T(s) - I]^r (f_n - f)\|)^q \frac{ds}{s} < \varepsilon^q$$

for all $n \geqq N$. From this it follows immediately that $\{f_n\}_{n=1}^\infty$ is a Cauchy sequence in $\mathsf{X}_{\alpha,r;q}$ having the limit f.

In the proof of the completeness we have already made use of the fact that for all $f \in \mathsf{X}_{\alpha,r;q}$, $\|f\| \leqq \|f\|_{\alpha,r;q}$, which proves the second inclusion relation of (3.1.2). Now, if $f \in \mathsf{D}(A^r)$, then we obtain by relation (1.1.11) that $\|[T(s) - I]^r f\| \leqq M \|A^r f\| s^r$ for all $s > 0$. On the other hand, $\|[T(s) - I]^r f\| \leqq (M+1)^r \|f\|$ $(s > 0)$. Thus

(3.1.3) $$\|[T(s) - I]^r f\| \leqq (M+1)^r \min(1, s^r)\,(\|f\| + \|A^r f\|),$$

where $\|f\| + \|A^r f\|$ is an equivalent norm on $\mathsf{D}(A^r)$ (see (1.1.13)). Consequently, for all $f \in \mathsf{D}(A^r)$ and $1 \leqq q < \infty$

(3.1.4)

$$\|f\|_{\alpha,r;q} \leqq \left[1 + (M+1)^r \left\{\int_0^\infty (s^{-\alpha} \min(1, s^r))^q \frac{ds}{s}\right\}^{1/q}\right] (\|f\| + \|A^r f\|) \qquad (0 < \alpha < r),$$

and for $q = \infty$

(3.1.5)

$$\|f\|_{\alpha,r;\infty} \leqq [1 + (M+1)^r \sup_{0<s<\infty} (s^{-\alpha} \min(1, s^r))]\,(\|f\| + \|A^r f\|) \qquad (0 < \alpha \leqq r).$$

Since the integral and the supremum on the right-hand side of the latter two inequalities are finite, (3.1.2) follows.

We have just proved that the spaces $\mathsf{X}_{\alpha,r;q}$ generated by the semi-group $\{T(t); 0 \leqq t < \infty\}$ are continuously embedded between $\mathsf{D}(A^r)$

and X. In this case, we say the spaces $\mathsf{X}_{\alpha,r;q}$ form *intermediate spaces* of $\mathsf{D}(A^r)$ and X. In the following proposition we shall prove some simple properties for these spaces.

Proposition 3.1.4. (a) $\mathsf{X}_{\beta,r;q} \subset \mathsf{X}_{\alpha,r;q} \qquad (\beta \geqq \alpha > 0;\ 1 \leqq q \leqq \infty)$.

(b) *For* $0 < \alpha < r$ *and* $1 \leqq q < \infty$, $\mathsf{D}(A^r)$ *is a dense subspace of* $\mathsf{X}_{\alpha,r;q}$.

Proof. Since $s^{-\alpha} \leqq s^{-\beta}$ for $0 < s \leqq 1$ and all $\beta \geqq \alpha > 0$, one readily sees that for each $f \in \mathsf{X}_{\beta,r;q}$

$$\|f\|_{\alpha,r;q} \leqq \|f\| + \left\{\int_0^1 (s^{-\alpha}\,\|[T(s)-I]^r f\|)^q \frac{ds}{s}\right\}^{1/q} + \\ + \left\{\int_1^\infty (s^{-\alpha}\,\|[T(s)-I]^r f\|)^q \frac{ds}{s}\right\}^{1/q}$$

$$\leqq \|f\| + \left\{\int_0^1 (s^{-\beta}\,\|[T(s)-I]^r f\|)^q \frac{ds}{s}\right\}^{1/q} + \frac{(M+1)^r}{(\alpha q)^{1/q}}\,\|f\|$$

$$\leqq \left(1 + \frac{(M+1)^r}{(\alpha q)^{1/q}}\right)\|f\|_{\beta,r;q}$$

in case $1 \leqq q < \infty$. For $q = \infty$

$$\|f\|_{\alpha,r;\infty} \leqq \left(1 + (M+1)^r\right)\|f\|_{\beta,r;\infty}.$$

To prove part (b), we set for $f \in \mathsf{X}_{\alpha,r;q}$, $t > 0$

$$(3.1.6)\qquad f_t = \frac{1}{t^r}\int_0^t\int_0^t\cdots\int_0^t T(\tau_1+\tau_2+\cdots+\tau_r)\,f\,d\tau_1\,d\tau_2\ldots d\tau_r.$$

Obviously, $f_t \in \mathsf{D}(A^r)$ for each $t > 0$ and $A^r f_t = t^{-r}[T(t)-I]^r f$. Then for some fixed positive δ

$$\left\{\int_0^\infty (s^{-\alpha}\,\|[T(s)-I]^r(f-f_t)\|)^q\frac{ds}{s}\right\}^{1/q} \leqq \left\{\int_0^\delta\cdots\right\}^{1/q} + \left\{\int_\delta^\infty\cdots\right\}^{1/q} = I_1 + I_2.$$

Since $\|[T(s)-I]^r f_t\| \leqq M\,\|[T(s)-I]^r f\|$ for each $t > 0$, we see that

$$I_1 \leqq (M+1)\left\{\int_0^\delta (s^{-\alpha}\,\|[T(s)-I]^r f\|)^q\frac{ds}{s}\right\}^{1/q}.$$

For I_2 we obtain

$$I_2 \leqq \frac{(M+1)^r}{(\alpha q)^{1/q}}\,\delta^{-\alpha}\,\|f - f_t\|.$$

Now, given $\varepsilon > 0$, we can choose $\delta > 0$ such that the integral $\left\{\int_0^\delta (s^{-\alpha} \| [T(s) - I]^r f \|)^q \, ds/s\right\}^{1/q} < \varepsilon/(M+1)$. Thus by our evaluations and the fact that $\lim_{t\to 0+} \| f - f_t \| = 0$, we have $\limsup_{t\to 0+} \| f - f_t \|_{\alpha,r;q} \leqq \varepsilon$, i.e. the elements $f_t \in \mathsf{D}(A^r)$, $t > 0$, converge strongly in $\mathsf{X}_{\alpha,r;q}$ to f as $t \to 0+$ for each $f \in \mathsf{X}_{\alpha,r;q}$. This proves the proposition.

The intermediate spaces $\mathsf{X}_{\alpha,r;q}$, $0 < \alpha < r$, $1 \leqq q \leqq \infty$ and/or $\alpha = r$, $q = \infty$ $(r = 1, 2, \ldots)$, are *invariant* under the semi-group $\{T(t); 0 \leqq t < \infty\}$. This means that

$$T(t)\,[\mathsf{X}_{\alpha,r;q}] \subset \mathsf{X}_{\alpha,r;q} \qquad (t \geqq 0); \tag{3.1.7}$$

in particular,

$$\| T(t) f \|_{\alpha,r;q} \leqq M \| f \|_{\alpha,r;q} \qquad (f \in \mathsf{X}_{\alpha,r;q};\ t \geqq 0).$$

Thus the restriction of $\{T(t); 0 \leqq t < \infty\}$ on $\mathsf{X}_{\alpha,r;q}$ defines an equibounded semi-group of operators in $\mathscr{E}(\mathsf{X}_{\alpha,r;q})$. The question now is to determine those elements $f \in \mathsf{X}_{\alpha,r;q}$ for which this restriction has the $(\mathscr{C}_0)$-property.

Definition 3.1.5. *We denote by* $\mathsf{X}^0_{\alpha,r;q}$, $0 < \alpha < r$, $1 \leqq q \leqq \infty$ *and/or* $\alpha = r$, $q = \infty$ $(r = 1, 2, \ldots)$, *the set of all elements* $f \in \mathsf{X}_{\alpha,r;q}$ *for which*

$$\lim_{t\to 0+} \| T(t) f - f \|_{\alpha,r;q} = 0. \tag{3.1.8}$$

By the semi-group property of $\{T(t); 0 \leqq t < \infty\}$ an element $f \in \mathsf{X}$ belongs to $\mathsf{X}^0_{\alpha,r;q}$ if and only if the mapping $t \to T(t) f$ on $[0, \infty)$ into $\mathsf{X}_{\alpha,r;q}$ is strongly continuous (see Proposition 1.1.2 (b)).

We now investigate the classes $\mathsf{X}^0_{\alpha,r;q}$. In analogy with Plessner's theorem concerning the group of translations on function spaces (see Remark 1.4.10 and Example 1.5.9) we call such problems "problems of Plessner type".

Proposition 3.1.6. *The set* $\mathsf{X}^0_{\alpha,r;q}$ *defines a closed linear subspace in* $\mathsf{X}_{\alpha,r;q}$, *equal to the closure of* $\mathsf{D}(A^r)$ *in* $\mathsf{X}_{\alpha,r;q}$.

Proof. Clearly, $\mathsf{X}^0_{\alpha,r;q}$ is a linear manifold in $\mathsf{X}_{\alpha,r;q}$. To prove that it is closed, suppose $\{f_n\}_{n=1}^\infty$ is a sequence in $\mathsf{X}^0_{\alpha,r;q}$ which converges to an element g of the closure of $\mathsf{X}^0_{\alpha,r;q}$ in $\mathsf{X}_{\alpha,r;q}$. Given $\varepsilon > 0$, there exists an n and a $\delta > 0$ such that $\| f_n - g \|_{\alpha,r;q} < \varepsilon/2(M+1)$ and $\| T(t) f_n - f_n \|_{\alpha,r;q} < \varepsilon/2$ for $0 < t < \delta$. Hence we obtain for the limit g

$$\begin{aligned} \| T(t) g - g \|_{\alpha,r;q} &\leqq \| T(t) g - T(t) f_n \|_{\alpha,r;q} + \| T(t) f_n - f_n \|_{\alpha,r;q} + \\ &+ \| f_n - g \|_{\alpha,r;q} \leqq (M+1) \, \| f_n - g \|_{\alpha,r;q} + \| T(t) f_n - f_n \|_{\alpha,r;q} < \varepsilon \end{aligned}$$

for $0 < t < \delta$, i.e. $g \in \mathsf{X}^0_{\alpha,r;q}$, and consequently this subspace is closed. By Proposition 3.1.3, $\mathsf{D}(A^r) \subset \mathsf{X}_{\alpha,r;q}$. Moreover, $\mathsf{D}(A^r)$ belongs to the subspace $X^0_{\alpha,r;q}$. Indeed, since $D(A^r)$ is continuously embedded in $X_{\alpha,r;q}$ one has using the estimates (3.1.4) and (3.1.5)

$$\|T(t)f - f\|_{\alpha,r;q} \leqq C(\|T(t)f - f\| + \|T(t)A^r f - A^r f\|),$$

where $C = C(\alpha, r, q; M) > 0$. But the right-hand side of this inequality tends to zero as $t \to 0+$.

It remains to prove that $D(A^r)$ is dense in $X^0_{\alpha,r;q}$. Since for an $f \in X^0_{\alpha,r;q}$ the vector-valued function $T(\tau)f$ on $[0,\infty)$ in $X_{\alpha,r;q}$ is strongly continuous, the integral f_t defined in (3.1.6) exists in the sense of Riemann (App. 2) and

$$\|f_t - f\|_{\alpha,r;q}$$

$$\leqq \frac{1}{t^r}\int_0^t\int_0^t \cdots \int_0^t \|T(\tau_1+\tau_2+\cdots+\tau_r)f - f\|_{\alpha,r;q}\,d\tau_1\,d\tau_2\ldots d\tau_r < \varepsilon$$

for t sufficiently small. On the other hand, $f_t \in D(A^r)$ for each $t > 0$, proving the proposition.

Corollary 3.1.7. *The subspace* $X^0_{\alpha,r;q}$ *is equal to* $X_{\alpha,r;q}$ *for* $0 < \alpha < r$, $1 \leqq q < \infty$.

The proof follows immediately by Propositions 3.1.4 (b) and 3.1.6.

Corollary 3.1.8. $D(A^r)$ *is equal to* $X^0_{r,r;\infty}$.

Proof. One proves easily that $D(A^r)$ is a closed linear subspace in $X_{r,r;\infty}$. Indeed,

$$\|f\| + \|A^r f\| \leqq \|f\|_{r,r;\infty} \leqq M(\|f\| + \|A^r f\|)$$

for all $f \in D(A^r)$ and, as $D(A^r)$ is dense in $X^0_{r,r;\infty}$, these two spaces are equal.

We know from Corollary 2.2.15 that if X is reflexive, then $D(A^r)$ and $X_{r,r;\infty}$ are equal. In general, however, $D(A^r)$ is a proper subspace of $X_{r,r;\infty}$ and the assertion given in Corollary 3.1.8 is a Plessner type characterization for the domain of A^r. Furthermore, we shall see that in case $0 < \alpha < r$, $q = \infty$ the spaces $X^0_{\alpha,r;\infty}$ are also, in general, proper subspaces of $X_{\alpha,r;\infty}$.

Having given the definition and several simple properties of the intermediate spaces $X_{\alpha,r;q}$ of X and $D(A^r)$ ($0 < \alpha < r$, $1 \leqq q < \infty$ and/or $\alpha = r$, $q = \infty$), we now wish to treat these spaces more thoroughly. But to this end we require important and deep results concerning the theory of intermediate spaces. This theory is developed as far as needed in the next section.

3.2 Intermediate Spaces and Interpolation

3.2.1 Definitions

Let X_1 and X_2 be two Banach spaces contained in a linear Hausdorff space $\mathscr{X}$ such that the identity mapping of X_i $(i = 1, 2)$ in $\mathscr{X}$ is continuous. Thus $X_i \subset \mathscr{X}$ $(i = 1; 2)$. We denote the elements of X_i by f_i and their norms by $\|f_i\|_i$.

We introduce the intersection $X_1 \cap X_2$ and the algebraic sum $X_1 + X_2$ (the space of all elements $f \in \mathscr{X}$ of the form $f = f_1 + f_2$, $f_1 \in X_1$ and $f_2 \in X_2$) of X_1 and X_2.

Proposition 3.2.1. *The spaces* $X_1 \cap X_2$ *and* $X_1 + X_2$ *are Banach spaces under the norms*

$$\|f\|_{X_1 \cap X_2} = \max(\|f\|_1, \|f\|_2) \tag{3.2.1}$$

and

$$\|f\|_{X_1 + X_2} = \inf_{f = f_1 + f_2} (\|f_1\|_1 + \|f_2\|_2), \tag{3.2.2}$$

respectively. Furthermore,

$$X_1 \cap X_2 \subset X_i \subset X_1 + X_2 (\subset \mathscr{X}) \qquad (i = 1, 2). \tag{3.2.3}$$

Proof. Clearly, $X_1 \cap X_2$ is a normed vector space under the norm described. To prove that it is complete, suppose $\{f^n\}_{n=1}^{\infty}$ is a Cauchy sequence in $X_1 \cap X_2$. Since

$$\|f\|_i \leqq \|f\|_{X_1 \cap X_2} \qquad (f \in X_1 \cap X_2;\ i = 1, 2) \tag{3.2.4}$$

and since the spaces X_i are Banach spaces continuously embedded in $\mathscr{X}$, $\{f^n\}$ is a Cauchy sequence in both X_1 and X_2 with one and the same limit f^0. The inequality $\|f^0 - f^n\|_{X_1 \cap X_2} \leqq \|f^0 - f^n\|_1 + \|f^0 - f^n\|_2$ finally shows that the sequence $\{f^n\}$ also converges to f^0 as $n \to \infty$ with respect to the norm of $X_1 \cap X_2$.

Concerning $X_1 + X_2$, this space is obviously linear. Furthermore, the norm introduced in (3.2.2) satisfies the homogeneity and the triangle property. We show that $f = \theta$ if and only if $\|f\|_{X_1 + X_2} = 0$. The "only if" part is trivial. Hence assume $\|f\|_{X_1 + X_2} = 0$. By definition of the norm there exist two sequences $\{f_1^n\}_{n=1}^{\infty}$ and $\{f_2^n\}_{n=1}^{\infty}$ in X_1 and X_2, respectively, such that $f = f_1^n + f_2^n$ for all $n = 1, 2, \ldots$ and $\|f_1^n\|_1 + \|f_2^n\|_2 < 1/n$, i.e. the sequence $\{f_i^n\}$ is a null sequence in X_i $(i = 1, 2)$. But the space X_i $(i = 1, 2)$ is continuously embedded in $\mathscr{X}$; thus $f_i^n \to \theta$ $(i = 1, 2)$, and consequently $f = f_1^n + f_2^n \to \theta$ in the Hausdorff topology of $\mathscr{X}$. Therefore $f = \theta$ and $X_1 + X_2$ is a normed linear space.

To prove that $X_1 + X_2$ is a Banach space it suffices to show that every absolutely summable sequence $\{f^n\}_{n=1}^{\infty}$ is summable. Let by assumption $\sum_{n=1}^{\infty} \|f^n\|_{X_1 + X_2} < \infty$. For each f^n there exist two elements f_1^n and f_2^n

in X_1 and X_2, respectively, such that $f^n = f_1^n + f_2^n$ and $\|f_1^n\|_1 + \|f_2^n\|_2 \leqq \leqq \|f^n\|_{X_1+X_2} + 1/2^n$ $(n = 1, 2, \ldots)$. Hence

$$\sum_{n=1}^{\infty} (\|f_1^n\|_1 + \|f_2^n\|_2) \leqq \sum_{n=1}^{\infty} \|f^n\|_{X_1+X_2} + 1 < \infty .$$

Since X_i $(i = 1, 2)$ is complete, the series $\sum_{n=1}^{\infty} f_i^n$ is summable to an element f_i^0, and consequently for $f^0 = f_1^0 + f_2^0$

$$\left\| f^0 - \sum_{n=1}^{N} f^n \right\|_{X_1+X_2} \leqq \left\| f_1^0 - \sum_{n=1}^{N} f_1^n \right\|_1 + \left\| f_2^0 - \sum_{n=1}^{N} f_2^n \right\|_2 ,$$

the two terms on the right hand side converging to zero as $N \to \infty$. Thus the sequence $\{f^n\}$ is summable to f^0.

Since X_1 and X_2 are continuously embedded in $\mathscr{X}$ it is evident that $X_1 \cap X_2$ and $X_1 + X_2$ are also continuously embedded in $\mathscr{X}$.

Finally,

(3.2.5) $$\|f_i\|_{X_1+X_2} \leqq \|f_i\|_i \qquad (f_i \in X_i;\ i = 1, 2),$$

which, together with (3.2.4), proves the relation (3.2.3).

Definition 3.2.2. *We call each Banach space* $X \subset \mathscr{X}$ *satisfying*

(3.2.6) $$X_1 \cap X_2 \subset X \subset X_1 + X_2$$

an intermediate space (of X_1 *and* X_2*).*

In the following subsection we shall discuss two general methods for generating intermediate spaces of X_1 and X_2.

3.2.2 The K- and J-Methods for Generating Intermediate Spaces

Let Y be any Banach space with elements g and norm $\|\cdot\|$. We denote by $L_*^q(Y)$ the Banach space of all (classes of) functions $t \to g(t)$, $t \in (0, \infty)$ and $g(t) \in Y$, for which the mapping $t \to g(t)$ is strongly measurable with respect to the measure dt/t (Haar measure with respect to the multiplicative group of the points t in $(0, \infty)$) and the norm $\|g(\cdot)\|_{L_*^q(Y)}$ is finite, where

(3.2.7) $$\|g(\cdot)\|_{L_*^q(Y)} = \begin{cases} \left\{ \int_0^\infty \|g(t)\|^q \frac{dt}{t} \right\}^{1/q} & (1 \leqq q < \infty), \\ \operatorname*{ess\,sup}_{0<t<\infty} \{\|g(\cdot)\|\} & (q = \infty). \end{cases}$$

If Y is the real or complex number system, for $L_*^q(Y)$ we write briefly L_*^q (App. 2).

For what is to follow, we introduce the *function norms*

(3.2.8) $$\mathrm{J}(t; f) = \max(\|f\|_1, t\,\|f\|_2) \qquad (0 < t < \infty)$$

on $X_1 \cap X_2$ and

(3.2.9) $$K(t; f) = \inf_{f=f_1+f_2} (\|f_1\|_1 + t\,\|f_2\|_2) \qquad (0 < t < \infty),$$

on $X_1 + X_2$.

Proposition 3.2.3. (a) *For each element* $f \in X_1 \cap X_2$ $J(t; f)$ *is a continuous, monotone increasing and convex function on* $(0, \infty)$ *and*

(3.2.10) $$\min(1, t)\,\|f\|_{X_1 \cap X_2} \leqq J(t; f) \leqq \max(1, t)\,\|f\|_{X_1 \cap X_2}.$$

(b) *For each element* $f \in X_1 + X_2$ $K(t; f)$ *is a continuous, monotone increasing and concave function on* $(0, \infty)$ *and*

(3.2.11) $$\min(1, t)\,\|f\|_{X_1 + X_2} \leqq K(t; f) \leqq \max(1, t)\,\|f\|_{X_1 + X_2}.$$

(c) *For each* $f \in X_1 \cap X_2$

(3.2.12) $$K(t; f) \leqq \min\left(1, \frac{t}{s}\right) J(s; f) \qquad (0 < t, s < \infty).$$

Proof. The inequalities (3.2.10) and (3.2.11) of parts (a) and (b) follow immediately by definitions (3.2.8) and (3.2.9), respectively. So do the other properties of $J(t; f)$ stated in part (a).

Therefore we just prove the properties given for the function norm $K(t; f)$. By definition, $K(t; f)$ is monotone increasing with respect to t and upper semi-continuous on $(0, \infty)$. Thus $K(t+; f) \leqq K(t; f) \leqq \leqq K(t+; f)$ for each fixed $t > 0$. On the other hand,

$$K(t-\varepsilon; f) \leqq K(t; f) \leqq \frac{t}{t-\varepsilon} K(t-\varepsilon; f) \qquad (0 < \varepsilon < t < \infty),$$

and consequently $K(t-; f) \leqq K(t; f) \leqq K(t-; f)$, proving the continuity of the function $K(t; f)$ on $(0, \infty)$. Since for every choice of $f = f_1 + f_2$ the functions $\|f_1\|_1 + t\,\|f_2\|_2$ on $(0, \infty)$ are linear, one obtains immediately by definition (3.2.9)

$$\frac{b-t}{b-a} K(a; f) + \frac{t-a}{b-a} K(b; f) \leqq K(t; f) \qquad (0 < a \leqq t \leqq b < \infty),$$

which proves that $K(t; f)$ is concave.

It remains to show part (c). Indeed, if $f \in X_1 \cap X_2$, then on the one hand $K(t; f) \leqq \|f\|_1 \leqq J(s; f)$ for all $0 < t, s < \infty$ and on the other hand $K(t; f) \leqq t\,\|f\|_2 \leqq (t/s)\, J(s; f)$ for all $0 < t, s < \infty$, proving (3.2.12).

Definition 3.2.4. *We define* $(X_1, X_2)_{\theta, q; K}$, $-\infty < \theta < \infty$, $1 \leqq q \leqq \infty$, *to be the space of all elements* $f \in X_1 + X_2$ *for which* $t^{-\theta} K(t; f) \in L^q_*$.

Proposition 3.2.5. *The spaces* $(X_1, X_2)_{\theta,q;K}$ *are meaningful for* $0 < \theta < 1$, $1 \leqq q < \infty$ *and/or* $0 \leqq \theta \leqq 1$, $q = \infty$. *They are Banach spaces under the norms*

$$\|f\|_{\theta,q;K} = \|t^{-\theta} K(t; f)\|_{L^q_*} \equiv \left\{ \int_0^\infty (t^{-\theta} K(t; f))^q \frac{dt}{t} \right\}^{1/q}. \tag{3.2.13}$$

Furthermore,

$$X_1 \cap X_2 \subset (X_1, X_2)_{\theta,q;K} \subset X_1 + X_2. \tag{3.2.14}$$

In all other cases the spaces $(X_1, X_2)_{\theta,q;K}$ *only contain the zero element.*

Proof. Applying inequality (3.2.11) for an $f \neq \theta$ in $X_1 + X_2$, we obtain

$$(\|t^{-\theta} \min(1, t)\|_{L^q_*}) \|f\|_{X_1+X_2} \leqq \|t^{-\theta} K(t; f)\|_{L^q_*}.$$

But the scalar-valued function $t^{-\theta} \min(1, t)$ belongs to L^q_* if and only if $0 < \theta < 1$, $1 \leqq q < \infty$ and/or $0 \leqq \theta \leqq 1$, $q = \infty$, and consequently f may belong to $(X_1, X_2)_{\theta,q;K}$ in these cases only.

Obviously, the spaces $(X_1, X_2)_{\theta,q;K}$ are normed linear spaces under the norms (3.2.13) for the given values of θ and q. We prove completeness. If $\{f^n\}_{n=1}^\infty$ is any absolutely summable sequence in $(X_1, X_2)_{\theta,q;K}$, then by the latter inequality $\sum_{n=1}^\infty K(t; f^n) < \infty$ for each $0 < t < \infty$. Since $X_1 + X_2$ is complete, there exists a unique element f^0 in $X_1 + X_2$ such that $\sum_{n=1}^N f^n \to f^0$ in $K(t; \cdot)$-norm as $N \to \infty$ and $K(t; f^0) \leqq \leqq \sum_{n=1}^\infty K(t; f^n)$. Consequently, f^0 belongs to $(X_1, X_2)_{\theta,q;K}$ too, and $\|f^0 - \sum_{n=1}^N f^n\|_{\theta,q;K} \to 0$ as $N \to \infty$, proving that $\{f^n\}$ is summable to f^0.

It remains to prove the inclusion relation (3.2.14). We have already seen that for all $f \in (X_1, X_2)_{\theta,q;K}$, $0 < \theta < 1$, $1 \leqq q < \infty$ and/or $0 \leqq \theta \leqq 1$, $q = \infty$,

$$\|f\|_{X_1+X_2} \leqq \frac{1}{\|t^{-\theta} \min(1, t)\|_{L^q_*}} \|f\|_{\theta,q;K}. \tag{3.2.15}$$

On the other hand, for all f in $X_1 \cap X_2$ we have by inequality (3.2.12) with $s = 1$ that $K(t; f) \leqq \min(1, t) \|f\|_{X_1 \cap X_2}$. Hence

$$\|f\|_{\theta,q;K} \leqq (\|t^{-\theta} \min(1, t)\|_{L^q_*}) \|f\|_{X_1 \cap X_2}, \tag{3.2.16}$$

which proves (3.2.14).

We have thus seen that the non-trivial spaces $(X_1, X_2)_{\theta,q;K}$ define intermediate spaces of X_1 and X_2. Furthermore, $X_1 \subset (X_1, X_2)_{0,\infty;K}$ and $X_2 \subset (X_1, X_2)_{1,\infty;K}$.

Definition 3.2.6. *We define* $(X_1, X_2)_{\theta,q;J}$ *to be the space of all elements* $f \in X_1 + X_2$ *for which there exists a strongly measurable function* $u = u(t)$ *with values in* $X_1 \cap X_2$ *such that*

$$(3.2.17)\qquad \begin{cases} f = \int\limits_0^\infty u(t)\,\frac{dt}{t} \qquad \left(u(\cdot) \in L^1_*(X_1 + X_2)\right) \\ t^{-\theta}\, J\big(t; u(t)\big) \in L^q_*, \end{cases}$$

where $-\infty < \theta < \infty$ *and* $1 \leqq q \leqq \infty$.

Proposition 3.2.7. *For* $0 \leqq \theta \leqq 1$, $q = 1$ *and/or* $0 < \theta < 1$, $1 < q \leqq \infty$ *the spaces* $(X_1, X_2)_{\theta,q;J}$ *are meaningful. They are Banach spaces under the norms*

$$(3.2.18)\qquad \begin{cases} \|f\|_{\theta,q;J} = \inf\limits_{f=\int_0^\infty u(t)\frac{dt}{t}} \left(\|t^{-\theta} J(t; u(t))\|_{L^q_*}\right) \\ \qquad = \inf\limits_{f=\int_0^\infty u(t)\frac{dt}{t}} \left\{\int\limits_0^\infty \left(t^{-\theta} J(t; u(t))\right)^q \frac{dt}{t}\right\}^{1/q}. \end{cases}$$

Furthermore,

$$(3.2.19)\qquad X_1 \cap X_2 \subset (X_1, X_2)_{\theta,q;J} \subset X_1 + X_2.$$

Proof. We only prove relation (3.2.19). If $f \in (X_1, X_2)_{\theta,q;J}$, then we obtain by inequality (3.2.12) for $t = 1$ and Hölder's inequality

$$\|f\|_{X_1+X_2} \leqq \int\limits_0^\infty \|u(s)\|_{X_1+X_2} \frac{ds}{s} \leqq \int\limits_0^\infty \min\left(1, \frac{1}{s}\right) J(s; u(s))\,\frac{ds}{s}$$

$$\leqq \left\{\int\limits_0^\infty \left(s^\theta \min\left(1, \frac{1}{s}\right)\right)^{q'} \frac{ds}{s}\right\}^{1/q'} \left\{\int\limits_0^\infty \left(s^{-\theta} J(s; u(s))\right)^q \frac{ds}{s}\right\}^{1/q},$$

where $q^{-1} + q'^{-1} = 1$. For $0 \leqq \theta \leqq 1$, $q = 1$ and/or $0 < \theta < 1$, $1 < q \leqq \infty$ the factor $\|s^\theta \min(1, s^{-1})\|_{L^{q'}_*}$ on of the right-hand side of the latter inequality is finite, and since this inequality holds for all representations $f = \int\limits_0^\infty u(t)\,dt/t$ we obtain

$$\|f\|_{X_1+X_2} \leqq \left(\|t^{-\theta} \min(1, t)\|_{L^{q'}_*}\right) \|f\|_{\theta,q;J}$$

for all $f \in (X_1, X_2)_{\theta,q;J}$. On the other hand, if f is any element in $X_1 \cap X_2$, then $f \in (X_1, X_2)_{\theta,q;J}$ and

$$\|f\|_{\theta,q;J} \leqq \frac{1}{\|t^{-\theta} \min(1, t)\|_{L^{q'}_*}} \|f\|_{X_1 \cap X_2}.$$

Indeed, there always exist scalar-valued functions $\psi(t) \geqq 0$ such that $\| t^{-\theta} \psi(t) \|_{L_*^{q'}} = 1$. Then, putting

$$u(t) = \frac{\psi(t) \min\left(1, \frac{1}{t}\right)}{\int\limits_0^\infty \psi(s) \min\left(1, \frac{1}{s}\right) \frac{ds}{s}} f,$$

we have by inequality (3.2.10)

$$\left(\int\limits_0^\infty \psi(s) \min\left(1, \frac{1}{s}\right) \frac{ds}{s}\right) \| f \|_{\theta, q; J}$$

$$\leqq \left(\int\limits_0^\infty \psi(s) \min\left(1, \frac{1}{s}\right) \frac{ds}{s}\right) \left\{\int\limits_0^\infty \left(t^{-\theta} J(t; u(t))\right)^q \frac{dt}{t}\right\}^{1/q}$$

$$= \left\{\int\limits_0^\infty \left(t^{-\theta} \psi(t) \min\left(1, \frac{1}{t}\right) J(t; f)\right)^q \frac{dt}{t}\right\}^{1/q}$$

$$\leqq \| t^{-\theta} \psi(t) \|_{L_*^q} \| f \|_{X_1 \cap X_2} = \| f \|_{X_1 \cap X_2}.$$

Taking the supremum over all possible functions ψ on the left-hand side of this estimate we obtain the desired result by the Riesz representation theorem.

Next we shall give a somewhat weaker definition for an element $f \in X_1 + X_2$ to belong to the intermediate space $(X_1, X_2)_{\theta, q; J}$ and, as a consequence, we prove one basic property for these spaces.

Proposition 3.2.8. (a) *A necessary and sufficient condition for an element f to belong to $(X_1, X_2)_{\theta, q; J}$ ($0 \leqq \theta \leqq 1, q = 1$ and/or $0 < \theta < 1$, $1 < q \leqq \infty$) is that there exists an infinitely often strongly continuously differentiable function $v = v(t)$ on $(0, \infty)$ in $X_1 \cap X_2$ such that*

$$f = \int\limits_0^\infty v(t) \frac{dt}{t} \quad (v(\cdot) \in L_*^1(X_1 + X_2)) \text{ and } t^{-\theta} J(t; v(t)) \in L_*^q.$$

(b) *For $0 \leqq \theta \leqq 1$, $q = 1$ and/or $0 < \theta < 1$, $1 < q < \infty$, $X_1 \cap X_2$ is a dense subspace of $(X_1, X_2)_{\theta, q; J}$.*

Proof. (a) Let ψ be any function in $C_{00}^\infty(E_1^+)$ with $\int\limits_0^\infty \psi(t)\, dt/t = 1$. If $f \in (X_1, X_2)_{\theta, q; J}$, then by definition there exists a strongly measurable function $u = u(t)$ in $X_1 \cap X_2$ such that $f = \int\limits_0^\infty u(t)\, dt/t$ $(u(\cdot) \in L_*^1(X_1 + X_2))$ and $t^{-\theta} J(t; u(t)) \in L_*^q$. Hence

$$v(t) = \int\limits_0^\infty \psi\left(\frac{t}{s}\right) u(s) \frac{ds}{s}$$

defines an infinitely often strongly continuously differentiable function on $(0, \infty)$ in $X_1 \cap X_2$ and $\int_0^\infty v(t)\, dt/t = \int_0^\infty u(t)\, dt/t = f$. It is not too difficult to see that

$$\|f\|_{\theta,q;J} = \inf_{f=\int_0^\infty v(t)\frac{dt}{t}} \left(\|t^{-\theta} J(t; v(t))\|_{L^q_*}\right).$$

(b) To prove this part, there exists by part (a) for each element $f \in (X_1, X_2)_{\theta,q;J}$ a strongly continuous function $v = v(t)$ on $(0, \infty)$ in $X_1 \cap X_2$ such that $t^{-\theta} J(t; v(t)) \in L^q_*$. Then

$$f_\varepsilon = \int_0^\infty v_\varepsilon(t) \frac{dt}{t} = \int_\varepsilon^{1/\varepsilon} v(t) \frac{dt}{t} \qquad (0 < \varepsilon < 1)$$

belongs to $X_1 \cap X_2$, and consequently to $(X_1, X_2)_{\theta,q;J}$ too. Furthermore, $J(t; v(t) - v_\varepsilon(t)) \to 0$ for all $0 < t < \infty$ as $\varepsilon \to 0+$ and $J(t; v_\varepsilon(t)) \leqq J(t; v(t))$ uniformly in $0 < \varepsilon < 1$. Thus

$$\|f - f_\varepsilon\|_{\theta,q;J} \leqq \|t^{-\theta} J(t; v(t) - v_\varepsilon(t))\|_{L^q_*} \to 0$$

as $\varepsilon \to 0+$ for $1 \leqq q < \infty$, proving the proposition.

3.2.3 On the Equivalence of the K- and J-Methods

We start with the following inclusion theorem.

Proposition 3.2.9. *For* $0 < \theta < 1$, $1 \leqq q \leqq \infty$

$$(X_1, X_2)_{\theta,q;J} \subset (X_1, X_2)_{\theta,q;K}. \tag{3.2.20}$$

More generally,

$$(X_1, X_2)_{\theta,p;J} \subset (X_1, X_2)_{\theta,q;K} \qquad (1 \leqq p \leqq q). \tag{3.2.21}$$

Proof. We prove relation (3.2.21). By inequality (3.2.12) one obtains for an element $f \in (X_1, X_2)_{\theta,p;J}$

$$K(t; f) \leqq \int_0^\infty K(t; u(s)) \frac{ds}{s} \leqq \int_0^\infty \min\left(1, \frac{t}{s}\right) J(s, u(s)) \frac{ds}{s},$$

and consequently by Young's inequality

$$\|t^{-\theta} K(t; f)\|_{L^q_*} \leqq \|t^{-\theta} \min(1, t)\|_{L^r_*} \; \|t^{-\theta} J(t; u(t))\|_{L^p_*}$$
$$\left(\frac{1}{r} = 1 - \left(\frac{1}{p} - \frac{1}{q}\right)\right)$$

for all representations $f = \int_0^\infty u(t)\, dt/t$. Thus

$$\|f\|_{\theta,q;\mathrm{K}} \leqq (\|t^{-\theta} \min(1, t)\|_{L^r_*})\, \|f\|_{\theta,p;\mathrm{J}},$$

proving (3.2.21) and, in particular, relation (3.2.20).

In the next proposition we show that the inclusion (3.2.20) may be reversed. For this purpose we need the following

Lemma 3.2.10. *Let f be in $X_1 + X_2$ such that*

$$\text{(3.2.22)} \qquad \mathrm{K}(t; f) \to 0 \text{ as } t \to 0+ \text{ and } \frac{\mathrm{K}(t; f)}{t} \to 0 \text{ as } t \to \infty.$$

Then there exists a strongly measurable function $u = u(t)$ in $X_1 \cap X_2$ satisfying

$$\text{(3.2.23)} \qquad f = \operatorname*{s-lim}_{\varepsilon \to 0+} \int_\varepsilon^{1/\varepsilon} u(t) \frac{dt}{t} \qquad (\text{in } X_1 + X_2)$$

and

$$\text{(3.2.24)} \qquad \mathrm{J}(t; u(t)) \leqq 4e\, \mathrm{K}(t; f) \qquad (0 < t < \infty).$$

Proof. For each integer n there exist, by definition of $\mathrm{K}(t; f)$, elements $f_1^n \in X_1$ and $f_2^n \in X_2$ such that

$$f = f_1^n + f_2^n \quad \text{and} \quad \|f_1^n\|_1 + e^n \|f_2^n\|_2 \leqq 2\mathrm{K}(e^n; f).$$

Thus we obtain by (3.2.22)

$$\text{(3.2.25)} \qquad \|f_1^n\|_1 \to 0 \quad \text{as} \quad n \to -\infty \quad \text{and} \quad \|f_2^n\|_2 \to 0 \quad \text{as} \quad n \to \infty.$$

Setting

$$u(t) = u_n \equiv f_1^{n+1} - f_1^n = f_2^n - f_2^{n+1}$$

for $e^n \leqq t < e^{n+1}$, then $u(t)$ is obviously a strongly measurable function in $X_1 \cap X_2$ and

$$\int_{e^{-N}}^{e^N} u(t) \frac{dt}{t} = \sum_{n=-N}^{N-1} u_n = f - f_1^{-N} - f_2^N,$$

proving, together with (3.2.25), relation (3.2.23). Furthermore, for $e^n \leqq t < e^{n+1}$

$$\begin{aligned} \mathrm{J}(t; u(t)) &\leqq \max(\|f_1^n\|_1 + \|f_1^{n+1}\|_1,\ t\,\|f_2^n\|_2 + t\,\|f_2^{n+1}\|_2) \\ &\leqq (\|f_1^n\|_1 + t\,\|f_2^n\|_2) + (\|f_1^{n+1}\|_1 + t\,\|f_2^{n+1}\|_2) \\ &\leqq 2e\,\mathrm{K}(e^n; f) + 2\mathrm{K}(e^{n+1}; f). \end{aligned}$$

Since $\mathrm{K}(t; f)$ is monotone increasing and $\mathrm{K}(e^{n+1}; f) \leqq e \cdot \mathrm{K}(e^n; f)$ we finally obtain (3.2.24).

Proposition 3.2.11. *For* $0 < \theta < 1$, $1 \leqq q \leqq \infty$

$$(X_1, X_2)_{\theta,q;K} \subset (X_1, X_2)_{\theta,q;J}. \tag{3.2.26}$$

Proof. Because $K(t; f)$ is monotone in t, we have for an $f \in (X_1, X_2)_{\theta,q;K}$

$$K(t; f) \left\{ \int_t^\infty s^{-\theta q} \frac{ds}{s} \right\}^{1/q} \leqq \left\{ \int_t^\infty (s^{-\theta} K(s; f))^q \frac{ds}{s} \right\}^{1/q} \leqq \|f\|_{\theta,q;K}.$$

Therefore,

$$K(t; f) \leqq (\theta q)^{1/q} t^\theta \|f\|_{\theta,q;K} \qquad (0 < t < \infty). \tag{3.2.27}$$

For $0 < \theta < 1$, $1 \leqq q \leqq \infty$ this estimate then implies that $K(t; f) \to 0$ as $t \to 0+$ and $t^{-1} K(t; f) \to 0$ as $t \to \infty$ for each $f \in (X_1, X_2)_{\theta,q;K}$. Thus the hypotheses of Lemma 3.2.10 are satisfied, and consequently there exists a strongly measurable function $u = u(t)$ in $X_1 \cap X_2$ such that

$$f = \operatorname*{s-lim}_{\varepsilon \to 0+} \int_\varepsilon^{1/\varepsilon} u(t) \frac{dt}{t} \quad (\text{in } X_1 + X_2) \quad \text{and} \quad J(t; u(t)) \leqq 4e\, K(t; f).$$

Hence

$$\|t^{-\theta} J(t; u(t))\|_{L_*^q} \leqq 4e \|t^{-\theta} K(t; f)\|_{L_*^q},$$

and by methods used in the first part of Proposition 3.2.7

$$\|u(\cdot)\|_{L_*^1(X_1+X_2)} \leqq \|t^{-\theta} \min(1, t)\|_{L_*^{q'}} \|t^{-\theta} J(t; u(t))\|_{L_*^q} < \infty \, (q^{-1} + q'^{-1} = 1),$$

which shows that

$$f = \int_0^\infty u(t) \frac{dt}{t} \quad (u(\cdot) \in L_*^1(X_1 + X_2)) \quad \text{and} \quad \|f\|_{\theta,q;J} \leqq 4e \|f\|_{\theta,q;K}.$$

This completes the proof.

Combining the results of the latter two propositions we obtain part (i) of Theorem 3.2.12 below. Part (ii) is evident.

Theorem 3.2.12. *The intermediate spaces* $(X_1, X_2)_{\theta,q;K}$ *and* $(X_1, X_2)_{\theta,q;J}$ *of* X_1 *and* X_2 *are related in the following way:*

(i) *For* $0 < \theta < 1$, $1 \leqq q \leqq \infty$

$$(X_1, X_2)_{\theta,q;J} = (X_1, X_2)_{\theta,q;K}.$$

(ii)

$$(X_1, X_2)_{0,1;J} \subset X_1 \subset (X_1, X_2)_{0,\infty;K};$$

$$(X_1, X_2)_{1,1;J} \subset X_2 \subset (X_1, X_2)_{1,\infty;K}.$$

There is one further consequence of Propositions 3.2.9 and 3.2.11.

Corollary 3.2.13. *For* $0 < \theta < 1$, $1 \leqq q \leqq \infty$

$$(X_1, X_2)_{\theta,p;K} \subset (X_1, X_2)_{\theta,q;K} \qquad (1 \leqq p \leqq q).$$

In particular,

$$(X_1, X_2)_{\theta,q;K} \subset (X_1, X_2)_{\theta,\infty;K} \qquad (1 \leqq q \leqq \infty)$$

and

$$K(t; f) \leqq C(\theta, q)\, t^\theta \, \|f\|_{\theta,q;K},$$

where $C(\theta, q)$ is a positive constant independent of f.

We have seen in Proposition 3.2.3 (b) that for each $f \in X_1 + X_2$ the function norm $K(t; f)$ is a continuous, monotone increasing and concave function on $(0, \infty)$. Thus, by a classical theorem in real variable theory $K(t; f)$ can be represented as the integral of a non-negative, non-increasing function $k(t; f)$. As a consequence we have

Proposition 3.2.14. *Let $X_1 \cap X_2$ be dense in X_1. For $0 < \theta < 1$, $1 \leqq q \leqq \infty$ an element $f \in X_1 + X_2$ belongs to $(X_1, X_2)_{\theta,q;K}$ if and only if $t^{1-\theta} k(t; f) \in L^q_*$. Furthermore,*

$$\text{(3.2.28)} \qquad \|t^{1-\theta} k(t; f)\|_{L^q_*} \leqq \|f\|_{\theta,q;K} \leqq \frac{1}{\theta} \|t^{1-\theta} k(t; f)\|_{L^q_*}.$$

Proof. As $X_1 \cap X_2$ is dense in X_1, $\lim_{t\to 0+} K(t; f) = 0$ for all $f \in X_1 + X_2$. Indeed, given $\varepsilon > 0$ there are $f_1 \in X_1$ and $f_2 \in X_2$ such that $f = f_1 + f_2$ with $\|f_1\|_1 \leqq \varepsilon$. Thus $\lim_{t\to 0+} K(t; f) \leqq \varepsilon$ for every $\varepsilon > 0$. Therefore,

$$\text{(3.2.29)} \qquad K(t; f) = \int_0^t k(s; f)\, ds \qquad (f \in X_1 + X_2).$$

Now suppose $f \in (X_1, X_2)_{\theta,q;K}$. Since $t\, k(t; f) \leqq K(t; f)$,

$$\|t^{1-\theta} k(t; f)\|_{L^q_*} \leqq \|t^{-\theta} K(t; f)\|_{L^q_*} = \|f\|_{\theta,q;K},$$

which proves the "only if" part.

On the other hand,

$$t^{-\theta} K(t; f) = \int_0^t t^{-\theta} k(s; f)\, ds = \int_1^\infty s^{-\theta} \left(\frac{t}{s}\right)^{1-\theta} k\left(\frac{t}{s}; f\right) \frac{ds}{s},$$

and thus

$$\|t^{-\theta} K(t; f)\|_{L^q_*} \leqq \left(\int_1^\infty s^{-\theta} \frac{ds}{s}\right) \|t^{1-\theta} k(t; f)\|_{L^q_*} = \frac{1}{\theta} \|t^{1-\theta} k(t; f)\|_{L^q_*},$$

the "if" part of the proposition.

The functional $\|t^{1-\theta} k(t; f)\|_{L^q_*}$ on $(X_1, X_2)_{\theta,q;K}$ does in general not possess the properties of a norm as the triangle inequality need not be fulfilled.

3.2.4 A Theorem of Reiteration

We begin with

Definition 3.2.15. *We say an intermediate space* X *of* X_1 *and* X_2 *belongs to*

(i) *the class* $\mathscr{K}(\theta; \mathsf{X}_1, \mathsf{X}_2)$, $0 \leqq \theta \leqq 1$, *if*

$$\mathrm{K}(t; f) \leqq C_1 t^{\theta} \|f\|_{\mathsf{X}} \qquad (f \in \mathsf{X}), \tag{3.2.30}$$

where C_1 *is a constant;*

(ii) *the class* $\mathscr{J}(\theta; \mathsf{X}_1, \mathsf{X}_2)$, $0 \leqq \theta \leqq 1$, *if*

$$\|f\|_{\mathsf{X}} \leqq C_2 t^{-\theta} \mathrm{J}(t; f) \qquad (f \in \mathsf{X}_1 \cap \mathsf{X}_2), \tag{3.2.31}$$

where C_2 *is a constant;*

(iii) *the class* $\mathscr{H}(\theta; \mathsf{X}_1, \mathsf{X}_2)$, $0 \leqq \theta \leqq 1$, *if it belongs to* $\mathscr{K}(\theta; \mathsf{X}_1, \mathsf{X}_2)$ *as well as to* $\mathscr{J}(\theta; \mathsf{X}_1, \mathsf{X}_2)$.

The next proposition gives necessary and sufficient conditions for an intermediate space X of X_1 and X_2 to belong to one of the classes defined above.

Proposition 3.2.16. *An intermediate space* X *of* X_1 *and* X_2 *belongs to*

(a) $\mathscr{K}(\theta; \mathsf{X}_1, \mathsf{X}_2)$, $0 \leqq \theta \leqq 1$, *if and only if*

$$\mathsf{X} \subset (\mathsf{X}_1, \mathsf{X}_2)_{\theta, \infty; \mathrm{K}}; \tag{3.2.32}$$

(b) $\mathscr{J}(\theta; \mathsf{X}_1, \mathsf{X}_2)$, $0 \leqq \theta \leqq 1$, *if and only if*

$$(\mathsf{X}_1, \mathsf{X}_2)_{\theta, 1; \mathrm{J}} \subset \mathsf{X}; \tag{3.2.33}$$

(c) $\mathscr{H}(\theta; \mathsf{X}_1, \mathsf{X}_2)$, $0 \leqq \theta \leqq 1$, *if and only if*

$$(\mathsf{X}_1, \mathsf{X}_2)_{\theta, 1; \mathrm{J}} \subset \mathsf{X} \subset (\mathsf{X}_1, \mathsf{X}_2)_{\theta, \infty; \mathrm{K}}. \tag{3.2.34}$$

Proof. By definition it is evident that $\mathsf{X} \in \mathscr{K}(\theta; \mathsf{X}_1, \mathsf{X}_2)$ if and only if $\mathsf{X} \subset (\mathsf{X}_1, \mathsf{X}_2)_{\theta, \infty; \mathrm{K}}$, i.e. there exists a constant C_1 such that

$$\|f\|_{\theta, \infty; \mathrm{K}} = \sup_{0 < t < \infty} \left(t^{-\theta} \mathrm{K}(t; f)\right) \leqq C_1 \|f\|_{\mathsf{X}} \qquad (f \in \mathsf{X}),$$

proving part (a). To prove part (b), we first show that if $\mathsf{X} \in \mathscr{J}(\theta; \mathsf{X}_1, \mathsf{X}_2)$, then $(\mathsf{X}_1, \mathsf{X}_2)_{\theta, 1; \mathrm{J}} \subset \mathsf{X}$. Indeed, if $f \in (\mathsf{X}_1, \mathsf{X}_2)_{\theta, 1; \mathrm{J}}$, then there is a strongly measurable function $u = u(t)$ in $\mathsf{X}_1 \cap \mathsf{X}_2$ such that $f = \int_0^\infty u(t) \frac{dt}{t}$ $(u(\cdot) \in \mathsf{L}^1_*(\mathsf{X}_1 + \mathsf{X}_2))$ and $t^{-\theta} \mathrm{J}(t; u(t)) \in \mathsf{L}^1_*$. Hence, by condition (3.2.31)

$$\|f\|_{\mathsf{X}} \leqq \int_0^\infty \|u(t)\|_{\mathsf{X}} \frac{dt}{t} \leqq C_2 \int_0^\infty t^{-\theta} \mathrm{J}(t; u(t)) \frac{dt}{t}$$

for all representations $f = \int_0^\infty u(t) \frac{dt}{t}$, and thus

$$\|f\|_X \leqq C_2 \|f\|_{\theta,1;J} \qquad (f \in (X_1, X_2)_{\theta,1;J}). \tag{3.2.35}$$

On the other hand, setting

$$\psi_n(s) = \begin{cases} n & t\,e^{-1/n} \leqq s \leqq t \\ 0 & \text{otherwise} \end{cases} \qquad (0 < t < \infty;\ n = 1, 2, \ldots),$$

we obtain for each $f \in X_1 \cap X_2$ with $u_n = u_n(s) = \psi_n(s) \cdot f$

$$\|f\|_{\theta,1;J} \leqq \int_0^\infty s^{-\theta} J(s; u_n(s)) \frac{ds}{s} = n \int_{te^{-1/n}}^t \psi_n(s)\, s^{-\theta} J(s; f) \frac{ds}{s} \to t^{-\theta} J(t; f)$$

as $n \to \infty$. Now, if we assume that (3.2.33) is valid, i.e. there exists a constant C_2 with (3.2.35) holding, then

$$\|f\|_X \leqq C_2 \|f\|_{\theta,1;J} \leqq C_2 t^{-\theta} J(t; f) \qquad (f \in X_1 \cap X_2),$$

proving part (b). Parts (a) and (b) give part (c).

Corollary 3.2.17. *For* $0 < \theta < 1$, $1 \leqq q \leqq \infty$

$$(X_1, X_2)_{\theta,q;K} \in \mathscr{H}(\theta; X_1, X_2). \tag{3.2.36}$$

Furthermore,

$$X_1 \in \mathscr{H}(0; X_1, X_2) \quad \textit{and} \quad X_2 \in \mathscr{H}(1; X_1, X_2). \tag{3.2.37}$$

Proof. By Theorem 3.2.12 and Corollary 3.2.13 it follows immediately that for $0 < \theta < 1$

$$(X_1, X_2)_{\theta,1;J} \subset (X_1, X_2)_{\theta,q;J} = (X_1, X_2)_{\theta,q;K} \subset (X_1, X_2)_{\theta,\infty;K},$$

proving (3.2.34) and thus (3.2.36). Relation (3.2.37) has already been shown in Theorem 3.2.12.

Now let X_{θ_1} and X_{θ_2} be two intermediate spaces of X_1 and X_2. We denote by

$$(X_{\theta_1}, X_{\theta_2})_{\theta',q;K'} \qquad (0 < \theta' < 1,\ 1 \leqq q < \infty \text{ and/or } 0 \leqq \theta' \leqq 1,\ q = \infty)$$

and

$$(X_{\theta_1}, X_{\theta_2})_{\theta',q;J'} \qquad (0 \leqq \theta' \leqq 1,\ q = 1 \text{ and/or } 0 < \theta' < 1,\ 1 < q \leqq \infty)$$

the intermediate spaces of X_{θ_1} and X_{θ_2} defined in the usual way. In the next two propositions we shall study connections between the intermediate spaces $(X_{\theta_1}, X_{\theta_2})_{\theta',q;K'}$ and $(X_1, X_2)_{\theta,q;K}$ as well as between the spaces $(X_{\theta_1}, X_{\theta_2})_{\theta',q;J'}$ and $(X_1, X_2)_{\theta,q;J}$, respectively, under general assumptions upon X_{θ_1} and X_{θ_2}.

Proposition 3.2.18. *Let the intermediate spaces X_{θ_1} and X_{θ_2} of X_1 and X_2, $0 \leqq \theta_1 < \theta_2 \leqq 1$, belong to $\mathscr{K}(\theta_1; X_1, X_2)$ and $\mathscr{K}(\theta_2; X_1, X_2)$, respectively. Then for $\theta = (1-\theta')\,\theta_1 + \theta'\,\theta_2$*

$$(X_{\theta_1}, X_{\theta_2})_{\theta', q; K'} \subset (X_1, X_2)_{\theta, q; K} \tag{3.2.38}$$
$$(0 < \theta' < 1,\ 1 \leqq q < \infty \text{ and/or } 0 \leqq \theta' \leqq 1,\ q = \infty).$$

Proof. If $f \in (X_{\theta_1}, X_{\theta_2})_{\theta', q; K'}$, then f has a representation $f = f_{\theta_1} + f_{\theta_2}$ and by assumption

$$\begin{aligned} K(t; f) &\leqq K(t; f_{\theta_1}) + K(t; f_{\theta_2}) \leqq C_{\theta_1} t^{\theta_1} \| f_{\theta_1} \|_{\theta_1} + C_{\theta_2} t^{\theta_2} \| f_{\theta_2} \|_{\theta_2} \\ &\leqq C_{\theta_1} t^{\theta_1} \Big(\| f_{\theta_1} \|_{\theta_1} + \frac{C_{\theta_2}}{C_{\theta_1}} t^{\theta_2 - \theta_1} \| f_{\theta_2} \|_{\theta_2} \Big) \end{aligned}$$

for all forms $f = f_{\theta_1} + f_{\theta_2}$, where C_{θ_1} and C_{θ_2} are constants. Thus

$$K(t; f) \leqq C_{\theta_1} t^{\theta_1} K'\Big(\frac{C_{\theta_2}}{C_{\theta_1}} t^{\theta_2 - \theta_1}; f \Big),$$

and consequently for $\theta = (1-\theta')\,\theta_1 + \theta'\,\theta_2$

$$\begin{aligned} \| t^{-\theta} K(t; f) \|_{L^q_*} &\leqq C_{\theta_1} \Big\| t^{-(\theta - \theta_1)} K'\Big(\frac{C_{\theta_2}}{C_{\theta_1}} t^{\theta_2 - \theta_1}; f \Big) \Big\|_{L^q_*} \\ &= \frac{C_{\theta_1}^{1-\theta'} C_{\theta_2}^{\theta'}}{(\theta_2 - \theta_1)^{1/q}} \| s^{-\theta'} K'(s; f) \|_{L^q_*}, \end{aligned}$$

i.e.

$$\| f \|_{\theta, q; K} \leqq \frac{C_{\theta_1}^{1-\theta'} C_{\theta_2}^{\theta'}}{(\theta_2 - \theta_1)^{1/q}} \| f \|_{\theta', q; K'} \qquad \big(f \in (X_{\theta_1}, X_{\theta_2})_{\theta', q; K'}\big), \tag{3.2.39}$$

which proves the proposition.

Proposition 3.2.19. *Let X_{θ_1} and X_{θ_2}, $0 \leqq \theta_1 < \theta_2 \leqq 1$, be two intermediate spaces of X_1 and X_2 which belong to $\mathscr{J}(\theta_1; X_1, X_2)$ and $\mathscr{J}(\theta_2; X_1, X_2)$, respectively. Then for $\theta = (1-\theta')\,\theta_1 + \theta'\,\theta_2$*

$$(X_1, X_2)_{\theta, q; J} \subset (X_{\theta_1}, X_{\theta_2})_{\theta', q; J'} \tag{3.2.40}$$
$$(0 \leqq \theta' \leqq 1,\ q = 1 \text{ and/or } 0 < \theta' < 1,\ 1 < q \leqq \infty).$$

Proof. If $f \in (X_1, X_2)_{\theta, q; J}$, then there exists a strongly measurable function $u = u(s)$ in $X_1 \cap X_2$ such that

$$f = \int_0^\infty u(s) \frac{ds}{s} \quad \big(u(\cdot) \in L^1_*(X_1 + X_2)\big) \quad \text{and} \quad s^{-\theta} J(s; u(s)) \in L^q_*.$$

Obviously, $u = u(s)$ is a strongly measurable function in $X_{\theta_1} \cap X_{\theta_2}$ and by hypothesis

$$\begin{aligned} J'(s; u(s)) &\equiv \max\big(\| u(s) \|_{\theta_1}, s \| u(s) \|_{\theta_2}\big) \\ &\leqq \max\big(C_{\theta_1} t^{-\theta_1} J(t; u(s));\ C_{\theta_2} t^{-\theta_2} s\, J(t; u(s))\big) \\ &= C_{\theta_1} t^{-\theta_1} \max\Big(1, \frac{C_{\theta_2}}{C_{\theta_1}} t^{-(\theta_2 - \theta_1)} s\Big) J(t; u(s)), \end{aligned}$$

where C_{θ_1} and C_{θ_2} are positive constants. Now we choose t such that $t^{\theta_2-\theta_1} = \frac{C_{\theta_2}}{C_{\theta_1}} s$. Thus

$$J'(s; u(s)) \leqq C_{\theta_1} \left(\frac{C_{\theta_2}}{C_{\theta_1}} s\right)^{-\frac{\theta_1}{\theta_2-\theta_1}} J\left(\left(\frac{C_{\theta_2}}{C_{\theta_1}} s\right)^{\frac{1}{\theta_2-\theta_1}}; u(s)\right)$$

for almost all s, and consequently

$$\| s^{-\theta'} J'(s; u(s)) \|_{L_*^q} \leqq C_{\theta_1}^{1-\theta'} C_{\theta_2}^{\theta'} \left\| \left(\frac{C_{\theta_2}}{C_{\theta_1}} s\right)^{-\frac{\theta}{\theta_2-\theta_1}} J\left(\left(\frac{C_{\theta_2}}{C_{\theta_1}} s\right)^{\frac{1}{\theta_2-\theta_1}}; u(s)\right)\right\|_{L_*^q}$$

$$\leqq C_{\theta_1}^{1-\theta'} C_{\theta_2}^{\theta'} (\theta_2 - \theta_1)^{1/q} \left\| s^{-\theta} J\left(s; u\left(\frac{C_{\theta_1}}{C_{\theta_2}} s^{\theta_2-\theta_1}\right)\right)\right\|_{L_*^q} < \infty.$$

Moreover,

$$\| f \|_{X_{\theta_1}+X_{\theta_2}} \leqq \int_0^\infty \| u(s) \|_{X_{\theta_1}+X_{\theta_2}} \frac{ds}{s} \leqq \int_0^\infty \min\left(1, \frac{1}{s}\right) J'(s; u(s)) \frac{ds}{s}$$

$$\leqq \left\| s^{\theta'} \min\left(1, \frac{1}{s}\right)\right\|_{L_*^{q'}} \| s^{-\theta'} J'(s; u(s)) \|_{L_*^q} < \infty \qquad (q^{-1} + q'^{-1} = 1),$$

giving $f \in (X_{\theta_1}, X_{\theta_2})_{\theta', q; J'}$. Finally,

$$\frac{f}{\theta_2 - \theta_1} = \frac{1}{\theta_2 - \theta_1} \int_0^\infty u(s) \frac{ds}{s} = \int_0^\infty u\left(\frac{C_{\theta_1}}{C_{\theta_2}} s^{\theta_2-\theta_1}\right) \frac{ds}{s}$$

and

$$\| f \|_{\theta', q; J'} \leqq \frac{C_{\theta_1}^{1-\theta'} C_{\theta_2}^{\theta'}}{(\theta_2 - \theta_1)^{1-1/q}} \| f \|_{\theta, q; J} \qquad (f \in (X_1, X_2)_{\theta, q; J}), \tag{3.2.41}$$

where $\theta = (1 - \theta')\,\theta_1 + \theta'\,\theta_2$. This completes the proof.

Both Propositions 3.2.18 and 3.2.19 lead to the so-called *theorem of reiteration.*

Theorem 3.2.20. *If the intermediate spaces* X_{θ_1} *and* X_{θ_2} *of* X_1 *and* X_2, $0 \leqq \theta_1 < \theta_2 \leqq 1$, *belong to* $\mathscr{H}(\theta_1; X_1, X_2)$ *and* $\mathscr{H}(\theta_2; X_1, X_2)$, *respectively, then for* $\theta = (1 - \theta')\,\theta_1 + \theta'\,\theta_2$, $0 < \theta' < 1$ *and* $1 \leqq q \leqq \infty$,

$$(X_{\theta_1}, X_{\theta_2})_{\theta', q; K'} = (X_1, X_2)_{\theta, q; K} \tag{3.2.42}$$

with equivalent norms. Furthermore,

$$(X_1, X_2)_{\theta_1, 1; J} \subset (X_{\theta_1}, X_{\theta_2})_{0, 1; J'} \subset X_{\theta_1} \subset (X_{\theta_1}, X_{\theta_2})_{0, \infty; K'} \subset (X_1, X_2)_{\theta_1, \infty; K}$$

and

$$(X_1, X_2)_{\theta_2, 1; J} \subset (X_{\theta_1}, X_{\theta_2})_{1, 1; J'} \subset X_{\theta_2} \subset (X_{\theta_1}, X_{\theta_2})_{1, \infty; K'} \subset (X_1, X_2)_{\theta_2, \infty; K}.$$

Corollary 3.2.21. *The assertion of Proposition* 3.2.14 *also holds in case* $X_1 \cap X_2$ *is not dense in* X_1.

Indeed, the closure of $X_1 \cap X_2$ in X_1, denoted by X_1^0, is equal to $(X_1, X_2)_{0,1;J}$. One proves easily that

$$\|f\|_1 \leqq \|f\|_{0,1;J} \leqq \|f\|_1,$$

the first inequality being valid for all $f \in (X_1, X_2)_{0,1;J}$ and the second one for all $f \in X_1 \cap X_2$. Since by Proposition 3.2.8 (b) $X_1 \cap X_2$ is dense in $(X_1, X_2)_{0,1;J}$, the spaces X_1^0 and $(X_1, X_2)_{0,1;J}$ are equal to another. Thus X_1^0 belongs to the class $\mathscr{H}(0; X_1, X_2)$, and consequently by Theorem 3.2.20

$$(X_1^0, X_2)_{\theta,q;K} = (X_1, X_2)_{\theta,q;K}$$

for $0 < \theta < 1$, $1 \leqq q \leqq \infty$.

3.2.5 Interpolation Theorems

An *interpolation pair* (X_1, X_2) is a couple of Banach spaces X_1 and X_2, continuously contained in a linear Hausdorff space $\mathscr{X}$.

Let (X_1, X_2) and (Y_1, Y_2) be two interpolation pairs in $\mathscr{X}$ and $\mathscr{Y}$, respectively. We denote by $\mathscr{T}(\mathscr{X}, \mathscr{Y})$ the space of all linear transformations from $X_1 + X_2$ to $Y_1 + Y_2$ such that for a $T \in \mathscr{T}(\mathscr{X}, \mathscr{Y})$, $f_i \in X_i$ implies $T f_i \in Y_i$ and

$$\|T f_i\|_i \leqq M_i \|f_i\|_i \qquad (i = 1, 2), \tag{3.2.43}$$

i.e. the restriction of T on X_i is a bounded linear transformation from X_i to Y_i with norm M_i.

Definition 3.2.22. *Let X and Y be two intermediate spaces of X_1 and X_2 and of Y_1 and Y_2, respectively. We say X and Y have the* i n t e r p o l a t i o n p r o p e r t y *if for each $T \in \mathscr{T}(\mathscr{X}, \mathscr{Y})$ the restriction of T on X is a bounded linear transformation on X to Y.*

We then call X and Y i n t e r p o l a t i o n s p a c e s *with respect to (X_1, X_2) and (Y_1, Y_2). More precisely, X and Y are called interpolation spaces of* t y p e *θ, $0 \leqq \theta \leqq 1$, if for the norm M of T on X to Y the convexity inequality*

$$M \leqq C M_1^{1-\theta} M_2^{\theta} \tag{3.2.44}$$

holds for all $T \in \mathscr{T}(\mathscr{X}, \mathscr{Y})$, where C is a constant $\geqq 1$, but independent of T. For $C = 1$ the inequality (3.2.44) is said to be e x a c t.

If $X_1 = Y_1$, $X_2 = Y_2$ and $X = Y$ and if I is the identity mapping of $X_1 + X_2$ into itself, then for an intermediate space X of X_1 and X_2 the inequality (3.2.44) is valid for $C = 1$ and all θ. Thus $C = 1$ is best possible.

The following theorems are concerned with the intermediate spaces defined and studied in the previous subsections in connection with interpolation.

Theorem 3.2.23. *Let (X_1, X_2) and (Y_1, Y_2) be two interpolation pairs of $\mathscr{X}$ and $\mathscr{Y}$, respectively.*

(a) *The intermediate spaces $(X_1, X_2)_{\theta,q;K}$ and $(Y_1, Y_2)_{\theta,q;K}$ $(0<\theta<1,$ $1 \leqq q < \infty$ and/or $0 \leqq \theta \leqq 1$, $q=\infty)$ are interpolation spaces of (X_1, X_2) and (Y_1, Y_2) of type θ and*

$$M \leqq M_1^{1-\theta} M_2^{\theta} \qquad (T \in \mathscr{T}(\mathscr{X}, \mathscr{Y})).$$

(b) *The intermediate spaces $(X_1, X_2)_{\theta,q;J}$ and $(Y_1, Y_2)_{\theta,q;J}$ $(0 \leqq \theta \leqq 1$, $q=1$ and/or $0<\theta<1$, $1<q \leqq \infty)$ are interpolation spaces of (X_1, X_2) and (Y_1, Y_2) of type θ and*

$$M \leqq M_1^{1-\theta} M_2^{\theta} \qquad (T \in \mathscr{T}(\mathscr{X}, \mathscr{Y})).$$

Proof. (a) Let T be an operator in $\mathscr{T}(\mathscr{X}, \mathscr{Y})$. Then by (3.2.43) for an $f \in X_1 + X_2$

$$\begin{aligned} K(t; Tf) &= \inf_{f=f_1+f_2} (\|Tf_1\|_1 + t\,\|Tf_2\|_2) \\ &\leqq M_1 \inf_{f=f_1+f_2} \left(\|f_1\|_1 + \frac{M_2}{M_1} t\,\|f_2\|_2\right) = M_1\, K\left(\frac{M_2}{M_1} t; f\right). \end{aligned}$$

Therefore, if $f \in (X_1, X_2)_{\theta,q;K}$ we obtain

$$\begin{aligned} \|Tf\|_{\theta,q;K} &= \|t^{-\theta} K(t; Tf)\|_{L_*^q} \leqq M_1 \left\| t^{-\theta} K\left(\frac{M_2}{M_1} t; f\right)\right\|_{L_*^q} \\ &= M_1^{1-\theta} M_2^{\theta}\, \|t^{-\theta} K(t; f)\|_{L_*^q} = M_1^{1-\theta} M_2^{\theta}\, \|f\|_{\theta,q;K}, \end{aligned}$$

which proves part (a).

To establish part (b), we remark that for all $g \in X_1 \cap X_2$

$$\begin{aligned} J(t; Tg) &= \max(\|Tg\|_1, t\,\|Tg\|_2) \\ &\leqq M_1 \max\left(\|g\|_1, \frac{M_2}{M_1} t\,\|g\|_2\right) = M_1\, J\left(\frac{M_2}{M_1} t; g\right). \end{aligned}$$

Now, for an $f \in (X_1, X_2)_{\theta,q;J}$ there exists, by definition, a measurable function $u = u(t)$ in $X_1 \cap X_2$ such that $f = \int_0^\infty u(t) \frac{dt}{t}$ $(u(\cdot) \in L_*^1(X_1 + X_2))$ and $t^{-\theta} J(t; u(t)) \in L_*^q$. Thus

$$\begin{aligned} \|Tf\|_{\theta,q;J} &\leqq \|t^{-\theta} J(t; Tu(t))\|_{L_*^q} \leqq M_1 \left\| t^{-\theta} J\left(\frac{M_2}{M_1} t; u(t)\right)\right\|_{L_*^q} \\ &= M_1^{1-\theta} M_2^{\theta} \left\| t^{-\theta} J\left(t; u\left(\frac{M_1}{M_2} t\right)\right)\right\|_{L_*^q}. \end{aligned}$$

This inequality holds for all representations $f = \int_0^\infty u\left(\frac{M_1}{M_2} t\right) \frac{dt}{t}$, and consequently

$$\|Tf\|_{\theta,q;J} \leqq M_1^{1-\theta} M_2^{\theta}\, \|f\|_{\theta,q;J}.$$

In the theory of interpolation this theorem expresses a result of M. Riesz-Thorin type, while the second theorem following below expresses one of Marcinkiewicz type.

Theorem 3.2.24. *The intermediate spaces* $(X_1, X_2)_{\theta,q;J}$ *and* $(Y_1, Y_2)_{\theta,q;K}$ $(0 < \theta < 1, 1 \leqq q \leqq \infty)$ *are interpolation spaces of* (X_1, X_2) *and* (Y_1, Y_2) *of type* θ. *In particular, for the functional* $\| t^{1-\theta} k(t; T f) \|_{L^q_*}$ *on* $(Y_1, Y_2)_{\theta,q;K}$ *there holds the estimate*

$$\| t^{1-\theta} k(t; T f) \|_{L^q_*} \leqq \frac{M_1^{1-\theta} M_2^{\theta}}{(1-\theta)\,\theta} \| f \|_{\theta,q;J}. \tag{3.2.45}$$

Proof. Let $T \in \mathcal{T}(\mathcal{X}, \mathcal{Y})$. By assumption T transforms $X_1 \cap X_2$ into $Y_1 \cap Y_2$ and, applying inequality (3.2.12), one obtains for an element $g \in X_1 \cap X_2$

$$\begin{aligned} t\, k(t; T g) &\leqq K(t; T g) \leqq \min\left(1, \frac{t}{s}\right) J(s; T g) \\ &\leqq \min\left(1, \frac{t}{s}\right) \max(M_1 \| g \|_1, s M_2 \| g \|_2) \\ &\leqq M_1 \min\left(1, \frac{t}{s}\right) J\left(\frac{M_2}{M_1} s; g\right) \qquad (0 < s,\ t < \infty). \end{aligned}$$

Now, if $f \in (X_1, X_2)_{\theta,q;J}$, then there exists a measurable function $u = u(t)$ in $X_1 \cap X_2$ such that $f = \int_0^\infty u(s) \frac{ds}{s}$ $(u(\cdot) \in L^1_*(X_1 + X_2))$ and $s^{-\theta} J(s; u(s)) \in L^q_*$. Therefore,

$$T f = \int_0^\infty T u(s) \frac{ds}{s}$$

and by the above estimate

$$t\, k(t; T f) \leqq M_1 \int_0^\infty \min\left(1, \frac{t}{s}\right) J\left(\frac{M_2}{M_1} s; u(s)\right) \frac{ds}{s}.$$

Consequently,

$$\begin{aligned} \| t^{1-\theta} k(t; T f) \|_{L^q_*} &\leqq M_1 \| t^{-\theta} \min(1, t) \|_{L^1_*} \left\| s^{-\theta} J\left(\frac{M_2}{M_1} s; u(s)\right) \right\|_{L^q_*} \\ &\leqq \frac{M_1^{1-\theta} M_2^{\theta}}{(1-\theta)\,\theta} \| s^{-\theta} J(s; u(s)) \|_{L^q_*}. \end{aligned}$$

This inequality holds for all representations of f, which proves the desired estimate (3.2.45) and therefore the theorem.

3.3 Lorentz Spaces and Convexity Theorems

3.3.1 Lorentz Spaces

This section is concerned with function spaces of complex-valued functions f defined on a *totally σ-finite measure space* (R, μ).

Let $\mathcal{L}(\mu)$ be the space of all measurable functions f which are finite almost everywhere (two functions coinciding almost everywhere will be identified). $\mathscr{L}(\mu)$ becomes a linear Hausdorff space under convergence in measure on each measurable set E in R of finite measure $\mu(\mathrm{E})$. Moreover, we denote by $L^p(\mu)$, $1 \leqq p \leqq \infty$, the space of all functions $f \in \mathscr{L}(\mu)$ for which

$$\int_{\mathrm{R}} |f|^p \, d\mu < \infty \qquad (1 \leqq p < \infty),$$

$$\mu\{x \in \mathrm{R}; |f(x)| > C\} = 0 \quad \text{for some } C > 0 \qquad (p = \infty).$$

The Lebesgue spaces $L^p(\mu)$ are Banach spaces under the usual norms, continuously embedded in $\mathscr{L}(\mu)$.

Definition 3.3.1. *For an $f \in \mathscr{L}(\mu)$ the distribution function $D(f;\sigma)$ on $0 < \sigma < \infty$ is defined by the extended real-valued function*

$$D(f;\sigma) = \mu\{x \in \mathrm{R}; |f(x)| > \sigma\}. \tag{3.3.1}$$

There is the following

Lemma 3.3.2. *Let $f \in \mathscr{L}(\mu)$.*

(a) *$D(f;\sigma)$ is non-increasing and continuous from the right on $(0, \infty)$.*

(b) *If $f \in L^p(\mu)$, $1 \leqq p \leqq \infty$, then*

$$\|f\|^p_{L^p(\mu)} = \int_{\mathrm{R}} |f|^p \, d\mu = p \int_0^\infty \sigma^{p-1} D(f;\sigma) \, d\sigma \quad (1 \leqq p < \infty),$$

$$\|f\|_{L^\infty(\mu)} = \operatorname*{ess\,sup}_{x \in \mathrm{R}} |f(x)| = \inf\{\sigma; D(f;\sigma) = 0\} \quad (p = \infty),$$

the integral on the right-hand side defined on the semi-infinite interval $(0, \infty)$ being understood in the sense of Lebesgue with Lebesgue measure $d\sigma$.

Definition 3.3.3. *Let $f \in \mathscr{L}(\mu)$ and let $D(f;\sigma)$ be its distribution on $(0, \infty)$. The non-increasing rearrangement of f on $(0, \infty)$ is given by*

$$f^*(t) = \inf\{\sigma; D(f;\sigma) \leqq t\}. \tag{3.3.2}$$

Lemma 3.3.4. *Let $f \in \mathscr{L}(\mu)$.*

(a) *$f^*(t)$ is non-increasing and continuous from the right on $(0, \infty)$.*

(b) *If $D(f;\sigma) < \infty$, then $f^*(D(f;\sigma)) \leqq \sigma$. Moreover, if $f^*(t)$ is continuous at $t = D(f;\sigma)$, then $f^*(D(f;\sigma)) = \sigma$.*

(c) *The functions f and f^* are equi-measurable, i.e. $D(f;\sigma)$ is equal to the Lebesgue measure of the set $\{t \in (0, \infty); f^*(t) > \sigma\}$ for each $\sigma > 0$.*

(d) *If $f \in L^p(\mu)$, $1 \leqq p \leqq \infty$, then*

$$\|f\|_{L^p(\mu)} = \|f\|_p = \left\{\int_0^\infty f^*(t)^p \, dt\right\}^{1/p} \qquad (1 \leqq p < \infty),$$

$$\|f\|_{L^\infty(\mu)} = \|f\|_\infty = \sup_{0<t<\infty} (f^*(t)) \qquad (p = \infty).$$

(e) *For each measurable set* E *in* R *with* $\mu(E) \leqq t$ $(0 < t < \infty)$

$$\int_E |f|\, d\mu \leqq \int_0^t f^*(s)\, ds.$$

In particular, if $E_\sigma = \{x \in R; |f(x)| > \sigma\}$, *then*

$$\int_{E_\sigma} |f|\, d\mu = \int_0^{D(f;\sigma)} f^*(s)\, ds.$$

(f) *If, in addition, the measure* μ *on* E *is non-atomic, then given any* $t > 0$ *there exists a measurable set* E_t *in* R *such that* $\mu(E_t) = t$ *and*

$$\int_{E_t} |f|\, d\mu = \int_0^t f^*(s)\, ds.$$

In particular,

$$\sup_{\mu(E)=t} \int_E |f|\, d\mu = \int_0^t f^*(s)\, ds.$$

(g) *If* f *and* g *are two functions in* $\mathscr{L}(\mu)$, *then*

$$\int_R |f g|\, d\mu \leqq \int_0^\infty f^*(t)\, g^*(t)\, dt.$$

Finally, let us introduce the *average function*

$$f^{**}(t) = \frac{1}{t} \int_0^t f^*(s)\, ds \tag{3.3.3}$$

of the non-increasing rearrangement of an f in $\mathscr{L}(\mu)$. We are now able to consider the Lorentz spaces.

Definition 3.3.5. *The Lorentz spaces* $L^{pq}(\mu)$ *are defined to be the collection of all functions* $f \in \mathscr{L}(\mu)$ *for which either the integral or the supremum*

$$\int_0^\infty \left(t^{1/p} f^{**}(t)\right)^q \frac{dt}{t} \qquad (1 < p < \infty,\ 1 \leqq q < \infty),$$

$$\sup_{0<t<\infty} \left(t^{1/p} f^{**}(t)\right) \qquad (1 \leqq p \leqq \infty,\ q = \infty)$$

is finite.

For the spaces $L^{pq}(\mu)$, we shall refer to p as the principal index. There is the following

Theorem 3.3.6. *The spaces* $L^{pq}(\mu)$ *are Banach spaces continuously embedded in* $\mathscr{L}(\mu)$ *under the norms*

$$\|f\|_{L^{pq}(\mu)} = \begin{cases} \left\{ \int_0^t \left(t^{1/p} f^{**}(t)\right)^q \frac{dt}{t} \right\}^{1/q} & (1 \leqq q < \infty) \\ \sup_{0<t<\infty} \left(t^{1/p} f^{**}(t)\right) & (q = \infty). \end{cases} \tag{3.3.4}$$

Furthermore, for $1 < p < \infty$ *the Lebesgue spaces* $L^p(\mu)$ *are equivalent to* $L^{pp}(\mu)$:

$$\|f\|_{L^p(\mu)} \leqq \|f\|_{L^{pp}(\mu)} \leqq \frac{1}{1-1/p} \|f\|_{L^p(\mu)}.$$

The spaces $L^1(\mu)$ *and* $L^{1\infty}(\mu)$ *as well as the spaces* $L^\infty(\mu)$ *and* $L^{\infty\infty}(\mu)$ *are equal to each other with*

$$\|f\|_{L^1(\mu)} = \lim_{t\to\infty} \int_0^t f^*(s)\, ds = \sup_{0<t<\infty} (t\, f^{**}(t)) = \|f\|_{L^{1\infty}(\mu)},$$

$$\|f\|_{L^\infty(\mu)} = \lim_{t\to 0+} f^{**}(t) = \sup_{0<t<\infty} (f^{**}(t)) = \|f\|_{L^{\infty\infty}(\mu)}.$$

Theorem 3.3.6 is a direct consequence of Theorem 3.3.8 following below.

From this point of view the Lorentz spaces are natural generalizations of the classical Lebesgue spaces. In case $1 < p < \infty$, $q = \infty$ the spaces $L^{p\infty}(\mu)$ are often known as Marcinkiewicz spaces and denoted by $M^p(\mu)$. Usually, these spaces are defined to be the set of all functions $f \in \mathscr{L}(\mu)$ such that the functional

$$\sup_{0<t<\infty} (t^{1/p} f^*(t)) \qquad (1 \leqq p \leqq \infty) \tag{3.3.5}$$

is finite. Note that except for $p = \infty$ the latter functional does not define a norm but only a quasi-norm, since the triangle inequality fails. We shall however see that for $1 < p < \infty$ the Marcinkiewicz spaces $M^p(\mu)$ (defined by (3.3.5)) are normable by (3.3.4) for $q = \infty$, while $M^\infty(\mu)$ and $L^\infty(\mu)$ are equal to another by definition. In case $p = 1$, $L^{1\infty}(\mu) = L^1(\mu)$ is a proper subspace of the quasi-linear space $M^1(\mu)$. In the following we do not distinguish between the spaces $M^p(\mu)$ and $L^{p\infty}(\mu)$, $1 < p \leqq \infty$.

The object now is to study the Lorentz spaces $L^{pq}(\mu)$ in connection with the intermediate spaces of $L^{p_1}(\mu)$ and $L^{p_2}(\mu)$, $1 \leqq p_1 < p_2 \leqq \infty$ generated, in particular, by the K-method. Moreover, in the following subsection we shall prove the convexity theorems of M. Riesz-Thorin, Marcinkiewicz and Calderón for these spaces.

The fundamental relation in this section will be proved in the following

Proposition 3.3.7. *If* f *is an element in* $L^1(\mu) + L^\infty(\mu)$, *then the function norm*

$$K(t; f) = \int_0^t f^*(s)\, ds \qquad (0 < t < \infty), \tag{3.3.6}$$

f^* *being the non-increasing rearrangement of* f *on* $(0, \infty)$. *In particular, the functions* $k(t; f)$ *(defined at the end of Sec. 3.2.3) and* $f^*(t)$ *are equal almost everywhere.*

Proof. Since $f \in L^1(\mu) + L^\infty(\mu)$ implies $|f| \in L^1(\mu) + L^\infty(\mu)$ and $K(t; f) = K(t; |f|)$ for each $t > 0$, we may assume that f is real and non-negative. Now, let f be given by $f = g + h$, $g \in L^1(\mu)$ and $h \in L^\infty(\mu)$. Then $f(x) = \operatorname{Re} g(x) + \operatorname{Re} h(x)$. Since $|\operatorname{Re} g(x)| \leqq |g(x)|$ and $|\operatorname{Re} h(x)| \leqq |h(x)|$, and consequently $\|\operatorname{Re} g\|_{L^1(\mu)} \leqq \|g\|_{L^1(\mu)}$ and $\|\operatorname{Re} h(x)\|_{L^\infty(\mu)} \leqq \|h\|_{L^\infty(\mu)}$, we conclude that in order to calculate

$$K(t; f) = \inf_{f=g+h} (\|g\|_{L^1(\mu)} + t\,\|h\|_{L^\infty(\mu)}), \tag{3.3.7}$$

we may restrict the discussion to real-valued functions g and h.

Furthermore, setting $g'(x) = \min(\chi(x)\, g(x), f(x))$, where χ is the characteristic function of the set of points in R upon which g is positive, and $h'(x) = f(x) - g'(x)$, then

$$0 \leqq g'(x) \leqq |g(x)|, \quad 0 \leqq h'(x) \leqq |f(x) - g(x)| = |h(x)|,$$

i.e. the infimum in (3.3.7) is not changed by imposing on g and h the additional hypothesis of being non-negative.

Under these assumptions we define

$$f_\sigma(x) = \min(\sigma, f(x)), \quad \text{where} \quad \sigma = \|h\|_{L^\infty(\mu)}.$$

Since $h(x) \leqq \sigma$ and $h(x) \leqq f(x)$, we have $h(x) \leqq f_\sigma(x)$ and $f(x) - f_\sigma(x) \leqq f(x) - h(x) = g(x)$. Therefore,

$$\|f - f_\sigma\|_{L^1(\mu)} + t\,\|f_\sigma\|_{L^\infty(\mu)} = \|f - f_\sigma\|_{L^1(\mu)} + t\,\sigma \leqq \|g\|_{L^1(\mu)} + t\,\|h\|_{L^\infty(\mu)},$$

i.e.

$$K(t; f) = \inf_{0<\sigma<\infty} (\|f - f_\sigma\|_{L^1(\mu)} + t\,\sigma). \tag{3.3.8}$$

We now prove that $\|f - f_\sigma\|_{L^1(\mu)} + t\,\sigma$ achieves its infimum at $\sigma_0 = \inf\{\sigma; D(f; \sigma) < t\}$. Indeed, if $\sigma > \sigma_0$ then, since $D(f; \sigma_0) \leqq t$,

$$\begin{aligned}&(\|f - f_\sigma\|_{L^1(\mu)} + t\,\sigma) - (\|f - f_{\sigma_0}\|_{L^1(\mu)} + t\,\sigma_0)\\ &= -\int_R (f_\sigma - f_{\sigma_0})\, d\mu + t(\sigma - \sigma_0) \geqq -D(f; \sigma_0)\,(\sigma - \sigma_0) + t(\sigma - \sigma_0) \geqq 0.\end{aligned}$$

On the other hand, if $\|f - f_\sigma\|_{L^1(\mu)} + t\,\sigma$ is finite for some σ, then $\|f - f_\tau\|_{L^1(\mu)} + t\,\tau$ is a continuous function in $\tau \geqq \sigma$. Supposing $\|f - f_\sigma\|_{L^1(\mu)} + t\,\sigma < \infty$ for some $\sigma < \sigma_0$, then, given $\varepsilon > 0$, there is a τ, $\sigma \leqq \tau < \sigma_0$, such that

$$|(\|f - f_\tau\|_{L^1(\mu)} + t\,\tau) - (\|f - f_{\sigma_0}\|_{L^1(\mu)} + t\,\sigma_0)| < \varepsilon.$$

Furthermore, since $D(f; \tau) \geqq t$,

$$\begin{aligned}&(\|f - f_\sigma\|_{L^1(\mu)} + t\,\sigma) - (\|f - f_\tau\|_{L^1(\mu)} + t\,\tau)\\ &= \int_R (f_\tau - f_\sigma)\, d\mu - t(\tau - \sigma) \geqq D(f; \tau)\,(\tau - \sigma) - t(\tau - \sigma) \geqq 0.\end{aligned}$$

Thus

$$(\|f - f_\sigma\|_{L^1(\mu)} + t\,\sigma) - (\|f - f_{\sigma_0}\|_{L^1(\mu)} + t\,\sigma_0) \geqq -\varepsilon$$

for every $\varepsilon > 0$, and consequently

$$K(t; f) = \|f - f_{\sigma_0}\|_{L^1(\mu)} + t\,\sigma_0 .$$

Finally, since $D(f; \sigma)$ is continuous from the right (Lemma 3.3.2 (a)), $f^*(s) = \sigma_0$ for $D(f; \sigma_0) \leqq s \leqq t$. Thus by Lemma 3.3.4 (e)

$$\begin{aligned} K(t; f) &= \int_{E_{\sigma_0}} f\,d\mu + \sigma_0(t - D(f; \sigma_0)) \\ &= \int_0^{D(f;\sigma_0)} f^*(s)\,ds + \sigma_0(t - D(f; \sigma_0)) = \int_0^t f^*(s)\,ds. \end{aligned}$$

This proves the proposition.

As an immediate consequence of this proposition as well as Propositions 3.2.5 and 3.2.14 of the foregoing section and Lemma 3.3.4 (d) we have

Theorem 3.3.8. *The Lorentz spaces* $L^{pq}(\mu)$ $(1 < p < \infty,\ 1 \leqq q < \infty$ *and/or* $1 \leqq p \leqq \infty,\ q = \infty)$ *are intermediate spaces of* $L^1(\mu)$ *and* $L^\infty(\mu)$. *They are equal to the spaces* $(L^1(\mu), L^\infty(\mu))_{\theta,q;K}$, $\theta = 1 - 1/p$, *and*

$$\|f\|_{L^{pq}(\mu)} = \|f\|_{1-1/p,q;K} .$$

Moreover, for $1 < p < \infty$, $1 \leqq q \leqq \infty$ *there is a bounded functional on* $(L^1(\mu), L^\infty(\mu))_{1-1/p,q;K}$ *defined by* $\|t^{1/p} f^*(t)\|_{L^q_*}$ *satisfying*

$$(3.3.9)\qquad \|t^{1/p} f^*(t)\|_{L^q_*} \leqq \|f\|_{1-1/p,q;K} \leqq \frac{1}{1-1/p}\, \|t^{1/p} f^*(t)\|_{L^q_*} .$$

In particular we have for $1 < p < \infty$, $L^p(\mu) = (L^1(\mu), L^\infty(\mu))_{1-1/p,p;K}$ *with the equivalent norm:*

$$\|f\|_{L^p(\mu)} \leqq \|f\|_{1-1/p;p;K} \leqq \frac{1}{1-1/p}\, \|f\|_{L^p(\mu)} .$$

Also, $L^1(\mu) = (L^1(\mu), L^\infty(\mu))_{0,\infty;K}$ *and* $L^\infty(\mu) = (L^1(\mu), L^\infty(\mu))_{1,\infty;K}$ *and*

$$\|f\|_{L^1(\mu)} = \|f\|_{0,\infty;K}, \qquad \|f\|_{L^\infty(\mu)} = \|f\|_{1,\infty;K} .$$

A further consequence of Theorem 3.3.8 and Corollary 3.2.13 is given by

Theorem 3.3.9. (a) *For* $1 < p < \infty$, $1 \leqq q < \infty$, *the space* $L^1(\mu) \cap \cap L^\infty(\mu)$ *is a dense subset of* $L^{pq}(\mu)$.

(b) *For* $1 < p < \infty$ *and* $1 \leqq q_1 \leqq q_2 \leqq \infty$

$$L^{pq_1}(\mu) \subset L^{pq_2}(\mu) .$$

In particular, $L^{pq}(\mu)$, $1 \leqq q \leqq p$, *is a dense continuously embedded subspace of* $L^p(\mu)$. *Moreover,*

$$L^{pq}(\mu) \subset M^p(\mu)$$

for all $q \geqq 1$. *For* $q = p$

$$L^p(\mu) \subset M^p(\mu)$$

and

$$\sup_{0<t<\infty} \left(t^{1/p} f^*(t)\right) \leqq \|f\|_{L^p(\mu)} \qquad (f \in L^p(\mu)),$$

holding for all $1 \leqq p \leqq \infty$.

By Corollary 3.2.17 of Sec. 3.2.4 we know that the Lebesgue spaces $L^p(\mu)$, $1 \leqq p \leqq \infty$, belong to the class $\mathscr{H}(1 - 1/p; L^1(\mu), L^\infty(\mu))$. Thus, together with Theorem 3.2.20, we have the following generalization of Theorem 3.3.8.

Theorem 3.3.10. *For* $1 \leqq p_1 < p_2 \leqq \infty$, $1 \leqq q \leqq \infty$ *the Lorentz spaces* $L^{pq}(\mu)$ *are equal to the intermediate spaces* $(L^{p_1}(\mu), L^{p_2}(\mu))_{\theta, q; K}$ *of* $L^{p_1}(\mu)$ *and* $L^{p_2}(\mu)$, *where*

$$\frac{1}{p} = \frac{1-\theta}{p_1} + \frac{\theta}{p_2} \qquad (0 < \theta < 1),$$

both spaces having equivalent norms.

3.3.2 The Theorems of M. Riesz-Thorin and Marcinkiewicz

We conclude this section with a brief discussion of three interpolation theorems between Lebesgue spaces which play an important role in the study of linear operators between these spaces. In particular, we formulate and prove the fundamental convexity theorems.

Let (R, μ) and (S, ν) be two totally σ-finite measure spaces and let $L^p(\mu)$ and $L^p(\nu)$, $1 \leqq p \leqq \infty$, be the Lebesgue spaces on (R, μ) and (S, ν), respectively. As a first theorem we have

Theorem 3.3.11. *Let* $1 \leqq p_1 < p_2 \leqq \infty$ *and* $1 \leqq q_1, q_2 \leqq \infty$, $q_1 \neq q_2$, *and let* T *be a linear transformation defined on* $L^1(\mu) + L^\infty(\mu)$ *with values in* $L^1(\nu) + L^\infty(\nu)$. *If for each* $f \in L^{p_i}(\mu)$ $(i = 1, 2)$

$$\|Tf\|_{L^{q_i}(\nu)} \leqq M_i \|f\|_{L^{p_i}(\mu)}, \tag{3.3.10}$$

then T *defines a bounded linear transformation*

(a) *on* $(L^{p_1}(\mu), L^{p_2}(\mu))_{\theta, r; K}$ *into* $(L^{q_1}(\nu), L^{q_2}(\nu))_{\theta, r; K}$ $(0 < \theta < 1$, $1 \leqq r < \infty$ *and/or* $0 \leqq \theta \leqq 1$, $r = \infty)$ *such that*

$$\|Tf\|_{\theta, r; K} \leqq M_1^{1-\theta} M_2^{\theta} \|f\|_{\theta, r; K} \qquad (f \in (L^{p_1}(\mu), L^{p_2}(\mu))_{\theta, r; K});$$

(b) *on* $(L^{p_1}(\mu), L^{p_2}(\mu))_{\theta,r;J}$ *into* $(L^{q_1}(\nu), L^{q_2}(\nu))_{\theta,r;J}$ $(0 \leq \theta \leq 1, r = 1$ *and/or* $0 < \theta < 1,\ 1 < r \leq \infty)$ *such that*

$$\|Tf\|_{\theta,r;J} \leq M_1^{1-\theta} M_2^{\theta} \|f\|_{\theta,r;J} \qquad (f \in (L^{p_1}(\mu), L^{p_2}(\mu))_{\theta,r;J}).$$

This interpolation theorem is a direct consequence of Theorem 3.2.23.

Since by Theorem 3.3.10 the intermediate spaces $(L^{p_1}(\mu), L^{p_2}(\mu))_{\theta,r;K}$ $(0 < \theta < 1, 1 \leq r \leq \infty)$ of $L^{p_1}(\mu)$ and $L^{p_2}(\mu)$ are equal to the Lorentz spaces $L^{pr}(\mu)$, $1/p = (1-\theta)/p_1 + \theta/p_2$, both having equivalent norms, and since a similar situation holds for the intermediate spaces of $L^{q_1}(\nu)$ and $L^{q_2}(\nu)$, Theorem 3.3.11 has the following

Corollary 3.3.12. *Under the hypotheses of Theorem* 3.3.11 *the restriction of the linear transformation T on $L^{pr}(\mu)$ is continuous from $L^{pr}(\mu)$ into $L^{qr}(\nu)$,*

$$\frac{1}{p} = \frac{1-\theta}{p_1} + \frac{\theta}{p_2}, \quad \frac{1}{q} = \frac{1-\theta}{q_1} + \frac{\theta}{q_2} \qquad (0 < \theta < 1), \quad 1 \leq r \leq \infty,$$

and

$$\|Tf\|_{L^{qr}(\nu)} \leq C\, M_1^{1-\theta} M_2^{\theta} \|f\|_{L^{pr}(\mu)} \qquad (f \in L^{pr}(\mu)),$$

where $C = C(p_1, p_2, q_1, q_2, \theta) \geq 1$.

In particular, if $p_1 \leq q_1$ and $p_2 \leq q_2$, then T transforms $L^p(\mu)$ to $L^q(\nu)$ and

$$\|Tf\|_{L^q(\nu)} \leq C'\, M_1^{1-\theta} M_2^{\theta} \|f\|_{L^p(\mu)}.$$

Proof. It remains to prove the last part of the corollary. Setting $r = q$, then T transforms $L^{pq}(\mu)$ to $L^{qq}(\nu) = L^q(\nu)$. But by Theorem 3.3.9 (b) $L^p(\mu) = L^{pp}(\mu)$ is continuously contained in $L^{pq}(\mu)$ whenever $p \leq q$, thus if and only if $p_i \leq q_i$ $(i = 1, 2)$.

The latter part of Corollary 3.3.12 is nothing but the theorem of M. Riesz-Thorin with two restrictions: The constant C', given above, is not the "best" possible $(= 1)$, and the assertion of the corollary is not proven for arbitrary $1 \leq p_i, q_i \leq \infty$ $(i = 1, 2)$ but with the additional restriction $p_i \leq q_i$ $(i = 1, 2)$.

For the sake of completeness we will formulate the *theorem of M. Riesz-Thorin* in a slightly stronger form than given above. For this purpose, we denote by $\mathcal{S}(\mu)$ the set of all simple functions in $\mathcal{L}(\mu)$:

Let $1 \leq p_i, q_i \leq \infty$ $(i = 1, 2)$ and let T be a linear transformation defined on $\mathcal{S}(\mu)$ with values in $\mathcal{L}(\nu)$.

If for each $f \in \mathcal{S}(\mu)$

$$\|Tf\|_{L^{q_i}(\nu)} \leq M_i \|f\|_{L^{p_i}(\mu)} \qquad (i = 1, 2),$$

then T has a bounded linear extension on $L^p(\mu)$ into $L^q(\nu)$,

$$\frac{1}{p}=\frac{1-\theta}{p_1}+\frac{\theta}{p_2}, \qquad \frac{1}{q}=\frac{1-\theta}{q_1}+\frac{\theta}{q_2} \qquad (0 \leqq \theta \leqq 1),$$

such that

$$\|Tf\|_{L^q(\nu)} \leqq M_1^{1-\theta} M_2^{\theta} \|f\|_{L^p(\mu)} \qquad (f \in L^p(\mu))$$

(the extension being unique whenever $\mathscr{S}(\mu)$ is dense in $L^p(\mu)$).

Concluding the discussion of the first convexity theorem we remark that in interpolation theory a bounded linear operator T from $L^p(\mu)$ into $L^q(\nu)$ is said to be of *(strong) type* (p, q).

Now to the second interpolation theorem.

Theorem 3.3.13. *Let $1 \leqq p_1 < p_2 \leqq \infty$ and $1 < q_1, q_2 \leqq \infty$, $q_1 \neq q_2$ and let T be a linear transformation defined on $L^1(\mu) + L^\infty(\mu)$ into $L^1(\nu) + L^\infty(\nu)$. If for each $f \in L^{p_i}(\mu)$*

$$\text{(3.3.11)} \qquad \sup_{0<t<\infty} \left(t^{1/q_i}[Tf]^*(t)\right) \leqq M_i' \|f\|_{L^{p_i}(\mu)} \qquad (i = 1, 2),$$

then T defines a bounded linear transformation from $\left(L^{p_1}(\mu), L^{p_2}(\mu)\right)_{\theta, r; J}$ into $\left(M^{q_1}(\nu), M^{q_2}(\nu)\right)_{\theta, r; K}$ $(0 < \theta < 1,\ 1 \leqq r \leqq \infty)$ such that

$$\|t^{1-\theta} k(t; Tf)\|_{L_*^r} \leqq \frac{M_1'^{(1-\theta)} M_2'^{\theta}}{(1-\theta)\theta} \|f\|_{\theta, r; J} \qquad \left(f \in \left(L^{p_1}(\mu), L^{p_2}(\mu)\right)_{\theta, r; J}\right).$$

The proof follows by Theorem 3.2.24.

Again from Theorems 3.3.9 and 3.3.10 we obtain

Corollary 3.3.14. *Under the hypotheses of Theorem 3.3.13 the restriction of the transformation T on $L^{pr}(\mu)$ is continuous from $L^{pr}(\mu)$ into $L^{qr}(\nu)$,*

$$\frac{1}{p}=\frac{1-\theta}{p_1}+\frac{\theta}{p_2}, \qquad \frac{1}{q}=\frac{1-\theta}{q_1}+\frac{\theta}{q_2} \qquad (0 < \theta < 1), \qquad 1 \leqq r \leqq \infty,$$

and

$$\|Tf\|_{L^{qr}(\nu)} \leqq C\, M_1'^{(1-\theta)} M_2'^{\theta} \|f\|_{L^{pr}(\mu)} \qquad (f \in L^{pr}(\mu)),$$

the constant $C = C(p_1, p_2, q_1, q_2, \theta)$ tending to infinity as θ tends to zero or to one.

In particular, if $p_1 \leqq q_1$ and $p_2 \leqq q_2$, then T transforms $L^p(\mu)$ into $L^q(\nu)$ and

$$\|Tf\|_{L^q(\nu)} \leqq C'\, M_1'^{(1-\theta)} M_2'^{\theta} \|f\|_{L^p(\mu)}.$$

The second part of the above corollary is the so-called second convexity theorem or the *theorem of Marcinkiewicz* with the only exception that the case $p_1 = q_1 = 1$ is not included. Indeed, we know that the space $M^1(\nu)$ is not normable. So, if one restricts the treatment of the theory of interpolation to Banach spaces, as we have done, this case is excluded.

The classical formulation of the theorem of Marcinkiewicz is the following:

Let $1 \leqq p_i \leqq q_i \leqq \infty$ $(i = 1, 2)$, $p_1 < p_2$ *and* $q_1 \neq q_2$ *and let* T *be a linear transformation defined on* $\mathscr{S}(\mu)$ *with values in* $\mathscr{L}(\nu)$.

If T *is such that*

$$\sup_{0<\sigma<\infty} \left(\sigma \left\{\int_{|[Tf](y)|>\sigma} d\nu\right\}^{1/q_i}\right) \leqq M'_i \, \|f\|_{L^{p_i}(\mu)} \qquad (i = 1, 2) \tag{3.3.12}$$

for all $f \in \mathscr{S}(\mu)$, *then* T *has a bounded linear extension on* $L^p(\mu)$ *into* $L^q(\nu)$,

$$\frac{1}{p} = \frac{1-\theta}{p_1} + \frac{\theta}{p_2}, \qquad \frac{1}{q} = \frac{1-\theta}{q_1} + \frac{\theta}{q_2} \qquad (0 < \theta < 1),$$

and

$$\|Tf\|_{L^q(\nu)} \leqq C\, M_1'^{(1-\theta)}\, M_2'^{\theta}\, \|f\|_{L^p(\mu)},$$

where the constant $C = C(\theta)$ *tends to infinity as* θ *tends to zero or to one.*

The conditions (3.3.11) and (3.3.12) are identical. Indeed, by the properties of the non-increasing rearrangement of a function $f \in L^1(\mu) + L^\infty(\mu)$ given in Lemma 3.3.4 one can show that

$$\sup_{0<\sigma<\infty} \left(\sigma \left\{\int_{|f(x)|>\sigma} d\mu\right\}^{1/p}\right) = \sup_{0<t<\infty} \{t^{1/p} f^*(t)\} \qquad (1 \leqq p \leqq \infty). \tag{3.3.13}$$

We remark that a bounded linear transformation T from $\mathscr{S}(\mu)$ into $\mathscr{L}(\nu)$ such that (3.3.12) holds is said to be of *weak type* (p, q).

Finally, let us rewrite Corollary 3.3.14 in a weaker form being due to A. P. Calderón.

Corollary 3.3.15. *Let* $1 < p_1 < p_2 < \infty$ *and* $1 < q_1, q_2 \leqq \infty$, $q_1 \neq q_2$ *and let* T *be a linear transformation from* $L^1(\mu) + L^\infty(\mu)$ *to* $L^1(\nu) + L^\infty(\nu)$. *If for each* $f \in L^{p_i 1}(\mu)$

$$\sup_{0<t<\infty} (t^{1/q_i} [Tf]^*(t)) \leqq M''_i \, \|f\|_{L^{p_i 1}(\mu)} \qquad (i = 1, 2), \tag{3.3.14}$$

then the same conclusion holds as in Corollary 3.3.14.

Indeed, condition (3.3.14) weakens condition (3.3.11) of Theorem 3.3.13, since $L^{p1}(\mu)$ is continuously embedded in $L^p(\mu)$, $1 < p < \infty$. The proof is obvious by Theorem 3.2.24 and 3.3.13.

Corollary 3.3.15 is nothing but a weaker version of the second interpolation theorem which goes back to E. M. Stein–G. Weiss:

Let $1 \leqq p_i \leqq q_i \leqq \infty$ $(i = 1, 2)$, $p_1 < p_2$ and $q_1 \neq q_2$ and let T be a linear transformation from $\mathscr{S}(\mu)$ into $\mathscr{L}(\nu)$ such that for all characteristic functions χ_E of a measurable set E in R with finite measure $\mu(E)$

$$(3.3.15)\qquad \sup_{0<\sigma<\infty}\left(\sigma\left\{\int_{|[T\chi_E](y)|>\sigma} d\nu\right\}^{1/q_i}\right) \leqq M_i''\,\mu(E)^{1/p_i} \qquad (i = 1, 2),$$

then the same conclusion holds as in the theorem of Marcinkiewicz.

The equivalence of (3.3.14) and (3.3.15) for $1 < p < \infty$, $1 < q \leqq \infty$ follows by relation (3.3.13) and the fact that each simple function f in $\mathscr{S}(\mu)$ has a representation $f = \sum_{k=1}^{n} f_k$ such that $\|f\|_{L^{p_1}(\mu)} = \sum_{k=1}^{n} \|f_k\|_{L^{p_1}(\mu)}$, where $\{f_k\}_{k=1}^{n}$ are characteristic functions multiplied by a constant.

A linear transformation T from $\mathscr{S}(\mu)$ into $\mathscr{L}(\nu)$ such that (3.3.15) holds for some constants M'' and p, q $(1 \leqq p, q \leqq \infty)$ is said to be of *restricted weak type* (p, q).

3.4 Intermediate Spaces of X and $D(A^r)$

We continue the investigations begun in Sec. 3.1. Let X be a Banach space and let $\{T(t); 0 \leqq t < \infty\}$ be an equi-bounded semi-group of class $(\mathscr{C}_0)$ in $\mathscr{E}(X)$ (the bound of the semi-group being denoted by M).

3.4.1 An Equivalence Theorem for the Intermediate Spaces $X_{\alpha,r;q}$

In the first section of this chapter we have defined and studied the Banach subspace $X_{\alpha,r;q}$ $(0 < \alpha < r,\ 1 \leqq q \leqq \infty$ and/or $\alpha = r$, $q = \infty$; $r = 1, 2, \ldots)$ of X, generated by the semi-group $\{T(t); 0 \leqq t < \infty\}$. We have already seen that these subspaces are intermediate between the Banach space X and the domain $D(A^r)$ of the r-th power of the infinitesimal generator A of $\{T(t); 0 \leqq t < \infty\}$. The object now is to incorporate the spaces $X_{\alpha,r;q}$ into the theory of intermediate spaces of X and $D(A^r)$ as developed in Sec. 3.2. so as to obtain a deeper and wider theory.

Using the notations of Sec. 3.2, we identify the spaces X_1 and X_2 with the spaces X and $D(A^r)$, respectively. The norm of an element $f \in X$ will usually be denoted by $\|f\|$, sometimes however by $\|f\|_X$. $D(A^r)$ becomes a Banach space under the norm of the graph, but mainly we use for $\mathsf{D}(A^r)$ the equivalent norm: $\|f\|_{\mathsf{D}(A^r)} = \|f\| + \|A^r f\|$ (cf. Sec. 1.1.1).

By definition, $\mathsf{D}(A^r)$ is a continuously embedded subspace of X and $\|f\|_{\mathsf{X}} \leqq \|f\|_{\mathsf{D}(A^r)}$ for all $f \in \mathsf{D}(A^r)$. Thus the norms of $\mathsf{D}(A^r)$ and X as defined in (3.2.1) and (3.2.2), respectively, are equal to the norms described above. Moreover, we introduce on $\mathsf{D}(A^r)$ and X the function norms $\mathrm{J}(t; f)$ and $\mathrm{K}(t; f)$ $(0 < t < \infty)$, respectively, defined in (3.2.8) and (3.2.9).

With these preliminaries we may consider the intermediate spaces

$$(\mathsf{X}, \mathsf{D}(A^r))_{\theta, q; \mathrm{K}} \qquad (0 < \theta < 1,\ 1 \leqq q < \infty \text{ and/or } 0 \leqq \theta \leqq 1,\ \ q = \infty)$$

and

$$(\mathsf{X}, \mathsf{D}(A^r))_{\theta, q; \mathrm{J}} \qquad (0 \leqq \theta \leqq 1,\ q = 1 \text{ and/or } 0 < \theta < 1,\ 1 < q \leqq \infty)$$

(cf. Definitions 3.2.4 and 3.2.6). By Theorem 3.2.12

$$(3.4.1) \quad (\mathsf{X}, \mathsf{D}(A^r))_{\theta, q; \mathrm{J}} = (\mathsf{X}, \mathsf{D}(A^r))_{\theta, q; \mathrm{K}} \qquad (0 < \theta < 1,\ 1 \leqq q \leqq \infty),$$

and

$$(3.4.2) \qquad (\mathsf{X}, \mathsf{D}(A^r))_{0, 1; \mathrm{J}} \subset \mathsf{X} = (\mathsf{X}, \mathsf{D}(A^r))_{0, \infty; \mathrm{K}},$$

$$(3.4.3) \qquad (\mathsf{X}, \mathsf{D}(A^r))_{1, 1; \mathrm{J}} = \mathsf{D}(A^r) \subset (\mathsf{X}, \mathsf{D}(A^r))_{1, \infty; \mathrm{K}}.$$

Concerning the inclusion relation (3.4.2), it is easy to see that

$$\|f\|_{\mathsf{X}} \leqq \|f\|_{0, 1; \mathrm{J}} \leqq \|f\|_{\mathsf{X}},$$

the first inequality being valid for every $f \in (\mathsf{X}, \mathsf{D}(A^r))_{0, 1; \mathrm{J}}$ and the second one for every $f \in \mathsf{D}(A^r)$. As $\mathsf{D}(A^r)$ is a dense subspace of $(\mathsf{X}, \mathsf{D}(A^r))_{0, 1; \mathrm{J}}$ and X, respectively, we obtain (cf. the proof of Corollary 3.2.21)

$$(3.4.4) \qquad (\mathsf{X}, \mathsf{D}(A^r))_{0, 1; \mathrm{J}} = \mathsf{X} = (\mathsf{X}, \mathsf{D}(A^r))_{0, \infty; \mathrm{K}}$$

instead of (3.4.2). Concerning (3.4.3) we shall soon see that the inclusion in general is proper.

The next two theorems reveal that the intermediate spaces $\mathsf{X}_{\alpha, r; q}$ of X and $\mathsf{D}(A^r)$ are equal to the spaces $(\mathsf{X}, \mathsf{D}(A^r))_{\theta, r; \mathrm{K}}$, where $\theta = \alpha/r$. For this purpose we introduce a modulus of continuity of order r

$$(3.4.5) \qquad \omega_r(t^r; f) = \sup_{0 \leqq s \leqq t} (\|[T(s) - I]^r f\|) \qquad (f \in \mathsf{X}).$$

Proposition 3.4.1. *There exists a constant $C > 0$, $C = C(M, r)$, such that*

$$(3.4.6) \qquad \mathrm{K}(t^r; f) \leqq C(\omega_r(t^r; f) + \min(1, t^r)\, \|f\|)$$

for all $f \in X$. *Furthermore,*

(3.4.7) $$\omega_r(t^r; f) \leqq (M+1)^r \, \mathrm{K}(t^r; f) \qquad (0 < t < \infty;\ f \in X)$$

and

(3.4.8) $$\omega_r(t^r; f) \leqq (M+1)^r \min\left(1, \left(\frac{t}{s}\right)^r\right) \mathrm{J}(s^r; f) \qquad (0 < s, t < \infty;\ f \in D(A^r)).$$

Proof. At first we remark that

(3.4.9) $$\mathrm{K}(t; f) \leqq \|f\| \qquad (0 < t < \infty;\ f \in X).$$

We prove inequality (3.4.6) for $r = 2$; this indicates the method for general r. If $f \in X$, then

$$f = \frac{1}{(t/2)^2} \int_0^{t/2} \int_0^{t/2} [T(2\tau_1 + 2\tau_2) - 2T(\tau_1 + \tau_2) + I] f \, d\tau_1 \, d\tau_2 -$$

$$- \frac{1}{(t/2)^2} \int_0^{t/2} \int_0^{t/2} T(2\tau_1 + 2\tau_2) f \, d\tau_1 \, d\tau_2 + \frac{2}{(t/2)^2} \int_0^{t/2} \int_0^{t/2} T(\tau_1 + \tau_2) f \, d\tau_1 \, d\tau_2$$

$$= \frac{1}{(t/2)^2} \int_0^{t/2} \int_0^{t/2} [T(\tau_1 + \tau_2) - I]^2 f \, d\tau_1 \, d\tau_2 +$$

$$+ \left(-\frac{1}{t^2} \int_0^{t} \int_0^{t} T(\tau_1 + \tau_2) f \, d\tau_1 \, d\tau_2 + \frac{2}{(t/2)^2} \int_0^{t/2} \int_0^{t/2} T(\tau_1 + \tau_2) f \, d\tau_1 \, d\tau_2\right)$$

$$= f_1 + f_2 \qquad (0 < t < \infty),$$

where $f_1 \in X$ and $f_2 \in D(A^2)$. One easily verifies that

$$\|f_1\| \leqq \omega_2(t^2; f); \qquad \|f_2\| \leqq 3M \|f\|$$

and

$$\|A^2 f_2\| = \|-\frac{1}{t^2}[T(t) - I]^2 f + \frac{8}{t^2}[T(t/2) - I]^2 f\| \leqq \frac{9}{t^2} \omega_2(t^2; f).$$

Therefore,

$$\mathrm{K}(t^2; f) \leqq \|f_1\|_X + t^2 \|f_2\|_{D(A^2)} = \|f_1\| + t^2(\|f_2\| + \|A^2 f_2\|)$$
$$\leqq 10\omega_2(t^2; f) + 3M t^2 \|f\| \leqq \max(10, 3M)\big(\omega_2(t^2; f) + t^2 \|f\|\big).$$

Combining this result together with the estimate given in (3.4.9), we have (3.4.6) for $r = 2$.

To prove (3.4.8), we have already seen in Sec. 3.1 that $\|[T(s) - I]^r f\|$ is bounded by $(M+1)^r \|f\|_X$ for all $f \in X$ and $0 < s < \infty$ and by $(M+1)^r s^r \|f\|_{D(A^r)}$ for all $f \in D(A^r)$ and $0 < s < \infty$. Thus, if $f \in X$ is such that $f = f_1 + f_2$, $f_1 \in X$ and $f_2 \in D(A^r)$, then

$$\omega_r(t^r; f) \leqq \omega_r(t^r; f_1) + \omega_r(t^r; f_2)$$
$$\leqq (M+1)^r (\|f_1\|_X + t^r \|f_2\|_{D(A^r)}) \qquad (0 < t < \infty)$$

for all representations $f = f_1 + f_2$, which proves (3.4.7). Inequality (3.4.8) follows from (3.4.7) and (3.2.12). This completes the proof.

We are now able to prove

Theorem 3.4.2. *The intermediate spaces* $X_{\alpha,r;q}$ $(0<\alpha<r, 1\leq q\leq\infty;$ $r=1,2,\ldots)$ *of* X *and* $D(A^r)$ *are equal to the spaces* $(X, D(A^r))_{\theta,q;K} = (X, D(A^r))_{\theta,q;J}$, $\theta=\alpha/r$. *Furthermore, for* $X_{\alpha,r;q}$ *there are the following equivalent norms:*

$$\text{(i)} \quad \|f\| + \left\{\int_0^\infty (t^{-\alpha}\,\|[T(t)-I]^r f\|)^q \frac{dt}{t}\right\}^{1/q};$$

$$\text{(ii)} \quad \|f\| + \left\{\int_0^\infty (t^{-\alpha}\,\omega_r(t^r; f))^q \frac{dt}{t}\right\}^{1/q};$$

$$\text{(iii)} \quad \left\{\int_0^\infty (t^{-\alpha/r}\,\mathrm{K}(t; f))^q \frac{dt}{t}\right\}^{1/q};$$

$$\text{(iv)} \quad \inf_{f=\int_0^\infty u(t)\frac{dt}{t}} \left\{\int_0^\infty (t^{-\alpha/r}\,\mathrm{J}(t; u(t)))^q \frac{dt}{t}\right\}^{1/q},$$

where $u=u(t)$ *is a strongly measurable function in* $D(A^r)$ *and* $u(\cdot)\in L^1_*(X)$.

Proof. It is not hard to see that the norms (i) and (ii) for $X_{\alpha,r;q}$ are equivalent.

Suppose, $f\in (X, D(A^r))_{\theta,q;K}$, $\theta=\alpha/r$. By relation (3.4.7)

$$\|t^{-\alpha}\,\omega_r(t^r; f)\|_{L^q_*} \leq (M+1)^r\,\|t^{-\alpha}\,\mathrm{K}(t^r; f)\|_{L^q_*} = \frac{(M+1)^r}{r^{1/q}}\,\|f\|_{\theta,q;K}.$$

Furthermore, since $(X, D(A^r))_{\theta,q;K}$ is continuously embedded in X, by (3.2.15)

$$\|f\| \leq (\|t^{-\theta}\min(1,t)\|_{L^q_*})^{-1}\,\|f\|_{\theta,q;K}.$$

Thus, $(X, D(A^r))_{\theta,q;K}$ is contained in $X_{\alpha,r;q}$, $\alpha=\theta r$, and

$$\|f\| + \|t^{-\alpha}\,\omega_r(t^r; f)\|_{L^q_*} \leq \left\{(\|t^{-\theta}\min(1,t)\|_{L^q_*})^{-1} + \frac{(M+1)^r}{r^{1/q}}\right\}\|f\|_{\theta,q;K}.$$

On the other hand, applying the estimate (3.4.6) one verifies without difficulty that $X_{\alpha,r;q}\subset (X, D(A^r))_{\theta,q;K}$, $\theta=\alpha/r$, and

$$\|f\|_{\theta,q;K} \leq C\max(r^{1/q}, \|t^{-\theta}\min(1,t)\|_{L^q_*})\,\{\|f\| + \|t^{-\alpha}\,\omega_r(t^r; f)\|_{L^q_*}\}.$$

The equivalence of the norms (iii) and (iv) for $X_{\alpha,r;q}$ has already been shown in Theorem 3.2.12, in particular in relation (3.4.1).

For the saturation case we have

Theorem 3.4.3. *The r-th Favard class $X_{r,r;\infty}$ ($r = 1, 2, \ldots$) is equal to the intermediate space $(X, D(A^r))_{1,\infty;K}$ of X and $D(A^r)$. For $X_{r,r;\infty}$ the following norms are equivalent:*

(i) $\|f\| + \sup_{0<t<\infty} \left(t^{-r} \|[T(t) - I]^r f\|\right)$;

(ii) $\|f\| + \sup_{0<t<\infty} \left(t^{-r} \omega_r(t^r; f)\right)$;

(iii) $\sup_{0<t<\infty} \left(t^{-1} K(t; f)\right)$.

Proof. One easily verifies the equivalence of the norms (i) and (ii) for $X_{r,r;\infty}$. Hence for an $f \in X_{r,r;\infty}$ we obtain by (3.4.6) that

$$\|f\|_{1,\infty;K} \leqq C\left\{\|f\| + \sup_{0<t<\infty} \left(t^{-r} \omega_r(t^r; f)\right)\right\},$$

which shows that $X_{r,r;\infty} \subset (X, D(A^r))_{1,\infty;K}$. On the other hand, by (3.4.7)

$$\|f\| + \sup_{0<t<\infty} \left(t^{-r} \omega_r(t^r; f)\right) \leqq \left(1 + (M+1)^r\right) \|f\|_{1,\infty;K}$$

for all $f \in (X, D(A^r))_{1,\infty;K}$, proving that $(X, D(A^r))_{1,\infty;K} \subset X_{r,r;\infty}$.

As a consequence of Theorems 3.4.2 and 3.4.3, Proposition 3.1.4 and Corollary 3.2.13 there is the following generalization of Proposition 3.1.4.

Theorem 3.4.4. *For $\beta \geqq \alpha > 0$ and $1 \leqq p \leqq q \leqq \infty$*

$$X_{\beta,r;p} \subset X_{\alpha,r;q}.$$

In particular,

$$X_{\beta,r;p} \subset X^0_{\alpha,r;\infty} \quad (\beta \geqq \alpha > 0,\ 1 \leqq p < \infty),$$

where $X^0_{\alpha,r;\infty}$ is the closure of $D(A^r)$ in $X_{\alpha,r;\infty}$.

3.4.2 Theorems of Reduction for the Spaces $X_{\alpha,r;q}$

At first we shall study the behavior of the spaces $D(A^k)$, $k = 1, 2, \ldots, r-1$, as intermediate spaces of X and $D(A^r)$.

Proposition 3.4.5. *The space $D(A^k)$, $k = 0, 1, \ldots, r$, belongs to the class $\mathscr{H}(k/r; X, D(A^r))$. In particular, for $k = 1, 2, \ldots, r-1$*

$$X_{k,r;1} \subset D(A^k) \subset X_{k,r;\infty}. \tag{3.4.10}$$

Proof. For k equal to 0 or r the assertion has already been established in (3.4.2) and (3.4.3). Now, if $f \in D(A^k)$, $k = 1, 2, \ldots, r-1$, then by the estimate given in (3.1.3)

$$\begin{aligned}\|[T(t) - I]^r f\| &\leqq \|[T(t) - I]^{r-k}\| \; \|[T(t) - I]^k f\| \\ &\leqq (M+1)^r \min(1, t^k) \left(\|f\| + \|A^k f\|\right),\end{aligned}$$

and consequently

$$\|f\|_{k,r;\infty} \leqq (1 + (M+1)^r)\, \|f\|_{D(A^k)} \qquad (f \in D(A^k)),$$

which proves the second inclusion in (3.4.10).

On the other hand, if $f \in X_{k,r;1}$, $k = 1, 2, \ldots, r-1$, then, as will be shown below, $f \in D(A^k)$ and

$$(3.4.11) \qquad (-A)^k f = \frac{1}{C_{k,r}} \int_0^\infty t^{-k} [T(t) - I]^r f \frac{dt}{t},$$

where

$$(3.4.12) \qquad C_{k,r} = \int_0^\infty t^{-k} (e^{-t} - 1)^r \frac{dt}{t}.$$

Thus

$$\|f\|_{D(A^k)} \leqq \max\left(1, \frac{1}{|C_{k,r}|}\right) \|f\|_{k,r;1} \qquad (f \in X_{k,r;1}),$$

proving the proposition.

It remains to show the important relation (3.4.11). Here we need the following identity:

$$(3.4.13) \qquad \sum_{j=1}^{r} (-1)^{r-j} \binom{r}{j} j^k \int_{j\varepsilon}^{r\varepsilon} t^{n-k} \frac{dt}{t} = 0$$

for $n = 1, 2, \ldots, k-1$, $k = 1, 2, \ldots, r-1$ $(r = 1, 2, \ldots)$ and $\varepsilon > 0$, which follows immediately from the identities given in (2.2.6).

Let $f \in X_{k,r;1}$, $k = 1, 2, \ldots, r-1$. By Theorem 3.4.4 f belongs to $X_{n,r;1}$ for each $n = 1, 2, \ldots, k-1$, i.e. the integral

$$\int_0^\infty t^{-n} \|[T(t) - I]^r f\| \frac{dt}{t}$$

is finite. Introducing the integrals

$$f_{n,\varepsilon} = \int_\varepsilon^\infty t^{-n} [T(t) - I]^r f \frac{dt}{t} \qquad (0 \leqq \varepsilon < \infty)$$

and applying the identities (2.2.6), we obtain for $f_{n,\varepsilon}$ with $\varepsilon > 0$

$$f_{n,\varepsilon} = \sum_{j=1}^{r} (-1)^{r-j} \binom{r}{j} \int_\varepsilon^\infty t^{-n} [T(jt) - I] f \frac{dt}{t}$$

$$= \sum_{j=1}^{r} (-1)^{r-j} \binom{r}{j} j^n \int_{j\varepsilon}^{r\varepsilon} t^{-n} [T(t) - I] f \frac{dt}{t}.$$

For $n = 1$ we have with $0 < s < \infty$

$$\int_0^s T(\sigma)\, f_{1,\varepsilon}\, d\sigma = \sum_{j=1}^{r} (-1)^{r-j} \binom{r}{j} j \int_{j\varepsilon}^{r\varepsilon} t^{-1} \frac{dt}{t} \int_0^s T(\sigma)\, [T(t) - I]\, f\, d\sigma$$

$$= \sum_{j=1}^{r} (-1)^{r-j} \binom{r}{j} j \int_{j\varepsilon}^{r\varepsilon} \left(\frac{1}{t} \int_0^t T(\sigma)\, [T(s) - I]\, f\, d\sigma \right) \frac{dt}{t}.$$

Since on the one hand $f_{1,\varepsilon}$ converges in the norm to $f_{1,0}$ as $\varepsilon \to 0+$, and since on the other hand $(1/t) \int_0^t T(\sigma)\, [T(s) - I]\, f\, d\sigma \to [T(s) - I]\, f$ strongly as $t \to 0+$ and thus

$$\operatorname*{s-lim}_{\varepsilon \to 0+} \int_{j\varepsilon}^{r\varepsilon} \left(\frac{1}{t} \int_0^t T(\sigma)\, [T(s) - I]\, f\, d\sigma \right) \frac{dt}{t} = \left(\log \frac{r}{j} \right) [T(s) - I]\, f$$

$$(j = 1, 2, \ldots, r),$$

the latter equation gives

$$\int_0^s T(\sigma)\, f_{1,0}\, d\sigma = \left(\sum_{j=1}^{r} (-1)^{r-j} \binom{r}{j} j \log \frac{r}{j} \right) [T(s) - I]\, f$$

for each $s > 0$, or $f \in \mathsf{D}(A)$ and

$$\int_0^\infty t^{-1}\, [T(t) - I]^r\, f \frac{dt}{t} = \left(\sum_{j=1}^{r} (-1)^{r-j} \binom{r}{j} j \log \frac{r}{j} \right) A\, f.$$

Using this result, we obtain for $n = 2$ by the identity (3.4.13) with $0 < s < \infty$

$$\int_0^s T(\sigma)\, f_{2,\varepsilon}\, d\sigma = \sum_{j=1}^{r} (-1)^{r-j} \binom{r}{j} \frac{j^2}{2!} \int_{j\varepsilon}^{r\varepsilon} \frac{dt}{t} \int_0^s T(\sigma)\, B_t^2\, f\, d\sigma,$$

where $B_t^2 f$ is the second Taylor difference (cf. Definition 2.2.1). By Lemma 2.2.3 this leads to

$$\int_0^s T(\sigma)\, f_{2,0}\, d\sigma = \left(\sum_{j=1}^{r} (-1)^{r-j} \binom{r}{j} \frac{j^2}{2!} \log \frac{r}{j} \right) [T(s) - I]\, A\, f$$

as $\varepsilon \to 0+$, i.e. $f \in \mathsf{D}(A^2)$ and

$$\int_0^\infty t^{-2}\, [T(t) - I]^r\, f \frac{dt}{t} = \left(\sum_{j=1}^{r} (-1)^{r-j} \binom{r}{j} \frac{j^2}{2!} \log \frac{r}{j} \right) A^2\, f.$$

Proceeding successively, we finally have that $f \in \mathsf{D}(A^k)$ and

$$\int_0^\infty t^{-k}\, [T(t) - I]^r\, f \frac{dt}{t} = \left(\sum_{j=1}^{r} (-1)^{r-j} \binom{r}{j} \frac{j^k}{k!} \log \frac{r}{j} \right) A^k\, f.$$

The proof will be completed if the constant

$$(3.4.14)\quad C_{k,r} \equiv \int_0^\infty t^{-k}(e^{-t}-1)^r \frac{dt}{t} = (-1)^k \sum_{j=1}^{r} (-1)^{r-j} \binom{r}{j} \frac{j^k}{k!} \log \frac{r}{j}.$$

Indeed, if the Banach space X is equal to the complex number system and if the semi-group is defined by multiplication of the elements f by e^{-t}, then for the element $f_0 = 1$ one has the desired equality (3.4.14).

We now prove the *first theorem of reduction* in the case of non-optimal approximation: $0 < \alpha < r$, $1 \leqq q \leqq \infty$.

Theorem 3.4.6. *Let f belong to the intermediate space $\mathsf{X}_{\alpha,r;q}$ $(0 < \alpha < r$, $1 \leqq q \leqq \infty$; $r = 1, 2, \ldots)$ of X and $\mathsf{D}(A^r)$. Then for $\alpha = k + \beta$ $(k = 0, 1, \ldots, r-1; 0 < \beta \leqq 1)$ f belongs to $\mathsf{D}(A^k)$ and $A^k f$ to the intermediate space $\mathsf{X}_{\beta,1;q}$ of X and $\mathsf{D}(A)$ for $0 < \beta < 1$ and to $\mathsf{X}_{1,2;q}$ of X and $\mathsf{D}(A^2)$ for $\beta = 1$, and vice versa.*

Furthermore, for $\mathsf{X}_{\alpha,r;q}$ there are defined the equivalent norms:

$$\text{(i)}\quad \|f\| + \left\{\int_0^\infty (t^{-\alpha}\, \|[T(t) - I]^r f\|)^q \frac{dt}{t}\right\}^{1/q};$$

$$\text{(ii)}\quad \begin{cases} \|f\|_{\mathsf{D}(A^k)} + \left\{\int_0^\infty (t^{-\beta}\, \|[T(t) - I]\, A^k f\|)^q \frac{dt}{t}\right\}^{1/q} & (0 < \beta < 1), \\ \|f\|_{\mathsf{D}(A^k)} + \left\{\int_0^\infty (t^{-1}\, \|[T(t) - I]^2\, A^k f\|)^q \frac{dt}{t}\right\}^{1/q} & (\beta = 1). \end{cases}$$

Proof. By Proposition 3.4.5 $\mathsf{D}(A^k)$, $k = 0, 1, \ldots, r$, belongs to the class $\mathscr{H}(k/r; \mathsf{X}, \mathsf{D}(A^r))$. Consequently, for $0 \leqq k_1 < k_2 \leqq r$ Theorem 3.2.20 states that

$$(\mathsf{X}, \mathsf{D}(A^r))_{\frac{\alpha}{r},q;\mathrm{K}} = (\mathsf{D}(A^{k_1}), \mathsf{D}(A^{k_2}))_{\frac{\alpha'}{k_2-k_1},q;\mathrm{K}'}$$

for $\alpha = k_1 + \alpha'$, $0 < \alpha' < k_2 - k_1$ and $1 \leqq q \leqq \infty$.

Firstly, let $\alpha = k + \beta$ $(k = 0, 1, \ldots, r-1; 0 < \beta < 1)$. Then by the latter equation the space $\mathsf{X}_{\alpha,r;q}$ is contained in $\mathsf{D}(A^k)$ and

$$\mathsf{X}_{\alpha,r;q} = (\mathsf{X}, \mathsf{D}(A^r))_{\frac{k+\beta}{r},q;\mathrm{K}} = (\mathsf{D}(A^k), \mathsf{D}(A^{k+1}))_{\beta,q;\mathrm{K}'}.$$

Furthermore, there is an isomorphism between $\mathsf{D}(A^k)$ and X as well as between $\mathsf{D}(A^{k+1})$ and $\mathsf{D}(A)$, and consequently by the interpolation theorem (Theorem 3.2.23) also between $(D(A^k), D(A^{k+1}))_{\beta,q;K'}$ and $(X, D(A))_{\beta,q;K}$, $0 < \beta < 1$, $1 \leqq q \leqq \infty$. For instance, the transformation $(I - A)^k$ defines such an isomorphism (see Sec. 1.3).

Secondly, let $\alpha = k + \beta$ $(k = 0, 1, \ldots, r-2; \beta = 1)$. As shown above, the space $X_{\alpha,r;q}$ is embedded into $D(A^k)$ and

$$X_{\alpha,r;q} = (X, D(A^r))_{\frac{k+1}{r},q;K} = (D(A^k), D(A^{k+2}))_{\frac{1}{2},q;K'}.$$

But the transformation $(I - A)^k$ again defines an isomorphism between

$$(D(A^k), D(A^{k+2}))_{\frac{1}{2},q;K'} \quad \text{and} \quad (X, D(A^2))_{\frac{1}{2},q;K}.$$

With these observations it is obvious that an element $f \in X$ belongs to $X_{\alpha,r;q}$, $\alpha = k + \beta$ $(k = 0, 1, \ldots, r-1;\ 0 < \beta \leqq 1)$ if and only if $f \in D(A^k)$ and $A^k f$ belongs to $X_{\beta,1;q}$ for $0 < \beta < 1$ and to $X_{1,2;q}$ for $\beta = 1$ and that the norms described in the theorem are equivalent.

Remark. For $r = 2$ there is an elementary proof of the latter theorem which does not make any use of the theory of intermediate spaces. For this purpose we need two lemmas.

Lemma 3.4.7. *Let $\alpha > 0$, $1 \leqq q \leqq \infty$. If $\psi(s)$ is a non-negative measurable function on $(0, \infty)$ (measurable with respect to the measure ds/s), then*

$$\left\{\int_0^\infty \left(t^{-\alpha} \int_0^t \psi(s) \frac{ds}{s}\right)^q \frac{dt}{t}\right\}^{1/q} \leqq \frac{1}{\alpha} \left\{\int_0^\infty (s^{-\alpha} \psi(s))^q \frac{ds}{s}\right\}^{1/q} \tag{3.4.15}$$

and

$$\left\{\int_0^\infty \left(t^{\alpha} \int_t^\infty \psi(s) \frac{ds}{s}\right)^q \frac{dt}{t}\right\}^{1/q} \leqq \frac{1}{\alpha} \left\{\int_0^\infty (s^{\alpha} \psi(s))^q \frac{ds}{s}\right\}^{1/q}. \tag{3.4.16}$$

The relations (3.4.15) and (3.4.16) are well-known inequalities due to G. H. Hardy.

Lemma 3.4.8. *The semi-group operators $T(t)$, $0 \leqq t < \infty$, satisfy the following identities for $0 \leqq t < \infty$, $n = 0, 1, 2, \ldots$*

$$T(t) = \sum_{j=0}^{n} T(2^j t)\,[I - T(2^j t)] + T(2^{n+1} t), \tag{3.4.17}$$

$$[T(t) - I] = -\sum_{j=0}^{n} \frac{1}{2^{j+1}} [T(2^j t) - I]^2 + \frac{1}{2^{n+1}} [T(2^{n+1} t) - I]. \tag{3.4.18}$$

Proof. The first identity (3.4.17) is evident. To prove the second one, we remark that for each $f \in \mathsf{D}(A)$

$$[T(t) - I]f = \int_0^t T(\tau) A f \, d\tau$$

$$= \sum_{j=0}^{n} \int_0^t T(2^j \tau)[I - T(2^j \tau)] A f \, d\tau + \int_0^t T(2^{n+1}\tau) A f \, d\tau$$

$$= -\sum_{j=0}^{n} \frac{1}{2^{j+1}} [T(2^j t) - I]^2 f + \frac{1}{2^{n+1}} [T(2^{n+1} t) - I] f$$

$$(0 \leqq t < \infty).$$

Since $\mathsf{D}(A)$ is dense in X, the latter relation holds for all $f \in \mathsf{X}$, proving (3.4.18).

Proof of Theorem 3.4.6 for $r = 2$. At first, let $0 < \alpha < 1$ and $1 \leqq q \leqq \infty$. Using the identity

$$[T(t) - I]^2 = [T(2t) - I] - 2[T(t) - I],$$

one easily obtains that $\mathsf{X}_{\alpha,1;q} \subset \mathsf{X}_{\alpha,2;q}$ and

$$\|f\|_{\alpha,2;q} \leqq (2 + 2^\alpha) \|f\|_{\alpha,1;q} \qquad (f \in \mathsf{X}_{\alpha,1;q}).$$

On the other hand, if $f \in \mathsf{X}_{\alpha,2;q}$, then by (3.4.18)

$$\|[T(t) - I]f\| \leqq \sum_{j=0}^{n} \frac{1}{2^{j+1}} \|[T(2^j t) - I]^2 f\| + \frac{1}{2^{n+1}} \|[T(2^{n+1}t) - I]f\|,$$

and consequently for an $\varepsilon > 0$

$$\left\{\int_\varepsilon^\infty (t^{-\alpha} \|[T(t) - I]f\|)^q \frac{dt}{t}\right\}^{1/q}$$

$$\leqq \sum_{j=0}^{n} \frac{1}{2^{j+1}} \left\{\int_\varepsilon^\infty (t^{-\alpha} \|[T(2^j t) - I]^2 f\|)^q \frac{dt}{t}\right\}^{1/q} +$$

$$+ \frac{1}{2^{n+1}} \left\{\int_\varepsilon^\infty (t^{-\alpha} \|[T(2^{n+1} t) - I]f\|)^q \frac{dt}{t}\right\}^{1/q}$$

$$\leqq \frac{1}{2} \sum_{j=0}^{n} 2^{(\alpha-1)j} \left\|(t^{-\alpha} \|[T(t) - I]^2 f\|)\right\|_{L^q_*} + \frac{(M+1)\|f\|}{2^{n+1}} \frac{\varepsilon^{-\alpha}}{(\alpha q)^{1/q}}$$

$$\leqq \frac{1}{2 - 2^\alpha} \left\{\int_0^\infty (t^{-\alpha} \|[T(t) - I]^2 f\|)^q \frac{dt}{t}\right\}^{1/q}$$

as $n \to \infty$. Since ε was arbitrary, it follows that $f \in \mathsf{X}_{\alpha,1;q}$ and

$$\|f\|_{\alpha,1;q} \leqq \frac{1}{2 - 2^\alpha} \|f\|_{\alpha,2;q} \qquad (f \in \mathsf{X}_{\alpha,2;q}).$$

For $\alpha = 1$ and $1 \leqq q \leqq \infty$ there is nothing to prove.

It remains to discuss the case $1 < \alpha < 2$ and $1 \leqq q \leqq \infty$. If $f \in D(A)$ and $Af \in X_{\alpha-1,1;q}$, then $f \in X_{\alpha,2;q}$ and

$$\|f\|_{\alpha,2;q} \leqq \frac{2+2^\alpha}{\alpha}\left\{\|f\|_{D(A)} + \left\|\left(t^{-(\alpha-1)}\,\|[T(t)-I]\,Af\|\right)\right\|_{L^q_*}\right\}.$$

Indeed,

$$[T(t) - I - tA]\,f = \int_0^t [T(\tau) - I]\,Af\,d\tau,$$

and applying inequality (3.4.15) this gives

$$\left\|\left(t^{-\alpha}\,\|[T(t) - I - tA]\,f\|\right)\right\|_{L^q_*} \leqq \frac{1}{\alpha}\left\|\left(t^{-(\alpha-1)}\,\|[T(t)-I]\,Af\|\right)\right\|_{L^q_*}.$$

Furthermore,

$$[T(t) - I]^2 f = [T(2t) - I - 2tA]\,f - 2[T(t) - I - tA]\,f$$

and

$$\left\|\left(t^{-\alpha}\,\|[T(t)-I]^2 f\|\right)\right\|_{L^q_*} \leqq (2+2^\alpha)\left\|\left(t^{-\alpha}\,\|[T(t) - I - tA]\,f\|\right)\right\|_{L^q_*}.$$

This proves the result in one direction.

Conversely, suppose $f \in X_{\alpha,2;q}$. Then f is also an element of $X_{1,2;1}$ and

$$\|f\|_{1,2;1} \leqq \left\{1 + (M+1)^2 + \frac{1}{\{(\alpha-1)\,q'\}^{1/q}}\right\}\|f\|_{\alpha,2;q} \quad (q^{-1} + q'^{-1} = 1).$$

Thus by relation (3.4.11) of Proposition 3.4.5 $f \in D(A)$ and

$$(-A)\,f = \frac{1}{2\log 2}\int_0^\infty s^{-1}[T(s) - I]^2 f\,\frac{ds}{s}.$$

Therefore,

$$\|[T(t)-I]^2 Af\| \leqq \frac{1}{2\log 2}\int_0^\infty s^{-1}\,\|[T(t)-I]^2\,[T(s)-I]^2 f\|\,\frac{ds}{s}$$

$$\leqq \frac{(M+1)^2}{2\log 2}\left(\int_0^t s^{-1}\,\|[T(s)-I]^2 f\|\,\frac{ds}{s} + t^{-1}\,\|[T(t)-I]^2 f\|\right).$$

Applying once more inequality (3.4.15) of Lemma 3.4.7 we obtain that $Af \in X_{\alpha-1,2;q}$ and

$$\left\|\left(t^{-(\alpha-1)}\,\|[T(t)-I]^2 Af\|\right)\right\|_{L^q_*} \leqq \frac{(M+1)^2}{2\log 2}\;\frac{\alpha}{\alpha-1}\left\|\left(t^{-\alpha}\,\|[T(t)-I]^2 f\|\right)\right\|_{L^q_*}.$$

But then $Af \in X_{\alpha-1,1;q}$, as was shown in the first part of the proof, and

$$\|f\|_{D(A)} + \left\|\left(t^{-(\alpha-1)}\,\|[T(t)-I]\,Af\|\right)\right\|_{L^q_*} \leqq C\,\|f\|_{\alpha,2;q} \qquad (f \in X_{\alpha,2;q}),$$

where C is a positive constant depending on α, q and M. (The value of this constant C is rather poor compared with the others appearing n the above proof.)

As a consequence of the first theorem of reduction there is the following equivalence theorem.

Corollary 3.4.9. *Let* $0 < \alpha < r$, $1 \leqq q \leqq \infty$ $(r = 1, 2, \ldots)$ *and let* $\alpha = k + \beta$ $(k = 0, 1, \ldots, r-1; 0 < \beta \leqq 1)$. *For an element* $f \in \mathsf{X}$ *the following assertions are equivalent:*

(i) $f \in \mathsf{X}_{\alpha, r; q}$, *i.e.*

$$t^{-\alpha} \| [T(t) - I]^r f \| \in \mathsf{L}^q_*;$$

(ii) $f \in \mathsf{D}(A^k)$ *and* $A^k f \in \mathsf{X}_{\beta, 1; q}$, *i.e.*

$$t^{-(j+\beta)} \left\| \left[T(t) - \sum_{n=0}^{j} \frac{t^n}{n!} A^n \right] A^{k-j} f \right\| \in \mathsf{L}^q_* \quad (\text{any } 0 \leqq j \leqq k;\ 0 < \beta < 1);$$

(iii) $f \in \mathsf{D}(A^{k-j})$ *and* $A^{k-j} f \in \mathsf{X}_{j+\beta, j+1; q}$, *i.e.*

$$t^{-(j+\beta)} \| [T(t) - I]^{j+1} A^{k-j} f \| \in \mathsf{L}^q_* \qquad (\text{any } 0 \leqq j \leqq k;\ 0 < \beta < 1),$$

and $A^{k-j} f \in \mathsf{X}_{j+1, j+2; q}$, *i.e.*

$$t^{-(j+1)} \| [T(t) - I]^{j+2} A^{k-j} f \| \in \mathsf{L}^q_* \qquad (\text{any } 0 \leqq j \leqq k;\ \beta = 1).$$

We have just established a number of characterizations for the intermediate spaces $\mathsf{X}_{\alpha, r; q}$ $(0 < \alpha < r$ and $1 \leqq q \leqq \infty)$ of X and $\mathsf{D}(A^r)$. The basic theorem of the subject has been the theorem of reiteration in the theory of intermediate spaces, namely Theorem 3.2.20. But this theorem does not apply to the Favard classes $\mathsf{X}_{r, r; \infty}$. In the case of optimal approximation: $\alpha = r$, $q = \infty$, we prove as a *second theorem of reduction*

Theorem 3.4.10. *An element* $f \in \mathsf{X}$ *belongs to the Favard class* $\mathsf{X}_{r, r; \infty}$ $(r = 1, 2, \ldots)$ *if and only if* $f \in \mathsf{D}(A^{r-1})$ *and* $A^{r-1} f$ *belongs to the Favard class* $\mathsf{X}_{1, 1; \infty}$.

For $\mathsf{X}_{r, r; \infty}$ *there are the equivalent norms:*

(i) $\|f\| + \sup_{0 < t < \infty} (t^{-r} \| [T(t) - I]^r f \|)$;

(ii) $\|f\|_{\mathsf{D}(A^{r-1})} + \sup_{0 < t < \infty} (t^{-1} \| [T(t) - I] A^{r-1} f \|)$.

Proof. Suppose $f \in \mathsf{X}_{r, r; \infty}$. By Lemma 2.2.10

$$\int_0^{s_1} \int_0^{s_2} \cdots \int_0^{s_r} T(\sigma_1 + \sigma_2 + \cdots + \sigma_r) [T(\tau) - I]^r f \, d\sigma_1 \, d\sigma_2 \ldots d\sigma_r$$

$$= \int_0^{\tau} \int_0^{\tau} \cdots \int_0^{\tau} T(\sigma_1 + \sigma_2 + \cdots + \sigma_r) [T(s_1) - I] [T(s_2) - I] \ldots [T(s_r) - I] f \times$$
$$\times \, d\sigma_1 \, d\sigma_2 \ldots d\sigma_r$$

for arbitrary $s_k, \tau > 0$. Putting $s_1 = t$ and $s_2 = s_3 = \cdots = s_r = s$, we obtain

(3.4.19) $\| [T(t) - I] [T(s) - I]^{r-1} f \|$

$$= \lim_{\tau \to 0+} \left\| \frac{1}{\tau^r} \int_0^\tau \int_0^\tau \cdots \int_0^\tau T(\sigma_1 + \sigma_2 + \cdots + \sigma_r) [T(t) - I] [T(s) - I]^{r-1} f \times d\sigma_1 \, d\sigma_2 \ldots d\sigma_r \right\|$$

$$= \lim_{\tau \to 0+} \left\| \int_0^t \int_0^s \cdots \int_0^s T(\sigma_1 + \sigma_2 + \cdots + \sigma_r) \{\tau^{-r} [T(\tau) - I]^r f\} \, d\sigma_1 \, d\sigma_2 \ldots d\sigma_r \right\|$$

$$\leq M \sup_{0<\tau<\infty} \left(\tau^{-r} \| [T(\tau) - I]^r f \|\right) t \, s^{r-1}$$

for all $t, s > 0$. From this it follows easily that $f \in X_{r-1, r-1; \infty}$ and that

$$\sup_{0<s<\infty} \left(s^{-(r-1)} \| [T(t) - I] [T(s) - I]^{r-1} f \|\right) \leq M \sup_{0<\tau<\infty} \left(\tau^{-r} \| [T(\tau) - I]^r f \|\right) t.$$

This means that the mapping $t \to T(t) f$ on $(0, \infty)$ to $X_{r-1, r-1; \infty}$ is strongly continuous and, consequently, by Corollary 3.1.8 $f \in D(A^{r-1})$. Furthermore, relation (3.4.19) gives

$\| [T(t) - I] A^{r-1} f \|$

$$= \lim_{s \to 0+} \left\| \frac{1}{s^{r-1}} \int_0^s \int_0^s \cdots \int_0^s T(\sigma_1 + \sigma_2 + \cdots + \sigma_{r-1}) [T(t) - I] A^{r-1} f \times d\sigma_1 \, d\sigma_2 \ldots d\sigma_{r-1} \right\|$$

$$= \lim_{s \to 0+} \left(s^{-(r-1)} \| [T(s) - I]^{r-1} [T(t) - I] f \|\right)$$

$$\leq M \sup_{0<\tau<\infty} \left(\tau^{-r} \| [T(\tau) - I]^r f \|\right) t$$

and

$$\sup_{0<t<\infty} \left(t^{-1} \| [T(t) - I] A^{r-1} f \|\right) \leq M \sup_{0<\tau<\infty} \left(\tau^{-r} \| [T(\tau) - I]^r f \|\right),$$

proving that $f \in D(A^{r-1})$ and $A^{r-1} f \in X_{1,1;\infty}$.

The proof of the converse is easily obtained by the inequality

$$\| [T(t) - I]^r f \| \leq M \, t^{r-1} \| [T(t) - I] A^{r-1} f \| \qquad (0 < t < \infty;\ f \in D(A^{r-1})),$$

which follows by the identity (1.1.11).

Corollary 3.4.11. *Let* $r = 1, 2, \ldots$ *For an element* $f \in X$ *the following assertions are equivalent:*

(i) $f \in X_{r, r; \infty}$, *i.e.*

$$\sup_{0<t<\infty} \left(t^{-r} \| [T(t) - I]^r f \|\right) < \infty;$$

(ii) $f \in \mathsf{D}(A^{r-1})$ *and* $A^{r-1} f \in \mathsf{X}_{1,1;\infty}$, *i.e.*

$$\sup_{0<t<\infty} \left(t^{-k} \left\| \left[T(t) - \sum_{n=0}^{k-1} \frac{t^n}{n!} A^n\right] A^{r-k} f \right\|\right) < \infty \qquad (\text{any } 1 \leq k \leq r);$$

(iii) $f \in \mathsf{D}(A^{r-k})$ *and* $A^{r-k} f \in \mathsf{X}_{k,k;\infty}$, *i.e.*

$$\sup_{0<t<\infty} (t^{-k} \| [T(t) - I]^k A^{r-k} f \|) < \infty \qquad (\text{any } 1 \leq k \leq r).$$

If in addition X *is reflexive, then each of the latter three assertions is equivalent to*

(iv) $f \in \mathsf{D}(A^r)$.

This corollary is more general than Corollary 2.2.16 of Sec. 2.2.2 which is valid for reflexive Banach spaces X. Indeed, from the former one it follows that the characterizations (ii), (iii) and (iv) of Corollary 2.2.16 for an element $f \in \mathsf{X}$ are equivalent for an arbitrary Banach space X, and not only for reflexive ones.

3.4.3 The Spaces $\mathsf{X}^0_{\alpha,r;\infty}$

We conclude this section with a study of the Banach subspaces $\mathsf{X}^0_{\alpha,r;\infty}$ of X, $0 < \alpha < r$ $(r = 1, 2, \ldots)$.

By Definition 3.1.5, an element $f \in \mathsf{X}_{\alpha,r;q}$ $(0 < \alpha < r,\ 1 \leq q \leq \infty$ and/or $\alpha = r,\ q = \infty)$ belongs to the closed linear subspace $\mathsf{X}^0_{\alpha,r;q}$ if and only if

$$\lim_{t\to 0+} \| [T(t) - I] f \|_{\alpha,r;q} = 0.$$

We have already seen in Sec. 3.1 that the space $\mathsf{X}^0_{\alpha,r;q}$ is an invariant subspace of $\mathsf{X}_{\alpha,r;q}$ under the semi-group and that the domain $\mathsf{D}(A^r)$ of the r-th power of the infinitesimal generator is dense in it. Furthermore, we know by Corollaries 3.1.7 and 3.1.8 that in case $0 < \alpha < r$, $1 \leq q < \infty$ the spaces $\mathsf{X}^0_{\alpha,r;q}$ are equal to $\mathsf{X}_{\alpha,r;q}$ and that in case of saturation the space $\mathsf{X}^0_{r,r;\infty}$ forms the Plessner type characterization of $\mathsf{D}(A^r)$. Thus our discussion can be restricted to the spaces $\mathsf{X}^0_{\alpha,r;\infty}$, $0 < \alpha < r$.

Proposition 3.4.12. *An element* $f \in \mathsf{X}$ *belongs to the intermediate space* $\mathsf{X}^0_{\alpha,1;\infty}$ $(0 < \alpha < 1)$ *of* X *and* $\mathsf{D}(A)$ *if and only if*

$$\| [T(t) - I] f \| = o(t^\alpha) \qquad (t \to 0+). \tag{3.4.20}$$

Proof. Let us denote by lip$(\alpha; \mathsf{X})$ (cf. Sec. 2.3.2) the set of all elements $f \in \mathsf{X}$ such that condition (3.4.20) is valid. Since $\{T(t);\, 0 \leq t < \infty\}$ is an equi-bounded semi-group of class $(\mathscr{C}_0)$ in $\mathscr{E}(\mathsf{X})$, the set lip$(\alpha; \mathsf{X})$ is obviously a linear subspace of $\mathsf{X}_{\alpha,1;\infty}$. Moreover it is closed, as may be seen by a classical argument. Furthermore, $\operatorname{lip}(\alpha; X)$ is contained in $X^0_{\alpha,1;\infty}$. Indeed, if $f \in \operatorname{lip}(\alpha; X)$ then

$$\sup_{0<s\leqq t} (s^{-\alpha} \| [T(s) - I] [T(t) - I] f \|) \leqq (M+1) \sup_{0<s\leqq t} (s^{-\alpha} \| [T(s) - I] f \|)$$

and

$$\sup_{t<s<\infty} (s^{-\alpha} \| [T(s) - I] [T(t) - I] f \|) \leqq (M+1)\, t^{-\alpha} \| [T(t) - I] f \| .$$

Therefore,

$$\| [T(t) - I] f \|_{\alpha,1;\infty} \leqq \| [T(t) - I] f \| + (M+1) \sup_{0<s\leqq t} (s^{-\alpha} \| [T(s) - I] f \|),$$

which tends to zero as $t \to 0+$. On the other hand, $D(A) \subset \operatorname{lip}(\alpha; X)$, because

$$t^{-\alpha} \| [T(t) - I] f \| = \left\| t^{-\alpha} \int_0^t T(\tau)\, A f\, d\tau \right\| \leqq M \| A f \| \, t^{1-\alpha}$$

for all $t > 0$ and each $f \in D(A)$.

Combining the results, we have

$$X^0_{\alpha,1;\infty} = \overline{D(A)} \subset \operatorname{lip}(\alpha; X) \subset X^0_{\alpha,1;\infty},$$

proving the proposition.

There is one further

Proposition 3.4.13. *An element $f \in X$ belongs to the intermediate space $X^0_{1,2;\infty}$ of X and $D(A^2)$ if and only if*

$$\| [T(t) - I]^2 f \| = o(t) \qquad (t \to 0+). \tag{3.4.21}$$

Proof. We now denote by $\operatorname{lip}^*(1; X)$ (cf. Sec. 2.3.2) the space of all elements $f \in X$ such that (3.4.21) holds. The reader will have little difficulty in proving that this space is a closed linear subspace of $X_{1,2;\infty}$. Furthermore,

$$D(A) \subset X^0_{1,2;\infty} \subset \operatorname{lip}^*(1; X). \tag{3.4.22}$$

The first inclusion of (3.4.22) is obvious. To verify the second one, it suffices to show that $D(A) \subset \operatorname{lip}^*(1; X)$, since $\overline{D(A)} = X^0_{1,2;\infty}$ and $\operatorname{lip}^*(1; X)$ is closed in $X_{1,2;\infty}$. Indeed, for each $f \in D(A)$

$$[T(t) - I]^2 f = 2 \int_0^t T(\tau) [T(\tau) - I] A f\, d\tau \qquad (0 < t < \infty)$$

and, consequently, given an $\varepsilon > 0$ there is a $\delta = \delta(\varepsilon; f) > 0$ such that

$$t^{-1} \| [T(t) - I]^2 f \| \leqq 2M \sup_{0\leqq \tau \leqq t} \| [T(\tau) - I] A f \| < \varepsilon$$

for $0 < t < \delta$, proving (3.4.22).

It remains to show that $\mathrm{lip}^*(1; X) \subset X^0_{1,2;\infty}$. For this purpose, we introduce a further subspace of $X_{1,2;\infty}$:

$$X^{0,2}_{1,2;\infty} = \{f \in X_{1,2;\infty};\ \lim_{t\to 0+} \|[T(t) - I]^2 f\|_{1,2;\infty} = 0\}.$$

It is not hard to see that this subset of $X_{1,2;\infty}$ is closed and linear. Moreover, $X^0_{1,2;\infty}$ is contained in $X^{0,2}_{1,2;\infty}$. We shall prove that $D(A)$ is dense in $X^{0,2}_{1,2;\infty}$. Clearly, if $f \in X^{0,2}_{1,2;\infty}$, then for a $\delta > 0$ the element $f_\delta = \frac{1}{\delta}\int_0^\delta [2T(\tau) - T(2\tau)]\, f\, d\tau$ belongs to $D(A)$ and $f - f_\delta = = \frac{1}{\delta}\int_0^\delta [T(\tau) - I]^2 f\, d\tau$. Therefore,

$$\|f - f_\delta\|_{1,2;\infty} \leqq \sup_{0<\tau<\delta} \|[T(\tau) - I]^2 f\|_{1,2;\infty} < \varepsilon$$

for δ sufficiently small. Consequently, the spaces $X^0_{1,2;\infty}$ and $X^{0,2}_{1,2;\infty}$ are equal to another.

Now suppose $f \in \mathrm{lip}^*(1; X)$. Then one shows similarly as in the proof of Proposition 3.4.12 that

$$\|[T(t) - I]^2 f\|_{1,2;\infty} \leqq \|[T(t) - I]^2 f\| + \\ + (M+1)^2 \sup_{0<s\leqq t} \left(s^{-1} \|[T(s) - I]^2 f\|\right),$$

which tends to zero as $t \to 0+$. Thus

$$\mathrm{lip}^*(1; X) \subset X^{0,2}_{1,2;\infty} = X^0_{1,2;\infty}. \tag{3.4.23}$$

Both relations (3.4.22) and (3.4.23) prove the proposition.

Propositions 3.4.12 and 3.4.13 together with Theorem 3.4.6 give

Theorem 3.4.14. *Let $0 < \alpha < r$ $(r = 1, 2, \ldots)$ and let $\alpha = k + \beta$, $k = 0, 1, \ldots, r-1$ with $0 < \beta \leqq 1$. For an element $f \in X$ the following statements are equivalent:*

(i) $f \in X^0_{\alpha,r;\infty}$;

(ii) $f \in D(A^k)$ *and*

$$\|[T(t) - I]\, A^k f\| = o(t^\beta) \qquad (0 < \beta < 1;\ t \to 0+),$$
$$\|[T(t) - I]^2 A^k f\| = o(t) \qquad (\beta = 1;\ t \to 0+).$$

As a final corollary we have

Corollary 3.4.15. *Let $0 < \alpha < r$, $1 \leqq q < \infty$ $(r = 1, 2, \ldots)$ and let $\alpha = k + \beta$, $k = 0, 1, \ldots, r-1$ with $0 < \beta \leqq 1$. If an element*

$f \in X$ belongs to $X_{\alpha,r;q}$, then f belongs to $D(A^k)$ and

$$\|[T(t) - I]\, A^k f\| = o(t^\beta) \qquad (0 < \beta < 1;\ t \to 0+),$$
$$\|[T(t) - I]^2\, A^k f\| = o(t) \qquad (\beta = 1;\ t \to 0+).$$

By Theorem 3.4.4 the intermediate space $X_{\alpha,r;q}$ $(0 < \alpha < r,$ $1 \leqq q < \infty)$ is contained in $X^0_{\alpha,r;\infty}$, proving Corollary 3.4.15.

3.5 Equivalent Characterizations of $X_{\alpha,r;q}$ Generated by Holomorphic Semi-Groups

As in Sec. 3.1 and 3.4 let X be a Banach space and $\{T(t);\, 0 \leqq t < \infty\}$ an equi-bounded semi-group (with bound M) of class $(\mathscr{C}_0)$ in $\mathscr{E}(X)$. In addition we assume that the semi-group is holomorphic, i.e. $T(t)\,[X] \subset D(A)$ for each $t > 0$ and $t\,\|A\,T(t)\| \leqq N$ for all $t > 0$, N being some positive constant. Again r is some fixed positive integer.

It is our purpose in this section to reformulate the results of Sec. 2.3 in the terminology of the intermediate spaces $X_{\alpha,r;q}$ and to generalize and prove these in the spirit of the previous section.

Definition 3.5.1. *We denote by $X'_{\alpha,r;q}$ the space of all elements $f \in X$ such that*

$$\int_0^\infty (t^{r-\alpha}\, \|A^r T(t) f\|)^q \frac{dt}{t} < \infty \qquad (0 < \alpha < r;\ 1 \leqq q < \infty),$$

$$\sup_{0<t<\infty} (t^{r-\alpha}\, \|A^r\, T(t) f\|) < \infty \qquad (0 < \alpha \leqq r;\ q = \infty).$$

By standard arguments we have

Proposition 3.5.2. *The spaces $X'_{\alpha,r;q}$, $0 < \alpha < r$, $1 \leqq q \leqq \infty$ and/or $\alpha = r$, $q = \infty$, are Banach spaces under the norms*

$$(3.5.1)\qquad \|f\|'_{\alpha,r;q} = \begin{cases} \|f\| + \left\{\displaystyle\int_0^\infty (t^{r-\alpha}\, \|A^r\, T(t) f\|)^q \frac{dt}{t}\right\}^{1/q} & (1 \leqq q < \infty),\\[2ex] \|f\| + \displaystyle\sup_{0<t<\infty} (t^{r-\alpha}\, \|A^r\, T(t) f\|) & (q = \infty).\end{cases}$$

Moreover, these spaces are intermediate between X and $D(A^r)$.

We shall now formulate the main theorem of this section.

Theorem 3.5.3. *The intermediate spaces $X_{\alpha,r;q}$ and $X'_{\alpha,r;q}$ $(0 < \alpha < r,$ $1 \leqq q \leqq \infty$ and/or $\alpha = r$, $q = \infty)$ of X and $D(A^r)$ are equal to another with equivalent norms.*

Proof of Theorem 3.5.3 for $r = 1$. In this case we give a direct proof independent of the theory of intermediate spaces.

Firstly, let $f \in X_{\alpha,1;q}$, $0 < \alpha < 1$, $1 \leqq q \leqq \infty$. Applying the identity (3.4.17) of Lemma 3.4.8, we obtain

$$\|A\,T(t)\,f\| \leqq \sum_{k=0}^{n} \|A\,T(2^k t)\|\ \|[T(2^k t) - I]\,f\| + \|A\,T(2^{n+1}t)\|\ \|f\|$$

and, since by assumption $t\,\|A\,T(t)\| \leqq N$ for all $t > 0$,

$$t^{1-\alpha}\,\|A\,T(t)\,f\| \leqq N \sum_{k=0}^{n} 2^{(\alpha-1)k}\,(2^k t)^{-\alpha}\,\|[T(2^k t) - I]\,f\| + \frac{N}{2^{n+1}}\,\|f\|\,t^{-\alpha}.$$

Therefore, given any $\varepsilon > 0$ we have for $n \to \infty$

$$\left\{\int_{\varepsilon}^{\infty} (t^{1-\alpha}\,\|A\,T(t)\,f\|)^q\,\frac{dt}{t}\right\}^{1/q}$$

$$\leqq N \sum_{k=0}^{n} 2^{(\alpha-1)k} \left\{\int_{2^k\varepsilon}^{\infty} (t^{-\alpha}\,\|[T(t) - I]\,f\|)^q\,\frac{dt}{t}\right\}^{1/q} + \frac{N}{2^{n+1}}\,\|f\| \left\{\int_{\varepsilon}^{\infty} t^{-\alpha q}\,\frac{dt}{t}\right\}^{1/q}$$

$$\leqq \frac{N}{1 - 2^{(\alpha-1)}}\,\|(t^{-\alpha}\,\|[T(t) - I]\,f\|)\|_{L^q_*}$$

Since ε was arbitrary, f belongs to $X'_{\alpha,1;q}$ and

$$\|f\|'_{\alpha,1;q} \leqq \max\left(1, \frac{2N}{2 - 2^{\alpha}}\right)\|f\|_{\alpha,1;q},$$

which proves one direction. On the other hand, if $f \in X'_{\alpha,r;q}$, then

$$[T(t) - I]\,f = \int_0^t A\,T(\tau)\,f\,d\tau,$$

the right-hand integral existing in the sense of Bochner. Then, by inequality (3.4.15) of Lemma 3.4.7,

$$\left\{\int_0^{\infty} (t^{-\alpha}\,\|[T(t) - I]\,f\|)^q\,\frac{dt}{t}\right\}^{1/q} \leqq \left\{\int_0^{\infty}\left(t^{-\alpha}\int_0^t \tau\,\|A\,T(\tau)\,f\|\,\frac{d\tau}{\tau}\right)^q \frac{dt}{t}\right\}^{1/q}$$

$$\leqq \frac{1}{\alpha}\left\{\int_0^{\infty} (\tau^{1-\alpha}\,\|A\,T(\tau)\,f\|)^q\,\frac{d\tau}{\tau}\right\}^{1/q},$$

i.e. $f \in X_{\alpha,1;q}$ and

$$\|f\|_{\alpha,1;q} \leqq \frac{1}{\alpha}\,\|f\|'_{\alpha,1;q},$$

which completes the proof in case of non-optimal approximation. For $\alpha = r = 1$, $q = \infty$ see Proposition 2.3.1.

In case $0 < \alpha < 1$, $q = \infty$ this argument gives a second proof of the assertion of Corollary 2.3.4 (a). Although the proof of the relation

$X_{\alpha,1;\infty} \subset X'_{\alpha,1;\infty}$ of Proposition 2.3.3 depends upon a classical construction of S. Bernstein which in turn essentially rests upon the commutativity of the semi-group operators, the above method of proof makes use of the important identity (3.4.17) and the semi-group property per se of the operators $T(t)$, $0 \leqq t < \infty$. The proof of the converse result is the same for both methods and is again based upon the semi-group property.

Now to the proof of Theorem 3.5.3 for arbitrary integers $r \geqq 1$. To this end we need two lemmas.

Lemma 3.5.4. *For each* $f \in X$ *with* $M_r = \max((r\,N)^r, M)$

$$t^r \| A^r T(t) f \| \leqq M_r \, \mathrm{K}(t^r; f) \qquad (0 < t < \infty). \tag{3.5.2}$$

Proof. Obviously

$$t^r \| A^r T(t) f \| \leqq r^r \left(\frac{t}{r} \left\| A\, T\left(\frac{t}{r}\right) \right\| \right)^r \| f \| \leqq (r\,N)^r \| f \|_X .$$

Furthermore, if $f \in D(A^r)$, then trivially

$$t^r \| A^r T(t) f \| \leqq M\, t^r \| f \|_{D(A^r)} .$$

Now, let $f \in X$, $f = f_1 + f_2$, where $f_1 \in X$ and $f_2 \in D(A^r)$. Then

$$\begin{aligned} t^r \| A^r T(t) f \| &\leqq t^r \| A^r T(t) f_1 \| + t^r \| A^r T(t) f_2 \| \\ &\leqq (r\,N)^r \| f_1 \|_X + M\, t^r \| f_2 \|_{D(A^r)} \\ &\leqq M_r \big(\| f_1 \|_X + t^r \| f_2 \|_{D(A^r)} \big) \end{aligned}$$

for all representations $f = f_1 + f_2$. This proves the desired estimate (3.5.2).

Lemma 3.5.5. *For each* $f \in X$

$$\| [T(t) - I]^r f \| \leqq r\,M \int_0^t \tau^{r-1} \| A^r T(\tau) f \| \, d\tau \tag{3.5.3}$$

$$(r = 1, 2, \ldots;\ 0 < t < \infty).$$

Proof. By the holomorphic property of the semi-group we see that for each integer $r \geqq 1$ and all $f \in X$.

$$[T(t) - I]^r f = \underset{\varepsilon \to 0+}{\text{s-lim}}\ r \int_\varepsilon^t A\, T(\tau)\, [T(\tau) - I]^{r-1} f \, d\tau . \tag{3.5.4}$$

Thus

$$[T(t) - I]^r f = \underset{\varepsilon \to 0+}{\text{s-lim}}\ r! \int_\varepsilon^t A\, T(\tau_r)\, d\tau_r \int_\varepsilon^{\tau_r} A\, T(\tau_{r-1}) \ldots d\tau_2 \int_\varepsilon^{\tau_2} A\, T(\tau_1)\, f \, d\tau_1 .$$

But

$$\left\| r! \int_\varepsilon^t d\tau_r \int_\varepsilon^{\tau_r} \cdots d\tau_2 \int_\varepsilon^{\tau_2} A^r T(\tau_r + \tau_{r-1} + \cdots + \tau_1) f \, d\tau_1 \right\|$$

$$\leqq M\, r! \int_\varepsilon^t \| A^r T(\tau_r) f \| \, d\tau_r \int_\varepsilon^{\tau_r} \cdots d\tau_2 \int_\varepsilon^{\tau_2} d\tau_1 \leqq r\, M \int_0^t \tau^{r-1} \| A^r T(\tau) f \| \, d\tau ,$$

which gives the proof.

Proof of Theorem 3.5.3 for $r \geqq 1$. Suppose $f \in X_{\alpha, r; q}$, $0 < \alpha < r$, $1 \leqq q < \infty$ and/or $\alpha = r$, $q = \infty$. At first we remark that for $f \in X$ $\min(1, t^r) \|f\| \leqq \mathrm{K}(t^r; f)$, and consequently

$$(\| t^{-\alpha} \min(1, t^r) \|_{L^q_*}) \|f\| \leqq \| t^{-\alpha} \mathrm{K}(t^r; f) \|_{L^q_*} .$$

Now, using inequality (3.5.2) of Lemma 3.5.4, we obtain

$$\| (t^{r-\alpha} \| A^r T(t) f \|) \|_{L^q_*} \leqq M_r \| t^{-\alpha} \mathrm{K}(t^r; f) \|_{L^q_*} .$$

Thus $f \in X'_{\alpha, r; q}$ and

$$\|f\|'_{\alpha, r; q} \leqq ((\| t^{-\alpha} \min(1, t^r) \|_{L^q_*})^{-1} + M_r) \| t^{-\alpha} \mathrm{K}(t^r; f) \|_{L^q_*} ,$$

proving one direction.

Conversely, if $f \in X'_{\alpha, r; q}$, then by relation (3.5.3) and inequality (3.4.15)

$$\| (t^{-\alpha} \| [T(t) - I]^r f \|) \|_{L^q_*} \leqq \frac{r\, M}{\alpha} \| (t^{r-\alpha} \| A^r T(\tau) f \|) \|_{L^q_*} ,$$

i.e. $f \in X_{\alpha, r; q}$ and

$$\|f\|_{\alpha, r; q} \leqq \frac{r\, M}{\alpha} \|f\|'_{\alpha, r; q} .$$

This establishes Theorem 3.5.3.

Combining the results of Theorems 3.4.6 and 3.5.3 we have in case of non-optimal approximation

Corollary 3.5.6. *Let* $0 < \alpha < r$, $1 \leqq q \leqq \infty$ *and* $\alpha = k + \beta$, $0 < \beta \leqq 1$ *with* $k = 0, 1, \ldots, r-1$. *For an element* $f \in X$ *there are the following equivalent assertions:*

(i) $f \in X_{\alpha, r; q}$, *i.e.* $t^{-\alpha} \| [T(t) - I]^r f \| \in L^q_*$;

(ii) $t^{(r-\alpha)} \| A^r T(t) f \| \in L^q_*$;

(iii) $\begin{cases} t^{1-\beta} \| A^{k+1} T(t) f \| \in L^q_* & (0 < \beta < 1), \\ t \| A^{k+2} T(t) f \| \in L^q_* & (\beta = 1). \end{cases}$

Corollary 3.5.6 is an essential generalization of Corollary 2.3.4 (a) (the particular case $r = 1$, $q = \infty$). Its proof depends upon deep results on intermediate spaces (Theorem 3.4.6). This is one of the important reasons for the introduction of intermediate space theory in our study of semi-group operators. The reader may easily formulate further assertions equivalent to (i)—(iii) of Corollary 3.5.6 for the Taylor as well as Peano operator by making use of Corollary 3.4.9.

In the case of saturation we have the further corollary, a result already established in Theorem 2.3.2, namely

Corollary 3.5.7. *For the Favard class* $X_{r,r;\infty}$, *there are the equivalent norms*

(i) $\|f\| + \sup_{0<t<\infty} \left(t^{-r} \|[T(t) - I]^r f\|\right)$;

(ii) $\|f\| + \sup_{0<t<\infty} \left(\|A^r T(t) f\|\right)$.

We conclude this section with a brief discussion of the spaces $X^0_{\alpha,r;\infty}$, $0 < \alpha < r$, $r = 1, 2, \ldots$ Analogously to Propositions 3.4.12 and 3.4.13 we have

Proposition 3.5.8. *An element* $f \in X$ *belongs to*

(a) $X^0_{\alpha,1;\infty}$ $(0 < \alpha < 1)$ *if and only if*

$$\|A\,T(t)\,f\| = o(t^{\alpha-1}) \qquad (t \to 0+); \tag{3.5.5}$$

(b) $X^0_{1,2;\infty}$ *if and only if*

$$\|A^2\,T(t)\,f\| = o(t^{-1}) \qquad (t \to 0+). \tag{3.5.6}$$

Proof. To prove part (a), one easily verifies that the set of all elements $f \in X$ having property (3.5.5) forms a closed linear manifold in $X_{\alpha,1;\infty}$. On the one hand this space contains $D(A)$ (follows trivially) and on the other hand it is contained in $X^0_{\alpha,1;\infty}$. But $D(A)$ is dense in $X^0_{\alpha,1;\infty}$. Part (b) can be shown similarly.

More generally, we obtain by Theorem 3.4.14 for arbitrary integers $r \geqq 1$

Theorem 3.5.9. *Let* $0 < \alpha < r$ *and* $\alpha = k + \beta$, $0 < \beta \leqq 1$ *with* $k = 0, 1, \ldots, r - 1$. *An element* $f \in X$ *belongs to the space* $X^0_{\alpha,r;\infty}$ *if and only if*

$$\|A^{k+1}\,T(t)\,f\| = o(t^{\beta-1}) \qquad (0 < \beta < 1),$$
$$\|A^{k+2}\,T(t)\,f\| = o(t^{-1}) \qquad (\beta = 1).$$

The proof is obvious by the foregoing proposition.

3.6 Notes and Remarks

3.6.1. The subspaces $X_{\alpha,r;q}$ $(0 < \alpha < r$ and $1 \leqq q \leqq \infty$; $r = 1, 2, \ldots)$ of a Banach space X generated by an equi-bounded semi-group $\{T(t);\ 0 \leqq t < \infty\}$ of class $(\mathscr{C}_0)$ in $\mathscr{E}(X)$ (Definition 3.1.1) were introduced by J. L. Lions [3, I] (for $r = 1$) in 1959 and studied by him in connection with trace theorems and interpolation. For arbitrary positive integers r they are treated thoroughly by J. L. LIONS–J. PEETRE [2, Ch. VII § 2] as an application of a general method of constructing interpolation spaces ("espaces de moyennes"); see the remarks in Sec. 3.6.2 below. The Favard spaces $X_{r,r;\infty}$, $r = 1, 2, \ldots$, given in Definition 3.1.2 were first considered from the point of view of approximation by P. L. BUTZER [3; 4] (for $r = 1$) in 1956 and for arbitrary integers $r > 0$ by H. BERENS [2]; see the remarks in Sec. 2.7.1 and 2.7.2. Propositions 3.1.3 and 3.1 4 are immediate consequences of the assertions given in J. L. LIONS–J. PEETRE [2]. But—as we have seen—these simple properties are easily proved directly. The problems of Plessner type for the semi-group of operators on these spaces (Prop. 3.1.6, Cor. 3.1.7 and 3.1.8) were discussed by H. BERENS–P. L. BUTZER [4]. For the problems of Plessner type in connection with the group of translations on periodic function spaces see H. MIRKIL [1] (also the remarks in Sec. 4.4.1).

3.6.2. The subject matter of Sec. 3.2 is the development of an interpolation method between Banach spaces due to J. PEETRE [1; 2; 3; 4; 6; 9]. Our treatment is partially based upon the lecture notes [4] of Peetre given at the University of Brasília in 1963. But before going into a more detailed discussion concerning this and further interpolation methods as well as on general interpolation theory, let us cite the first paragraph of the introduction to the paper: *Interpolation spaces and interpolation methods,* by N. ARONSZAJN–E. GAGLIARDO [1], which gives a good survey on the historical background and recent research on the subject: "The beginning of what we now call interpolation methods between Banach spaces was the convexity theorem of M. RIESZ [1] in the late 1920's. This theorem gives an interpolation method for couples $(L^p(\mu), L^q(\mu))$. In the late 1930's, MARCINKIEWICZ [2] obtained an extension of the M. Riesz interpolation method to couples formed by weak L^p-spaces. In the 1950's, E. M. STEIN and G. WEISS [1] extended the method further by admitting couples $(L^p(\mu), L^q(\nu))$ with different measures μ and ν. Until the late 1950's, the research in interpolation methods between spaces remained essentially within the frame of couples of L^p-spaces. At the end of 1958, J. L. LIONS [1] gave the first proof of the interpolation theorem for quadratic interpolation between Hilbert spaces. This work gave impetus to the research on interpolation methods for arbitrary couples of Banach spaces. Since then several authors have introduced and developed a number of different interpolation methods for couples of general Banach spaces."

At first we shall briefly consider and compare the different interpolation methods for a couple of Banach spaces X_1 and X_2 continuously contained in a linear Hausdorff space $\mathcal{X}$, which were introduced by various authors. The notation is that of Sec. 3.2.1.

The method of J. PEETRE (*introduced in* 1963 — *the youngest of the various methods*): The K and J-methods due to J. Peetre of constructing intermediate spaces of X_1 and X_2 are in fact more general than presented in Sec. 3.2. Let $J(t; f)$ and $K(t; f)$ $(0 < t < \infty)$ be the function norms on $X_1 \cap X_2$ and $X_1 + X_2$ as defined in (3.2.8) and (3.2.9), respectively. A *functional norm* $\Psi = \Psi[\psi]$ is a positive functional (finite or not) defined on the set $\mathcal{M}_*^+$ of all non-negative (finite or infinite) functions ψ on $(0, \infty)$ measurable with respect to dt/t such that the following conditions are satisfied:

$$\Psi[0] = 0; \quad \Psi[\alpha\,\psi] = \alpha\,\Psi[\psi] \qquad (0 < \alpha < \infty); \tag{3.6.1}$$

$$\psi(t) \leqq \sum_{k=1}^{\infty} \psi_k(t) \quad \text{a.e.} \quad \Longrightarrow \Psi[\psi] \leqq \sum_{k=1}^{\infty} \Psi[\psi_k]; \tag{3.6.2}$$

$$\Psi[\psi] = 0 \Longrightarrow \psi(t) = 0 \quad \text{a.e.}; \quad \Psi[\psi] < \infty \Longrightarrow \psi(t) < \infty \quad \text{a.e.} \tag{3.6.3}$$

J. Peetre then denotes by $(X_1, X_2)_{\Psi;\,K}$ the set of all elements $f \in X_1 + X_2$ for which

$$\Psi[K(t; f)] < \infty,$$

and by $(X_1, X_2)_{\Psi;\,J}$ the set of $f \in X_1 + X_2$ for which there exists a measurable function $u = u(t)$ with values in $X_1 \cap X_2$ such that

$$f = \int_0^\infty u(t)\,\frac{dt}{t} \quad (u(\cdot) \in L_*^1(X_1 + X_2)), \qquad \Psi[J(t; u(t))] < \infty.$$

Obviously, these spaces are linear. They can be normed by setting

$$\|f\|_{\Psi;\,K} = \Psi[K(t; f)] \quad \text{and} \quad \|f\|_{\Psi;\,J} = \inf_{f = \int_0^\infty u(t) \frac{dt}{t}} (\Psi[J(t; u(t))]), \tag{3.6.4}$$

respectively. Let

$$c_K = (\Psi[\min(1, t)])^{-1} \quad \text{and} \quad c_J = \sup_{\Psi[\psi]=1} \left(\int_0^\infty \min\left(1, \frac{1}{t}\right) \psi(t)\,\frac{dt}{t} \right),$$

then one has the following theorem:

If $0 < c_K < \infty$ $(0 < c_J < \infty)$, *then the space* $(X_1, X_2)_{\Psi;\,K}$ $((X_1, X_2)_{\Psi;\,J})$ *normed by* (3.6.4) *is an intermediate space of* X_1 *and* X_2.

Of all possible functional norms the following is of greatest importance in the applications:

$$\Psi_{\theta,q}[\psi] = \begin{cases} \left\{ \int_0^\infty (t^{-\theta}\,\psi(t))^q\,\frac{dt}{t} \right\}^{1/q} & (-\infty < \theta < \infty;\ 1 \leqq q < \infty) \\ \operatorname*{ess\,sup}_{0<t<\infty} (t^{-\theta}\,\psi(t)) & (-\infty < \theta < \infty;\ q = \infty). \end{cases} \tag{3.6.5}$$

It is this particular instance of a functional norm which generates the intermediate spaces $(X_1, X_2)_{\theta,q;K}$ $(0 < \theta < 1, 1 \leqq q < \infty$ and/or $0 \leqq \theta \leqq 1, q = \infty)$ and $(X_1, X_2)_{\theta,q;J}$ $(0 \leqq \theta \leqq 1, q = 1$ and/or $0 < \theta < 1, 1 < q \leqq \infty)$ of X_1 and X_2 given in Definitions 3.2.4 and 3.2.6. For these spaces we have formulated and proved the main theorems such as the theorem on the identification of the K and J-methods (Theorem 3.2.12), the theorem of reiteration or stability (Theorem 3.2.20) and the interpolation theorems (Theorems 3.2.23 and 3.2.24). We should complete our results by stating the theorem of duality:

If $0 < \theta < 1$, $1 \leqq q < \infty$ *and if* $X_1 \cap X_2$ *is dense in* X_1 *as well as in* X_2, *then the dual space* $(X_1, X_2)^*_{\theta,q;K}$ *is equal to* $(X_2^*, X_1^*)_{1-\theta,q';J}$ $(q^{-1} + q'^{-1} = 1)$ *with equivalent norms. In particular, if* X_1 *and* X_2 *are reflexive, then the space* $(X_1, X_2)_{\theta,q;K}$ *is reflexive for* $0 < \theta < 1$, $1 < q < \infty$. For a proof see J. PEETRE [9, Ch. III].

The K-method was also independently but later introduced by E. T. OKLANDER [1; 2; 3].

The method of E. GAGLIARDO [3; 4; 6; 7; 8] (*introduced in* 1959): Let $f \in X_1 + X_2$. In the first quadrant of the plane E_2 E. Gagliardo considered the set

$$(3.6.6)\quad \Lambda(f) = \{(x_1, x_2);\ \text{there exist } f_1 \in X_1 \text{ and } f_2 \in X_2 \text{ with } f = f_1 + f_2,\ \|f_1\|_1 \leqq x_1 \text{ and } \|f_2\|_2 \leqq x_2\}.$$

The set $\Lambda = \Lambda(f)$ has the following properties:

(3.6.7) Λ *is convex.*

(3.6.8) *If* $(x_1, x_2) \in \Lambda$, *then* $(x_1 + h_1, x_2 + h_2) \in \Lambda$ *for every* $h_1, h_2 \geqq 0$.

(3.6.9) $\Lambda(\alpha f) = |\alpha|\, \Lambda(f)$, *where* $\alpha\Lambda \equiv \{(\alpha x_1, \alpha x_2);\ (x_1, x_2) \in \Lambda\}$.

(3.6.10) $\Lambda(f_1 + f_2) \supset \Lambda(f_1) + \Lambda(f_2)$, *where*

$$\Lambda_1 + \Lambda_2 \equiv \{(x_1 + y_1, x_2 + y_2);\ (x_1, x_2) \in \Lambda_1, (y_1, y_2) \in \Lambda_2\}.$$

Moreover, if $X_1 \cap X_2$ *is dense in* X_1, *one has*

$$(3.6.11)\qquad \inf_{(x_1, x_2) \in \Lambda} x_1 = 0,$$

and if $X_1 \cap X_2$ *is dense in* X_2, *one has*

$$(3.6.12)\qquad \inf_{(x_1, x_2) \in \Lambda} x_2 = 0.$$

The boundary of Λ is denoted by $\partial\Lambda$ from which possible sections lying on the positive half-axes have been removed.

There is a close connection between the set of points $\Lambda(f)$ in E_2 and the function norm $K(t; f)$ as was noted by J. PEETRE [6]. Indeed, he remarked that the family of tangents to the convex boundary $\partial\Lambda(f)$ is given by the straight lines

$$x_1 + t\, x_2 = K(t; f) \qquad (0 < t < \infty).$$

One has the following theorem:

Let $\mathfrak{F}[\Lambda]$ *be a functional (finite or not) defined for the domain* $\Lambda(f)$, $f \in X_1 + X_2$, *such that:*

$$\mathfrak{F}[\Lambda(\alpha f)] \leqq C_1 |\alpha| \, \mathfrak{F}[\Lambda(f)], \tag{3.6.13}$$

$$\mathfrak{F}[\Lambda(\textstyle\sum_k f^k)] \leqq C_2 \sum_k \mathfrak{F}[\Lambda(f^k)], \tag{3.6.14}$$

$$C_3' \, \|f\|_{X_1+X_2} \leqq \mathfrak{F}[\Lambda(f)] \leqq C_3'' \, \|f\|_{X_1 \cap X_2}; \tag{3.6.15}$$

if $\mathfrak{F}[\Lambda(f^n - f^m)] \to 0$ *as* $n, m \to \infty$, *then*

$$\mathfrak{F}[\Lambda(f^0)] \leqq C_4 \sup_n \mathfrak{F}[\Lambda(f^n)], \tag{3.6.16}$$

where f^0 *is the limit in* $X_1 + X_2$ *of* $\{f^n\}$ *which exists by* (3.6.15).

Then the subset $\mathfrak{F}(X_1, X_2)$ *of those elements* $f \in X_1 + X_2$ *for which* $\mathfrak{F}[\Lambda(f)] < \infty$ *is an intermediate space of* X_1 *and* X_2 *with the norm*

$$\|f\|_{\mathfrak{F}} = \inf \textstyle\sum_k \mathfrak{F}[\Lambda(f^k)] \qquad (f = \sum_k f^k), \tag{3.6.17}$$

which is equivalent to $\mathfrak{F}[\Lambda(f)]$:

$$\|f\|_{\mathfrak{F}} \leqq \mathfrak{F}[\Lambda(f)] \leqq C_2 \, \|f\|_{\mathfrak{F}}. \tag{3.6.18}$$

Of particular interest are the functionals

$$\mathfrak{F}^\theta[\Lambda] = \sup_{(x_1, x_2) \in \partial\Lambda} (x_1^{1-\theta} x_2^\theta) \qquad (0 \leqq \theta \leqq 1) \tag{3.6.19}$$

and

(3.6.20)

$$\mathfrak{F}_{\alpha,\beta,\gamma,\delta}[\Lambda] = \begin{cases} \infty, & \text{if } \Lambda \text{ does not satisfy (3.6.11) and (3.6.12),} \\ \left\{\int_{\partial\Lambda} x_1^\alpha x_2^\beta |dx_1|^\gamma |dx_2|^\delta\right\}^{\frac{1}{\alpha+\beta+1}}, \ (\leqq \infty), & \text{if } \Lambda \text{ satisfies (3.6.11) and (3.6.12),} \end{cases}$$

where $\alpha, \beta, \gamma, \delta$ are real non-negative numbers with $\gamma + \delta = 1$, $\alpha + \gamma > 0, \beta + \delta > 0$ and $|dx_1|^\gamma |dx_2|^\delta = |x_2'|^\delta \, dx_1$ (if $\partial\Lambda$ is considered oriented in the direction of increasing x_1).

It was shown by P. Arduini [1] that the functional (3.6.20) does in fact only depend on two independent parameters $0 < \theta < 1$, $1 \leqq q < \infty$, where $\theta = (\beta + \delta)/(\alpha + \beta + 1)$ and $q = \alpha + \beta + 1$. If we set

$$\mathfrak{F}_q^\theta[\Lambda] = \begin{cases} \mathfrak{F}_{(q-1)(1-\theta),(q-1)\theta,1-\theta,\theta}[\Lambda] & (0 < \theta < 1,\ 1 \leqq q < \infty) \\ \mathfrak{F}^\theta[\Lambda] & (0 \leqq \theta \leqq 1,\ q = \infty) \end{cases}$$

then, T. Holmstedt has further proved the important equivalence between the spaces $\mathfrak{F}_q^\theta(X_1, X_2)$ and $(X_1, X_2)_{\theta,q;K}$ (see J. Peetre [9, Ch. V; 10]).

The method of J. L. Lions–J. Peetre [1; 2]: In 1961 these authors introduced the so-called *method of means* of constructing intermediate spaces of X_1 and X_2. Indeed, let α_1, α_2 be two real parameters such that $\alpha_1 \alpha_2 < 0$ and let $1 \leqq q_1, q_2 \leqq \infty$. J. L. Lions–J. Peetre denoted by $S(\alpha_1, q_1; X_1; \alpha_2, q_2; X_2)$ the set of all elements $f \in X_1 + X_2$ such that the following two *equivalent* conditions are satisfied:

(J) there exists a measurable function $u = u(t)$ on $(0, \infty)$ with values in $X_1 \cap X_2$ such that

$$f = \int_0^\infty u(t) \frac{dt}{t} \quad (u(\cdot) \in L^1_*(X_1 + X_2)); \quad t^{\alpha_1} u(t) \in L^{q_1}_*(X_1); \quad t^{\alpha_2} u(t) \in L^{q_2}_*(X_2);$$

(K) there exist measurable functions $v_1 = v_1(t)$ and $v_2 = v_2(t)$ with values in X_1 and X_2, respectively, such that

$$f = v_1(t) + v_2(t) \ \text{a.e.} \ (\text{in } X_1 + X_2); \quad t^{\alpha_1} v_1(t) \in L^{q_1}_*(X_1); \quad t^{\alpha_2} v_2(t) \in L^{q_2}_*(X_2).$$

It is easy to see that these spaces are linear. The above authors called them *spaces of means* ("espaces de moyennes"). One has:

$S(\alpha_1, q_1; X_1; \alpha_2, q_2; X_2)$ *is an intermediate space of* X_1 *and* X_2 *under the two equivalent norms*

$$(3.6.21) \qquad \|f\|_S^{(J)} = \inf_{f = \int_0^\infty u(t) \frac{dt}{t}} \left\{\max\left(\|t^{\alpha_1} u(t)\|_{L^{q_1}_*}; \|t^{\alpha_2} u(t)\|_{L^{q_2}_*}\right)\right\}$$

and

$$(3.6.22) \qquad \|f\|_S^{(K)} = \inf_{f = v_1(t) + v_2(t) \ \text{a.e.}} \left\{\max\left(\|t^{\alpha_1} v_1(t)\|_{L^{q_1}_*}; \|t^{\alpha_2} v_2(t)\|_{L^{q_2}_*}\right)\right\}.$$

It was shown by J. PEETRE [3] that the space $S(\alpha_1, q_1; X_1; \alpha_2, q_2; X_2)$ depends on two parameters θ and q, $0 < \theta < 1$, $1 \leqq q \leqq \infty$, whereby $\theta = \alpha_1/(\alpha_1 - \alpha_2)$ and $1/q = (1-\theta)/q_1 + \theta/q_2$, and that

$$S(\alpha_1, q_1; X_1; \alpha_2, q_2; X_2) = S(\theta, q; X_1; \theta - 1, q; X_2) = S(\theta, q; X_1, X_2).$$

Furthermore, J. PEETRE, ibidem, proved that

$$(3.6.23) \qquad S(\theta, q; X_1, X_2) = (X_1, X_2)_{\theta, q; K} = (X_1, X_2)_{\theta, q; J}$$

with equivalent norms.

The method of J. L. LIONS [2; 3; 6; 8]: J. L. Lions has introduced this method, known as the *method of traces*, in 1959. He denotes by $\mathscr{W}(\theta, q; X_1, X_2)$ the space of functions $u = u(t)$ on $(0, \infty)$ with values in $X_1 + X_2$ such that

$$t^\theta u(t) \in L^q_*(X_1), \qquad t^\theta \frac{du}{dt} \in L^q_*(X_2),$$

where $0 < \theta < 1$, $1 \leqq q \leqq \infty$, normed by

$$(3.6.24) \qquad \|u(\cdot)\|_{\mathscr{W}} = \max\left\{\|t^\theta u(t)\|_{L^q_*(X_1)}; \left\|t^\theta \frac{du}{dt}\right\|_{L^q_*(X_2)}\right\}.$$

The derivative du/dt is to be understood in the distributional sense with values in $X_1 + X_2$. Under these hypotheses $u(t)$ converges in

$X_1 + X_2$ as $t \to 0+$ or u admits a trace at the origin:

$$\text{trace of } u = \lim_{t \to 0+} u(t) = u(0).$$

J. L. Lions then denotes by $T(\theta, q; X_1, X_2)$ the space of all elements $f = u(0)$ in $X_1 + X_2$, when u spans $\mathscr{W}(\theta, q; X_1, X_2)$. $T(\theta, q; X_1, X_2)$ becomes a Banach space, if it is provided with the norm

$$\|f\|_T = \inf_{f = u(0)} \|u(\cdot)\|_{\mathscr{W}}. \tag{3.6.25}$$

Moreover, $T(\theta, q; X_1, X_2)$ is an intermediate space of X_1 and X_2.

In [2] J. L. Lions–J. Peetre studied the connections between the mean spaces $S(\theta, q; X_1, X_2)$ and the trace spaces $T(\theta, q; X_1, X_2)$ and they proved that these spaces are also equal to another with equivalent norms. Moreover, it must be remarked that J. L. Lions [6] formulated and first proved the theorem of duality for trace spaces.

The methods treated above are so-called *real interpolation methods*. Inspired by the method of proof of M. Riesz' convexity theorem by G. O. Thorin, A. P. Calderón [2; 3], S. G. Kreĭn [1; 2] and J. L. Lions [5; 8] introduced independently in 1960 the so-called *complex interpolation method*. We shall briefly indicate the method of A. P. Calderón and J. L. Lions: Let $\mathscr{A}(X_1, X_2)$ be the space of functions $u(\zeta)$, $\zeta = \xi + i\eta$, $0 \leqq \xi \leqq 1$, holomorphic in the strip $0 < \xi < 1$ with values in $X_1 + X_2$ such that $u(i\eta)$ is continuous and bounded with values in X_1 and $u(1 + i\eta)$ is continuous and bounded with values in X_2. Provided with the norm

$$\|u\|_{\mathscr{A}} = \max\left\{\sup_\eta \|u(i\eta)\|_1; \sup_\eta \|u(1 + i\eta)\|_2\right\}, \tag{3.6.26}$$

$\mathscr{A}(X_1, X_2)$ becomes a Banach space.

Then the range of the mapping $u \to u(\theta)$, $0 < \theta < 1$, from $\mathscr{A}(X_1, X_2)$ to $X_1 + X_2$ is denoted by $[X_1, X_2]_\theta$. Under the norm

$$\|f\|_\theta = \inf_{f = u(\theta)} \|u\|_{\mathscr{A}} \tag{3.6.27}$$

$[X_1, X_2]_\theta$ becomes a Banach space. Moreover, it is intermediate between X_1 and X_2.

It was shown by J. L. Lions–J. Peetre in [2] that

$$[X_1, X_2]_\theta \in \mathscr{H}(\theta; X_1, X_2);$$

moreover, these authors proved that if $X_1 \subset X_2$ then for $\varepsilon > 0$ sufficiently small

$$(X_1, X_2)_{\theta - \varepsilon, q; \mathrm{K}} \subset [X_1, X_2]_\theta \subset (X_1, X_2)_{\theta + \varepsilon, q; \mathrm{K}} \quad (1 \leqq q \leqq \infty).$$

It happens that in particular examples (cf. E. Magenes [1])

$$(X_1, X_2)_{\theta, q; \mathrm{K}} = [X_1, X_2]_\theta, \tag{3.6.28}$$

but it would be of interest to obtain general sufficient conditions under which (3.6.28) is true, as was noted by J. L. LIONS [8] (cf. M. SCHECHTER [1]).

So far we have considered real and complex interpolation methods of constructing intermediate spaces for an interpolation pair $(\mathsf{X}_1, \mathsf{X}_2)$, i.e. a couple of Banach spaces X_1 and X_2 continuously contained in a linear Hausdorff space $\mathscr{X}$. Moreover, these methods lead to the so-called *interpolation spaces* of X_1 and X_2, an intermediate space X of X_1 and X_2 being called an interpolation space, if for each linear transformation $T \in \mathscr{T}(\mathscr{X}, \mathscr{X}) \equiv \mathscr{T}(\mathscr{X})$ its restriction on X is a continuous mapping from X to itself. (Compare this definition with Definition 3.2.22 of Sec. 3.2.5).

Setting $\mathscr{S}(\mathscr{X}, \mathscr{Y}) = \{T \in \mathscr{T}(\mathscr{X}, \mathscr{Y});\ \|T f_1\|_1 \leqq \|f_1\|_1 \text{ and } \|T f_2\|_2 \leqq \leqq \|f_2\|_2\}$, then there is the following equivalent definition: *An intermediate space X of X_1 and X_2 is said to be an interpolation space, if for every $T \in \mathscr{S}(\mathscr{X})$ T is a continuous operator from X to itself with $\|T f\|_{\mathsf{X}} \leqq \|f\|_{\mathsf{X}}$.*

Moreover, independently of any particular interpolation method, we generally admit the following definition: *An interpolator $\mathfrak{F}$ is a function defined on the class of interpolation pairs, whose values are interpolation spaces of their arguments, such that if $\mathfrak{F}(\mathsf{X}_1, \mathsf{X}_2) = \mathsf{X}$ and $\mathfrak{F}(\mathsf{Y}_1, \mathsf{Y}_2) = \mathsf{Y}$, then every $T \in \mathscr{S}(\mathscr{X}, \mathscr{Y})$ transforms X to Y and satisfies $\|T f\|_{\mathsf{Y}} \leqq \|f\|_{\mathsf{X}}$.*

In this general setting the following interpolation theorem, due to N. ARONSZAJN–E. GAGLIARDO [1], holds:

Theorem. *Given an interpolation pair $(\mathsf{X}_1, \mathsf{X}_2)$ and an interpolation space X of X_1 and X_2, there exist two interpolators $\mathfrak{F}_1$ and $\mathfrak{F}_2$ such that*

(i) $\mathfrak{F}_1(\mathsf{X}_1, \mathsf{X}_2) = \mathsf{X}$, $\mathfrak{F}_2(\mathsf{X}_1, \mathsf{X}_2) = \mathsf{X}$;

(ii) *$\mathfrak{F}_1$ is minimal: if $\mathfrak{F}$ is any interpolator such that $\mathfrak{F}(\mathsf{X}_1, \mathsf{X}_2) = \mathsf{X}$, then $\mathfrak{F}_1(\mathsf{Y}_1, \mathsf{Y}_2)$ is continuously contained in $\mathfrak{F}(\mathsf{Y}_1, \mathsf{Y}_2)$ for every interpolation pair $(\mathsf{Y}_1, \mathsf{Y}_2)$;*

(iii) *$\mathfrak{F}_2$ is maximal: if $\mathfrak{F}$ is any interpolator such that $\mathfrak{F}(\mathsf{X}_1, \mathsf{X}_2) = \mathsf{X}$, then $\mathfrak{F}(\mathsf{Y}_1, \mathsf{Y}_2)$ is continuously contained in $\mathfrak{F}_2(\mathsf{Y}_1, \mathsf{Y}_2)$ for every interpolation pair $(\mathsf{Y}_1, \mathsf{Y}_2)$.*

This theorem may be interpreted as the M. Riesz interpolation theorem for Banach spaces. For a proof we also refer to E. T. OKLANDER [2], whose exposition we have followed. We further refer to E. GAGLIARDO [6; 7; 8].

Having given a brief introduction to the various interpolation methods as well as to the main theorem on general interpolation theory, the reader is refered to the cited literature for a detailed treatment on the subject. In particular we mention the articles of E. MAGENES [1], S. G. KREĬN–JU. I. PETUNIN [1] and N. ARONSZAJN–E. GAGLIARDO [1].

In the first part of his excellent paper E. Magenes gave a detailed historical introduction and discussed in particular the method of traces, the complex method and that of E. Gagliardo. This paper is endowed with a lengthy list of references. S. G. Kreĭn–Ju. I. Petunin mainly studied the work of the first author and his collaborators. N. Aronszajn–E. Gagliardo gave an extensive treatment on general interpolation theory. All in all the theory is developing at an explosive rate in several directions at the present time.

The theory of interpolation has many applications in modern analysis and various interpolation methods often spring from these applications.

A standard example is the investigation of the interpolation spaces between Lebesgue spaces. This especially leads to the Lorentz spaces and to the classical convexity theorems of M. Riesz-Thorin and Marcinkiewicz and generalizations thereof; see Sec. 3.3 and Sec. 3.6.3 below for remarks.

For another application we refer to the main object of this chapter which is an intensive study from the point of view of interpolation of the subspaces $X_{\alpha,r;q}$ $(0 < \alpha < r, 1 \leqq q \leqq \infty$ and/or $\alpha = r, q = \infty)$ of a Banach space X defined in Sec. 3.1. For this see Sec. 3.4 and 3.5 as well as the corresponding Sec. 3.6.4 and 3.6.5.

If X is one of the Lebesgue spaces on the real axis and if the subspaces $X_{\alpha,r;q}$ are generated by the semi-group of left translations, then these spaces are in particular the generalized Lipschitz spaces of X. In the n-dimensional case one obtains the so-called Besov spaces. See Sec. 4.1.1, where the Lipschitz spaces are discussed for periodic function spaces, while Sec. 4.3.1 is concerned with the general case in E_n.

For the applications to the theory of partial differential equations (connected with the names of J. L. Lions, E. Magenes, M. Schechter, G. Stampachia, S. G. Kreĭn, etc.) see the second part of E. Magenes [1].

Interpolation methods as applied to the theory of best approximation were considered by J. Peetre [1; 4; 6; 9]. He obtains results due to S. M. Nikolskiĭ [1] and his school. Finally, let us mention the applications to the theory of multipliers in $L^p(\mathrm{E}_n)$. In this respect see L. Hörmander [1], W. Littman [2] and J. Peetre [11; 12].

So far we have discussed interpolation theory for Banach spaces; in particular, for Hilbert spaces, where the theory was first developed, see J. L. Lions [1], C. Foiaş–J. L. Lions [1], J. Peetre [8], etc. For interpolation theory in locally convex spaces see e.g. N. Deutsch [1; 2].

3.6.3. The identification of the Lorentz spaces $L^{pq}(\mu)$ $(1 < p < \infty$, $1 \leqq q < \infty$ and/or $1 \leqq p \leqq \infty, q = \infty)$ on a totally σ-finite measure space (R, μ) (Definition 3.3.5) as intermediate spaces of $L^1(\mu)$ and $L^\infty(\mu)$ forms an impressive application to interpolation theory. In particular, the characterization by the K-method via the fundamental relation (3.3.6) of Proposition 3.3.7 was first formulated by J. PEETRE [2] in 1963. Independently, but a year later, relation (3.3.6) was also formulated and established by E. T. OKLANDER [1; 2] whose proof we have followed. For measure theoretical results we refer e.g. to P. R. HALMOS [1], while the proofs of the Lemmata 3.3.2 and 3.3.4 can be seen in G. H. HARDY–J. E. LITTLEWOOD–G. PÓLYA [1, Ch. X], A. ZYGMUND [5, Vol. I pp. 29–33] or the recent lecture notes of E. T. OKLANDER [2] at the University of Buenos Aires.

The Lorentz spaces $L^{pq}(\mu)$, introduced by A. P. CALDERÓN in the present notation (see R. O'NEIL [1]), were first defined and studied by G. G. LORENTZ [1] in 1950 on the unit interval $(0, 1)$ with respect to the Lebesgue measure λ and for the particular cases $1 < p < \infty$, $q = 1, \infty$ and $1 \leqq q \leqq p < \infty$. Using the somewhat different notation of G. G. LORENTZ [1; 2; 3; 4] a function f on $(0, 1)$ belongs to the class $\Lambda(\phi; r)$, $r \geqq 1$, provided the norm

$$\|f\|_{\Lambda(\phi;r)} = \left\{\int_0^1 \phi(t)\, f^*(t)^r\, dt\right\}^{1/r} \tag{3.6.29}$$

is finite. Here $\phi(t) > 0$ is a decreasing integrable function on $(0, 1)$ with $\int_0^1 \phi(t)\, dt = 1$ and $f^*(t)$ the non-increasing rearrangement of f on $(0, 1)$. The most interesting special case, besides $\phi(t) = 1$ when $\Lambda(\phi; r) = L^r(0, 1)$, is $\phi(t) = \alpha\, t^{\alpha-1}$ for some $0 < \alpha \leqq 1$, the corresponding space being denoted by $\Lambda(\alpha; r)$. If $\alpha = q/p$ and $r = q$, thus for $1 \leqq q \leqq p < \infty$, the spaces $\Lambda(q/p; q)$ are identical with $L^{pq}(0, 1)$ of Definition 3.3.5 in view of the inequalities (3.3.9) (which also hold on $(0, 1)$) and the fact that

$$\left\{\int_0^1 (t^{1/p} f^*(t))^q \frac{dt}{t}\right\}^{1/q} = (p/q)^{1/q}\, \|f\|_{\Lambda(q/p;q)}\,.$$

(Note that for $q \leqq p$ the functional $\|t^{1/p} f^*(t)\|_{L^q_*}$ defines a norm on $L^{pq}(\mu)$, but fails to do so for $q > p$, as was shown by G. G. LORENTZ [2].)

Another space introduced by G. G. Lorentz is the class $M(\phi; r)$, $r \geqq 1$, of all functions f for which

$$\|f\|_{M(\phi;r)} = \sup_{E \subset (0,1)} \left\{(1/\Phi(\lambda(E))) \int_E |f(t)|^r\, dt\right\}^{1/r} \tag{3.6.30}$$

is finite. Here $\Phi(t) = \int_0^t \phi(s)\,ds$. For $\Phi(t) = t^\alpha, 0 \leqq \alpha \leqq 1$, this space is denoted by $M(\alpha; r)$. If $\alpha = 1 - 1/p$, $r = 1$ the space $M(1 - 1/p; 1)$ is identical with $L^{p\infty}(0, 1)$ of Definition 3.3.5, since

$$\|f\|_{M(1-1/p;1)} = \sup_{E \subset (0,1)} \left\{\lambda(E)^{1/p-1} \int_E |f(t)|\,dt\right\} = \sup_{0<t<1} \left\{t^{1/p} f^{**}(t)\right\}.$$

We should mention that G. G. LORENTZ [1, p. 41] remarked that spaces of the type $\Lambda(\alpha; r)$ had been considered indirectly before, and that the well-known theorems of Hardy-Littlewood and Paley (cf. A. ZYGMUND [5, Vol. II p. 128]) may be regarded as to refer to the space $\Lambda(p - 1; p)$, $p > 1$. Furthermore, it should be noted that the spaces $\Lambda(\phi; r)$ and $M(\phi; r)$ are particular instances of Köthe spaces; see G. G. LORENTZ [3, pp. 66—67], G. G. LORENTZ–D. G. WERTHEIM [1]. General Köthe spaces of integrable functions were first considered by J. DIEUDONNÉ [1] and J. L. B. COOPER [1]; Köthe and Toeplitz in a series of papers beginning in 1934 dealt with spaces of sequences of similar type (see e.g. G. KÖTHE [1; 2, Kap. 6 § 30]). In this connection we should further mention the papers of I. HALPERIN [1; 2; 3], H. W. ELLIS–I. HALPERIN [1], and especially the series of papers on "Banach function spaces" in Nederl. Akad. Wetensch. Indag. Math. by W. A. J. LUXEMBURG–A. C. ZAANEN, the first [1] of which appeared in 1963, where problems of this type are considered from a very general point of view.

In our notation, G. G. LORENTZ [1] has shown that the spaces $L^{p1}(0, 1)$ and $L^{p\infty}(0, 1)$, $1 < p < \infty$, are Banach spaces under the norms (3.6.29) and (3.6.30), respectively. Moreover, $L^{p'\infty}(0, 1)$ is the dual space to $L^{p1}(0, 1)$, but the dual to $L^{p\infty}(0, 1)$ does not prove to be $L^{p'1}(0,1)$. This follows by the fact that $L^{p1}(0, 1)$ is separable, while $L^{p\infty}(0, 1)$ is not. In this respect E. M. SEMENOV [1] proved in 1962 the following result: If $L_0^{p\infty}(0,1)$, $1 < p < \infty$, denotes the set of elements in $L^{p\infty}(0, 1)$ such that

$$\lim_{t \to 0+} t^{1/p} f^{**}(t) = 0,$$

then $L_0^{p\infty}(0, 1)$ is a closed linear subspace of $L^{p\infty}(0, 1)$ and the dual to $L_0^{p\infty}(0, 1)$ is given by $L^{p'1}(0, 1)$. Thus the second dual of $L_0^{p\infty}(0, 1)$ is $L^{p\infty}(0, 1)$. Moreover, G. G. Lorentz also proved the inclusion $L^{p1}(0, 1) \subset \subset L^{p}(0, 1) \subset L^{p\infty}(0, 1)$. Concerning the spaces $L^{pq}(0, 1)$, I. HALPERIN [1] has shown that for $1 < q \leqq p < \infty$ these spaces are reflexive. In general we have that the dual to $L^{pq}(0, 1)$, $1 < p, q < \infty$, is equal to $L^{p'q'}(0, 1)$. For this latter result as well as for generalizations to arbitrary measure spaces $(\mathrm{R}; \mu)$ see the cited papers, in particular we refer to G. G. LORENTZ [3], A. P. CALDERÓN [3], J. L. LIONS–J. PEETRE

[2], J. PEETRE [4], E. T. OKLANDER [2] and S. G. KREĬN–JU. I. PETUNIN [1].

The first convexity theorem, originally due to M. RIESZ [1] (1926) and extended by G. O. THORIN [1] in 1939, is one of the corner stones of analysis. For the various classical proofs, extensions and applications (cf. Sec. 4.2.1), the reader may consult A. ZYGMUND [5, Vol. II Ch. XII and the Notes attached thereto], G. H. HARDY–J. E. LITTLEWOOD–G. PÓLYA [1, Ch. VIII], G. O. THORIN [2], M. COTLAR–M. BRUSCHI [1], A. P. CALDERÓN–A. ZYGMUND [1; 4], E. M. STEIN [1], E. M. STEIN–G. WEISS [1], etc. The second interpolation theorem, due to J. MARCINKIEWICZ [2] (1939), is a deep extension of the theorem of M. Riesz-Thorin having many applications for which that of Riesz-Thorin cannot be applied (cf. Sec. 4.2.2). Other classical proofs, extensions and applications can be found in A. ZYGMUND [5, Vol. II Ch. XII and the Notes], M. COTLAR–M. BRUSCHI [1], E. M. STEIN–G. WEISS [2], etc. The extension of the theorem of Marcinkiewicz given by E. M. Stein and G. Weiss to operators of restricted weak type seems to be of great importance from the point of view of Sec. 3.3.

Essentially new proofs and extensions to Lorentz spaces of the convexity theorems were given in 1959—1964, based upon the various methods of interpolation (see Sec. 3.6.2 above). These theorems are connected with the names of E. GAGLIARDO [4; 6; 7; 8], J. L. LIONS [5; 6], A. P. CALDERÓN [2; 3], S. G. KREĬN [1; 2], S. G. KREĬN–E. M. SEMENOV [1], E. M. SEMENOV [1], J. L. LIONS–J. PEETRE [2], J. PEETRE [4; 6; 9], R. A. HUNT [1], R. A. HUNT–G. WEISS [1], E. T. OKLANDER [2], N. ARONSZAJN–E. GAGLIARDO [1], S. G. KREĬN–JU. I. PETUNIN [1], etc. One of the most general forms of an interpolation theorem between Lorentz spaces is given in R. A. HUNT [1]. In our discussion we had the lecture notes of E. T. OKLANDER [2] at our disposal to which we refer to for proofs not given in Sec. 3.3.

The main results concerning interpolation theorems may be summarized as follows: Let X and Y be one of the Lorentz spaces $\mathsf{L}^{pr}(\mu)$ and $\mathsf{L}^{pr}(\nu)$ ($1 < p < \infty$, $1 \leqq r \leqq \infty$ and/or $1 \leqq p \leqq \infty$, $r = \infty$) on (R, μ) and (S, ν), respectively, and let T be a bounded linear transformation from X to Y, in short, $T: \mathsf{X} \to \mathsf{Y}$.

(a) T is of *(strong) type* (p, q), $1 \leqq p, q \leqq \infty$, if and only if $T: \mathsf{L}^p(\mu) \to \mathsf{L}^q(\nu)$. The corresponding interpolation theorem is that of M. Riesz-Thorin.

(b) T is of *restricted (strong) type* (p, q), $1 < p < \infty$, $1 \leqq q \leqq \infty$, if and only if $T: \mathsf{L}^{p1}(\mu) \to \mathsf{L}^q(\nu)$. The interpolation theorem is that of Stein–Weiss.

(c) T is of *weak type* (p, q), $1 \leqq p \leqq \infty$, $1 < q \leqq \infty$, if and only if $T: \mathsf{L}^p(\mu) \to \mathsf{L}^{q\infty}(\nu)$. The interpolation theorem is that of Marcinkiewicz.

(d) T is of *restricted weak type* (p, q), $1 < p < \infty$, $1 < q \leqq \infty$, if and only if $T: L^{p1}(\mu) \to L^{q\infty}(\nu)$. The interpolation theorem is that of Marcinkiewicz–Stein–Weiss–Calderón–Kreĭn–Semenov.

3.6.4. In Sec. 3.6.1 we have already mentioned that J. L. LIONS [3, I] was the first (1959) to treat the intermediate spaces $X_{\alpha,r;q}$ of X and $D(A^r)$ $(0 < \alpha < r, 1 \leqq q \leqq \infty; r = 1, 2, \ldots)$ via interpolation methods by means of the method of traces for the case $r = 1$, while the general case goes back to J. L. LIONS–J. PEETRE [2, Ch. VII § 2] using the method of means. The construction of the spaces $X_{\alpha,r;q}$ by the K-method was given by J. PEETRE [4; 7; 9] in 1963—1965. In this respect Proposition 3.4.1, due to J. PEETRE [4; 7], is the connecting link from which the identification of the spaces $X_{\alpha,r;q}$ and $(X, D(A^r))_{\alpha/r,q;K}$ (Theorems 3.4.2 and 3.4.3) follows. The inclusion theorem (Theorem 3.4.4) is also due to J. L. LIONS–J. PEETRE, loc. cit. The fundamental theorems of Sec. 3.4 are the two theorems of reduction, namely, Theorem 3.4.6 for non-optimal approximation, due to J. L. LIONS–J. PEETRE, loc. cit., and Theorem 3.4.10 for saturation, due to H. BERENS–P. L. BUTZER [4]. Moreover we remark that the direct proof of Theorem 3.4.6 for $r = 2$ is due to J. PEETRE (personal communication).

Concerning Proposition 3.4.5, J. L. Lions–J. Peetre gave a proof based on a lemma, which is formulated at the end of Sec. 2.7.6 (see also H. BERENS–P. L. BUTZER–U. WESTPHAL [1]). For the inequalities of Lemma 3.4.7 see G. H. HARDY–J. E. LITTLEWOOD–G. PÓLYA [1, p. 245]; however, they follow easily from Young's inequality for functions in L^q_*, $1 \leqq q \leqq \infty$. The identities (3.4.17) and (3.4.18) of Lemma 3.4.8 are given by H. BERENS [1] and J. PEETRE (personal communication), respectively.

Theorem 3.4.10 is a far-reaching generalization of the results of Sec. 2.2.2 concerning saturation for the Taylor, Peano and Riemann differences. One may formulate another equivalent characterization of the Favard classes $X_{r,r;\infty}$, $r = 1, 2, \ldots$:

An element $f \in X$ belongs to $X_{r,r;\infty}$ if and only if

$$\left\| \int_{\varepsilon}^{\infty} t^{-r}[T(t) - I]^{r+1} f \frac{dt}{t} \right\| = O(1) \qquad (\varepsilon \to 0+).$$

The characterization given is of interest with respect to fractional powers of the infinitesimal generator A, a problem which was brought up in Sec. 2.7.6.

There is one further interesting characterization of the Favard space $X_{r,r;\infty}$ $(r = 1, 2, \ldots)$. In [5] E. GAGLIARDO introduced the notion of *relative completion:* Let X be a Banach space and Y a Banach subspace of X. *The completion of Y relative to X, denoted by $\tilde{Y}^X$, is the space of all elements $f \in X$ which are contained in the closure with respect to X of some bounded sphere in Y, i.e.* $\tilde{Y}^X = \bigcup_{\varrho > 0} \overline{S_Y(\varrho)}^X$, *where* $S_Y(\varrho) = \{f \in Y; \|f\|_Y < \varrho\}$. It is easy to see that $\tilde{Y}^X$ becomes a Banach subspace of X under the norm

$$\|f\|_{\tilde{Y}^X} = \inf\{\varrho; f \in \overline{S_Y(\varrho)}^X\}.$$

N. Aronszajn–E. Gagliardo [1] gave a formula expressing $\tilde{Y}^X$ in terms of the conjugate spaces of Y and X, when Y is dense in X. In particular they proved that Y is relative complete with respect to X, whenever Y is reflexive (see also E. Gagliardo [6]). With these concepts it is possible to solve the saturation problem for the r-th Riemann difference of a semi-group of operators $\{T(t); 0 \leqq t < \infty\}$ on a Banach space X in general terms: *The Favard space $X_{r,r;\infty}$ is equal to the relative completion of $D(A^r)$ in X, the spaces having equivalent norms. Moreover, if X is reflexive, then $X_{r,r;\infty}$ and $D(A^r)$ are equal to another* (cf. Corollaries 2.2.15 and 3.4.11). The former part of this result may be proved directly or by intermediate space methods as developed in Sec. 3.2, while the latter one then follows by the reflexivity of X. For details see H. Berens [3].

From Theorems 3.4.6 and 3.4.10 there springs a number of equivalent characterizations of the spaces $X_{\alpha,r;q}$. These are considered in Corollaries 3.4.9 and 3.4.11. One may easily formulate further assertions concerning Peano differences equivalent to those of the latter corollaries. The fact that Corollary 3.4.11 holds for arbitrary Banach spaces (instead of reflexive ones, Corollary 2.2.16) is an important generalization. As a whole the assertions on the Taylor and Peano differences in these corollaries are new.

Problems of Plessner type for the intermediate spaces $X_{\alpha,r;q}$ were discussed by H. Berens–P. L. Butzer [4]. In the case of the group of translations on the periodical function spaces this was considered earlier by H. Mirkil [1]. The proof of Proposition 3.4.12 is exactly that of H. Mirkil, loc. cit., for the Lipschitz classes $\text{Lip}(\alpha; X)$, $0 < \alpha < 1$; while that of Proposition 3.4.13 is the extension to the Zygmund class $\text{Lip}^*(1; X)$, X being equal to $C_{2\pi}$ or $L^p_{2\pi}$, $1 \leqq p < \infty$.

Concerning the dual of the intermediate space $X_{\alpha,r;q}$ we have by the theorem of duality, formulated in Sec. 3.6.2, that for $0 < \alpha < r$, $1 \leqq q < \infty$,

$$X^*_{\alpha,r;q} = (X, D(A^r))^*_{\frac{\alpha}{r},q;K} = (D(A^r)^*; X^*)_{1-\frac{\alpha}{r},q';J} \qquad (q^{-1} + q'^{-1} = 1).$$

In particular for *reflexive* spaces X, J. L. Lions [6] has shown the following. Since $D(A)$ is dense in X, the dual of X can be considered as a subspace of the dual of $\mathsf{D}(A)$: $\mathsf{X}^* \subset \mathsf{D}(A)^*$, with continuous injection. Now, if $\{S(t); 0 \leqq t < \infty\}$ denotes the dual semi-group of (the restriction of) $\{T(t); 0 \leqq t < \infty\}$ (on $\mathsf{D}(A)$) in $\mathscr{E}(\mathsf{D}(A)^*)$, then $\{S(t); 0 \leqq t < \infty\}$ is an equi-bounded strongly continuous semi-group on $\mathsf{D}(A)^*$ and the domain of its infinitesimal generator B is equal to $\mathsf{X}^*: \mathsf{D}(B) = \mathsf{X}^*$, where B is the dual of A, A to be considered as a bounded linear transformation from $\mathsf{D}(A)$ to X. Under these hypotheses J. L. Lions proved: *Let* $0 < \alpha < 1$, $1 < q < \infty$. *The dual of* $\mathsf{X}_{\alpha,1;q}$ *coincides algebraically and topologically with the space of elements* $g \in \mathsf{D}(A)^*$ *such that*

$$\| g \|_{\mathsf{D}(A)^*} + \left\{ \int_0^\infty (t^{-(1-\theta)} \| S(t)\, g - g \|_{\mathsf{D}(A)^*})^{q'} \frac{dt}{t} \right\}^{1/q'}$$

is finite.

3.6.5. The intermediate spaces $\mathsf{X}'_{\alpha,r;q}$ of X and $\mathsf{D}(A^r)$ $(0 < \alpha < r$, $1 \leqq q \leqq \infty$ and/or $\alpha = r$, $q = \infty$; $r = 1, 2, \ldots)$ generated by a holomorphic semi-group $\{T(t); 0 \leqq t < \infty\}$ were introduced for integral $r \geqq 1$ by J. Peetre [7] and for $r = 1$ by H. Berens–P. L. Butzer [2] simultaneously in 1964. For the particular case $\mathsf{X} = L^p(\mathrm{E}_n)$, $1 \leqq p \leqq \infty$, and $\{T(t); 0 \leqq t < \infty\}$ equal to the singular integral of Poisson or Gauss–Weierstrass these spaces had, except for the saturation case, already been defined by M. H. Taibleson [1] in 1963, (see also J. Peetre [6]). The basic Theorem 3.5.3, which establishes the equivalence of the spaces $\mathsf{X}_{\alpha,r;q}$ and $\mathsf{X}'_{\alpha,r;q}$, is due to J. Peetre [7]; his proof using intermediate space methods rests upon Lemmata 3.5.4 and 3.5.5. A direct proof of Theorem 3.5.3 for $0 < \alpha < 1$, $1 \leqq q \leqq \infty$ was given by H. Berens [1], and for the particular singular integrals of Poisson and Gauss–Weierstrass in $L^p(\mathrm{E}_n)$ by M. H. Taibleson [2, I]. As a consequence of Theorem 3.5.3 as well as the two theorems of reduction (Theorems 3.4.6 and 3.4.10) we have the Corollaries 3.5.6 and 3.5.7, the case for non-optimal and optimal approximation, respectively Corollary 3.5.6 generalizes results obtained in Sec. 2.3.1, especially Corollary 2.3.6. Proposition 3.5.8 and the general Theorem 3.5.9 are the extensions of Propositions 3.4.12 and 3.4.13 and Theorem 3.4.14 to holomorphic semi-groups.

Chapter Four

Applications to Singular Integrals

4.0 Orientation

In the preceding chapter, using intermediate space theory, we presented a general theory concerning the subspace $X_{\alpha,r;q}$ $(0 < \alpha < r, 1 \leqq q \leqq \infty$ and/or $\alpha = r, q = \infty; r = 1, 2, \ldots)$ of a Banach space X, generated by a uniformly bounded semi-group $\{T(t); 0 \leqq t < \infty\}$ of class $(\mathscr{C}_0)$ in $\mathscr{E}(X)$. Here we shall apply this theory to three characteristic examples, namely, to the singular integral of Abel–Poisson for periodic functions already familiar to us, to the integral of Cauchy–Poisson for functions in $L^p(\mathrm{E}_1)$, $1 \leqq p < \infty$, and to the integral of Gauss–Weierstrass for functions defined on Euclidean n-space E_n. This chapter will, in fact, serve to show a constant interplay between functional analysis and "hard" analysis.

Sec. 4.1.1 is concerned with a study of the generalized Lipschitz spaces $\mathrm{Lip}(\alpha, r, q; X)$, X being one of the function spaces $C_{2\pi}$, $L^p_{2\pi}$, $1 \leqq p < \infty$. In case $q = \infty$ these are the classical Lipschitz spaces for the r-th difference. In particular, we may mention Theorems 4.1.4 and 4.1.6, which provide a simple and direct characterization of these spaces, and Proposition 4.1.8, which is concerned with the spaces $\mathrm{lip}(\alpha, r, \infty; X)$. Sec. 4.1.2 is devoted to the spaces $X_{\alpha,r,q;\mathrm{V}}$ generated by the Abel–Poisson singular integral. In case of non-optimal approximation the spaces $X_{\alpha,r,q;\mathrm{V}}$ turn out to be equal to the spaces $\mathrm{Lip}(\alpha, r, q; X)$ (Theorem 4.1.10), while in the saturation case a function $f \in X$ belongs to the Favard space $X_{r,r,\infty;\mathrm{V}}$ if and only if $f \in \mathrm{Lip}(r, r, \infty; X)$ for r even, and $f^{\sim} \in X$ with $f^{\sim} \in \mathrm{Lip}(r, r, \infty; X)$ for r odd (Theorem 4.1.13). In Sec. 4.1.3 the counterparts of these results are briefly stated for the periodic singular integral of Weierstrass.

Sec. 4.2 is concerned with the non-periodic integral of Cauchy–Poisson for functions in $L^p(\mathrm{E}_1)$, $1 \leqq p < \infty$. In the first subsection we state (mainly without proof) classical theorems concerning Fourier and Fourier–Stieltjes transforms on the real line. The second subsection deals with the Hilbert transform for functions in $L^p(\mathrm{E}_1)$, $1 \leqq p < \infty$. Following a method of E. M. Stein and G. Weiss, the Hilbert transform is shown to be of restricted weak type (p, p), $1 \leqq p < \infty$, (Proposition 4.2.4), and from this result the well-known M. Riesz theorem (Theorem 4.2.5) is shown to follow by applying a weak version of the Marcinkiewicz interpolation theorem (Corollary 3.3.15). Lemmas 4.2.8 and 4.2.9, needed in the discussion on the Poisson integral, are of independent interest. Sec. 4.2.3 then deals with the Cauchy–Poisson integral itself. Theorem 4.2.10 is the basic result here, while Theorems 4.2.12, 4.2.13 and 4.2.15 are concerned with problems of non-optimal and optimal approximation.

The final section of the chapter is devoted to the Gauss–Weierstrass integral in Euclidean n-space E_n. For this purpose, generalized Lipschitz spaces $\mathrm{Lip}(\alpha, r, q; p)$ of functions in $L^p(E_n)$, $1 \leqq p < \infty$, are introduced. In the literature these spaces are known as fractional Sobolev or Besov spaces. It is shown (Proposition 4.3.5) that they are intermediate between the Sobolev space $W^{r,p}(E_n)$ and the original space $L^p(E_n)$ and, furthermore, that they can be generated by the K-interpolation method (cf. Theorem 4.3.6). The fundamental theorems of reduction are given by Theorems 4.3.8 and 4.3.9. Theorem 4.3.11 of Sec. 4.3.2 shows that the Weierstrass integral $W(t) f$ $(f \in L^p(E_n)$, $1 \leqq p < \infty)$ is a holomorphic contraction semi-group of class $(\mathscr{C}_0)$, the infinitesimal generator being the Laplacian operator Δ. This enables one to treat the intermediate spaces $[L^p(E_n)]_{\alpha, r, q; W}$ between $L^p(E_n)$ and $D(\Delta^r; p)$. Theorem 4.3.12 gives an equivalent characterization of $[L^p(E_n)]_{\alpha, r, q; W}$ for all possible α, q, r by the spherical means which play an important role in the study of the heat equation in Euclidean n-space. In the case of non-optimal approximation, Theorem 4.3.14 then shows that $[L^p(E_n)]_{\alpha, r, q; W}$ is equal to the Lipschitz space $\mathrm{Lip}(2\alpha, 2r, q; p)$. Finally, Theorem 4.3.17 characterizes the saturation space $[L^p(E_n)]_{1,1,\infty; W}$ for $p = 1$ and separately for $1 < p < \infty$.

The chapter concludes with Sec. 4.4 on "Notes and Remarks".

4.1 Periodic Functions

4.1.1 Generalized Lipschitz Spaces

The semi-group of translations in the classical function spaces on E_1 (or E_1^+) is perhaps the simplest application to the theory of semi-groups of operators. Nevertheless it is quite instructive, as we already saw in Sec. 2.1.2 and 2.2.3. Here it is our purpose to apply intermediate space theory to this particular example and thus to obtain and generalize a number of classical results in real and complex analysis.

In the following the basic space X is one of the spaces $C_{2\pi}$ or $L^p_{2\pi}$, $1 \leqq p < \infty$. As we saw in Example 1.5.5 the left translations in X

define a contraction semi-group of class $(\mathscr{C}_0)$ with infinitesimal generator d/dx and domain $X^{(1)} = \{f \in X; f \in AC_{2\pi}$ and $f' \in X\}$. More generally,

$$X^{(r)} = \{f \in X; f, f', \ldots, f^{(r-1)} \in AC_{2\pi} \text{ and } f^{(r)} \in X\} \qquad (r = 1, 2, \ldots).$$

$X^{(r)}$ itself becomes a Banach space under the norm $\|f\| + \|f^{(r)}\|$. As a matter of fact, the operator d/dx generates the group of translations for the function spaces in question.

Let $r = 1, 2, \ldots$ We denote by $\Delta_t^r f$ the r-th right difference of an element $f \in X$ with increment $t \geqq 0$. $\Delta_t^r f$ is a strongly continuous and 2π-periodic vector-valued function of t (cf. Sec. 1.2.1).

Definition 4.1.1. *The* ***generalized Lipschitz space*** $\mathrm{Lip}(\alpha, r, q; X)$ *is defined as the collection of all functions* $f \in X$ *for which the integral and supremum*

$$\int_0^\infty (t^{-\alpha}\|\Delta_t^r f\|)^q \frac{dt}{t} \qquad (0 < \alpha < r,\ 1 \leqq q < \infty),$$

$$\sup_{0<t<\infty} (t^{-\alpha}\|\Delta_t^r f\|) \qquad (0 \leqq \alpha \leqq r,\ q = \infty),$$

respectively, are finite.

Obviously, for $r = 1$ and $q = \infty$ we have the classical Lipschitz classes, well-known in approximation theory and already familiar to us.

Theorem 4.1.2. *The subspace* $\mathrm{Lip}(\alpha, r, q; X)$ *of* X *becomes a Banach space with respect to the norm*

$$\|f\|_{\mathrm{Lip}(\alpha,r,q;X)} = \|f\| + \left\{\int_0^\infty (t^{-\alpha}\|\Delta_t^r f\|)^q \frac{dt}{t}\right\}^{1/q}$$

(the modification for $q = \infty$ *being evident). Moreover,* $\mathrm{Lip}(\alpha, r, q; X)$ *is continuously embedded between* $X^{(r)}$ *and* X*:*

$$X^{(r)} \subset \mathrm{Lip}(\alpha, r, q; X) \subset X.$$

It is evident that the Lipschitz space $\mathrm{Lip}(0, r, \infty; X)$ is equal to X. To avoid trivialities this case will be excluded in the following.

The proof of this theorem as well as all the following results are immediate consequences of the theory of intermediate spaces (of X and $X^{(r)}$) as developed in the previous chapter, in particular in Sec. 3.1 and 3.4.

In the next proposition we assemble some simple properties of Lipschitz spaces.

Proposition 4.1.3. (a) *A function* $f \in X$ *belongs to* $\mathrm{Lip}(\alpha, r, q; X)$ $(0 < \alpha < r,\ 1 \leqq q \leqq \infty$ *and/or* $\alpha = r,\ q = \infty)$ *if and only if*

$t^{-\alpha}\,\omega_r(t; f; \mathsf{X}) \in \mathsf{L}^q_*$, *where* $\omega_r(t; f; \mathsf{X})$ *is the* r*-th modulus of continuity:*

$$\omega_r(t; f; \mathsf{X}) = \sup_{0<s<t} (\|\Delta^r_s f\|).$$

(b) *For* $0 < \alpha < r$, $1 \leqq q < \infty$ $\mathsf{X}^{(r)}$ *is a dense subset in* $\mathrm{Lip}(\alpha, r, q; \mathsf{X})$.

(c) $\mathrm{Lip}(\alpha_2, r, q_2; \mathsf{X}) \subset \mathrm{Lip}(\alpha_1, r, q_1; \mathsf{X})$, *whenever* $0 < \alpha_1 \leqq \alpha_2 \leqq r$ *and* $1 \leqq q_2 \leqq q_1 \leqq \infty$. *In particular,*

$$\mathrm{Lip}(\alpha, r, q; \mathsf{X}) \subset \mathrm{Lip}^0(\alpha, r, \infty; \mathsf{X}) \quad (0 < \alpha < r,\ 1 \leqq q < \infty),$$

where $\mathrm{Lip}^0(\alpha, r, \infty; \mathsf{X})$ *is the closure of* $\mathsf{X}^{(r)}$ *in* $\mathrm{Lip}(\alpha, r, \infty; \mathsf{X})$.

As a first far-reaching result in case of non-saturation there is the following theorem of reduction.

Theorem 4.1.4. *Let* $0 < \alpha < r$, $1 \leqq q \leqq \infty$ *and* $\alpha = k + \beta$ $(0 < \beta \leqq 1,\ k = 0, 1, \ldots, r-1)$. *A function* $f \in \mathsf{X}$ *belongs to the Lipschitz space* $\mathrm{Lip}(\alpha, r, q; \mathsf{X})$ *if and only if* $f \in \mathsf{X}^{(k)}$ *and* $f^{(k)}$ *belongs to* $\mathrm{Lip}(\beta, 1, q; \mathsf{X})$ *for* $0 < \beta < 1$ *and to* $\mathrm{Lip}(1, 2, q; \mathsf{X})$ *for* $\beta = 1$. *For* $\mathrm{Lip}(\alpha, r, q; \mathsf{X})$ *the following norms are equivalent:*

(i) $\|f\|_{\mathrm{Lip}(\alpha, r, q; \mathsf{X})}$;

(ii) $$\begin{cases} \|f\|_{\mathsf{X}} + \|f^{(k)}\|_{\mathrm{Lip}(\beta, 1, q; \mathsf{X})} & (0 < \beta < 1), \\ \|f\|_{\mathsf{X}} + \|f^{(k)}\|_{\mathrm{Lip}(1, 2, q; \mathsf{X})} & (\beta = 1). \end{cases}$$

Hence for non-saturation the two basic Lipschitz classes are the spaces $\mathrm{Lip}(\alpha, 1, q; \mathsf{X})$, $0 < \alpha < 1$, $1 \leqq q \leqq \infty$, and $\mathrm{Lip}(1, 2, q; \mathsf{X})$, $1 \leqq q \leqq \infty$. The generalizations for the r-th difference can thus be characterized through derivatives and the two basic classes in question.

As a consequence of Theorem 4.1.4 one obtains

Corollary 4.1.5. *Let* $0 < \alpha < r$, $1 \leqq q \leqq \infty$ *and* $\alpha = k + \beta$ $(0 < \beta \leqq 1,\ k = 0, 1, \ldots, r-1)$. *For an element* $f \in \mathsf{X}$ *the following assertions are equivalent:*

(i) $f \in \mathrm{Lip}(\alpha, r, q; \mathsf{X})$;

(ii) $f \in \mathsf{X}^{(k-j)}$ *and* $$\begin{cases} t^{-(j+\beta)}\, \|\Delta^{j+1}_t f^{(k-j)}\| \in \mathsf{L}^q_* & (\text{any } 0 \leqq j \leqq k,\ 0 < \beta < 1), \\ t^{-(j+1)}\, \|\Delta^{j+2}_t f^{(k-j)}\| \in \mathsf{L}^q_* & (\text{any } 0 \leqq j \leqq k,\ \beta = 1); \end{cases}$$

(iii) $f \in \mathsf{X}^{(k)}$ *and* $t^{-(j+\beta)}\, \|\nabla^{j+1}_t f^{(k-j)}\| \in \mathsf{L}^q_*$

$$(\text{any } 0 \leqq j \leqq k,\ 0 < \beta < 1),$$

where $\nabla^{j+1}_t f$ *is the* $(j+1)$*-th right Taylor difference of* f.

For the saturation case we have

Theorem 4.1.6. *An element $f \in \mathsf{X}$ belongs to* $\mathrm{Lip}(r, r, \infty; \mathsf{X})$ *if and only if $f \in \mathsf{X}^{(r-1)}$ and $f^{(r-1)} \in \mathrm{Lip}(1, 1, \infty; \mathsf{X})$. Moreover,*

$$\mathrm{Lip}(r, r, \infty; C_{2\pi}) = \{f \in C_{2\pi};\, f, f', \ldots, f^{(r-1)} \in AC_{2\pi} \text{ and } f^{(r)} \in L^{\infty}_{2\pi}\},$$
$$\mathrm{Lip}(r, r, \infty; L^{1}_{2\pi}) = \{f \in L^{1}_{2\pi};\, f, f', \ldots, f^{(r-2)} \in AC_{2\pi} \text{ and } f^{(r-1)} \in NBV_{2\pi}\},$$
$$\mathrm{Lip}(r, r, \infty; L^{p}_{2\pi}) = [L^{p}_{2\pi}]^{(r)} \quad (1 < p < \infty).$$

The following norms are equivalent:

(i) $\|f\|_{\mathrm{Lip}(r, r, \infty; \mathsf{X})}$;

(ii) $\|f\|_{\mathsf{X}} + \|f^{(r-1)}\|_{\mathrm{Lip}(1, 1, \infty; \mathsf{X})}$

(iii) $\begin{cases} \text{for } \mathsf{X} = C_{2\pi}: & \|f\|_{C_{2\pi}} + \|f^{(r)}\|_{L^{\infty}_{2\pi}}, \\ \text{for } \mathsf{X} = L^{1}_{2\pi}: & \|f\|_{L^{1}_{2\pi}} + \|f^{(r-1)}\|_{NBV_{2\pi}}, \\ \text{for } \mathsf{X} = L^{p}_{2\pi} \quad (1 < p < \infty): & \|f\|_{L^{p}_{2\pi}} + \|f^{(r)}\|_{L^{p}_{2\pi}}. \end{cases}$

Theorem 4.1.6 has already been established by the methods of classical approximation theory discussed in Chapter II, in particular, in connection with saturation problems for the r-th Riemann difference defined by the left translations on X (Sec. 2.2.3: Theorem 2.2.26). Theorem 2.2.26 is actually concerned with the analogous problem for the function spaces $UCB(\mathrm{E}_1^+)$ and $L^p(\mathrm{E}_1^+)$, $1 \leq p < \infty$. In case $r = 1$ one has the well-known results of G. H. Hardy and J. E. Littlewood (Sec. 2.1.2). However, both methods of proof of the theorem in question are different. While the proof of Theorem 2.2.26 is based upon a generalization of the first right difference to the r-th right difference, the assertion concerning the r-th difference in Theorem 4.1.6 is reduced to an equivalent one in the first difference (the equivalence of (i) and (ii) is a consequence of the general Theorem 3.4.10) and then the Hardy–Littlewood result for $r = 1$ is applied to obtain the equivalence (iii).

For the sake of completeness some further equivalent characterizations of $\mathrm{Lip}(r, r, \infty; \mathsf{X})$ are collected in

Corollary 4.1.7. *For a function $f \in \mathsf{X}$ the following are equivalent:*

(i) $f \in \mathsf{X}^{(r-k)}$ *and* $\sup_{0<t<\infty} (t^{-k} \|\Delta_t^k f^{(r-k)}\|) < \infty$ *(any $1 \leq k \leq r$);*

(ii) $f \in \mathsf{X}^{(r-1)}$ *and* $\sup_{0<t<\infty} (t^{-k} \|\nabla_t^k f^{(r-k)}\|) < \infty$ *(any $1 \leq k \leq r$).*

It is evident that the restrictions of the left translations on the Lipschitz space $\mathrm{Lip}(\alpha, r, q; \mathsf{X})$ $(0 < \alpha < r,\ 1 \leq q \leq \infty$ and/or $\alpha = r$, $q = \infty)$ again define a contraction semi-group in $\mathscr{E}(\mathrm{Lip}(\alpha, r, q; \mathsf{X}))$. Let us denote by $\mathrm{Lip}^0(\alpha, r, q; \mathsf{X})$ the subspace of all functions f in $\mathrm{Lip}(\alpha, r, q; \mathsf{X})$ which are continuous under left translations in the

Lipschitz norm, i.e. for which

$$\lim_{t\to 0+} \|\Delta_t f\|_{\mathrm{Lip}(\alpha, r, q; X)} = 0.$$

By Proposition 3.1.6 of Sec. 3.1 it follows that $\mathrm{Lip}^0(\alpha, r, q; X)$ is a closed subspace of $\mathrm{Lip}(\alpha, r, q; X)$ and $X^{(r)}$ is dense in it. Consequently, by Proposition 4.1.3 (b) the spaces $\mathrm{Lip}(\alpha, r, q; X)$ and $\mathrm{Lip}^0(\alpha, r, q; X)$ are equal to another for $0 < \alpha < r$, $1 \leqq q < \infty$. For $q = \infty$ we have in case of non-saturation

Proposition 4.1.8. *Let* $0 < \alpha < r$ *and* $\alpha = k + \beta$ $(0 < \beta \leqq 1$, $k = 0, 1, \ldots, r-1)$. *For an element* $f \in X$ *the following are equivalent:*

(i) $f \in \mathrm{Lip}^0(\alpha, r, \infty; X)$;

(ii) $f \in \mathrm{lip}(\alpha, r, \infty; X)$, *i.e.* $\|\Delta_t^r f\| = o(t^\alpha)$ $\quad (t \to 0+)$;

(iii) $f \in X^{(k)}$ *and* $\begin{cases} \|\Delta_t f^{(k)}\| = o(t^\beta) & (0 < \beta < 1;\ t \to 0+), \\ \|\Delta_t^2 f^{(k)}\| = o(t) & (\beta = 1;\ t \to 0+). \end{cases}$

On the other hand, in case of saturation we have

Proposition 4.1.9. *The space* $\mathrm{Lip}^0(r, r, \infty; X)$ *is equal to* $X^{(r)}$, *both having equivalent norms. Furthermore, for* $1 < p < \infty$

$$[L^p_{2\pi}]^{(r)} = \mathrm{Lip}^0(r, r, \infty; L^p_{2\pi}) = \mathrm{Lip}(r, r, \infty; L^p_{2\pi}).$$

Proposition 4.1.9 is nothing but the Plessner type characterization of $X^{(r)}$.

We have already mentioned (cf. Definition 2.3.8) that the class of functions $\mathrm{Lip}(1, 2, \infty; X)$ is often known as the *Zygmund class*. Therefore, the generalization $\mathrm{Lip}(1, 2, q; X)$ may be referred to as the generalized Zygmund class. One has (Proposition 3.4.5)

$$\mathrm{Lip}(1, 2, 1; X) \subset X^{(1)} \subset \mathrm{Lip}(1, 2, \infty; X)$$

with continuous injections. More generally, for $k = 1, 2, \ldots, r-1$ with $r = 2, 3, \ldots$

$$\mathrm{Lip}(k, r, 1; X) \subset X^{(k)} \subset \mathrm{Lip}(k, r, \infty; X). \tag{4.1.1}$$

The Zygmund space $\mathrm{Lip}(1, 2, \infty; X)$ may be regarded as a cogent generalization of the Lipschitz space $\mathrm{Lip}(1, 1, \infty; X)$ in the theory of approximation and Fourier series. (Obviously, $f \in \mathrm{Lip}(1, 2, \infty; X)$ whenever $f \in \mathrm{Lip}(1, 1, \infty; X)$). Furthermore, from the same point of view the space $\mathrm{lip}(1, 2, \infty; X)$ is a generalization of $X^{(1)}$. However, these generalizations are rather deep. If for instance X is equal to $C_{2\pi}$, then by the theorem of Hardy-Littlewood a function $f \in \mathrm{Lip}(1, 1, \infty; C_{2\pi})$ is absolutely continuous and its derivative f' is essentially bounded (see Theorem 4.1.6). But a function in $\mathrm{Lip}(1, 2, \infty; C_{2\pi})$ may be nowhere differentiable. A particular example is the special Weierstrass function

$$\sum_{k=1}^{\infty} 2^{-k} \cos 2^k x$$

which belongs to the Zygmund class but has no finite derivative at any point. For the class $\mathrm{lip}(1, 2, \infty; C_{2\pi})$ the situation is quite different. By a theorem of A. Rajchman a function in $\mathrm{lip}(1, 2, \infty; C_{2\pi})$ has a pointwise derivative on an everywhere dense set of points in E_1. However, the function

$$\sum_{k=1}^{\infty} \frac{2^{-k} \cos 2^k x}{\sqrt{k}}$$

belongs to $\mathrm{lip}(1, 2, \infty; C_{2\pi})$, but has no pointwise derivative except on a set of measure zero.

We conclude with the remark that all assertions given above are valid in an appropriate sense if the basic space X is equal to one of the spaces $UCB(E_1)$, $L^p(E_1)$ $(1 \leqq p < \infty)$, or $UCB(E_1^+)$, $L^p(E_1^+)$ $(1 \leqq p < \infty)$; see also Sec. 2.1 and 2.2.

4.1.2 The Singular Integral of Abel-Poisson

As in the foregoing subsection the basic space X is one of the spaces $C_{2\pi}$ or $L^p_{2\pi}$, $1 \leqq p < \infty$.

In Sec. 1.5.4 we discussed in detail Dirichlet's problem for the unit disk with boundary functions f belonging to X. We saw that the unique solution $v(\varrho; f)$, $0 \leqq \varrho \leqq 1$, is given by the singular integral of Abel–Poisson

$$[v(\varrho; f)](x) = [V(\varrho) f](x) = \frac{1}{2\pi} \int_0^{2\pi} f(u)\, p(\varrho; x-u)\, du$$

$$p(\varrho; u) = \frac{1-\varrho^2}{1 - 2\varrho \cos u + \varrho^2} \qquad (0 \leqq \varrho < 1),$$

where $\{V(e^{-t}); 0 \leqq t < \infty\}$ is a holomorphic contraction semi-group of class $(\mathscr{C}_0)$ in $\mathscr{E}(X)$ with infinitesimal generator A: $Af = -(f^\sim)'$, and domain $X^{\{1\}} = \{f \in X; f^\sim \in AC_{2\pi}$ and $(f^\sim)' \in X\}$. In general, the domain of A^r: $A^r f = (-1)^{[(r+1)/2]} f^{\{r\}}$ $(r = 1, 2, \ldots)$, is given by

$$X^{\{r\}} = \left\{ f \in X; \begin{array}{ll} f, f', \ldots, f^{(r-1)} \in AC_{2\pi} \text{ and } f^{(r)} \in X, & \text{if } r \text{ is even}, \\ f^\sim, (f^\sim)', \ldots, (f^\sim)^{(r-1)} \in AC_{2\pi} \text{ and } (f^\sim)^{(r)} \in X, & \text{if } r \text{ is odd} \end{array} \right\}.$$

Then, in Sec. 2.4.1 and 2.4.2 we treated the approximation behavior of $\|[V(\varrho) - I] f\|$ as $\varrho \to 1-$. The saturation problem was solved, and problems of non-optimal approximation were discussed.

The object now is to study the intermediate spaces $(X, X^{\{r\}})_{\alpha/r, q; K}$ of X and $X^{\{r\}}$, $0 < \alpha < r$, $1 \leqq q \leqq \infty$ and/or $\alpha = r$, $q = \infty$ $(r = 1, 2, \ldots)$.

For simplicity we write $V(t)$ instead of $V(e^{-t})$, $0 \leqq t < \infty$, and denote the intermediate space $(X, X^{\{r\}})_{\alpha/r, q; K}$ by $X_{\alpha, r, q; V}$. By Theorems 3.4.2 and 3.4.3 an element $f \in X$ belongs to $X_{\alpha, r, q; V}$ if and only if $t^{-\alpha} \| [V(t) - I]^r f \| \in L^q_*$, and

$$\|f\|_{\alpha, r, q; V} = \|f\| + \left\{ \int_0^\infty (t^{-\alpha} \| [V(t) - I]^r f \|)^q \frac{dt}{t} \right\}^{1/q}$$

(the modification for $q = \infty$ being evident) defines an equivalent norm.

Theorem 4.1.10. *If a function $f \in X$ belongs to* $\mathrm{Lip}(\alpha, r, q; X)$ $(0 < \alpha < r,\ 1 \leqq q \leqq \infty)$, *then f is in $X_{\alpha, r, q; V}$, and vice versa.*

Proof. If r is even, then $X^{\{r\}}$ is equal to $X^{(r)}$. Applying Theorem 3.4.2, on the one hand the intermediate space $(X, X^{\{r\}})_{\alpha/r, q; K}$ is equal to $\mathrm{Lip}(\alpha, r, q; X)$, and on the other hand to $X_{\alpha, r, q; V}$ for all possible parameters α and q (even for the Favard space $X_{r, r, \infty; V}$, cf. Theorem 3.4.3). If r is odd, then $\mathrm{Lip}(\alpha, r+1, q; X) = X_{\alpha, r+1, q; V}$. But by the theorem of reiteration (Theorem 3.2.20), for $0 < \alpha < r$, $1 \leqq q \leqq \infty$ the space $(X, X^{\{r+1\}})_{\alpha/(r+1), q; K}$ is equal to $(X, X^{\{r\}})_{\alpha/r, q; K}$, proving the theorem.

The proof of the theorem given above is elementary. It is an impressive example of what can be shown in applying methods of the theory of intermediate spaces to approximation theory. Theorem 4.1.10 includes Corollary 2.4.10 (a), the theorem for $0 < \alpha < 1$ and $q = \infty$, the proof of which was given by classical approximation theoretical methods. Furthermore, in Corollary 2.4.10 (b) we showed that a function $f \in X$ satisfying $\| [V(\varrho) - I] f \| = O(1 - \varrho)$ $(\varrho \to 1-)$ belongs to the Zygmund space $\mathrm{Lip}(1, 2, \infty; X)$. Clearly, this assertion holds only in the given direction, but from Theorem 4.1.10 it follows that $f \in \mathrm{Lip}(1, 2, \infty; X)$ if and only if $\| [V(\varrho) - I]^2 f \| = O(1 - \varrho)$ as $\varrho \to 1-$.

The generalization of Theorem 2.4.13 from $0 < \alpha < 1$, $q = \infty$ to $0 < \alpha < r$, $1 \leqq q \leqq \infty$ $(r = 1, 2, \ldots)$ is given in the following

Corollary 4.1.11. *Let* $0 < \alpha < r$, $1 \leqq q \leqq \infty$ *and* $\alpha = k + \beta$ $(0 < \beta \leqq 1,\ k = 0, 1, \ldots, r-1)$. *The following are equivalent:*

(i) $f \in X_{\alpha, r, q; V}$;

(ii) $$\begin{cases} t^{-\alpha} \| [V(t) - I]^{k+1} f \| \in L^q_* & (0 < \beta < 1), \\ t^{-\alpha} \| [V(t) - I]^{k+2} f \| \in L^q_* & (\beta = 1); \end{cases}$$

(iii) $f \in X^{\{k\}}$ *and* $t^{-\alpha}\left\| V(t)\, f - \sum_{j=0}^{k} \frac{t^j}{j!} (-1)^{[(j+1)/2]} f^{\{j\}} \right\| \in L_*^q$ $(0 < \beta < 1)$;

(iv) $t^{r-\alpha} \| [V(t)\, f]^{\{r\}} \| \in L_*^q$;

(v) $\begin{cases} t^{1-\beta} \| [V(t)\, f]^{\{k+1\}} \| \in L_*^q & (0 < \beta < 1), \\ t \| [V(t)\, f]^{\{k+2\}} \| \in L_*^q & (\beta = 1); \end{cases}$

(vi) $f \in X^{(k)}$ *and* $\begin{cases} f^{(k)} \in \mathrm{Lip}(\beta, 1, q; X) & (0 < \beta < 1), \\ f^{(k)} \in \mathrm{Lip}(1, 2, q; X) & (\beta = 1). \end{cases}$

Proof. The equivalences of (i), (ii) and (iii) are direct applications of the first theorem of reduction (Theorem 3.4.6). Since $\{V(t); 0 \leqq t < \infty\}$ is holomorphic, by Corollary 3.5.6 we obtain the equivalence with the assertions (iv) and (v), whereas (vi) follows from Theorem 4.1.10 and Corollary 4.1.5.

As a second consequence of Theorem 4.1.10 we have

Corollary 4.1.12. *Let* $0 < \alpha < r$, $1 \leqq q \leqq \infty$. *If* $f \in \mathrm{Lip}(\alpha, r, q; X)$ *then* $f^\sim$ *belongs to* X *and as a function of* X *to* $\mathrm{Lip}(\alpha, r, q; X)$.

This means that in case of non-saturation the generalized Lipschitz spaces defined in Sec. 4.1.1 are closed with respect to the operation of conjugacy.

Now to the saturation case.

Theorem 4.1.13. *An element* $f \in X$ *belongs to the Favard space* $X_{r, r, \infty; V}$ $(r = 1, 2, \ldots)$ *if and only if* $f \in \mathrm{Lip}(r, r, \infty; X)$ $(r$ *even*$)$ *and* $f^\sim$ *belongs to* X *and as a function of* X *to* $\mathrm{Lip}(r, r, \infty; X)$ $(r$ *odd*$)$.

Proof. In case r is even the theorem has already been shown in the proof of Theorem 4.1.10. Let r be odd. Then, applying the second theorem of reduction (Theorem 3.4.10), $f \in X^{(r-1)}$ and $f^{(r-1)}$ belongs to $X_{1,1,\infty; V}$, i.e. $(f^{(r-1)})^\sim$ belongs to X and as a function of X to $\mathrm{Lip}(1, 1, \infty; X)$ (see Theorem 2.4.1). But under these hypotheses $f^\sim, (f^\sim)', \ldots, (f^\sim)^{(r-2)} \in AC_{2\pi}$, $(f^\sim)^{(r-1)} \in X$ and $(f^\sim)^{(r-1)} = (f^{(r-1)})^\sim$, which proves the theorem.

Theorem 4.1.13 asserts nothing but the fact that the statements (a) and (b) of Theorem 2.4.5 are equivalent. The proof given above again uses methods of the theory of intermediate spaces. For further equivalent characterizations of the Favard space $X_{r,r,\infty; V}$ we refer to the remaining assertions of Theorem 2.4.5.

We conclude the discussion of the periodic Poisson integral with a characterization of the subspace $X^0_{\alpha, r, \infty; V}$ of $X_{\alpha, r, \infty; V}$, $0 < \alpha < r$.

By definition, a function f belongs to $X^0_{\alpha,r,\infty;V}$ if the map $t \to V(t) f$ from $[0, \infty)$ into $X_{\alpha,r,\infty;V}$ is strongly continuous. In this respect we have by Theorems 3.4.14 and 3.5.9

Proposition 4.1.14. *Let* $0 < \alpha < r$ *and* $\alpha = k + \beta$ $(0 < \beta \leqq 1$, $k = 0, 1, \ldots, r-1)$. *For an* $f \in X$ *the following are equivalent:*

(i) $f \in X^0_{\alpha,r,\infty;V}$;

(ii) $\|[V(t) - I]^r f\| = o(t^\alpha)$ $\qquad (t \to 0+)$;

(iii) $\|[V(t) f]^{\{r\}}\| = o(t^{\alpha-r})$ $\qquad (t \to 0+)$;

(iv) $f \in X^{(k)}$ *and* $\begin{cases} \|\Delta_t f^{(k)}\| = o(t^\beta) & (0 < \beta < 1;\ t \to 0+), \\ \|\Delta_t^2 f^{(k)}\| = o(t) & (\beta = 1;\ t \to 0+). \end{cases}$

4.1.3 The Singular Integral of Weierstrass

In Sec. 1.5.2 and 2.4.3 we already became familiar with the periodic Weierstrass singular integral and its classical approximation properties. These shall now be considered from the point of view of the theory of intermediate spaces. Proofs are omitted.

If X is one of the spaces $C_{2\pi}$ or $L^p_{2\pi}$, $1 \leqq p < \infty$, the Weierstrass singular integral on X is given by

$$[W(t) f](x) = \frac{1}{2\pi} \int_0^{2\pi} f(u)\, \vartheta_3(x-u; t)\, du \qquad (0 < t < \infty),$$

$\vartheta_3(u; t)$ being the Jacobi-theta function. Under the convention $W(0) = I$, the family of operators $\{W(t); 0 \leqq t < \infty\}$ forms a contraction semi-group of class $(\mathscr{C}_0)$ in $\mathscr{E}(X)$ with $D(A^r) = X^{(2r)}$ and $A^r f = f^{(2r)}$, $r = 1, 2, \ldots$

We denote by $X_{\alpha,r,q;W}$ the intermediate spaces of X and $X^{(2r)}$ generated by $\{W(t); 0 \leqq t < \infty\}$, $0 < \alpha < r$, $1 \leqq q \leqq \infty$ and/or $\alpha = r$, $q = \infty$. Our main result is the following

Theorem 4.1.15. *An element* $f \in X$ *belongs to the intermediate space* $X_{\alpha,r,q;W}$ *if and only if* $f \in \mathrm{Lip}(2\alpha, 2r, q; X)$.

Regarding the non-saturation as well as the saturation case for the Weierstrass singular integral we have more specifically:

Corollary 4.1.16. *Let* $0 < \alpha < r$, $1 \leqq q \leqq \infty$ *and* $\alpha = k + \beta$ $(0 < \beta \leqq 1$, $k = 0, 1, \ldots, r-1)$. *For an* $f \in X$ *the following are equiv-*

alent:

(i) $f \in X_{\alpha, r, q; W}$;

(ii) $f \in X^{(2k)}$ *and* $\begin{cases} f^{(2k)} \in X_{\beta, 1, q; W} & (0 < \beta < 1), \\ f^{(2k)} \in X_{1, 2, q; W} & (\beta = 1); \end{cases}$

(iii) $f \in X^{(2k)}$ *and* $\begin{cases} f^{(2k)} \in \mathrm{Lip}(2\beta, 1, q; X) & (0 < \beta < 1/2), \\ f^{(2k)} \in \mathrm{Lip}(1, 2, q; X) & (\beta = 1/2), \end{cases}$

$f \in X^{(2k+1)}$ *and* $\begin{cases} f^{(2k+1)} \in \mathrm{Lip}(2\beta - 1, 1, q; X) & (1/2 < \beta < 1), \\ f^{(2k+1)} \in \mathrm{Lip}(1, 2, q; X) & (\beta = 1). \end{cases}$

Corollary 4.1.17. *The following assertions are equivalent:*

(i) $f \in X_{r, r, \infty; W}$;

(ii) $f \in X^{(2r-2)}$ *and* $f^{(2r-2)} \in X_{1, 1, \infty; W}$;

(iii) $f \in X^{(2r-1)}$ *and* $f^{(2r-1)} \in \mathrm{Lip}(1, 1, \infty; X)$;

(iv) *for* $X = C_{2\pi}$: $f, f', \ldots, f^{(2r-1)} \in AC_{2\pi}$ *and* $f^{(2r)} \in L^{\infty}_{2\pi}$,
for $X = L^1_{2\pi}$: $f, f', \ldots, f^{(2r-2)} \in AC_{2\pi}$ *and* $f^{(2r-1)} \in NBV_{2\pi}$,
for $X = L^p_{2\pi}$, $1 < p < \infty$:
$f, f', \ldots, f^{(2r-1)} \in AC_{2\pi}$ *and* $f^{(2r)} \in L^p_{2\pi}$.

4.2 The Hilbert Transform and the Cauchy-Poisson Singular Integral

4.2.1 Foundations on the Fourier Transform

If f is a function in $L^1(E_1)$, the *Fourier transform* of f is defined by

$$f^{\wedge}(v) = [\mathfrak{F} f](v) \equiv \int_{-\infty}^{\infty} e^{-ivx} f(x)\, dx \qquad (-\infty < v < \infty). \tag{4.2.1}$$

It is easy to see that $f^{\wedge}(v)$ is a bounded uniformly continuous function, with bound $\|f\|_1$. Moreover, the Riemann–Lebesgue theorem holds:

$$\lim_{|v| \to \infty} f^{\wedge}(v) = 0.$$

Hence, $\mathfrak{F}$ transforms $L^1(E_1)$ continuously and linearly into $C_0(E_1)$, with norm of $\mathfrak{F}$ equal to one. By the inversion formula

$$f(x) = \frac{1}{2\pi} \lim_{N \to \infty} \int_{-N}^{N} \left(1 - \frac{|v|}{N}\right) e^{ivx} f^{\wedge}(v)\, dv,$$

the limit existing in the mean of order one (in Fourier transform theory briefly: $\overset{(1)}{\text{l.i.m.}}$) and pointwise almost everywhere, it follows that the

Fourier transform is a one-to-one mapping, and it is not difficult to construct a counter-example showing that $\mathfrak{F}$ transforms $L^1(E_1)$ *into* $C_0(E_1)$.

Furthermore, we state *Parseval's formula*

$$\int_{-\infty}^{\infty} f^{\wedge}(v)\, g(v)\, dv = \int_{-\infty}^{\infty} f(x)\, g^{\wedge}(x)\, dx,$$

f and g being any two functions in $L^1(E_1)$.

We may remark that for each fixed $v \in E_1$ $f^{\wedge}(v) = \langle f_v^*, f\rangle$ forms a linear functional on $L^1(E_1)$ with $\|f_v^*\| = 1$; by the uniqueness theorem for the Fourier transform the family of functionals $\{f_v^*; v \in E_1\}$, in addition, separates the functions in $L^1(E_1)$.

The Fourier transform considered as a transformation on $L^1(E_1)$ into $C_0(E_1)$ possesses a generalization for functions f in $L^p(E_1)$, $1 < p \leqq 2$, in the following sense: If f belongs to $L^p(E_1)$, its L^p-Fourier transform is defined by

$$\text{(4.2.2)} \qquad f^{\wedge}(v) = [\mathfrak{F}_p f](v) = \underset{N\to\infty}{\overset{(p')}{\text{l.i.m.}}} \int_{-N}^{N} e^{-ivx} f(x)\, dx \qquad (p^{-1} + p'^{-1} = 1).$$

This means that the limit in the mean of order p' as defined on the right-hand side of the equation exists for each $f \in L^p(E_1)$ and the mean limit is called the Fourier transform of f. It can be seen that $\mathfrak{F}_p$ forms a one-to-one continuous linear mapping of $L^p(E_1)$ into $L^{p'}(E_1)$ with $\|\mathfrak{F}_p\| \leqq 1$. In particular, for $p = 2$ the Fourier transform is an isometric isomorphism of $L^2(E_1)$ onto itself.

To justify the terminology of a generalized Fourier transform, we remark that for functions $f \in L^1(E_1) \cap L^p(E_1)$, $1 < p \leqq 2$, $[\mathfrak{F} f](v) = [\mathfrak{F}_p f](v)$ almost everywhere. More precisely, one can prove by different methods that the transform $f^{\wedge}(v)$ of a function $f \in L^1(E_1) \cap L^2(E_1)$ satisfies the famous *Parseval relation*

$$\int_{-\infty}^{\infty} |f^{\wedge}(v)|^2\, dv = \int_{-\infty}^{\infty} |f(x)|^2\, dx.$$

Since $L^1(E_1) \cap L^2(E_1)$ is dense in $L^p(E_1)$, $1 \leqq p \leqq 2$, the Fourier transform defined on $L^1(E_1) \cap L^2(E_1)$ on the one hand is of strong type $(1, \infty)$ and on the other hand of strong type $(2, 2)$. Therefore, by the theorem of M. Riesz (Corollary 3.3.12) it has a unique extension $\mathfrak{F}_p$ on $L^p(E_1)$ into $L^{p'}(E_1)$, $1 \leqq p \leqq 2$ and $p^{-1} + p'^{-1} = 1$, with norm $\|\mathfrak{F}_p\| \leqq 1$, and the definitions (4.2.1) and (4.2.2) are nothing but the representations of the extensions $\mathfrak{F}_p$. Clearly, $\mathfrak{F}_1$ is equal to $\mathfrak{F}$.

Corresponding to the Fourier transform on $L^1(E_1)$ the following inversion formula is valid for $1 < p \leqq 2$:

$$f(x) = \frac{1}{2\pi} \lim_{N\to\infty} \int_{-N}^{N} \left(1 - \frac{|v|}{N}\right) e^{ivx} [\mathfrak{F}_p f](v)\, dv,$$

whereby the limit exists in the mean of order p and pointwise almost everywhere. Moreover,

$$f(x) = \frac{1}{2\pi} \operatorname*{l.i.m.}^{(p)}_{N\to\infty} \int_{-N}^{N} e^{ivx} [\mathfrak{F}_p f](v)\, dv.$$

For $1 < p < 2$ this formula is a famous result of E. Hille–J. D. Tamarkin. Furthermore, as a Parseval formula:

$$\int_{-\infty}^{\infty} [\mathfrak{F}_p f](v)\, g(v)\, dv = \int_{-\infty}^{\infty} f(x)\, [\mathfrak{F}_p g](x)\, dx.$$

Henceforth we denote the Fourier transform of an $f \in L^p(\mathrm{E}_1)$, $1 \leqq p \leqq 2$, by the single notation $f^\wedge$, unless ambiguities may arise.

Let f belong to $L^p(\mathrm{E}_1)$, $1 \leqq p < \infty$, and g to $L^1(\mathrm{E}_1)$. We define the convolution of f and g by

$$[f * g](x) = \int_{-\infty}^{\infty} f(x-u)\, g(u)\, du.$$

The convolution integral exists for almost all x, belongs to $L^p(\mathrm{E}_1)$ and $\|f * g\|_p \leqq \|f\|_p \|g\|_1$ (see also Sec. 1.3.3). If, in particular, p is restricted to $1 \leqq p \leqq 2$, then the Fourier transform of $f * g$ is the product of the Fourier transforms of f and g:

$$[f * g]^\wedge = f^\wedge g^\wedge.$$

For the discussion of the singular integral of Cauchy–Poisson on $L^p(\mathrm{E}_1)$ we need a lemma concerning the Fourier transform of derivatives of functions.

Lemma 4.2.1. *Let $r = 1, 2, \ldots$, and let f and g be two functions in $L^p(\mathrm{E}_1)$, $1 \leqq p \leqq 2$, such that*

$$(iv)^r f^\wedge(v) = g^\wedge(v).$$

Then $f, f', \ldots, f^{(r-1)} \in AC_{\mathrm{loc}}(\mathrm{E}_1) \cap L^p(\mathrm{E}_1)$, $f^{(r)} \in L^p(\mathrm{E}_1)$ with $f^{(r)} = g$, and conversely.

We do not prove this lemma, which is by no means trivial; we only mention that for the space $L^1(\mathrm{E}_1)$ the assertion can be written in the more precise form: $f, f', \ldots, f^{(r-1)} \in AC(\mathrm{E}_1)$ and $f^{(r)} = g$.

We conclude this subsection with the definition and some basic properties of the *Fourier–Stieltjes transform*. If μ is a function of bounded variation on E_1, the function $\mu^\vee$ defined by

$$\mu^\vee(v) = \int_{-\infty}^{\infty} e^{-ivx}\, d\mu(x) \qquad (-\infty < v < \infty) \tag{4.2.3}$$

is called the Fourier–Stieltjes transform of μ, in notation: $\mu^\vee \equiv \mathfrak{F}\mathfrak{S}\mu \equiv \mathfrak{F}\, d\mu$. The function $\mu^\vee(v)$ is uniformly continuous on E_1 and bounded by the total variation of μ. The following inversion formula is due to P. Lévy:

$$\mu(x) - \mu(0) = \frac{1}{2\pi} \lim_{N\to\infty} \int_{-N}^{N} \frac{e^{ivx} - 1}{iv}\, \mu^\vee(v)\, dv.$$

Thus $\mathfrak{F}\mathfrak{S}$ is a one-to-one, continuous linear mapping from $\mathsf{NBV}(E_1)$ into $\mathsf{UCB}(E_1)$ with $\|\mathfrak{F}\mathfrak{S}\| = 1$. If, in particular, μ is absolutely continuous, then $\mu^\vee$ is equal to the Fourier transform of μ'.

Let μ and ν be two elements of $\mathsf{NBV}(E_1)$. The convolution of μ and ν is defined by

$$[\mu * \nu](x) = \int_{-\infty}^{\infty} \mu(x - u)\, d\nu(u).$$

The integral exists for all x except for a countable set of points $\Pi_{\mu,\nu} = \{x \in E_1;\, x = x_\mu + x_\nu,\, x_\mu$ and x_ν being the points of discontinuity of μ and ν, respectively$\}$. However, $\mu * \nu$ can be extended to a function of bounded variation by setting $[\mu * \nu](x) = ([\mu * \nu](x+) + [\mu * \nu](x-))/2$ for $x \in \Pi_{\mu,\nu}$ (the limites on the right-hand side of the equation exist), $[\mu * \nu](-\infty) = 0$ and $[\mu * \nu](\infty) = \mu(\infty)\,\nu(\infty)$. Under these conventions $\mu * \nu$ is also normalized. Furthermore, convolution is commutative, $[\mathrm{Var}\,\mu * \nu](E_1) \leqq [\mathrm{Var}\,\mu](E_1) \cdot [\mathrm{Var}\,\nu](E_1)$, and

$$[\mu * \nu]^\vee(v) = \mu^\vee(v)\, \nu^\vee(v).$$

The Parseval formula for the Fourier–Stieltjes transform takes on the form

$$\int_{-\infty}^{\infty} \mu^\vee(v)\, d\nu(v) = \int_{-\infty}^{\infty} \nu^\vee(x)\, d\mu(x).$$

Finally, we formulate a generalization of Lemma 4.2.1 for functions in $\mathsf{L}^1(E_1)$.

Lemma 4.2.2. *Let $r = 1, 2, \ldots$ If for an $f \in \mathsf{L}^1(E_1)$ and a $\mu \in \mathsf{NBV}(E_1)$*

$$(iv)^r f^\wedge(v) = \mu^\vee(v),$$

then $f, f', \ldots, f^{(r-2)} \in \mathsf{AC}(E_1)$, $f^{(r-1)} \in \mathsf{NBV}(E_1)$ with $f^{(r-1)} = \mu$, and conversely.

The preceding résumé on the classical Fourier as well as Fourier–Stieltjes transform is by no means complete. We have just considered their definitions and some of their fundamental properties, concentrating upon those which are of importance for the study of the Cauchy–Poisson singular integral by means of Fourier transform methods.

4.2.2 The Hilbert Transform

For a function $f(x)$ defined on the real line the *Hilbert transform* $f^{\sim}(x)$ is given by the Cauchy principal value:

$$(4.2.4)\quad f^{\sim}(x) = \frac{1}{\pi}\,\mathrm{PV}\int_{-\infty}^{\infty} \frac{f(u)}{x-u}\,du = -\frac{1}{\pi}\lim_{\varepsilon\to 0+}\int_{\varepsilon}^{\infty} \frac{f(x+u)-f(x-u)}{u}\,du.$$

One of the fundamental results on the subject is that $f^{\sim}(x)$ exists for almost every x if f belongs to $L^p(\mathrm{E}_1)$, $1 \leqq p < \infty$. We shall return to this result later on. In the meantime our aim will be to give a meaning of $f^{\sim}$ for simple functions f (briefly: $f \in \mathscr{S}(\mathrm{E}_1)$), to prove that the Hilbert transform on $\mathscr{S}(\mathrm{E}_1)$ is of restricted weak type (p, p), $1 \leqq p < \infty$, and, as a consequence of this and the second convexity theorem, to obtain the famous theorem of M. Riesz: the Hilbert transform on $\mathscr{S}(\mathrm{E}_1)$ has a unique continuous linear extension on $L^p(\mathrm{E}_1)$ into itself for $1 < p < \infty$.

If $\chi_{(a,b)}$ is the characteristic function of the finite interval (a, b), it follows directly from (4.2.4) that

$$\chi^{\sim}_{(a,b)}(x) = \frac{1}{\pi}\log\left|\frac{x-a}{x-b}\right|.$$

More generally, if F is the union of a finite number of mutually disjoint intervals (a_k, b_k), $k = 1, 2, \ldots, n$, then the Hilbert transform of χ_F has the representation

$$(4.2.5)\qquad \chi^{\sim}_F(x) = \frac{1}{\pi}\log\prod_{k=1}^{n}\left|\frac{x-a_k}{x-b_k}\right|.$$

The following lemma is basic.

Lemma 4.2.3. *Let F be the union of a finite number of mutually disjoint intervals (a_k, b_k), $k = 1, 2, \ldots, n$. Then the distribution function of $\chi^{\sim}_F$ is given by*

$$(4.2.6)\qquad D(\chi^{\sim}_F; \sigma) = \frac{2\lambda(F)}{\sinh(\pi\sigma)} \qquad (0 < \sigma < \infty),$$

where $\lambda(F)$ is the sum of the lengths of the intervals.

Proof. Without loss of generality assume that

$$a_1 < b_1 < a_2 < b_2 < \cdots < a_n < b_n.$$

The distribution function $D(\chi^{\sim}_F; \sigma)$ is defined to be the measure of the set

$$G_\sigma = \left\{x; \frac{1}{\pi}\left|\log \prod_{k=1}^{n}\left|\frac{x-a_k}{x-b_k}\right|\right| > \sigma\right\}.$$

Setting

$$G_\sigma^+ = \left\{x; \frac{1}{\pi}\log \prod_{k=1}^{n}\left|\frac{x-a_k}{x-b_k}\right| > \sigma\right\} = \left\{x; \prod_{k=1}^{n}\left(\frac{x-a_k}{x-b_k}\right)^2 > e^{2\pi\sigma}\right\}$$

and

$$G_\sigma^- = \left\{x; \frac{1}{\pi}\log \prod_{k=1}^{n}\left|\frac{x-a_k}{x-b_k}\right| < -\sigma\right\} = \left\{x; \prod_{k=1}^{n}\left(\frac{x-a_k}{x-b_k}\right)^2 < e^{-2\pi\sigma}\right\},$$

then $D(\chi_F^\sim; \sigma) = \lambda(G_\sigma^+) + \lambda(G_\sigma^-)$.

We first examine $\lambda(G_\sigma^+)$ and observe that the polynomial equation

$$\prod_{k=1}^{n}\left(\frac{x-a_k}{x-b_k}\right)^2 = e^{2\pi\sigma} \tag{4.2.7}$$

has at most $2n$ roots. Since the rational function on the left-hand side of the equation tends to $+\infty$ as $x \to b_k$ and to 1 as $x \to +\infty$, we find at least one root of (4.2.7) in each of the intervals $(a_1, b_1), (b_1, a_2), \ldots, (a_n, b_n), (b_n, \infty)$. There are $2n$ such intervals. Thus, there is exactly one root in each of these intervals, and this gives all of the roots of the polynomial equation. We number the $2n$ roots by $\alpha_1, \alpha_2, \ldots, \alpha_n$ and $\beta_1, \beta_2, \ldots, \beta_n$ in such a way that

$$a_1 < \alpha_1 < b_1 < \beta_1 < a_2 < \alpha_2 < \cdots < \beta_{n-1} < a_n < \alpha_n < b_n < \beta_n.$$

Since $(\beta_j - a_k)/(\beta_j - b_k) > 0$ for all j and k, while $(\alpha_j - a_k)/(\alpha_j - b_k) > 0$ for $j \neq k$ and $(\alpha_k - a_k)/(\alpha_k - b_k) < 0$, it follows that $\beta_1, \beta_2, \ldots, \beta_n$ are the roots of

$$\prod_{k=1}^{n}\frac{x-a_k}{x-b_k} = e^{\pi\sigma}, \tag{4.2.8}$$

and $\alpha_1, \alpha_2, \ldots, \alpha_n$ are those of

$$\prod_{k=1}^{n}\frac{x-a_k}{x-b_k} = -e^{\pi\sigma}. \tag{4.2.9}$$

Now, $\lambda(G_\sigma^+)$ is the sum of the lengths of the intervals (α_k, β_k), $k = 1, 2, \ldots, n$, i.e.

$$\lambda(G_\sigma^+) = \sum_{k=1}^{n}(\beta_k - \alpha_k).$$

To evaluate this sum, we rewrite the two equations (4.2.8) and (4.2.9) as follows: Let

$$p_\beta(x) = \frac{\prod_{k=1}^{n}(x-a_k) - e^{\pi\sigma}\prod_{k=1}^{n}(x-b_k)}{1-e^{\pi\sigma}} = x^n + \frac{e^{\pi\sigma}\sum_{k=1}^{n} b_k - \sum_{k=1}^{n} a_k}{1-e^{\pi\sigma}}x^{n-1} + \cdots$$

and

$$p_\alpha(x) = \frac{\prod_{k=1}^{n}(x-a_k) + e^{\pi\sigma}\prod_{k=1}^{n}(x-b_k)}{1+e^{\pi\sigma}} = x^n + \frac{-e^{\pi\sigma}\sum_{k=1}^{n} b_k - \sum_{k=1}^{n} a_k}{1+e^{\pi\sigma}}x^{n-1} + \cdots$$

Then the roots of the polynomial $p_\beta(x)$ are $\beta_1, \beta_2, \ldots, \beta_n$ and those of $p_\alpha(x)$ are $\alpha_1, \alpha_2, \ldots, \alpha_n$. Consequently,

$$p_\beta(x) = \prod_{k=1}^{n} (x - \beta_k) = x^n + \left(-\sum_{k=1}^{n} \beta_k\right) x^{n-1} + \cdots$$

and

$$p_\alpha(x) = \prod_{k=1}^{n} (x - \alpha_k) = x^n + \left(-\sum_{k=1}^{n} \alpha_k\right) x^{n-1} + \cdots$$

Comparing the coefficients of x^{n-1}, we immediately obtain that

$$\lambda(G_\sigma^+) = \sum_{k=1}^{n} (\beta_k - \alpha_k) = -\frac{e^{\pi\sigma}\sum_{k=1}^{n} b_k - \sum_{k=1}^{n} a_k}{1 - e^{\pi\sigma}} - \frac{e^{\pi\sigma}\sum_{k=1}^{n} b_k + \sum_{k=1}^{n} a_k}{1 + e^{\pi\sigma}}$$

$$= 2\,\frac{\sum_{k=1}^{n} (b_k - a_k)}{e^{\pi\sigma} - e^{-\pi\sigma}} = \frac{\lambda(F)}{\sinh \pi\sigma}.$$

Analogously, we have

$$\lambda(G_\sigma^-) = \frac{\lambda(F)}{\sinh \pi\sigma}.$$

Since the distribution function $D(\tilde{\chi}_F; \sigma)$ of $\tilde{\chi}_F$ is the sum of $\lambda(G_\sigma^+)$ and $\lambda(G_\sigma^-)$, the proof of relation (4.2.6) follows and thus the lemma.

There is one simple consequence of the lemma: *If F is the union of a finite number of mutually disjoint intervals, then $\tilde{\chi}_F$ belongs to $\mathsf{L}^2(\mathrm{E}_1)$ and*

$$\|\tilde{\chi}_F\|_2 = \|\chi_F\|_2. \tag{4.2.10}$$

Indeed, by Lemma 3.3.2 (b)

$$\|\tilde{\chi}_F\|_2 = \left\{2\int_0^\infty \sigma\, D(\tilde{\chi}_F;\sigma)\, d\sigma\right\}^{1/2} = 2\sqrt{\lambda(F)}\left\{\int_0^\infty \frac{\sigma}{\sinh \pi\sigma}\, d\sigma\right\}^{1/2} = \|\chi_F\|_2.$$

The latter equality holds because $\int_0^\infty (\sigma/\sinh \pi\sigma)\, d\sigma = 1/4$.

Now, let F be an arbitrary measurable set in E_1 of finite measure $\lambda(F)$. We can find a sequence of sets $\{F_n\}_{n=1}^\infty$, each member F_n being the union of a finite number of mutually disjoint intervals, such that $\|\chi_F - \chi_{F_n}\|_2 \to 0$ as $n \to \infty$. Since by (4.2.4) $\tilde{\chi}_{F_n}(x) - \tilde{\chi}_{F_m}(x)$ is equal to $\tilde{\chi}_{F_n - F_m}(x) - \tilde{\chi}_{F_m - F_n}(x)$ for each pair of n and m, except for a finite number of points, we obtain by (4.2.10)

$$\|\tilde{\chi}_{F_n} - \tilde{\chi}_{F_m}\|_2 = \|\tilde{\chi}_{F_n - F_m} - \tilde{\chi}_{F_m - F_n}\|_2$$
$$\leqq \|\chi_{F_n - F_m}\|_2 + \|\chi_{F_m - F_n}\|_2 \leqq 2\,\|\chi_{F_n} - \chi_{F_m}\|_2$$

for every n and m, i.e. $\{\tilde{\chi}_{F_n}\}_{n=1}^\infty$ is a Cauchy sequence of functions in $\mathsf{L}^2(\mathrm{E}_1)$. Therefore, by the theorem of Riesz–Fischer, the sequence

$\{\chi_{F_n}^{\sim}\}$ has a limit in $L^2(E_1)$. We denote this limit by $\chi_F^{\sim}$ and call it the Hilbert transform of χ_F. It is not hard to see that $\chi_F^{\sim}$ is well-defined in this way.

We are now able to give a definition of the Hilbert transform $f^{\sim}$ for a simple function $f = \sum_{k=1}^{n} c_k \chi_{F_k}$, where $c_1, c_2, \ldots, c_n$ are real or complex numbers and $F_1, F_2, \ldots, F_n$ are mutually disjoint measurable sets of finite measure, by

$$f^{\sim} = \sum_{k=1}^{n} c_k \chi_{F_k}^{\sim}.$$

Clearly, the Hilbert transform defined in this way is a linear operator on $\mathscr{S}(E_1)$ into the class of measurable functions $\mathscr{L}(E_1)$. The following proposition states that the Hilbert transform is of restricted weak type (p, p), $1 \leqq p < \infty$, generalizing at the same time the result of Lemma 4.2.3.

Proposition 4.2.4. *Let F be a measurable set in E_1 having finite measure $\lambda(F)$. Then the distribution function of $\chi_F^{\sim}$ is given by*

$$D(\chi_F^{\sim}; \sigma) = \frac{2\lambda(F)}{\sinh \pi\sigma} \qquad (0 < \sigma < \infty).$$

Moreover,

$$\sup_{0<t<\infty} \left(t^{1/p}[\chi_F^{\sim}]^*(t)\right) \leqq M_p \|\chi_F\|_p \qquad (1 \leqq p < \infty). \tag{4.2.11}$$

Proof. Let $\{F_n\}_{n=1}^{\infty}$ be a sequence of sets, each set being a finite union of mutually disjoint intervals, such that $\|\chi_F - \chi_{F_n}\|_2 \to 0$ as $n \to \infty$. By definition this implies that $\|\chi_F^{\sim} - \chi_{F_n}^{\sim}\|_2 \to 0$ as $n \to \infty$, too. We shall show that

(4.2.12)
$$D(\chi_F^{\sim}; \sigma) = \lim_{n\to\infty} D(\chi_{F_n}^{\sim}; \sigma) = \lim_{n\to\infty} \frac{2\lambda(F_n)}{\sinh \pi\sigma} = \frac{2\lambda(F)}{\sinh \pi\sigma} \quad (0 < \sigma < \infty)$$

for each point of continuity of $D(\chi_F^{\sim}; \sigma)$. Since the distribution function is non-increasing and continuous from the right it would then follow that (4.2.12) holds for all σ in $(0, \infty)$.

Let σ be a point of continuity of $D(\chi_F^{\sim}; \sigma)$. We set $G_\sigma = \{x; |\chi_F^{\sim}| > \sigma\}$ and $G_\sigma^{(n)} = \{x; |\chi_{F_n}^{\sim}| > \sigma\}$. Then $D(\chi_F^{\sim}; \sigma) = \lambda(G_\sigma)$ and $D(\chi_{F_n}^{\sim}; \sigma) = \lambda(G_\sigma^{(n)})$; furthermore

$$|\lambda(G_\sigma) - \lambda(G_\sigma^{(n)})| \leqq \lambda(G_\sigma - G_\sigma^{(n)}) + \lambda(G_\sigma^{(n)} - G_\sigma).$$

If $0 < \varepsilon < \sigma$,

$$G_\sigma - G_\sigma^{(n)} = \{G_\sigma - G_{\sigma-\varepsilon}^{(n)}\} \cup \{G_\sigma \cap (G_{\sigma-\varepsilon}^{(n)} - G_\sigma^{(n)})\}$$

and

$$G_\sigma^{(n)} - G_\sigma = \{G_\sigma^{(n)} - G_{\sigma-\varepsilon}\} \cup \{G_\sigma^{(n)} \cap (G_{\sigma-\varepsilon} - G_\sigma)\};$$

thus

$$\begin{aligned}\lambda(G_\sigma - G_\sigma^{(n)}) &= \lambda(G_\sigma - G_{\sigma-\varepsilon}^{(n)}) + \lambda\bigl(G_\sigma \cap (G_{\sigma-\varepsilon}^{(n)} - G_\sigma^{(n)})\bigr)\\ &\leqq \lambda(G_\sigma - G_{\sigma-\varepsilon}^{(n)}) + \lambda(G_{\sigma-\varepsilon}^{(n)}) - \lambda(G_\sigma^{(n)})\end{aligned}$$

and, correspondingly,

$$\lambda(G_\sigma^{(n)} - G_\sigma) \leqq \lambda(G_\sigma^{(n)} - G_{\sigma-\varepsilon}) + \lambda(G_{\sigma-\varepsilon}) - \lambda(G_\sigma).$$

But

$$\lambda(G_{\sigma-\varepsilon}^{(n)}) - \lambda(G_\sigma^{(n)}) = \frac{2\lambda(F_n)}{\sinh(\pi(\sigma-\varepsilon))} - \frac{2\lambda(F_n)}{\sinh \pi\sigma} \to 0$$

as $\varepsilon \to 0+$ uniformly with respect to n, because the sequence $\{\lambda(F_n)\}$ is convergent as $n \to \infty$ and thus bounded. Also, since σ is a point of continuity of $\lambda(G_\sigma)$, $\lambda(G_{\sigma-\varepsilon}) - \lambda(G_\sigma) \to 0$ as $\varepsilon \to 0+$. It remains to prove that, for $\varepsilon > 0$ fixed, both $\lambda(G_\sigma - G_{\sigma-\varepsilon}^{(n)})$ and $\lambda(G_\sigma^{(n)} - G_{\sigma-\varepsilon})$ tend to zero as $n \to \infty$.

If $x \in (G_\sigma - G_{\sigma-\varepsilon}^{(n)})$, then

$$|\widetilde{\chi_F}(x) - \widetilde{\chi_{F_n}}(x)| \geqq |\widetilde{\chi_F}(x)| - |\widetilde{\chi_{F_n}}(x)| > \sigma - (\sigma - \varepsilon) = \varepsilon,$$

while for an $x \in (G_\sigma^{(n)} - G_{\sigma-\varepsilon})$

$$|\widetilde{\chi_{F_n}}(x) - \widetilde{\chi_F}(x)| \geqq |\widetilde{\chi_{F_n}}(x)| - |\widetilde{\chi_F}(x)| > \sigma - (\sigma - \varepsilon) = \varepsilon.$$

Hence, setting $G = (G_\sigma - G_{\sigma-\varepsilon}^{(n)}) \cup (G_\sigma^{(n)} - G_{\sigma-\varepsilon})$,

$$\varepsilon^2 \lambda(G) = \int_G \varepsilon^2\, dx \leqq \int_G |\widetilde{\chi_F}(x) - \widetilde{\chi_{F_n}}(x)|^2\, dx \leqq \|\widetilde{\chi_F} - \widetilde{\chi_{F_n}}\|_2^2,$$

which tends to zero as $n \to \infty$. Since $\lambda(G) = \lambda(G_\sigma - G_{\sigma-\varepsilon}^{(n)}) + \lambda(G_\sigma^{(n)} - G_{\sigma-\varepsilon})$, this proves relation (4.2.12) and thus generalizes Lemma 4.2.3 to arbitrary measurable sets F with finite measure.

Obviously, by the representation of $D(\widetilde{\chi_F}; \sigma)$ the rearrangement function of $\widetilde{\chi_F}$ is given by

$$[\widetilde{\chi_F}]^*(t) = \frac{1}{\pi}\sinh^{-1}(2\lambda(F)/t) \qquad (0 < t < \infty). \tag{4.2.13}$$

Observing, in addition, that $\sup_{0<\tau<\infty}\left(\frac{\sinh^{-1}\tau}{\tau^{1/p}}\right) < \infty$ for $1 \leqq p < \infty$, one has immediately

$$\sup_{0<t<\infty}\left(t^{1/p}[\widetilde{\chi_F}]^*(t)\right) = \frac{(2\lambda(F))^{1/p}}{\pi}\sup_{0<t<\infty}\left(\frac{\sinh^{-1}(2\lambda(F)/t)}{(2\lambda(F)/t)^{1/p}}\right) = M_p\|\chi_F\|_p,$$

where
$$M_p = \frac{2^{1/p}}{\pi}\sup_{0<\tau<\infty}\left(\frac{\sinh^{-1}\tau}{\tau^{1/p}}\right),$$

i.e. the Hilbert transform as defined on $\mathscr{S}(\mathrm{E}_1)$ is of restricted weak type (p, p), $1 \leqq p < \infty$.

Now we can prove the famous theorem of M. Riesz, given by

Theorem 4.2.5. *The Hilbert transform on $\mathscr{S}(\mathrm{E}_1)$ has a unique extension as a continuous linear operator on $L^p(\mathrm{E}_1)$, $1 < p < \infty$, into itself.*

Proof. Indeed, by the foregoing proposition the Hilbert transform is a linear map from $\mathscr{S}(E_1)$ into $\mathscr{L}(E_1)$ of restricted weak type (p, p), $1 \leqq p < \infty$. Therefore, we can apply the convexity theorem of Marcinkiewicz in the version of Stein and Weiss (Corollary 3.3.15) to deduce that the Hilbert transform has a unique continuous linear extension on $L^p(E_1)$, $1 < p < \infty$, into itself. If f is a function in $L^p(E_1)$, we again denote its Hilbert transform by $f^\sim$.

Our study on the definition of the Hilbert transform will be complete if we show that $f^\sim(x)$ is almost everywhere equal to the representation given by (4.2.4). The proof of this fact will be postponed.

In the following we shall at first prove the so-called *Riesz formula* for the Hilbert transform, namely (4.2.14) below, and then investigate the Fourier transform of $f^\sim$ for functions $f \in L^p(E_1)$, $1 < p \leqq 2$.

Proposition 4.2.6. *For all functions* $f \in L^p(E_1)$, $1 < p < \infty$, *and all* $F \in L^{p'}(E_1)$, $p^{-1} + p'^{-1} = 1$,

$$\int_{-\infty}^{\infty} F(x)\, f^\sim(x)\, dx = - \int_{-\infty}^{\infty} F^\sim(x)\, f(x)\, dx. \tag{4.2.14}$$

Proof. Let both G_1 and G_2 be the union of a finite number of mutually disjoint intervals. One evaluates directly from the representations (4.2.5) given for $\chi_{G_1}^\sim$ and $\chi_{G_2}^\sim$ that

$$\int_{G_2} \chi_{G_1}^\sim(x)\, dx = - \int_{G_1} \chi_{G_2}^\sim(x)\, dx. \tag{4.2.15}$$

But then by the definition of the Hilbert transform of the characteristic function χ_G, G being an arbitrary measurable set in E_1 of finite measure, relation (4.2.15) is valid for any pair G_1 and G_2 of measurable sets of finite measure. More generally, (4.2.14) holds for all simple functions f and F. Since $\mathscr{S}(E_1)$ is dense in $L^p(E_1)$ as well as in $L^{p'}(E_1)$, and since the Hilbert transform is continuous and linear, equation (4.2.14) even holds for all $f \in L^p(E_1)$ and $F \in L^{p'}(E_1)$. This completes the proof.

One can prove the first part of the next proposition using similar methods. The second part is a classical result in Fourier transform theory, the proof of which will therefore be omitted.

Proposition 4.2.7. *For a function* $f \in L^p(E_1)$, $1 < p \leqq 2$, *the Fourier transform of* $f^\sim$ *is given by*

$$[f^\sim]^\wedge(v) = (-i \operatorname{sgn} v)\, f^\wedge(v). \tag{4.2.16}$$

Moreover,

$$(4.2.17)\qquad \lim_{N\to\infty}\left\{\frac{1}{2\pi}\int_{-N}^{N}\left(1-\frac{|v|}{N}\right)e^{ivx}(-i\operatorname{sgn}v)\,f^{\wedge}(v)\,dv+\right.$$
$$\left.+\frac{1}{\pi}\int_{1/N}^{\infty}\frac{f(x+u)-f(x-u)}{u}\,du\right\}=0$$

a.e. for each $f\in L^p(E_1)$, $1\leqq p\leqq 2$.

Concerning the second part of the proposition we remark that the following more precise assertion is known: If f belongs to $L^p(E_1)$, $1\leqq p<\infty$, then

$$(4.2.18)\qquad \lim_{N\to\infty}\left\{-\frac{1}{\pi}\int_{0}^{\infty}\frac{f(x+u)-f(x-u)}{u}\left(1-\frac{\sin Nu}{Nu}\right)du+\right.$$
$$\left.+\frac{1}{\pi}\int_{1/N}^{\infty}\frac{f(x+u)-f(x-u)}{u}\,du\right\}=0$$

whenever $\int_0^{\delta}|f(x+u)-f(x-u)|\,du=o(\delta)$, i.e. almost everywhere. The reader will have no difficulties in proving this fact. Moreover, for functions $f\in L^p(E_1)$, $1\leqq p\leqq 2$, both terms within the curly brackets of (4.2.17) and (4.2.18) are identical by Parseval's formula.

Let us now restrict the discussion to the space $L^p(E_1)$, $1<p<\infty$. Then, applying formula (4.2.14), the first integral of (4.2.18) can be rewritten in the form

$$\frac{2}{\pi N}\int_{-\infty}^{\infty}f^{\sim}(x-u)\,\frac{\sin^2 Nu/2}{u^2}\,du.$$

This is the well-known singular integral of Fejér which converges to $f^{\sim}(x)$ for almost every x. Thus by (4.2.18) the principal value of

$$\frac{1}{\pi}\int_{-\infty}^{\infty}\frac{f(u)}{x-u}\,du$$

exists almost everywhere and is equal to $f^{\sim}(x)$ as defined through Theorem 4.2.5.

There is yet to show that this assertion even holds for L^1-functions. For this we refer the reader to the available literature on the subject (see Sec. 4.4.2).

We conclude with two lemmas.

Lemma 4.2.8. *If f and g are two functions in $\mathsf{L}^1(\mathrm{E}_1)$ such that*

$$|v|\, f^\wedge(v) = g^\wedge(v) \qquad (-\infty < v < \infty), \tag{4.2.19}$$

then $f^\sim \in \mathsf{AC}(\mathrm{E}_1)$ with $f^\sim(x) = \int_{-\infty}^{x} g(u)\,du$, and vice versa.

More generally, if $f \in \mathsf{L}^1(\mathrm{E}_1)$ and $\mu \in \mathsf{NBV}(\mathrm{E}_1)$ is such that

$$|v|\, f^\wedge(v) = \mu^\vee(v) \qquad (-\infty < v < \infty), \tag{4.2.20}$$

then $f^\sim \in \mathsf{NBV}(\mathrm{E}_1)$ with $f^\sim = \mu$, and vice versa.

Proof. It suffices to prove the more general second part of the lemma. First to the "if" part. Clearly, a function $f \in \mathsf{L}^1(\mathrm{E}_1)$ which satisfies (4.2.20) for a function $\mu \in \mathsf{NBV}(\mathrm{E}_1)$ belongs to $\mathsf{L}^2(\mathrm{E}_1)$ and

$$[f^\sim]^\wedge(v) = (-i \operatorname{sgn} v)\, f^\wedge(v) \tag{4.2.21}$$

a.e. On the other hand, let $q(x) = \mu(x + x_0) - \mu(x)$, x_0 being arbitrary but fixed $\neq 0$. Then $q \in \mathsf{L}^1(\mathrm{E}_1) \cap \mathsf{L}^2(\mathrm{E}_1)$ and

$$q^\wedge(v) = \frac{e^{i v x_0} - 1}{i v}\, \mu^\vee(v). \tag{4.2.22}$$

Combining relations (4.2.21) and (4.2.22) with assumption (4.2.20), we obtain

$$(e^{i v x_0} - 1)\, [f^\sim]^\wedge(v) = q^\wedge(v),$$

and thus by the uniqueness of the Fourier transform

$$f^\sim(x + x_0) - f^\sim(x) = \mu(x + x_0) - \mu(x)$$

a.e. To show that $f^\sim(x) = \mu(x)$ a.e., we integrate the latter equation with respect to x from 0 to y, y being an arbitrary but fixed real number. Since

$$\int_0^y f^\sim(x + x_0)\, dx = \int_{x_0}^{x_0 + y} f^\sim(x)\, dx \to 0 \qquad (x_0 \to -\infty)$$

and, similarly,

$$\int_0^y \mu(x + x_0)\, dx = \int_{x_0}^{x_0 + y} \mu(x)\, dx \to 0 \qquad (x_0 \to -\infty),$$

we obtain

$$\int_0^y (f^\sim(x) - \mu(x))\, dx = 0$$

for all real y. This completes the proof in one direction.

Now to the "only if" part. We recall that for a function $f \in \mathsf{L}^1(\mathrm{E}_1)$, its Hilbert transform $f^\sim(x)$ exists almost everywhere. By assumption $f^\sim$ belongs to $\mathsf{NBV}(\mathrm{E}_1)$, but then $f^\sim(\cdot + x_0) - f^\sim(\cdot)$ belongs to $\mathsf{L}^1(\mathrm{E}_1) \cap \mathsf{L}^2(\mathrm{E}_1)$

for each fixed $x_0 \neq 0$. Consequently, $(f(\cdot + x_0) - f(\cdot)) \in L^1(E_1) \cap L^2(E_1)$, too. The rest of the proof is obvious.

Lemma 4.2.9. *If f and g belong to $L^p(E_1)$, $1 < p \leqq 2$, such that*

$$|v| f^\wedge(v) = g^\wedge(v)$$

a.e. then $f^\sim \in AC_{loc}(E_1) \cap L^p(E_1)$ with $(f^\sim)' = g$, and conversely.

The proof is an immediate consequence of Proposition 4.2.7 and Lemma 4.2.1.

4.2.3 The Singular Integral of Cauchy-Poisson

We now consider the solution of Dirichlet's problem for the half-plane $E_2^+ = \{(x, y) \in E_2; 0 < y < \infty\}$, known as the *singular integral of Cauchy–Poisson*. Let X be one of the Lebesgue spaces $L^p(E_1)$, $1 \leqq p < \infty$. The Cauchy–Poisson singular integral for $f \in X$ is given by

$$[V(y) f](x) = \frac{y}{\pi} \int_{-\infty}^{\infty} \frac{f(x-u)}{y^2 + u^2} du \qquad (0 < y < \infty). \tag{4.2.23}$$

Under the convention $V(0) = I$, I being the identity mapping, there holds the following theorem for the family of operators $\{V(y); 0 \leqq y < \infty\}$:

Theorem 4.2.10. *The family of operators $\{V(y); 0 \leqq y < \infty\}$ forms a holomorphic contraction semi-group of class $(\mathscr{C}_0)$ in $\mathscr{E}(X)$ with infinitesimal generator A: $Af = -(f^\sim)'$, and domain*

$$D(A) = \{f \in X; f^\sim \in AC_{loc}(E_1) \text{ and } (f^\sim)' \in X\}. \tag{4.2.24}$$

Proof. We observe that the Poisson kernel

$$p(y; x) = \frac{1}{\pi} \frac{y}{y^2 + x^2}$$

is non-negative with $\int_{-\infty}^{\infty} p(y; x)\, dx = 1$ for all $y > 0$. Since $p(y; \cdot)$ belongs to $L^1(E_1) \cap C_0(E_1)$ for each positive y, $V(y)$ defines a contraction operator on X into itself; moreover, $V(y)[X] \subset C_0(E_1)$. The semi-group property of $\{V(y); 0 \leqq y < \infty\}$ follows by the Chapman–Kolmogorov functional equation

$$p(y_1 + y_2; x) = \int_{-\infty}^{\infty} p(y_1; x - u)\, p(y_2; u)\, du \qquad (0 < y_1, y_2 < \infty),$$

whereas the strong continuity of $\{V(y); 0 \leqq y < \infty\}$ at the origin ($(\mathscr{C}_0)$-property) is a well-known fact in the theory of singular convolution integrals. Also, it is not difficult to see that the operator function $V(y)$, $0 < y < \infty$, is differentiable in the strong operator topology and

$$\frac{d}{dy} V(y) f = A\, V(y) f = \frac{1}{\pi} \int_{-\infty}^{\infty} f(x-u) \frac{\partial}{\partial y} \left(\frac{y}{y^2+u^2} \right) du$$

$$= -\frac{1}{\pi} \int_{-\infty}^{\infty} f(x-u) \frac{y^2-u^2}{(y^2+u^2)^2}\, du \qquad (f \in \mathsf{X};\, 0 < y < \infty).$$

Hence, $V(y)\,[\mathsf{X}] \subset \mathsf{D}(A)$ for each $y > 0$ and

$$\| A\, V(y) \| \leq \frac{1}{\pi} \int_{-\infty}^{\infty} \left| \frac{y^2-u^2}{(y^2+u^2)^2} \right| du \leq \frac{2}{\pi} y^{-1},$$

i.e. the semi-group is holomorphic.

Thus $\{V(y), 0 \leq y < \infty\}$ is a holomorphic contraction semi-group of class $(\mathscr{C}_0)$ in $\mathscr{E}(\mathsf{X})$. It remains to determine the infinitesimal generator A, which is the delicate part of the proof. For this purpose we need the following

Lemma 4.2.11. *Let* $\mathsf{X} = \mathsf{L}^p(\mathrm{E}_1)$, $1 \leq p \leq 2$. *An element* $f \in \mathsf{X}$ *belongs to the domain of* A *if and only if* $|v|\, f^\wedge(v)$ *is the Fourier transform of a function in* X. *Moreover,*

(4.2.25) $$[A f]^\wedge(v) = -|v|\, f^\wedge(v).$$

Proof. We prove this lemma for $p = 1$ only. Supposing $f \in \mathsf{D}(A)$, then there is an element $g \in \mathsf{X}$ such that $\lim_{y \to 0+} \| (V(y) f - f)/y - g \|_1 = 0$. Observing that the Fourier transform of the Poisson kernel $p(y; \cdot)$ is equal to $e^{-y|v|}$, we obtain for each $v \in \mathrm{E}_1$

$$\left[\frac{V(y) f - f}{y} - g \right]^\wedge (v) = \frac{e^{-y|v|} - 1}{y} f^\wedge(v) - g^\wedge(v),$$

which converges to zero as $y \to 0+$, i.e.

$$[A f]^\wedge(v) = g^\wedge(v) = -|v|\, f^\wedge(v).$$

This proves the lemma in one direction. Conversely, if f and g belong to $\mathsf{L}^1(\mathrm{E}_1)$ and satisfy $-|v|\, f^\wedge(v) = g^\wedge(v)$, then

$$[V(y) f - f]^\wedge(v) = (e^{-y|v|} - 1) f^\wedge(v) = \int_0^y e^{-\sigma|v|} g^\wedge(v)\, d\sigma$$

$$= \int_0^y [V(\sigma) g]^\wedge(v)\, d\sigma = \left[\int_0^y V(\sigma) g\, d\sigma \right]^\wedge (v),$$

and by the uniqueness of the Fourier transform

$$V(y)\,f - f = \int_0^y V(\sigma)\,g\,d\sigma .$$

But this means that $f \in \mathsf{D}(A)$ and $A\,f = g$.

The proof for the spaces $\mathsf{L}^p(\mathrm{E}_1)$, $1 < p \leqq 2$, follows by a refinement of the above argument.

We continue the proof of the theorem. At first, let $\mathsf{X} = \mathsf{L}^1(\mathrm{E}_1)$. Then by the characterization of A and its domain given in the preceding lemma and by the first part of Lemma 4.2.8 we have immediately that

$$\mathsf{D}(A) = \{f \in \mathsf{L}^1(\mathrm{E}_1)\,;\, f^\sim \in \mathsf{AC}(\mathrm{E}_1)\}$$

and $A\,f = -(f^\sim)'$. More generally, it can be shown that a function $f \in \mathsf{L}^1(\mathrm{E}_1)$ belongs to $\mathsf{D}(A^r)$, $r = 1, 2, \ldots$, if and only if $|v|^r f^\wedge(v)$ is the Fourier transform of a function in $\mathsf{L}^1(\mathrm{E}_1)$ and $[A^r f]^\wedge(v) = (-|v|)^r f^\wedge(v)$. This means,

$$\mathsf{D}(A^r) = \left\{ f \in \mathsf{L}^1(\mathrm{E}_1)\,;\, \begin{matrix} f, f', \ldots, f^{(r-1)} \in \mathsf{AC}(\mathrm{E}_1), & r \text{ even}, \\ f^\sim, (f^\sim)', \ldots, (f^\sim)^{(r-1)} \in \mathsf{AC}(\mathrm{E}_1), & r \text{ odd} \end{matrix} \right\} \tag{4.2.26}$$

and

$$A^r f = (-1)^{[(r+1)/2]} \begin{cases} f^{(r)}, & r \text{ even}, \\ (f^\sim)^{(r)}, & r \text{ odd}. \end{cases} \tag{4.2.27}$$

Similarly, for $\mathsf{X} = \mathsf{L}^p(\mathrm{E}_1)$, $1 < p \leqq 2$, one obtains by Lemmata 4.2.1, 4.2.9 and 4.2.11 that a function f is in the domain of A^r if and only if there exists a $g \in \mathsf{L}^p(\mathrm{E}_1)$ such that $|v|^r f^\wedge(v) = g^\wedge(v)$ and $[A^r f]^\wedge(v) = (-|v|)^r f^\wedge(v)$, or

$$\mathsf{D}(A^r) = \left\{ f \in \mathsf{L}^p(\mathrm{E}_1)\,;\, \begin{matrix} f, f', \ldots, f^{(r-1)} \in \mathsf{AC}_{\mathrm{loc}}(\mathrm{E}_1) \cap \mathsf{L}^p(\mathrm{E}_1) \text{ and} \\ f^{(r)} \in \mathsf{L}^p(\mathrm{E}_1), \quad r \text{ even} \\ f^\sim, (f^\sim)', \ldots (f^\sim)^{(r-1)} \in \mathsf{AC}_{\mathrm{loc}}(\mathrm{E}_1) \cap \mathsf{L}^p(\mathrm{E}_1) \text{ and} \\ (f^\sim)^{(r)} \in \mathsf{L}^p(\mathrm{E}_1), \quad r \text{ odd} \end{matrix} \right\}. \tag{4.2.28}$$

It remains to prove that the characterization of $\mathsf{D}(A^r)$ given in (4.2.28) for functions in $\mathsf{L}^p(\mathrm{E}_1)$, $1 < p \leqq 2$, is valid for all p, $1 < p < \infty$. Indeed, for $2 < p < \infty$ this follows by the fact that $\mathsf{L}^p(\mathrm{E}_1)$ is isometrically isomorphic to the dual space of $\mathsf{L}^{p'}(\mathrm{E}_1)$, $p^{-1} + p'^{-1} = 1$, and by the Riesz formula, established in Proposition 4.2.6. This completes the proof of Theorem 4.2.10.

For the sake of completeness let us briefly consider the *conjugate Cauchy–Poisson singular integral*. For this purpose we evaluate the Hilbert transform of the Poisson kernel $p(y;\cdot)$, $0 < y < \infty$, known as the conjugate Poisson kernel $q(y;\cdot)$. Since the Fourier transform of $p(y;\cdot)$ is integrable on E_1 (being equal to $e^{-y|v|}$)

$$q(y;x) = \frac{1}{2\pi}\int_{-\infty}^{\infty} e^{ivx}(-i\,\mathrm{sgn}\,v)\, e^{-y|v|}\, dv$$

$$= \frac{1}{\pi}\int_0^{\infty} e^{-yv}\sin vx\, dv = \frac{1}{\pi}\frac{x}{y^2+x^2} \qquad (0<y<\infty).$$

The kernel $q(y;\cdot)$ belongs to $L^p(E_1)\cap C_0(E_1)$, $1<p<\infty$; moreover, $q(y;\cdot)\in AC(E_1)$ and its Fourier–Stieltjes transform is

$$[q(y;\cdot)]^{\vee}(v) = |v|\, e^{-y|v|}.$$

The singular integral

$$[V^{\sim}(y) f](x) = \int_{-\infty}^{\infty} f(x-u)\, q(y;u)\, du \qquad (0<y<\infty) \tag{4.2.29}$$

is called the conjugate singular integral of Cauchy–Poisson on X. Clearly, $V^{\sim}(y)$ is a continuous linear transformation from X into $C_0(E_1)$, and $[V^{\sim}(y) f](x)$ converges to $f^{\sim}(x)$ pointwise almost everywhere as $y\to 0+$. If, in particular, $X = L^p(E_1)$, $1<p<\infty$, then $\{V^{\sim}(y);\, 0<y<\infty\}$ is a family of operators in $\mathscr{E}(L^p(E_1))$ and $V^{\sim}(y) f$ also converges in L^p-norm to $f^{\sim}$ for all $f\in L^p(E_1)$ as $y\to 0+$. Furthermore, for each $f\in X$

$$[A\, V(y) f](x) = -\int_{-\infty}^{\infty} f(x-u)\, d_u q(y;u)$$

$$= -\frac{1}{\pi}\int_{-\infty}^{\infty} f(x-u)\frac{y^2-u^2}{(y^2+u^2)^2}\, du \qquad (0<y<\infty).$$

If $f\in D(A)$, then the latter integral converges in norm to $A f = -(f^{\sim})'$ as $y\to 0+$.

In the following we denote the domain of A^r $(r = 1, 2, \ldots)$ by $X^{\{r\}}$ and write $A^r f = (-1)^{[(r+1)/2]} f^{\{r\}}$.

We now investigate the intermediate spaces $X_{\alpha,r,q;V}$ of X and $X^{\{r\}}$, generated by the singular integral of Cauchy–Poisson, where $0<\alpha<r$, $1\leqq q\leqq\infty$ and/or $\alpha = r$, $q=\infty$ $(r = 1, 2, \ldots)$. By definition, $f\in X$ belongs to $X_{\alpha,r,q;V}$ if $y^{-\alpha}\,\|[V(y) - I]^r f\|\in L^q_*$, and $X_{\alpha,r,q;V}$ is a Banach space with respect to the norm

$$\|f\| + \left\{\int_0^{\infty} (y^{-\alpha}\,\|[V(y)-I]^r f\|)^q \frac{dy}{y}\right\}^{1/q}.$$

Our first result concerning these intermediate spaces is

Theorem 4.2.12. *A function $f \in X$ belongs to the intermediate space $X_{\alpha,r,q;V}$, $0 < \alpha < r$ and $1 \leqq q \leqq \infty$, if and only if f belongs to the Lipschitz space* $\mathrm{Lip}(\alpha, r, q; X)$. *The norms on $X_{\alpha,r,q;V}$ and* $\mathrm{Lip}(\alpha, r, q; X)$ *are equivalent.*

In Sec. 4.1.2 we studied this theorem for the singular integral of Poisson on the periodic function spaces $L^p_{2\pi}$, $1 \leqq p < \infty$. If we now compare Theorem 4.1.10 with Theorem 4.2.12 we see that the above theorem is the counterpart of Theorem 4.1.10 for the spaces $L^p(E_1)$, $1 \leqq p < \infty$. The notations being identical, the proof of the above theorem is word for word the same as that of Theorem 4.1.10. Similarly we may deduce the corresponding interpretation of Corollary 4.1.11 giving further equivalent characterizations of the intermediate spaces $X_{\alpha,r,q;V}$. Moreover, Corollary 4.1.12 on the Hilbert transform holds in case $p > 1$, while for $p = 1$ $f^\sim$ need not belong to X but it satisfies the Lipschitz condition in question.

In the following we shall restrict our discussion to the Favard spaces $X_{r,r,\infty;V}$, which were introduced in Sec. 2.2.2 under the notation $\mathscr{F}\{[V(y) - I]^r; X\}$. Since the Lebesgue spaces $L^p(E_1)$, $1 < p < \infty$, are reflexive we have immediately by Corollary 3.4.11

Theorem 4.2.13. *Let $r = 1, 2, \ldots$ For $X = L^p(E_1)$, $1 < p < \infty$, the Favard space $X_{r,r,\infty;V}$ is equal to $X^{\{r\}}$. The norms are equivalent.*

Thus it remains to study the saturation problem for the non-reflexive space $L^1(E_1)$. Here we have as our basic result

Proposition 4.2.14. *An element $f \in L^1(E_1)$ belongs to the Favard space $\mathscr{F}\{[V(y) - I]; L^1(E_1)\}$ if and only if the Hilbert transform $f^\sim$ belongs to $NBV(E_1)$. Also*

$$\|f\|_{L^1(E_1)} + \|f^\sim\|_{NBV(E_1)}$$

defines an equivalent norm for this Favard space.

Proof. We recall that $NBV(E_1)$ is isometrically isomorphic to the dual space of $C_0(E_1)$. It is easy to see that the Cauchy–Poisson singular integral on $C_0(E_1)$ forms a holomorphic contraction semi-group of class $(\mathscr{C}_0)$ and that the dual semi-group $\{V^*(y); 0 \leqq y < \infty\}$ on $NBV(E_1)$ is given by

$$d[V^*(y)\,\mu](x) = \left(\int_{-\infty}^{\infty} p(y; x-u)\, d\mu(u)\right) dx \quad (0 < y < \infty). \tag{4.2.30}$$

We observe that $V^*(y)\,\mu$ belongs to $AC(E_1)$ for all $\mu \in NBV(E_1)$ and each $y > 0$. Thus the maximal subspace in $NBV(E_1)$ upon which the restriction of $\{V^*(y); 0 \leqq y < \infty\}$ is of class $(\mathscr{C}_0)$ is $\mathsf{AC}(\mathrm{E}_1)$. But by the isomorphism $\mu' \leftrightarrow f$ between $\mathsf{AC}(\mathrm{E}_1)$ and $\mathsf{L}^1(\mathrm{E}_1)$, the restriction of the semi-group on $\mathsf{AC}(\mathrm{E}_1)$ is nothing but the Cauchy–Poisson singular integral on $\mathsf{L}^1(\mathrm{E}_1)$. The saturation problem for dual semi-groups was solved in general in Theorem 2.1.4. In particular, Corollary 2.1.5 states that the Favard class is equal to $\mathsf{D}(A^*)$ and $(V^*(y)\,\mu - \mu)/y$ is weakly* convergent to $A^*\mu$ as $y \to 0+$.

Let $\mu \in \mathsf{D}(A^*)$ and $A^*\mu = \nu$. Then by Parseval's formula,

$$\frac{1}{y}\int_{-\infty}^{\infty} \varphi^\wedge(x)\, d[V^*(y)\,\mu - \mu](x) = \int_{-\infty}^{\infty} \varphi(v)\,\frac{e^{-y|v|}-1}{y}\,\mu^\vee(v)\,dv$$

for all $\varphi \in \mathsf{C}_{00}^{\infty}(\mathrm{E}_1)$. Since $\varphi^\wedge \in \mathsf{C}_0(\mathrm{E}_1)$, the left-hand side of the latter equation converges to

$$\int_{-\infty}^{\infty} \varphi^\wedge(x)\, d\nu(x) = \int_{-\infty}^{\infty} \varphi(v)\,\nu^\vee(v)\,dv$$

as $y \to 0+$, while

$$\lim_{y\to 0+} \int_{-\infty}^{\infty} \varphi(v)\,\frac{e^{-y|v|}-1}{y}\,\mu^\vee(v)\,dv = \int_{-\infty}^{\infty} \varphi(v)\,(-|v|)\,\mu^\vee(v)\,dv.$$

Therefore,

$$\int_{-\infty}^{\infty} \varphi(v)\,(-|v|)\,\mu^\vee(v)\,dv = \int_{-\infty}^{\infty} \varphi(v)\,\nu^\vee(v)\,dv$$

for all $\varphi \in \mathsf{C}_{00}^{\infty}(\mathrm{E}_1)$, i.e.

$$-|v|\,\mu^\vee(v) = \nu^\vee(v) \qquad (-\infty < v < \infty). \tag{4.2.31}$$

Conversely, if relation (4.2.31) holds for some $\mu \in \mathsf{AC}(\mathrm{E}_1)$ and $\nu \in \mathsf{NBV}(\mathrm{E}_1)$, then for $0 < \varepsilon < y$

$$[V^*(y)\,\mu - V^*(\varepsilon)\,\mu]^\vee(v) = (e^{-y|v|} - e^{-\varepsilon|v|})\,\mu^\vee(v) = \int_{\varepsilon}^{y} e^{-\sigma|v|}\,\nu^\vee(v)\,d\sigma$$

$$= \int_{\varepsilon}^{y} [V^*(\sigma)\,\nu]^\vee(v)\,d\sigma = \left[\int_{\varepsilon}^{y} V^*(\sigma)\,\nu\,d\sigma\right]^\vee(v),$$

and by the uniqueness of the Fourier–Stieltjes transform

$$\|V^*(y)\,\mu - V^*(\varepsilon)\,\mu\|_{\mathsf{V}} = \left\|\int_{\varepsilon}^{y} V^*(\sigma)\,\nu\,d\sigma\right\|_{\mathsf{V}} \leqq \|\nu\|_{\mathsf{V}}\,y.$$

Since $V^*(\varepsilon)\,\mu \to \mu$ in norm as $\varepsilon \to 0+$

$$\sup_{0<y<\infty} (y^{-1}\,\|V^*(y)\,\mu - \mu\|_{\mathsf{V}}) \leqq \|\nu\|_{\mathsf{V}},$$

i.e. μ belongs to the Favard class of $\{V^*(y);\, 0 \leqq y < \infty\}$. Finally, by Lemma 4.2.8 relation (4.2.31) states that the Hilbert transform of μ' is in $NBV(E_1)$. This proves the proposition.

In general we obtain by the theorem of reduction and the above proposition

Theorem 4.2.15. *Let* $r = 1, 2, \ldots$ *For an* $f \in L^1(E_1)$ *the following are equivalent:*

(i) $f \in \mathscr{F}\{[V(y) - I]^r;\, L^1(E_1)\}$;

(ii) $\begin{cases} f, f', \ldots, f^{(r-2)} \in AC(E_1) \text{ and } f^{(r-1)} \in NBV(E_1), & \text{if } r \text{ is even},\\ f^\sim, (f^\sim)', \ldots, (f^\sim)^{(r-2)} \in AC(E_1) \text{ and } (f^\sim)^{(r-1)} \in NBV(E_1), & \text{if } r \text{ is odd}. \end{cases}$

Finally, we remark that the singular integral of Gauss–Weierstrass on $L^p(E_1)$, $1 \leqq p < \infty$, can be treated in much the same way, which we omit here. But in the next section we shall discuss the more general case of the Weierstrass singular integral for functions on Euclidean n-space.

4.3 The Weierstrass Integral on Euclidean n-Space

Let us conclude this chapter with a discussion of the approximation behavior of the singular integral of Gauss–Weierstrass for functions belonging to the Lebesgue space $L^p(E_n)$, $1 \leqq p < \infty$. We are already familiar with an heuristic treatment of Weierstrass' integral for functions in $UCB(E_1)$, presented in the two introductory Sec. 1.0 and 2.0 as a motivation for the study of approximation problems in semi-group theory. Moreover, in Sec. 1.5.2, 2.4.3 and 4.1.3 we treated the integral of Weierstrass for periodic functions intensively, so that we are well acquainted with the problem in the one dimensional case. But before going into details we need several results concerning Lipschitz classes of functions of several variables.

4.3.1 Sobolev and Besov Spaces

We begin with some notations and conventions. Let E_n be the n-dimensional Euclidean space, thus $E_n = \{x = (x_1, x_2, \ldots, x_n);\, x_i \in E_1,\, i = 1, 2, \ldots, n\}$ provided with the norm $|x| = (x_1^2 + x_2^2 + \cdots + x_n^2)^{1/2}$, the Euclidean distance function of the vector x from the origin. E_1 is the real number system.

Throughout this section $f(x)$ will be a complex-valued Lebesgue-measurable function on E_n which is finite a.e. (briefly: $f \in \mathscr{L}(E_n)$). By $\mathscr{L}_{\text{loc}}(E_n)$ we mean the set of all locally integrable functions in

$\mathscr{L}(E_n)$, and by $L^p(E_n)$, $1 \leqq p \leqq \infty$, the classical Lebesgue spaces under the norms

$$\|f\|_p = \begin{cases} \left\{ \int\limits_{E_n} |f(x)|^p \, dx \right\}^{1/p} & (1 \leqq p < \infty) \\ \operatorname*{ess\,sup}\limits_{x \in E_n} |f(x)| & (p = \infty), \end{cases}$$

respectively. Furthermore, $C_0(E_n)$ denotes the space of all complex-valued continuous functions on E_n which tend to zero as $|x| \to \infty$. $C_0(E_n)$ becomes a Banach space under the supremum norm. $C_{00}^\infty(E_n)$ is the set of all functions $\varphi(x)$ with compact support having continuous partial derivatives of all orders. As it is well-known, $C_{00}^\infty(E_n)$ is a dense subspace in $C_0(E_n)$ and $L^p(E_n)$, $1 \leqq p < \infty$, respectively. Finally, let $M(E_n)$ be the space of all bounded (complex-valued) Borel measures μ on E_n, this space being the dual of $C_0(E_n)$.

Let $j = (j_1, j_2, \ldots, j_n)$ be a multi-index of non-negative integers. We set

$$D^j = \frac{\partial^{|j|}}{\partial x_1^{j_1} \partial x_2^{j_2} \ldots \partial x_n^{j_n}}, \quad |j| = j_1 + j_2 + \cdots + j_n,$$

$|j|$ being called the order of the differential operator D^j. For each $\varphi \in C_{00}^\infty(E_n)$, $D^j \varphi$ is well-defined in the classical sense.

Definition 4.3.1. *Let f be a function in $\mathscr{L}_{\mathrm{loc}}(E_n)$. If there exists a $g_j \in \mathscr{L}_{\mathrm{loc}}(E_n)$ such that*

$$(-1)^{|j|} \int\limits_{E_n} f(x) \, [D^j \varphi](x) \, dx = \int\limits_{E_n} g_j(x) \, \varphi(x) \, dx \quad (\varphi \in C_{00}^\infty(E_n)),$$

then f is said to have a generalized j-derivative g_j in the sense of Sobolev, and we write $g_j = D^j f$.

This definition is meaningful since the generalized derivative, if it exists, is uniquely determined except on a set of measure zero. For $n = 1$ the existence of a generalized derivative $D^j f$ $(j = 1, 2, \ldots)$ of a function $f \in \mathscr{L}_{\mathrm{loc}}(E_1)$ is equivalent to $f, f', \ldots, f^{(j-1)} \in AC_{\mathrm{loc}}(E_1)$ and $D^j f = f^{(j)}$, where $f^{(k)}$ $(k = 1, 2, \ldots, j)$ is the k-th ordinary derivative of f (compare Sec. 1.3.3 and 1.4.2). This shows moreover that the existence almost everywhere of the ordinary derivative does not imply the existence of the generalized derivative.

Now to the definition of the fundamental *Sobolev spaces* $W^{r,p}(E_n)$, $1 \leqq p < \infty$, $r = 1, 2, \ldots$

Definition 4.3.2. *A function $f \in L^p(E_n)$, $1 \leqq p < \infty$, is said to belong to the Sobolev space $W^{r,p}(E_n)$, $r = 1, 2, \ldots$, if f has generalized derivatives $D^j f$ in $L^p(E_n)$ for all j with $|j| \leqq r$.*

Proposition 4.3.3. (a) *The Sobolev space* $W^{r,p}(E_n)$ *is a Banach space under the norm*

(4.3.1) $$\|f\|_{r,p} = \sum_{|j| \leqq r} \|D^j f\|_p .$$

(b) $C_{00}^{\infty}(E_n)$ *is a dense subspace in* $W^{r,p}(E_n)$.

We do not prove this proposition explicitly. However, we shall see that in particular part (a) is an immediate consequence of the following. Let $\{T(h); h \in E_n\}$ be the n-parameter group of translation operators on $L^p(E_n)$, $1 \leqq p < \infty$:

$$[T(h) f](x) = f(x+h) \qquad (h = (h_1, h_2, \ldots, h_n)).$$

Obviously, $\{T(h); h \in E_n\}$ is a strongly continuous contraction group. Moreover, it is the direct product of the n one-parameter groups of translation operators

$$[T_i(h_i) f](x) = f(x + h_i e_i) \qquad (h_i \in E_1, i = 1, 2, \ldots, n),$$

where e_i is the i-th unit vector in E_n. Thus

$$T(h) = \prod_{i=1}^{n} T_i(h_i).$$

The operators $T_i(h_i)$, $h_i \in E_1$ $(i = 1, 2, \ldots, n)$, commute with each other (see Proposition 1.1.8 for n-parameter semi-groups of operators on Banach spaces).

If D_i denotes the infinitesimal generator of $\{T_i(h_i); h_i \in E_1\}$ $(i = 1, 2, \ldots, n)$, then it is easy to see (cf. Sec. 1.3.3, 1.4.2) that its domain is given by

$$D(D_i; p) = \{f \in L^p(E_n); \partial f/\partial x_i \text{ exists in the generalized sense and belongs to } L^p(E_n)\}$$

and that $D_i f = \partial f/\partial x_i$.

Thus the differential operator D^j can be rewritten in the form

$$D^j = D_1^{j_1} D_2^{j_2} \ldots D_n^{j_n} \qquad (j = (j_1, j_2, \ldots, j_n)),$$

and consequently (by Proposition 1.1.9)

$$W^{r,p}(E_n) = \bigcap_{|j|=r} D(D^j; p),$$

which is obviously a Banach space under the norm (4.3.1). For the following, however, it will be more convenient to use the equivalent norm

(4.3.2) $$\|f\|_p + \sum_{|j|=r} \|D^j f\|_p .$$

We may now define and study generalized Lipschitz spaces of functions in $L^p(E_n)$, $1 \leqq p < \infty$, from the point of view considered in the one-dimensional case in Sec. 4.1.1. On account of the similarity with the results in Sec. 4.1.1 we shall be brief in what is to follow.

Let

$$\Delta_h^r f = [T(h) - I]^r f = \sum_{l=0}^{r} (-1)^{r-l} \binom{r}{l} f(\cdot + l h) \qquad (h \in E_n)$$

be the r-th right difference of a function f in $L^p(E_n)$, and

$$\omega_r(t; f; p) = \sup_{0<|h|\leqq t} (\|\Delta_h^r f\|_p) \qquad (0 < t < \infty)$$

its r-th modulus of continuity.

Definition 4.3.4. *Let* $r = 1, 2, \ldots$ *A function* $f \in L^p(E_n)$, $1 \leqq p < \infty$, *belongs to the generalized Lipschitz space* $\mathrm{Lip}(\alpha, r, q; L^p(E_n))$[1] *if the functional*

$$\begin{cases} \displaystyle\int_{E_n} (|h|^{-\alpha} \|\Delta_h^r f\|_p)^q \frac{dh}{|h|^n} & (0 < \alpha < r,\ 1 \leqq q < \infty) \\ \displaystyle\sup_{h \in E_n} (|h|^{-\alpha} \|\Delta_h^r f\|_p) & (0 \leqq \alpha \leqq r,\ q = \infty) \end{cases}$$

is finite.

For these generalized Lipschitz spaces we have

Proposition 4.3.5. *The Lipschitz spaces* $\mathrm{Lip}(\alpha, r, q; p)$ *are Banach spaces under the equivalent norms*

$$\text{(i)} \quad \|f\|_p + \left\{ \int_{E_n} (|h|^{-\alpha} \|\Delta_h^r f\|_p)^q \frac{dh}{|h|^n} \right\}^{1/q},$$

$$\text{(ii)} \quad \|f\|_p + \left\{ \int_0^\infty (t^{-\alpha} \omega_r(t; f; p))^q \frac{dt}{t} \right\}^{1/q}$$

(with an evident modification for $q = \infty$*). Moreover, these spaces are intermediate between* $W^{r,p}(E_n)$ *and* $L^p(E_n)$*:*

$$W^{r,p}(E_n) \subset \mathrm{Lip}(\alpha, r, q; p) \subset L^p(E_n). \tag{4.3.3}$$

We only sketch the proof of the inclusions (4.3.3). While the second one is obvious, the first will follow from

$$\omega_r(t; f; p) \leqq 2^r \min(1, t^r) \|f\|_{r,p} \qquad (f \in W^{r,p}(E_n)).$$

Indeed,

$$\omega_r(t; f; p) \leqq \begin{cases} 2^r \|f\|_p & (f \in L^p(E_n)), \\ t^r \displaystyle\sum_{|j|=r} \|D^j f\|_p & (f \in W^{r,p}(E_n)), \end{cases}$$

[1] For the sake of brevity we denote the space $\mathrm{Lip}(\alpha, r, q; L^p(E_n))$ by $\mathrm{Lip}(\alpha, r, q; p)$ for what is to follow.

the second estimate following by

$$[\Delta_h^r f](x)$$

$$= r! \int_0^s d s_r \int_0^{s_r} d s_{r-1} \ldots d s_2 \int_0^{s_2} [(e_\sigma, \nabla)^r f]\,(x + (s_r + s_{r-1} + \cdots + s_1)\, e_\sigma)\, d s_1,$$

where $s = |h|$, $e_\sigma = (\sigma_1, \sigma_2, \ldots, \sigma_n)$, $\sum_{i=1}^{n} \sigma_i^2 = 1$, is the unit vector in the direction of h $(h = s\, e_\sigma)$, and $(e_\sigma, \nabla) = \sigma_1 D_1 + \cdots + \sigma_n D_n$.

In this respect we remark that the Lipschitz space $\mathrm{Lip}(0, r, \infty; p)$ is equal to the initial space $L^p(\mathrm{E}_n)$, both having equivalent norms. In the literature the generalized Lipschitz spaces of functions on E_n are more familiarly known as *fractional Sobolev spaces* or *Besov spaces*. We now formulate the basic theorem of this subsection.

Theorem 4.3.6. *The generalized Lipschitz spaces* $\mathrm{Lip}(\alpha, r, q; p)$ *are equal to the intermediate spaces* $(L^p, W^{r,p})_{\alpha/r, q; \mathrm{K}}$ *of* $L^p(\mathrm{E}_n)$ *and* $W^{r,p}(\mathrm{E}_n)$ *generated by the* K*-method. Their norms are equivalent.*

Proof. Consider the function norm

$$\mathrm{K}_r(t; f) = \mathrm{K}(t; f; L^p, W^{r,p}) \equiv \inf_{f = f_1 + f_2} (\|f_1\|_p + t\, \|f_2\|_{r,p}) \qquad (0 < t < \infty)$$

defined on $L^p(\mathrm{E}_n)$. The proof of the theorem is an obvious consequence of inequality

$$\frac{1}{C_r} \mathrm{K}_r(t^r; f) \leqq \min(1, t^r)\, \|f\|_p + \omega_r(t; f; p) \leqq C_r\, \mathrm{K}_r(t^r; f), \tag{4.3.4}$$

valid for all $f \in L^p(\mathrm{E}_n)$, where C_r is a positive constant depending only on r (and n). We shall prove (4.3.4) for $r = 1$. At first we remark that

$$\mathrm{K}_1(t; f) \leqq \|f\|_p \qquad (0 < t < \infty;\ f \in L^p(\mathrm{E}_n)). \tag{4.3.5}$$

Now, if f is any function in $L^p(\mathrm{E}_n)$, then

$$f(x) = \left(\frac{\sqrt{n}}{t}\right)^n \int\limits_{\substack{0 \leqq u_i \leqq t/\sqrt{n} \\ i = 1, 2, \ldots, n}} (f(x) - f(x+u))\, d u + \left(\frac{\sqrt{n}}{t}\right)^n \int\limits_{\substack{0 \leqq u_i \leqq t/\sqrt{n} \\ i = 1, 2, \ldots, n}} f(x+u)\, d u$$

$$= f_1(x) + f_2(x)$$

say, with $f_1 \in L^p(\mathrm{E}_n)$ and $f_2 \in W^{1,p}(\mathrm{E}_n)$. Since $\|f_1\|_p \leqq \omega_1(t; f; p)$, $\|f_2\|_p \leqq \|f\|_p$ and $\|D_i f_2\|_p \leqq (\sqrt{n}/t)\, \omega_1(t; f; p)$ $(i = 1, 2, \ldots, n)$, we have

$$\mathrm{K}_1(t; f) \leqq (\|f_1\|_p + t\, \|f_2\|_{r,p}) \leqq \omega_1(t; f; p) + t(\|f\|_p + (n^{3/2}/t)\, \omega_1(t; f; p)),$$

which, together with (4.3.5), gives

$$\text{(4.3.6)} \qquad K_1(t; f) \leqq (1 + n^{3/2}) \big(\min(1, t) \, \|f\|_p + \omega_1(t; f; p)\big).$$

On the other hand,

$$\omega_1(t; f; p) \leqq \begin{cases} 2\|f\|_p & (f \in L^p(E_n)), \\ t \, \|f\|_{1,p} & (f \in W^{1,p}(E_n)), \end{cases}$$

and, consequently, for $f = f_1 + f_2$

$$\omega_1(t; f; p) \leqq \omega_1(t; f_1; p) + \omega_1(t; f_2; p) \leqq 2(\|f_1\|_p + t \, \|f_2\|_{1,p})$$

for all possible representations $f = f_1 + f_2$, $f_1 \in L^p(E_n)$ and $f_2 \in W^{1,p}(E_n)$. This, together with $\min(1, t) \, \|f\|_p \leqq K_1(t; f)$, gives

$$\text{(4.3.7)} \qquad \min(1, t) \, \|f\|_p + \omega_1(t; f; p) \leqq 3 K_1(t; f).$$

The inequalities (4.3.6) and (4.3.7) prove relation (4.3.4) for $r = 1$. The above method of proof leads the way for arbitrary $r \geqq 1$.

As a consequence of Theorem 4.3.6 as well as by methods of proof similar to those in the one-dimensional case one obtains

Proposition 4.3.7. (a) *For $0 < \alpha < r$, $1 \leqq q < \infty$ the space $C_{00}^{\infty}(E_n)$ is dense in* $\mathrm{Lip}(\alpha, r, q; p)$.

(b) $\mathrm{Lip}(\alpha_2, r, q_2; p) \subset \mathrm{Lip}(\alpha_1, r, q_1; p)$ *whenever* $0 < \alpha_1 \leqq \alpha_2 \leqq r$, $1 \leqq q_2 \leqq q_1 \leqq \infty$. *In particular,*

$$\mathrm{Lip}(\alpha, r, q; p) \subset \mathrm{lip}(\alpha, r, \infty; p) \qquad (0 < \alpha < r, \ 1 \leqq q < \infty),$$

where $\mathrm{lip}(\alpha, r, \infty; p)$ *is the closed linear subspace of* $\mathrm{Lip}(\alpha, r, \infty; p)$ *with elements satisfying*

$$\|\Delta_h^r f\|_p = o(|h|^\alpha) \qquad (|h| \to 0+).$$

(c) *For $k = 1, 2, \ldots, r - 1$*

$$\mathrm{Lip}(k, r, 1; p) \subset W^{k,p}(E_n) \subset \mathrm{Lip}(k, r, \infty; p).$$

In particular, part (c) of the foregoing proposition in connection with the theorem of reiteration (Theorem 3.2.20) leads us to the first theorem of reduction for non-optimal approximation.

Theorem 4.3.8. *Let $0 < \alpha < r$, $1 \leqq q \leqq \infty$ and $\alpha = k + \beta$, $0 < \beta \leqq 1$, $k = 0, 1, 2, \ldots, r - 1$. For a function $f \in L^p(E_n)$ the following are equivalent:*

(i) $f \in \mathrm{Lip}(\alpha, r, q; p)$;

(ii) $f \in W^{k,p}(E_n)$ *and for all j with $|j| = k$*

$$D^j f \in \begin{cases} \mathrm{Lip}(\beta, 1, q; p) & (0 < \beta \leqq 1), \\ \mathrm{Lip}(1, 2, q; p) & (\beta = 1). \end{cases}$$

For the saturation case we have as the second theorem of reduction

Theorem 4.3.9. *For a function $f \in L^p(E_n)$ the following assertions are equivalent:*

(i) $f \in \mathrm{Lip}(r, r, \infty; p)$;

(ii) $f \in W^{r-1,p}(E_n)$ *and* $D^j f \in \mathrm{Lip}(1, 1, \infty; p)$ *for all* j *with* $|j| = r-1$;

(iii) *for* $p = 1$: $f \in L^1(E_n)$ *and for each* j *with* $|j| = r$ *there exists a measure* $\mu_j \in M(E_n)$ *such that*

$$(-1)^{|j|} \int_{E_n} f(x)\,[D^j \varphi]\,(x)\,dx = \int_{E_n} \varphi(x)\,d\mu_j(x) \qquad (\varphi \in C_{00}^{\infty}(E_n)),$$

for $1 < p < \infty$: $f \in W^{r,p}(E_n)$.

Remark 4.3.10. By a theorem of S. G. Mikhlin concerning multipliers of Fourier integrals one can prove that for $1 < p < \infty$

$$\|f\|_p + \sum_{i=1}^{n} \|D_i^r f\|_p \tag{4.3.8}$$

defines an equivalent norm for the Sobolev spaces $W^{r,p}(E_n)$, $r = 1, 2, \ldots$ Thus, if for an $f \in L^p(E_n)$, $1 < p < \infty$, ${}^{(i)}\Delta_{h_i}^r f \equiv [T_i(h_i) - I]^r f$ denotes the r-th right difference of f with respect to the i-th component of its argument and if $\omega_r^{(i)}(t; f; p)$ is the related modulus of continuity, then one obtains as an immediate consequence the following equivalent definition of the generalized Lipschitz spaces $\mathrm{Lip}(\alpha, r, q; p)$:

A function $f \in L^p(E_n)$, $1 < p < \infty$, belongs to $\mathrm{Lip}(\alpha, r, q; p)$ if and only if for each $i = 1, 2, \ldots, n$ the functionals

$$\int_{-\infty}^{\infty} (|h_i|^{-\alpha}\, \|{}^{(i)}\Delta_{h_i}^r f\|_p)^q \frac{dh_i}{|h_i|} \qquad (0 < \alpha < r,\ 1 \leqq q < \infty),$$

$$\sup_{-\infty < h_i < \infty} (|h_i|^{-\alpha}\, \|{}^{(i)}\Delta_{h_i}^r f\|_p) \qquad (0 \leqq \alpha \leqq r,\ q = \infty)$$

are finite.

Moreover, on $\mathrm{Lip}(\alpha, r, q; p)$ *there are defined the equivalent norms*

$$\text{(i)} \quad \|f\|_p + \sum_{i=1}^{n} \left\{ \int_{-\infty}^{\infty} (|h_i|^{-\alpha}\, \|{}^{(i)}\Delta_{h_i}^r f\|_p)^q \frac{dh_i}{|h_i|} \right\}^{1/q};$$

$$\text{(ii)} \quad \|f\|_p + \sum_{i=1}^{n} \left\{ \int_{0}^{\infty} (t^{-\alpha}\, \omega_r^{(i)}(t; f; p))^q \frac{dt}{t} \right\}^{1/q}$$

(with an evident modification for $q = \infty$*).*

One can reformulate the two theorems of reduction (Theorems 4.3.8 and 4.3.9) in a similar fashion. Finally we remark that just the reduced form of (ii) was introduced by O.V. Besov in his definition of the generalized Lipschitz spaces.

4.3.2 The Gauss-Weierstrass Integral

If f is a function in $L^p(\mathrm{E}_n)$, $1 \leqq p < \infty$, then the Gauss–Weierstrass singular integral associated with the function f is defined by

$$(4.3.9)\quad [W(t)f](x) = \begin{cases} \dfrac{1}{(4\pi t)^{n/2}} \displaystyle\int_{\mathrm{E}_n} f(x-u)\exp(-|u|^2/4t)\,du & (0 < t < \infty), \\ f(x) & (t = 0). \end{cases}$$

This integral is known to be the solution $w = w(x, t)$ of Cauchy's problem for the heat conduction equation in E_n

$$\frac{\partial w}{\partial t} = \Delta w, \quad \Delta = \frac{\partial^2}{\partial x_1^2} + \frac{\partial^2}{\partial x_2^2} + \cdots + \frac{\partial^2}{\partial x_2^n} \qquad (0 < t < \infty),$$

$$w = f \qquad (t = 0).$$

The problem is to be understood in the abstract sense as defined in Sec. 1.0 and Δ is the Laplace operator with domain given in (4.3.10) below (compare also Sec. 1.5.2). The following theorem will make this more precise.

Theorem 4.3.11. *The family of operators $\{W(t); 0 \leqq t < \infty\}$ forms a holomorphic contraction semi-group of class $(\mathscr{C}_0)$ in $\mathscr{E}(L^p(\mathrm{E}_n))$ with infinitesimal generator Δ: $\Delta f = \left(\sum_{i=1}^{n} D_i^2\right) f$, and domain*

$$(4.3.10)\quad D(\Delta; p) = \{f \in L^p(\mathrm{E}_n);\ \Delta f \text{ exists in the sense of Sobolev and belongs to } L^p(\mathrm{E}_n)\}.$$

Moreover,

$$(4.3.11)\quad \|\Delta W(t) f\|_p \leqq \frac{n}{t} \|f\|_p \qquad (f \in L^p(\mathrm{E}_n);\ 0 < t < \infty).$$

Proof. We omit the proof that the singular integral of Gauss–Weierstrass defines a strongly continuous contraction semi-group of operators on $L^p(\mathrm{E}_n)$, but we determine its infinitesimal generator. At first we notice that for all $\varphi \in C_{00}^{\infty}(\mathrm{E}_n)$ and $1 \leqq p' \leqq \infty$

$$(4.3.12)\quad \lim_{t\to 0+} \left\| \frac{W(t)\varphi - \varphi}{t} - \Delta\varphi \right\|_{p'} = 0 \qquad \left(\Delta\varphi = \sum_{i=1}^{n} D_i^2 \varphi\right),$$

i.e. $C_{00}^{\infty}(\mathrm{E}_n) \subset D(\Delta; p)$ for $1 \leqq p < \infty$. This follows easily by evaluation. Now, if $f \in D(\Delta; p)$, by definition there exists a $g \in L^p(\mathrm{E}_n)$ such that

$\lim_{t\to 0+} \|t^{-1}[W(t)f - f] - g\|_p = 0$, and, in view of the fact that

$$\int_{E_n} g(x)\,\varphi(x)\,dx = \lim_{t\to 0+} \int_{E_n} \frac{[W(t)f](x) - f(x)}{t}\,\varphi(x)\,dx$$
$$= \lim_{t\to 0+} \int_{E_n} f(x)\,\frac{[W(t)\varphi](x) - \varphi(x)}{t}\,dx$$
$$= \int_{E_n} f(x)\,[\Delta\varphi](x)\,dx \qquad (\varphi \in C_{00}^{\infty}(E_n)),$$

f belongs to the domain described by the right-hand side of (4.3.10). Conversely, if for an $f \in L^p(E_n)$ Δf exists in the generalized sense and belongs to $L^p(E_n)$, then one obtains for each $t > 0$ with $\Delta f = g$

$$\int_{E_n}\left[\int_0^t W(\tau)\,g\,d\tau\right](x)\,\varphi(x)\,dx = \int_0^t \left(\int_{E_n} [W(\tau)\,g](x)\,\varphi(x)\,dx\right)d\tau$$
$$= \int_0^t \left(\int_{E_n} f(x)\,[W(\tau)\,\Delta\varphi](x)\,dx\right)d\tau = \int_{E_n} f(x)\left[\int_0^t W(\tau)\,\Delta\varphi\,d\tau\right](x)\,dx$$
$$= \int_{E_n} f(x)\,([W(t)\,\varphi](x) - \varphi(x))\,dx = \int_{E_n} ([W(t)\,f](x) - f(x))\,\varphi(x)\,dx$$

for all $\varphi \in C_{00}^{\infty}(E_n)$. Therefore, $W(t)f - f = \int_0^t W(\tau)\,g\,d\tau$, or $f \in D(\Delta; p)$ and $\Delta f = g$.

The fact that $\{W(t); 0 \leqq t < \infty\}$ is holomorphic is now easy to verify, and so is the inequality (4.3.11).

The object now is to study the intermediate spaces $[L^p(E_n)]_{\alpha,r,q;W}$ of $L^p(E_n)$ and $D(\Delta^r; p)$ generated by $\{W(t); 0 \leqq t < \infty\}$, by characterizing their elements more directly. By definition, a function $f \in L^p(E_n)$ belongs to $[L^p(E_n)]_{\alpha,r,q;W}$ $(0 < \alpha < r,\ 1 \leqq q \leqq \infty$ and/or $\alpha = r$, $q = \infty$; $r = 1, 2, \ldots)$ whenever the functional

$$\|f\|_p + \left\{\int_0^\infty (t^{-\alpha}\,\|[W(t) - I]^r f\|_p)^q\,\frac{dt}{t}\right\}^{1/q}$$

is finite. (The modification for $q = \infty$ is evident.) By the general theory developed in Sec. 3.1, 3.4 and 3.5, in particular by the two theorems of reduction, namely Theorems 3.4.6 and 3.4.10, it suffices to investigate the spaces $[L^p(E_n)]_{\alpha,1,q;W}$, $0 < \alpha < 1$, and $[L^p(E_n)]_{1,2,q;W}$, $1 \leqq q \leqq \infty$, in the case of non-optimal approximation as well as the space $[L^p(E_n)]_{1,1,\infty;W}$ in the case of saturation. However, we shall formulate our next theorem in the non-reduced form. To this end, let us denote by

$$\text{(4.3.13)} \qquad [S(\varrho)\,f](x) = \frac{1}{|\Sigma_n|}\int_{\Sigma_n} f(x + \varrho\,e_\sigma)\,d\sigma \qquad (0 < \varrho < \infty)$$

the *spherical means* of the function $f \in L^p(E_n)$, $1 \leqq p < \infty$, where Σ_n is the unit sphere of E_n, e_σ are its elements and $|\Sigma_n|$ is its area (dimension $n \geqq 2$). Setting $S(0) = I$, one easily verifies that $\|S(\varrho) f\|_p \leqq \|f\|_p$ for all $f \in L^p(E_n)$ and all parameters $\varrho \geqq 0$ and that $S(\varrho) f$ is a strongly continuous vector-valued function on $0 \leqq \varrho < \infty$ for all $f \in L^p(E_n)$. In addition, $S(\varrho) f$ is a solution (in the sense of Sobolev) of the Euler–Poisson–Darboux equation

$$\frac{d^2}{d\varrho^2} S(\varrho) f + \frac{n-1}{\varrho} \frac{d}{d\varrho} S(\varrho) f = \Delta S(\varrho) f \qquad (0 < \varrho < \infty) \tag{4.3.14}$$

whenever $f \in W^{2,p}(E_n)$, in particular for all functions in $C_{00}^\infty(E_n)$.

Theorem 4.3.12. *A function $f \in L^p(E_n)$ belongs to $[L^p(E_n)]_{\alpha,r,q;W}$ if and only if*

$$\begin{cases} \displaystyle\int_0^\infty \left(\varrho^{-2\alpha} \left\| \sum_{l=0}^{r} (-1)^{r-l} \binom{r}{l} S(l^{1/2}\varrho) f \right\|_p\right)^q \frac{d\varrho}{\varrho} \\ \qquad\qquad (0 < \alpha < r,\ 1 \leqq q < \infty), \\ \displaystyle\sup_{0<\varrho<\infty} \left(\varrho^{-2\alpha} \left\| \sum_{l=0}^{r} (-1)^{r-l} \binom{r}{l} S(l^{1/2}\varrho) f \right\|_p\right) \\ \qquad\qquad (0 < \alpha \leqq r,\ q = \infty) \end{cases} \tag{4.3.15}$$

is finite. Moreover, for $[L^p(E_n)]_{\alpha,r,q;W}$ there are defined the following equivalent norms

(i) $$\|f\|_p + \left\{\int_0^\infty (t^{-\alpha} \|[W(t) - I]^r f\|_p)^q \frac{dt}{t}\right\}^{1/q},$$

(ii) $$\|f\|_p + \left\{\int_0^\infty (t^{r-\alpha} \|\Delta^r W(t) f\|_p)^q \frac{dt}{t}\right\}^{1/q},$$

(iii) $$\|f\|_p + \left\{\int_0^\infty \left(\varrho^{-2\alpha} \left\| \sum_{l=0}^{r} (-1)^{r-l} \binom{r}{l} S(l^{1/2}\varrho) f \right\|_p\right)^q \frac{d\varrho}{\varrho}\right\}^{1/q}$$

(with an evident modification for $q = \infty$).

Proof. At first we remark that by Theorem 3.5.3 the functionals defined by (i) and (ii) form equivalent norms for $[L^p(E_n)]_{\alpha,r,q;W}$. Also, it is not difficult to see that the set of all $f \in L^p(E_n)$ for which (4.3.15) is finite defines a linear subspace of $L^p(E_n)$. We have to prove that this subspace is equal to $[L^p(E_n)]_{\alpha,r,q;W}$ and that the functional (iii) defines a further equivalent norm.

Let us at first restrict the discussion to the case $r = 1$. By the definitions of the Gauss-Weierstrass integral and of the spherical means one obtains immediately the representation

$$[W(t) - I]\,f = \frac{|\Sigma_n|}{(4\pi t)^{n/2}} \int_0^\infty \varrho^n \{S(\varrho)\,f - f\}\, e^{-\varrho^2/4t} \frac{d\varrho}{\varrho} \qquad (f \in \mathsf{L}^p(\mathrm{E}_n)).$$

Thus

$$t^{-2\alpha} \|[W(t^2) - I]\,f\|_p \leqq \frac{|\Sigma_n|}{(4\pi)^{n/2}} \int_0^\infty \left(\frac{\varrho}{t}\right)^{n+2\alpha} e^{-\varrho^2/4t^2}\, \varrho^{-2\alpha} \|S(\varrho)\,f - f\|_p \frac{d\varrho}{\varrho}$$

and furthermore

$$\|(t^{-2\alpha}\|[W(t^2) - I]\,f\|_p)\|_{\mathsf{L}^q_*} \leqq \frac{|\Sigma_n|}{(4\pi)^{n/2}} \|(t^{n+2\alpha} e^{-t^2/4})\|_{\mathsf{L}^1_*} \|(\varrho^{-2\alpha}\|S(\varrho)\,f - f\|_p)\|_{\mathsf{L}^q_*},$$

i.e. the set $\{f \in \mathsf{L}^p(\mathrm{E}_n);\ \|(\varrho^{-2\alpha}\|S(\varrho)\,f - f\|_p)\|_{\mathsf{L}^q_*} < \infty\}$ is contained in $[\mathsf{L}^p(\mathrm{E}_n)]_{\alpha,1,q;W}$. Moreover, there is a constant $C_1 = C_1(\alpha, q, n) > 0$ such that

(4.3.16)

$$\|f\|_p + \|(t^{-\alpha}\|[W(t) - I]\,f\|_p)\|_{\mathsf{L}^q_*} \leqq C_1\left(\|f\|_p + \|(\varrho^{-2\alpha}\|S(\varrho)\,f - f\|_p)\|_{\mathsf{L}^q_*}\right).$$

Conversely, for each $f \in \mathsf{L}^p(\mathrm{E}_n)$ and each value of the two parameters ϱ and t $(0 < \varrho, t < \infty)$

$$S(\varrho)\,f - f = [S(\varrho) - I]\,[I - W(t)]\,f + [S(\varrho) - I]\,W(t)\,f$$

giving

$$\|S(\varrho)\,f - f\|_p \leqq 2\|[W(t) - I]\,f\|_p + \|[S(\varrho) - I]\,W(t)\,f\|_p.$$

Since $W(t)\,f \in \mathsf{W}^{2,p}(\mathrm{E}_n)$, we obtain by the differential equation (4.3.14) for the second term on the right-hand side of the latter inequality the estimate

$$\|[S(\varrho) - I]\,W(t)\,f\|_p = \left\| \int_0^\varrho \varrho_1^{-n+2} \frac{d\varrho_1}{\varrho_1} \int_0^{\varrho_1} \varrho_2^n\, \Delta S(\varrho_2)\, W(t)\,f \frac{d\varrho_2}{\varrho_2} \right\|_p \leqq \frac{\varrho^2}{2n} \|\Delta W(t)\,f\|_p$$

and thus, setting $t = \varrho^2$,

$$\|S(\varrho)\,f - f\|_p \leqq 2\left(\int_0^{\varrho^2} \|\Delta W(\tau)\,f\|_p\, d\tau + \varrho^2 \|\Delta W(\varrho^2)\,f\|_p\right).$$

Hence, by the inequality (3.4.15) of Hardy

$$\|(\varrho^{-2\alpha}\|S(\varrho)\,f - f\|_p)\|_{\mathsf{L}^q_*} \leqq 2^{1-1/p}\left(\frac{1}{\alpha} + 1\right) \|(t^{1-\alpha}\|\Delta W(t)\,f\|_p)\|_{\mathsf{L}^q_*},$$

i.e. there is a second constant $C_2 = C_2(\alpha, q) > 0$ such that for all $f \in [L^p(E_n)]_{\alpha,1,q;W}$

(4.3.17)

$$\|f\|_p + \|(\varrho^{-2\alpha}\|S(\varrho)f - f\|_p)\|_{L^q_*} \leq C_2\left(\|f\|_p + \|(t^{1-\alpha}\|\Delta W(t)f\|_p)\|_{L^q_*}\right).$$

The estimates (4.3.16) and (4.3.17) give the proof of the theorem for $r = 1$, since trivially the functional $\|f\|_p + \|(\varrho^{-2\alpha}\|S(\varrho)f - f\|_p)\|_{L^q_*}$ defines a norm for $[L^p(E_n)]_{\alpha,1,q;W}$.

For arbitrary integers $r \geq 1$ the theorem follows in the same way from the inequalities

$$\|[W(t) - I]^r f\|_p \leq \frac{|\Sigma_n|}{(4\pi t)^{n/2}} \int_0^\infty \varrho^n \left\|\sum_{l=0}^r (-1)^{r-l}\binom{r}{l} S(l^{1/2}\varrho) f\right\|_p e^{-\varrho^2/4t}\frac{d\varrho}{\varrho},$$

$$\left\|\sum_{l=0}^r (-1)^{r-l}\binom{r}{l} S(l^{1/2}\varrho) f\right\|_p \leq 2^r r\left(\int_0^{\varrho^2} \tau^r \|\Delta^r W(\tau) f\|_p \frac{d\tau}{\tau} + \varrho^{2r}\|\Delta^r W(\varrho^2) f\|_p\right),$$

valid for all $f \in L^p(E_n)$ and $0 < t < \infty$, $0 < \varrho < \infty$. An explicit proof will be left to the reader.

Next we need the following

Lemma 4.3.13. *Let $\beta > 0$. For all $f \in L^p(E_n)$ there hold*

(4.3.18)

$$\sup_{|j|=2}\left\{\int_0^\infty (t^\beta \|D^j W(t) f\|_p)^q \frac{dt}{t}\right\}^{1/q} \leq \frac{2^{1+\beta}}{\beta}\left\{\int_0^\infty (t^\beta \|\Delta W(t) f\|_p)^q \frac{dt}{t}\right\}^{1/q},$$

(4.3.19)

$$\sup_{|j|=4}\left\{\int_0^\infty (t^\beta \|D^j W(t) f\|_p)^q \frac{dt}{t}\right\}^{1/q} \leq \left(\frac{2^{1+\beta}}{\beta}\right)^2\left\{\int_0^\infty (t^\beta \|\Delta^2 W(t) f\|_p)^q \frac{dt}{t}\right\}^{1/q}.$$

Proof. We only prove the inequality (4.3.18). One easily verifies that for each multi-index j with $|j| = 2$

(4.3.20) $$\|D^j W(t) f\|_p \leq \frac{1}{t}\|f\|_p \qquad (0 < t < \infty;\ f \in L^p(E_n)).$$

Consequently, $\lim_{t\to\infty}\|D^j W(t) f\|_p = 0$ for these indices j and for each $f \in L^p(E_n)$. Since $D^j W(t_2) f - D^j W(t_1) f = \int_{t_1}^{t_2} D^j \Delta W(\tau) f\, d\tau$, $0 < t_1 <$

$< t_2 < \infty$, this leads to the estimate

$$\| D^j W(2t) f \|_p \leqq \int_{2t}^{\infty} \| D^j \Delta W(\tau) f \|_p \, d\tau = \int_{2t}^{\infty} \left\| D^j W\left(\frac{\tau}{2}\right) \Delta W\left(\frac{\tau}{2}\right) f \right\|_p d\tau$$

$$\leqq \int_{2t}^{\infty} \left(\frac{\tau}{2}\right)^{-1} \left\| \Delta W\left(\frac{\tau}{2}\right) f \right\|_p d\tau = 2 \int_{t}^{\infty} \| \Delta W(\tau) f \|_p \frac{d\tau}{\tau}$$

$$(0 < t < \infty;\ \text{any } j \text{ with } |j| = 2;\ f \in \mathsf{L}^p(\mathrm{E}_n)).$$

Hence, applying Hardy's inequality (3.4.16) to the latter estimate multiplied by $(2t)^{\beta}$, we obtain (4.3.18).

We are now able to formulate and prove the equivalence theorem in case of non-optimal approximation.

Theorem 4.3.14. (a) *For* $0 < \alpha < 1$, $1 \leqq q \leqq \infty$ *the intermediate spaces* $[\mathsf{L}^p(\mathrm{E}_n)]_{\alpha,1,q;W}$ *are equal to the generalized Lipschitz spaces* $\mathrm{Lip}(2\alpha, 2, q; p)$. *Moreover, for these spaces the following norms are equivalent:*

(i) $$\|f\|_p + \left\{ \int_0^{\infty} (t^{-\alpha} \, \| [W(t) - I] f \|_p)^q \frac{dt}{t} \right\}^{1/q};$$

(ii) $$\|f\|_p + \left\{ \int_0^{\infty} (\varrho^{-2\alpha} \, \| S(\varrho) f - f \|_p)^q \frac{d\varrho}{\varrho} \right\}^{1/q};$$

(iii) $$\|f\|_p + \left\{ \int_0^{\infty} (t^{-2\alpha} \, \omega_2(t; f; p))^q \frac{dt}{t} \right\}^{1/q};$$

(iv) $$\begin{cases} \|f\|_p + \left\{ \displaystyle\int_{\mathrm{E}_n} (|h|^{-2\alpha} \, \| f(\cdot + h) - f(\cdot) \|_p)^q \frac{dh}{|h|^n} \right\}^{1/q} & (0 < \alpha < 1/2), \\ \|f\|_p + \left\{ \displaystyle\int_{\mathrm{E}_n} (|h|^{-1} \, \| f(\cdot + 2h) - 2f(\cdot + h) + f(\cdot) \|_p)^q \frac{dh}{|h|^n} \right\}^{1/q} & (\alpha = 1/2), \\ \|f\|_{1,p} + \displaystyle\sum_{i=1}^{n} \left\{ \int_{\mathrm{E}_n} (|h|^{-(2\alpha-1)} \, \| [D_i f](\cdot + h) - [D_i f](\cdot) \|_p)^q \frac{dh}{|h|^n} \right\}^{1/q}. & (1/2 < \alpha < 1). \end{cases}$$

(b) *The spaces* $[L^p(E_n)]_{1,2,q;W}$ *and* Lip$(2, 4, q; p)$, $1 \leqq q \leqq \infty$, *are equal to another; the following norms are equivalent:*

$$\text{(i)}\quad \|f\|_p + \left\{\int_0^\infty (t^{-1}\,\|[W(t) - I]^2 f\|_p)^q \frac{dt}{t}\right\}^{1/q};$$

$$\text{(ii)}\quad \|f\|_p + \left\{\int_0^\infty (\varrho^{-2}\,\|S(2^{1/2}\varrho) f - 2S(\varrho) f + f\|_p)^q \frac{d\varrho}{\varrho}\right\}^{1/q};$$

$$\text{(iii)}\quad \|f\|_p + \left\{\int_0^\infty (t^{-2}\,\omega_4(t; f; p))^q \frac{dt}{t}\right\}^{1/q};$$

$$\text{(iv)}\quad \|f\|_{1,p} + \sum_{i=1}^n \left\{\int_{E_n} (|h|^{-1}\,\|[D_i f](\cdot + 2h) - 2[D_i f](\cdot + h) + [D_i f](\cdot)\|_p)^q \frac{dh}{|h|^n}\right\}^{1/q}.$$

Proof. (a) Obviously, $W^{2,p}(E_n)$ is continuously contained in $D(\Delta; p)$, and for $f \in W^{2,p}(E_n)$

$$\|f\|_{D(\Delta;p)} = \|f\|_p + \|\Delta f\|_p \leqq \|f\|_p + \sum_{|j|=2} \|D^j f\|_p = \|f\|_{2,p}.$$

Hence, for the two function norms $K_1(t; f; L^p, D(\Delta; p))$ and $K_2(t; f; L^p, W^{2,p})$ defined on $L^p(E_n)$

$$K_1(t; f; L^p, D(\Delta; p)) \leqq K_2(t; f; L^p, W^{2,p}),$$

and consequently Lip$(2\alpha, 2, q; p) \subset [L^p(E_n)]_{\alpha,1,q;W}$, $0 < \alpha < 1$, $1 \leqq q \leqq \infty$ and/or $\alpha = 1$, $q = \infty$.

Conversely, let f be any function in $L^p(E_n)$. Setting $f = [I - W(t)]f + W(t)f = f_1 + f_2$ $(0 < t < \infty)$, we obtain with $\|f_1\|_p = \|[W(t) - I]f\|_p \leqq \int_0^t \|\Delta W(\tau) f\|_p\, d\tau$, $\|f_2\|_p \leqq \|f\|_p$ and $\|D^j f_2\|_p = \|D^j W(t) f\|_p$ for each j with $|j| = 2$

$$\begin{aligned} K_2(t; f; L^p, W^{2,p}) &\leqq \|f_1\|_p + t(\|f_2\|_p + \sum_{|j|=2} \|D^j f_2\|_p) \\ &\leqq \int_0^t \|\Delta W(\tau) f\|_p\, d\tau + t\,\|f\|_p + \sum_{|j|=2} t\,\|D^j W(t) f\|_p. \end{aligned}$$

Since $K_2(t; f; L^p, W^{2,p}) \leqq \|f\|_p$ for all $t > 0$, the latter estimate gives

$$K_2(t; f; L^p, W^{2,p}) \leqq \min(1, t)\,\|f\|_p + \int_0^t \|\Delta W(\tau) f\|_p\, d\tau + \sum_{|j|=2} t\,\|D^j W(t) f\|_p \quad (0 < t < \infty;\ f \in L^p(E_n)).$$

Therefore, by the inequality (4.3.18) with $\beta = 1 - \alpha$ as well as Hardy's inequality (3.4.15)

$$\|(t^{-\alpha} K_2(t; f; L^p, W^{2,p}))\|_{L^q_*}$$
$$\leq \|(t^{-\alpha} \min(1, t))\|_{L^q_*} \|f\|_p + \left(\frac{1}{\alpha} + \frac{n^2}{1-\alpha} 2^{2-\alpha}\right) \|(t^{1-\alpha} \|\Delta W(t) f\|_p)\|_{L^q_*},$$

i.e. for $0 < \alpha < 1$, $1 \leq q \leq \infty$ we have $[L^p(E_n)]_{\alpha,1,q;W} \subset \mathrm{Lip}(2\alpha, 2, q; p)$. The fact that the norms (i)—(iv) are equivalent for $[L^p(E_n)]_{\alpha,1,q;W}$ now follows by Theorems 4.3.8 and 4.3.12.

(b) Analogously as in the proof of part (a) this part follows from the inequalities

$$K_2(t; f; L^p, D(\Delta^2; p)) \leq K_4(t; f; L^p, W^{4,p}) \qquad (0 < t < \infty;\ f \in L^p(E_n))$$

and

$$K_4(t^2; f; L^p, W^{4,p}) \leq 3\left(\min(1, t^2) \|f\|_p + \int_0^{t^2} \tau \|\Delta^2 W(\tau) f\|_p \, d\tau + \right.$$
$$\left. + \sum_{|j|=4} t^2 \|D^j W(t) f\|_p\right) \quad (0 < t < \infty;\ f \in L^p(E_n)).$$

This theorem in connection with the first theorem of reduction, namely Theorem 3.4.6, enables one to formulate complete characterizations of the intermediate spaces $[L^p(E_n)]_{\alpha,r,q;W}$, $0 < \alpha < r$, $1 \leq q \leq \infty$, for all integers $r = 1, 2, \ldots$ Moreover, it is not difficult to state further equivalent characterizations of these spaces by means of the various Taylor or Peano differences with respect to the Gauss–Weierstrass integral, the spherical means or the group of translation operators. In this respect see Sec. 4.4.3.

Remark 4.3.15. By a theorem of S. G. Mikhlin concerning multipliers of Fourier integrals—already noted in Remark 4.3.10—it even follows that for $1 < p < \infty$ the spaces $D(\Delta^r; p)$ and $W^{2r,p}(E_n)$, $r = 1, 2, \ldots$, are equal to another with equivalent norms. Thus, for $1 < p < \infty$ the equality of the spaces $[L^p(E_n)]_{\alpha,r,q;W}$ and $\mathrm{Lip}(2\alpha, 2r, q; p)$ follows directly by intermediate space theory, even in the saturation case $\alpha = r$, $q = \infty$.

The next corollary characterizes the spaces $[L^p(E_n)]^0_{\alpha,1,\infty;W}$, $0 < \alpha < 1$ and $[L^p(E_n)]^0_{1,2,\infty;W}$. The proof is obvious by the foregoing Theorem 4.3.14 as well as Propositions 3.4.12, 3.4.13, and 3.5.8.

Corollary 4.3.16. (a) *Let* $0 < \alpha < 1$. *For an element* $f \in L^p(E_n)$ *the following assertions are equivalent:*

(i) $\|[W(t) - I] f\|_p = o(t^\alpha)$, (ii) $\|\Delta W(t) f\|_p = o(t^{\alpha-1})$ $(t \to 0+)$;

(iii) $\|[S(\varrho) - I] f\|_p = o(\varrho^{2\alpha})$ $(\varrho \to 0+)$;

(iv) $\omega_2(t; f; p) = o(t^{2\alpha})$ $(t \to 0+)$;

(v) $\| f(\cdot + h) - f(\cdot) \|_p = o(|h|^{2\alpha})$ $(0 < \alpha < 1/2;\ |h| \to 0+)$,

$\| f(\cdot + 2h) - 2f(\cdot + h) + f(\cdot) \|_p = o(|h|)$ $(\alpha = 1/2;\ |h| \to 0+)$,

$\| [D_i f](\cdot + h) - [D_i f](\cdot) \|_p = o(|h|^{2\alpha - 1})$ *with* $f \in \mathsf{W}^{1,p}(\mathrm{E}_n)$

$(1/2 < \alpha < 1;\ |h| \to 0+;\ i = 1, 2, \ldots, n)$.

(b) *For an* $f \in \mathsf{L}^p(\mathrm{E}_n)$ *the following are equivalent:*

(i) $\| [W(t) - I]^2 f \|_p = o(t)$ (ii) $\| \Delta^2 W(t) f \|_p = o(t^{-1})$ $(t \to 0+)$;

(iii) $\| [S(2^{1/2}\varrho) - 2S(\varrho) + I] f \|_p = o(\varrho^2)$ $(\varrho \to 0+)$;

(iv) $\omega_4(t; f; p) = o(t^2)$ $(t \to 0+)$;

(v) $\| [D_i f](\cdot + 2h) - 2[D_i f](\cdot + h) + [D_i f](\cdot) \|_p = o(|h|)$ *with*

$f \in \mathsf{W}^{1,p}(\mathrm{E}_n)$ $(|h| \to 0+;\ i = 1, 2, \ldots, n)$.

We conclude with the determination of the Favard space $[\mathsf{L}^p(\mathrm{E}_n)]_{1,1,\infty;W}$, the case of optimal approximation.

Theorem 4.3.17. *A function* $f \in \mathsf{L}^p(\mathrm{E}_n)$ *belongs to the Favard space* $[\mathsf{L}^p(\mathrm{E}_n)]_{1,1,\infty;W}$ *if and only if one of the following conditions is satisfied:*

(i) $\sup_{0<t<\infty} \left(t^{-1} \| [W(t) - I] f \|_p\right) < \infty$;

(ii) $\sup_{0<\varrho<\infty} \left(\varrho^{-2} \| [S(\varrho) - I] f \|_p\right) < \infty$;

(iii) *for* $p = 1$: *there exists a* $\mu \in \mathsf{M}(\mathrm{E}_n)$ *such that for all* $\varphi \in \mathsf{C}_{00}^{\infty}(\mathrm{E}_n)$

$$\int_{\mathrm{E}_n} f(x)\, [\Delta \varphi](x)\, dx = \int_{\mathrm{E}_n} \varphi(x)\, d\mu(x),$$

for $1 < p < \infty$: $f \in \mathsf{D}(\Delta; p)$.

Moreover, for $1 < p < \infty$ *there are the further equivalences:*

(iv) $\sup_{0<t<\infty} \left(t^{-2} \omega_2(t; f; p)\right) < \infty$;

(v) $f \in \mathsf{W}^{1,p}(\mathrm{E}_n)$ *and for each* $i = 1, 2, \ldots, n$

$$\sup_{h \in \mathrm{E}_n} \left(|h|^{-1} \| [D_i f](\cdot + h) - [D_i f](\cdot) \|_p\right) < \infty;$$

(vi) $f \in \mathsf{W}^{2,p}(\mathrm{E}_n)$.

Proof. The equivalence of the assertions (i) and (ii) is obvious by Theorem 4.3.12. Let us prove (iii). At first for $p = 1$. We recall that $\mathsf{M}(\mathrm{E}_n)$ is isometrically isomorphic to the dual space of $\mathsf{C}_0(\mathrm{E}_n)$. Moreover, it is easy to prove (cf. Theorem 4.3.11) that $\{W(t);\, 0 \leq t < \infty\}$ forms a holomorphic contraction semi-group of operators of class $(\mathscr{C}_0)$ on the space $\mathsf{C}_0(\mathrm{E}_n)$ with infinitesimal generator Δ and domain $\{f \in \mathsf{C}_0(\mathrm{E}_n);$

Δf exists in the sense of Sobolev and belongs to $C_0(\mathrm{E}_n)\}$. Now, the dual semi-group $\{W^*(t); 0 \leqq t < \infty\}$ on $M(\mathrm{E}_n)$ has the representation

(4.3.21)
$$d[W^*(t)\,\mu](x) = \left(\frac{1}{(4\pi t)^{n/2}} \int_{\mathrm{E}_n} \exp(-|x-u|^2/4t)\, d\mu(u)\right) dx \quad (0 < t < \infty),$$

i.e. for each $\mu \in M(\mathrm{E}_n)$ $W^*(t)\,\mu$ defines an absolutely continuous measure with respect to the Lebesgue measure dx. Thus the maximal subspace of $M(\mathrm{E}_n)$ upon which the restriction of $\{W^*(t); 0 \leqq t < \infty\}$ is strongly continuous is the space $AC(\mathrm{E}_n)$, which is isometrically isomorphic to $L^1(\mathrm{E}_n)$.

The saturation problem for dual semi-groups, however, was solved in general in Sec. 2.1.1: Theorem 2.1.4, which states that the Favard class is equal to the domain of the dual of the infinitesimal generator. Now the assertion (iii) for $p = 1$ is nothing but the definition of the dual of the Laplace operator. This proves the case $p = 1$.

By the reflexivity of $L^p(\mathrm{E}_n)$, $1 < p < \infty$, it follows immediately by Theorem 2.1.2 that $[L^p(\mathrm{E}_n)]_{1,1,\infty;W}$ is equal to $D(\Delta; p)$. Finally, the equivalences (iv)—(vi) are direct consequences of the Remarks 4.3.10 and 4.3.15.

4.4 Notes and Remarks

4.4.1. In Sec. 4.1 we treated the singular integrals of Abel-Poisson and Weierstrass for functions f in $C_{2\pi}$ or $L^p_{2\pi}$, $1 \leqq p < \infty$, in particular their behavior when f belongs to a generalized Lipschitz space. The results obtained are direct consequences of the theory as developed in Chapter III, especially since all of the preliminary results are already given in Sec. 1.5. Moreover, these results are deep generalizations of those obtained in Sec. 2.4 by more classical methods—if one may express it in this way.

In Sec. 2.3.2 we already defined the classical Lipschitz spaces of periodic functions and in Sec. 2.7.3 we noted their connection with the theory of best approximation as well as recent results concerning them. While the definition of the generalized Lipschitz spaces $\mathrm{Lip}(\alpha, r, q; X)$ $(0 < \alpha < r,\ 1 \leqq q < \infty$ and/or $\alpha = r, q = \infty$; $r = 1, 2, \ldots)$ — X being one of the spaces $C_{2\pi}$ or $L^p_{2\pi}$, $1 \leqq p < \infty$ — is practically evident for $q = \infty$ and already well-known in the theory of trigonometric series and of best approximation (let us just mention A. F. Timan [1] in this respect), the extension for $1 \leqq q < \infty$ may probably be said to have its roots in the function

$$(4.4.1)\qquad \mu_q(x; f) = \left\{\int_0^{\pi} t^{-q-1}\, |f(x+t) - 2f(x) + f(x-t)|^q\, dt\right\}^{1/q}$$

considered by J. MARCINKIEWICZ [1] in 1938 (cf. A. ZYGMUND [1]). But the definition in its full generality seems to go back to O. V. BESOV [1; 2] (1959–1961); see also I. I. HIRSCHMAN [1] (1953) for intermediate results.

One of the most important results concerning the generalized Lipschitz spaces of Sec. 4.1.1 is the fact that one may restrict the discussion to the reduced spaces $\mathrm{Lip}(\alpha, 1, q; X)$, $0 < \alpha < 1$, $1 \leqq q \leqq \infty$ and/or $\alpha = 1, q = \infty$, and $\mathrm{Lip}(1, 2, q; X)$, $1 \leqq q \leqq \infty$ (Theorems 4.1.4 and 4.1.6). For $q = \infty$ this was already known, see e.g. A. F. TIMAN [1, Ch. V—VI]. Theorem 4.1.6 in addition contains the theorem of Hardy-Littlewood (Theorem 2.1.7) for $\mathrm{Lip}(r, r, \infty; X)$. The Plessner type characterization of $\mathrm{lip}(\alpha, r, \infty; X)$, $0 < \alpha < r$, and $X^{(r)}$ in the case $r = 1$ is due to H. MIRKIL [1]; see also the article of S. G. KREĬN–JU. I. PETUNIN [1] for the development in the Soviet Union.

In the theory of best approximation the theorems of Jackson and Bernstein combined read as follows (see Sec. 2.7.3): *A function $f \in X$ belongs to* $\mathrm{Lip}(\alpha, r, q; X)$ $(0 < \alpha < r, 1 \leqq q \leqq \infty)$ *if and only if* $\sum_{n=0}^{\infty} (2^{\alpha n} E_{2^n}[f; X])^q < \infty$. *Moreover,*

$$\|f\| + \left\{\sum_{n=0}^{\infty} (2^{\alpha n} E_{2^n}[f; X])^q\right\}^{1/q}$$

defines an equivalent norm, see e.g. O. V. BESOV [2]. But in the case of saturation no characterization is known for $\mathrm{Lip}(r, r, \infty; X)$ in terms of $E_n[f; X]$.

Already in 1951 S. B. STEČKIN [1] and A. F. TIMAN [1, p. 334] showed that for all $f \in X^{(k)}$ $(k = 1, 2, \ldots)$

$$C_{1,k} \sup_{n=1,2,\ldots} (2^{kn} E_{2^n}[f; X]) \leqq \|f^{(k)}\|_X \leqq C_{2,k} \sum_{n=0}^{\infty} 2^{kn} E_{2^n}[f; X],$$

where $C_{1,k}$ and $C_{2,k}$ are two positive constants. This result, together with the above theorem, proves the inclusions (4.1.1). Moreover, for $1 < p < \infty$ these inclusion relations may be generalized as

$$(4.4.2)\qquad \mathrm{Lip}(k, r, \min[p, 2]; L^p_{2\pi}) \subset [L^p_{2\pi}]^{(k)} \subset \mathrm{Lip}(k, r, \max[p, 2]; L^p_{2\pi}) \quad (k = 1, 2, \ldots, r-1),$$

all three spaces being equal for $p = 2$. For a proof see O. V. BESOV [2]. Earlier partial results concerning (4.4.2) already follow from those of J. Marcinkiewicz, see A. ZYGMUND [1]. Furthermore, (4.1.1) and

(4.4.2) even hold when the integer k is replaced by the continuous parameter α, $0 < \alpha < r$, where

$$X^{(\alpha)} = \left\{ f \in X;\, f^{(\alpha)} \sim \sum_{l=-\infty}^{\infty} (i\,l)^{\alpha} f^{\wedge}(l)\, e^{i l x} \in X \right\}$$

with norm $\|f\| + \|f^{(\alpha)}\|$. $f^{(\alpha)}$ is called the *fractional derivative* of f of order α. For fractional derivatives and integrals of periodic functions see e.g. A. ZYGMUND [5, Vol. II pp. 133–142]. The definitions go back to H. WEYL, while the main results are due to G. H. HARDY, J. E. LITTLEWOOD, R. E. A. C. PALEY, A. ZYGMUND, J. MARCINKIEWICZ and I. I. HIRSCHMAN, JR. For a proof of (4.4.2) for $0 < \alpha < 1$ see I. I. HIRSCHMAN [1]; see also M. H. TAIBLESON [2, I]. For a detailed presentation see P. L. BUTZER–K. SCHERER [1].

In recent years the investigations concerning generalized Lipschitz spaces for periodic functions have made great further progress. In particular, this is true for the definition of Lipschitz spaces for arbitrary real parameters α, for their dual spaces, their connections with the Bessel, Riesz and Weyl (Liouville) potentials for periodic functions, for multiplier transforms on these spaces as well as for generalizations of these problems to functions defined on an n-dimensional torus. For these facts we refer to N. DU PLESSIS [2], A. ZYGMUND [6], I. I. HIRSCHMAN [2], M. H. TAIBLESON [2], S. WAINGER [2], S. G. KREĬN–JU. I. PETUNIN [1] and others. We also refer to the literature cited in Sec. 4.4.3, concerning generalized Lipschitz spaces of functions on Euclidean n-space, this literature sometimes containing information on the periodic case.

The investigations on Lipschitz spaces of periodic functions are in many cases intimately tied up with the investigations on the singular integral of Abel-Poisson for these functions. Many of the proofs of just the deep theorems concerning Lipschitz spaces follow by introducing the Abel-Poisson integral, see the literature cited above. In this respect let us only mention the function

$$g_q(x; f) = \left\{ \int_0^1 (1-\varrho)^{q-1}\, |f'(\varrho\, e^{ix})|^q\, d\varrho \right\}^{1/q}, \tag{4.4.3}$$

where $\operatorname{Re} f(\varrho\, e^{ix}) = [V(\varrho)\, f](x)$ and $\operatorname{Im} f(0) = 0$, introduced by J. E. LITTLEWOOD–R. E. A. C. PALEY [1] in 1936 (cf. A. ZYGMUND [1]), which is closely related to the Marcinkiewicz function $\mu_q(x; f)$ defined above. Here see Sec. 2.4.1 and 2.4.2 and the notes attached thereto in Sec. 2.7.4.

The methods of proof of the main results in Sec. 4.1.2, formulated in Theorems 4.1.10 and 4.1.13, are new. See also J. PEETRE [6]. Yet Theorem 4.1.10 giving the equivalence of the space $X_{\alpha,r,q;V}$ with the Lipschitz space $\operatorname{Lip}(\alpha, r, q; X)$ in the case of non-optimal approximation ($0 < \alpha < r$, $1 \leqq q \leqq \infty$; $r = 1, 2, \ldots$) was already obtained independently for $r = 1$ by M. H. TAIBLESON [2, I] and H. BERENS [1]; the former even proved the theorem for $r = 1$ for functions on the n-dimensional torus. Here we may remark that M. H. Taibleson used condition (v) of Corollary 4.1.11 for his definition of the Lipschitz spaces; he did not introduce powers of the operator $[V(t) - I]$ by means of which we defined the spaces $X_{\alpha, r, q; V}$ (condition (i) of the corollary in question). Taibleson followed the notations of HIRSCHMAN [1]. Corollary 4.1.12 is nothing but the generalization of a well-known theorem of I. I. Privalov and A. Zygmund, concerning the fact that the Lipschitz spaces $\mathrm{Lip}(\alpha, 1, \infty; X)$, $0 < \alpha < 1$, and $\mathrm{Lip}(1, 2, \infty; X)$ are closed with respect to the operation of conjugacy, to the space $\mathrm{Lip}(\alpha, r, q; X)$ ($\alpha = r, q = \infty$ being excluded), see A. ZYGMUND [5, Vol. I p. 121]. For the saturation theorem: Theorem 4.1.13, see the notes and remarks in Sec. 2.7.4; for Proposition 4.1.14 see also A. ZYGMUND [5, Vol. I Ch. VII] and the notes appended thereto.

Further results, in particular those which are connected with problems indicated above for the generalized Lipschitz spaces, can be found in the literature cited above; we mention here especially the papers of I. I. Hirschman and M. H. Taibleson.

For the singular integral of Weierstrass of periodic functions (Sec. 4.1.3) which was treated only too briefly in the literature in comparison with the Abel-Poisson integral, we refer to Sec. 1.6.5 and 2.7.4 as well as to the cited papers of M. H. Taibleson.

4.4.2. For Sec. 4.2.1, which gives a brief introduction to the foundations on the classical Fourier and Fourier-Stieltjes transforms for functions on the real line, we refer to the standard books of S. BOCHNER [1], E. C. TITCHMARSH [2], S. BOCHNER-K. CHANDRASEKHARAN [1] and A. ZYGMUND [5, Vol. II Ch. XVI].

Our presentation concerning the classical Hilbert transform in Sec. 4.2.2 follows E. M. STEIN–G. WEISS [2] (1959). In their fine paper on an extension of the interpolation theorem of Marcinkiewicz (Corollary 3.3.15) these authors gave as an application thereto a new proof of the famous M. Riesz' theorem on the Hilbert transform (Theorem 4.2.5, M. RIESZ [2] 1927) via the basic Proposition 4.2.4.

For general aspects of the theory, for historical remarks and a bibliography see E. C. TITCHMARSH [2, Ch. V] and A. ZYGMUND [5, Vol. II Ch. XVI]. Regarding Propositions 4.2.6 and 4.2.7 and for the explanations following them we refer to the book by E. C. Titchmarsh. A newer, more elegant proof of the existence almost everywhere of the integral (4.2.4) for functions belonging to $L^1(E_1)$ was given by L. H. LOOMIS [1]. Lemma 4.2.8, raised by P. L. BUTZER [7], was proved by J. L. B. COOPER [3].

For Hilbert transforms or more general singular integrals for functions on E_n we mention A. P. CALDERÓN-A. ZYGMUND [2; 3]. A. ZYGMUND [4], and A. P. CALDERÓN [4] and the literature cited there. Their results may be found in book-form under the heading "Inequalities of Calderón–Zygmund Type" in N. DUNFORD–J. T. SCHWARTZ [1, Vol. II pp 1044—1073] and C. B. MORREY, JR. [1,. pp. 55—61]. Concerning the Hilbert transform we further mention R O'NEIL–G. WEISS [1] and P. L. BUTZER–W. TREBELS [1; 2].

Finally, we remark that the conjugate function in the theory of Fourier series, defined in Sec. 1.5.1, may be treated in much the same way as the Hilbert transform in Sec. 4.2.2, see E. M. STEIN–G. WEISS [2].

The semi-group character of the Cauchy-Poisson operators $\{V(y); 0 \leqq y < \infty\}$ of (4.2.23) seems to have been first emphazised by E. HILLE [1] in 1936. H. POLLARD [1] even proved the semi-group property for this transform in case $f(x)$ is only integrable on each finite interval of E_1 such that the integrals $\int^{\infty} (f(x)/x^2)\,dx$ and $\int_{-\infty} (f(x)/x^2)\,dx$ converge. While Lemma 4.2.11, which determines as a pre-result the infinitesimal generator A of $\{V(y); 0 \leqq y < \infty\}$ on $L^p(E_1)$, $1 \leqq p \leqq 2$, in terms of the Fourier transform, is essentially given in E. HILLE [4, pp. 370, 386 and 411] (see also H.-PH. [1, p. 576]), the direct characterization of A and its domain, as established in Theorem 4.2.10, is due to E. HILLE [6] for $1 < p < \infty$. For $p = 1$ it is a consequence of Lemmas 4.2.11 and 4.2.8; see also J. ELLIOT—W. FELLER [1], G. SUNOUCHI [1]. HILLE [6] moreover solved the Dirichlet problem for the halfplane $E_2^+ = \{(x, y) \in E_2; 0 < y < \infty\}$ with boundary values f in $L^p(E_1)$, $1 < p < \infty$:

$$\begin{cases} \dfrac{\partial^2 v}{\partial x^2}(x, y) + \dfrac{\partial^2 v}{\partial y^2}(x, y) = 0 & ((x, y) \in E_2^+) \\ v(x, 0) = f(x), & \end{cases}$$

considered as an abstract Cauchy problem (cf. Sec. 1.0), via the Hille-Yosida theorem (Corollary 1.3.7). The solution $v(x, y)$ turns out to be the Poisson integral $[V(y) f](x)$.

For proofs of the results given concerning the conjugate Cauchy-Poisson integral, see E. C. TITCHMARSH [2, Ch. V], also G. WEISS [1] who moreover treated the n-dimensional case. Theorem 4.2.12, in particular for $r = 1$, was first shown by M. H. TAIBLESON [2, I] (in n dimensions) without using semi-group theory; the general case $r \geqq 1$ is stated by J. PEETRE [6; 7]. The saturation theorems (Theorems 4.2.13 and 4.2.15, the cases $1 < p < \infty$ and $p = 1$, respectively) are new for $r > 1$. The case $r = 1$ for the reflexive space

$L^p(E_1)$, $1 < p < \infty$, was first shown by P. L. BUTZER [3; 4] as an application of Theorem 2.1.2, while for the non-reflexive space $L^1(E_1)$ (Proposition 4.2.14) it was obtained by P. L. BUTZER [5; 7] as an application of a general theorem on singular integrals, the proof using Fourier transform methods, and independently and almost simultaneously by G. SUNOUCHI [1]. The generalization to arbitrary integers $r \geqq 1$ is then an immediate consequence of Theorem 3.4.10 and the results for $r = 1$. The proof given for Proposition 4.2.14 is a modified form of that of K. DE LEEUW [2] and based upon Theorem 2.1.4. For the saturation problem of the n-dimensional Cauchy-Poisson integral see P. L. BUTZER [9], P. L. BUTZER–R. J. NESSEL [1; 2; 3], R. J. NESSEL [1; 2], E. GÖRLICH [2].

Regarding the counterparts of the Littlewood–Paley and Marcinkiewicz functions (4.4.3) and (4.4.1) for functions on the real line, the Bessel, Riesz and Liouville potentials, the connections with the Lipschitz spaces $\mathrm{Lip}(\alpha, r, q; L^p(E_1))$ and related problems as mentioned in Sec. 4.4.1 we refer to N. DU PLESSIS [1], D. WATERMAN [1; 2], M. H. TAIBLESON [2] as well as to the literature cited in Sec. 4.4.3.

4.4.3. The definition of the Sobolev spaces $W^{r,p}(E_n)$, $1 \leqq p < \infty$ $(r = 1, 2, \ldots)$, in Sec. 4.3.1 was given by S. L. SOBOLEV [1] in 1938 and he popularized them in his book [2] of 1950. However, the definition has its roots in earlier papers by B. LEVI (1906), G. C. EVANS, L. TONELLI and R. RELLICH, as C. B. MORREY, JR. [1, p. 19] remarks. In the meantime many others studied these spaces, we mention only N. ARONSZAJN–K. T. SMITH [1]. Their use is now standard in many mathematical disciplines, in particular in the theory of partial differential equations, see J. L. LIONS [7], L. HÖRMANDER [2], A. FRIEDMAN [1], also C. B. MORREY, JR. [1].

The development of the theory of Sobolev spaces to spaces with fractional indices $r = \alpha > 0$ or, more generally, for any real α, thus the development to Besov spaces (here called the generalized Lipschitz spaces on E_n and denoted by $\mathrm{Lip}(\alpha, r, q; p)$) is closely connected with the names of many mathematicians. For the contributions of the Soviet mathematicians we refer to the survey article of S. M. NIKOLSKIĬ [1] (1961), which is certainly the best source for the work done by S. M. NIKOLSKIĬ, O. V. BESOV, V. P. IL'IN, L. D. KUDRYAVCEV, P. I. LIZORKIN, L. N. SLOBODECKIĬ, V. A. SOLONNIKOV, S. V. USPENSKIĬ and others. See also E. GAGLIARDO [1]. Nikolskiĭ and his school incorporate especially the theory of best approximation into their investigations, see also J. PEETRE [1; 6].

Closely related in concept are the *spaces of Bessel potentials* $L^{\alpha,p}(E_n)$, α real, $1 \leqq p < \infty$, introduced by N. ARONSZAJN–K. T. SMITH [2] in the L^2-theory and generalized by A. P. CALDERÓN [1] (see also

E. GAGLIARDO [2]). By definition, $L^{\alpha,p}(E_n)$ is the space of all tempered distributions f for which

$$(1 + |v|^2)^{\alpha/2} f^\wedge(v) \qquad (v = (v_1, v_2, \ldots, v_n))$$

is the Fourier transform of a function $f^{\langle\alpha\rangle}$ in $L^p(E_n)$ (in the sense of L. SCHWARTZ [1]). $L^{\alpha,p}(E_n)$ is normed by $\|f^{\langle\alpha\rangle}\|_p$. The fundamental relations between the spaces of Bessel potentials and the Sobolev and Besov spaces are the following: For $1 < p < \infty$ and $r = 1, 2, \ldots$

$$L^{r,p}(E_n) = W^{r,p}(E_n). \tag{4.4.4}$$

Moreover, for $0 < \alpha < r$ $(r = 1, 2, \ldots)$ and $1 \leqq p < \infty$

$$\text{Lip}(\alpha, r, 1; p) \subset L^{\alpha,p}(E_n) \subset \text{Lip}(\alpha, r, \infty; p), \tag{4.4.5}$$

and more generally for $1 < p < \infty$

$$\text{Lip}(\alpha, r, \min[p, 2]; p) \subset L^{\alpha,p}(E_n) \subset \text{Lip}(\alpha, r, \max[p, 2]; p) \tag{4.4.6}$$

(compare (4.1.1) and (4.4.2)). The equality (4.4.4) is due to A. P. CALDERÓN [1]; for proofs of the inclusions (4.4.5) and (4.4.6) see e.g. M. H. TAIBLESON [2, I], N. ARONSZAJN–F. MULLA–P. SZEPTYCKI [1]. For an intensive treatment we mention the cited papers of M. H. Taibleson, N. Aronszajn–F. Mulla–P. Szeptycki as well as E. MAGENES [1], N. ARONSZAJN [1]. Regarding the Littlewood-Paley and Marcinkiewicz functions on E_n as well as for connections between the Bessel and Riesz potentials, we refer to E. M. STEIN [2; 3].

For a characterization of the Lipschitz spaces $\text{Lip}(\alpha, r, q; p)$ as intermediate spaces between $W^{r,p}(E_n)$ and $L^p(E_n)$ and for investigations concerning them by means of the various interpolation methods (cf. Sec. 3.6.2), see E. GAGLIARDO [4], J. L. LIONS [3, I], J. L. LIONS–E. MAGENES [1], J. L. LIONS–J. PEETRE [2], A. P. CALDERÓN [3], J. PEETRE [6]. For further results as well as for other papers of these and further authors see the cited survey article of E. Magenes. Moreover, for recent developments concerning the theory we refer to K. GRÖGER [1; 2; 3], S. M. NIKOLSKIĬ–J. L. LIONS–P. I. LIZORKIN [1], P. I. LIZORKIN [1], M. H. TAIBLESON [2, II—III], J. PEETRE [13], etc.

The presentation given in Sec. 4.3.1 follows that of J. L. LIONS–J. PEETRE [2] and J. PEETRE [11]. For the theorem of S. G Mikhlin on multipliers of Fourier integrals (Remark 4.3.10) see S. G. MIKHLIN [1, p. 232].

In his lecture notes [7] R. S. PHILLIPS showed via the Hille–Yosida theorem that the Cauchy problem of the heat-conduction equation on E_n has a unique semi-group solution for a given function in $C_0(E_n)$ or $L^1(E_n)$. This initial value problem may also be considered for functions in $L^p(E_n)$, $1 < p < \infty$, the same methods of proof carrying over. The L^2-case had already been considered by E. HILLE [4, p. 403].

With these results it is not difficult to show using Fourier transform theory that the unique solution is given by the singular integral (4.3.9) of Gauss–Weierstrass. For a general treatment of linear partial differential equations of the heat equation type we recall H.–PH. [1, Ch. XXIII], G. HELLWIG [1, Part I] as well as K. YOSIDA [10, Ch. XIII–XIV] (cf. Sec. 1.6.5).

For the significance of the spherical means in connection with the heat conduction equation and in particular with the wave equation, see F. JOHN [1] and L. BERS–F. JOHN–M. SCHECHTER [1]. Theorem 4.3.12 for $r = 1$ was established by M. H. TAIBLESON [2, I] in the case of non-optimal approximation and by R. J. NESSEL [1] (see P. L. BUTZER–R. J. NESSEL [1; 2]) in the saturation case. Theorem 4.3.14, proving equality between $[L^p(E_n)]_{\alpha,1,q;W}$ and $\text{Lip}(2\alpha, 2, q; p)$, $0 < \alpha < 1$, $1 \leqq q \leqq \infty$ (part (a)) as well as between $[L^p(E_n)]_{1,2,q;W}$ and $\text{Lip}(2, 4, q; p)$, $1 \leqq q \leqq \infty$ (part (b)), and also the basic Lemma 4.3.13 hereto are due to M. H. TAIBLESON [2, I] (in particular part (a) of the theorem and the lemma). However, the method of proof given here is quite different. Using Theorem 4.3.14 it is now not difficult to formulate and prove various types of equivalent characterizations of the spaces $[L^p(E_n)]_{\alpha,r,q;W}$ $(0 < \alpha < r,\ 1 \leqq q \leqq \infty;\ r = 1, 2, \ldots)$ by means of the Taylor, Peano and Riemann differences. Let us only state those by the Taylor differences: *If* $\alpha = k + \beta$, $0 < \beta < 1$ *and* $k = 0, 1, \ldots, r-1$, *then for an* $f \in [L^p(E_n)]_{\alpha,r,q;W}$ *the following are equivalent:*

(i) $f \in D(\Delta^k; p)$ *and* $t^{-\alpha} \left\| W(t) f - \sum_{l=0}^{k} \frac{t^l}{l!} \Delta^l f \right\|_p \in L^q_*$;

(ii) $f \in D(\Delta^k; p)$ *and* $\varrho^{-2\alpha} \left\| S(\varrho) f - \sum_{l=0}^{k} \frac{\Gamma(n/2)}{\Gamma(n/2+1)} \frac{(\varrho/2)^{2l}}{l!} \Delta^l f \right\|_p \in L^q_*$;

(iii)
$$\begin{cases} f \in W^{2k,p}(E_n) \ \textit{and} \ t^{-2\alpha} \sup\limits_{0<|h|<t} \left\| f(\cdot + h) - \sum\limits_{l=0}^{2k} \frac{1}{l!} (h, \nabla)^l f \right\|_p \in L^q_* & (0 < \beta < 1/2), \\ f \in W^{2k+1,p}(E_n) \ \textit{and} \ t^{-2\alpha} \sup\limits_{0<|h|<t} \left\| f(\cdot + h) - \sum\limits_{l=0}^{2k+1} \frac{1}{l!} (h, \nabla)^l f \right\|_p \in L^q_* & (1/2 < \beta < 1). \end{cases}$$

The equivalences (i), (ii), and (iii) of Theorem 4.3.17 (the saturation theorem) were first given by R. J. NESSEL [1] for $1 \leqq p \leqq 2$ using Fourier transform methods. For the theorem in general see E. GÖRLICH [2], who applied distribution theory in his proofs. Moreover, the latter author gave a number of further equivalent characterizations for the case $1 < p < \infty$. We mention only one by the symmetrical means: *A function* $f \in L^p(E_n)$, $1 < p < \infty$, *belongs to (the Favard space)*

$[L^p(\mathrm{E}_n)]_{1,1,\infty;W}$ *if and only if*

$$\sup_{0<\varrho<\infty} (\varrho^{-2} \| \sum_{e_\sigma} (f(\cdot + \varrho\, e_\sigma) - f(\cdot)) \|_p) < \infty,$$

where $e_\sigma = (\sigma_1, \sigma_2, \ldots, \sigma_n)$, $\sigma_i = \pm 1$ $(i = 1, 2, \ldots, n)$, *and the sum is taken for all possible permutations of* e_σ. E. Görlich [2], in addition, treated the generalized Weierstrass integral for functions on E_n, which includes as a particular case the singular integral of Cauchy–Poisson. The Poisson integral on E_n may be discussed similarly as the Weierstrass integral in Sec. 4.3.2; for results see M. H. Taibleson [2, I] (in the case of non-optimal approximation), P. L. Butzer–R. J. Nessel [2], R. J. Nessel [2], P. L. Butzer–E. Görlich [2] and E. Görlich [2] (in the saturation case).

Appendix

The purpose of this appendix is to give the reader a survey of the material on functional analysis that will be assumed as known. This will also clarify terminology and notation. For detailed information we refer the reader to the standard literature on the subject, thus the corresponding paragraphs in the books by S. BANACH [1], J. DIEUDONNÉ [2], N. DUNFORD–J. T. SCHWARTZ [1, Vol. I], R. E. EDWARDS [1], E. HILLE [4, Ch. I—III], E. HILLE–R. S. PHILLIPS [1, Ch. I—III], J. HORVÁTH [1], L. V. KANTOROVICH–G. P. AKILOV [1], G. KÖTHE [2], L. A. LJUSTERNIC–V. I. SOBOLEV [1], F. RIESZ–B. SZ.-NAGY [1], H. L. ROYDEN [1], H. H. SCHAEFER [1], A. E. TAYLOR [1], K. YOSIDA [10], A. C. ZAANEN [1], etc.

I.

Sets and Mappings. The notion of a set is obvious from a naive viewpoint. Its members are called elements or points. The *empty* set is denoted by $\emptyset$. We shall use freely the conventional notations of elementary set theory. Thus $f \in \mathcal{X}$ means that the element f belongs to the set $\mathcal{X}$, $\mathcal{A} \subset \mathcal{X}$ means that $\mathcal{A}$ is a *subset* of $\mathcal{X}$. If $\mathcal{A}$ and $\mathcal{B}$ are both subsets of $\mathcal{X}$, then $\mathcal{A} \cup \mathcal{B}$ is their *union*, $\mathcal{A} \cap \mathcal{B}$ their *intersection*, $\mathcal{A} - \mathcal{B}$ their *difference* and $\complement_{\mathcal{X}} \mathcal{A}$ the *complement* of $\mathcal{A}$ with respect to $\mathcal{X}$. The *cartesian product* $\mathcal{X} \times \mathcal{Y}$ of two sets $\mathcal{X}$ and $\mathcal{Y}$ is the set of all ordered pairs (f, g) with $f \in \mathcal{X}$, $g \in \mathcal{Y}$; thus, $\mathcal{X} \times \mathcal{Y} = \{(f, g);\ f \in \mathcal{X} \text{ and } g \in \mathcal{Y}\}$. One says that Φ is a *mapping* (transformation or function) from (on) $\mathcal{X}$ into (to) $\mathcal{Y}$, if for each $f \in \mathcal{X}$, there is determined a unique element $g = \Phi(f)$ in $\mathcal{Y}$, in notation: $f \to \Phi(f)$. $\mathcal{X}$ is called the *domain* of Φ, the image of $\mathcal{X}$ under Φ the *range* of Φ; the *graph* of Φ is the subset $\{(f, \Phi(f));\ f \in \mathcal{X}\}$ of $\mathcal{X} \times \mathcal{Y}$. For any $\mathcal{A} \subset \mathcal{X}$ we write $\Phi(\mathcal{A})$ to denote the set $\{\Phi(f);\ f \in \mathcal{A}\}$. If $\mathcal{Y} = \Phi(\mathcal{X})$ then Φ maps $\mathcal{X}$ *onto* $\mathcal{Y}$. If $\mathcal{B}$ is any subset of $\mathcal{Y}$, we define the *inverse image* $\Phi^{-1}(\mathcal{B}) = \{f \in \mathcal{X};\ \Phi(f) \in \mathcal{B}\}$. Φ is said to be *one-to-one* if $\Phi(f_1) = \Phi(f_2)$ implies $f_1 = f_2$. If Φ is one-to-one from $\mathcal{X}$ into $\mathcal{Y}$, the corresponding mapping $g \to f = \Phi^{-1}(\{g\})$ from $\Phi(\mathcal{X})$ onto $\mathcal{X}$ is called the *inverse* of Φ and simply written by Φ^{-1}. If Λ is a non-empty set and $\mathcal{X}$ another set, a mapping $\lambda \to f_\lambda$ of Λ into $\mathcal{X}$ is sometimes called a *family of elements* in $\mathcal{X}$ and denoted by $\{f_\lambda;\ \lambda \in \Lambda\}$. In this setting Λ is said to be an *index set.* A *sequence* is a family $\{f_n\}_{n=1}^{\infty}$ in $\mathscr{X}$ with the set of natural numbers as the index set.

Topological Notions. A collection $\mathfrak{T}$ of subsets of some set $\mathscr{X}$ defines a *topology for* $\mathscr{X}$ if $\mathfrak{T}$ contains the empty set $\emptyset$ and $\mathscr{X}$ itself, the union of any number of members of $\mathfrak{T}$ (even uncountably many), and the intersection of any finite number of members of $\mathfrak{T}$. The members $\mathscr{O}$ of $\mathfrak{T}$ are called the *open sets* of the *topological space* $(\mathscr{X}, \mathfrak{T})$. $\mathfrak{T}$ is said to be a *Hausdorff topology* if it satisfies the *separation axiom*: for each pair of distinct points f_1, f_2 in $\mathscr{X}$ there exist disjoint open sets $\mathscr{O}_1$, $\mathscr{O}_2$ of $\mathfrak{T}$ such that $f_1 \in \mathscr{O}_1$ and $f_2 \in \mathscr{O}_2$. The complement of an open set is called *closed*. Given a subset $\mathscr{A} \subset \mathscr{X}$, the union of all open sets in $\mathscr{A}$ is called the *interior* of $\mathscr{A}$, denoted by $\mathring{\mathscr{A}}$, an open set; the intersection of all closed sets containing $\mathscr{A}$ is called the *closure* of $\mathscr{A}$, denoted by $\bar{\mathscr{A}}$, a closed set. If $\mathscr{A}_1$ and $\mathscr{A}_2$ are subsets of $\mathscr{X}$, $\mathscr{A}_1$ is *dense relative to* $\mathscr{A}_2$ if $\mathscr{A}_2 \subset \bar{\mathscr{A}}_1$ (*dense* in $\mathscr{A}_2$ if $\mathscr{A}_1 \subset \mathscr{A}_2$ and $\mathscr{A}_2 \subset \bar{\mathscr{A}}_1$). A topological space $\mathscr{X}$ is *separable* if $\mathscr{X}$ contains a countable dense subset. The topology in a subset $\mathscr{A} \subset \mathscr{X}$ inherited from the collection of sets $\{\mathscr{A} \cap \mathscr{O}; \mathscr{O} \in \mathfrak{T}\}$ is called the *relative topology* for $\mathscr{A}$ induced by $\mathfrak{T}$.

A subset $\mathscr{U} \subset \mathscr{X}$ is called a *neighborhood* of a point f if $f \in \mathring{\mathscr{U}}$. A point $f \in \mathscr{X}$ is a *limit* (or *accumulation*) *point* of a subset $\mathscr{A}$ of $\mathscr{X}$ if every neighborhood of f contains at least one point $g \in \mathscr{A}$ other than f. A collection $\mathfrak{N}$ of open sets $\mathscr{N}$ is called a *neighborhood base* of the point f if $f \in \mathscr{N}$ whenever $\mathscr{N} \in \mathfrak{N}$ and if to each neighborhood $\mathscr{U}$ of f corresponds some $\mathscr{N} \in \mathfrak{N}$ such that $\mathscr{N} \subset \mathscr{U}$. A family $\mathfrak{B}$ of open sets of $(\mathscr{X}, \mathfrak{T})$ is called a *base* for the topology $\mathfrak{T}$ if the following is satisfied: (i) to each $f \in \mathscr{X}$ there corresponds some $\mathscr{B} \in \mathfrak{B}$ such that $f \in \mathscr{B}$; (ii) if $\mathscr{B}_1, \mathscr{B}_2 \in \mathfrak{B}$ and $f \in \mathscr{B}_1 \cap \mathscr{B}_2$, there exists some $\mathscr{B}_3 \in \mathfrak{B}$ such that $f \in \mathscr{B}_3 \subset (\mathscr{B}_1 \cap \mathscr{B}_2)$. Let $\mathfrak{T}_1$ and $\mathfrak{T}_2$ be two topologies for the same set $\mathscr{X}$. We say that $\mathfrak{T}_1$ is *finer* (stronger) than $\mathfrak{T}_2$ if every open set of $\mathfrak{T}_2$ is an open set of $\mathfrak{T}_1$; $\mathfrak{T}_2$ is *coarser* (weaker) than $\mathfrak{T}_1$. If $(\mathscr{X}, \mathfrak{T})$ and $(\mathscr{Y}, \mathfrak{S})$ are two topological spaces, we define a topology on the product $\mathscr{X} \times \mathscr{Y}$ by taking as a base the collection of all sets of the form $\mathscr{O} \times \mathscr{P}$, where $\mathscr{O}$, $\mathscr{P}$ are open sets of $\mathfrak{T}$ and $\mathfrak{S}$, respectively. This topology is called the *product topology* for $\mathscr{X} \times \mathscr{Y}$.

Let $\mathscr{X}$ and $\mathscr{Y}$ be two topological spaces. A mapping Φ from $\mathscr{X}$ into $\mathscr{Y}$ is called *continuous at* $f \in \mathscr{X}$ if for each neighborhood $\mathscr{V}$ of $g = \Phi(f)$, $\Phi^{-1}(\mathscr{V})$ is a neighborhood of f. Φ is *continuous on* $\mathscr{X}$ if it is continuous at each $f \in \mathscr{X}$. If Φ is a one-to-one mapping of $\mathscr{X}$ onto $\mathscr{Y}$ and if both Φ and Φ^{-1} are continuous, then Φ is called a *homeomorphic mapping* or a *homeomorphism*. We note that the topology $\mathfrak{T}_1$ is finer than $\mathfrak{T}_2$ for the same set $\mathscr{X}$ if and only if the identity mapping $f \to f$ of $(\mathscr{X}, \mathfrak{T}_1)$ onto $(\mathscr{X}, \mathfrak{T}_2)$ is continuous.

Let $\mathscr{X}$ be a topological space. A subset $\mathscr{A}$ of $\mathscr{X}$ is called *nowhere dense* if its closure $\bar{\mathscr{A}}$ has an empty interior; $\mathscr{A}$ is called of *first category* in $\mathscr{X}$ if $\mathscr{A}$ is the union of a countable set of nowhere dense sets. If $\mathscr{A}$ is not of first category then $\mathscr{A}$ is of *second category*.

By an *open covering* of a set $\mathscr{X}$ we mean a collection of open subsets of $\mathscr{X}$ the union of which is $\mathscr{X}$. A topological space $\mathscr{X}$ is called *compact* if every open covering of $\mathscr{X}$ has a finite subcovering (*Heine-Borel property*) or, equivalently, if a family of closed subsets of $\mathscr{X}$ has non-empty intersection whenever each finite subfamily has non-empty intersection (*finite intersection property*). A closed subset of a compact set is compact. A compact subset of a Hausdorff topological space is closed.

Metric Spaces. A *metric* ϱ for a (non-empty) set $\mathscr{X}$ is a real-valued function defined on $\mathscr{X} \times \mathscr{X}$ such that for all f, g and $h \in \mathscr{X}$: (i) $\varrho(f, g) \geqq 0$ and $\varrho(f, g) = 0$ if and only if $f = g$; (ii) $\varrho(f, g) = \varrho(g, f)$; (iii) $\varrho(f, g) \leqq \leqq \varrho(f, h) + \varrho(h, g)$. $\varrho(f, g)$ is called the *distance* between f and g. The collection of all *open spheres* $\{g; \varrho(g, f) < n^{-1}, n = 1, 2, \ldots\}$ forms a countable neighborhood base at the point f, while the collection of open spheres in $\mathscr{X}$ constitutes a base of a topology for $\mathscr{X}$. Thus topologized the set $\mathscr{X}$ is called a *metric space*, in notation $(\mathscr{X}, \varrho)$. This topology separates points in $\mathscr{X}$ (a Hausdorff space), moreover, it separates disjoint closed sets in $\mathscr{X}$ (a normal space). A metric space is separable if and only if it has a countable base. A homeomorphism between two metric spaces which leaves distance invariant is called an *isometry*.

In a metric space a sequence $\{f_n\}_{n=1}^{\infty}$ converges to a limit point f if and only if $\lim_{n\to\infty} \varrho(f_n, f) = 0$; any convergent sequence satisfies the *Cauchy-condition*: $\varrho(f_n, f_m) \to 0$ as $n, m \to \infty$. A metric space is said to be *complete* if every Cauchy sequence has a limit point. To each incomplete metric space $\mathscr{X}$ one can construct a complete metric space (or completion) $\tilde{\mathscr{X}}$ in which $\mathscr{X}$ is isometrically imbedded as a dense subset. The completion $\tilde{\mathscr{X}}$ is unique up to an isometry. A complete metric space is of second category (*Baire category theorem*).

A metric space $\mathscr{X}$ is said to be *totally bounded* (*precompact*) if for each $\varepsilon > 0$ there is a finite collection of open spheres of radius ε which cover $\mathscr{X}$. A metric space $\mathscr{X}$ is compact if and only if it is both complete and totally bounded or, equivalently, if it is *sequentially compact*, i.e. every sequence $\{f_n\}_{n=1}^{\infty}$ in $\mathscr{X}$ has a convergent subsequence. A compact metric space is separable.

Linear Spaces. Let $\mathscr{X}$ be a (non-empty) set and K the field of real (or complex) numbers. Suppose, there are defined a mapping $(f, g) \to f + g$ on $\mathscr{X} \times \mathscr{X}$ into $\mathscr{X}$, called *addition*, and a mapping $(\alpha, f) \to \alpha f$ on $\mathrm{K} \times \mathscr{X}$

into $\mathscr{X}$, called *scalar multiplication*, such that the following axioms for the elements $f, g, h, \dots \in \mathscr{X}$ and $\alpha, \beta, \dots \in \mathrm{K}$ are satisfied:

(1) $f + g = g + f$;
(2) $(f + g) + h = f + (g + h)$;
(3) there is an element θ in $\mathscr{X}$ such that $f + \theta = f$ for all $f \in \mathscr{X}$;
(4) $\alpha (f + g) = \alpha f + \alpha g$;
(5) $(\alpha + \beta) f = \alpha f + \beta f$;
(6) $\alpha (\beta f) = (\alpha \beta) f$;
(7) $0 \cdot f = \theta$, $1 \cdot f = f$.

Under the structure so defined, $\mathscr{X}$ is called a real (or complex) *linear system*. A linear system, with or without an imposed topology, is usually referred to as a *linear vector space*. It should be noted that the element θ (zero element) is unique. The element $(-1) f$ is called the negative of f and written by $-f$. One has $f + (-1) f = 1 \cdot f + (-1) f = (1 - 1) f = 0 \cdot f = \theta$.

A non-empty subset $\mathscr{M}$ in $\mathscr{X}$ is a *linear manifold* in $\mathscr{X}$, if $\alpha f_1 + \beta f_2$ belongs to $\mathscr{M}$ whenever $f_1, f_2 \in \mathscr{M}$ and $\alpha, \beta \in \mathrm{K}$. If $\mathscr{A}$ is any (non-empty) subset of $\mathscr{X}$, the linear manifold $\mathscr{M}$ of $\mathscr{X}$ with elements $\sum_{k=1}^{n} \alpha_k f_k$, where n is any positive integer (not fixed), $f_k \in \mathscr{A}$ and $\alpha_k \in \mathrm{K}$ $(k = 1, 2, \dots, n)$, is called the *linear hull* of $\mathscr{X}$ *spanned* by $\mathscr{A}$. If $\mathscr{A}$ and $\mathscr{B}$ are any two sets in $\mathscr{X}$, then the *translate* of $\mathscr{A}$ by f: $\mathscr{A} + f = \{g; g = h + f, h \in \mathscr{A}\}$, and the *algebraic su m*of $\mathscr{A}$ and $\mathscr{B}$: $\mathscr{A} + \mathscr{B} = \{g; g = h + f, h \in \mathscr{A}$ and $f \in \mathscr{B}\}$. $\mathscr{A}$ is *convex* if, whenever it contains f and g, it also contains $\alpha f + (1 - \alpha) g$ for $0 \leqq \alpha \leqq 1$.

Let $\mathscr{X}$ and $\mathscr{Y}$ be two linear systems (over the same field K). A mapping Φ from $\mathscr{X}$ into $\mathscr{Y}$ is called a *linear transformation* (or linear map) if $\Phi(\alpha f + \beta g) = \alpha \Phi(f) + \beta \Phi(g)$ for all $\alpha, \beta \in \mathrm{K}$ and $f, g \in \mathscr{X}$. A linear map Φ on $\mathscr{X}$ to $\mathscr{Y}$ has an inverse if and only if $\Phi(f) = \theta$ implies $f = \theta$. Defining addition by $(\Phi_1 + \Phi_2)(f) = \Phi_1(f) + \Phi_2(f)$ and scalar multiplication by $(\alpha \Phi)(f) = \Phi(\alpha f)$, the set of all linear transformations from $\mathscr{X}$ into $\mathscr{Y}$ also generates a linear system. In the special case where $\mathscr{Y}$ is the field K, the linear transformations are called *linear functionals*. $\mathscr{X}$ and $\mathscr{Y}$ are said to be *isomorphic*, if there exists a one-to-one linear transformation of $\mathscr{X}$ onto $\mathscr{Y}$; such a mapping is called an *isomorphism*.

A *topological linear space* is a linear system $\mathscr{X}$ having a Hausdorff topology such that addition is a continuous mapping from $\mathscr{X} \times \mathscr{X}$ into $\mathscr{X}$ and scalar multiplication is a continuous mapping from $\mathrm{K} \times \mathscr{X}$ into $\mathscr{X}$. Since the translate of $\mathscr{X}$ by g, g any fixed point in $\mathscr{X}$, is a homeomorphism from $\mathscr{X}$ onto itself, the topology is completely determined by a neighborhood base of the zero element θ. A topological linear space is called *locally convex* if every neighborhood of θ contains a convex neighborhood of θ. Two topological linear spaces $\mathscr{X}$ and $\mathscr{Y}$ over the same field K are called *topologically isomorphic* if there is an isomorphism of $\mathscr{X}$ onto $\mathscr{Y}$ which is also a homeomorphism. Moreover, two metric linear spaces $\mathscr{X}$ and $\mathscr{Y}$ are *isometrically isomorphic* if there is a one-to-one correspondence between the elements of $\mathscr{X}$ and $\mathscr{Y}$ which makes the two spaces isomorphic as well as isometric.

A linear system (over K) is said to be an *algebra* (over K) if there is defined a mapping $(f, g) \to f \cdot g$ on $\mathscr{X} \times \mathscr{X}$ into $\mathscr{X}$, called the *product* "f times g", such that the following axioms are satisfied:

(8) $(f g) h = f(g h)$;

(9) $f(g + h) = f g + f h, \ (f + g) h = f h + g h$;

(10) $(\alpha f) (\beta g) = (\alpha \beta) f g$.

If the algebra $\mathscr{X}$ contains an element e such that $e f = f e = f$ for every $f \in \mathscr{X}$, e is called the *unit element* of $\mathscr{X}$; e is necessarily unique if it exists. An algebra is called *commutative* or *abelian* if $f g = g f$ for each pair (f, g) in $\mathscr{X} \times \mathscr{X}$. A *topological algebra* is a topological linear space such that the product $f g$ on $\mathscr{X} \times \mathscr{X}$ into $\mathscr{X}$ is continuous in f and g separately.

Banach Spaces. Let $\mathscr{X}$ be a linear system over the real (or complex) number field. A non-negative real-valued function $\|\cdot\|$ defined on $\mathscr{X}$ is called a *norm* if for $f, g \in \mathscr{X}$, $\alpha \in$ K:

(1) $\|f\| = 0$ if and only if $f = \theta$,

(2) $\|\alpha f\| = |\alpha| \, \|f\|$,

(3) $\|f + g\| \leqq \|f\| + \|g\|$.

A linear system $\mathscr{X}$ for which a norm is defined becomes a metric space if we define $\varrho(f, g) = \|f - g\|$. Under this metric, $\mathscr{X}$ becomes a locally convex space, and the topology is called the *strong topology* for $\mathscr{X}$. A linear system that carries the topology generated by the above metric is said to be a *normed linear space*. If such a space is complete it is called a *Banach space*. A sequence $\{f_n\}_{n=1}^{\infty}$ in $\mathscr{X}$ is said to be *strongly convergent* to $f \in \mathscr{X}$ if $\|f_n - f\|$ tends to zero as $n \to \infty$; in notation, $\operatorname{s-lim}_{n\to\infty} f_n = f$ or $f_n \to f$ in the norm as $n \to \infty$. A normed linear space $\mathscr{X}$ is complete if and only if every absolutely summable sequence is summable, i.e. if $\{f_n\}_{n=1}^{\infty}$ is any sequence in $\mathscr{X}$ such that $\sum_{n=1}^{\infty} \|f_n\| < \infty$, then $\sum_{k=1}^{n} f_k$ converges in the norm to an element of $\mathscr{X}$. It is obvious that a closed linear manifold of a Banach space is again a Banach space. Let $\mathscr{X}$ be a linear system, and suppose two norms $\|f\|_1$ and $\|f\|_2$ are defined on

$\mathscr{X}$. These norms are said to be *equivalent* (or define the same topology) on $\mathscr{X}$, if there exist two positive constants c, C such that $c \|f\|_1 \leqq \leqq \|f\|_2 \leqq C \|f\|_1$ $(f \in \mathscr{X})$, in other words, if the identity mapping $f \to f$ of $(\mathscr{X}, \|\cdot\|_1)$ onto $(\mathscr{X}, \|\cdot\|_2)$ is a linear homeomorphism. If $\mathscr{X}$ and $\mathscr{Y}$ are two normed linear spaces, a suitable norm for the linear system $\mathscr{X} \times \mathscr{Y}$ is given by $\|(\cdot,\cdot)\|_{\mathscr{X}\times\mathscr{Y}} = \|\cdot\|_{\mathscr{X}} + \|\cdot\|_{\mathscr{Y}}$.

If $\mathscr{X}$ is a real (or complex) algebra as well as a normed linear space such that $\|f g\| \leqq \|f\| \, \|g\|$, then $\mathscr{X}$ is called a *normed algebra*. If $\mathscr{X}$ is in addition a complete normed linear space then $\mathscr{X}$ is said to be a *Banach algebra*.

In the following, normed linear spaces will always be complete, thus Banach spaces, and we denote them by X or Y. Let X and Y be two real (or complex) Banach spaces. A linear transformation (or operator) T with domain D in X and range R in Y (D is assumed to be a linear manifold of X) is *bounded* on D if there is a constant C such that $\|T f\| \leqq C \|f\|$ for all $f \in \mathsf{D}$. We call the smallest such constant C the *norm* of T and denote it by $\|T\|$. Thus $\|T\| = \sup\{\|T f\|; f \in \mathsf{D}$ with $\|f\| \leqq 1\}$. A bounded linear operator T on D always has a bounded linear *extension* $\bar{T}$ on $\bar{\mathsf{D}}$ (also a linear manifold of X) which preserves norms: $\|\bar{T}\| = \|T\|$. For a linear operator T on $\mathsf{D} \subset \mathsf{X}$ to Y the following three assertions are equivalent: (i) T is bounded on D; (ii) T is continuous at one point of D; (iii) T is *uniformly continuous* on D, i.e. given $\varepsilon > 0$ there is a $\delta = \delta(\varepsilon) > 0$ such that $\|T f_1 - T f_2\| < \varepsilon$ whenever $\|f_1 - f_2\| < \delta$.

The linear system of all bounded linear transformations on X to Y forms a Banach space, denoted by $\mathscr{E}(\mathsf{X}, \mathsf{Y})$.

If T is a linear operator on $\mathsf{D} \subset \mathsf{X}$ onto $\mathsf{R} \subset \mathsf{Y}$, then the inverse T^{-1} exists and is bounded if and only if there exists a $c > 0$ such that $\|T f\| \geqq c \|f\|$ for all $f \in \mathsf{D}$. The supremum of all admissible values of c is the reciprocal of $\|T^{-1}\|$. A linear transformation T on $\mathsf{D} \subset \mathsf{X}$ to Y is said to be *closed* if its graph $\{(f, T f); f \in \mathsf{D}\}$ is a closed subspace of $\mathsf{X} \times \mathsf{Y}$ or, in other words, if whenever $f_n \to f$, $f_n \in \mathsf{D}$, and $T f_n \to g$ in the norm of X and Y, respectively, it follows that $f \in \mathsf{D}$ and $T f = g$. A linear transformation on $\mathsf{D} \subset \mathsf{X}$ to Y has a closed extension if and only if no pair of the form (θ, g), $g \neq \theta$, belongs to the closure of the graph of T in $\mathsf{X} \times \mathsf{Y}$. In this case, the closure of the graph of T defines the smallest closed linear extension of T. A bounded linear transformation on a closed domain $\mathsf{D} \subset \mathsf{X}$ to Y is closed. The inverse of a closed linear operator, if it exists, is closed.

The main theorems concerning linear transformations between Banach spaces are the following:

A continuous linear transformation T from X onto Y transforms open sets into open sets. In particular, if T is one-to-one it is an isomorphism (*open mapping theorem*).

A closed linear transformation on X to Y is continuous (*closed graph theorem*).

Let $\{T_\lambda; \lambda \in \Lambda\}$ be a family of operators in $\mathscr{E}(\mathsf{X}, \mathsf{Y})$. If for each $f \in \mathsf{X}$ there is a constant C_f such that $\sup_{\lambda \in \Lambda} \| T_\lambda f \| \leqq C_f$, then the operators T_λ are uniformly bounded, i.e. there exists a constant C such that $\sup_{\lambda \in \Lambda} \| T_\lambda \| \leqq C$ (*uniform-boundedness principle*).

Let $\{T_n\}_{n=1}^{\infty}$ be a sequence of operators in $\mathscr{E}(\mathsf{X}, \mathsf{Y})$ such that (i) $\| T_n \| \leqq C$ for all n and (ii) $\lim_{n \to \infty} T_n f$ exists for a dense subset of X. Then $\lim_{n \to \infty} T_n f$ exists for all $f \in \mathsf{X}$ and the limit defines a linear transformation T with $\| T \| \leqq \liminf_{n \to \infty} \| T_n \|$ (*Banach-Steinhaus theorem*).

A bounded linear transformation on X to itself is called an *endomorphism* of X. The space of all endomorphisms of X forms a Banach algebra $\mathscr{E}(\mathsf{X})$, where $\mathscr{E}(\mathsf{X})$ is an algebra with respect to the operations $T_1 + T_2$, αT and $T_1 T_2$. $\mathscr{E}(\mathsf{X})$ has the identity transformation I as unit element and is in general non-commutative.

By a real (or complex) *Hilbert space* H we mean a real (or complex) Banach space for which there is defined on $\mathsf{H} \times \mathsf{H}$ a real (or complex) valued function $\langle f, g \rangle$, called the *inner product* of f and g, with the following properties: (i) $\langle \alpha_1 f_1 + \alpha_2 f_2, g \rangle = \alpha_1 \langle f_1, g \rangle + \alpha_2 \langle f_2, g \rangle$; (ii) $\langle f, g \rangle = \langle g, f \rangle$ (or $= \overline{\langle g, f \rangle}$, the complex conjugate of $\langle g, f \rangle$); (iii) $\langle f, f \rangle = \| f \|^2$.

Linear Functionals and Dual Spaces. The principal result on linear functionals on Banach spaces is the *Hahn-Banach extension theorem:* Given a Banach space X and a bounded linear functional F defined on a linear manifold D of X, then there exists a bounded linear functional f^* on X such that $f^*(f) = F(f)$ for all $f \in \mathsf{D}$, and the norm of f^* on X is equal to the norm of F on D.

The Hahn–Banach theorem has two important corollaries (*existence theorems for bounded linear functionals*):

To each point $f_0 \in \mathsf{X}$, $f_0 \neq \theta$, there exists a bounded linear functional f^* on X such that $f^*(f_0) = \| f_0 \|$ and $\| f^* \| = 1$.

Given a linear manifold D in X and a point $f_1 \in \mathsf{X}$ such that f_1 has positive distance d from D: $d = \inf\{\| f_1 - f \|; f \in \mathsf{D}\}$, then there exists a bounded linear functional f^* on X such that (i) $f^*(\mathsf{D}) = \{0\}$, (ii) $f^*(f_1) = 1$, and $\| f^* \| = 1/d$.

A bounded linear functional on X that vanishes on a dense manifold vanishes identically. Moreover, given two distinct points f_1 and f_2 in X, then there exists at least one bounded linear functional f^* such that $f^*(f_1) \neq f^*(f_2)$, i.e. if f is an element of X such that $f^*(f) = 0$ for all bounded linear functionals on X then $f = \theta$. The norm $\|\cdot\|$ is a continuous real functional on X.

The space X^* of all bounded linear functionals on X is called the *dual* (or *adjoint*) space of X; X^* is a Banach space. The values of the functionals $f^* \in X^*$ at the points $f \in X$, in the following denoted by $\langle f^*, f\rangle$, may be considered as a *bilinear form*

$$\langle f^*, \alpha_1 f_1 + \alpha_2 f_2\rangle = \alpha_1 \langle f^*, f_1\rangle + \alpha_2 \langle f^*, f_2\rangle,$$

$$\langle \alpha_1 f_1^* + \alpha_2 f_2^*, f\rangle = \alpha_1 \langle f_1^*, f\rangle + \alpha_2 \langle f_2^*, f\rangle,$$

$$|\langle f^*, f\rangle| \leqq \|f^*\| \, \|f\|.$$

The dual space of X^*, also called the *second dual* of X, is denoted by X^{**} and its elements by f^{**}. The correspondence $\langle f_0^{**}, f^*\rangle = \langle f^*, f_0\rangle$ $(f^* \in X^*)$ establishes a *natural mapping* $f_0 \to f_0^{**}$ of X onto a linear manifold X_0^{**} of X^{**}. This mapping is one-to-one and norm-preserving and thus an isometric isomorphism of X onto X_0^{**}. In this sense $X \subset X^{**}$. If $X = X^{**}$ under the natural embedding, then X is called *reflexive.* If X^* is separable, so is X. If X is reflexive, the same is true for X^*; also each closed linear manifold of a reflexive space is reflexive.

Let A be any subset of X. The *annihilator* of A in X^* is the set $A^0 = \{f^* \in X^*; \langle f^*, f\rangle = 0 \text{ if } f \in A\}$. If $B \subset X^*$, the annihilator of B in X is the set ${}^0B = \{f \in X; \langle f^*, f\rangle = 0 \text{ if } f^* \in B\}$. If $A \subset X$, ${}^0(A^0)$ is the closed linear hull M spanned by A. Moreover, if $B \subset X^*$ and N is the closed linear hull spanned by B, then $N \subset ({}^0B)^0$. A linear manifold N in X^* is called *saturated* if $N = ({}^0N)^0$. There do exist saturated manifolds of X^* as, for instance, $\{\theta^*\}$, X^* and A^0, where A is any non-empty set in X.

Let H be a Hilbert space. To each bounded linear functional f^* on H there is a $g \in H$ such that $f^*(f) = \langle g, f\rangle$ for all $f \in H$. Moreover $\|f^*\| = \|g\|$. Thus the dual H^* is isometrically isomorphic to H.

Weak Topologies. In addition to the strong topology of a Banach space X we make use of a further topology called the *weak topology* of X. This topology is obtained by taking as a neighborhood base at the zero-element θ all sets of X of the form

$$\mathcal{N}(\theta; f_1^*, f_2^*, \ldots, f_n^*; \varepsilon) = \{f; |\langle f_k^*, f\rangle| < \varepsilon,\ k = 1, 2, \ldots, n\},$$

where $f_1^*, \ldots, f_n^*$ is any finite set in X^* and $\varepsilon > 0$. X is a locally convex space under the weak topology, which is coarser than the strong topology. Specifically, the linear functionals on X which are continuous in the weak topology are precisely the functionals in X^*. We speak of strongly open sets, strong compactness, strong convergence, etc. or simply, of open sets, compactness, convergence, etc. when referring to the strong topology of X, and of weakly open sets, weak compactness, weak convergence, etc. for the weak topology. A sequence $\{f_n\}_{n=1}^{\infty}$ in X is weakly convergent to an $f \in X$: $\underset{n\to\infty}{\text{w-lim}} f_n = f$, if and only if $\langle f^*, f_n\rangle \to \langle f^*, f\rangle$ as $n \to \infty$ for all $f^* \in X^*$. If $\{f_n\}_{n=1}^{\infty}$ converges weakly in X then $\sup_n \|f_n\| < \infty$.

Every strongly convergent sequence in X is weakly convergent. Every weakly closed set in X is strongly closed, but not conversely. However, a linear manifold in X or, more generally, a convex subset in X is weakly closed if and only if it is strongly closed (*theorem of Mazur*). A subset of X is weakly compact if and only if it is weakly sequentially compact (*theorem of Eberlein*). If T is a linear transformation from X to Y, then T is continuous with respect to the strong topologies in X and Y if and only if it is continuous with respect to the weak topologies (*theorem of Banach–Dunford*).

Analogously, one may consider the weak topology of the dual X^* of a Banach space X. However, this topology turns out to be less useful than that obtained when we restrict the functionals to $X \subset X^{**}$; the latter defines the *weak* topology* of X^* for which a neighborhood base at θ^* consists of all sets of the form

$$\mathcal{N}(\theta^*; f_1, f_2, \ldots, f_n; \varepsilon) = \{f^*; |\langle f^*, f_k\rangle| < \varepsilon,\ k = 1, 2, \ldots, n\},$$

where $f_1, \ldots, f_n$ is any finite set in X and $\varepsilon > 0$. The weak* topology for X^* is even coarser than the weak topology. X^* is a locally convex space under the weak* topology, and the linear functionals on X^* which are *weakly* continuous* are precisely the elements of X under the natural mapping. If X is reflexive, then the weak and weak* topology of X^* coincide.

A sequence $\{f_n^*\}_{n=1}^{\infty}$ in X^* is *weakly* convergent* to an $f^* \in X^*$: $\underset{n\to\infty}{\text{w*-lim}} f_n^* = f^*$, if and only if $\langle f_n^*, f\rangle \to \langle f^*, f\rangle$ as $n \to \infty$ for all $f \in X$. If $\{f_n^*\}_{n=1}^{\infty}$ converges weakly* in X^* then $\sup_n \|f_n^*\| < \infty$. A linear manifold N in X^* is *weakly* closed* if and only if it is saturated or, equivalently, if and only if it is *regulary closed*, i.e. to each $f_0^* \notin N$ there exists an $f_0 \in X$ such that $\langle f_0^*, f_0\rangle = 1$ and $\langle f^*, f_0\rangle = 0$ for all $f^* \in N$ (*Taylor–Banach*).

If X is separable, then the unit sphere $\{f^*; \|f^*\| \leqq 1\}$ in X^* is sequentially compact in the weak* topology of X^* (*Banach*). In general, the closed unit sphere of X^* is compact in the weak* topology (*theorem of Alaoglu*). A subset of X^* is *weakly* compact* if and only if it is (strongly) bounded and weakly* closed. A Banach space is reflexive if and only if its closed unit sphere is weakly compact or, more generally, if and only if every bounded set is sequentially weakly compact (*theorems of Kakutani and Eberlein*). A reflexive space X is weakly sequentially complete, i.e. every weak Cauchy sequence has a weak limit point.

Operator Topologies. The linear system of all endomorphisms on a Banach space X was made into a Banach algebra by introducing the topology obtained by the operator norm, in this connection usually called the *uniform operator topology*. Apart from this topology there are two further ones of interest, namely the *strong* and the *weak operator topologies*, under which $\mathscr{E}(\mathsf{X})$ is a locally convex topological algebra in each case. A *strong operator neighborhood base* at the zero operator O is the collection of all sets in $\mathscr{E}(\mathsf{X})$ of the form

$$\mathscr{N}(O; f_1, \ldots, f_n; \varepsilon) = \{T; \|T f_k\| < \varepsilon, \ k = 1, 2, \ldots, n\},$$

where $f_1, f_2, \ldots, f_n$ are n arbitrary elements of X and $\varepsilon > 0$ is arbitrary. Similarly, a *weak operator neighborhood* at O is any set of the form

$$\mathscr{N}(O; f_1, \ldots, f_n; f_1^*, \ldots, f_n^*; \varepsilon) = \{T; |\langle f_k^*, T f_k\rangle| < \varepsilon, \ k = 1, 2, \ldots, n\},$$

where $f_1, \ldots, f_n$ and $f_1^*, \ldots, f_n^*$ are arbitrary elements of X and X^*, respectively. Clearly, the uniform operator topology of $\mathscr{E}(\mathsf{X})$ is finer than the strong operator topology which, in turn, is finer than the weak operator topology.

$\mathscr{E}(\mathsf{X})$ is sequentially complete in the strong operator topology; if, however, X is weakly sequentially complete, then $\mathscr{E}(\mathsf{X})$ is sequentially complete in the weak operator topology. If X is reflexive, then the closed unit sphere in $\mathscr{E}(\mathsf{X})$ is compact in the weak operator topology.

II.

Vector-valued Functions. Let X be a real (or complex) Banach space. A vector-valued function defined on a set E of the real line is a mapping $t \to f(t)$ from E into X. We say that the function $f(t)$ on an open interval (a, b) (which may be finite or infinite) to X is (i) *strongly continuous* at $t = t_0$ if $\lim_{t \to t_0} \|f(t) - f(t_0)\| = 0$, and (ii) *weakly continuous* at $t = t_0$ if $\lim_{t \to t_0} |\langle f^*, f(t) - f(t_0)\rangle| = 0$ for each $f^* \in \mathsf{X}^*$. The vector function $f(t)$ is strongly (weakly) continuous on (a, b) if it is strongly (weakly) continuous at each point $t_0 \in (a, b)$. It is clear from the hierarchy of the two topologies on X that a strongly continuous vector function on (a, b) is weakly continuous. If $t \to f(t)$ is weakly continuous on (a, b) to X, then the scalar-valued function $\langle f^*, f(t)\rangle$ is continuous and thus bounded on each closed finite subinterval $[c, d]$ in (a, b) for each $f^* \in \mathsf{X}^*$. Hence by the uniform-boundedness principle $\|f(t)\|$ is likewise bounded on $[c, d]$. Furthermore, the range of $f(t)$ for $t \in (a, b)$ is contained in the *separable* closed linear hull of X spanned by $\{f(t); t \text{ rational in } (a, b)\}$. A vector-valued function $f(t)$ on (a, b) to X is *strongly (weakly) differentiable* at $t = t_0$ if there exists an element $f'(t_0)$ in X such that the difference quotient $h^{-1}[f(t + h) - f(t)]$ converges strongly (weakly) to $f'(t_0)$ as $h \to 0$. If $f(t)$ is weakly differentiable at $t = t_0$, then $\langle f^*, f(t)\rangle$ is a differentiable scalar-valued function at $t = t_0$ for all $f^* \in X^*$, the converse being in general not true. A strongly (weakly) differentiable vector function is necessarily strongly (weakly) continuous. If $f(t)$ is weakly differentiable on (a, b) and if the weak derivative equals θ on (a, b), then $f(t)$ is a constant vector function.

Likewise the Riemann integral can be extended to vector-valued functions. Let Π denote any partition of the finite closed interval $[a, b]$, $a = t_0 < t_1 < \cdots < t_n = b$ together with the arbitrary points s_k in $t_{k-1} \leqq s_k \leqq t_k$ $(k = 1, 2, \ldots, n)$ and the norm $|\Pi| = \max_k (t_k - t_{k-1})$. If for a vector-valued function $f(t)$ defined on $[a, b]$ to X the limit

$$\lim_{|\Pi|\to 0+} S_\Pi(f; t) = \lim_{|\Pi|\to 0+} \sum_{k=1}^{n} f(s_k)\,(t_k - t_{k-1})$$

exists (independently of the choice of the partition Π) in a given topology of X, we define this limit to be the Riemann integral

$$\int_a^b f(t)\,dt$$

of $f(t)$ over $[a, b]$ relative to the topology of X. In the following we restrict our discussion to the *strong Riemann integral* for vector-valued functions $f(t)$ on $[a, b]$ to X. In this respect one can show in the usual manner: If $t \to f(t)$ on $[a, b]$ to X is strongly continuous, then the strong Riemann integral over $[a, b]$ exists. Moreover:

(a) $\displaystyle\int_a^b [\alpha_1 f_1(t) + \alpha_2 f_2(t)]\,dt = \alpha_1 \int_a^b f_1(t)\,dt + \alpha_2 \int_a^b f_2(t)\,dt \quad (\alpha_1, \alpha_2 \in K)$.

(b) $\displaystyle\int_a^b f(t)\,dt = \int_a^c f(t)\,dt + \int_c^b f(t)\,dt$, where $a < c < b$.

(c) $\displaystyle\left\| \int_a^b f(t)\,dt \right\| \leqq (b - a) \max_{a \leqq t \leqq b} \|f(t)\|$.

(d) $\displaystyle F(t) = \int_a^t f(s)\,ds$ is strongly differentiable and the derivative is again $f(t)$.

(e) If $f_n(t)$ converges to $f(t)$ on $[a, b]$ in the norm as $n \to \infty$ uniformly with respect to t, then

$$\operatorname*{s-lim}_{n\to\infty} \int_a^b f_n(t)\,dt = \int_a^b f(t)\,dt.$$

(f) If T is a closed linear operator with domain $\mathsf{D} \subset \mathsf{X}$ to Y, if $f(t) \in \mathsf{D}$ for each $t \in [a, b]$, and if $[Tf](t)$ is also strongly continuous on $[a, b]$ to Y then

$$T\left[\int_a^b f(t)\,dt\right] = \int_a^b [Tf](t)\,dt.$$

In the case where the Banach space is the Banach algebra $\mathscr{E}(\mathsf{X})$ we speak of the mapping $t \to T(t)$ from a set E of the real line to $\mathscr{E}(\mathsf{X})$ as an *operator-valued function*. Analogously as for vector functions, the operator function $T(t)$ on (a, b) to $\mathscr{E}(\mathsf{X})$ is (i) *continuous in the uniform operator topology at* $t = t_0$ if $\lim_{t \to t_0} \| T(t) - T(t_0) \| = 0$, (ii) *continuous in the strong operator topology at* $t = t_0$ if $\lim_{t \to t_0} \| T(t) f - T(t_0) f \| = 0$ for all $f \in \mathsf{X}$, and (iii) *continuous in the weak operator topology at* $t = t_0$ if $\lim_{t \to t_0} |\langle f^*, T(t) f - T(t_0) f \rangle| = 0$ for all $f^* \in \mathsf{X}^*$ and all $f \in \mathsf{X}$. If $T(t)$ is an operator function continuous in the weak operator topology on (a, b), then $\| T(t) \|$ is bounded on each closed finite subinterval of (a, b). However, in contrast to vector functions the range need not be contained in a separable manifold of $\mathscr{E}(\mathsf{X})$. For an operator function on (a, b) to $\mathscr{E}(\mathsf{X})$ there are the three possibilities for defining a derivative at a point $t = t_0$ according to the three types of operator topologies of $\mathscr{E}(\mathsf{X})$. Also, if $t \to T(t)$ is continuous in the uniform operator topology from the finite interval $[a, b]$ to $\mathscr{E}(\mathsf{X})$, then the Riemann integral

$$\int_a^b T(t)\,dt$$

of $T(t)$ over $[a, b]$ exists in the uniform operator topology. Obviously, this integral possesses the properties (a)—(e) (to be understood in the appropriate sense) formulated above for the strong Riemann integral of vector-valued functions. Moreover, if $T(t)$ is continuous in the strong operator topology on $[a, b]$, then the Riemann integral $\int_a^b T(t)\,dt$ of $T(t)$ over $[a, b]$ exists in the strong operator topology and

$$\left[\int_a^b T(t)\,dt\right] f = \int_a^b T(t) f\,dt \qquad (f \in \mathsf{X}).$$

The latter assertions hold, since $T(t) f$ is a strongly continuous vector-valued function on $[a, b]$ to X for each $f \in \mathsf{X}$. If $T(t)$ is continuous in the strong operator topology on $[a, b]$ to $\mathscr{E}(\mathsf{X})$, then for $t, t + h \in [a, b]$

$$\operatorname*{s-lim}_{h \to 0} \frac{1}{h} \int_t^{t+h} T(u) f\,du = T(t) f \qquad (f \in \mathsf{X}).$$

The extensions of the above definitions to *Riemann–Stieltjes integrals* for vector (or operator) valued functions: $\int_a^b f(t)\,d\mu(t)$ $\left(\text{or} \int_a^b T(t)\,d\mu(t)\right)$, where μ is a scalar-valued function of bounded variation on $[a, b]$, are immediate.

Vector-valued Holomorphic Functions. Here we assume X to be a complex Banach space. Let G be a given open domain in the complex ζ-plane, and $f(\zeta)$ be a vector-valued function on G to X, $T(\zeta)$ an operator-valued function on G to $\mathscr{E}(X)$. From the foregoing paragraph it is obvious what we mean when speaking of strong (weak) continuity or strong (weak) differentiability with respect to the complex variable ζ of $f(\zeta)$ at $\zeta = \zeta_0$ in G. Similar remarks apply to continuity, differentiability of $T(\zeta)$ at $\zeta = \zeta_0$ in G in the uniform (strong, weak) operator topology for $\mathscr{E}(X)$. The function $f(\zeta)$ on G to X is said to be *strongly* (*weakly*) *holomorphic* on G if it is strongly (weakly) differentiable at each point ζ of G; $T(\zeta)$ on G to $\mathscr{E}(X)$ is said to be *holomorphic in the uniform* (*strong, weak*) *operator topology* on G if it is differentiable on G in the uniform (strong, weak) operator topology. The remarkable fact here is that the various definitions of a holomorphic vector (or operator) function on a domain G in the ζ-plane are equivalent to another. Moreover, one has: The function $f(\zeta)$ is strongly holomorphic on G if and only if the complex-valued function $\langle f^*, f(\zeta)\rangle$ is holomorphic in the usual sense for all $f^* \in X^*$; $T(\zeta)$ is holomorphic on G in the uniform operator topology if and only if $\langle f^*, T(\zeta)\, f\rangle$ is holomorphic on G in the usual sense for all $f \in X$ and $f^* \in X^*$ (*Dunford–Hille–Taylor*). The proof of this result is a beautiful application of the uniform-boundedness principle. Thus in the following we may simply speak of a holomorphic vector (or operator) function. Furthermore, we may restrict ourselves to vector-valued holomorphic functions.

Many results of the classical theory of analytic functions carry over to vector-valued holomorphic functions. We only formulate those which are of importance in the book. For this purpose, let C be a rectifiable curve in the ζ-plane given by $\zeta(t)$, $0 \leqq t \leqq 1$, where $\zeta(t)$ is continuous and of bounded variation on $[0, 1]$. If $f(\zeta)$ is strongly continuous on C to X, then the strong vector-valued Riemann–Stieltjes integral

$$\int_0^1 f[\zeta(t)]\,d\zeta(t) \equiv \int_C f(\zeta)\,d\zeta$$

exists and

$$\langle f^*, \int_C f(\zeta)\,d\zeta\rangle = \int_C \langle f^*, f(\zeta)\rangle\,d\zeta \qquad (f^* \in X^*).$$

If $f(\zeta)$ is holomorphic on G to X, then

$$\int_C f(\zeta)\,d\zeta = 0$$

for every rectifiable Jordan curve C in G such that the interior of C also belongs to G (*Cauchy's integral theorem*).

Under the same hypotheses upon $f(\zeta)$ on C and the curve C, having in addition positive orientation, we have

$$f^{(n)}(\zeta_0) = \frac{n!}{2\pi i} \int_C \frac{f(\zeta)}{(\zeta - \zeta_0)^{n+1}} d\zeta \qquad (n = 0, 1, \ldots)$$

for any point ζ_0 in the interior of C (*Cauchy's integral formula*).

Let $f(\zeta)$ be holomorphic on G to X. The *Taylor expansion* of $f(\zeta)$ at a point ζ_0 of G converges strongly in a suitable neighborhood sphere $\{\zeta; |\zeta - \zeta_0| < \varrho\}$ of ζ_0, where $\varrho = \varrho(\zeta_0) > 0$:

$$f(\zeta) = \sum_{n=0}^{\infty} \frac{f^{(n)}(\zeta_0)}{n!} (\zeta - \zeta_0)^n.$$

If $f(\zeta)$ is holomorphic in the whole ζ-plane such that $\sup_{\zeta} \| f(\zeta) \| < \infty$, then $f(\zeta)$ reduces to a constant vector function (*Liouville's theorem*).

Mutatis mutandis, all the fundamental theorems of classical function theory have their counterparts for holomorphic vector functions.

The Bochner Integral. Let X be a real (or complex) Banach space, and let (R, μ) be a totally σ-finite measure space (see P. R. HALMOS [1], A. C. ZAANEN [2]). A vector-valued function $f(t)$ defined on R with values in X is said to be *finitely-valued* in R if it is a constant vector $\neq \theta$ on each of a finite number of disjoint measurable sets E_k and equal to θ on $R - \bigcup_k E_k$. If the set of R for which $\| f(t) \| > 0$ is of finite measure then $f(t)$ is a *simple function*. A function $f(t)$ on R to X is called *separably-valued* in R if its range $f(R)$ is separable, and *almost separably-valued* if there is a set E_0 of measure zero such that $f(R - E_0)$ is separable. Moreover, $f(t)$ is said to be *strongly measurable* on R if there is a sequence $\{f_n(t)\}_{n=1}^{\infty}$ of simple functions which converges strongly almost everywhere in R to $f(t)$ (i.e. there is a set E_0 of measure zero such that $\lim_{n\to\infty} \| f(t) - f_n(t) \| = 0$ for each $t \in R - E_0$) and $f(t)$ is *weakly measurable* if the scalar-valued function $\langle f^*, f(t) \rangle$ is measurable for each $f^* \in X^*$. The basic result in this respect is: A vector-valued function $f(t)$ on R to X is strongly measurable if and only if it is weakly measurable and almost separably-valued (*Pettis*). If $f(t)$ is strongly measurable we have as a consequence that the scalar-valued function $\| f(t) \|$ is measurable. Also, if X is separable, then strong and weak measurability of a vector-valued function are equivalent notions.

If $f(t)$ is a simple function on R to X: $f(t) = \sum_{k=1}^{n} f_k \chi_{E_k}(t)$, $\chi_{E_k}(t)$ being the characteristic function of the set E_k, we define the Bochner integral (B) $\int_E f(t)\, d\mu$ of $f(t)$ over an arbitrary measurable set E of R by the sum $\sum_{k=1}^{n} f_k \mu(E \cap E_k)$. In general, a function $f(t)$ on R to X is said to be *Bochner integrable,* if there exists a sequence $\{f_n(t)\}_{n=1}^{\infty}$ of simple functions on R to X which converges strongly almost everywhere to $f(t)$ in such a way that

$$\lim_{n\to\infty} \int_{\mathrm{R}} \| f(t) - f_n(t) \| \, d\mu = 0.$$

By definition, the *Bochner integral* of $f(t)$ over E (any measurable set in R) is

$$(\mathrm{B}) \int_E f(t) \, d\mu = \operatorname*{s\text{-}lim}_{n\to\infty} (\mathrm{B}) \int_E f_n(t) \, d\mu.$$

This definition is meaningful, since $f(t)$ is strongly measurable in R, and consequently the scalar-valued functions $\| f(t) - f_n(t) \|$, $n = 1, 2, \ldots$, are measurable, since the strong limit of $(\mathrm{B}) \int_E f_n(t) \, dt$ exists, and since this limit is independent of the particular sequence of simple functions. A necessary and sufficient condition that $f(t)$ on R to X is Bochner integrable ist that $f(t)$ is strongly measurable and that $\int_R \| f(t) \| \, dt < \infty$ (*Bochner*).

We denote the set of all Bochner integrable functions on R to X (with respect to the measure μ) by $\mathscr{L}(\mathrm{R}; \mathsf{X}; \mu)$. If, in particular, X is the field of the real (or complex) numbers, the Bochner integral reduces to the classical Lebesgue integral; in this case we simply write $\mathscr{L}(\mathrm{R}; \mu)$ for the set of all Lebesgue integrable functions on R. $\mathscr{L}(\mathrm{R}; \mathsf{X}; \mu)$ forms a real (or complex) linear system under the natural definitions of addition and scalar multiplication, and the integral $(\mathrm{B}) \int_E f(t) \, dt$, E a measurable set in R, defines a linear transformation from $\mathscr{L}(\mathrm{R}; \mathsf{X}; \mu)$ to X. Moreover, the following theorems hold for the Bochner integral:

If $f(t) \in \mathscr{L}(\mathrm{R}; \mathsf{X}; \mu)$, then

$$\left\| (\mathrm{B}) \int_E f(t) \, d\mu \right\| \leq \int_E \| f(t) \| \, d\mu.$$

If $\{f_n(t)\}_{n=1}^{\infty} \subset \mathscr{L}(\mathrm{R}; \mathsf{X}; \mu)$ and

$$\lim_{n, m\to\infty} \int_{\mathrm{R}} \| f_n(t) - f_m(t) \| \, d\mu = 0,$$

then there exists a function $f(t) \in \mathscr{L}(\mathrm{R}; \mathsf{X}; \mu)$, uniquely determined except on a set of measure zero, such that

$$\lim_{n\to\infty} \int_{\mathrm{R}} \| f(t) - f_n(t) \| \, d\mu = 0.$$

If the sequence $\{f_n(t)\}_{n=1}^{\infty}$ in $\mathscr{L}(\mathrm{R}; \mathsf{X}; \mu)$ converges strongly almost everywhere to a limit function $f(t)$, and if there is a scalar-valued function $F(t) \in \mathscr{L}(\mathrm{R}; \mu)$ such that $\|f_n(t)\| \leqq |F(t)|$ for almost all t and all $n = 1, 2, \ldots$, then $f(t) \in \mathscr{L}(\mathrm{R}; \mathsf{X}; \mu)$ and

$$(\mathrm{B}) \int_E f(t)\, d\mu = \operatorname*{s-lim}_{n\to\infty} (\mathrm{B}) \int_E f_n(t)\, d\mu$$

(*dominated convergence theorem*).

Let $\{E_n\}_{n=1}^{\infty}$ be a sequence of mutually disjoint measurable sets in R. Then for any $f(t) \in \mathscr{L}(\mathrm{R}; \mathsf{X}; \mu)$

$$(\mathrm{B}) \int_{\bigcup_{n=1}^{\infty} E_n} f(t)\, d\mu = \sum_{n=1}^{\infty} (\mathrm{B}) \int_{E_n} f(t)\, d\mu,$$

where the sum on the right-hand side is absolutely summable.

If $f(t) \in \mathscr{L}(\mathrm{R}; \mathsf{X}; \mu)$, then the integral $(\mathrm{B}) \int_E f(t)\, d\mu$ is *absolutely continuous*, i.e. $\lim_{\mu(E)\to 0+} \|(\mathrm{B}) \int_E f(t)\, d\mu\| = 0$.

Let T be a closed linear operator with domain $\mathsf{D} \subset \mathsf{X}$ and range in Y. If $f(t) \in \mathscr{L}(\mathrm{R}; \mathsf{X}; \mu)$ with values in D and $[Tf](t) \in \mathscr{L}(\mathrm{R}; \mathsf{Y}; \mu)$, then $(\mathrm{B}) \int_E f(t)\, d\mu$ is in D and

$$T\left[(\mathrm{B}) \int_E f(t)\, d\mu\right] = (\mathrm{B}) \int_E [Tf](t)\, d\mu.$$

If we identify (pairwise) strongly measurable functions on R to X which differ only on sets of measure zero, then (the linear system) $\mathscr{L}(\mathrm{R}; \mathsf{X}; \mu)$ becomes a Banach space under the norm

$$\|f(\cdot)\| = \int_{\mathrm{R}} \|f(t)\|\, d\mu.$$

In this setting we write $\mathsf{L}(\mathrm{R}; \mathsf{X}; \mu)$ instead of $\mathscr{L}(\mathrm{R}; \mathsf{X}; \mu)$. More generally, the linear system of all (classes of) strongly measurable functions $f(t)$ on R to X (which are equal to another almost everywhere) such that $\int_{\mathrm{R}} \|f(t)\|^p\, d\mu < \infty$ for $1 \leqq p < \infty$ and $\operatorname*{ess\,sup}_{t\in\mathrm{R}} \|f(t)\| < \infty$ for $p = \infty$, forms a Banach space $\mathsf{L}^p(\mathrm{R}; \mathsf{X}; \mu)$ under the norm

$$\|f(\cdot)\|_p = \left\{\int_{\mathrm{R}} \|f(t)\|^p\, d\mu\right\}^{1/p}, \quad \|f(\cdot)\|_\infty = \operatorname*{ess\,sup}_{t\in\mathrm{R}} \|f(t)\|.$$

If X is reflexive and $1 < p < \infty$, so is $\mathsf{L}^p(\mathrm{R}; \mathsf{X}; \mu)$ and the dual to $\mathsf{L}^p(\mathrm{R}; \mathsf{X}; \mu)$ is simply $\mathsf{L}^{p'}(\mathrm{R}; \mathsf{X}^*; \mu)$, $p^{-1} + p'^{-1} = 1$ (*Phillips*).

It is possible to extend the above considerations to Bochner integrals of operator-valued functions.

Bibliography

ACHIESER, N. I.
[1] *Theory of Approximation.* New York: Frederick Ungar 1956, x + 307 pp. (Transl. of the Russian edition, Moscow 1947)

AKILOV, G. P.: *see Kantorovich, L. V.*

APPELL, P.
[1] Sur l'équation $\partial^2 z/\partial x^2 - \partial z/\partial y = 0$ et la théorie de la chaleur. *J. de Math.* (4) **8,** 187—216 (1892).

ARDUINI, P.
[1] Sull'equivalenza di certi funzionali della teoria dell'interpolazione tra spazi di Banach. *Ricerche Mat.* **11,** 51—60 (1962).

ARONSZAJN, N.
[1] Potentiels besseliens. *Ann. Inst. Fourier (Grenoble)* **15,** 43—58 (1965).

ARONSZAJN, N. – E. GAGLIARDO
[1] Interpolation spaces and interpolation methods. *Ann. Mat. Pura Appl.* (4) **68,** 51—118 (1965).

ARONSZAJN, N. – F. MULLA – P. SZEPTYCKI
[1] On spaces of potentials connected with L^p classes. *Ann. Inst. Fourier (Grenoble)* **13,** 211—306 (1963).

ARONSZAJN, N. – K. T. SMITH
[1] Functional spaces and functional completion. *Ann. Inst. Fourier (Grenoble)* **6,** 125—185 (1955—1956).
[2] Theory of Bessel potentials I. (French summary) *Ann. Inst. Fourier (Grenoble)* **11,** 385—475 (1961).

BALAKRISHNAN, A. V.
[1] An operational calculus for infinitesimal generators of semigroups. *Trans. Amer. Math. Soc.* **91,** 330—353 (1959).
[2] Fractional powers of closed operators and the semigroups generated by them. *Pacific. J. Math.* **10,** 419—437 (1960).

BANACH, S.
[1] *Théorie des opérations linéaires.* Warsaw 1932. Reprinted by Chelsea Publ. Co., New York, xii + 259 pp.

BERENS, H.
[1] Approximationssätze für Halbgruppenoperatoren in intermediären Räumen. *Schr. Math. Inst. Univ. Münster* **32** (1964), 59 pp. (Dissertation, Aachen)
[2] Equivalent representations for the infinitesimal generator of higher orders in semi-group theory. *Nederl. Akad. Wetensch. Indag. Math.* **27,** 497—512 (1965).
[3] Interpolationsmethoden bei der Behandlung von Approximationsproblemen für Halbgruppen von Operatoren auf Banachräumen. (in preparation)

BERENS, H. – P. L. BUTZER
[1] On the best approximation for singular integrals by Laplace-transform methods. *Bull. Amer. Math. Soc.* **70,** 180—184 (1964).

[2] Approximation theorems for semi-group operators in intermediate spaces. *Bull. Amer. Math. Soc.* **70,** 689—692 (1964).

[3] On the best approximation for singular integrals by Laplace-transform methods. (Proceedings of a Conference at Oberwolfach 1963.) In *On Approximation Theory*, edited by P. L. BUTZER and J. KOREVAAR, ISNM 5, pp. 24—42. Basel: Birkhäuser 1964.

[4] Über die Stetigkeit von Halbgruppen von Operatoren in intermediären Räumen. *Math. Ann.* **163,** 204—211 (1966).

BERENS, H. – P. L. BUTZER – U. WESTPHAL

[1] Representation of fractional powers of infinitesimal generators of semi-groups. *Bull. Amer. Math. Soc.* **74** (1968). (in print)

BERENS, H. – E. GÖRLICH

[1] Über einen Darstellungssatz für Funktionen als Fourierintegrale und Anwendungen in der Fourieranalysis. *Tôhoku Math. J.* **18,** 429—453 (1966).

BERENS, H. – U. WESTPHAL

[1] Zur Charakterisierung von Ableitungen nichtganzer Ordnung im Rahmen der Laplacetransformation. *Math. Nachr.* (in print)

[2] A Cauchy problem for a generalized wave equation. (in preparation)

BERNSTEIN, F.

[1] Die Integralgleichung der elliptischen Thetanullfunktion. *S.-B. Preuss. Akad. Wiss. Phys.-Math. Kl.*, pp. 735—747 (1920).

BERNSTEIN, S. N.

[1] Démonstration du théorème de Weierstrass, fondée sur le calcul des probabilitiés. *Commun. Soc. Math. Kharkov* (2) **13,** 1—2 (1912/13).

BERS, L. – F. JOHN – M. SCHECHTER

[1] *Partial Differential Equations*. Lectures in Applied Mathematics, Vol. III. New York/London/Sydney: Interscience 1964, xiii + 343 pp.

BESOV, O. V.

[1] On some families of functional spaces. Imbedding and extension theorems. (Russian) *Dokl. Akad. Nauk SSSR* **126,** 1163—1165 (1959).

[2] Investigation of a family of function spaces in connection with theorems of imbedding and extension. (Russian) *Trudy. Mat. Inst. Steklov* **60,** 42—81 (1961) = *Amer. Math. Soc. Transl.* (2) **40,** 85—126 (1964).

BOAS, R. P., JR.

[1] *Integrability Theorems for Trigonometric Transforms*. Berlin/Heidelberg/New York: Springer 1967, 65 pp.

BOCHNER, S.

[1] *Vorlesung über Fouriersche Integrale*. Leipzig: Akademie-Verlag 1932. Reprinted by Chelsea Publ. Co., New York 1948, viii + 227 pp.

[2] Diffusion equation and stochastic processes. *Proc. Nat. Acad. Sci. USA* **35,** 368—370 (1949).

[3] Quasi-analytic functions, Laplace operator, positive kernels. *Ann. of Math.* (2) **51,** 68—91 (1950).

BOCHNER, S. – K. CHANDRASEKHARAN

[1] *Fourier Transforms*. Annals of Mathematics Studies, no. 19. Princeton, N. J.: Princeton University Press 1949, ix + 219 pp.

BOHMAN, H.

[1] On approximation of continuous and of analytic functions. *Ark. Mat.* **2,** 43—56 (1952).

BRUCKNER, A. M. – J. L. LEONARD

[1] Derivatives. *Amer. Math. Monthly* **73,** 24—56 (1966).

Bruschi, M.: *see Cotlar, M.*

Buchwalter, H.

[*1*] Saturation de certains procédés de sommation. *C. R. Acad. Sci. Paris* **248,** 909—912 (1959).

[*2*] Saturation et distributions. *C. R. Acad. Sci. Paris* **250,** 3562—3564 (1960).

Butzer, P. L.: *see also Berens, H.*

[*1*] Linear combinations of Bernstein polynomials. *Canad. J. Math.* **5,** 559—567 (1953).

[*2*] On the extensions of Bernstein polynomials to the infinite interval. *Proc. Amer. Math. Soc.* **5,** 547—553 (1954).

[*3*] Sur la théorie des demi-groupes et classes de saturation de certaines intégrales singulières. *C. R. Acad. Sci. Paris* **243,** 1473—1475 (1956).

[*4*] Über den Grad der Approximation des Identitätsoperators durch Halbgruppen von linearen Operatoren und Anwendungen auf die Theorie der singulären Integrale. *Math. Ann.* **133,** 410—425 (1957).

[*5*] Sur le rôle de la transformation de Fourier dans quelques problèmes d'approximation. *C. R. Acad. Sci. Paris* **249,** 2467—2469 (1959).

[*6*] Representation and approximation of functions by general singular integrals. *Nederl. Akad. Wetensch. Indag. Math.* **22,** 1—24 (1960).

[*7*] Fourier-transform methods in the theory of approximation. *Arch. Rational Mech. Anal.* **5,** 390—415 (1960).

[*8*] On some theorems of Hardy, Littlewood and Titchmarsh. *Math. Ann.* **142,** 259—269 (1961).

[*9*] On Dirichlet's problem for the half-space and the behavior of its solution on the boundary. *J. Math. Anal. Appl.* **2,** 86—96 (1961).

[*10*] Beziehungen zwischen den Riemannschen, Taylorschen und gewöhnlichen Ableitungen reellwertiger Funktionen. *Math. Ann.* **144,** 275—298 (1961).

[*11*] Saturation and Approximation. *SIAM J. Numer. Anal. Ser. B*, **1,** 2—10 (1964).

[*12*] Integral transform methods in the theory of approximation. (Proceedings of a Conference at Oberwolfach 1963.) In *On Approximation Theory,* edited by: P. L. Butzer and J. Korevaar, ISNM 5, pp. 12—23. Basel: Birkhäuser 1964.

[*13*] Semi-groups of bounded linear operators and approximation. *Séminaire d'Analyse Harmonique,* Université de Paris, Faculté des Sciences d'Orsay, Exposé n⁰ 15, 1965/66, pp. 1—15.

Butzer, P. L. – E. Görlich

[*1*] Saturationsklassen und asymptotische Eigenschaften trigonometrischer singulärer Integrale. *Festschr. Gedächtnisfeier K. Weierstrass,* pp. 339—392. Köln: Westdeutscher Verlag 1966.

[*2*] Characterizations of Favard classes for functions of several variables. *Bull. Amer. Math. Soc.* **74** (1968). (in print)

Butzer, P. L. – J. Korevaar

[*1*] *On Approximation Theory.* Proceedings of a Conference at Oberwolfach 1963. ISNM Vol. 5. Basel: Birkhäuser 1964, xvi + 261 pp.

Butzer, P. L. – W. Kozakiewicz

[*1*] On the Riemann derivatives for integrable functions. *Canad. J. Math.* **6,** 572—581 (1954).

Butzer, P. L. – R. J. Nessel

[*1*] Favard classes for n-dimensional singular integrals. *Bull. Amer. Math. Soc.* **72,** 493—498 (1966).

[*2*] Contributions to the theory of saturation for singular integrals in several variables I. General theory. *Nederl. Akad. Wetensch. Indag. Math.* **28,** 515—531 (1966).

[*3*] *Fourier Analysis and Approximation.* (book in preparation)

BUTZER, P. L. – S. PAWELKE

[*1*] Semi-groups and resolvent operators. (in preparation)

BUTZER, P. L. – K. SCHERER

[*1*] *Interpolationsmethoden in der Theorie der Besten Approximation und der linearen Summationsprozesse.* Forschungsberichte des Landes Nordrhein-Westfalen. Köln: Westdeutscher Verlag. (monograph in print)

BUTZER, P. L. – G. SUNOUCHI

[*1*] Approximation theorems for the solution of Fourier's problem and Dirichlet's problem. *Math. Ann.* **155,** 316—330 (1964).

BUTZER, P. L. – H. G. TILLMANN

[*1*] An approximation theorem for semi-groups of operators. *Bull. Amer. Math. Soc.* **66,** 191—193 (1960).

[*2*] Approximation theorems for semi-groups of bounded linear transformations. *Math. Ann.* **140,** 256—262 (1960).

BUTZER, P. L. – W. TREBELS

[*1*] *Hilberttransformation, gebrochene Integration und Differentiation.* Forschungsberichte des Landes Nordrhein-Westfalen, Nr. 1889. Köln: Westdeutscher Verlag 1967, 82 pp.

[*2*] Hilbert transforms, fractional integration and differentiation. *Bull. Amer. Math. Soc.* **74** (1968). (in print)

CALDERÓN, A. P.

[*1*] Lebesgue spaces of differentiable functions and distributions. *Proc. Sympos. Pure Math., Vol. IV*, pp. 33—49. Providence, R. I.: Amer. Math. Soc. 1961.

[*2*] Intermediate spaces and interpolation. (Conference on *Functional Analysis,* Warsaw 1960) *Studia Math.* (*Ser. Specjalna*) *Zeszyt* **1,** 31—34 (1963).

[*3*] Intermediate spaces and interpolation, the complex method. *Studia Math.* **24,** 113—190 (1964).

[*4*] Singular integrals. *Bull. Amer. Math. Soc.* **72,** 427—465 (1966).

CALDERÓN, A. P. – A. ZYGMUND

[*1*] A note on the interpolation of linear operations. *Studia Math.* **12,** 194—204 (1951).

[*2*] On the existence of certain singular integrals. *Acta Math.* **88,** 85—139 (1952).

[*3*] Singular integrals and periodic functions. *Studia Math.* **14,** 249—271 (1954).

[*4*] A note on the interpolation of sublinear operations. *Amer. J. Math.* **78,** 282—288 (1956).

CARSLAW, H. S.

[*1*] *Introduction to the Theory of Fourier's Series and Integrals and the Mathematical Theory of the Conduction of Heat.* London 1906, xvii + 434 pp.

CATON, W. B. – E. HILLE

[*1*] Laguerre polynomials and Laplace integrals. *Duke Math. J.* **12,** 217—242 (1945).

CESÀRO, E.

[*1*] Sur un problème de propagation de la chaleur. *Acad. Roy. Belg. Bull. Cl. Sci.* 1902, pp. 387—404.

CHANDRASEKHARAN, K.: *see Bochner, S.*

CHAUNDY, TH.

[*1*] *The Differential Calculus.* Oxford: Oxford University Press 1935, xiv + 459 pp.

CHENEY, E. W.

[*1*] *Introduction to Approximation Theory.* New York/St. Louis/San Francisco/Toronto/London/Sydney: McGraw-Hill 1966, xii + 259 pp.

CHENEY, E. W. – A. SHARMA

[*1*] Bernstein power series. *Canad. J. Math.* **16,** 241—252 (1964).

CHUNG, K. L.
[1] On the exponential formulas of semi-group theory. *Math. Scand.* **10,** 153—162 (1962).
CIESIELSKI, Z.
[1] On the isomorphisms of the spaces H_α and m. *Bull. Acad. Polon. Sci. Sér. Sci. Math. Astronom. Phys.* **8,** 217—222 (1960).
CLIFFORD, A. H. – G. B. PRESTON
[1] *The Algebraic Theory of Semigroups, Vol. I.* Mathematical Surveys, No. 7. Providence, R. I.: Amer. Math. Soc. 1961, xv + 224 pp.
COOPER, J. L. B.
[1] One-parameter semi-groups of isometric operators in Hilbert space. *Ann. of Math.* (2) **48,** 827—842 (1947).
[2] Coordinated linear spaces. *Proc. London Math. Soc.* (3) **3,** 305—327 (1953).
[3] Some problems in the theory of Fourier transforms. *Arch. Rational Mech. Anal.* **14,** 213—216 (1963).
COTLAR, M. – M. BRUSCHI
[1] On the convexity theorems of Riesz-Thorin and Marcinkiewicz. *Rev. Un. Mat. Argentina* **18,** 162—172 (1957).
COURANT, R. – D. HILBERT
[1] *Methods of Mathematical Physics. Vol. I and Vol. II: Partial Differential Equations.* New York: Interscience 1953, xv + 561 pp. and 1962, xxii + 830pp.
CUPELLO, L.
[1] Sulla condizione di Hölder in forma integrale. *Riv. Mat. Univ. Parma* (2) **4,** 221—253 (1963).
DAVIS, P. J.
[1] *Interpolation and Approximation.* New York/Toronto/London: Blaisdell 1963, xiv + 393 pp.
DEUTSCH, N.
[1] Interpolation dans les espaces vectoriels topologiques localement convexes. *C. R. Acad. Sci. Paris* **257,** 3796—3799 (1963).
[2] Construction duale de la construction d'une note précédente. *C. R. Acad. Sci. Paris* **257,** 4114—4116 (1963).
DIEUDONNÉ, J.
[1] Sur les espaces de Köthe. *J. Analyse Math.* **1,** 81—115 (1951).
[2] *Foundations of Modern Analysis.* New York/London: Academic Press 1960, xiv + 361 pp.
DOETSCH, G.
[1] Transzendente Additionstheoreme der elliptischen Thetafunktionen und andere Thetarelationen vom Faltungstypus. *Math. Ann.* **90,** 19—25 (1923).
[2] Probleme aus der Theorie der Wärmeleitung. 3. Mitteilung: Der lineare Wärmeleiter mit beliebiger Anfangstemperatur. Die zeitliche Fortsetzung des Wärmezustandes. *Math. Z.* **25,** 608—626 (1926).
[3] Thetarelationen als Konsequenzen des Huygensschen und Eulerschen Prinzips in der Theorie der Wärmeleitung. *Math. Z.* **40,** 613—628 (1935).
[4] Integration von Differentialgleichungen vermittels der endlichen Fourier-Transformationen. *Math. Ann.* **112,** 52—68 (1935).
[5] *Theorie und Anwendung der Laplace-Transformation.* Berlin: Springer 1937, 436 pp.
[6] *Handbuch der Laplace-Transformation. Bd. I: Theorie der Laplace-Transformation, Bd. II und III: Anwendungen der Laplace-Transformation.* Basel: Birkhäuser 1950—1956, 581, 436 und 300 pp.

DUNFORD, N.
[1] On one-parameter groups of linear transformations. *Ann. of Math.* (2), **39**, 569—573 (1938).
DUNFORD, N. – J. T. SCHWARTZ
[1] *Linear Operators. Vol. I: General Theory, and Vol. II: Spectral Theory.* New York: Interscience 1958, xiv + 858 pp. and 1963, ix + pp. 859—1923.
DUNFORD, N. – I. E. SEGAL
[1] Semi-groups of operators and the Weierstrass theorem. *Bull. Amer. Math. Soc.* **52**, 911—914 (1946).
DYNKIN, E. B.
[1] Markov processes and semi-groups of operators. (Russian) *Teor. Veroyatnost. i Primenen.* **1**, 25—37 (1956).
[2] *Markov Processes. Vol. I.* Berlin/Göttingen/Heidelberg: Springer 1965, viii + 365 pp. (Transl. of the Russian edition, 1962)
EDWARDS, R. E.
[1] *Functional Analysis: Theory and Applications.* New York/Chicago/San Francisco/Toronto/London: Holt, Rinehart and Winston 1965, xiii + 781 pp.
ELLIOT, J. – W. FELLER
[1] Stochastic processes connected with harmonic functions. *Trans. Amer. Math. Soc.* **82**, 392—420 (1956).
ELLIS, H. W. – I. HALPERIN
[1] Function spaces determined by a levelling length function. *Canad. J. Math.* **5**, 576—592 (1953).
EVANS, G. C.
[1] *The Logarithmic Potential. Discontinuous Dirichlet and Neumann Problems.* Amer. Math. Soc. Colloq. Publ. Vol. 6, New York 1927, viii + 150 pp.
FAVARD, J.
[1] Sur les multiplicateurs d'interpolation. *J. Math. Pures Appl.* (9) **23**, 219—247 (1944).
[2] Sur l'approximation des fonctions d'une variable réelle. (Colloques Internationaux d'Analyse Harmonique 1947) *Publ. Centre National de la Recherche Scientifique, Paris* **15**, 97—100 (1949).
[3] Sur l'approximation dans les espaces vectoriels. *Ann. Mat. Pura Appl.* (4) **29**, 259—291 (1949).
FELLER, W.: *see also Elliot, J.*
[1] The parabolic differential equations and the associated semi-groups of transformations. *Ann. of Math.* (2) **55**, 468—519 (1952).
[2] On a generalization of Marcel Riesz' potentials and the semi-groups generated by them. *Comm. Sém. Math. Univ. Lund. Tome Supplémentaire,* 72—81 (1952).
[3] Semi-groups of transformations in general weak topologies. *Ann. of Math.* (2) **57**, 287—308 (1953).
[4] On the generation of unbounded semi-groups of bounded linear operators. *Ann. of Math.* (2) **58**, 166—174 (1953).
[5] *An Introduction to Probability Theory and Its Applications. Vol. I* (2nd edition) *and Vol. II.* New York/London: John Wiley & Sons 1957, xv + 461 pp. and 1966, xviii + 626 pp.
FOIAŞ, C.: *see also Sz.-Nagy, B.*
[1] Remarques sur les semi-groupes distributions d'opérateurs normaux. *Portugal. Math.* **19**, 227—242 (1960).
FOIAŞ, C. – G. GUSSI – V. POENARU
[1] On the basic approximation theorem for semigroups of linear operators. *Proc. Nat. Acad. Sci. USA* **43**, 616—618 (1957).

FOIAŞ, C. – J. L. LIONS
[1] Sur certains théorèmes d'interpolation. *Acta Sci. Math.* (*Szeged*) **22,** 269—282 (1961).
FRIEDMAN, A.
[1] *Generalized Functions and Partial Differential Equations.* Englewood Cliffs: Prentice-Hall 1963, xii + 340 pp.
FUKAMIYA, M.
[1] On one-parameter groups of operators. *Proc. Imp. Acad. Tokyo* **16,** 262—265 (1940).
GAGLIARDO, E.: *see also Aronszajn, N.*
[1] Caratterizzazioni delle tracce sulla frontiera relative ad alcune classi di funzioni in *n* variabili. *Rend. Sem. Mat. Univ. Padova* **27,** 284—305 (1957).
[2] Proprietà di alcune classi di funzioni in più variabili. *Ricerche Mat.* **7,** 102—137 (1958).
[3] Interpolation d'espaces de Banach et applications I—III. *C. R. Acad. Sci. Paris* **248,** 1912—1914, 3388—3390, 3517—3518 (1959).
[4] Interpolazione di spazi di Banach e applicazioni. *Ricerche Mat.* **9,** 58—81 (1960).
[5] A unified structure in various families of function spaces. Compactness and closure theorems. Proc. Internat. Sympos. *Linear Spaces* (Jerusalem, 1960), pp. 237—241. Jerusalem: Jerusalem Academic Press, and Oxford/London/New York/Paris: Pergamon Press 1961.
[6] Una struttura unitaria in diverse famiglie di spazi funzionali I. *Ricerche Mat.* **10,** 244—281 (1961).
[7] *Quasi linear interpolation spaces.* Tech. Report 1, University of Kansas, Lawrence, 1962, 34 pp.
[8] A common structure in various families of functional spaces. II. Quasilinear interpolation spaces. *Ricerche Mat.* **12,** 87—107 (1963).
GÅRDING, L.
[1] Some trends and problems in linear partial differential equations. *Proc. Internat. Congress Math.* 1958, pp. 87—102. New York/London: Cambridge University Press 1960.
GELFAND, I. M.
[1] On one-parametrical groups of operators in a normed space. *C. R.* (*Doklady*) *Acad. Sci. URSS* (*N. S.*) **25,** 713—718 (1939).
GOLOMB, M.
[1] *Lectures on Theory of Approximation.* Argonne National Laboratory Applied Math. Division 1962, 289 pp.
GÖRLICH, E.: *see also Berens, H., and Butzer, P. L.*
[1] *Saturationssätze und Charakterisierung der Saturationsklassen für Limitierungsverfahren von Fourierreihen.* Staatsexamensarbeit, TH Aachen 1964, 137 pp.
[2] *Distributionentheoretische Methoden in der Saturationstheorie.* Dissertation, TH Aachen 1967, 69 pp.
GÖRLICH, E. – R. J. NESSEL
[1] Über Peano- und Riemann-Ableitungen in der Norm. *Arch. Math.* **18,** 399—410 (1967).
GRÖGER, K.
[1] Einführung und Anwendung Sobolewscher Räume für beliebige Gebiete. *Math. Nachr.* **28,** 123—144 (1964/65).
[2] Nichtlineare ausgearbeitete elliptische Differentialgleichungen. *Math. Nachr.* **28,** 181—205 (1964/65).
[3] Einbettungssätze für die Sobolewschen Räume zu unbeschränkten Gebieten. *Math. Nachr.* **31,** 73—88 (1966).

GUSSI, G.: *see Foiaş, C.*

HADAMARD, J.

[*1*] Sur un problème mixte aux derivées partielles. *Bull. Soc. Math. France* **31,** 208—224 (1903).

[*2*] *Lectures on Cauchy's Problem in Linear Partial Differential Equations.* New Haven: Yale University Press 1923, viii + 316 pp. Reprinted by Dover Publications, New York 1952.

[*3*] Principe de Huygens et prolongement analytique. *Bull. Soc. Math. France* **52,** 241—278, 610—640 (1924).

HALMOS, P. R.

[*1*] *Measure Theory.* New York: D. Van Nostrand 1950, xi + 304 pp.

HALPERIN, I.: *see also Ellis, H. W.*

[*1*] Function spaces. *Canad. J. Math.* **5,** 273—288 (1953).

[*2*] Uniform convexity in function spaces. *Duke Math. J.* **21,** 195—204 (1954).

[*3*] Reflexivity in the L^λ function spaces. *Duke Math. J.* **21,** 205—208 (1954).

HARDY, G. H. – J. E. LITTLEWOOD

[*1*] Some properties of fractional integrals I, II. *Math. Z.* **27,** 565—606 (1928); **34,** 403—439 (1932).

[*2*] A convergence criterion for Fourier series. *Math. Z.* **28,** 612—634 (1928).

[*3*] Theorems concerning mean values of analytic or harmonic functions. *Quart. J. Math. Oxford Series* **12,** 221—256 (1941).

HARDY, G. H. – J. E. LITTLEWOOD – G. PÓLYA

[*1*] *Inequalities.* Cambridge: Cambridge University Press 1934, xii + 314 pp.

HARDY, G. H. – W. W. ROGOSINSKI

[*1*] *Fourier Series.* (3rd edition) Cambridge: Cambridge University Press 1956, x + 100 pp.

HELLWIG, G.

[*1*] *Partial Differential Equations.* New York/Toronto/London: Blaisdell 1964, xiii + 263 pp. (Transl. of the German edition, Stuttgart 1960)

HILBERT, D.: *see Courant, R.*

HILLE, E.: *see also Caton, W. B.*

[*1*] Notes on linear transformations I. *Trans. Amer. Math. Soc.* **39,** 131—153 (1936).

[*2*] On semi-groups of transformations in Hilbert space. *Proc. Nat. Acad. Sci. USA* **24,** 159—161 (1938).

[*3*] Representation of one-parameter semi-groups of linear transformations. *Proc. Nat. Acad. Sci. USA* **28,** 175—178 (1942).

[*4*] *Functional Analysis and Semi-Groups.* Amer. Math. Soc. Colloq. Publ. Vol. 31, New York 1948, xii + 528 pp.

[*5*] On the differentiability of semi-group operators. *Acta Sci. Math.* (*Szeged*) **12,** 19—24 (1950).

[*6*] On the generation of semi-groups and the theory of conjugate functions. *Proc. R. Physiogr. Soc. Lund* **21** : **14,** 130—142 (1951).

[*7*] Une généralisation du problème de Cauchy. *Ann. Inst. Fourier* (*Grenoble*) **4,** 31—48 (1952).

[*8*] Le problème abstrait de Cauchy. *Univ. e Politecnico Torino Rend. Sem. Mat.* **12,** 95—103 (1953).

[*9*] The abstract Cauchy problem and Cauchy's problem for parabolic differential equations. *J. Analyse Math.* **3,** 81—196 (1954).

HILLE, E. – R. S. PHILLIPS

[*1*] *Functional Analysis and Semi-Groups.* (revised edition) Amer. Math. Soc. Colloq. Publ. Vol. 31, Providence, R. I. 1957, xii + 808 pp.

HIRSCHMAN, I. I., JR.

[1] Fractional integration. *Amer. J. Math.* **75,** 531—546 (1953).

[2] On multiplier transformations I, II, III. *Duke Math. J.* **26,** 221—242 (1959); *ibidem* **28,** 45—56 (1961); *Proc. Amer. Math. Soc.* **71,** 764—766 (1965).

HIRSCHMAN, I. I., JR. – D. V. WIDDER

[1] Generalized Bernstein polynomials. *Duke Math. J.* **16,** 433—438 (1949).

HOFMANN, K. H. – P. S. MOSTERT

[1] *Elements of Compact Semigroups.* Columbus, Ohio: C. E. Merrill Books, Inc. 1966, xiii + 384 pp.

HÖRMANDER, L.

[1] Estimates for translation invariant operators in L^p spaces. *Acta Math.* **104,** 93—140 (1960).

[2] *Linear Partial Differential Operators.* Berlin/Göttingen/Heidelberg: Springer 1963, vii + 287 pp.

HORVÁTH, J.

[1] *Topological Vector Spaces and Distributions. Vol. I.* Reading, Mass./Palo Alto/London/Don Mills, Ont.: Addison-Wesley 1966, xii + 449 pp.

HSU, L. C.

[1] An estimation for the first exponential formula in the theory of semi-groups of linear operations. *Czechoslovak Math. J.* **10** (85), 323—328 (1960).

HUNT, R. A.

[1] An extension of the Marcinkiewicz interpolation theorem to Lorentz spaces. *Bull. Amer. Math. Soc.* **70,** 803—807 (1964). Addendum, *ibidem* **71,** 396 (1965).

HUNT, R. A. – G. WEISS

[1] The Marcinkiewicz interpolation theorem. *Proc. Amer. Math. Soc.* **15,** 996—998 (1964).

IL'IN, V. P.

[1] On a theorem of G. H. Hardy and J. E. Littlewood. (Russian) *Trudy Mat. Inst. Steklov.* **53,** 128—144 (1959).

ITÔ, K. – H. MCKEAN

[1] *Diffusion Processes and Their Sample Paths.* Berlin/Heidelberg/New York: Springer 1965, xiii + 321 pp.

IVANOVA, O. A.

[1] Certain theorems on an n-parametric semigroup of bounded linear operators and their application in the theory of functions. (Russian) *Teor. Funkcii Funkcional. Anal. i Priložen. Vyp.* **2,** 34—41 (1966).

JOHN, F.: *see also Bers, L.*

[1] *Plane Waves and Spherical Means Applied to Partial Differential Equations.* New York/London: Interscience 1955, viii + 172 pp.

KANTOROVICH, L. V. – G. P. AKILOV

[1] *Functional Analysis in Normed Spaces.* Oxford/London/Edinburgh/New York/Paris/Frankfurt: Pergamon Press 1964, xiii + 771 pp. (Transl. of the Russian edition, Moscow 1959)

KASSIMATIS, C.

[1] Functions which have generalized Riemann derivatives. *Canad. J. Math.* **10,** 413—420 (1958).

KATO, T.

[1] Remarks on pseudo-resolvents and infinitesimal generators of semi-groups. *Proc. Japan Acad.* **35,** 467—468 (1959).

[2] Note on fractional powers of linear operators. *Proc. Japan Acad.* **36,** 94—96 (1960).

[3] *Perturbation Theory for Linear Operators.* Berlin/Heidelberg/New York: Springer 1966, xix + 592 pp.

KENDALL, D. G.

[1] Bernstein polynomials and semi-groups of operators. *Math. Scand.* **2,** 185—186 (1954).

KOMATSU, H.

[1] Semi-groups of operators in locally convex spaces. *J. Math. Soc. Japan* **16,** 230—262 (1964).

[2] Fractional powers of operators I. *Pacific J. Math.* **19,** 285—346 (1966).

KOREVAAR, J.: *see Butzer, P. L.*

KÖTHE, G.

[1] Die Teilräume eines linearen Koordinatenraumes. *Math. Ann.* **114,** 99—125 (1937).

[2] *Topologische lineare Räume. Bd. I.* Berlin/Göttingen/Heidelberg: Springer 1960, xii + 456 pp.

KOZAKIEWICZ, W.: *see Butzer, P. L.*

KREĬN, S. G.

[1] On an interpolation theorem in operator theory. (Russian) *Dokl. Akad. Nauk SSSR* **130,** 491—494 (1960) = *Soviet Math. Dokl.* **1,** 61—64 (1960).

[2] On the concept of a normal scale of spaces. (Russian) *Dokl. Akad. Nauk SSSR* **132,** 510—513 (1960) = *Soviet Math. Dokl.* **1,** 586—589 (1960).

KREĬN, S. G. – JU. I. PETUNIN

[1] Scales of Banach Spaces. (Russian) *Uspehi Mat. Nauk* **21,** no. 2 (128), 89—168 (1966).

KREĬN, S. G. – E. M. SEMENOV

[1] On a space scale. (Russian) *Dokl. Akad. Nauk SSSR* **138,** 763—766 (1961) = *Soviet Math. Dokl.* **2,** 706—710 (1961).

LANGLANDS, R. P.

[1] On Lie semi-groups. *Canad. J. Math.* **12,** 686—693 (1960).

LAX, P. D. – R. S. PHILLIPS

[1] *Scattering Theory.* New York/London: Academic Press 1967, xii + 276 pp.

DE LEEUW, K.

[1] Linear spaces with a compact group of operators. *Illinois J. Math.* **2,** 367—377 (1958).

[2] On the adjoint semi-group and some problems in the theory of approximation. *Math. Z.* **73,** 219—234 (1960).

[3] Banach spaces of Lipschitz functions. *Studia Math.* **21,** 55—66 (1961).

LEIS, R.

[1] Über das Randverhalten harmonischer Funktionen. *Arch. Rational Mech. Anal.* **7,** 168—180 (1961). Addendum. *ibidem* **8,** 444—445 (1961).

[2] Approximationssätze für stetige Operatoren. *Arch. Math.* **14,** 120—129 (1963).

[3] Zur Approximation der Randwerte von Potentialfunktionen. *Arch. Math.* **16,** 378—387 (1965).

LEONARD, J. L.: *see Bruckner, A. M.*

LIONS, J. L.: *see also Foiaş, C., and Nikolskiĭ, S. M.*

[1] Espaces intermédiaires entre espaces hilbertiens et applications. *Bull. Math. Soc. Sci. Math. Phys. R. P. Roumaine (N. S.)* **2** (50), 419—432 (1958).

[2] Un théorème de traces; applications. *C. R. Acad. Sci. Paris* **249,** 2259—2261 (1959).

[3] Théorèmes de trace et d'interpolation, I—V. *Ann. Scuola Norm. Sup. Pisa* (3) **13,** 389—403 (1959); *ibidem* **14,** 317—331 (1960); *J. Math. Pures Appl.* (9) **42,** 195—203 (1963); *Math. Ann.* **151,** 42—56 (1963); *An. Acad. Brasil. Ci.*

[4] Les semi-groupes distributions. *Portugal. Math.* **19,** 141—164 (1960).
[5] Une construction d'espaces d'interpolation. *C. R. Acad. Sci. Paris* **251,** 1853—1855 (1961).
[6] Sur les espaces d'interpolation; dualité. *Math. Scand.* **9,** 147—177 (1961).
[7] *Équations différentielles opérationnelles et problèmes aux limites.* Berlin/Göttingen/Heidelberg: Springer 1961, ix + 292 pp.
[8] Properties of some interpolation spaces. *J. Math. Mech.* **11,** 969—977 (1962).

LIONS, J. L. – E. MAGENES
[1] Problemi ai limiti non omogenei III. *Ann. Scuola Norm. Sup. Pisa* (3) **15,** 41—103 (1961).

LIONS, J. L. – J. PEETRE
[1] Propriétés d'espaces d'interpolation. *C. R. Acad. Sci. Paris* **253,** 1747—1749 (1961).
[2] Sur une classe d'espaces d'interpolation. *Inst. Hautes Études Sci. Publ. Math.* **19,** 5—68 (1964).

LITTLEWOOD, J. E.: *see Hardy, G. H.*

LITTLEWOOD, J. E. – R. E. A. C. PALEY
[1] Theorems on Fourier series and power series II. *Proc. London Math. Soc.* **42,** 52—89 (1936).

LITTMAN, W.
[1] The wave operator and L_p norms. *J. Math. Mech.* **12,** 55—68 (1963).
[2] Multipliers in L^p and interpolation. *Bull. Amer. Math. Soc.* **71,** 764—766 (1965).

LIZORKIN, P. I.: *see also Nikolskiĭ, S. M.*
[1] On the Fourier transform in Besov spaces. The zero scale $B^0_{p,\theta}$. (Russian) *Dokl. Akad. Nauk SSSR* **163,** 1318—1321 (1965) = *Soviet Math. Dokl.* **6,** 1110—1113 (1965).

LJAPIN, E. S.
[1] *Semigroups.* Transl. of Math. Monogr. Vol. 3, Amer. Math. Soc., Providence, R. I. 1963, vii + 447 pp. (Transl. of the Russian edition, Moscow 1960)

LJUBIČ, JU. I.
[1] The classical and local Laplace transform in the abstract Cauchy problem. (Russian) *Uspehi Mat. Nauk* **21,** no. 3 (129), 3—51 (1966) = *Russian Math. Surveys* **21,** 1—52 (1966).

LJUSTERNIC, L. A. – V. I. SOBOLEV
[1] *Elemente der Funktionalanalysis.* Berlin: Akademie-Verlag 1955, xi + 256 pp. (German transl. of the Russian edition, USSR 1951)

LÖFSTRÖM, J.
[1] On certain interpolation spaces related to generalized semi-groups. *Math. Scand.* **16,** 41—54 (1965).
[2] Some theorems on interpolation spaces with applications to approximation in L_p. *Math. Ann.* **172,** 176—196 (1967).

LOOMIS, L. H.
[1] A note on the Hilbert transform. *Bull. Amer. Math. Soc.* **52,** 1082—1086 (1946).

LORENTZ, G. G.
[1] Some new functional spaces. *Ann. of Math.* (2) **51,** 37—55 (1950).
[2] On the theory of spaces Λ. *Pacific J. Math.* **1,** 411—429 (1951).
[3] *Bernstein polynomials.* Mathematical Expositions, no. 8. Toronto, Ont.: University of Toronto Press 1953, x + 130 pp.
[4] Majorants in spaces of integrable functions. *Amer. J. Math.* **77,** 484—492 (1955).
[5] *Approximation of Functions.* New York/Chicago/San Francisco/Toronto/London: Holt, Rinehart and Winston 1966, ix + 188 pp.

LORENTZ, G. G. – D. G. WERTHEIM

[1] Representation of linear functionals on Köthe spaces. *Canad. J. Math.* **5,** 568—575 (1953).

LUPAŞ, A. – M. MÜLLER

[1] Approximationseigenschaften der Gammaoperatoren. *Math. Z.* **98,** 208—226 (1967).

LUXEMBURG, W. A. J. – A. C. ZAANEN

[1] Notes on Banach function spaces I. *Nederl. Akad. Wetensch. Indag. Math.* **25,** 135—147 (1963).

MAGENES, E.: *see also Lions, J. L.*

[1] Spazi di interpolazione ed equazioni a derivate parziali. *Atti del VII Congresso dell'Unione Matematica Italiana, Genova* 1963, pp. 134—197. Roma: Edizioni Cremonese 1964.

MARCHAUD, A.

[1] Sur les dérivées et sur les différences des fonctions des variables réelles. *J. Math. Pures Appl.* (9) **6,** 337—425 (1927).

MARCINKIEWICZ, J.

[1] Sur quelques intégrales du type de Dini. *Ann. de la Soc. Polonaise de Math.* **17,** 42—50 (1938).

[2] Sur l'interpolation d'opérations. *C. R. Acad. Sci. Paris* **208,** 1272—1273 (1939).

MCKEAN, H.: *see Itô, K.*

MEINARDUS, G.

[1] *Approximation von Funktionen und ihre numerische Behandlung.* Berlin/Heidelberg/New York: Springer 1964, viii + 180 pp.

MIKHLIN, S. G.

[1] *Multidimensional Singular Integrals and Integral Equations.* Oxford/London/Edinburgh/New York/Paris/Frankfurt: Pergamon Press 1965, xii + 255 pp. (Transl. of the Russian edition, Moscow 1962)

MINAKSHISUNDARAM, S.

[1] Studies in Fourier Ansatz and parabolic equations. *J. Madras Univ.* **14,** 73—142 (1942).

MIRKIL, H.

[1] Continuous translation of Hölder and Lipschitz functions. *Canad. J. Math.* **12,** 674—685 (1960).

MIYADERA, I.

[1] Generation of a strongly continuous semi-group of operators. *Tôhoku Math. J.* (2) **4,** 109—114 (1952).

MLAK, W.

[1] *Unitary Dilations of Contraction Operators.* Rozprawy Matematyczne XLVI, Warzaw 1965, 88 pp.

MORREY, C. B., JR.

[1] *Multiple Integrals in the Calculus of Variations.* Berlin/Heidelberg/New York: Springer 1966, ix + 506 pp.

MOSCO, U.: *see da Prato, G.*

MOSTERT, P. S.: *see Hofmann, K. H.*

MULLA, F.: *see Aronszajn, N.*

MÜLLER, M.: *see Lupaş, A.*

NACHBIN, L.

[1] *Elements of Approximation Theory.* Notas de Matemática no. 33. University of Rio de Janeiro 1965, v + 121 pp. (= Princeton, N. J.: Van Nostrand 1967)

NATANSON, I. P.

[1] *Konstruktive Funktionentheorie*. Berlin: Akademie-Verlag 1955, xiv + 515 pp. (German transl. of the Russian edition, SSSR 1951)

[2] On the approximation of multiple differentiable periodic functions by means of singular integrals. (Russian) *Dokl. Akad. Nauk SSSR (N. S.)* **82,** 337—339 (1952).

NESSEL, R. J.: *see also Butzer, P. L., and Görlich, E.*

[1] *Das Saturationsproblem für mehrdimensionale singuläre Integrale und seine Lösung mit Hilfe der Fourier-Transformation*. Dissertation, TH Aachen 1965, 145 pp.

[2] Contributions to the theory of saturation for singular integrals in several variables II. Applications, III. Radial kernels. *Nederl. Akad. Wetensch. Indag. Math.* **29,** 52—73 (1967).

VON NEUMANN, J.

[1] Über die analytischen Eigenschaften von Gruppen linearer Transformationen und ihrer Darstellungen. *Math. Z.* **30,** 3—42 (1929).

NEVEU, J.

[1] *Mathematical Foundations of the Calculus of Probability*. San Francisco/London/Amsterdam: Holden-Day 1965, xiii + 223 pp. (Transl. of the French edition, Paris 1964)

NIKOLSKIĬ, S. M.

[1] On imbedding, continuation and approximation theorems for differentiable functions of several variables. (Russian) *Uspehi Mat. Nauk* **16,** no. 5 (101), 63—114 (1961) = *Russian Math. Surveys* **16,** 55—104 (1961).

NIKOLSKIĬ, S. M. – J. L. LIONS – P. I. LIZORKIN

[1] Integral representations and isomorphism properties of some classes of functions. *Ann. Scuola Norm. Sup. Pisa* **19,** 127—178 (1965).

OKLANDER, E. T.

[1] *On Interpolation of Banach Spaces*. Dissertation, University of Chicago 1964, 38 pp.

[2] *Interpolacion, Espacios de Lorentz y Teorema de Marcinkiewicz*. Cursos y seminarios Fasc. 20, Universidad de Buenos Aires, 1965, 111 pp.

[3] L_{pq} interpolators and the theorem of Marcinkiewicz. *Bull. Amer. Math. Soc.* **72,** 49—53 (1966).

O'NEIL, R.

[1] Convolution operators and $L(p, q)$ spaces. *Duke Math. J.* **30,** 129—142 (1963).

O'NEIL, R. – G. WEISS

[1] The Hilbert transform and rearrangement of functions. *Studia Math.* **23,** 189—198 (1963).

PALEY, R. E. A. C.: *see Littlewood, J.E.*

PAWELKE, S.: *see also Butzer, P. L.*

[1] *Approximationsaussagen über das singuläre Integral von Weierstrass*. Staatsexamensarbeit, TH Aachen 1965, 56 pp.

PEANO, G.

[1] *Opere Scelte. Vol. I.* Roma: Edizioni Cremonese 1957, vii + 530 pp.

PEETRE, J.: *see also Lions, J. L.*

[1] Espaces intermédiaires et la théorie constructive des fonctions. *C. R. Acad. Sci. Paris* **256,** 54—55 (1963).

[2] Nouvelles propriétés d'espaces d'interpolation. *C. R. Acad. Sci. Paris* **256,** 1424—1426 (1963).

[3] Sur le nombre de paramètres dans la définition de certains espaces d'interpolation. *Ricerche Mat.* **12,** 248—261 (1963).

[4] *A Theory of Interpolation of Normed Spaces.* Notes Universidade de Brasilia, 1963, 88 pp.
[5] *Generation of Distribution Semi-Groups.* Mimeographed Note, Lund Inst. Tech., Lund 1963, 38 pp.
[6] Espaces d'interpolation, généralisations, applications. *Rend. Sem. Mat. Fis. Milano* **34,** 133—164 (1964).
[7] On an equivalence theorem of Taibleson. Lund 1964 (unpublished manuscript), 9 pp.
[8] On an interpolation theorem of Foiaş and Lions. *Acta Sci. Math.* (*Szeged*) **25,** 255—261 (1964).
[9] *Étude de quelques espaces d'interpolation.* Lund 1965. (unpublished book-manuscript)
[10] Relations entre deux méthodes d'interpolation. *Inst. Hautes Études Sci. Publ. Math.* **29,** 305—309 (1966).
[11] Espaces d'interpolation et théorème de Soboleff. *Ann. Inst. Fourier* (*Grenoble*) **16,** 279—317 (1966).
[12] Applications de la théorie des espaces d'interpolation dans l'analyse harmonique. *Ricerche Mat.* **15,** 3—36 (1966).
[13] Sur les espaces de Besov. *C. R. Acad. Sci. Paris Sér. A* **264,** 281—283 (1967).

PEŁCZYŃSKI, A.
[1] On the isomorphism of the spaces *m* and *M*. *Bull. Acad. Polon. Sci. Sér. Math. Astronom. Phys.* **6,** 695—696 (1958).

PETUNIN, JU. I.: *see Kreĭn, S. G.*

PHILLIPS, R. S.: *see also Hille, E., and Lax, P. D.*
[1] On one-parameter semi-groups of linear transformations. *Proc. Amer. Math. Soc.* **2,** 234—237 (1951).
[2] Spectral theory for semi-groups of linear operators. *Trans. Amer. Math. Soc.* **71,** 393—415 (1951).
[3] On the generation of semi-groups of linear operators. *Pacific J. Math.* **2,** 343—369 (1952).
[4] Perturbation theory for semi-groups of linear operators. *Trans. Amer. Math. Soc.* **74,** 199—221 (1953).
[5] An inversion formula for Laplace transforms and semi-groups of linear operators. *Ann. of Math.* (2) **59,** 325—356 (1954).
[6] A note on the abstract Cauchy problem. *Proc. Nat. Acad. Sci. USA* **40,** 244—248 (1954).
[7] *Applications of the Theory of Semi-Group Operators.* Lecture Notes, Stanford University 1954, 82 pp.
[8] Semi-groups of operators. *Bull. Amer. Math. Soc.* **61,** 16—33 (1955).
[9] The adjoint semi-group *Pacific J. Math.* **5,** 269—283 (1955).

DU PLESSIS, N.
[1] Some theorems about the Riesz fractional integral. *Trans. Amer. Math. Soc.* **80,** 124—134 (1955).
[2] Spherical fractional integrals. *Trans. Amer. Math. Soc.* **84,** 262—272 (1957).

PLESSNER, A. I.
[1] Eine Kennzeichnung der totalstetigen Funktionen. *J. Reine Angew. Math.* **160,** 26—32 (1929).

POENARU, V.: *see Foiaş, C.*

POLLARD, H.
[1] The semi-group property of Poisson transformation and Snow's inversion formula. *Proc. Amer. Math. Soc.* **14,** 285—290 (1963).

PÓLYA, G.: *see Hardy, G. H.*
DA PRATO, G. – U. MOSCO
[*1*] Semigruppi distribuzioni analitici. *Ann. Scuola Norm. Sup. Pisa* (3) **19,** 367—396 (1965).
[*2*] Regolarizzazione dei semigruppi distribuzioni analitici. *Ann. Scuola Norm. Sup. Pisa* (3) **19,** 563—576 (1965).
PRESTON, G. B.: *see Clifford, A. H.*
PRIVALOV, I. I.
[*1*] Sur les fonctions conjuguées. *Bull. Soc. Math. France* **44,** 100—103 (1916).
REID, W. T.
[*1*] Integral criteria for solutions of linear differential equations. *Duke Math. J.* **12,** 685—694 (1945).
RICE, J. R.
[*1*] *The Approximation of Functions. Vol. I: Linear Theory.* Reading, Mass.: Addison-Wesley 1964, x + 203 pp.
RIESZ, M.
[*1*] Sur les maxima des formes bilinéaires et sur les fonctionnelles linéaires. *Acta Math.* **49,** 465—497 (1926).
[*2*] Sur les fonctions conjuguées. *Math. Z.* **27,** 218—244 (1927).
RIESZ, F. – B. SZ.-NAGY
[*1*] *Functional Analysis.* New York: Frederick Ungar 1955, xii + 468 pp. (Transl. of the French edition, Budapest 1952)
ROGOSINSKI, W. W.: *see Hardy, G. H.*
ROMANOV, N. P.
[*1*] On one-parameter groups of linear transformations I. *Ann. of Math.* (2) **48,** 216—233 (1947).
ROYDEN, H. L.
[*1*] *Real Analysis.* New York: Macmillan 1963, xvi + 284 pp.
SAKS, S.
[*1*] On the generalized derivatives. *J. London Math. Soc.* **7,** 247—251 (1932).
SALEM, R. – A. ZYGMUND
[*1*] Capacity of sets and Fourier series. *Trans. Amer. Math. Soc.* **59,** 23—41 (1946).
SARD, A.
[*1*] *Linear Approximation.* Mathematical Surveys, No. 9. Providence, R. I. Amer. Math. Soc. 1963, xi + 544 pp.
SCHAEFER, H. H.
[*1*] *Topological Vector Spaces.* New York/London: Macmillan 1966, ix + 294 pp.
SCHECHTER, M.: *see also Bers, L.*
[*1*] Interpolation spaces by complex methods. *Bull. Amer. Math. Soc.* **72**, 526—533 (1966).
SCHERER, K.: *see Butzer, P. L.*
SCHWARTZ, J. T.: *see Dunford, N.*
SCHWARTZ, L.
[*1*] *Théorie des Distributions.* Tomes I et II. Paris: Hermann & Cie. 1950, 148 pp. et 1951, 169 pp.
[*2*] *Lectures on Mixed Problems in Partial Differential Equations and the Representation of Semi-Groups.* Bombay: Tata Inst. of Fund. Research 1958.
SEGAL, I. E.: *see Dunford, N.*
DE SÉGUIER, J. A.
[*1*] *Éléments de la théorie des groupes abstraits.* Paris: Gauthier-Villars 1904, ii + 176 pp.

SEMENOV, E. M.: *see also Kreĭn, S. G.*

[*1*] A scale of spaces with an interpolation property. (Russian) *Dokl. Akad. Nauk SSSR* **148,** 1038—1041 (1963) = *Soviet Math. Dokl.* **4,** 235—239 (1963).

SHARMA, A.: *see Cheney, E. W.*

SINGBAL-VEDAK, K.

[*1*] A note on semigroups of operators on a locally convex space. *Proc. Amer. Math. Soc.* **16,** 696—702 (1965).

SMITH, K. T.: *see Aronszajn, N.*

SMITH, T. L.: *see Sternberg, W. J.*

SNEDDON, I. N.

[*1*] *Functional Analysis.* Encyclopedia of Physics, Vol. II, Mathematical Methods II, edited by S. Flügge, pp. 198—348. Berlin/Göttingen/Heidelberg: Springer 1955.

SOBOLEV, S. L.

[*1*] Sur un théorème d'analyse fonctionelle. (Russian, French summary) *Mat. Sbornik* **4,** 471—496 (1938).

[*2*] *Applications of Functional Analysis in Mathematical Physics.* Translations of Mathematical Monographs Vol. 7. Providence, R. I.: Amer. Math. Soc. 1963, vii + 239 pp. (Transl. of the Russian edition, Leningrad 1950)

SOBOLEV, V. I.: *see Ljusternic, L. A.*

STEČKIN, S. B.

[*1*] On the order of the best approximations of continuous functions. (Russian) *Izv. Akad. Nauk SSSR. Ser. Mat.* **15,** 219—242 (1951).

STEIN, E. M.

[*1*] Interpolation of linear operators. *Trans. Amer. Math. Soc.* **83,** 482—492 (1956).

[*2*] On the functions of Littlewood-Paley, Lusin and Marcinkiewicz. *Trans. Amer. Math. Soc.* **88,** 430—466 (1958). Correction. *ibidem* **98,** 186 (1961).

[*3*] The characterization of functions arising as potentials I, II. *Bull. Amer. Math. Soc.* **67,** 102—104 (1961); **68**, 577—582 (1962).

STEIN, E. M. – G. WEISS

[*1*] Interpolation of operators with change of measures. *Trans. Amer. Math. Soc.* **87,** 159—172 (1958).

[*2*] An extension of a theorem of Marcinkiewicz and some of its applications. *J. Math. Mech.* **8,** 263—284 (1959).

STERNBERG, W. J. – T. L. SMITH

[*1*] *The Theory of Potential and Spherical Harmonics.* Mathematical Expositions, no. 3. Toronto, Ont.: University of Toronto Press, 1944. xii + 312 pp.

STONE, M. H.

[*1*] Linear transformations in Hilbert space III. *Proc. Nat. Acad. Sci. USA* **16,** 172—175 (1930).

[*2*] On one parameter unitary groups in Hilbert space. *Ann. of Math.* (2) **33,** 643—648 (1932).

[*3*] A generalized Weierstrass approximation theorem. In *Studies in Modern Analysis, Vol. I,* edited by R. C. Buck, pp. 30—87. Englewood Cliffs, N. J.: Prentice-Hall 1962.

SUNOUCHI, G.: *see also Butzer, P. L.*

[*1*] On the class of saturation in the theory of approximation I. *Tôhoku Math. J.* (2) **12,** 339—344 (1960).

[*2*] Saturation in the theory of best approximation. (Proceedings of a Conference at Oberwolfach, 1963) In *On Approximation Theory,* edited by P. L. BUTZER–J. KOREVAAR, ISNM 5, pp. 72—88. Basel: Birkhäuser 1964.

SUNOUCHI, G. – C. WATARI

[1] On determination of the class of saturation in the theory of approximation of functions. I, II. *Proc. Japan Acad.* **34,** 477—481 (1958); *Tôhoku Math. J.* (2) **11,** 480—488 (1959).

SZÁSZ, O.

[1] Generalization of S. Bernstein's polynomials to the infinite interval. *J. Research Nat. Bur. Standards* **45,** 239—245 (1950).

SZEPTYCKI, P.: *see Aronszajn, N.*

SZ.-NAGY, B.: *see also Riesz, F.*

[1] Über meßbare Darstellungen Liescher Gruppen. *Math. Ann.* **112,** 286—296 (1936).

[2] On semi-groups of self-adjoint transformations in Hilbert-space. *Proc. Nat. Acad. Sci.* **24,** 559—560 (1938).

SZ.-NAGY, B. – C. FOIAŞ

[1] Sur les contractions de l'espace de Hilbert III. *Acta Sci. Math. Szeged* **19,** 26—45 (1958).

[2] *Analyse harmonique des opérateurs de l'espace de Hilbert.* Budapest: Akadémiai Kiadó et Paris: Masson et Cie 1967, xi + 374 pp.

TABERSKI, R.

[1] On singular integrals. *Ann. Polon. Math.* **4,** 249—268 (1958).

TAIBLESON, M. H.

[1] Lipschitz classes of functions and distributions in E_n. *Bull. Amer. Math. Soc.* **69,** 487—493 (1963).

[2] On the theory of Lipschitz spaces of distributions on Euclidean n-space. I. Principal properties; II. Translation invariant operators, duality, and interpolation; III. Smoothness and integrability of Fourier transforms, smoothness of convolution kernels. *J. Math. Mech.* **13,** 407—479 (1964); **14,** 821—839 (1965); **15,** 973—981 (1966).

TAYLOR, A. E.

[1] *Introduction to Functional Analysis.* New York: John Wiley & Sons 1958, xvi + 423 pp.

THORIN, G. O.

[1] An extension of a convexity theorem due to M. Riesz. *Comm. Sém. Math. Univ. Lund* **4,** 1—5 (1939).

[2] Convexity theorems generalizing those of M. Riesz and Hadamard with some applications. *Comm. Sém. Math. Univ. Lund* **9,** 1—58 (1948). (Dissertation, Lund)

TILLMANN, H. G.: *see also Butzer, P. L.*

[1] Approximationssätze für Halbgruppen von Operatoren in topologischen Vektorräumen. *Arch. Math.* **11,** 194—199 (1960).

TIMAN, A. F.

[1] *Theory of Approximation of Functions of a Real Variable.* Oxford/London/New York/Paris: Pergamon Press 1963, xii + 631 pp. (Transl. of the Russian edition, Moscow 1960)

TITCHMARSH, E. C.

[1] A theorem on Lebesgue integrals. *J. London Math. Soc.* **2,** 36—37 (1927).

[2] *Introduction to the Theory of Fourier Integrals.* (second edition) Oxford: Oxford University Press 1948, viii + 395 pp.

[3] *The Theory of Functions.* Oxford: Oxford University Press 1939, x + 454 pp.

TREBELS, W.: *see Butzer, P. L.*

TURECKIĬ, A. H.

[1] On classes of saturation for certain methods of summation of Fourier series of continuous periodic functions. (Russian) *Uspehi Mat. Nauk.* **15,** no. 6 (96) 149—156 (1960) = *Amer. Math. Soc. Transl.* (2) **26,** 263—272 (1963).

DE LA VALLÉE-POUSSIN, CH. J.
[1] *Leçons sur l'approximation des fonctions d'une variable réelle.* Paris: Gauthier-Villars 1919, vi + 150 pp.
VERBLUNSKY, S.
[1] The generalized fourth derivative. *J. London Math. Soc.* **6,** 82—84 (1931).
WAINGER, S.
[1] Special trigonometric series in *k*-dimensions. *Mem. Amer. Math. Soc.* **59** (1965), 102 pp.
WATARI, C.: *see Sunouchi, G.*
WATERMAN, D.
[1] On functions analytic in a half-plane. *Trans. Amer. Math. Soc.* **81,** 167—194 (1956).
[2] On an integral of Marcinkiewicz. *Trans. Amer. Math. Soc.* **91,** 129—138 (1959).
WEIERSTRASS, K.
[1] Über die analytische Darstellbarkeit sogenannter willkürlicher Funktionen reeller Argumente. *S.-B. Königl. Akad. d. Wiss.* pp. 633—639, 789—805 (1885) (cf. Mathematische Werke, Band III, Berlin 1903).
WEISS, G.: *see also Hunt, R. A., O'Neil, R., and Stein, E. M.*
[1] *Analisis armonico en varias variables. Teoria de los espacios H^p.* Cursos y Seminarios de Matemática, Fasc. 9. Universidad de Buenos Aires 1960, 139 pp.
WERTHEIM, D. G.: *see Lorentz, G. G.*
WESTPHAL, U.: *see Berens, H.*
WIDDER, D. V.: *see also Hirschman, I. I., Jr.*
[1] *The Laplace Transform.* Princeton Mathematical Series, No. 6. Princeton, N. J.: Princeton University Press 1941, x + 406 pp.
[2] Some analogies from classical analysis in the theory of heat conduction. *Arch. Rational Mech. Anal.* **21,** 108—119 (1966).
YOSHINAGA, K.
[1] Ultra-distributions and semi-group distributions. *Bull. Kyushu Inst. Tech. Math. Natur. Sci.* **10,** 1—24 (1963).
[2] Values of vector-valued distributions and smoothness of semi-group distributions. *Bull. Kyushu Inst. Tech. Math. Natur. Sci.* **12,** 1—27 (1965).
YOSIDA, K.
[1] On the group embedded in the metrical complete ring. *Japan J. Math.* **13,** 7—26, 459—472 (1936).
[2] On the differentiability and the representation of one-parameter semi-groups of linear operators. *J. Math. Soc. Japan* **1,** 15—21 (1948).
[3] An operator-theoretical treatment of temporally homogeneous Markoff processes. *J. Math. Soc. Japan* **1,** 244—253 (1949).
[4] On Cauchy's problem in the large for wave equations. *Proc. Japan Acad.* **28,** 396—403 (1952).
[5] Semi-group theory and the integration problem of diffusion equations. *Proceedings of the Internat. Congress of Math.*, Amsterdam, 1954, Vol. 1, pp. 405—420.
[6] An operator-theoretical integration of the wave equation. *J. Math. Soc. Japan* **8,** 79—92 (1956).
[7] *Lectures on Semi-Group Theory and its Application to Cauchy's Problem in Partial Differential Equations.* Bombay: Tata Inst. of Fund. Research 1957, iv + 131 pp.

[8] Fractional powers of infinitesimal generators and the analyticity of the semi-groups generated by them. *Proc. Japan Acad.* **36,** 86—89 (1960).
[9] Ergodic theorems for pseudo-resolvents. *Proc. Japan Acad.* **37,** 422—425 (1961).
[10] *Functional Analysis.* Berlin/Göttingen/Heidelberg: Springer 1965, xi + 458 pp.
ZAANEN, A. C.: *see also Luxemburg, W. A. J.*
[1] *Linear Analysis.* Amsterdam: North-Holland Publ. Co. 1953, vii + 601 pp.
[2] *An Introduction to the Theory of Integration.* Amsterdam: North Holland Publ. Co. 1958, ix + 254 pp.
ZAMANSKY, M.
[1] Classes de saturation de certains procédés d'approximation des séries de Fourier des fonctions continues et applications à quelques problèmes d'approximation. *Ann. Sci École Norm. Sup.* (3) **66,** 19—93 (1949).
ZELLER, K.
[1] *Theorie der Limitierungsverfahren.* Berlin/Wien: Springer 1958, viii + 242 pp.
ZYGMUND, A.: *see also Calderón, A. P., and Salem, R.*
[1] On certain integrals. *Trans. Amer. Math. Soc.* **55,** 170—204 (1944).
[2] Smooth functions. *Duke Math. J.* **12,** 47—76 (1945).
[3] The approximation of functions by typical means of their Fourier series. *Duke Math. J.* **12,** 695—704 (1945).
[4] On singular integrals. *Rend. Mat. e Appl.* (5) **16,** 468—505 (1957).
[5] *Trigonometric Series. Vol. I and II* (2nd edition). London/New York: Cambridge University Press 1959, xii + 383 pp. and vii + 354 pp.
[6] On the preservation of classes of functions. *J. Math. Mech.* **8,** 889—895 (1959). Erratum. *ibidem* **9,** 663 (1960).

Index

721/7/68 — III/18/203

Die Grundlehren der mathematischen Wissenschaften in Einzeldarstellungen mit besonderer Berücksichtigung der Anwendungsgebiete